Avizandum Statutes on

Scots Public Law

Fifth edition

Avizandum Statutes on

Scots Public Law

Fifth edition

Editor

Navraj Singh Ghaleigh LLB, LLM, Barrister

Head of Public Law Subject Area

University of Edinburgh

EDINBURGH

University Press

Edinburgh University Press is one of the leading university presses in the UK. We publish academic books and journals in our selected subject areas across the humanities and social sciences, combining cutting-edge scholarship with high editorial and production values to produce academic works of lasting importance. For more information visit our website: edinburghuniversitypress.com

First published 2006
5th edition 2020

Edinburgh University Press Ltd
The Tun – Holyrood Road
12 (2f) Jackson's Entry
Edinburgh EH8 8PJ

Typeset by Servis Filmsetting Ltd, Stockport, Cheshire

A CIP record for this book is available from the British Library

ISBN 978 1 4744 8361 2 (paperback)
ISBN 978 1 4744 8362 9 (pdf)
ISBN 978 1 4744 8363 6 (epub)

EDITOR'S PREFACE

Public law is an increasingly codified subject, arguably more so in Scotland than in the rest of the United Kingdom. As well as Acts of Parliament and instruments of supranational law, Acts of the Scottish Parliament and Court of Session Rules substantially structure the body of public law in Scotland – materials usually missed in the UK-wide public law books. Close textual facility with the primary materials is essential for the university-level study of law, as it is for legal practice. The purpose of this collection is to provide students of Scots public law with a convenient collection of the texts essential to the study of the subject, as well as a representative sample of materials bearing upon widely studied sub-topics and cognate areas.

Any collection of this sort is bound to be characterised as much by its exclusions as its inclusions. The War Damage Act 1965 and Foreign Compensation Act 1969 fail to make the cut despite their relevance to watershed moments in UK public law, owing to their limited broader relevance. Disappointed readers might be interested in the estimable S S Juss and M Sunkin (eds), *Landmark Cases in Public Law* (Hart Publishing, 2017). Much of the material included in previous editions of this book on the criminal/ public law boundary, or pertaining to immigration law, has been omitted as these topics are often taught in non-public law courses. Readers who take exception or spot omissions, glaring or otherwise, are invited to contact the editor.

Many of the decisions regarding inclusions have been informed by the selection of materials taken in Edinburgh Law School's two ordinary courses, Public Law of the United Kingdom and Scotland, and Public Law and Individual Rights. Accordingly, I should like to acknowledge the help and assistance of my colleagues, past and present, in shaping these courses. Colleagues at the law schools of Queen Mary University of London and Aberdeen University, where I have served as external examiner, have also provided invaluable insights into the practice of teaching public law. Thanks are also owed to Jenny Brown and Hannah Smethurst who provided excellent research assistance, and to the editors of previous editions of these statutes, whose basic choices have often been followed. I am particularly grateful to Margaret Cherry who has been the model of efficiency, help, and encouragement.

At 11 pm on 31 January 2020 the UK ceased to be a member of the European Union, commencing a 'transitional period' during which the long-term relationship between the UK and EU will be renegotiated. That transitional period is due to expire on 31 December 2020, but may be subject to change owing to the impact of the Covid-19 pandemic on the negotiations. For the duration of the transition period the UK remains within the EU single market and customs union, and EU law continues to apply in the UK. The current position as at summer 2020 is governed by the European Communities Act 1972, the European Union (Withdrawal) Act 2018, and the European Union (Withdrawal Agreement) Act 2020. Properly called 'tortuous and confusing' by Mark Elliott and Robert Thomas (*Public Law*, (4th edn, 2017, OUP), this marks not the end but only the beginning of the UK's legal disentanglement from the EU.

Amendments made since the statutes were originally enacted are indicated by the use of square brackets. Prospective amendments appear in italic type. Every attempt has been made to update the materials to the end of July 2018.

Navraj Singh Ghaleigh
Head of Public Law Subject Area
Edinburgh Law School
August 2020

CONTENTS

PART II: OTHER MATERIALS

PART I
STATUTES

BILL OF RIGHTS 1688
(1688, c 2)

Article 4: Levying money
By Levying Money for and to the use of the Crowne by preference of Prerogative for other time and in other manner then the same was granted by Parlyament.

THE UNION WITH ENGLAND ACT 1707
(1707, c 7)

I. That the Two Kingdoms of Scotland and England shall upon the first day of May next ensuing the date hereof and forever after be United into One Kingdom by the Name of Great Britain And that the Ensigns Armorial of the said United Kingdom be such as Her Majesty shall appoint and the Crosses of St Andrew and St George be conjoined in such manner as Her Majesty shall think fit and used in all Flags Banners Standards and Ensigns both at Sea and Land.

II. That the Succession to the Monarchy of the United Kingdom of Great Britain and of the Dominions thereunto belonging after Her Most Sacred Majesty and in default of Issue of Her Majesty be, remain and continue to the Most Excellent Princess Sophia Electoress and Dutchess Dowager of Hanover and the Heirs of Her body being Protestants upon whom the Crown of England is settled by an Act of Parliament made in England in the twelth year of the Reign of His late Majesty King William the Third entituled An Act for the further Limitation of the Crown and better securing the Rights and Liberties of the Subject And that all Papists and persons marrying Papists shall be excluded from and for ever incapable to inherit possess or enjoy the Imperial Crown of Great Britain and the Dominions thereunto belonging or any part thereof And in every such case the Crown and Government shall from time to time descend to and be enjoyed by such person being a Protestant as should have inherited and enjoyed the same in case such Papists or person marrying a Papist was naturally dead according to the provision for the Descent of the Crown of England made by another Act of Parliament in England in the first year of the Reign of their late Majesties King William and Queen Mary entituled An Act declaring the Rights and Liberties of the Subject and settling the Succession of the Crown.

III. That the United Kingdom of Great Britain be Represented by one and the same Parliament to be stiled the Parliament of Great Britain.

VI. That all parts of the United Kingdom for ever from and after the Union shall have the same Allowances Encouragements and Drawbacks and be under the same Prohibitions Restrictions and Regulations of Trade and lyable to the same Customs and Duties on Import and Export And that the Allowances Encouragements and Drawbacks Prohibitions Restrictions and Regulations of Trade and the Customs and Duties on Import and Export settled in England when the Union commences shall from and after the Union take place throughout the whole United Kingdom [. . .].

XVIII. That the Laws concerning Regulation of Trade, Customs and such Excises to which Scotland is by virtue of this Treaty to be lyable be the same in Scotland from and after the Union as in England and that all other Lawes in use within the Kingdom of Scotland do after the Union and notwithstanding thereof remain in the same force as before (except such as are contrary to or inconsistent with this Treaty) but alterable by the Parliament of Great Britain With this difference betwixt the Laws concerning publick Right, Policy and Civil Government and those which concern private Right That the Laws which concern publick Right Policy and Civil Government may be made the same throughout the whole United Kingdom but that no alteration be made in Laws which concern private Right except for evident utility of the subjects within Scotland.

XIX. That the Court of Session or Colledge of Justice do after the Union and notwithstanding thereof remain in all time coming within Scotland as it is now constituted by the Laws of that Kingdom and with the same Authority and Priviledges as before the Union subject nevertherless to such Regulations for the better Administration of Justice as shall be made by the Parliament of Great Britain And that hereafter none shall be named by Her Majesty or Her Royal Successors to be Ordinary Lords of Session but such who have served in the Colledge of Justice as Advocats or Principal Clerks of Session for the space of five years or as Writers to the Signet for the space of ten years With this provision That no Writer to the Signet be capable to be admitted a Lord of the Session unless he undergo a private and publick Tryal on the Civil Law before the Faculty of Advocats and be found by them qualified for the said Office two years before he be named to be a Lord of the Session yet so as the Qualifications made or to be made for capacitating persons to be named Ordinary Lords of Session may be altered by the Parliament of Great Britain And that the Court of Justiciary do also after the Union and notwithstanding thereof remain in all time coming within Scotland as it is now constituted by the Laws of that Kindom and with the same Authority and Priviledges as before the Union subject nevertherless to such Regulations as shall be made by the Parliament of Great Britain and without prejudice of other Rights of Justiciary [. . .] And that the Heritable Rights of Admiralty and Vice-Admiralties in Scotland be reserved to the respective Proprietors as Rights of Property subject nevertherless as to the manner of Exercising such Heritable Rights to such Regulations and Alterations as shall be thought proper to be made by the Parliament of Great Britain And that all other Courts now in being within the Kingdom of Scotland do remain but subject to Alterations by the Parliament of Great Britain And that all Inferior Courts within the said Limits do remain subordinate as they are now to the Supream Courts of Justice within the same in all time coming And that no Causes in Scotland be cognoscible by the Courts of Chancery, Queens-Bench, Common-Pleas or any other Court in Westminster-hall And that the said Courts or any other of the like nature after the Unions shall have no power to Cognosce Review or Alter the Acts or Sentences of the Judicatures within Scotland or stop the Execution of the same [. . .].

XXV. That all Laws and Statutes in either Kingdom so far as they are contrary to or inconsistent with the Terms of these Articles or any of them shall from and after the Union cease and become void and shall be so declared to be by the respective Parliaments of the said Kingdoms.

PARLIAMENT ACT 1911
(1911, c 13)

1 Powers of House of Lords as to Money Bills

(1) If a Money Bill, having been passed by the House of Commons, and sent up to the House of Lords at least one month before the end of the session, is not passed by the House of Lords without amendment within one month after it is so

sent up to that House, the Bill shall, unless the House of Commons direct to the contrary, be presented to His Majesty and become an Act of Parliament on the Royal Assent being signified, notwithstanding that the House of Lords have not consented to the Bill.

(2) A Money Bill means a Public Bill which in the opinion of the Speaker of the House of Commons contains only provisions dealing with all or any of the following subjects, namely, the imposition, repeal, remission, alteration, or regulation of taxation; the imposition for the payment of debt or other financial purposes of charges on the Consolidated Fund, [the National Loans Fund] or on money provided by Parliament, or the variation or repeal of any such charges; supply; the appropriation, receipt, custody, issue, or audit of accounts of public money; the raising or guarantee of any loan or the repayment thereof; or subordinate matters incidental to those subjects or any of them. In this subsection the expressions 'taxation,' 'public money,' and 'loan' respectively do not include any taxation, money, or loan raised by local authorities or bodies for local purposes.

(3) There shall be endorsed on every Money Bill when it is sent up to the House of Lords and when it is presented to His Majesty for assent the certificate of the Speaker of the House of Commons signed by him that it is a Money Bill. Before giving his certificate the Speaker shall consult, if practicable, two members to be appointed from the Chairmen's Panel at the beginning of each Session by the Committee of Selection.

2 Restriction of the powers of the House of Lords as to Bills other than Money Bills

(1) If any Public Bill (other than a Money Bill or a Bill containing any provision to extend the maximum duration of Parliament beyond five years) is passed by the House of Commons [in two successive sessions] (whether of the same Parliament or not), and, having been sent up to the House of Lords at least one month before the end of the session, is rejected by the House of Lords in each of those sessions, that Bill shall, on its rejection [for the second time] by the House of Lords, unless the House of Commons direct to the contrary, be presented to His Majesty and become an Act of Parliament on the Royal Assent being signified thereto, notwithstanding that the House of Lords have not consented to the Bill: Provided that this provision shall not take effect unless [one year has elapsed] between the date of the second reading in the first of those sessions of the Bill in the House of Commons and the date on which it passes the House of Commons [in the second of these sessions].

(2) When a Bill is presented to His Majesty for assent in pursuance of the provisions of this section, there shall be endorsed on the Bill the certificate of the Speaker of the House of Commons signed by him that the provisions of this section have been duly complied with.

(3) A Bill shall be deemed to be rejected by the House of Lords if it is not passed by the House of Lords either without amendment or with such amendments only as may be agreed to by both Houses.

(4) A Bill shall be deemed to be the same Bill as a former Bill sent up to the House of Lords in the preceding session if, when it is sent up to the House of Lords, it is identical with the former Bill or contains only such alterations as are certified by the Speaker of the House of Commons to be necessary owing to the time which has elapsed since the date of the former Bill, or to represent any amendments which have been made by the House of Lords in the former Bill in the preceding session, and any amendments which are certified by the Speaker to have been made by the House of Lords [in the second session] and agreed to by the House of Commons shall be inserted in the Bill as presented for Royal Assent in pursuance of this section:

Provided that the House of Commons may, if they think fit, on the passage of such a Bill through the House [in the second session], suggest any further amendments without inserting the amendments in the Bill, and any such suggested amendments shall be considered by the House of Lords, and, if agreed to by that House, shall be treated as amendments made by the House of Lords and agreed to by the House of Commons; but the exercise of this power by the House of Commons shall not affect the operation of this section in the event of the Bill being rejected by the House of Lords.

3 Certificate of Speaker

Any certificate of the Speaker of the House of Commons given under this Act shall be conclusive for all purposes, and shall not be questioned in any court of law.

4 Enacting words

(1) In every Bill presented to His Majesty under the preceding provisions of this Act, the words of enactment shall be as follows, that is to say:—

'Be it enacted by the King's most Excellent Majesty, by and with the advice and consent of the Commons in this present Parliament assembled, in accordance with the provisions of [the Parliament Acts 1911 and 1949], and by authority of the same, as follows.'

(2) Any alteration of a Bill necessary to give effect to this section shall not be deemed to be an amendment of the Bill.

5 Provisional Order Bills excluded

In this Act the expression 'Public Bill' does not include any Bill for confirming a Provisional Order.

6 Saving for existing rights and privileges of the House of Commons

Nothing in this Act shall diminish or qualify the existing rights and privileges of the House of Commons.

[. . .]

8 Short title

This Act may be cited as the Parliament Act, 1911.

OFFICIAL SECRETS ACT 1911
(1911, c 28)

1 Penalties for spying

(1) If any person for any purpose prejudicial to the safety or interests of the State—

(a) approaches, [inspects, passes over] or is in the neighbourhood of, or enters any prohibited place within the meaning of this Act; or

(b) makes any sketch, plan, model, or note which is calculated to be or might be or is intended to be directly or indirectly useful to an enemy; or

(c) obtains, [collects, records, or publishes,] or communicates to any other person [any secret official code word, or pass word, or] any sketch, plan, model, article, or note, or other document or information which is calculated to be or might be or is intended to be directly or indirectly useful to an enemy;

he shall be guilty of felony [. . .].

(2) On a prosecution under this section, it shall not be necessary to show that the accused person was guilty of any particular act tending to show a purpose prejudicial to the safety or interests of the State, and, notwithstanding that no such act is proved against him, he may be convicted if, from the circumstances of the case, or his conduct, or his known character as proved, it appears that his purpose was a purpose prejudicial to the safety or interests of the State; and if any sketch, plan, model, article, note, document, or information relating to or used in any prohibited place within the meaning of this Act, or anything in such a place [or any secret official code word or pass word], is made, obtained, [collected, recorded, published], or communicated by any person other than a person acting under

lawful authority, it shall be deemed to have been made, obtained, [collected, recorded, published] or communicated for a purpose prejudicial to the safety or interests of the State unless the contrary is proved.

3 Definition of prohibited place

For the purposes of this Act, the expression 'prohibited place' means—

[(a) any work of defence, arsenal, naval or air force establishment or station, factory, dockyard, mine, minefield, camp, ship, or aircraft belonging to or occupied by or on behalf of His Majesty, or any telegraph, telephone, wireless or signal station, or office so belonging or occupied, and any place belonging to or occupied by or on behalf of His Majesty and used for the purpose of building, repairing, making, or storing any munitions of war, or any sketches, plans, models or documents relating thereto, or for the purpose of getting any metals, oil, or minerals of use in time of war];

(b) any place not belonging to His Majesty where any [munitions of war], or any [sketches, models, plans] or documents relating thereto, are being made, repaired, [gotten,] or stored under contract with, or with any person on behalf of, His Majesty, or otherwise on behalf of His Majesty; and

(c) any place belonging to [or used for the purposes of] His Majesty which is for the time being declared [by order of a Secretary of State] to be a prohibited place for the purposes of this section on the ground that information with respect thereto, or damage thereto, would be useful to an enemy; and

(d) any railway, road, way, or channel, or other means of communication by land or water (including any works or structures being part thereof or connected therewith), or any place used for gas, water, or electricity works or other works for purposes of a public character, or any place where any [munitions of war], or any [sketches, models, plans] or documents relating thereto, are being made, repaired, or stored otherwise than on behalf of His Majesty, which is for the time being declared [by order of a Secretary of State] to be a prohibited place for the purposes of this section, on the ground that information with respect thereto, or the destruction or obstruction thereof, or interference therewith, would be useful to an enemy.

8 Restriction on prosecution

A prosecution for an offence under this Act shall not be instituted except by or with the consent of the Attorney-General [. . .]

10 Extent of Act and place of trial of offence

(1) This Act shall apply to all acts which are offences under this Act when committed in any part of His Majesty's dominions, or when committed by British officers or subjects elsewhere.

(2) An offence under this Act, if alleged to have been committed out of the United Kingdom, may be inquired of, heard, and determined, in any competent British court in the place where the offence was committed, or [. . .] in England [. . .].

(3) An offence under this Act shall not be tried [. . .] by the sheriff court in Scotland, nor by any court out of the United Kingdom which has not jurisdiction to try crimes which involve the greatest punishment allowed by law.

[. . .]

STATUTE OF WESTMINSTER 1931
(1931, c 4)

WHEREAS the delegates of His Majesty's Governments in the United Kingdom, the Dominion of Canada, the Commonwealth of Australia, the Dominion of New Zealand, the Union of South Africa, the Irish Free State and Newfoundland, at Imperial Conferences holden at Westminster in the years of our Lord nineteen hundred and twenty-six and nineteen hundred and thirty did concur in making the declarations and resolutions set forth in the Reports of the said Conferences:

And whereas it is meet and proper to set out by way of preamble to this Act that, inasmuch as the Crown is the symbol of the free association of the members of the British Commonwealth of Nations, and as they are united by a common allegiance to the Crown, it would be in accord with the established constitutional position of all the members of the Commonwealth in relation to one another that any alteration in the law touching the Succession to the Throne or the Royal Style and Titles shall hereafter require the assent as well of the Parliaments of all the Dominions as of the Parliament of the United Kingdom:

And whereas it is in accord with the established constitutional position that no law hereafter made by the Parliament of the United Kingdom shall extend to any of the said Dominions as part of the law of that Dominion otherwise than at the request and with the consent of that Dominion:

And whereas it is necessary for the ratifying, confirming and establishing of certain of the said declarations and resolutions of the said Conferences that a law be made and enacted in due form by authority of the Parliament of the United Kingdom:

And whereas the Dominion of Canada, the Commonwealth of Australia, the Dominion of New Zealand, the Union of South Africa, the Irish Free State and Newfoundland have severally requested and consented to the submission of a measure to the Parliament of the United Kingdom for making such provision with regard to the matters aforesaid as is hereafter in this Act contained:

1 Meaning of 'Dominion' in this Act

In this Act the expression 'Dominion' means any of the following Dominions, that is to say, the Dominion of Canada, the Commonwealth of Australia, the Dominion of New Zealand, [. . .] the Irish Free State and Newfoundland.

2 Validity of laws made by Parliament of a Dominion

(1) The Colonial Laws Validity Act, 1865, shall not apply to any law made after the commencement of this Act by the Parliament of a Dominion.

(2) No law and no provision of any law made after the commencement of this Act by the Parliament of a Dominion shall be void or inoperative on the ground that it is repugnant to the law of England, or to the provisions of any existing or future Act of Parliament of the United Kingdom, or to any order, rule or regulation made under any such Act, and the powers of the Parliament of a Dominion shall include the power to repeal or amend any such Act, order, rule or regulation in so far as the same is part of the law of the Dominion.

3 Power of Parliament of Dominion to legislate extra-territorially

It is hereby declared and enacted that the Parliament of a Dominion has full power to make laws having extra-territorial operation.

4 Parliament of United Kingdom not to legislate for Dominion except by consent

No Act of Parliament of the United Kingdom passed after the commencement of this Act shall extend, or be deemed to extend, to a Dominion as part of the law of that Dominion, unless it is expressly declared in that Act that that Dominion has requested, and consented to, the enactment thereof.

PUBLIC ORDER ACT 1936
(1936, c 6)

1 Prohibition of uniforms in connection with political objects

(1) Subject as hereinafter provided, any person who in any public place or at any public meeting wears uniform signifying his association with any political

organisation or with the promotion of any political object shall be guilty of an offence:

Provided that, if the chief officer of police is satisfied that the wearing of any such uniform as aforesaid on any ceremonial, anniversary, or other special occasion will not be likely to involve risk of public disorder, he may, with the consent of a Secretary of State, by order permit the wearing of such uniform on that occasion either absolutely or subject to such conditions as may be specified in the order.

(2) Where any person is charged before any court with an offence under this section, no further proceedings in respect thereof shall be taken against him without the consent of the Attorney-General [except such as are authorised by section 6 of the Prosecution of Offences Act 1979] so, however, that if that person is remanded in custody he shall, after the expiration of a period of eight days from the date on which he was so remanded, be entitled to be [released on bail] without sureties unless within that period the Attorney-General has consented to such further proceedings as aforesaid.

2 Prohibition of quasi-military organisations

(1) If the members or adherents of any association of persons, whether incorporated or not, are—

(a) organised or trained or equipped for the purpose of enabling them to be employed in usurping the functions of the police or of the armed forces of the Crown; or

(b) organised and trained or organised and equipped either for the purpose of enabling them to be employed for the use or display of physical force in promoting any political object, or in such manner as to arouse reasonable apprehension that they are organised and either trained or equipped for that purpose;

then any person who takes part in the control or management of the association, or in so organising or training as aforesaid any members or adherents thereof, shall be guilty of an offence under this section:

Provided that in any proceedings against a person charged with the offence of taking part in the control or management of such an association as aforesaid it shall be a defence to that charge to prove that he neither consented to nor connived at the organisation, training, or equipment of members or adherents of the association in contravention of the provisions of this section.

(2) No prosecution shall be instituted under this section without the consent of the Attorney-General.

(3) If upon application being made by the Attorney-General it appears to the High Court that any association is an association of which members or adherents are organised, trained, or equipped in contravention of the provisions of this section, the Court may make such order as appears necessary to prevent any disposition without the leave of the Court of property held by or for the association and in accordance with rules of court may direct an inquiry and report to be made as to any such property as aforesaid and as to the affairs of the association and make such further orders as appear to the Court to be just and equitable for the application of such property in or towards the discharge of the liabilities of the association lawfully incurred before the date of the application or since that date with the approval of the Court, in or towards the repayment of moneys to persons who became subscribers or contributors to the association in good faith and without knowledge of any such contravention as aforesaid, and in or towards any costs incurred in connection with any such inquiry and report as aforesaid or in winding-up or dissolving the association, and may order that any property which is not directed by the Court to be so applied as aforesaid shall be forfeited to the Crown.

(4) In any criminal or civil proceedings under this section proof of things done or of words written, spoken or published (whether or not in the presence of any

party to the proceedings) by any person taking part in the control or management of an association or in organising, training or equipping members or adherents of an association shall be admissible as evidence of the purposes for which, or the manner in which, members or adherents of the association (whether those persons or others) were organised, or trained, or equipped.

(5) If a judge of the High Court is satisfied by information on oath that there is reasonable ground for suspecting that an offence under this section has been committed, and that evidence of the commission thereof is to be found at any premises or place specified in the information, he may, on an application made by an officer of police of a rank not lower than that of inspector, grant a search warrant authorising any such officer as aforesaid named in the warrant together with any other persons named in the warrant and any other officers of police to enter the premises or place at any time within [three months] from the date of the warrant, if necessary by force, and to search the premises or place and every person found therein, and to seize anything found on the premises or place or on any such person which the officer has reasonable ground for suspecting to be evidence of the commission of such an offence as aforesaid:

Provided that no woman shall, in pursuance of a warrant issued under this subsection, be searched except by a woman.

(6) Nothing in this section shall be construed as prohibiting the employment of a reasonable number of persons as stewards to assist in the preservation of order at any public meeting held upon private premises, or the making of arrangements for that purpose or the instruction of the persons to be so employed in their lawful duties as such stewards, or their being furnished with badges or other distinguishing signs.

7 Enforcement

(1) Any person who commits an offence under section two of this Act shall be liable on summary conviction to imprisonment for a term not exceeding six months or to a fine not exceeding one hundred pounds, or to both such imprisonment and fine, or, on conviction on indictment, to imprisonment for a term not exceeding two years or to a fine not exceeding five hundred pounds, or to both such imprisonment and fine.

(2) Any person guilty of [any offence under this Act other than an offence under section two] shall be liable on summary conviction to imprisonment for a term not exceeding three months or to a fine not exceeding [level 4 on the standard scale], or to both such imprisonment and fine.

[. . .]

8 Application to Scotland

This Act shall apply to Scotland subject to the following modifications:—

(1) Subsection (2) of section one and subsection (2) of section two of this Act shall not apply.

(2) In subsection (3) of section two the Lord Advocate shall be substituted for the Attorney-General and the Court of Session shall be substituted for the High Court.

(3) Subsection (5) of section two shall have effect as if for any reference to a judge of the High Court there were substituted a reference to the sheriff and any application for a search warrant under the said subsection shall be made by the procurator fiscal instead of such officer as is therein mentioned.

[. . .]

9 Interpretation, &c

(1) In this Act the following expressions have the meanings hereby respectively assigned to them, that is to say:—

[. . .]

'Meeting' means a meeting held for the purpose of the discussion of matters of public interest or for the purpose of the expression of views on such matters;

'Private premises' means premises to which the public have access (whether on payment or otherwise) only by permission of the owner, occupier, or lessee of the premises;

'Public meeting' includes any meeting in a public place and any meeting which the public or any section thereof are permitted to attend, whether on payment or otherwise;

['Public place' includes any highway, [or, in Scotland any road within the meaning of the Roads (Scotland) Act 1984] and any other premises or place to which at the material time the public have or are permitted to have access, whether on payment or otherwise.]

[. . .]

(3) Any order made under this Act [. . .] by a chief officer of police may be revoked or varied by a subsequent order made in like manner.

(4) The powers conferred by this Act on any chief officer of police may, in the event of a vacancy in the office or in the event of the chief officer of police being unable to act owing to illness or absence, be exercised by the person duly authorised in accordance with directions given by a Secretary of State to exercise those powers on behalf of the chief officer of police.

STATUTORY INSTRUMENTS ACT 1946
(1946, c 36)

1 Definition of 'Statutory Instrument'

(1) Where by this Act or any Act passed after the commencement of this Act power to make, confirm or approve orders, rules, regulations or other subordinate legislation is conferred on His Majesty in Council or on any Minister of the Crown then, if the power is expressed—

(a) in the case of a power conferred on His Majesty, to be exercisable by Order in Council;

(b) in the case of a power conferred on a Minister of the Crown, to be exercisable by statutory instrument,

any document by which that power is exercised shall be known as a 'statutory instrument' and the provisions of this Act shall apply thereto accordingly.

[(1A) Where by any Act power to make, confirm or approve orders, rules, regulations or other subordinate legislation is conferred on the Welsh Ministers and the power is expressed to be exercisable by statutory instrument, any document by which that power is exercised shall be known as a 'statutory instrument' and the provisions of this Act shall apply to it accordingly.]

(2) Where by any Act passed before the commencement of this Act power to make statutory rules within the meaning of the Rules Publication Act 1893, was conferred on any rule-making authority within the meaning of that Act, any document by which that power is exercised after the commencement of this Act shall, save as is otherwise provided by regulations made under this Act, be known as a 'statutory instrument' and the provisions of this Act shall apply thereto accordingly.

2 Numbering, printing, publication and citation

(1) Immediately after the making of any statutory instrument, it shall be sent to the King's printer of Acts of Parliament and numbered in accordance with regulations made under this Act, and except in such cases as may be provided by any Act passed after the commencement of this Act or prescribed by regulations made under this Act, copies thereof shall as soon as possible be printed and sold by [or under the authority of] the King's printer of Acts of Parliament.

(2) Any statutory instrument may, without prejudice to any other mode of

citation, be cited by the number given to it in accordance with the provisions of this section, and the calendar year.

3 Supplementary provisions as to publication

(1) Regulations made for the purposes of this Act shall make provision for the publication by His Majesty's Stationery Office of lists showing the date upon which every statutory instrument printed and sold by [or under the authority of] the King's printer of Acts of Parliament was first issued by [or under the authority of] that office; and in any legal proceedings a copy of any list so published [. . .] shall be received in evidence as a true copy, and an entry therein shall be conclusive evidence of the date on which any statutory instrument was first issued by [or under the authority of] His Majesty's Stationery Office.

(2) In any proceedings against any person for an offence consisting of a contravention of any such statutory instrument, it shall be a defence to prove that the instrument had not been issued by [or under the authority of] His Majesty's Stationery Office at the date of the alleged contravention unless it is proved that at that date reasonable steps had been taken for the purpose of bringing the purport of the instrument to the notice of the public, or of persons likely to be affected by it, or of the person charged.

(3) Save as therein otherwise expressly provided, nothing in this section shall affect any enactment or rule of law relating to the time at which any statutory instrument comes into operation.

4 Statutory instruments which are required to be laid before Parliament

(1) Where by this Act or any Act passed after the commencement of this Act any statutory instrument is required to be laid before Parliament after being made, a copy of the instrument shall be laid before each House of Parliament and, subject as hereinafter provided, shall be so laid before the instrument comes into operation:

Provided that if it is essential that any such instrument should come into operation before copies thereof can be so laid as aforesaid, the instrument may be made so as to come into operation before it has been so laid; and where any statutory instrument comes into operation before it is laid before Parliament, notification shall forthwith be sent [to the Speaker of the House of Commons and the Speaker of the House of Lords] drawing attention to the fact that copies of the instrument have yet to be laid before Parliament and explaining why such copies were not so laid before the instrument came into operation.

(2) Every copy of any such statutory instrument sold by [or under the authority of] the King's printer of Acts of Parliament shall bear on the face thereof:

(a) a statement showing the date on which the statutory instrument came or will come into operation; and

(b) either a statement showing the date on which copies thereof were laid before Parliament or a statement that such copies are to be laid before Parliament.

(3) Where any Act passed before the date of the commencement of this Act contains provisions requiring that any Order in Council or other document made in exercise of any power conferred by that or any other Act be laid before Parliament after being made, any statutory instrument made in exercise of that power shall by virtue of this Act be laid before Parliament and the foregoing provisions of this section shall apply thereto accordingly in substitution for any such provisions as aforesaid contained in the Act passed before the said date.

5 Statutory instruments which are subject to annulment by resolution of either House of Parliament

(1) Where by this Act or any Act passed after the commencement of this Act, it is provided that any statutory instrument shall be subject to annulment in pursuance of resolution of either House of Parliament, the instrument shall be laid before Parliament after being made and the provisions of the last foregoing section

shall apply thereto accordingly, and if either House within the period of forty days beginning with the day on which a copy thereof is laid before it, resolves that an Address be presented to His Majesty praying that the instrument be annulled, no further proceedings shall be taken thereunder after the date of the resolution, and His Majesty may by Order in Council revoke the instrument, so, however, that any such resolution and revocation shall be without prejudice to the validity of anything previously done under the instrument or to the making of a new statutory instrument.

(2) Where any Act passed before the date of the commencement of this Act contains provisions requiring that any Order in Council or other document made in exercise of any power conferred by that or any other Act shall be laid before Parliament after being made and shall cease to be in force or may be annulled, as the case may be, if within a specified period either House presents an address to His Majesty or passes a resolution to that effect, then, subject to the provisions of any Order in Council made under this Act, any statutory instrument made in exercise of the said power shall by virtue of this Act be subject to annulment in pursuance of a resolution of either House of Parliament and the provisions of the last foregoing subsection shall apply thereto accordingly in substitution for any such provisions as aforesaid contained in the Act passed before the said date.

6 Statutory instruments of which drafts are to be laid before Parliament

(1) Where by this Act or any Act passed after the commencement of this Act it is provided that a draft of any statutory instrument shall be laid before Parliament, but the Act does not prohibit the making of the instrument without the approval of Parliament, then, in the case of an Order in Council the draft shall not be submitted to His Majesty in Council, and in any other case the statutory instrument shall not be made, until after the expiration of a period of forty days beginning with the day on which a copy of the draft is laid before each House of Parliament, or, if such copies are laid on different days, with the later of the two days, and if within that period either House resolves that the draft be not submitted to His Majesty or that the statutory instrument be not made, as the case may be, no further proceedings shall be taken thereon, but without prejudice to the laying before Parliament of a new draft.

(2) Where any Act passed before the date of the commencement of this Act contains provisions requiring that a draft of any Order in Council or other document to be made in exercise of any power conferred by that or any other Act shall be laid before Parliament before being submitted to His Majesty, or before being made, as the case may be, and that it shall not be so submitted or made if within a specified period either House presents an address to His Majesty or passes a resolution to that effect, then, subject to the provisions of any Order in Council made under this Act, a draft of any statutory instrument made in exercise of the said power shall by virtue of this Act be laid before Parliament and the provisions of the last foregoing subsection shall apply thereto accordingly in substitution for any such provisions as aforesaid contained in the Act passed before the said date.

CROWN PROCEEDINGS ACT 1947
(1947, c 44)

1 Right to sue the Crown

Where any person has a claim against the Crown after the commencement of this Act, and, if this Act had not been passed, the claim might have been enforced, subject to the grant of His Majesty's fiat, by petition of right, or might have been enforced by a proceeding provided by any statutory provision repealed by this Act, then, subject to the provisions of this Act, the claim may be enforced as of right, and without the fiat of His Majesty, by proceedings taken against the Crown for that purpose in accordance with the provisions of this Act.

2 Liability of the Crown in tort

(1) Subject to the provisions of this Act, the Crown shall be subject to all those liabilities in tort to which, if it were a private person of full age and capacity, it would be subject:—

(a) in respect of torts committed by its servants or agents;

(b) in respect of any breach of those duties which a person owes to his servants or agents at common law by reason of being their employer; and

(c) in respect of any breach of the duties attaching at common law to the ownership, occupation, possession or control of property:

Provided that no proceedings shall lie against the Crown by virtue of paragraph (a) of this subsection in respect of any act or omission of a servant or agent of the Crown unless the act or omission would apart from the provisions of this Act have given rise to a cause of action in tort against that servant or agent or his estate.

(2) Where the Crown is bound by a statutory duty which is binding also upon persons other than the Crown and its officers, then, subject to the provisions of this Act, the Crown shall, in respect of a failure to comply with that duty, be subject to all those liabilities in tort (if any) to which it would be so subject if it were a private person of full age and capacity.

(3) Where any functions are conferred or imposed upon an officer of the Crown as such either by any rule of the common law or by statute, and that officer commits a tort while performing or purporting to perform those functions, the liabilities of the Crown in respect of the tort shall be such as they would have been if those functions had been conferred or imposed solely by virtue of instructions lawfully given by the Crown.

(4) Any enactment which negatives or limits the amount of the liability of any Government department [, part of the Scottish Administration] or officer of the Crown in respect of any tort committed by that department [, part] or officer shall, in the case of proceedings against the Crown under this section in respect of a tort committed by that department [, part] or officer, apply in relation to the Crown as it would have applied in relation to that department [, part] or officer if the proceedings against the Crown had been proceedings against that department [, part] or officer.

(5) No proceedings shall lie against the Crown by virtue of this section in respect of anything done or omitted to be done by any person while discharging or purporting to discharge any responsibilities of a judicial nature vested in him, or any responsibilities which he has in connection with the execution of judicial process.

(6) No proceedings shall lie against the Crown by virtue of this section in respect of any act, neglect or default of any officer of the Crown, unless that officer has been directly or indirectly appointed by the Crown and was at the material time paid in respect of his duties as an officer of the Crown wholly out of the Consolidated Fund of the United Kingdom, moneys provided by Parliament, [the Scottish Consolidated Fund] [. . .] or any other Fund certified by the Treasury or the purposes of this subsection or was at the material time holding an office in respect of which the Treasury certify that the holder thereof would normally be so paid.

17 Parties to proceedings

(1) The [Minister for the Civil Service] shall publish a list specifying the several Government departments which are authorised departments for the purposes of this Act, and the name and address for service of the person who is, or is acting for the purposes of this Act as, the solicitor for each such department, and may from time to time amend or vary the said list.

Any document purporting to be a copy of a list published under this section and purporting to be printed under the superintendence or the authority of His Majesty's Stationery Office shall in any legal proceedings be received as evidence for the purpose of establishing what departments are authorised departments for the purposes of this Act, and what person is, or is acting for the purposes of this Act as, the solicitor for any such department.

(2) Civil proceedings by the Crown may be instituted either by an authorised Government department in its own name, whether that department was or was not at the commencement of this Act authorised to sue, or by the Attorney General.

(3) Civil proceedings against the Crown shall be instituted against the appropriate authorised Government department, or, if none of the authorised Government departments is appropriate or the person instituting the proceedings has any reasonable doubt whether any and if so which of those departments is appropriate, against the Attorney General.

(4) Where any civil proceedings against the Crown are instituted against the Attorney General, an application may at any stage of the proceedings be made to the court by or on behalf of the Attorney General to have such of the authorised Government departments as may be specified in the application substituted for him as defendant to the proceedings; and where any such proceedings are brought against an authorised Government department, an application may at any stage of the proceedings be made to the court on behalf of that department to have the Attorney General or such of the authorised Government departments as may be specified in the application substituted for the applicant as the defendant to the proceedings.

Upon any such application the court may if it thinks fit make an order granting the application on such terms as the court thinks just; and on such an order being made the proceedings shall continue as if they had been commenced against the department specified in that behalf in the order, or, as the case may require, against the Attorney General.

(5) No proceedings instituted in accordance with this Part of this Act by or against the Attorney General or an authorised Government department shall abate or be affected by any change in the person holding the office of Attorney General or in the person or body of persons constituting the department.

21 Nature of relief

(1) In any civil proceedings by or against the Crown the court shall, subject to the provisions of this Act, have power to make all such orders as it has power to make in proceedings between subjects, and otherwise to give such appropriate relief as the case may require:

Provided that:—

(a) where in any proceedings against the Crown any such relief is sought as might in proceedings between subjects be granted by way of injunction or specific performance, the court shall not grant an injunction or make an order for specific performance, but may in lieu thereof make an order declaratory of the rights of the parties; and

(b) in any proceedings against the Crown for the recovery of land or other property the court shall not make an order for the recovery of the land or the delivery of the property, but may in lieu thereof make an order declaring that the plaintiff is entitled as against the Crown to the land or property, or to the possession thereof.

(2) The court shall not in any civil proceedings grant any injunction or make any order against an officer of the Crown if the effect of granting the injunction or making the order would be to give any relief against the Crown which could not have been obtained in proceedings against the Crown.

23 Scope of Part II

(1) Subject to the provisions of this section, any reference in this Part of this

Act to civil proceedings by the Crown shall be construed as a reference to the following proceedings only:—

(a) proceedings for the enforcement or vindication of any right or the obtaining of any relief which, if this Act had not been passed, might have been enforced or vindicated or obtained by any such proceedings as are mentioned in paragraph 1 of the First Schedule to this Act;

[. . .]

40 Savings

(1) Nothing in this Act shall apply to proceedings by or against, or authorise proceedings in tort to be brought against, His Majesty in His private capacity.

[. . .]

43 Interpretation for purposes of application to Scotland

In the application of this Act to Scotland:—

(a) for any reference to the High Court (except a reference to that Court as a prize court) there shall be substituted a reference to the Court of Session; for any reference to the county court there shall be substituted a reference to the sheriff court; the expression 'plaintiff' means pursuer; the expression 'defendant' means defender; the expression 'county court rules' means Act of Sederunt applying to the sheriff court; and the expression 'injunction' means interdict;

(b) the expression 'tort' means any wrongful or negligent act or omission giving rise to liability in reparation, and any reference to liability or right or action or proceedings in tort shall be construed accordingly; and for any reference to Part II of the Law Reform (Married Women and Tortfeasors) Act, 1935, there shall be substituted a reference to section three of the Law Reform (Miscellaneous Provisions) (Scotland) Act, 1940.

[. . .]

47 Recovery of documents in possession of Crown

Subject to and in accordance with Acts of Sederunt applying to the Court of Session and the sheriff court, commission and diligence for the recovery of documents in the possession of the Crown may be granted in any action whether or not the Crown is a party thereto, in like manner in all respects as if the documents were in the possession of a subject:

Provided that—

(i) this subsection shall be without prejudice to any rule of law which authorises or requires the withholding of any document on the ground that its disclosure would be injurious to the public interest; and

(ii) the existence of a document shall not be disclosed if, in the opinion of a Minister of the Crown, it would be injurious to the public interest to disclose the existence thereof.

PARLIAMENT ACT 1949
(1949, c 103)

2 Short title, construction and citation

(1) This Act may be cited as the Parliament Act 1949.

(2) This Act and the Parliament Act 1911, shall be construed as one and may be cited together as the Parliament Acts 1911 and 1949 [. . .].

LIFE PEERAGES ACT 1958
(1958, c 21)

1 Power to create life peerages carrying right to sit in House of Lords

(1) [. . .] Her Majesty shall have power by letters patent to confer on any

person a peerage for life having the incidents specified in subsection (2) of this section.

(2) A peerage conferred under this section shall, during the life of the person on whom it is conferred, entitle him—

(a) to rank as a baron under such style as may be appointed by the letters patent; and

(b) subject to subsection (4) of this section, to receive writs of summons to attend the House of Lords and sit and vote therein accordingly,

and shall expire on his death.

(3) A life peerage may be conferred under this section on a woman.

(4) Nothing in this section shall enable any person to receive a writ of summons to attend the House of Lords, or to sit and vote in that House, at any time when disqualified therefor by law.

MISUSE OF DRUGS ACT 1971
(1971, c 38)

23 Powers to search and obtain evidence

. . .

(2) If a constable has reasonable grounds to suspect that any person is in possession of a controlled drug in contravention of this Act or of any regulations [or orders] made thereunder, the constable may—

(a) search that person, and detain him for the purpose of searching him;

(b) search any vehicle or vessel in which the constable suspects that the drug may be found, and for that purpose require the person in control of the vehicle or vessel to stop it;

(c) seize and detain, for the purposes of proceedings under this Act, anything found in the course of the search which appears to the constable to be evidence of an offence under this Act.

In this subsection 'vessel' includes a hovercraft within the meaning of the Hovercraft Act 1968; and nothing in this subsection shall prejudice any power of search or any power to seize or detain property which is exercisable by a constable apart from this subsection.

(3) If a justice of the peace (or in Scotland a justice of the peace, a magistrate or a sheriff) is satisfied by information on oath that there is reasonable ground for suspecting—

(a) that any controlled drugs are, in contravention of this Act or of any regulations [or orders] made thereunder, in the possession of a person on any premises; or

(b) that a document directly or indirectly relating to, or connected with, a transaction or dealing which was, or an intended transaction or dealing which would if carried out be, an offence under this Act, or in the case of a transaction or dealing carried out or intended to be carried out in a place outside the United Kingdom, an offence against the provisions of a corresponding law in force in that place, is in the possession of a person on any premises, he may grant a warrant authorising any constable [. . .] at any time or times within one month from the date of the warrant, to enter, if need be by force, the premises named in the warrant, and to search the premises and any persons found therein and, if there is reasonable ground for suspecting that an offence under this Act has been committed in relation to any controlled drugs found on the premises or in the possession of any such persons, or that a document so found is such a document as is mentioned in paragraph (b) above, to seize and detain those drugs or that document, as the case may be.

. . .

(4) A person commits an offence if he—

(a) intentionally obstructs a person in the exercise of his powers under this section; or

(b) conceals from a person acting in the exercise of his powers under subsection (1) above any such books, documents, stocks or drugs as are mentioned in that subsection; or

(c) without reasonable excuse (proof of which shall lie on him) fails to produce any such books or documents as are so mentioned where their production is demanded by a person in the exercise of his power under that subsection.

[. . .]

28 Proof of lack of knowledge etc. to be a defence in proceedings for certain offences

. . .

(3) Where in any proceedings for an offence to which this section applies it is necessary, if the accused is to be convicted of the offence charged, for the prosecution to prove that some substance or product involved in the alleged offence was the controlled drug which the prosecution alleges it to have been, and it is proved that the substance or product in question was that controlled drug, the accused—

(a) shall not be acquitted of the offence charged by reason only of proving that he neither knew nor suspected nor had reason to suspect that the substance or product in question was the particular controlled drug alleged; but

(b) shall be acquitted thereof—

(i) if he proves that he neither believed nor suspected nor had reason to suspect that the substance or product in question was a controlled drug; or

(ii) if he proves that he believed the substance or product in question to be a controlled drug, or a controlled drug of a description, such that, if it had in fact been that controlled drug or a controlled drug of that description, he would not at the material time have been committing any offence to which this section applies.

EUROPEAN COMMUNITIES ACT 1972
(1972, c 68)

NOTE: This Act was repealed on 31 January 2020 subject to savings for implementation period: European Union (Withdrawal) Act 2018, ss 1A, 1B.

1 Short title and interpretation

(1) This Act may be cited as the European Communities Act 1972.

(2) In this Act [. . .]—

['the EU' means the European Union, being the Union established by the Treaty on European Union signed at Maastricht on 7th February 1992 (as amended by any later Treaty);]

'the Communities' means the European Economic Community, the European Coal and Steel Community and the European Atomic Energy Community;

'the Treaties' or '[*the EU Treaties*]' means, subject to subsection (3) below, the pre-accession treaties, that is to say, those described in Part I of Schedule 1 to this Act, taken with—

(a) the treaty relating to the accession of the United Kingdom to the European Economic Community and to the European Atomic Energy Community, signed at Brussels on the 22nd January 1972; and

(b) the decision, of the same date, of the Council of the European Communities relating to the accession of the United Kingdom to the European Coal and Steel Community; and

[(c) the treaty relating to the accession of the Hellenic Republic to the European Economic Community and to the European Atomic Energy Community, signed at Athens on 28th May 1979; and

(d) the decision, of 24th May 1979, of the Council relating to the accession of the Hellenic Republic to the European Coal and Steel Community;] and

(e) [the decisions of the Council of 7th May 1985, 24th June 1988, 31st October 1994, 29th September 2000 and 7th June 2007 on the Communities' system of own resources;] and

(f) [. . .]

(g) the treaty relating to the accession of the Kingdom of Spain and the Portuguese Republic to the European Economic Community and to the European Atomic Energy Community, signed at Lisbon and Madrid on 12th June 1985; and

(h) the decision, of 11th June 1985, of the Council relating to the accession of the Kingdom of Spain and the Portuguese Republic to the European Coal and Steel Community; and

[(j) the following provisions of the Single European Act signed at Luxembourg and The Hague on 17th and 28th February 1986, namely Title II (amendment of the treaties establishing the Communities) and, so far as they relate to any of the Communities or any Community institution, the preamble and Titles I (common provisions) and IV (general and final provisions);] [and

(k) Titles II, III and IV of the Treaty on European Union signed at Maastricht on 7th February 1992, together with the other provisions of the Treaty so far as they relate to those Titles, and the Protocols adopted at Maastricht on that date and annexed to the Treaty establishing the European Community with the exception of the Protocol on Social Policy on page 117 of Cm 1934] [and

(l) the decision, of 1st February 1993, of the Council amending the Act concerning the election of the representatives of the European Parliament by direct universal suffrage annexed to Council Decision 76/787/ECSC, EEC, Euratom of 20th September 1976] [and

(m) the Agreement on the European Economic Area signed at Oporto on 2nd May 1992 together with the Protocol adjusting that Agreement signed at Brussels on 17th March 1993] [and

(n) the treaty concerning the accession of the Kingdom of Norway, the Republic of Austria, the Republic of Finland and the Kingdom of Sweden to the European Union, signed at Corfu on 24th June 1994;] [and

(o) the following provisions of the Treaty signed at Amsterdam on 2nd October 1997 amending the Treaty on European Union, the Treaties establishing the European Communities and certain related Acts—

(i) Articles 2 to 9,

(ii) Article 12, and

(iii) the other provisions of the Treaty so far as they relate to those Articles, and the Protocols adopted on that occasion other than the Protocol on Article J.7 of the Treaty on European Union;] [and

(p) the following provisions of the Treaty signed at Nice on 26th February 2001 amending the Treaty on European Union, the Treaties establishing the European Communities and certain related Acts—

(i) Articles 2 to 10, and

(ii) the other provisions of the Treaty so far as they relate to those Articles, and the Protocols adopted on that occasion;] [

(q) the treaty concerning the accession of the Czech Republic, the Republic of Estonia, the Republic of Cyprus, the Republic of Latvia, the Republic of Lithuania, the Republic of Hungary, the Republic of Malta, the Republic of Poland, the Republic of Slovenia and the Slovak Republic to the European Union, signed at Athens on 16th April 2003;] [and

(r) the treaty concerning the accession of the republic of Bulgaria and Romania to the European Union, signed at Luxembourg on 25th April 2005;] [and

(s) the Treaty of Lisbon Amending the Treaty on European Union and the Treaty Establishing the European Community signed at Lisbon on 13th December 2007 (together with its Annex and protocols), excluding any provision that relates to, or in so far as it relates to or could be applied in relation to, the Common Foreign and Security Policy;] [and

(t) the Protocol amending the Protocol (No 36) on transitional provisions annexed to the Treaty on European Union, to the Treaty on the Functioning of the European Union and to the Treaty establishing the European Atomic Energy Community, signed at Brussels on 23 June 2010,] [and

(u) the Treaty concerning the accession of the Republic of Croatia to the European Union, signed at Brussels on 9 December 2011, and

(v) the Protocol on the concerns of the Irish people on the Treaty of Lisbon, adopted at Brussels on 16 May 2012.]

and [any other treaty entered into by the EU (except in so far as it relates to, or could be applied in relation to, the Common Foreign and Security Policy], with or without any of the member States, or entered into, as a treaty ancillary to any of the Treaties by the United Kingdom;

and any expression defined in Schedule 1 to this Act has the meaning there given to it.

(3) If Her Majesty by Order in Council declares that a treaty specified in the Order is to be regarded as one of [the EU Treaties] as herein defined, the Order shall be conclusive that it is to be so regarded; but a treaty entered into by the United Kingdom after the 22nd January 1972, other than a pre-accession treaty to which the United Kingdom accedes on terms settled on or before that date, shall not be so regarded unless it is so specified, nor be so specified unless a draft of the Order in Council has been approved by resolution of each House of Parliament.

(4) For purposes of subsections (2) and (3) above, 'treaty' includes any international agreement, and any protocol or annex to a treaty or international agreement.

2 General implementation of Treaties*

(1) All such rights, powers, liabilities, obligations and restrictions from time to time created or arising by or under the Treaties, and all such remedies and procedures from time to time provided for by or under the Treaties, as in accordance with the Treaties are without further enactment to be given legal effect or used in the United Kingdom shall be recognised and available in law, and be enforced, allowed and followed accordingly; and the expression ['enforceable EU right'] and similar expressions shall be read as referring to one to which this subsection applies.

(2) Subject to Schedule 2 to this Act, at any time after its passing Her Majesty may by Order in Council, and any designated Minister or department may [by orders, rules, regulations or scheme], make provision—

(a) for the purpose of implementing any [EU obligation] of the United Kingdom, or enabling any such obligation to be implemented, or of enabling any rights enjoyed or to be enjoyed by the United Kingdom under or by virtue of the Treaties to be exercised; or

(b) for the purpose of dealing with matters arising out of or related to any such obligation or rights or the coming into force, or the operation from time to time, of subsection (1) above;

and in the exercise of any statutory power or duty, including any power to give directions or to legislate by means of orders, rules, regulations or other subordinate instrument, the person entrusted with the power or duty may have regard to the [objects of the EU] and to any such obligation or rights as aforesaid.

In this subsection 'designated Minister or department' means such Minister of the Crown or government department as may from time to time be designated by Order in Council in relation to any matter or for any purpose, but subject to such restrictions or conditions (if any) as may be specified by the Order in Council.

(3) There shall be charged on and issued out of the Consolidated Fund or, if so

*Section 2 is modified by the Scotland Act 1998, Sch 8, para 15.

determined by the Treasury, the National Loans Fund the amounts required to meet any [EU obligation] to make payments to [the EU or a member State], or any [EU obligation] in respect of contributions to the capital or reserves of the European Investment Bank or in respect of loans to the Bank, or to redeem any notes or obligations issued or created in respect of any such [EU obligation]; and, except as otherwise provided by or under any enactment,—

(a) any other expenses incurred under or by virtue of the Treaties or this Act by any Minister of the Crown or government department may be paid out of moneys provided by Parliament; and

(b) any sums received under or by virtue of the Treaties or this Act by any Minister of the Crown or government department, save for such sums as may be required for disbursements permitted by any other enactment, shall be paid into the Consolidated Fund or, if so determined by the Treasury, the National Loans Fund.

(4) The provision that may be made under subsection (2) above includes, subject to Schedule 2 to this Act, any such provision (of any such extent) as might be made by Act of Parliament, and any enactment passed or to be passed, other than one contained in this Part of this Act, shall be construed and have effect subject to the foregoing provisions of this section; but, except as may be provided by any Act passed after this Act, Schedule 2 shall have effect in connection with the powers conferred by this and the following sections of this Act to make Orders in Council [or orders, rules, regulations or schemes].

[. . .]

3 Decisions on, and proof of, Treaties and [EU instruments] etc

(1) For the purposes of all legal proceedings any question as to the meaning or effect of any of the Treaties, or as to the validity, meaning or effect of any [EU instrument], shall be treated as a question of law (and, if not referred to the European Court, be for determination as such in accordance with the principles laid down by and any relevant [decision of [the European Court])].

(2) Judicial notice shall be taken of the Treaties, [of the Official Journal of the European Union] and of any decision of, or expression of opinion by, [the European Court] on any such question as aforesaid; and the Official Journal shall be admissible as evidence of any instrument or other act thereby communicated of [the EU] or of any [EU institution].

(3) Evidence of any instrument issued by [an EU institution], including any judgment or order of [the European Court], or of any document in the custody of [an EU institution], or any entry in or extract from such a document, may be given in any legal proceedings by production of a copy certified as a true copy by an official of that institution; and any document purporting to be such a copy shall be received in evidence without proof of the official position or handwriting of the person signing the certificate.

(4) Evidence of any [EU instrument] may also be given in any legal proceedings—

(a) by production of a copy purporting to be printed by the Queen's Printer;

(b) where the instrument is in the custody of a government department (including a department of the Government of Northern Ireland), by production of a copy certified on behalf of the department to be a true copy by an officer of the department generally or specially authorised so to do;

and any document purporting to be such a copy as is mentioned in paragraph (b) above of an instrument in the custody of a department shall be received in evidence without proof of the official position or handwriting of the person signing the certificate, or of his authority to do so, or of the document being in the custody of the department.

[. . .]

SCHEDULE 2
PROVISIONS AS TO SUBORDINATE LEGISLATION

1.—(1) The powers conferred by section 2(2) of this Act to make provision for the purposes mentioned in section 2(2)(a) and (b) shall not include power—

(a) to make any provision imposing or increasing taxation; or

(b) to make any provision taking effect from a date earlier than that of the making of the instrument containing the provision; or

(c) to confer any power to legislate by means of orders, rules, regulations or other subordinate instrument, other than rules of procedure for any court or tribunal; or

(d) to create any new criminal offence punishable with imprisonment for more than two years or punishable on summary conviction with imprisonment for more than three months or with a fine of more than [level 5 on the standard scale] (if not calculated on a daily basis) or with a fine of more than [£100 a day].

(2) Sub-paragraph (1)(c) above shall not be taken to preclude the modification of a power to legislate conferred otherwise than under section 2(2), or the extension of any such power to purposes of the like nature as those for which it was conferred; and a power to give directions as to matters of administration is not to be regarded as a power to legislate within the meaning of sub-paragraph (l)(c).

[1A.—(1) Where—

(a) subordinate legislation makes provision for a purpose mentioned in section 2(2) of this Act,

(b) the legislation contains a reference to an [EU instrument] or any provision of an [EU instrument], and

(c) it appears to the person making the legislation that it is necessary or expedient for the reference to be construed as a reference to that instrument or that provision as amended from time to time,

the subordinate legislation may make express provision to that effect.

(2) In this paragraph 'subordinate legislation' means any Order in Council, order, rules, regulations, scheme, warrant, byelaws or other instrument made after the coming into force of this paragraph under any Act, Act of the Scottish Parliament [, Measure or Act of the National Assembly for Wales] or Northern Ireland legislation passed or made before or after the coming into force of this paragraph.]

2.—(1) Subject to paragraph 3 below, where a provision contained in any section of this Act confers power to make [any orders, rules, regulations or scheme] (otherwise than by modification, or extension of an existing power), the power shall be exercisable by statutory instrument.

(2) Any statutory instrument containing an Order in Council or [any orders, rules, regulations or scheme] made in the exercise of a power so conferred, if made without a draft having been approved by resolution of each House of Parliament, shall be subject to annulment in pursuance of a resolution of either House.

[2A.—(1) This paragraph applies where, pursuant to paragraph 2(2) above, a draft of a statutory instrument containing provision made in exercise of the power conferred by section 2(2) of this Act is laid before Parliament for approval by resolution of each House of Parliament and—

(a) the instrument also contains provision made in exercise of a power conferred by any other enactment; and

(b) apart from this paragraph, any of the conditions in sub-paragraph (2) below applies in relation to the instrument so far as containing that provision.

(2) The conditions referred to in sub-paragraph (1)(b) above are that—

(a) the instrument, so far as containing the provision referred to in sub-paragraph (1)(a) above, is by virtue of any enactment subject to annulment in pursuance of a resolution of either House of Parliament;

(b) the instrument so far as containing that provision is by virtue of any enactment required to be laid before Parliament after being made and to be approved by resolution of each House of Parliament in order to come into or remain in force;

(c) in a case not falling within paragraph (a) or (b) above, the instrument so far as containing that provision is by virtue of any enactment required to be laid before Parliament after being made;

(d) the instrument or a draft of the instrument so far as containing that provision is not by virtue of any enactment required at any time to be laid before Parliament.

(3) Where this paragraph applies in relation to the draft of a statutory instrument—

(a) the instrument, so far as containing the provision referred to in sub-paragraph (1)(a) above, may not be made unless the draft is approved by a resolution of each House of Parliament;

(b) in a case where the condition in sub-paragraph (2)(a) above is satisfied, the instrument so far as containing that provision is not subject to annulment in pursuance of a resolution of either House of Parliament;

(c) in a case where the condition in sub-paragraph (2)(b) above is satisfied, the instrument is not required to be laid before Parliament after being made (and accordingly any requirement that the instrument be approved by each House of Parliament in order for it to come into or remain in force does not apply); and

(d) in a case where the condition in sub-paragraph (2)(c) above is satisfied, the instrument so far as containing that provision is not required to be laid before Parliament after being made.

(4) In this paragraph, references to an enactment are to an enactment passed or made before or after the coming into force of this paragraph.]

[2B.—(1) This paragraph applies where, pursuant to paragraph 2(2) above, a statutory instrument containing provision made in exercise of the power conferred by section 2(2) of this Act is laid before Parliament under section 5 of the Statutory Instruments Act 1946 (instruments subject to annulment) and—

(a) the instrument also contains provision made in exercise of a power conferred by any other enactment; and

(b) apart from this paragraph, either of the conditions in sub-paragraph (2) below applies in relation to the instrument so far as containing that provision.

(2) The conditions referred to in sub-paragraph (1)(b) above are that—

(a) the instrument so far as containing the provision referred to in sub-paragraph (1)(a) above is by virtue of any enactment required to be laid before Parliament after being made but—

(i) is not subject to annulment in pursuance of a resolution of either House of Parliament; and

(ii) is not by virtue of any enactment required to be approved by resolution of each House of Parliament in order to come into or remain in force;

(b) the instrument or a draft of the instrument so far as containing that provision is not by virtue of any enactment required at any time to be laid before Parliament.

(3) Where this paragraph applies in relation to a statutory instrument, the instrument, so far as containing the provision referred to in sub-paragraph (1)(a) above, is subject to annulment in pursuance of a resolution of either House of Parliament.

(4) In this paragraph, references to an enactment are to an enactment passed or made before or after the coming into force of this paragraph.]

[2C. Paragraphs 2A and 2B above apply to a Scottish statutory instrument containing provision made in the exercise of the power conferred by section 2(2) of this Act (and a draft of any such instrument) as they apply to any other statutory instrument containing such provision (or, as the case may be, any draft of such an instrument), but subject to the following modifications—

(a) references to Parliament and to each or either House of Parliament are to be read as references to the Scottish Parliament;

(b) references to an enactment include an enactment comprised in, or in an instrument made under, an Act of the Scottish Parliament; and

(c) the reference in paragraph 2B(1) to section 5 of the Statutory Instruments Act 1946 is to be read as a reference to [section 28 of the Interpretation and Legislative Reform (Scotland) Act 2010 (asp 10)].]

LOCAL GOVERNMENT (SCOTLAND) ACT 1973
(1973, c 65)

Proposals by Local Government Boundary Commission for Scotland

12 Local Government Boundary Commission for Scotland

(1) There shall be a Local Government Boundary Commission for Scotland (in this Part of this Act referred to as 'the Boundary Commission') who shall carry out the functions conferred on them by or under this Act.

(2) The provisions of Schedule 4 to this Act shall have effect with respect to the Boundary Commission.

13 Proposals for changes in local government areas

The Boundary Commission may, in consequence of a review conducted by them under this Part of this Act, make proposals to the Secretary of State for effecting changes appearing to the Commission desirable in the interests of effective and convenient local government by any of the following means or any combination of those means (including the application of any of the following paragraphs to an area constituted or altered under any of those paragraphs):

(a) the alteration of a local government area;

(b) the constitution of a new local government area;

(c) the abolition of a local government area;

(d) a change of electoral arrangements for any local government area which is either consequential on any change in local government areas proposed under this section or is a change (hereinafter in this Part of this Act referred to as a 'substantive change') which is independent of any change in local government areas so proposed.

16 Substantive changes in electoral arrangements

(1) No review shall be conducted under section 14 or 15 of this Act for the purpose of making proposals for a substantive change of electoral arrangements, but the following provisions of this section shall have effect with respect to the making of such proposals.

(2) It shall be the duty of the Boundary Commission not less than [eight] nor more than [twelve] years after the submission of the report on the [first] review of electoral arrangements for a local government area under [section 4(1) of the Local Governance (Scotland) Act 2004 (asp 9)] and thereafter, so far as is reasonably practicable, at intervals of not less than [eight] nor more than [twelve] years from the submission of the last report of the Commission under this subsection in relation to that area, to review the electoral arrangements for that area for the purpose of considering whether to make proposals to the Secretary of State for a substantive change in those arrangements and what proposals, if any, to make, and the Commission shall formulate any such proposals accordingly.

(3) Without prejudice to subsection (2) above, the Boundary Commission may at any time, whether at the request of a local authority or otherwise, review the electoral arrangements for a local government area for the purpose of considering whether to make proposals to the Secretary of State for a substantive change in

those arrangements and what proposals, if any, to make and the Commission shall formulate any such proposals accordingly.

56 Arrangements for discharge of functions by local authorities

(1) Subject to any express provision contained in this Act or any Act passed after this Act, a local authority may arrange for the discharge of any of their functions by a committee of the authority, a sub-committee, an officer of the authority or by any other local authority in Scotland.

[(2) Where by virtue of this section any function of a local authority may be discharged by any committee or sub-committee of theirs, then, unless the local authority otherwise direct—

(a) the committee may arrange for the discharge of any of those functions by a sub-committee or an officer of the authority; and

(b) the sub-committee, whether assigned the discharge of functions by the authority or by a committee, may arrange for the discharge of any such functions by an officer of the authority.]

(3) Where by virtue of this section any functions of a local authority may be discharged by another local authority, subsections (1) and (2) above shall apply in relation to those functions as they apply in relation to the functions of that other authority, except that—

(a) the foregoing provision shall have effect subject to the terms of the arrangement relating to the functions; and

(b) that other authority shall not, by virtue of this subsection, arrange for the discharge of those functions by some other local authority.

(4) Any arrangement made by a local authority or committee under this section for the discharge of any functions by a committee, sub-committee, officer or local authority shall not prevent the authority or committee by whom the arrangement is made from exercising those functions.

(5) Two or more local authorities may discharge any of their functions jointly and, where arrangements are in force for them to do so,—

(a) they may also arrange for the discharge of those functions by a joint committee of theirs or by an officer of one of them, and subsection (2) above shall apply in relation to those functions as it applies in relation to the functions of the individual authorities; and

(b) any enactment relating to those functions or the authorities by whom or the areas in respect of which they are to be discharged shall have effect subject to all necessary modifications in its application in relation to those functions and the authorities by whom and the areas in respect of which (whether in pursuance of the arrangements or otherwise) they are to be discharged.

[(6) A local authority's functions with respect to—

[. . .]

(b) setting an amount of council tax in accordance with section 93(1) of the Local Government Finance Act 1992, or setting a reduced amount of council tax under section 94 of that Act or paragraph 3 of Schedule 7 to that Act;

[. . .]

(d) borrowing money,

[(e) approval of any annual investment strategy or annual investment report required by any consent issued by the Scottish Ministers by virtue of section 40 of the Local Government in Scotland Act 2003 (asp 1),]

shall be discharged only by the authority.]

[. . .]

[(6B) The duty to carry out a review of a case imposed on an authority under section 86(2) of the Community Empowerment (Scotland) Act 2015 (reviews by local authorities of asset transfer requests) must be discharged only by the authority or a committee or sub-committee of the authority; and accordingly no such committee or sub-committee may arrange for the discharge under subsection (2) of the duty by an officer of the authority.

(6C) In subsection (6B), the reference to section 86(2) of the Community Empowerment (Scotland) Act 2015 includes a reference to that section as applied by subsection (2) of, and modified in such application by virtue of subsection (4) of, section 89 of that Act.]

(7) A local authority shall not make arrangements under this section for the discharge of any of their functions under [the Animal Health Act 1981] by any other local authority.

[(7A) A local authority is not to make arrangements under this section for the discharge of any functions conferred on it by the Public Bodies (Joint Working) (Scotland) Act 2014 by any other local authority.]

(8) Any enactment, except one mentioned in subsection (9) below, which contains any provision—

(a) which empowers or requires local authorities or any class of local authorities to establish committees (including joint committees) for any purpose or enables a Minister to make an instrument establishing committees of local authorities for any purpose, or empowering or requiring a local authority or any class of local authorities to establish committees for any purpose; or

(b) which empowers or requires local authorities or any class of local authorities to arrange or to join with other authorities in arranging for the exercise by committees so established or by officers of theirs of any of their functions or provides that any specified functions of theirs shall be discharged by such committees or officers, or enables any Minister to make an instrument conferring such a power, imposing such a requirement or containing such a provision;

shall, to the extent that it makes any such provision, cease to have effect.

(9) The following enactments are exempted from subsection (8) above—

[. . .]

(e) section 7 of the Superannuation Act 1972 (superannuation of persons employed in local government service, etc);

(f) section 9 of the said Act of 1972 (superannuation of teachers).

(10) This section shall not authorise a local authority to arrange for the discharge by any committee, sub-committee or local authority of any functions which, by any enactment mention in subsection (9) above, are required or authorised to be discharged by a specified committee, but the foregoing provision shall not prevent a local authority who are required by or under any such enactment to establish, or delegate functions to, a committee established by or under any such enactment from arranging under this section for the discharge of their functions by an officer of the local authority or committee, as the case may be.

[. . .]

(14) References in this section and section 57 below to the discharge of any of the functions of a local authority include references to the doing of anything which is calculated to facilitate, or is conducive or incidental to, the discharge of any of those functions.

(15) Nothing in this section affects the operation of the Local Authorities (Goods and Services) Act 1970.

[(16) In this section, 'Act' includes an Act of the Scottish Parliament.]

57 Appointment of committees

(1) For the purpose of discharging any functions of a local authority in pursuance of arrangements made under section 56 of this Act—

(a) the authority may appoint a committee of the authority; or

(b) two or more local authorities may appoint a joint committee of those authorities; or

(c) any such committee may appoint one or more sub-committees.

(2) Subject to the provisions of this section, the number of members of a

committee appointed under subsection (1) above, their term of office, and the area (if restricted) within which the committee are to exercise their authority, shall be fixed by the appointing authority or authorities or, in the case of a sub-committee, by the appointing committee.

(3) A committee appointed under subsection (1) above, other than a committee for regulating and controlling the finance of the local authority or of their area may, subject to section 59 below, include persons who are not members of the appointing authority or authorities or, in the case of a sub-committee, the authority or authorities of whom they are a sub-committee, [but at least two-thirds of the members appointed to any such committee (other than a sub-committee) shall be members of that authority or those authorities, as the case may be.]

(4) A local authority may appoint a committee, and two or more local authorities may join in appointing a committee, to advise the appointing authority or authorities on any matter relating to the discharge of their functions, and any such committee—

(a) may consist of such persons (whether members of the appointing authority or authorities or not) appointed for such term as may be determined by the appointing authority or authorities; and

(b) may appoint one or more sub-committees to advise the committee with respect to any such matter.

(5) Every member of a committee appointed under this section who at the time of his appointment was a member of the appointing authority or one of the appointing authorities shall, upon ceasing to be a member of that authority, also cease to be a member of the committee; but for the purposes of this section a member of a local authority shall not be deemed to have ceased to be a member of the authority by reason of retirement if he has been re-elected a member thereof not later than the day of his retirement.

69 Subsidiary powers of local authorities

(1) Without prejudice to any powers exercisable apart from this section but subject to the provisions of this Act and any other enactment passed before or after this Act, a local authority shall have power to do any thing (whether or not involving the expenditure, borrowing or lending of money or the acquisition or disposal of any property or rights) which is calculated to facilitate, or is conducive or incidental to, the discharge of any of their functions.

(2) A local authority shall not by virtue of this section raise money, whether by means of rates or borrowing, or lend money except in accordance with the enactments relating to those matters respectively.

(3) Without prejudice to section 53 of the Countryside (Scotland) Act 1967 (contributions by or to local authorities), two or more local authorities may make arrangements for defraying any expenditure incurred by one of them in exercising any functions exercisable by both or all of them.

[. . .]

HOUSE OF COMMONS DISQUALIFICATION ACT 1975
(1975, c 24)

1 Disqualification of holders of certain offices and places

(1) Subject to the provisions of this Act, a person is disqualified for membership of the House of Commons who for the time being—

[(za) is a Lord spiritual;]

(a) holds any of the judicial offices specified in Part I of Schedule 1 to this Act;

(b) is employed in the civil service of the Crown, whether in an established capacity or not, and whether for the whole or part of his time;

(c) is a member of any of the armed forces of the Crown;

(d) is a member of any police force maintained by [a local policing body or] a police authority;

[. . .]

(e) is a member of the legislature of any country or territory outside the Commonwealth [(other than Ireland)]; or

(f) holds any office described in Part II or Part III of Schedule 1.

(2) A person who for the time being holds any office described in Part IV of Schedule 1 is disqualified for membership of the House of Commons for any constituency specified in relation to that office in the second column of Part IV.

(3) In this section—

'civil service of the Crown' includes the civil service of Northern Ireland, Her Majesty's Diplomatic Service and Her Majesty's Overseas Civil Service;

'police authority' means any police authority within the meaning of [the Police Act 1996] [, the Scottish Police Authority], or the [Northern Ireland Policing Board]; and 'member' in relation to a police force means a person employed as a full-time constable;

'regular armed forces of the Crown' means the Royal Navy, [the Royal Marines, the regular army (as defined by section 374 of the Armed Forces Act 2006) or the Royal Air Force.]

(4) Except as provided by this Act, a person shall not be disqualified for membership of the House of Commons by reason of his holding an office or place of profit under the Crown or any other office or place; and a person shall not be disqualified for appointment to or for holding any office or place by reason of his being a member of that House.

CONTEMPT OF COURT ACT 1981
(1981, c 49)

1 The strict liability rule

In this Act 'the strict liability rule' means the rule of law whereby conduct may be treated as a contempt of court as tending to interfere with the course of justice in particular legal proceedings regardless of intent to do so.

2 Limitation of scope of strict liability

(1) The strict liability rule applies only in relation to publications, and for this purpose 'publication' includes any speech, writing, [programme included in a cable programme service] or other communication in whatever form, which is addressed to the public at large or any section of the public.

(2) The strict liability rule applies only to a publication which creates a substantial risk that the course of justice in the proceedings in question will be seriously impeded or prejudiced.

(3) The strict liability rule applies to a publication only if the proceedings in question are active within the meaning of this section at the time of the publication.

(4) Schedule 1 applies for determining the times at which proceedings are to be treated as active within the meaning of this section.

[(5) In this section 'programme service' has the same meaning as in the Broadcasting Act 1990.]

3 Defence of innocent publication or distribution

(1) A person is not guilty of contempt of court under the strict liability rule as the publisher of any matter to which that rule applies if at the time of publication (having taken all reasonable care) he does not know and has no reason to suspect that relevant proceedings are active.

(2) A person is not guilty of contempt of court under the strict liability rule as the distributor of a publication containing any such matter if at the time of

distribution (having taken all reasonable care) he does not know that it contains such matter and has no reason to suspect that it is likely to do so.

(3) The burden of proof of any fact tending to establish a defence afforded by this section to any person lies upon that person.

[. . .]

4 Contemporary reports of proceedings

(1) Subject to this section a person is not guilty of contempt of court under the strict liability rule in respect of a fair and accurate report of legal proceedings held in public, published contemporaneously and in good faith.

(2) In any such proceedings the court may, where it appears to be necessary for avoiding a substantial risk of prejudice to the administration of justice in those proceedings, or in any other proceedings pending or imminent, order that the publication of any report of the proceedings, or any part of the proceedings, be postponed for such period as the court thinks necessary for that purpose.

[(2A) Where in proceedings for any offence which is an administration of justice offence for the purposes of section 54 of the Criminal Procedure and Investigations Act 1996 (acquittal tainted by an administration of justice offence) it appears to the court that there is a possibility that (by virtue of that section) proceedings may be taken against a person for an offence of which he has been acquitted, subsection (2) of this section shall apply as if those proceedings were pending or imminent.]

(3) For the purposes of subsection (1) of this section [. . .] a report of proceedings shall be treated as published contemporaneously—

(a) in the case of a report of which publication is postponed pursuant to an order under subsection (2) of this section, if published as soon as practicable after that order expires;

[(b) in the case of a report of allocation or sending proceedings of which publication is permitted by virtue only of subsection (6) of section 52A of the Crime and Disorder Act 1998 ('the 1998 Act'), if published as soon as practicable after publication is so permitted;

(c) in the case of a report of an application of which publication is permitted by virtue only of sub-paragraph (5) or (7) of paragraph 3 of Schedule 3 to the 1998 Act, if published as soon as practicable after publication is so permitted.]

[. . .]

5 Discussion of public affairs

A publication made as or as part of a discussion in good faith of public affairs or other matters of general public interest is not to be treated as a contempt of court under the strict liability rule if the risk of impediment or prejudice to particular legal proceedings is merely incidental to the discussion.

6 Savings

Nothing in the foregoing provisions of this Act—

(a) prejudices any defence available at common law to a charge of contempt of court under the strict liability rule;

(b) implies that any publication is punishable as contempt of court under that rule which would not be so punishable apart from those provisions;

(c) restricts liability for contempt of court in respect of conduct intended to impede or prejudice the administration of justice.

. . .

8 Confidentiality of jury's deliberations[: Scotland and Northern Ireland]

[(1) [In Scotland and Northern Ireland], subject to subsection (2) below, it is a contempt of court to obtain, disclose or solicit any particulars of statements made, opinions expressed, arguments advanced or votes cast by members of a jury in the course of their deliberations in any legal proceedings.

(2) This section does not apply to any disclosure of any particulars—

(a) in the proceedings in question for the purpose of enabling the jury to arrive at their verdict, or in connection with the delivery of that verdict, or

(b) in evidence in any subsequent proceedings for an offence alleged to have been committed in relation to the jury in the first mentioned proceedings,

or to the publication of any particulars so disclosed.

(3) Proceedings for a contempt of court under this section (other than Scottish proceedings) shall not be instituted except by or with the consent of the Attorney General or on the motion of a court having jurisdiction to deal with it.]

9 Use of tape recorders

(1) Subject to subsection (4) below, it is a contempt of court—

(a) to use in court, or bring into court for use, any tape recorder or other instrument for recording sound, except with the leave of the court;

(b) to publish a recording of legal proceedings made by means of any such instrument, or any recording derived directly or indirectly from it, by playing it in the hearing of the public or any section of the public, or to dispose of it or any recording so derived, with a view to such publication;

(c) to use any such recording in contravention of any conditions of leave granted under paragraph (a).

[(d) to publish or dispose of any recording in contravention of any conditions of leave granted under subsection (1A)].

[(1A) In the case of a recording of Supreme Court proceedings, subsection (1)(b) does not apply to its publication or disposal with the leave of the Court.]

(2) Leave under paragraph (a) of subsection (1) [, or under subsection (1A)] may be granted or refused at the discretion of the court and [, if granted—

(a) may, in the case of leave under subsection (1)(a),] be granted subject to such conditions as the court thinks proper with respect to the use of any recording made pursuant to the leave; and

[(b) may, in the case of leave under subsection (1A) be granted subject to such conditions as the Supreme Court thinks proper with respect to publication or disposal to which the leave relates; and]

where leave has been granted the court may at the like discretion withdraw or amend it either generally or in relation to any particular part of the proceedings.

(3) Without prejudice to any other power to deal with an act of contempt under paragraph (a) of subsection (1), the court may order the instrument, or any recording made with it, or both, to be forfeited; and any object so forfeited shall (unless the court otherwise determines on application by a person appearing to be the owner) be sold or otherwise disposed of in such manner as the court may direct.

(4) This section does not apply to the making or use of sound recordings for purposes of official transcripts of proceedings.

[(5) See section 32 of the Crime and Courts Act 2013 for power to provide for further exceptions.]

10 Sources of information

No court may require a person to disclose, nor is any person guilty of contempt of court for refusing to disclose, the source of information contained in a publication for which he is responsible, unless it be established to the satisfaction of the court that disclosure is necessary in the interests of justice or national security or for the prevention of disorder or crime.

11 Publication of matters exempted from disclosure in court

In any case where a court (having power to do so) allows a name or other matter to be withheld from the public in proceedings before the court, the court may give such directions prohibiting the publication of that name or matter in connection with the proceedings as appear to the court to be necessary for the purpose for which it was so withheld.

15 Penalties for contempt of court in Scottish proceedings

(1) In Scottish proceedings, when a person is committed to prison for contempt of court the committal shall (without prejudice to the power of the court to order his earlier discharge) be for a fixed term.

(2) The maximum penalty which may be imposed by way of imprisonment or fine for contempt of court in Scottish proceedings shall be two years' imprisonment or a fine or both, except that—

(a) where the contempt is dealt with by the sheriff in the course of or in connection with proceedings other than criminal proceedings on indictment, such penalty shall not exceed three months' imprisonment or a fine of [level 4 on the standard scale] or both; and

(b) where the contempt is dealt with by the district court, such penalty shall not exceed sixty days' imprisonment or a fine of [level 4 on the standard scale] or both.

[(3) The following provisions of the Criminal Procedure (Scotland) Act 1995 shall apply in relation to persons found guilty of contempt of court in Scottish proceedings as they apply in relation to persons convicted of offences—

(a) in every case, section 207 (restrictions on detention of young offenders);

(b) in any case to which paragraph (b) of subsection (2) above does not apply, sections 58, 59 and 61 (persons suffering from mental disorder);

and in any case to which the said paragraph (b) does apply, subsection (5) below shall have effect.]

[. . .]

(5) Where a person is found guilty by a district court of contempt of court and it appears to the court that he may be suffering from mental disorder, it shall remit him to the sheriff in the manner provided [by section 7(9) and (10) of the Criminal Procedure (Scotland) Act 1995] and the sheriff shall, on such remit being made, have the like power to make an order under [section 58(1)] of the said Act in respect of him as if he had been convicted by the sheriff of an offence, or in dealing with him may exercise the like powers as the court making the remit.

[. . .]

19 Interpretation

In this Act—

[. . .]

'court' includes any tribunal or body exercising the judicial power of the State, and 'legal proceedings' shall be construed accordingly;

'publication' has the meaning assigned by subsection (1) of section 2, and 'publish' (except in section 9) shall be construed accordingly;

'Scottish proceedings' means proceedings before any court, including the [Court Martial Appeal Court], [. . .] and the Employment Appeal Tribunal, sitting in Scotland, and includes proceedings before the [Supreme Court] in the exercise of any appellate jurisdiction over proceedings in such a court;

'the strict liability rule' has the meaning assigned by section 1;

'superior court' means [the Supreme Court] the Court of Appeal, the High Court, the Crown Court, the [Court Martial Appeal Court], [. . .] the Employment Appeal Tribunal and any other court exercising in relation to its proceedings powers equivalent to those of the High Court [. . .].

20 Tribunals of Inquiry

(1) In relation to any tribunal to which the Tribunals of Inquiry (Evidence) Act 1921 applies, and the proceedings of such a tribunal, the provisions of this Act (except subsection (3) of section 9) apply as they apply in relation to courts and

legal proceedings; and references to the course of justice or the administration of justice in legal proceedings shall be construed accordingly.

(2) The proceedings of a tribunal established under the said Act shall be treated as active within the meaning of section 2 from the time when the tribunal is appointed until its report is presented to Parliament.

SCHEDULE 1

TIMES WHEN PROCEEDINGS ARE ACTIVE FOR PURPOSES OF SECTION 2

Section 2

Preliminary

1. In this Schedule 'criminal proceedings' means proceedings against a person in respect of an offence, not being appellate proceedings or proceedings commenced by motion for committal or attachment in England and Wales or Northern Ireland; and 'appellate proceedings' means proceedings on appeal from or for the review of the decision of a court in any proceedings.

[**1ZA.** Proceedings under the Double Jeopardy (Scotland) Act 2011 (asp 16) are criminal proceedings for the purposes of this Schedule.]

[**1A.** In paragraph 1 the reference to an offence includes a service offence within the meaning of the Armed Forces Act 2006.]

2. Criminal, appellate and other proceedings are active within the meaning of section 2 at the times respectively prescribed by the following paragraphs of this Schedule; and in relation to proceedings in which more than one of the steps described in any of those paragraphs is taken, the reference in that paragraph is a reference to the first of those steps.

Criminal proceedings

3. Subject to the following provisions of this Schedule, criminal proceedings are active from the relevant initial step specified in paragraph 4 [or 4A] until concluded as described in paragraph 5. [. . .]

4. The initial steps of criminal proceedings are:—

(a) arrest without warrant;

(b) the issue, or in Scotland the grant, of a warrant for arrest;

(c) the issue of a summons to appear, or in Scotland the grant of a warrant to cite;

(d) the service of an indictment or other document specifying the charge;

(e) except in Scotland, oral charge.

[(f) the making of an application under section 2(2) (tainted acquittals), 3(3)(b) (admission made or becoming known after acquittal), 4(3)(b) (new evidence), 11 (3) (eventual death of injured person) or 12(3) (nullity of previous proceedings) of the Double Jeopardy (Scotland) Act 2011 (asp 16).]

[**4A.** Where as a result of an order under section 54 of the Criminal Procedure and Investigations Act 1996 (acquittal tainted by an administration of justice offence) proceedings are brought against a person for an offence of which he has previously been acquitted, the initial step of the proceedings is a certification under subsection (2) of that section; and paragraph 4 has effect subject to this.]

5. Criminal proceedings are concluded—

(a) by acquittal or, as the case may be, by sentence;

(b) by any other verdict, finding, order or decision which puts an end to the proceedings;

(c) by discontinuance or by operation of law.

[(d) where the initial steps of the proceedings are as mentioned in paragraphs 4(f)—

(i) by refusal of the application;

(ii) if the application is granted and within the period of 2 months mentioned in section 6(3) of the Double Jeopardy (Scotland) Act 2011 (asp 16) a new prosecution is brought, by acquittal or, as the case may be, by sentence in the new prosecution.]

6. The reference in paragraph 5(a) to sentence includes any order or decision consequent on conviction or finding of guilt which disposes of the case, either absolutely or subject to future events, and a deferment of sentence under [section 1 of the Powers of Criminal Courts (Sentencing) Act 2000], section 219 or 432 of the Criminal Procedure (Scotland) Act 1975 or Article 14 of the Treatment of Offenders (Northern Ireland) Order 1976.

7. Proceedings are discontinued within the meaning of paragraph 5(c)—

. . .

(b) in Scotland, if the proceedings are expressly abandoned by the prosecutor or are deserted *simpliciter;*

. . .

[(d) where the initial steps of the proceedings are as mentioned in paragraph 4(f) and the application is granted, if no new prosecution is brought within the period of 2 months mentioned in section 6(3) of the Double Jeopardy (Scotland) Act 2011 (asp 16).]

[. . .]

9, 9A. [*Do not apply to Scotland.*]

10. Without prejudice to paragraph 5(b) above, criminal proceedings against a person cease to be active—

(a) if the accused is found to be under a disability such as to render him unfit to be tried or unfit to plead or, in Scotland, is found to be insane in bar of trial; or

(b) if a hospital order is made in his case under [section 51(5) of the Mental Health Act 1983] or paragraph (b) of subsection (2) of section 62 of the Mental Health Act (Northern Ireland) 1961 or, in Scotland, where [an assessment order or a treatment order ceases to have effect by virtue of sections 52H or 52R respectively of the Criminal Procedure (Scotland) Act 1995],

but become active again if they are later resumed.

11. Criminal proceedings against a person which become active on the issue or the grant of a warrant for his arrest cease to be active at the end of the period of twelve months beginning with the date of the warrant unless he has been arrested within that period, but become active again if he is subsequently arrested.

Other proceedings at first instance

12. Proceedings other than criminal proceedings and appellate proceedings are active from the time when arrangements for the hearing are made or, if no such arrangements are previously made, from the time the hearing begins, until the proceedings are disposed of or discontinued or withdrawn; and for the purposes of this paragraph any motion or application made in or for the purposes of any proceedings, and any pre-trial review in the county court, is to be treated as a distinct proceeding.

[. . .]

14. In Scotland arrangements for the hearing of proceedings to which paragraph 12 applies are made within the meaning of that paragraph—

(a) in the case of an ordinary action in the Court of Session or in the sheriff court, when the Record is closed;

(b) in the case of a motion or application, when it is enrolled or made;

(c) in any other case, when the date for a hearing is fixed or a hearing is allowed.

Appellate proceedings

15. Appellate proceedings are active from the time when they are commenced—

(a) by application for leave to appeal or apply for review, or by notice of such an application;

(b) by notice of appeal or of application for review;

(c) by other originating process,

until disposed of or abandoned, discontinued or withdrawn.

16. Where, in appellate proceedings relating to criminal proceedings, the court—

(a) remits the case to the court below; or

(b) orders a new trial or a *venire de novo*, or in Scotland grants authority to bring a new prosecution,

any further or new proceedings which result shall be treated as active from the conclusion of the appellate proceedings.

CIVIC GOVERNMENT (SCOTLAND) ACT 1982
(1982, c 45)

51 Obscene material

(1) Subject to subsection (4) below, any person who displays any obscene material in any public place or in any other place where it can be seen by the public shall be guilty of an offence under this section.

(2) Subject to subsection (4) below, any person who publishes, sells or distributes or, with a view to its eventual sale or distribution, makes, prints, has or keeps any obscene material shall be guilty of an offence under this section.

[(2A) Subject to subsection (4) below, any person who—

(a) is responsible for the inclusion of any obscene material in a programme included in a programme service; or

(b) with a view to its eventual inclusion in a programme so included, makes, prints, has or keeps any obscene material, shall be guilty of an offence under this section.]

[(3) A person guilty of an offence under this section is liable—

(a) on summary conviction, to imprisonment for a period not exceeding 12 months or to a fine not exceeding the statutory maximum or to both, or

(b) on conviction on indictment—

(i) in a case where the obscene material is or includes an extreme pornographic image, to imprisonment for a period not exceeding 5 years or to a fine or to both, or

(ii) in any other case, to imprisonment for a period not exceeding 3 years or to a fine or to both.]

(4) A person shall not be convicted of an offence under this section if he proves that he had used all due diligence to avoid committing the offence.

(5) Under an indictment for or on a complaint of a breach of subsection (1) above, the court may, if satisfied that the person accused is guilty of an offence under section 1(1) of the Indecent Displays (Control) Act 1981 (offence of public display of indecent matter), convict him of a breach of the said section 1(1).

(6) Nothing in this section applies in relation to any matter—

[. . .]

(b) included in a performance of a play (within the meaning of the Theatres Act 1968).

. . .

(8) In this section—

['extreme pornographic image' is to be construed in accordance with section 51A,]

'material' includes any book, magazine, bill, paper, print, film, tape, disc or other kind of recording (whether of sound or visual images or both), photograph, drawing, painting, representation, model or figure [. . .];

'photograph' includes the negative as well as the positive version;

['programme' and 'programme service' have the same meaning as in the Broadcasting Act 1990;]

'public place' has the same meaning as in section 133 of this Act except that it includes any place to which at the material time the public are permitted to have access, whether on payment or otherwise;

[. . .]

and the reference to publishing includes a reference to [. . .] playing, projecting or otherwise reproducing [, or, where the material is data stored electronically, transmitting that data].

[51A Extreme pornography

(1) A person who is in possession of an extreme pornographic image is guilty of an offence under this section.

(2) An extreme pornographic image is an image which is all of the following—

(a) obscene,

(b) pornographic,

(c) extreme.

(3) An image is pornographic if it is of such a nature that it must reasonably be assumed to have been made solely or principally for the purpose of sexual arousal.

(4) Where (as found in the person's possession) an image forms part of a series of images, the question of whether the image is pornographic is to be determined by reference to—

(a) the image itself, and

(b) where the series of images is such as to be capable of providing a context for the image, its context within the series of images,

and reference may also be had to any sounds accompanying the image or the series of images.

(5) So, for example, where—

(a) an image forms an integral part of a narrative constituted by a series of images, and

(b) having regard to those images as a whole, they are not of such a nature that they must reasonably be assumed to have been made solely or principally for the purpose of sexual arousal,

the image may, by virtue of being part of that narrative, be found not to be pornographic (even if it may have been found to be pornographic where taken by itself).

(6) An image is extreme if it depicts, in an explicit and realistic way any of the following—

(a) an act which takes or threatens a person's life,

(b) an act which results, or is likely to result, in a person's severe injury,

(c) rape or other non-consensual penetrative sexual activity,

(d) sexual activity involving (directly or indirectly) a human corpse,

(e) an act which involves sexual activity between a person and an animal (or the carcase of an animal).

(7) In determining whether (as found in the person's possession) an image depicts an act mentioned in subsection (6), reference may be had to—

(a) how the image is or was described (whether the description is part of the image itself or otherwise),

(b) any sounds accompanying the image,

(c) where the image forms an integral part of a narrative constituted by a series of images—

(i) any sounds accompanying the series of images,

(ii) the context provided by that narrative.

(8) A person guilty of an offence under this section is liable—

(a) on summary conviction, to imprisonment for a period not exceeding 12 months or to a fine not exceeding the statutory maximum or to both,

(b) on conviction on indictment, to imprisonment for a period not exceeding 3 years or to a fine or to both.

(9) In this section, an 'image' is—

(a) a moving or still image (made by any means), or

(b) data (stored by any means) which is capable of conversion into such an image.]

[51B Extreme pornography: excluded images

(1) An offence is not committed under section 51A if the image is an excluded image.

(2) An 'excluded image' is an image which is all or part of a classified work.

(3) An image is not an excluded image where—

(a) it has been extracted from a classified work, and

(b) it must be reasonably be assumed to have been extracted (whether with or without other images) from the work solely or principally for the purpose of sexual arousal.

(4) In determining whether (as found in the person's possession) the image was extracted from the work for the purpose mentioned in subsection (3)(b), reference may be had to—

(a) how the image was stored,

(b) how the image is or was described (whether the description is part of the image itself or otherwise),

(c) any sounds accompanying the image,

(d) where the image forms an integral part of a narrative constituted by a series of images—

(i) any sounds accompanying the series of images,

(ii) the context provided by that narrative.

(5) In this section—

'classified work' means a video work in respect of which a classification certificate has been issued by a designated authority,

'classification certificate' and 'video work' have the same meanings as in the Video Recordings Act 1984 (c 39),

'designated authority' means an authority which has been designated by the Secretary of State under section 4 of that Act,

'extract' includes an extract of a single image,

'image' is to be construed in accordance with section 51A.]

[51C Extreme pornography: defences

(1) Where a person ('A') is charged with an offence under section 51A, it is a defence for A to prove one or more of the matters mentioned in subsection (2).

(2) The matters are—

(a) that A had a legitimate reason for being in possession of the image concerned,

(b) that A had not seen the image concerned and did not know, nor had any cause to suspect, it to be an extreme pornographic image,

(c) that A—

(i) was sent the image concerned without any prior request having been made by or on behalf of A, and

(ii) did not keep it for an unreasonable time.

(3) Where A is charged with an offence under section 51A, it is a defence for A to prove that—

(a) A directly participated in the act depicted, and

(b) subsection (4) applies.

(4) This subsection applies—

(a) in the case of an image which depicts an act described in subsection (6)(a) of that section, if the act depicted did not actually take or threaten a person's life,

(b) in the case of an image which depicts an act described in subsection (6)(b) of that section, if the act depicted did not actually result in (nor was it actually likely to result in) a person's severe injury,

(c) in the case of an image which depicts an act described in subsection (6)(c) of that section, if the act depicted did not actually involve non-consensual activity,

(d) in the case of an image which depicts an act described in subsection (6)(d) of that section, if what is depicted as a human corpse was not in fact a corpse,

(e) in the case of an image which depicts an act described in subsection (6)(e) of that section, if what is depicted as an animal (or the carcase of an animal) was not in fact an animal (or a carcase).

(5) The defence under subsection (3) is not available if A shows, gives or offers for sale the image to any person who was not also a direct participant in the act depicted.

(6) In this section 'image' and 'extreme pornographic image' are to be construed in accordance with section 51A.]

59 Powers of arrest and apprehension

[. . .]

(3) The owner, tenant or occupier of any property in, upon, or in respect of, which an offence to which this section applies is being committed or any person authorised by him may apprehend any person whom the owner or, as the case may be, the tenant, occupier or authorised person finds committing that offence and detain the apprehended person until [the arrival] of a constable. In this subsection 'property' means heritable or moveable property.

(4) This section applies to offences under sections 50, 57 and 58 of this Act.

[. . .]

60 Powers of search and seizure

(1) Subject to subsection (2) and (3) below, if a constable has reasonable grounds to suspect that a person is in possession of any stolen property, the constable may without warrant—

(a) search that person or anything in his possession, and detain him for as long as is necessary for the purpose of that search;

(b) enter and search any vehicle or vessel in which the constable suspects that that thing may be found, and for that purpose require the person in control of the vehicle or vessel to stop it and keep it stopped;

(c) enter and search any premises occupied by a second-hand dealer or a metal dealer for the purposes of his business;

(d) seize and detain anything found in the course of any such search which appears to the constable to have been stolen or to be evidence of the commission of the crime of theft and may, in doing so, use reasonable force.

[. . .]

(2) The power under subsection (1)(b) above to require the person in charge of a vehicle or vessel to stop it shall be exercisable only by a constable in uniform.

(3) A constable who is not in uniform shall not be entitled to exercise the powers which he may exercise under subsection (1)(a) to (c) above until he has produced his identification

(a) in relation to the exercise of powers under subsection (1)(a) above, to the person in respect of whom the powers are exercised;

(b) in relation to the exercise of powers under subsections (1)(b) or (c) above, to the person for the time being in charge of the vehicle, vessel or premises and to any other person in or on the vehicle, vessel or premises who, having reasonable cause to do so, requests to see it.

(4) In subsection (1) above 'theft' includes any aggravation of theft including robbery.

(5) Nothing in [section 54(2A) of this Act or] this section prejudices any power of entry or search or any power to seize or detain property or any power to require any vehicle or vessel to be stopped [which is otherwise exercisable by a constable].

(6) Any person who, without reasonable excuse—

(a) fails to allow a constable [to enter and search—

(i) any premises in pursuance of section 54(2A) of this Act or of subsection (1) above; or

(ii) any vehicle or vessel in pursuance of the said subsection (1)], or seize and detain anything found in the course of such search;

(b) when required by a constable in pursuance of subsection (1) above to stop a vehicle or vessel and keep it stopped, fails to do so; or

(c) obstructs a constable in the exercise of his powers under [section 54(2A) of this Act] or subsection (1) above;

shall be guilty of an offence and liable, on summary conviction, to a fine not exceeding [level 3 on the standard scale].

62 Notification of processions

(1) A person proposing to hold a procession in public shall give written notice of that proposal in accordance with subsections (2) and (3) below—

[(a) to the [local authority] in whose area the procession is to be held, or if it is to be held in the areas of more than one such [authority], to each such [authority];

[(aa) if the procession is to be held to any extent in a National Park, to the National Park authority for the National Park;] and

(b) to the chief constable.]

(2) Notice shall be given for the purposes of subsection (1) above by—

(a) its being posted to the main office of [the local authority and (where subsection (1)(aa) above applies) of the National Park authority and to the office of the chief constable] so that in the normal course of post it might be expected to arrive not later than [28] days before the date when the procession is to be held; or

(b) its being delivered by hand to [those offices] not later than [28] days before that date.

(3) The notice to be given under subsection (1) above shall specify—

(a) the date and time when the procession is to be held;

(b) its route;

(c) the number of persons likely to take part in it;

(d) the arrangements for its control being made by the person proposing to hold it; and

(e) the name and address of that person.

(4) [A local authority] may, on application in accordance with subsection (5) below by a person proposing to hold a procession in public in their area [—

(a) made to them; and

[(aa) if the procession is to be held to any extent in a National Park, intimated to the National Park authority for the National Park;] and

(b) intimated to the chief constable,] within the period of [28] days before the date when the procession is to be held,

make an order dispensing with the requirements of subsection (2) above in relation to the time limits for the giving of notice of that proposal.

(5) An application under subsection (4) above shall—

[(a) set out the reason why notice of the proposal was not given in accordance with subsections (1) and (2) above; and

(b) specify the matters mentioned in subsection (3) above.]

[. . .]

(9) [The local authority] shall, before making an order under subsection (4) above [. . .] consult the chief constable.

[. . .]

[(11A) A local authority shall, as soon as possible after making an order under subsection (4) above, publicise that fact in such manner as they think fit and send a copy of the order to the applicant.

(11B) This section does not apply to a procession—

(a) which is a funeral procession organised by a funeral director acting in the ordinary course of his business; or

(b) which is specified in, or is within a description specified in, an order made by the Scottish Ministers.

(11C) In subsection (11B) above, a 'funeral director' is a person whose business consists of or includes the arrangement and conduct of funerals.

(11D) An order made for the purposes of subsection (11B)(b) above shall be made by statutory instrument subject to annulment in pursuance of a resolution of the Scottish Parliament.]

(12) In this section and in sections 63 to 65 of this Act—

'procession in public' means a procession in a public place;

['chief constable' means the chief constable of the Police Service of Scotland]; and

'public place' has the same meaning as in [Part II of the Public Order Act 1986].

63 Functions of [local authority] in relation to processions

(1) The [local authority] may, after consulting the chief constable [and (where section 62(1)(aa) of this Act applies) the National Park authority] in respect of a procession notice of which has been given or falls to be treated as having been given in accordance with section 62(1) of this Act, make an order—

(i) prohibiting the holding of the procession; or

(ii) imposing conditions on the holding of it.

[(1A) Where notice of a proposal to hold a procession has been given or falls to be treated as having been given in accordance with section 62(1) of this Act—

(a) if a [local authority] have made an order under subsection (1) above they may at any time thereafter, after consulting the chief constable [and (where subsection (1)(aa) of that section applies) the National Park authority], vary or revoke the order and, where they revoke it, make any order which they were empowered to make under that subsection;

(b) if they have decided not to make an order they may at any time thereafter, after consulting the chief constable [and (where subsection (1)(aa) of that section applies) the National Park authority], make any order which they were empowered to make under that subsection.]

[. . .]

(3) A [local authority] shall—

(a) where notice of a proposal to hold a procession has been given or falls to be treated as having been given in accordance with section 62(1) [or (1A) above] of this Act, deliver at least 2 days before the date when, in terms of the notice, the procession is to be held, to the person who gave the notice—

(i) where they have made an order under subsection (1) [or (1A)] above, a copy of it and a written statement of the reasons for it [. . .];

(ii) where they decide not to make [an order under subsection (1) above or to revoke an order already made under subsection (1) or (1A) above], notification of that fact;

[(iii) where they have, under subsection (1A) above, varied such an order, a copy of the order as varied and a written statement of the reasons for the variation; and]

(b) where they have made an order under subsection (1) [or (1A)] above in relation to a proposal to hold a procession, make such arrangements as will ensure that persons who might take or are taking part in that procession are made [and, if the order has been varied under subsection (1A) above, that it has been so varied] aware of the fact that the order has been made and of its effect; [and

(c) where they have revoked an order made under subsection (1) or (1A) above in relation to a proposal to hold a procession, make such arrangements as will ensure that persons who might take or are taking part in that procession are made aware of the fact that the order has been revoked.]

(4) The [local authority] shall comply with subsection (3) above—

(a) as early as possible;

(b) only insofar as it is reasonably practicable for them to do so.

[(5) The local authority may, after consulting the chief constable and (where section 62(1)(aa) of this Act applies) the National Parks Authority, make an order—

(a) imposing conditions on the holding of a procession to which paragraph (a) of subsection (11B) of section 62 of this Act relates;

(b) prohibiting or imposing conditions on the holding of a procession to which paragraph (b) of that subsection relates.

(6) Subsections (1A), (3) and (4) above apply in relation to an order made under subsection (5) above and to a decision not to make an order under that subsection as they apply to an order under subsection (1) above and to a decision not to make an order under that subsection respectively, but with the modifications set out in subsection (7) below.

(7) Those modifications are—

(a) the references to notice having been or falling to be treated as having been given shall be ignored;

(b) the reference to the person who gave the notice shall be treated as a reference to the person appearing to the local authority to be the person who is to hold the procession; and

(c) the words 'not to make an order under subsection (1) above or' in subsection (3)(a)(ii) shall be ignored.

(8) The considerations to which the local authority shall have regard when deciding whether to prohibit the holding of a procession or impose conditions on it under this section shall include—

(a) the likely effect of the holding of the procession in relation to—

(i) public safety;

(ii) public order;

(iii) damage to property;

(iv) disruption of the life of the community;

(b) the extent to which the containment of risks arising from the procession would (whether by itself or in combination with any other circumstances) place an excessive burden on the police;

(c) where the person proposing to hold the procession has previously held one in the area of the authority or the persons likely to take part in the procession, or some of them, are the same persons as took part in one previously held in that area, or some of them—

(i) whether the previous procession was held in breach of a prohibition under this section on its being held or of a condition so imposed on the holding of it;

(ii) whether any guidance or code of conduct issued by the authority as to the holding of the previous procession or as to the holding of processions generally was followed; and

(iii) the effect of the previous procession in relation to the matters mentioned in sub-paragraphs (i) to (iv) of paragraph (a) above and in paragraph (b) above.

(9) The local authority shall compile, maintain and make available to the public, free of charge, a list containing information about—

(a) processions which have, after the coming into force of this subsection, been held in their area;

(b) proposed processions which they have, after that time, prohibited under this section.

(10) A local authority shall make sufficient arrangements to secure that any person, body or other grouping resident in or otherwise present in their area who makes a request for the purposes of this subsection is enabled to receive information about processions which are to or might be held in that area or in any part of it specified in the request.]

64 Appeals against orders under section 63

(1) An appeal to the sheriff shall lie at the instance of a person who, in accordance with section 62 of this Act, has or falls to be treated as having given notice of a proposal to hold a procession in public [against—

(a) an order made under section 63(1) or (1A) of this Act; or

(b) a variation under section 63(1A) of this Act of an order made under section 63(1) or (1A),

in relation to the procession.]

(2) An appeal under this section shall be made by way of summary application and shall be lodged with the sheriff clerk within 14 days from the date on which the copy of the order and statement of reasons were received by the appellant.

(3) On good cause being shown, the sheriff may hear an appeal under this section notwithstanding that it was not lodged within the time mentioned in subsection (2) above.

(4) The sheriff may uphold an appeal under this section only if he considers that the [local authority] in arriving at their decision to make [or, as the case may be, to vary] the order—

(a) erred in law;

(b) based their decision on any incorrect material fact;

(c) exercised their discretion in an unreasonable manner; or

(d) otherwise acted beyond their powers.

(5) In considering an appeal under this section the sheriff may hear evidence by or on behalf of any party to the appeal.

(6) Subject to subsection (7) below, on an appeal under this section, the sheriff may—

(a) uphold the appeal and—

(i) remit the case, with the reasons for his decision, to the [local authority] for reconsideration of their decision, or

(ii) if he considers that there is insufficient time for the case to be remitted under sub-paragraph (i) above [quash] the order which is the subject of the appeal [, vary it] or make [in substitution for the order] any such order as the [authority] were empowered to make under section 63(1) of this Act; or

(b) dismiss the appeal,

and on remitting a case under [paragraph (a)(ii)] above, the sheriff may—

(i) specify a date by which the reconsideration by the [authority] must take place;

(ii) modify any procedural steps which otherwise would be required to be taken in relation to the matter by or under any enactment (including this Act).

(7) The sheriff shall not exercise any of his powers under subsection (6) above unless he is satisfied that all steps which in the circumstances were reasonable

have been taken with a view to securing that notice of the appeal and an opportunity of being heard with respect to it have been given to the [authority] whose order [or, as the case may be, the variation of whose order] under section 63 of this Act is the subject of the appeal.

(8) The sheriff may include in his decision on an appeal under this section such order as to the expenses of the appeal as he thinks proper.

(9) Any party to an appeal to the sheriff under this section may appeal on a point of law from the decision of the sheriff to the Court of Session within 28 days from the date of that decision.

65 Offences and enforcement

(1) Subject to subsection (3) below, a person who holds a procession in public—

(a) [not]—

(i) having given or being a person who is treated as having given notice in accordance with section 62 of this Act of his proposal to do so;

[. . .]

(b) in contravention of an order under section 63(1) [or (1A)] or 64(6)(a)(ii) of this Act prohibiting the holding of it;

(c) otherwise than in accordance with a condition imposed by an order under section 63(1) [or (1A)] or 64(6)(a)(ii) of this Act in relation to the procession; or

(d) otherwise than in accordance with the particulars of its date, time and route specified—

(i) in the notice given under section 62(1) to (3) of this Act; or

(ii) where an order has been made under subsection (4) of that section, in the application for the order,

except to the extent that a condition referred to in paragraph (c) above relates to its date, time or route,

shall be guilty of an offence and liable, on summary conviction, to a fine not exceeding [level 4 on the standard scale] or to imprisonment for a period not exceeding 3 months or to both.

(2) Subject to subsection (3) below, a person who takes part in a procession in public—

(a) in respect of which—

(i) notice has not been or is not treated as having been given in accordance with section 62 of this Act [. . .]

(b) in relation to which an order has been made under section 63(1) [or (1A)] or 64(6)(a)(ii) of this Act prohibiting the holding of it;

(c) which is held otherwise than in accordance with a condition imposed by an order under section 63(1) [or (1A)] or 64(6)(a)(ii) of this Act in relation to the procession; or

(d) which is held otherwise than in accordance with the particulars of its date, time and route specified—

(i) in the notice given under section 62(1) to (3) of this Act; or

(ii) where an order has been made under subsection (4) of that section, in the application for the order

except to the extent that a condition referred to in paragraph (c) above relates to its date, time or route

and refuses to desist when required to do so by a constable in uniform shall be guilty of an offence and liable, on summary conviction, to a fine not exceeding [level 3 on the standard scale].

(3) [This section applies to a procession of the description set out in section 62 (11B)(a) of this Act (funeral processions) only to the extent that the procession has been held otherwise than in accordance with conditions imposed under this Part of this Act.]

[(3A) This section applies to a procession which is within section 62(11B)(b) of this Act (processions specified by order) only if and to the extent that it has been prohibited or conditions imposed on it under this Part of this Act.]

[. . .]

[65A Guidance to local authorities
The local authority shall, in carrying out functions under this Part of this Act, have regard to any guidance in that respect issued by the Scottish Ministers.]

REPRESENTATION OF THE PEOPLE ACT 1983
(1983, c 2)

[1 Parliamentary electors

(1) A person is entitled to vote as an elector at a parliamentary election in any constituency if on the date of the poll he—

(a) is registered in the register of parliamentary electors for that constituency;

(b) is not subject to any legal incapacity to vote (age apart);

(c) is either a Commonwealth citizen or a citizen of the Republic of Ireland; and

(d) is of voting age (that is, 18 years or over).

(2) A person is not entitled to vote as an elector—

(a) more than once in the same constituency at any parliamentary election; or

(b) in more than one constituency at a general election.]

[75ZA Return of permitted expenditure: power to require return

(1) The returning officer or the Electoral Commission may, at any time during the period of 6 months beginning with the date of the poll at a parliamentary election, request a relevant person to deliver to the officer or Commission a return of permitted expenditure in relation to a candidate at the election who is specified in the request.

(2) 'Relevant person' means a person who—

(a) is not required to deliver a return under section 75(2) in relation to the candidate, and

(b) is not the candidate, the candidate's election agent, or a person engaged or employed for payment or promise of payment by the candidate or the candidate's election agent.

(3) 'Return of permitted expenditure' means a return—

(a) showing all permitted expenses incurred by the person in relation to the candidate, or

(b) stating that the person incurred no such expenses or that the total such expenses incurred by the person was £200 or less.

(4) 'Permitted expense', in relation to a candidate, means an expense incurred by the person in respect of the candidate which, if the person had been required to deliver a return under section 75(2) in relation to the candidate, would have been required to be included in that return.]

[75ZB Return of permitted expenditure: compliance and sanctions

(1) A person must comply with a request under section 75ZA(1) within the period of 21 days beginning with the day on which the request is received.

(2) A return of permitted expenditure must be accompanied by a declaration made by the person (or in the case of an association or body of persons, by a director, general manager, secretary or other similar officer of the association or body)—

(a) verifying the return, and

(b) in the case of a return of the kind mentioned in section 75ZA(3)(a), giving particulars of the matters for which the expenses were incurred.

(3) A person who fails to deliver a return or declaration in accordance with this section is guilty of an illegal practice.

(4) A person who knowingly makes a false declaration under subsection (2) is guilty of a corrupt practice.

(5) The court before whom a person is convicted under subsection (3) or (4) may, if they think it just in the special circumstances of the case, mitigate or entirely remit any incapacity imposed by virtue of section 173.

(6) Where any act or omission of an association or body of persons, corporate or unincorporate, is an offence declared to be a corrupt or illegal practice by this section, any person who at the time of the act or omission was a director, general manager, secretary or other similar officer of the association or body, or was purporting to act in any such capacity, shall be deemed to be guilty of that offence, unless he proves—

(a) that the act or omission took place without his consent or connivance, and

(b) that he exercised all such diligence to prevent the commission of the offence as he ought to have exercised having regard to the nature of his functions in that capacity and to all the circumstances.]

[75A Scottish local government elections: prohibition of expenses not authorised by election agent]

(1) This section applies in relation to a local government election in Scotland.

(2) No person other than a candidate at the election, his election agent or a person authorised in writing by the election agent shall, with a view to promoting or procuring the election of the candidate, incur any expenses on account of—

(a) holding public meetings or organising any public display;

(b) issuing advertisements, circulars or publications; or

(c) otherwise presenting to the electors the candidate or his views or the extent or nature of his backing or disparaging another candidate.

(3) Subsection (2)(c) above does not restrict the publication of any matter relating to the election in—

(a) a newspaper or other periodical;

(b) a broadcast made by the British Broadcasting Corporation; or

(c) a programme included in any service licensed under Part 1 or 3 of the Broadcasting Act 1990 (c 42) or Part 1 or 2 of the Broadcasting Act 1996 (c 55).

(4) Subsection (2) does not apply to expenses incurred by any person—

(a) which do not exceed in the aggregate the permitted sum (and are not incurred by that person as part of a concerted plan of action); or

(b) in travelling or in living away from home or similar personal expenses.

(5) For the purposes of subsection (4)(a) above—

(a) 'the permitted sum' means, in respect of each candidate, £50 together with an additional 0.5p for every entry in the register of local government electors for the electoral area in question as it has effect on the last day for publication of notice of the election; and

(b) expenses are to be regarded as incurred by a person 'as part of a concerted plan of action' if they are incurred by that person in pursuance of any plan or other arrangement whereby that person and one or more other persons are to incur, with a view to promoting or procuring the election of the same candidate, expenses which (disregarding subsection (4)(a)) fall within subsection (2) above.

(6) Where a person incurs any expenses required by subsection (2) above to be authorised by the election agent, that person shall, within 21 days after the day on which the result of the election is declared, deliver to the appropriate officer—

(a) a return of the amount of the expenses, stating the election at which, and the candidate in whose support they were incurred;

(b) a declaration by that person (or in the case of an association or body of persons, by a director, general manager, secretary or other similar officer of the association or body) verifying the return and giving particulars of the matters for which the expenses were incurred; and

(c) the authority received from the election agent (which, for the purposes of this section, is to be treated as forming part of the return).

(7) A person is guilty of a corrupt practice if he—

(a) incurs, or aids, abets, counsels or procures any other persons to incur, any expenses in contravention of subsection (2) above; or

(b) makes a declaration required by subsection (6)(b) above which he knows to be false.

(8) A person is guilty of an illegal practice if he fails to deliver any return or declaration as required by subsection (6) above.

(9) The court by or before which a person is convicted of a corrupt or illegal practice under subsection (7) or (8) above may, if the court thinks it just in the special circumstances of the case, mitigate or entirely remit any incapacity incurred under section 173 or 173A of this Act by virtue of the conviction.

(10) A candidate is not liable for, and his election is not void by reason of, a corrupt or illegal practice under subsection (7) or (8) above committed by an agent without his consent or connivance.

(11) Where any act or omission of an association or body of persons (whether corporate or unincorporate) is a corrupt or illegal practice under this section, any person who at the time of the act or omission was a director, general manager, secretary or other similar officer of the association or body, or was purporting to act in any such capacity, is also guilty of the corrupt or illegal practice, unless the person proves—

(a) that the act or omission took place without his consent or connivance; and

(b) that he exercised all such diligence to prevent the commission of the offence as he ought to have exercised having regard to the nature of his functions in that capacity and to all the circumstances.]

76 Limitation of election expenses

(1) [The election expenses incurred by or on behalf of a candidate at an election must not in the aggregate exceed the maximum amount specified in subsection (2) below or, in the case of any of the Authority elections mentioned in subsection (2A)(a) to (c) below, the maximum amount prescribed by order under that subsection.]

. . .

[(1B) Where any election expenses are incurred in excess of a maximum amount specified in subsection (2) below or prescribed by order under subsection (2A) below, any candidate or election agent who—

(a) incurred, or authorised the incurring of, the election expenses, and

(b) knew or ought reasonably to have known that the expenses would be incurred in excess of that maximum amount,

shall be guilty of an illegal practice.]

(2) That maximum amount is—

(a) for a candidate at a [parliamentary general election being an election]—

(i) in a county constituency [£7,150] together with an additional [7p] for every entry in the register of electors [. . .]; and

(ii) in a borough constituency [£7,150] together with an additional [5p] for every entry in the register of electors [. . .];

[(aa) for a candidate at a parliamentary by-election, £100,000;]

(b) for a candidate at a local government election [other than an Authority election]—

[. . .]

(ii) at any other local government election [£600] together with an additional [5p] for every entry in the register of electors [. . .].

. . .

[. . .]

(4) [In subsection (2) above 'the register of electors' means the register of parliamentary electors, or (as the case may be) local government electors, for the constituency or electoral area in question as it has effect on the last day for publication of notice of the election.]

(5) The maximum amount mentioned above for a candidate at a parliamentary election [or an Authority election (including the maximum amount for the purposes of subsection (1A) above)] is not required to cover the candidate's personal expenses.

[(5A) The maximum amount mentioned above for a candidate at a local government election in Scotland is not required to cover—

(a) the candidate's personal expenses;

(b) expenses that are reasonably attributable to the candidate having a physical or mental impairment that has a substantial and long-term adverse effect on the candidate's ability to carry out normal day-to-day activities.]

(6) Where at an election a poll is countermanded or abandoned by reason of a candidate's death, the maximum amount of election expenses shall, for any of the other candidates who then remain validly nominated, be twice or, if there has been a previous increase under this subsection, three times what it would have been but for any increase under this subsection; but the maximum amount shall not be affected for any candidate by the change in the timing of the election or of any step in the proceedings at the election.

92 Broadcasting from outside United Kingdom

[(1) No person shall, with intent to influence persons to give or refrain from giving their votes at a parliamentary or local government election, include, or aid, abet, counsel or procure the inclusion of, any matter relating to the election in any programme service (within the meaning of the Broadcasting Act 1990) provided from a place outside the United Kingdom otherwise than in pursuance of arrangements made with:—

(a) the British Broadcasting Corporation;

(b) Sianel Pedwar Cymru; or

(c) the holder of any licence granted by [the Office of Communications],

for the reception and re-transmission of that matter by that body or the holder of that licence] [or in pursuance of arrangements made with—

(i) the Independent Television Commission or the Radio Authority, or

(ii) any programme contractor whose contract continues in force by virtue of Part II or IV of Schedule 11 to the Broadcasting Act 1990,

for the matter to be received by that body or contractor and re-transmitted by that body in the provision of any broadcasting service in accordance with the said Schedule 11.]

(2) An offence under this section shall be an illegal practice, but the court before whom a person is convicted of an offence under this section may, if they think it just in the special circumstances of the case, mitigate or entirely remit any incapacity imposed by virtue of section 173 below.

(3) Where any act or omission of an association or body of persons, corporate or unincorporate, is an illegal practice under this section, any person who at the time of the act or omission was a director, general manager, secretary or other similar officer of the association or body, or was purporting to act in any such capacity, shall be deemed to be guilty of the illegal practice, unless he proves—

(a) that the act or omission took place without his consent or connivance; and

(b) that he exercised all such diligence to prevent the commission of the illegal practice as he ought to have exercised having regard to the nature of his functions in that capacity and to all the circumstances.

[93 Broadcasting of local items during election period

(1) Each broadcasting authority shall adopt a code of practice with respect to the participation of candidates at a parliamentary or local government election in items about the constituency or electoral area in question which are included in relevant services during the election period.

(2) The code for the time being adopted by a broadcasting authority under this section shall be either—

(a) a code drawn up by that authority, whether on their own or jointly with one or more other broadcasting authorities, or

(b) a code drawn up by one or more other such authorities;

and a broadcasting authority shall from time to time consider whether the code for the time being so adopted by them should be replaced by a further code falling within paragraph (a) or (b).

(3) Before drawing up a code under this section a broadcasting authority shall have regard to any views expressed by the Electoral Commission for the purposes of this subsection; and any such code may make different provision for different cases.

(4) [The Office of Communications] shall do all that they can to secure that the code for the time being adopted by them under this section is observed in the provision of relevant services; and the British Broadcasting Corporation and Sianel Pedwar Cymru shall each observe in the provision of relevant services the code so adopted by them.

(5) For the purposes of subsection (1) 'the election period', in relation to an election, means the period beginning—

(a) (if a parliamentary general election) with the date of the dissolution of Parliament or any earlier time at which Her Majesty's intention to dissolve Parliament is announced,

(b) (if a parliamentary by-election) with the date of the issue of the writ for the election or any earlier date on which a certificate of the vacancy is notified in the London Gazette in accordance with the Recess Elections Act 1975, or

(c) (if a local government election) with the last date for publication of notice of the election,

and ending with the close of the poll.

(6) In this section—

'broadcasting authority' means the British Broadcasting Corporation, [the Office of Communications] or Sianel Pedwar Cymru;

'candidate', in relation to an election, means a candidate standing nominated at the election or included in a list of candidates submitted in connection with it;

'relevant services'—

(a) in relation to the British Broadcasting Corporation or Sianel Pedwar Cymru, means services broadcast by that body;

(b) [in relation to the Office of Communications, means services licensed under Part 1 or 3 of the Broadcasting Act 1990 or Part 1 or 2 of the Broadcasting Act 1996.]]

100 Illegal canvassing by police officers

(1) No member of a police force shall by word, message, writing or in any other manner, endeavour to persuade any person to give, or dissuade any person from giving, his vote, whether as an elector or as proxy—

(a) at any parliamentary election for a constituency, or

(b) at any local government election for any electoral area,

wholly or partly within the police area.

(2) A person acting in contravention of subsection (1) above shall be liable [on summary conviction to a fine not exceeding level 3 on the standard scale but] nothing in that subsection shall subject a member of a police force to any penalty for anything done in the discharge of his duty as a member of the force.

(3) In this section references to a member of a police force and to a police area are to be taken in relation to Northern Ireland as references to a member of [the Police Service of Northern Ireland].

PUBLIC ORDER ACT 1986
(1986, c 64)

PART II
PROCESSIONS AND ASSEMBLIES

11 Advance notice of public processions

(1) Written notice shall be given in accordance with this section of any proposal to hold a public procession intended—

(a) to demonstrate support for or opposition to the views or actions of any person or body of persons,

(b) to publicise a cause or campaign, or

(c) to mark or commemorate an event,

unless it is not reasonably practicable to give any advance notice of the procession.

(2) Subsection (1) does not apply where the procession is one commonly or customarily held in the police area (or areas) in which it is proposed to be held or is a funeral procession organised by a funeral director acting in the normal course of his business.

(3) The notice must specify the date when it is intended to hold the procession, the time when it is intended to start it, its proposed route, and the name and address of the person (or of one of the persons) proposing to organise it.

(4) Notice must be delivered to a police station—

(a) in the police area in which it is proposed the procession will start, or

(b) where it is proposed the procession will start in Scotland and cross into England, in the first police area in England on the proposed route.

(5) If delivered not less than 6 clear days before the date when the procession is intended to be held, the notice may be delivered by post by the recorded delivery service; but section 7 of the Interpretation Act 1978 (under which a document sent by post is deemed to have been served when posted and to have been delivered in the ordinary course of post) does not apply.

(6) If not delivered in accordance with subsection (5), the notice must be delivered by hand not less than 6 clear days before the date when the procession is intended to be held or, if that is not reasonably practicable, as soon as delivery is reasonably practicable.

(7) Where a public procession is held, each of the persons organising it is guilty of an offence if—

(a) the requirements of this section as to notice have not been satisfied, or

(b) the date when it is held, the time when it starts, or its route, differs from the date, time or route specified in the notice.

(8) It is a defence for the accused to prove that he did not know of, and neither suspected nor had reason to suspect, the failure to satisfy the requirements or (as the case may be) the difference of date, time or route.

(9) To the extent that an alleged offence turns on a difference of date, time or route, it is a defence for the accused to prove that the difference arose from circumstances beyond his control or from something done with the agreement of a police officer or by his direction.

(10) A person guilty of an offence under subsection (7) is liable on summary conviction to a fine not exceeding level 3 on the standard scale.

12 Imposing conditions on public processions

(1) If the senior police officer, having regard to the time or place at which and the circumstances in which any public procession is being held or is intended to be held and to its route or proposed route, reasonably believes that—

(a) it may result in serious public disorder, serious damage to property or serious disruption to the life of the community, or

(b) the purpose of the persons organising it is the intimidation of others with a view to compelling them not to do an act they have a right to do, or to do an act they have a right not to do,

he may give directions imposing on the persons organising or taking part in the procession such conditions as appear to him necessary to prevent such disorder, damage, disruption or intimidation, including conditions as to the route of the procession or prohibiting it from entering any public place specified in the directions.

(2) In subsection (1) 'the senior police officer' means—

(a) in relation to a procession being held, or to a procession intended to be held in a case where persons are assembling with a view to taking part in it, the most senior in rank of the police officers present at the scene, and

(b) in relation to a procession intended to be held in a case where paragraph (a) does not apply, the chief officer of police.

(3) A direction given by a chief officer of police by virtue of subsection (2)(b) shall be given in writing.

(4) A person who organises a public procession and knowingly fails to comply with a condition imposed under this section is guilty of an offence, but it is a defence for him to prove that the failure arose from circumstances beyond his control.

(5) A person who takes part in a public procession and knowingly fails to comply with a condition imposed under this section is guilty of an offence, but it is a defence for him to prove that the failure arose from circumstances beyond his control.

(6) A person who incites another to commit an offence under subsection (5) is guilty of an offence.

[. . .]

(8) A person guilty of an offence under subsection (4) is liable on summary conviction to imprisonment for a term not exceeding 3 months or a fine not exceeding level 4 on the standard scale or both.

(9) A person guilty of an offence under subsection (5) is liable on summary conviction to a fine not exceeding level 3 on the standard scale.

(10) A person guilty of an offence under subsection (6) is liable on summary conviction to imprisonment for a term not exceeding 3 months or a fine not exceeding level 4 on the standard scale or both [. . .].

(11) In Scotland this section applies only in relation to a procession being held, and to a procession intended to be held in a case where persons are assembling with a view to taking part in it.

13 Prohibiting public processions

(1) If at any time the chief officer of police reasonably believes that, because of particular circumstances existing in any district or part of a district, the powers under section 12 will not be sufficient to prevent the holding of public processions in that district or part from resulting in serious public disorder, he shall apply to the council of the district for an order prohibiting for such period not exceeding 3 months as may be specified in the application the holding of all public processions (or of any class of public procession so specified) in the district or part concerned.

(2) On receiving such an application, a council may with the consent of the Secretary of State make an order either in the terms of the application or with such modifications as may be approved by the Secretary of State.

(3) Subsection (1) does not apply in the City of London or the metropolitan police district.

(4) If at any time the Commissioner of Police for the City of London or the Commissioner of Police of the Metropolis reasonably believes that, because of particular circumstances existing in his police area or part of it, the powers under section 12 will not be sufficient to prevent the holding of public processions in that area or part from resulting in serious public disorder, he may with the consent of the Secretary of State make an order prohibiting for such period not exceeding 3 months as may be specified in the order the holding of all public processions (or of any class of public procession so specified) in the area or part concerned.

(5) An order made under this section may be revoked or varied by a subsequent order made in the same way, that is, in accordance with subsections (1) and (2) or subsection (4), as the case may be.

(6) Any order under this section shall, if not made in writing, be recorded in writing as soon as practicable after being made.

(7) A person who organises a public procession the holding of which he knows is prohibited by virtue of an order under this section is guilty of an offence.

(8) A person who takes part in a public procession the holding of which he knows is prohibited by virtue of an order under this section is guilty of an offence.

(9) A person who incites another to commit an offence under subsection (8) is guilty of an offence.

[. . .]

(11) A person guilty of an offence under subsection (7) is liable on summary conviction to imprisonment for a term not exceeding 3 months or a fine not exceeding level 4 on the standard scale or both.

(12) A person guilty of an offence under subsection (8) is liable on summary conviction to a fine not exceeding level 3 on the standard scale.

(13) A person guilty of an offence under subsection (9) is liable on summary conviction to imprisonment for a term not exceeding 3 months or a fine not exceeding level 4 on the standard scale or both [. . .].

14 Imposing conditions on public assemblies

(1) If the senior police officer, having regard to the time or place at which and the circumstances in which any public assembly is being held or is intended to be held, reasonably believes that—

(a) it may result in serious public disorder, serious damage to property or serious disruption to the life of the community, or

(b) the purpose of the persons organising it is the intimidation of others with a view to compelling them not to do an act they have a right to do, or to do an act they have a right not to do,

he may give directions imposing on the persons organising or taking part in the assembly such conditions as to the place at which the assembly may be (or continue to be) held, its maximum duration, or the maximum number of persons who may constitute it, as appear to him necessary to prevent such disorder, damage, disruption or intimidation.

(2) In subsection (1) 'the senior police officer' means—

(a) in relation to an assembly being held, the most senior in rank of the police officers present at the scene, and

(b) in relation to an assembly intended to be held, the chief officer of police.

(3) A direction given by a chief officer of police by virtue of subsection (2)(b) shall be given in writing.

(4) A person who organises a public assembly and knowingly fails to comply

with a condition imposed under this section is guilty of an offence, but it is a defence for him to prove that the failure arose from circumstances beyond his control.

(5) A person who takes part in a public assembly and knowingly fails to comply with a condition imposed under this section is guilty of an offence, but it is a defence for him to prove that the failure arose from circumstances beyond his control.

(6) A person who incites another to commit an offence under subsection (5) is guilty of an offence.

[. . .]

(8) A person guilty of an offence under subsection (4) is liable on summary conviction to imprisonment for a term not exceeding 3 months or a fine not exceeding level 4 on the standard scale or both.

(9) A person guilty of an offence under subsection (5) is liable on summary conviction to a fine not exceeding level 3 on the standard scale.

(10) A person guilty of an offence under subsection (6) is liable on summary conviction to imprisonment for a term not exceeding 3 months or a fine not exceeding level 4 on the standard scale or both [. . .].

[14A Prohibiting trespassory assemblies

(1) If at any time the chief officer of police reasonably believes that an assembly is intended to be held in any district at a place on land to which the public has no right of access or only a limited right of access and that the assembly—

(a) is likely to be held without the permission of the occupier of the land or to conduct itself in such a way as to exceed the limits of any permission of his or the limits of the public's right of access, and

(b) may result—

(i) in serious disruption to the life of the community, or

(ii) where the land, or a building or monument on it, is of historical, architectural, archaeological or scientific importance, in significant damage to the land, building or monument,

he may apply to the council of the district for an order prohibiting for a specified, period the holding of all trespassory assemblies in the district or a part of it, as specified.

(2) On receiving such an application, a council may—

(a) in England and Wales, with the consent of the Secretary of State make an order either in the terms of the application or with such modifications as may be approved by the Secretary of State; or

(b) in Scotland, make an order in the terms of the application.

(3) Subsection (1) does not apply in the City of London or the metropolitan police district.

(4) If at any time the Commissioner of Police for the City of London or the Commissioner of Police of the Metropolis reasonably believes that an assembly is intended to be held at a place on land to which the public has no right of access or only a limited right of access in his police area and that the assembly—

(a) is likely to be held without the permission of the occupier of the land or to conduct itself in such a way as to exceed the limits of any permission of his or the limits of the public's right of access, and

(b) may result—

(i) in serious disruption to the life of the community, or

(ii) where the land, or a building or monument on it, is of historical, architectural, archaeological or scientific importance, in significant damage to the land, building or monument,

he may with the consent of the Secretary of State make an order prohibiting for a specified period the holding of all trespassory assemblies in the area or a part of it, as specified.

(5) An order prohibiting the holding of trespassory assemblies operates to prohibit any assembly which—

(a) is held on land to which the public has no right of access or only a limited right of access, and

(b) takes place in the prohibited circumstances, that is to say, without the permission of the occupier of the land or so as to exceed the limits of any permission of his or the limits of the public's right of access.

(6) No order under this section shall prohibit the holding of assemblies for a period exceeding 4 days or in an area exceeding an area represented by a circle with a radius of 5 miles from a specified centre.

(7) An order made under this section may be revoked or varied by a subsequent order made in the same way, that is, in accordance with subsection (1) and (2) or subsection (4), as the case may be.

(8) Any order under this section shall, if not made in writing, be recorded in writing as soon as practicable after being made.

(9) In this section and sections 14B and 14C—

'assembly' means an assembly of 20 or more persons;

'land' means land in the open air;

'limited', in relation to a right of access by the public to land, means that their use of it is restricted to use for a particular purpose (as in the case of a highway or road) or is subject to other restrictions;

'occupier' means—

(a) in England and Wales, the person entitled to possession of the land by virtue of an estate or interest held by him; or

(b) in Scotland, the person lawfully entitled to natural possession of the land, and in subsections (1) and (4) includes the person reasonably believed by the authority applying for or making the order to be the occupier;

'public' includes a section of the public; and

'specified' means specified in an order under this section.

[(9A) In relation to Scotland, the references in this section to the public's rights (or limited right) of access do not include any right which the public or any member of the public may have by way of access rights within the meaning of the Land Reform (Scotland) Act 2003 (asp 2).]

(10) In relation to Scotland, the references in subsection (1) above to a district and to the council of the district shall be construed—

(a) as respects applications before 1st April 1996, as references to the area of a regional or islands authority and to the authority in question; and

(b) as respects applications on and after that date, as references to a local government area and to the council for that area.

(11) In relation to Wales, the references in subsection (1) above to a district and to the council of the district shall be construed, as respects applications on and after 1st April 1996, as references to a county or county borough and to the council for that county or county borough.]

[14B Offences in connection with trespassory assemblies and arrest therefor

(1) A person who organises an assembly the holding of which he knows is prohibited by an order under section 14A is guilty of an offence.

(2) A person who takes part in an assembly which he knows is prohibited by an order under section 14A is guilty of an offence.

(3) In England and Wales, a person who incites another to commit an offence under subsection (2) is guilty of an offence.

[. . .]

(5) A person guilty of an offence under subsection (1) is liable on summary conviction to imprisonment for a term not exceeding 3 months or a fine not exceeding level 4 on the standard scale or both.

(6) A person guilty of an offence under subsection (2) is liable on summary conviction to a fine not exceeding level 3 on the standard scale.

(7) A person guilty of an offence under subsection (3) is liable on summary conviction to imprisonment for a term not exceeding 3 months or a fine not exceeding level 4 on the standard scale or both [. . .].

(8) Subsection (3) above is without prejudice to the application of any principle of Scots Law as respects art and part guilt to such incitement as is mentioned in that subsection.]

[14C Stopping persons from proceeding to trespassory assemblies

(1) If a constable in uniform reasonably believes that a person is on his way to an assembly within the area to which an order under section 14A applies which the constable reasonably believes is likely to be an assembly which is prohibited by that order, he may, subject to subsection (2) below—

(a) stop that person, and

(b) direct him not to proceed in the direction of the assembly.

(2) The power conferred by subsection (1) may only be exercised within the area to which the order applies.

(3) A person who fails to comply with a direction under subsection (1) which he knows has been given to him is guilty of an offence.

[. . .]

(5) A person guilty of an offence under subsection (3) is liable on summary conviction to a fine not exceeding level 3 on the standard scale.]

15 Delegation

(1) The chief officer of police may delegate, to such extent and subject to such conditions as he may specify, any of his functions under sections 12 to [14A] to [an] assistant chief constable; and references in those sections to the person delegating shall be construed accordingly.

(2) *[Does not apply to Scotland.]*

16 Interpretation

In this Part—

'the City of London' means the City as defined for the purposes of the Acts relating to the City of London police;

'the metropolitan police district' means that district as defined in section 76 of the London Government Act 1963;

'public assembly' means an assembly of [2] or more persons in a public place which is wholly or partly open to the air;

'public place' means—

(a) any highway, or in Scotland any road within the meaning of the Roads (Scotland) Act 1984, and

(b) any place to which at the material time the public or any section of the public has access, on payment or otherwise, as of right or by virtue of express or implied permission;

'public procession' means a procession in a public place.

PART III
RACIAL HATRED

Meaning of racial hatred

17 Meaning of 'racial hatred'

In this Part 'racial hatred' means hatred against a group of persons [. . .] defined by reference to colour, race, nationality (including citizenship) or ethnic or national origins.

Acts intended or likely to stir up racial hatred

18 Use of words or behaviour or display of written material

(1) A person who uses threatening, abusive or insulting words or behaviour, or displays any written material which is threatening, abusive or insulting, is guilty of an offence if—

(a) he intends thereby to stir up racial hatred, or

(b) having regard to all the circumstances racial hatred is likely to be stirred up thereby.

(2) An offence under this section may be committed in a public or a private place, except that no offence is committed where the words or behaviour are used, or the written material is displayed, by a person inside a dwelling and are not heard or seen except by other persons in that or another dwelling.

[. . .]

(4) In proceedings for an offence under this section it is a defence for the accused to prove that he was inside a dwelling and had no reason to believe that the words or behaviour used, or the written material displayed, would be heard or seen by a person outside that or any other dwelling.

(5) A person who is not shown to have intended to stir up racial hatred is not guilty of an offence under this section if he did not intend his words or behaviour, or the written material, to be, and was not aware that it might be, threatening, abusive or insulting.

(6) This section does not apply to words or behaviour used, or written material displayed, solely for the purpose of being [included in a programme service].

19 Publishing or distributing written material

(1) A person who publishes or distributes written material which is threatening, abusive or insulting is guilty of an offence if—

(a) he intends thereby to stir up racial hatred, or

(b) having regard to all the circumstances racial hatred is likely to be stirred up thereby.

(2) In proceedings for an offence under this section it is a defence for an accused who is not shown to have intended to stir up racial hatred to prove that he was not aware of the content of the material and did not suspect, and had no reason to suspect, that it was threatening, abusive or insulting.

(3) References in this Part to the publication or distribution of written material are to its publication or distribution to the public or a section of the public.

20 Public performance of play

(1) If a public performance of a play is given which involves the use of threatening, abusive or insulting words or behaviour, any person who presents or directs the performance is guilty of an offence if—

(a) he intends thereby to stir up racial hatred, or

(b) having regard to all the circumstances (and, in particular, taking the performance as a whole) racial hatred is likely to be stirred up thereby.

(2) If a person presenting or directing the performance is not shown to have intended to stir up racial hatred, it is a defence for him to prove—

(a) that he did not know and had no reason to suspect that the performance would involve the use of the offending words or behaviour, or

(b) that he did not know and had no reason to suspect that the offending words or behaviour were threatening, abusive or insulting, or

(c) that he did not know and had no reason to suspect that the circumstances in which the performance would be given would be such that racial hatred would be likely to be stirred up.

(3) This section does not apply to a performance given solely or primarily for one or more of the following purposes—

(a) rehearsal,

(b) making a recording of the performance, or

(c) enabling the performance to be [included in a programme service];

but if it is proved that the performance was attended by persons other than those directly connected with the giving of the performance or the doing in relation to it of the things mentioned in paragraph (b) or (c), the performance shall, unless the contrary is shown, be taken not to have been given solely or primarily for the purposes mentioned above.

(4) For the purposes of this section—

(a) a person shall not be treated as presenting a performance of a play by reason only of his taking part in it as a performer,

(b) a person taking part as a performer in a performance directed by another shall be treated as a person who directed the performance if without reasonable excuse he performs otherwise than in accordance with that person's direction, and

(c) a person shall be taken to have directed a performance of a play given under his direction notwithstanding that he was not present during the performance;

and a person shall not be treated as aiding or abetting the commission of an offence under this section by reason only of his taking part in a performance as a performer.

(5) In this section 'play' and 'public performance' have the same meaning as in the Theatres Act 1968.

(6) The following provisions of the Theatres Act 1968 apply in relation to an offence under this section as they apply to an offence under section 2 of that Act—

section 9 (script as evidence of what was performed),

section 10 (power to make copies of script),

section 15 (powers of entry and inspection).

21 Distributing, showing or playing a recording

(1) A person who distributes, or shows or plays, a recording of visual images or sounds which are threatening, abusive or insulting is guilty of an offence if—

(a) he intends thereby to stir up racial hatred, or

(b) having regard to all the circumstances racial hatred is likely to be stirred up thereby.

(2) In this Part 'recording' means any record from which visual images or sounds may, by any means, be reproduced; and references to the distribution, showing or playing of a recording are to its distribution, showing or playing to the public or a section of the public.

(3) In proceedings for an offence under this section it is a defence for an accused who is not shown to have intended to stir up racial hatred to prove that he was not aware of the content of the recording and did not suspect, and had no reason to suspect, that it was threatening, abusive or insulting.

(4) This section does not apply to the showing or playing of a recording solely for the purpose of enabling the recording to be [included in a programme service].

22 Broadcasting or including programme in cable programme service

(1) If a programme involving threatening, abusive or insulting visual images or sounds is [included in a programme service], each of the persons mentioned in subsection (2) is guilty of an offence if—

(a) he intends thereby to stir up racial hatred, or

(b) having regard to all the circumstances racial hatred is likely to be stirred up thereby.

(2) The persons are—

(a) the person providing the [. . .] programme service,

(b) any person by whom the programme is produced or directed, and

(c) any person by whom offending words or behaviour are used.

(3) If the person providing the service, or a person by whom the programme was produced or directed, is not shown to have intended to stir up racial hatred, it is a defence for him to prove that—

(a) he did not know and had not reason to suspect that the programme would involve the offending material, and

(b) having regard to the circumstances in which the programme was [included in a programme service], it was not reasonably practicable for him to secure the removal of the material.

(4) It is a defence for a person by whom the programme was produced or directed who is not shown to have intended to stir up racial hatred to prove that he did not know and had not reason to suspect—

(a) that the programme would be [included in a programme service], or

(b) that the circumstances in which the programme would be [. . .] so included would be such that racial hatred would be likely to be stirred up.

(5) It is a defence for a person by whom offending words or behaviour were used and who is not shown to have intended to stir up racial hatred to prove that he did not know and had no reason to suspect—

(a) that a programme involving the use of the offending material would be [included in a programme service], or

(b) that the circumstances in which a programme involving the use of the offending material would be [. . .] so included, or in which a programme [. . .] so included would involve the use of the offending material, would be such that racial hatred would be likely to be stirred up.

(6) A person who is not shown to have intended to stir up racial hatred is not guilty of an offence under this section if he did not know, and had no reason to suspect, that the offending material was threatening, abusive or insulting.

[. . .]

Racially inflammatory material

23 Possession of racially inflammatory material

(1) A person who has in his possession written material which is threatening, abusive or insulting, or a recording of visual images or sounds which are threatening, abusive or insulting, with a view to—

(a) in the case of written material, its being displayed, published, distributed, [or included in a cable programme service], whether by himself or another, or

(b) in the case of a recording, its being distributed, shown, played, [or included in a cable programme service], whether by himself or another,

is guilty of an offence if he intends racial hatred to be stirred up thereby or, having regard to all the circumstances, racial hatred is likely to be stirred up thereby.

(2) For this purpose regard shall be had to such display, publication, distribution, showing, playing, [or inclusion in a programme service] as he has, or it may reasonably be inferred that he has, in view.

(3) In proceedings for an offence under this section it is a defence for an accused who is not shown to have intended to stir up racial hatred to prove that he was not aware of the content of the written material or recording and did not suspect, and had no reason to suspect, that it was threatening, abusive or insulting.

[. . .]

24 Powers of entry and search

(1) [*Does not apply to Scotland.*]

(2) If in Scotland a sheriff or justice of the peace is satisfied by evidence on oath that there are reasonable grounds for suspecting that a person has possession of written material or a recording in contravention of section 23, the sheriff or justice may issue a warrant authorising any constable to enter and search the premises where it is suspected the material or recording is situated.

(3) A constable entering or searching premises in pursuance of a warrant issued under this section may use reasonable force if necessary.

(4) In this section 'premises' means any place and, in particular, includes—

(a) any vehicle, vessel, aircraft or hovercraft,

(b) any offshore installation as defined in section 1(3)(b) of the Mineral Workings (Offshore Installations) Act 1971, and

(c) any tent or movable structure.

25 Power to order forfeiture

(1) A court by or before which a person is convicted of—

(a) an offence under section 18 relating to the display of written material, or

(b) an offence under section 19, 21 or 23,

shall order to be forfeited any written material or recording produced to the court and shown to its satisfaction to be written material or a recording to which the offence relates.

(2) An order made under this section shall not take effect—

(a) in the case of an order made in proceedings in England and Wales, until the expiry of the ordinary time within which an appeal may be instituted or, where an appeal is duly instituted, until it is finally decided or abandoned;

(b) in the case of an order made in proceedings in Scotland, until the expiration of the time within which, by virtue of any statute, an appeal may be instituted or, where such an appeal is duly instituted, until the appeal is finally decided or abandoned.

(3) For the purposes of subsection (2)(a)—

(a) an application for a case stated or for leave to appeal shall be treated as the institution of an appeal, and

(b) where a decision on appeal is subject to a further appeal, the appeal is not finally determined until the expiry of the ordinary time within which a further appeal may be instituted or, where a further appeal is duly instituted, until the further appeal is finally decided or abandoned.

(4) For the purposes of subsection (2)(b) the lodging of an application for a stated case or note of appeal against sentence shall be treated as the institution of an appeal.

Supplementary proceedings

26 Savings for reports of parliamentary or judicial proceedings

(1) Nothing in this Part applies to a fair and accurate report of proceedings in Parliament [or in the Scottish Parliament or in the National Assembly for Wales].

(2) Nothing in this Part applies to a fair and accurate report of proceedings publicly heard before a court or tribunal exercising judicial authority where the report is published contemporaneously with the proceedings or, if it is not reasonably practicable or would be unlawful to publish a report of them contemporaneously, as soon as publication is reasonably practicable and lawful.

27 Procedure and punishment

(1), (2) [*Applies to England and Wales only.*]

(3) A person guilty of an offence under this Part is liable

(a) on conviction on indictment to imprisonment for a term not exceeding [seven years] or a fine or both;

(b) on summary conviction to imprisonment for a term not exceeding six months or a fine not exceeding the statutory maximum or both.

[PART IIIA
HATRED AGAINST PERSONS ON RELIGIOUS GROUNDS [OR GROUNDS OF SEXUAL ORIENTATION]

Meaning of 'religious hatred' [and hatred on the grounds of sexual orientation]

[29A Meaning of 'religious hatred'
In this Part 'religious hatred' means hatred against a group of persons defined by reference to religious belief or lack of religious belief.]

[29AB Meaning of 'hatred on the grounds of sexual orientation'
In this Part 'hatred on the grounds of sexual orientation' means hatred against a group of persons defined by reference to sexual orientation (whether towards persons of the same sex, the opposite sex or both).]

Acts intended to stir up religious hatred [or hatred on the grounds of sexual orientation]

[29B Use of words or behaviour or display of written material
(1) A person who uses threatening words or behaviour, or displays any written material which is threatening, is guilty of an offence if he intends thereby to stir up religious hatred [or hatred on the grounds of sexual orientation].
(2) An offence under this section may be committed in a public or a private place, except that no offence is committed where the words or behaviour are used, or the written material is displayed, by a person inside a dwelling and are not heard or seen except by other persons in that or another dwelling.
[. . .]
(4) In proceedings for an offence under this section it is a defence for the accused to prove that he was inside a dwelling and had no reason to believe that the words or behaviour used, or the written material displayed, would be heard or seen by a person outside that or any other dwelling.
(5) This section does not apply to words or behaviour used, or written material displayed, solely for the purpose of being included in a programme service.]

[29C Publishing or distributing written material
(1) A person who publishes or distributes written material which is threatening is guilty of an offence if he intends thereby to stir up religious hatred [or hatred on the grounds of sexual orientation].
(2) References in this Part to the publication or distribution of written material are to its publication or distribution to the public or a section of the public.]

[29D Public performance of play
(1) If a public performance of a play is given which involves the use of threatening words or behaviour, any person who presents or directs the performance is guilty of an offence if he intends thereby to stir up religious hatred [or hatred on the grounds of sexual orientation].
(2) This section does not apply to a performance given solely or primarily for one or more of the following purposes—
(a) rehearsal,
(b) making a recording of the performance, or
(c) enabling the performance to be included in a programme service;
but if it is proved that the performance was attended by persons other than those directly connected with the giving of the performance or the doing in relation to it of the things mentioned in paragraph (b) or (c), the performance shall, unless the contrary is shown, be taken not to have been given solely or primarily for the purpose mentioned above.
(3) For the purposes of this section—
(a) a person shall not be treated as presenting a performance of a play by reason only of his taking part in it as a performer,

(b) a person taking part as a performer in a performance directed by another shall be treated as a person who directed the performance if without reasonable excuse he performs otherwise than in accordance with that person's direction, and

(c) a person shall be taken to have directed a performance of a play given under his direction notwithstanding that he was not present during the performance;

and a person shall not be treated as aiding or abetting the commission of an offence under this section by reason only of his taking part in a performance as a performer.

(4) In this section 'play' and 'public performance' have the same meaning as in the Theatres Act 1968.

(5) The following provisions of the Theatres Act 1968 apply in relation to an offence under this section as they apply to an offence under section 2 of that Act—

section 9 (script as evidence of what was performed),
section 10 (power to make copies of script),
section 15 (powers of entry and inspection).]

[29E Distributing, showing or playing a recording

(1) A person who distributes, or shows or plays, a recording of visual images or sounds which are threatening is guilty of an offence if he intends thereby to stir up religious hatred [or hatred on the grounds of sexual orientation].

(2) In this Part 'recording' means any record from which visual images or sounds may, by any means, be reproduced; and references to the distribution, showing or playing of a recording are to its distribution, showing or playing to the public or a section of the public.

(3) This section does not apply to the showing or playing of a recording solely for the purpose of enabling the recording to be included in a programme service.]

[29F Broadcasting or including programme in programme service

(1) If a programme involving threatening visual images or sounds is included in a programme service, each of the persons mentioned in subsection (2) is guilty of an offence if he intends thereby to stir up religious hatred [or hatred on the grounds of sexual orientation].

(2) The persons are—

(a) the person providing the programme service,
(b) any person by whom the programme is produced or directed, and
(c) any person by whom offending words or behaviour are used.]

Inflammatory material

[29G Possession of inflammatory material

(1) A person who has in his possession written material which is threatening, or a recording of visual images or sounds which are threatening, with a view to—

(a) in the case of written material, its being displayed, published, distributed, or included in a programme service whether by himself or another, or

(b) in the case of a recording, its being distributed, shown, played, or included in a programme service, whether by himself or another,

is guilty of an offence if he intends [thereby to stir up religious hatred or hatred on the grounds of sexual orientation].

(2) For this purpose regard shall be had to such display, publication, distribution, showing, playing, or inclusion in a programme service as he has, or it may be reasonably be inferred that he has, in view.]

[29H Powers of entry and search

(1) [*Does not apply to Scotland.*]

(2) [. . .]

(3) A constable entering or searching premises in pursuance of a warrant issued under this section may use reasonable force if necessary.

(4) In this section 'premises' means any place and, in particular, includes—

(a) any vehicle, vessel, aircraft or hovercraft,

(b) any offshore installation as defined in section 12 of the Mineral Workings (Offshore Installations) Act 1971, and

(c) any tent or movable structure.]

. . .

[29J Protection of freedom of expression

Nothing in this Part shall be read or given effect in a way which prohibits or restricts discussion, criticism or expressions of antipathy, dislike, ridicule, insult or abuse of particular religions or the beliefs or practices of their adherents, or of any other belief system or the beliefs or practices of its adherents, or proselytising or urging adherents of a different religion or belief system to cease practising their religion or belief system.]

[29JA Protection of freedom of expression (sexual orientation)

[(1)] In this Part, for the avoidance of doubt, the discussion or criticism of sexual conduct or practices or the urging of persons to refrain from or modify such conduct or practices shall not be taken of itself to be threatening or intended to stir up hatred.]

[(2) In this Part, for the avoidance of doubt, any discussion or criticism of marriage which concerns the sex of the parties to marriage shall not be taken of itself to be threatening or intended to stir up hatred.]

Supplementary provisions

. . .

[29N Interpretation

In this Part—

'distribute', and related expressions, shall be construed in accordance with section 29C(2) (written material) and section 29E(2) (recordings);

'dwelling' means any structure or part of a structure occupied as a person's home or other living accommodation (whether the occupation is separate or shared with others) but does not include any part not so occupied, and for this purpose 'structure' includes a tent, caravan, vehicle, vessel or other temporary or movable structure;

['hatred on the grounds of sexual orientation' has the meaning given by section 29AB;]

'programme' means any item which is included in a programme service;

'programme service' has the same meaning as in the Broadcasting Act 1990;

'publish', and related expressions, in relation to written material, shall be construed in accordance with section 29C(2);

'religious hatred' has the meaning given by section 29A;

'recording' has the meaning given by section 29E(2), and 'play' and 'show', and related expressions, in relation to a recording, shall be construed in accordance with that provision;

'written material' includes any sign or other visible representation.']

PART V
MISCELLANEOUS AND SUPPLEMENTARY

. . .

40 Amendments, repeals and savings

. . .

(5) As respects Scotland, nothing in this Act affects any power of a constable under any rule of law.

COURT OF SESSION ACT 1988
(1988, c 36)

[Applications to the supervisory jurisdiction of the Court]

[27A Time limits

(1) An application to the supervisory jurisdiction of the Court must be made before the end of—

(a) the period of 3 months beginning with the date on which the grounds giving rise to the application first arise, or

(b) such longer period as the Court considers equitable having regard to all the circumstances.

(2) Subsection (1) does not apply to an application to the supervisory jurisdiction of the Court which, by virtue of any enactment, is to be made before the end of a period ending before the period of 3 months mentioned in that subsection (however that first-ending period may be expressed).]

[27B Requirement for permission

(1) No proceedings may be taken in respect of an application to the supervisory jurisdiction of the Court unless the Court has granted permission for the application to proceed.

(2) Subject to subsection (3), the Court may grant permission under subsection (1) for an application to proceed only if it is satisfied that—

(a) the applicant can demonstrate a sufficient interest in the subject matter of the application, and

(b) the application has a real prospect of success.

(3) Where the application relates to [a relevant decision of the Upper Tribunal], the Court may grant permission under subsection (1) for the application to proceed only if it is satisfied that—

(a) the applicant can demonstrate a sufficient interest in the subject matter of the application,

(b) the application has a real prospect of success, and

(c) either—

(i) the application would raise an important point of principle or practice, or

(ii) there is some other compelling reason for allowing the application to proceed.

(4) The Court may grant permission under subsection (1) for an application to proceed—

(a) subject to such conditions as the Court thinks fit,

(b) only on such of the grounds specified in the application as the Court thinks fit.

(5) The Court may decide whether or not to grant permission without an oral hearing having been held.]

[(6) In this section, 'a relevant Upper Tribunal decision' means—

(a) a decision of the Upper Tribunal for Scotland in an appeal from the First-tier Tribunal for Scotland under section 46 of the Tribunals (Scotland) Act 2014,

(b) a decision of the Upper Tribunal in an appeal from the First-tier Tribunal under section 11 of the Tribunals, Courts and Enforcement Act 2007.]

[27C Oral hearings where permission refused, etc

(1) Subsection (2) applies where, in relation to an application to the supervisory jurisdiction of the Court—

(a) the Court—

(i) refuses permission under subsection 27B(1) for the application to proceed, or

(ii) grants permission for the application to proceed subject to conditions or only on particular grounds, and

(b) the Court decides to refuse permission, or grant permission as mentioned in paragraph (a)(ii), without an oral hearing having been held.

(2) The person making the application may, within the period of 7 days beginning with the day on which that decision is made, request a review of the decision at an oral hearing.

(3) A request under subsection (2) must be considered by a different Lord Ordinary from the one who refused permission or granted permission as mentioned in subsection (1)(a)(ii).

(4) Where a request under subsection (2) is granted, the oral hearing must be conducted before a different Lord Ordinary from the one who refused or so granted permission.

(5) At a review following a request under subsection (2), the Court must consider whether to grant permission for the application to proceed; and subsections (2), (3) and (4) of section 27B apply for that purpose.

(6) Section 28 does not apply—

(a) where subsection (2) applies, or

(b) in relation to the refusal of a request made under subsection (2).]

[27D Appeals following oral hearings

(1) Subsection (2) applies where, after an oral hearing to determine whether or not to grant permission for an application to the supervisory jurisdiction of the Court to proceed, the Court—

(a) refuses permission for the application to proceed, or

(b) grants permission for the application to proceed subject to conditions or only on particular grounds.

(2) The person making the application may, within the period of 7 days beginning with the day on which the Court makes its decision, appeal under this section to the Inner House (but may not appeal under any other provision of this Act).

(3) In an appeal under subsection (2), the Inner House must consider whether to grant permission for the application to proceed; and subsections (2), (3) and (4) of section 27B apply for that purpose.

(4) In subsection (1), the reference to an oral hearing is to an oral hearing whether following a request under section 27C(2) or otherwise.]

SECURITY SERVICE ACT 1989
(1989, c 5)

1 The Security Service

(1) There shall continue to be a Security Service (in this Act referred to as 'the Service') under the authority of the Secretary of State.

(2) The function of the Service shall be the protection of national security and, in particular, its protection against threats from espionage, terrorism and sabotage, from the activities of agents of foreign powers and from actions intended to overthrow or undermine parliamentary democracy by political, industrial or violent means.

(3) It shall also be the function of the Service to safeguard the economic well-being of the United Kingdom against threats posed by the actions or intentions of persons outside the British Islands.

[(4) It shall also be the function of the Service to act in support of the activities of police forces, [the National Crime Agency] and other law enforcement agencies in the prevention and detection of serious crime.]

[(5) Section 81(5) of the Regulation of Investigatory Powers Act 2000 (meaning of 'prevention' and 'detection'), so far as it relates to serious crime, shall apply for the purposes of this Act as it applies for the purposes of that Act not contained in Chapter I of Part I.]

2 The Director-General

(1) The operations of the Service shall continue to be under the control of a Director-General appointed by the Secretary of State.

(2) The Director-General shall be responsible for the efficiency of the Service and it shall be his duty to ensure—

(a) that there are arrangements for securing that no information is obtained by the Service except so far as necessary for the proper discharge of its functions or disclosed by it except so far as necessary for that purpose or for the purpose of [the prevention or detection of] serious crime [or for the purpose of any criminal proceedings]; and

(b) that the Service does not take any action to further the interests of any political party[; and

(c) that there are arrangements agreed with the [Director General of the National Crime Agency], for co-ordinating the activities of the Service in pursuance of section 1(4) of this Act with the activities of police forces, [the National Crime Agency] and other law enforcement agencies.

(3) The arrangements mentioned in subsection (2)(a) above shall be such as to ensure that information in the possession of the Service is not disclosed for use in determining whether a person should be employed, or continue to be employed, by any person, or in any office or capacity, except in accordance with provisions in that behalf approved by the Secretary of State.

[(3A) Without prejudice to the generality of subsection (2)(a) above, the disclosure of information shall be regarded as necessary for the proper discharge of the functions of the Security Service if it consists of—

(a) the disclosure of records subject to and in accordance with the Public Records Act 1958; or

(b) the disclosure, subject to and in accordance with arrangements approved by the Secretary of State, of information to the Comptroller and Auditor General for the purposes of his functions.]

(4) The Director-General shall make an annual report on the work of the Service to the Prime Minister and the Secretary of State and may at any time report to either of them on any matter relating to its work.

OFFICIAL SECRETS ACT 1989
(1989, c 6)

1 Security and intelligence

(1) A person who is or has been—

(a) a member of the security and intelligence services; or

(b) a person notified that he is subject to the provisions of this subsection,

is guilty of an offence if without lawful authority he discloses any information, document or other article relating to security or intelligence which is or has been in his possession by virtue of his position as a member of any of those services or in the course of his work while the notification is or was in force.

(2) The reference in subsection (1) above to disclosing information relating to security or intelligence includes a reference to making any statement which purports to be a disclosure of such information or is intended to be taken by those to whom it is addressed as being such a disclosure.

(3) A person who is or has been a Crown servant or government contractor is guilty of an offence if without lawful authority he makes a damaging disclosure of any information, document or other article relating to security or intelligence which is or has been in his possession by virtue of his position as such but otherwise than as mentioned in subsection (1) above.

(4) For the purposes of subsection (3) above a disclosure is damaging if—

(a) it causes damage to the work of, or of any part of, the security and intelligence services; or

(b) it is of information or a document or other article which is such that its unauthorised disclosure would be likely to cause such damage or which falls within a class or description of information, documents or articles the unauthorised disclosure of which would be likely to have that effect.

(5) It is a defence for a person charged with an offence under this section to prove that at the time of the alleged offence he did not know, and had no reasonable cause to believe, that the information, document or article in question related to security or intelligence or, in the case of an offence under subsection (3), that the disclosure would be damaging within the meaning of that subsection.

(6) Notification that a person is subject to subsection (1) above shall be effected by a notice in writing served on him by a Minister of the Crown; and such a notice may be served if, in the Minister's opinion, the work undertaken by the person in question is or includes work connected with the security and intelligence services and its nature is such that the interests of national security require that he should be subject to the provisions of that subsection.

(7) Subject to subsection (8) below, a notification for the purposes of subsection (1) above shall be in force for the period of five years beginning with the day on which it is served but may be renewed by further notices under subsection (6) above for periods of five years at a time.

(8) A notification for the purposes of subsection (1) above may at any time be revoked by a further notice in writing served by the Minister on the person concerned; and the Minister shall serve such a further notice as soon as, in his opinion, the work undertaken by that person ceases to be such as is mentioned in subsection (6) above.

(9) In this section 'security or intelligence' means the work of, or in support of, the security and intelligence services or any part of them, and references to information relating to security or intelligence include references to information held or transmitted by those services or by persons in support of, or of any part of, them.

2 Defence

(1) A person who is or has been a Crown servant or government contractor is guilty of an offence if without lawful authority he makes a damaging disclosure of any information, document or other article relating to defence which is or has been in his possession by virtue of his position as such.

(2) For the purposes of subsection (1) above a disclosure is damaging if—

(a) it damages the capability of, or of any part of, the armed forces of the Crown to carry out their tasks or leads to loss of life or injury to members of those forces or serious damage to the equipment or installations of those forces; or

(b) otherwise than as mentioned in paragraph (a) above, it endangers the interests of the United Kingdom abroad, seriously obstructs the promotion or protection by the United Kingdom of those interests or endangers the safety of British citizens abroad; or

(c) it is of information or of a document or article which is such that its unauthorised disclosure would be likely to have any of those effects.

(3) It is a defence for a person charged with an offence under this section to prove that at the time of the alleged offence he did not know, and had no reasonable cause to believe, that the information, document or article in question related to defence or that its disclosure would be damaging within the meaning of subsection (1) above.

(4) In this section 'defence' means—

(a) the size, shape, organisation, logistics, order of battle, deployment, operations, state of readiness and training of the armed forces of the Crown;

(b) the weapons, stores or other equipment of those forces and the invention, development, production and operation of such equipment and research relating to it;

(c) defence policy and strategy and military planning and intelligence;

(d) plans and measures for the maintenance of essential supplies and services that are or would be needed in time of war.

3 International relations

(1) A person who is or has been a Crown servant or government contractor is guilty of an offence if without lawful authority he makes a damaging disclosure of—

(a) any information, document or other article relating to international relations; or

(b) any confidential information, document or other article which was obtained from a State other than the United Kingdom or an international organisation,

being information or a document or article which is or has been in his possession by virtue of his position as a Crown servant or government contractor.

(2) For the purposes of subsection (1) above a disclosure is damaging if—

(a) it endangers the interests of the United Kingdom abroad, seriously obstructs the promotion or protection by the United Kingdom of those interests or endangers the safety of British citizens abroad; or

(b) it is of information or of a document or article which is such that its unauthorised disclosure would be likely to have any of those effects.

(3) In the case of information or a document or article within subsection (1)(b) above—

(a) the fact that it is confidential, or

(b) its nature or contents,

may be sufficient to establish for the purposes of subsection (2)(b) above that the information, document or article is such that its unauthorised disclosure would be likely to have any of the effects there mentioned.

(4) It is a defence for a person charged with an offence under this section to prove that at the time of the alleged offence he did not know, and had no reasonable cause to believe, that the information, document or article in question was such as is mentioned in subsection (1) above or that its disclosure would be damaging within the meaning of that subsection.

(5) In this section 'international relations' means the relations between States, between international organisations or between one or more States and one or more such organisations and includes any matter relating to a State other than the United Kingdom or to an international organisation which is capable of affecting the relations of the United Kingdom with another State or with an international organisation.

(6) For the purposes of this section any information, document or article obtained from a State or organisation is confidential at any time while the terms on which it was obtained require it to be held in confidence or while the circumstances in which it was obtained make it reasonable for the State or organisation to expect that it would be so held.

4 Crime and special investigation powers

(1) A person who is or has been a Crown servant or government contractor is guilty of an offence if without lawful authority he discloses any information, document or other article to which this section applies and which is or has been in his possession by virtue of his position as such.

(2) This section applies to any information, document or other article—

(a) the disclosure of which—

(i) results in the commission of an offence; or

(ii) facilitates an escape from legal custody or the doing of any other act prejudicial to the safekeeping of persons in legal custody; or

(iii) impedes the prevention or detection of offences or the apprehension or prosecution of suspected offenders; or

(b) which is such that its unauthorised disclosure would be likely to have any of those effects.

(3) This section also applies to—

(a) any information obtained by reason of the interception of any communication in obedience to a warrant issued under section 2 of the Interception of Communications Act 1985 [or under the authority of an interception warrant under section 5 of the Regulation of Investigatory Powers Act 2000], any information relating to the obtaining of information by reason of any such interception and any document or other article which is or has been used or held for use in, or has been obtained by reason of, any such interception; and

(b) any information obtained by reason of action authorised by a warrant issued under section 3 of the Security Service Act 1989 [or under section 5 of the Intelligence Services Act 1994 or by an authorisation given under section 7 of that Act], any information relating to the obtaining of information by reason of any such action and any document or other article which is or has been used or held for use in, or has been obtained by reason of, any such action.

(4) It is a defence for a person charged with an offence under this section in respect of a disclosure falling within subsection (2)(a) above to prove that at the time of the alleged offence he did not know, and had no reasonable cause to believe, that the disclosure would have any of the effects there mentioned.

(5) It is a defence for a person charged with an offence under this section in respect of any other disclosure to prove that at the time of the alleged offence he did not know, and had no reasonable cause to believe, that the information, document or article in question was information or a document or article to which this section applies.

(6) In this section 'legal custody' includes detention in pursuance of any enactment or any instrument made under an enactment.

5 Information resulting from unauthorised disclosures or entrusted in confidence

(1) Subsection (2) below applies where—

(a) any information, document or other article protected against disclosure by the foregoing provisions of this Act has come into a person's possession as a result of having been—

(i) disclosed (whether to him or another) by a Crown servant or government contractor without lawful authority; or

(ii) entrusted to him by a Crown servant or government contractor on terms requiring it to be held in confidence or in circumstances in which the Crown servant or government contractor could reasonably expect that it would be so held; or

(iii) disclosed (whether to him or another) without lawful authority by a person to whom it was entrusted as mentioned in sub-paragraph (ii) above; and

(b) the disclosure without lawful authority of the information, document or article by the person into whose possession it has come is not an offence under any of those provisions.

(2) Subject to subsections (3) and (4) below, the person into whose possession the information, document or article has come is guilty of an offence if he discloses it without lawful authority knowing, or having reasonable cause to believe, that it is protected against disclosure by the foregoing provisions of this Act and that it has come into his possession as mentioned in subsection (1) above.

(3) In the case of information or a document or article protected against

disclosure by sections 1 to 3 above, a person does not commit an offence under subsection (2) above unless—

(a) the disclosure by him is damaging; and

(b) he makes it knowing, or having reasonable cause to believe, that it would be damaging;

and the question whether a disclosure is damaging shall be determined for the purposes of this subsection as it would be in relation to a disclosure of that information, document or article by a Crown servant in contravention of section 1(3), 2 (1) or 3(1) above.

(4) A person does not commit an offence under subsection (2) above in respect of information or a document or other article which has come into his possession as a result of having been disclosed—

(a) as mentioned in subsection (1)(a)(i) above by a government contractor; or

(b) as mentioned in subsection (1)(a)(iii) above,

unless that disclosure was by a British citizen or took place in the United Kingdom, in any of the Channel Islands or in the Isle of Man or a colony.

(5) For the purposes of this section information or a document or article is protected against disclosure by the foregoing provisions of this Act if—

(a) it relates to security or intelligence, defence or international relations within the meaning of section 1, 2 or 3 above or is such as is mentioned in section 3(1)(b) above; or

(b) it is information or a document or article to which section 4 above applies;

and information or a document or article is protected against disclosure by sections 1 to 3 above if it falls within paragraph (a) above.

(6) A person is guilty of an offence if without lawful authority he discloses any information, document or other article which he knows, or has reasonable cause to believe, to have come into his possession as a result of a contravention of section 1 of the Official Secrets Act 1911.

7 Authorised disclosures

(1) For the purposes of this Act a disclosure by—

(a) a Crown servant; or

(b) a person, not being a Crown servant or government contractor, in whose case a notification for the purposes of section 1(1) above is in force,

is made with lawful authority if, and only if, it is made in accordance with his official duty.

(2) For the purposes of this Act a disclosure by a government contractor is made with lawful authority if, and only if, it is made—

(a) in accordance with an official authorisation; or

(b) for the purposes of the functions by virtue of which he is a government contractor and without contravening an official restriction.

(3) For the purposes of this Act a disclosure made by any other person is made with lawful authority if, and only if, it is made—

(a) to a Crown servant for the purposes of his functions as such; or

(b) in accordance with an official authorisation.

(4) It is a defence for a person charged with an offence under any of the foregoing provisions of this Act to prove that at the time of the alleged offence he believed that he had lawful authority to make the disclosure in question and had no reasonable cause to believe otherwise.

(5) In this section 'official authorisation' and 'official restriction' mean, subject to subsection (6) below, an authorisation or restriction duly given or imposed by a Crown servant or government contractor or by or on behalf of a prescribed body or a body of a prescribed class.

(6) In relation to section 6 above 'official authorisation' includes an authorisation duly given by or on behalf of the State or organisation concerned or, in the case of an organisation, a member of it.

8 Safeguarding of information

(1) Where a Crown servant or government contractor, by virtue of his position as such, has in his possession or under his control any document or other article which it would be an offence under any of the foregoing provisions of this Act for him to disclose without lawful authority he is guilty of an offence if—

(a) being a Crown servant, he retains the document or article contrary to his official duty; or

(b) being a government contractor, he fails to comply with an official direction for the return or disposal of the document or article,

or if he fails to take such care to prevent the unauthorised disclosure of the document or article as a person in his position may reasonably be expected to take.

(2) It is a defence for a Crown servant charged with an offence under subsection (1)(a) above to prove that at the time of the alleged offence he believed that he was acting in accordance with his official duty and had no reasonable cause to believe otherwise.

(3) In subsections (1) and (2) above references to a Crown servant include any person, not being a Crown servant or government contractor, in whose case a notification for the purposes of section 1(1) above is in force.

(4) Where a person has in his possession or under his control any document or other article which it would be an offence under section 5 above for him to disclose without lawful authority, he is guilty of an offence if—

(a) he fails to comply with an official direction for its return or disposal; or

(b) where he obtained it from a Crown servant or government contractor on terms requiring it to be held in confidence or in circumstances in which that servant or contractor could reasonably expect that it would be so held, he fails to take such care to prevent its unauthorised disclosure as a person in his position may reasonably be expected to take.

(5) Where a person has in his possession or under his control any document or other article which it would be an offence under section 6 above for him to disclose without lawful authority, he is guilty of an offence if he fails to comply with an official direction for its return or disposal.

(6) A person is guilty of an offence if he discloses any official information, document or other article which can be used for the purpose of obtaining access to any information, document or other article protected against disclosure by the foregoing provisions of this Act and the circumstances in which it is disclosed are such that it would be reasonable to expect that it might be used for that purpose without authority.

(7) For the purposes of subsection (6) above a person discloses information or a document or article which is official if—

(a) he has or has had it in his possession by virtue of his position as a Crown servant or government contractor; or

(b) he knows or has reasonable cause to believe that a Crown servant or government contractor has or has had it in his possession by virtue of his position as such.

(8) Subsection (5) of section 5 above applies for the purposes of subsection (6) above as it applies for the purposes of that section.

(9) In this section 'official direction' means a direction duly given by a Crown servant or government contractor or by or on behalf of a prescribed body or a body of a prescribed class.

9 *[Does not apply to Scotland.]*

10 Penalties

(1) A person guilty of an offence under any provision of this Act other than section 8(1), (4) or (5) shall be liable—

(a) on conviction on indictment, to imprisonment for a term not exceeding two years or a fine or both;

(b) on summary conviction, to imprisonment for a term not exceeding six months or a fine not exceeding the statutory maximum or both.

(2) A person guilty of an offence under section 8(1), (4) or (5) above shall be liable on summary conviction to imprisonment for a term not exceeding [51 weeks] or a fine not exceeding level 5 on the standard scale or both.

11 *[Does not apply to Scotland.]*

12 'Crown servant' and 'government contractor'

(1) In this Act 'Crown servant' means—

(a) a Minister of the Crown;

[(aa) a member of the Scottish Executive or a Junior Scottish Minister;]

[(ab) the First Minister for Wales, a Welsh Minister appointed under section 48 of the Government of Wales Act 2006, the Counsel General to the Welsh Assembly Government or a Deputy Welsh Minister;]

(b) a person appointed under section 8 of the Northern Ireland Constitution Act 1973 (the Northern Ireland Executive etc);

(c) any person employed in the civil service of the Crown, including Her Majesty's Diplomatic Service, Her Majesty's Overseas Civil Service, the civil service of Northern Ireland and the Northern Ireland Court Service;

(d) any member of the naval, military or air forces of the Crown, including any person employed by an association established for the purposes of [Part XI of the Reserve Forces Act 1996];

(e) any constable and any other person employed or appointed in or for the purposes of any police force [(including the Police Service of Northern Ireland and the Police Service of Northern Ireland Reserve) or an NCA special (within the meaning of Part 1 of the Crime and Courts Act 2013).];

(f) any person who is a member or employee of a prescribed body or a body of a prescribed class and either is prescribed for the purposes of this paragraph or belongs to a prescribed class of members or employees of any such body;

(g) any person who is the holder of a prescribed office or who is an employee of such a holder and either is prescribed for the purposes of this paragraph or belongs to a prescribed class of such employees.

(2) In this Act 'government contractor' means, subject to subsection (3) below, any person who is not a Crown servant but who provides, or is employed in the provision of, goods or services—

(a) for the purposes of any Minister or person mentioned in paragraph (a) [, (ab)] or (b) of subsection (1) above, [of any office-holder in the Scottish Administration,] of any of the services, forces or bodies mentioned in that subsection or of the holder of any office prescribed under that subsection; or

[. . .]

(b) under an agreement or arrangement certified by the Secretary of State as being one to which the government of a State other than the United Kingdom or an international organisation is a party or which is subordinate to, or made for the purposes of implementing, any such agreement or arrangement.

(3) Where an employee or class of employees of any body, or of any holder of an office, is prescribed by an order made for the purposes of subsection (1) above—

(a) any employee of that body, or of the holder of that office, who is not prescribed or is not within the prescribed class; and

(b) any person who does not provide, or is not employed in the provision of, goods or services for the purposes of the performance of those functions of the body or the holder of the office in connection with which the employee or prescribed class of employees is engaged,

shall not be a government contractor for the purposes of this Act.

[(4) In this section 'office-holder in the Scottish Administration' has the same meaning as in section 126(7)(a) of the Scotland Act 1998.]

[(4A) In this section the reference to a police force includes a reference to the Civil Nuclear Constabulary.]

13 Other interpretation provisions

(1) In this Act—

'disclose' and 'disclosure', in relation to a document or other article, include parting with possession of it;

'international organisation' means, subject to subsections (2) and (3) below, an organisation of which only States are members and includes a reference to any organ of such an organisation;

'prescribed' means prescribed by an order made by the Secretary of State;

'State' includes the government of a State and any organ of its government and references to a State other than the United Kingdom include references to any territory outside the United Kingdom.

(2) In section 12(2)(b) above the reference to an international organisation includes a reference to any such organisation whether or not one of which only States are members and includes a commercial organisation.

(3) In determining for the purposes of subsection (1) above whether only States are members of an organisation, any member which is itself an organisation of which only States are members, or which is an organ of such an organisation, shall be treated as a State.

INTELLIGENCE SERVICES ACT 1994
(1994, c 13)

The Secret Intelligence Service

1 The Secret Intelligence Service

(1) There shall continue to be a Secret Intelligence Service (in this Act referred to as 'the Intelligence Service') under the authority of the Secretary of State; and, subject to subsection (2) below, its functions shall be—

(a) to obtain and provide information relating to the actions or intentions of persons outside the British Islands; and

(b) to perform other tasks relating to the actions or intentions of such persons.

(2) The functions of the Intelligence Service shall be exercisable only—

(a) in the interests of national security, with particular reference to the defence and foreign policies of Her Majesty's Government in the United Kingdom; or

(b) in the interests of the economic well-being of the United Kingdom; or

(c) in support of the prevention or detection of serious crime.

2 The Chief of the Intelligence Service

(1) The operations of the Intelligence Service shall continue to be under the control of a Chief of that Service appointed by the Secretary of State.

(2) The Chief of the Intelligence Service shall be responsible for the efficiency of that Service and it shall be his duty to ensure—

(a) that there are arrangements for securing that no information is obtained by the Intelligence Service except so far as necessary for the proper discharge of its functions and that no information is disclosed by it except so far as necessary—

(i) for that purpose;

(ii) in the interests of national security;

(iii) for the purpose of the prevention or detection of serious crime; or

(iv) for the purpose of any criminal proceedings; and

(b) that the Intelligence Service does not take any action to further the interests of any United Kingdom political party.

(3) Without prejudice to the generality of subsection (2)(a) above, the disclosure of information shall be regarded as necessary for the proper discharge of the functions of the Intelligence Service if it consists of—

(a) the disclosure of records subject to and in accordance with the Public Records Act 1958; or

(b) the disclosure, subject to and in accordance with arrangements approved by the Secretary of State, of information to the Comptroller and Auditor General for the purposes of his functions.

(4) The Chief of the Intelligence Service shall make an annual report on the work of the Intelligence Service to the Prime Minister and the Secretary of State and may at any time report to either of them on any matter relating to its work.

GCHQ

3 The Government Communications Headquarters

(1) There shall continue to be a Government Communications Headquarters under the authority of the Secretary of State; and, subject to subsection (2) below, its functions shall be—

(a) to monitor [, make use of] or interfere with electromagnetic, acoustic and other emissions and any equipment producing such emissions and to obtain and provide information derived from or related to such emissions or equipment and from encrypted material; and

(b) to provide advice and assistance about—

(i) languages, including terminology used for technical matters, and

(ii) cryptography and other matters relating to the protection of information and other material,

to the armed forces of the Crown, to Her Majesty's Government in the United Kingdom or to a Northern Ireland Department [or, in such cases as it considers appropriate, to other organisations or persons, or to the general public, in the United Kingdom or elsewhere].

(2) The functions referred to in subsection (1)(a) above shall be exercisable only—

(a) in the interests of national security, with particular reference to the defence and foreign policies of Her Majesty's Government in the United Kingdom; or

(b) in the interests of the economic well-being of the United Kingdom in relation to the actions or intentions of persons outside the British Islands; or

(c) in support of the prevention or detection of serious crime.

(3) In this Act the expression 'GCHQ' refers to the Government Communications Headquarters and to any unit or part of a unit of the armed forces of the Crown which is for the time being required by the Secretary of State to assist the Government Communications Headquarters in carrying out its functions.

4 The Director of GCHQ

(1) The operations of GCHQ shall continue to be under the control of a Director appointed by the Secretary of State.

(2) The Director shall be responsible for the efficiency of GCHQ and it shall be his duty to ensure—

(a) that there are arrangements for securing that no information is obtained by GCHQ except so far as necessary for the proper discharge of its functions and that no information is disclosed by it except so far as necessary for that purpose or for the purpose of any criminal proceedings; and

(b) that GCHQ does not take any action to further the interests of any United Kingdom political party.

(3) Without prejudice to the generality of subsection (2)(a) above, the disclosure of information shall be regarded as necessary for the proper discharge of the functions of GCHQ if it consists of—

(a) the disclosure of records subject to and in accordance with the Public Records Act 1958; or

(b) the disclosure, subject to and in accordance with arrangements approved by the Secretary of State, of information to the Comptroller and Auditor General for the purposes of his functions.

(4) The Director shall make an annual report on the work of GCHQ to the Prime Minister and the Secretary of State and may at any time report to either of them on any matter relating to its work.

CRIMINAL JUSTICE AND PUBLIC ORDER ACT 1994
(1994, c 33)

61 Power to remove trespassers on land

(1) If the senior police officer present at the scene reasonably believes that two or more persons are trespassing on land and are present there with the common purpose of residing there for any period, that reasonable steps have been taken by or on behalf of the occupier to ask them to leave and—

(a) that any of those persons has caused damage to the land or to property on the land or used threatening, abusive or insulting words or behaviour towards the occupier, a member of his family or an employee or agent of his, or

(b) that those persons have between them six or more vehicles on the land,

he may direct those persons, or any of them, to leave the land and to remove any vehicles or other property they have with them on the land.

(2) Where the persons in question are reasonably believed by the senior police officer to be persons who were not originally trespassers but have become trespassers on the land, the officer must reasonably believe that the other conditions specified in subsection (1) are satisfied after those persons became trespassers before he can exercise the power conferred by that subsection.

(3) A direction under subsection (1) above, if not communicated to the persons referred to in subsection (1) by the police officer giving the direction, may be communicated to them by any constable at the scene.

(4) If a person knowing that a direction under subsection (1) above has been given which applies to him—

(a) fails to leave the land as soon as reasonably practicable, or

(b) having left again enters the land as a trespasser within the period of three months beginning with the day on which the direction was given,

he commits an offence and is liable on summary conviction to imprisonment for a term not exceeding three months or a fine not exceeding level 4 on the standard scale, or both.

[(4A) Where, as respects Scotland, the reason why these persons have become trespassers is that they have ceased to be entitled to exercise access rights by virtue of—

(a) their having formed the common purpose mentioned in subsection (1) above; or

(b) one or more of the conditions specified in paragraphs (a) and (b) of that subsection having been satisfied,

the circumstances constituting that reason shall be treated, for the purposes of subsection (4) above, as having also occurred after these persons became trespassers.

(4B) In subsection (4A) above 'access rights' has the meaning given by the Land Reform (Scotland) Act 2003 (asp 2).]

(5) A constable in uniform who reasonably suspects that a person is committing an offence under this section may arrest him without a warrant.

(6) In proceedings for an offence under this section it is a defence for the accused to show—

(a) that he was not trespassing on the land, or

(b) that he had a reasonable excuse for failing to leave the land as soon as reasonably practicable or, as the case may be, for again entering the land as a trespasser.

(7), (8) [*Apply to England and Wales.*]

(9) In this section—

['common land' means—

(a) land registered as common land in a register of common land kept under Part 1 of the Commons Act 2006; and

(b) land to which Part 1 of that Act does not apply and which is subject to rights of common as defined in that Act.]

'commoner' means a person with rights of common [as so defined];

'land' does not include—

(a) buildings other than—

(i) agricultural buildings within the meaning of, in England and Wales, paragraphs 3 to 8 of Schedule 5 to the Local Government Finance Act 1988 or, in Scotland, section 7(2) of the Valuation and Rating (Scotland) Act 1956, or

(ii) scheduled monuments within the meaning of the Ancient Monuments and Archaeological Areas Act 1979;

(b) land forming part of—

[. . .]

(ii) a road within the meaning of the Roads (Scotland) Act 1984 unless it falls within the definitions in section 151(2)(a)(ii) or (b) (footpaths and cycle tracks) of that Act or is a bridleway within the meaning of section 47 of the Countryside (Scotland) Act 1967;

'the local authority', in relation to common land, means any local authority which has powers in relation to the land under [section 45 of the Commons Act 2006];

'occupier' [. . .] means—

[. . .]

(b) in Scotland, the person lawfully entitled to natural possession of the land;

'property', in relation to damage to property on land, means—

. . .

(b) in Scotland, either—

(i) heritable property other than land; or

(ii) corporeal moveable property,

and 'damage' includes the deposit of any substance capable of polluting the land;

'trespass' means, in the application of this section—

[. . .]

(b) in Scotland, entering, or as the case may be remaining on, land without lawful authority and without the occupier's consent; and

'trespassing' and 'trespasser' shall be construed accordingly;

'vehicle' includes—

(a) any vehicle, whether or not it is in a fit state for use on roads, and includes any chassis or body, with or without wheels, appearing to have formed part of such a vehicle, and any load carried by, and anything attached to, such a vehicle; and

(b) a caravan as defined in section 29(1) of the Caravan Sites and Control of Development Act 1960;

and a person may be regarded for the purposes of this section as having a purpose of residing in a place notwithstanding that he has a home elsewhere.

63 Powers to remove persons attending or preparing for a rave

(1) This section applies to a gathering on land in the open air of 100 or more persons (whether or not trespassers) at which amplified music is played during the night (with or without intermissions) and is such as, by reason of its loudness and duration and the time at which it is played, is likely to cause serious distress to the inhabitants of the locality; and for this purpose—

(a) such a gathering continues during intermissions in the music and, where the gathering extends over several days, throughout the period during which amplified music is played at night (with or without intermissions); and

(b) 'music' includes sounds wholly or predominantly characterised by the emission of a succession of repetitive beats.

(2) If, as respects any land [. . .], a police officer of at least the rank of superintendent reasonably believes that—

(a) two or more persons are making preparations for the holding there of a gathering to which this section applies,

(b) ten or more persons are waiting for such a gathering to begin there, or

(c) ten or more persons are attending such a gathering which is in progress,

he may give a direction that those persons and any other persons who come to prepare or wait for or to attend the gathering are to leave the land and remove any vehicles or other property which they have with them on the land.

(3) A direction under subsection (2) above, if not communicated to the persons referred to in subsection (2) by the police officer giving the direction, may be communicated to them by any constable at the scene.

(4) Persons shall be treated as having had a direction under subsection (2) above communicated to them if reasonable steps have been taken to bring it to their attention.

(5) A direction under subsection (2) above does not apply to an exempt person.

(6) If a person knowing that a direction has been given which applies to him—

(a) fails to leave the land as soon as reasonably practicable, or

(b) having left again enters the land within the period of 7 days beginning with the day on which the direction was given,

he commits an offence and is liable on summary conviction to imprisonment for a term not exceeding three months or a fine not exceeding level 4 on the standard scale, or both.

(7) In proceedings for an offence under this section it is a defence for the accused to show that he had a reasonable excuse for failing to leave the land as soon as reasonably practicable or, as the case may be, for again entering the land.

(8) A constable in uniform who reasonably suspects that a person is committing an offence under this section may arrest him without a warrant.

(9) This section does not apply—

[. . .]

(b) in Scotland, to a gathering in premises which, by virtue of section 41 of the Civic Government (Scotland) Act 1982, are licensed to be used as a place of public entertainment.

(10) In this section—

'entertainment licence' means a licence granted by a local authority under—

(a) Schedule 12 to the London Government Act 1963;

(b) section 3 of the Private Places of Entertainment (Licensing) Act 1967; or

(c) Schedule 1 to the Local Government (Miscellaneous Provisions) Act 1982;

'exempt person', in relation to land (or any gathering on land), means the occupier, any member of his family and any employee or agent of his and any person whose home is situated on the land;

'land in the open air' includes a place partly open to the air;

. . .

'occupier', 'trespasser' and 'vehicle' have the same meaning as in section 61.

(11) Until 1st April 1996, in this section 'local authority' means, in Wales, a district council.

65 Raves: power to stop persons from proceeding

(1) If a constable in uniform reasonably believes that a person is on his way to a gathering to which section 63 applies in relation to which a direction under section 63(2) is in force, he may, subject to subsections (2) and (3) below—

(a) stop that person, and

(b) direct him not to proceed in the direction of the gathering.

(2) The power conferred by subsection (1) above may only be exercised at a place within 5 miles of the boundary of the site of the gathering.

(3) No direction may be given under subsection (1) above to an exempt person.

(4) If a person knowing that a direction under subsection (1) above has been given to him fails to comply with that direction, he commits an offence and is liable on summary conviction to a fine not exceeding level 3 on the standard scale.

(5) A constable in uniform who reasonably suspects that a person is committing an offence under this section may arrest him without a warrant.

(6) In this section, 'exempt person' has the same meaning as in section 63.

CRIMINAL PROCEDURE (SCOTLAND) ACT 1995
(1995, c 46)

18 Prints, samples etc in criminal investigations

(1) This section applies where a person has been arrested and is in custody [. . .].

(2) A constable may take from the person [, or require the person to provide him with, such relevant physical data] as the constable may, having regard to the circumstances of the suspected offence [or the relevant offence (within the meaning of section 164(3) of the Extradition Act 2003)] in respect of which the person has been arrested [. . .], reasonably consider it appropriate to take [from him or require him to provide, and the person so required shall comply with that requirement].

[(3) Subject to [subsections (3A) and (4)] below [and sections 18A to 18G of this Act], all record of any relevant physical data taken from or provided by a person under subsection (2) above, all samples taken under subsection (6) [or (6A)] below and all information derived from such samples shall be destroyed as soon as possible following a decision not to institute criminal proceedings against the person or on the conclusion of such proceedings otherwise than with a conviction or an order under section 246(3) of this Act.]

[(3A) Subsection (3) does not apply to—

(a) relevant physical data taken under subsection (2) from, or provided under that subsection by, a person arrested under an extradition arrest power (within the meaning of section 174(2) of the Extradition Act 2003), and

(b) any sample, or any information derived from a sample, taken under subsection (6) or (6A) from a person arrested under such a power (but see section 18H).]

(4) The duty under subsection (3) above to destroy samples taken under subsection (6) [or (6A)] below and information derived from such samples shall not apply—

(a) where the destruction of the sample or the information could have the effect of destroying any sample, or any information derived therefrom, lawfully held in relation to a person other than the person from whom the sample was taken; or

(b) where the record, sample or information in question is of the same kind as a record, a sample or, as the case may be, information lawfully held by or on behalf of [the Police Service of Scotland] in relation to the person.

(5) No sample, or information derived from a sample, retained by virtue of subsection (4) above shall be used—

(a) in evidence against the person from whom the sample was taken; or

(b) for the purposes of the investigation of any offence.

(6) A constable may, with the authority of an officer of a rank no lower than inspector, take from the person—

(a) from the hair of an external part of the body other than pubic hair, by means of cutting, combing or plucking, a sample of hair or other material;

(b) from a fingernail or toenail or from under any such nail, a sample of nail or other material;

(c) from an external part of the body, by means of swabbing or rubbing, a sample of blood or other body fluid, of body tissue or of other material;

[. . .]

[(6A) A constable, or at a constable's direction a police custody and security officer, may take from the inside of the person's mouth, by means of swabbing, a sample of saliva or other material.]

[. . .]

[(7A) For the purposes of this section and [, subject to the modification in subsection (7AA), sections 18A to 19C] of this Act 'relevant physical data' means any—

(a) fingerprint;

(b) palm print;

(c) print or impression other than those mentioned in paragraph (a) and (b) above, of an external part of the body;

(d) record of a person's skin on an external part of the body created by a device approved by the Secretary of State.

[(7AA) The modification is that for the purposes of section 19C as it applies in relation to relevant physical data taken from or provided by a person outwith Scotland, subsection (7A) is to be read as if in paragraph (d) the words from 'created' to the end were omitted.]

[(7B) The Secretary of State by order made by statutory instrument may approve a device for the purpose of creating such records as are mentioned in paragraph (d) of subsection (7A) above.]

(8) Nothing in this section shall prejudice—

(a) any power of search;

(b) any power to take possession of evidence where there is imminent danger of its being lost or destroyed; or

(c) any power to take [relevant physical data] or samples under the authority of a warrant.

34 Petition for warrant

(1) A petition for warrant to arrest and commit a person suspected of or charged with crime may be in the forms—

(a) set out in Schedule 2 to this Act; or

(b) prescribed by Act of Adjournal,

or as nearly as may be in such form; and Schedule 3 to this Act shall apply to any such petition as it applies to the indictment.

(2) If on the application of the procurator fiscal, a sheriff is satisfied that there is reasonable ground for suspecting that an offence has been or is being committed by a body corporate, the sheriff shall have the like power to grant warrant for the citation of witnesses and the production of documents and articles as he would have if a petition charging an individual with the commission of the offence were presented to him.

47 Restriction on report of proceedings involving children

(1) Subject to subsection (3) below, no newspaper report of any proceedings in a court shall reveal the name, address or school, or include any particulars calculated to lead to the identification, of any person under the age of [18] years concerned in the proceedings, either—

(a) as being a person against or in respect of whom the proceedings are taken; or

(b) as being a witness in the proceedings.

(2) Subject to subsection (3) below, no picture which is, or includes, a picture of a person under the age of [18] years concerned in proceedings as mentioned in subsection (1) above shall be published in any newspaper in a context relevant to the proceedings.

[. . .]

(4) This section shall, with the necessary modifications, apply in relation to sound and television programmes included in a programme service (within the meaning of the Broadcasting Act 1990) as it applies in relation to newspapers.

(5) A person who publishes matter in contravention of this section shall be guilty of an offence and liable on summary conviction to a fine not exceeding level 4 of the standard scale.

(6) In this section, references to a court shall not include a court in England, Wales or Northern Ireland.

[Convention rights and EU law compatibility issues, and devolution issues]

[288ZA Right of Advocate General to take part in proceedings

(1) The Advocate General for Scotland may take part as a party in criminal proceedings so far as they relate to a compatibility issue.

(2) In this section 'compatibility issue' means a question, arising in criminal proceedings, as to—

(a) whether a public authority has acted (or proposes to act)—

(i) in a way which is made unlawful by section 6(1) of the Human Rights Act 1998, or

(ii) in a way which is [*made unlawful by section 57(4) of the Scotland Act 1998 (restriction on subordinate legislation modifying retained EU law)*], or

(b) whether an Act of the Scottish Parliament or any provision of an Act of the Scottish Parliament is incompatible with any of the Convention rights or [*in breach of the restriction in section 30A(1) of the Scotland Act 1998 (restriction on the modification of retained EU law)*].

(3) In subsection (2)—

(a) 'public authority' has the same meaning as in section 6 of the Human Rights Act 1998;

(b) references to acting include failing to act.]

[. . .]

[288ZB References of compatibility issues to the High Court or Supreme Court

(1) Where a compatibility issue has arisen in criminal proceedings before a court, other than a court consisting of two or more judges of the High Court, the court may, instead of determining it, refer the issue to the High Court.

(2) The Lord Advocate or the Advocate General for Scotland, if a party to criminal proceedings before a court, other than a court consisting of two or more judges of the High Court, may require the court to refer to the High Court any compatibility issue which has arisen in the proceedings.

(3) The High Court may, instead of determining a compatibility issue referred to it under subsection (2), refer it to the Supreme Court.

(4) Where a compatibility issue has arisen in criminal proceedings before a

court consisting of two or more judges of the High Court, otherwise than on a reference, the court may, instead of determining it, refer it to the Supreme Court.

(5) The Lord Advocate or the Advocate General for Scotland, if a party to criminal proceedings before a court consisting of two or more judges of the High Court, may require the court to refer to the Supreme Court any compatibility issue which has arisen in the proceedings otherwise than on a reference.

(6) On a reference to the Supreme Court under this section—

(a) the powers of the Supreme Court are exercisable only for the purpose of determining the compatibility issue;

(b) for that purpose the Court may make any change in the formulation of that issue that it thinks necessary in the interests of justice.

(7) When it has determined a compatibility issue on a reference under this section, the Supreme Court must remit the proceedings to the High Court.

(8) An issue referred to the High Court or the Supreme Court under this section is referred to it for determination.

(9) In this section 'compatibility issue' has the meaning given by section 288ZA.]

[288A Rights of appeal for Advocate General: [compatibility issues and] devolution issues

(1) This section applies where—

(a) a person is acquitted or convicted of a charge (whether on indictment or in summary proceedings), and

(b) the Advocate General for Scotland was a party to the proceedings [. . .]

[(2) Where the Advocate General for Scotland was a party in pursuance of paragraph 6 of Schedule 6 to the Scotland Act 1998 (devolution issues), the Advocate General may refer to the High Court for their opinion any devolution issue which has arisen in the proceedings.]

[(2A) Where the Advocate General for Scotland was a party in pursuance of section 288ZA, the Advocate General may refer to the High Court for their opinion any compatibility issue (within the meaning of that section) which has arisen in the proceedings.]

[(2B) If a reference is made under subsection (2) or (2A) the Clerk of Justiciary shall send to the person acquitted or convicted and to any solicitor who acted for that person at the trial a copy of the reference and intimation of the date fixed by the Court for a hearing.]

(3) The person may, not later than seven days before the date so fixed, intimate in writing to the Clerk of Justiciary and to the Advocate General for Scotland either—

(a) that he elects to appear personally at the hearing, or

(b) that he elects to be represented by counsel at the hearing,

but, except by leave of the Court on cause shown, and without prejudice to his right to attend, he shall not appear or be represented at the hearing other than by and in conformity with an election under this subsection.

(4) Where there is no intimation under subsection (3)(b), the High Court shall appoint counsel to act at the hearing as amicus curiae.

(5) The costs of representation elected under subsection (3)(b) or of an appointment under subsection (4) shall, after being taxed by the Auditor of the Court of Session, be paid by the Advocate General for Scotland out of money provided by Parliament.

(6) The opinion on the point referred under subsection (2) [or (2A)] shall not affect the acquittal or (as the case may be) conviction in the trial.]

[288AA Appeals to the Supreme Court: compatibility issues

(1) For the purpose of determining any compatibility issue an appeal lies to the

Supreme Court against a determination in criminal proceedings by a court of two or more judges of the High Court.

(2) On an appeal under this section—

(a) the powers of the Supreme Court are exercisable only for the purpose of determining the compatibility issue;

(b) for that purpose the Court may make any change in the formulation of that issue that it thinks necessary in the interests of justice.

(3) When it has determined the compatibility issue the Supreme Court must remit the proceedings to the High Court.

(4) In this section 'compatibility issue' has the same meaning as in section 288ZA.

(5) An appeal under this section against a determination lies only with the permission of the High Court or, failing that permission, with the permission of the Supreme Court.

(6) Subsection (5) does not apply if it is an appeal by the Lord Advocate or the Advocate General for Scotland against a determination by the High Court of a compatibility issue referred to it under section 288ZB(2).

(7) An application to the High Court for permission under subsection (5) must be made—

(a) within 28 days of the date of the determination against which the appeal lies, or

(b) within such longer period as the High Court considers equitable having regard to all the circumstances.

(8) An application to the Supreme Court for permission under subsection (5) must be made—

(a) within 28 days of the date on which the High Court refused permission under that subsection, or

(b) within such longer period as the Supreme Court considers equitable having regard to all the circumstances.]

[288B [Appeals to the Supreme Court: general]

(1) This section applies where the [Supreme Court] determines an appeal under [section 288AA of this Act or] paragraph 13(a) of Schedule 6 to the Scotland Act 1998 against a determination [. . .] by the High Court in the ordinary course of proceedings.

(2) The determination of the appeal shall not affect any earlier acquittal or earlier quashing of any conviction in the proceedings.

(3) Subject to subsection (2) above, the High Court shall have the same powers in relation to the proceedings when remitted to it by the [Supreme Court] as it would have if it were considering the proceedings otherwise than as a trial court.]

DEFAMATION ACT 1996
(1996, c 31)

1 Responsibility for publication

. . .

(3) A person shall not be considered the author, editor or publisher of a statement if he is only involved—

(a) in printing, producing, distributing or selling printed material containing the statement;

(b) in processing, making copies of, distributing, exhibiting or selling a film or sound recording (as defined in Part I of the Copyright, Designs and Patents Act 1988) containing the statement;

(c) in processing, making copies of, distributing or selling any electronic medium in or on which the statement is recorded, or in operating or providing any equipment, system or service by means of which the statement is retrieved, copied, distributed or made available in electronic form;

(d) as the broadcaster of a live programme containing the statement in circumstances in which he has no effective control over the maker of the statement;

(e) as the operator of or provider of access to a communications system by means of which the statement is transmitted, or made available, by a person over whom he has no effective control.

In a case not within paragraphs (a) to (e) the court may have regard to those provisions by way of analogy in deciding whether a person is to be considered the author, editor or publisher of a statement.

. . .

15 Reports, &c protected by qualified privilege

(1) The publication of any report or other statement mentioned in Schedule 1 to this Act is privileged unless the publication is shown to be made with malice, subject as follows.

(2) In defamation proceedings in respect of the publication of a report or other statement mentioned in Part II of that Schedule, there is no defence under this section if the plaintiff shows that the defendant—

(a) was requested by him to publish in a suitable manner a reasonable letter or statement by way of explanation or contradiction, and

(b) refused or neglected to do so.

For this purpose 'in a suitable manner' means in the same manner as the publication complained of or in a manner that is adequate and reasonable in the circumstances.

(3) This section does not apply to the publication to the public, or a section of the public, of matter which is not of public concern and the publication of which is not for the public benefit.

(4) Nothing in this section shall be construed—

(a) as protecting the publication of matter the publication of which is prohibited by law, or

(b) as limiting or abridging any privilege subsisting apart from this section.

CRIME AND DISORDER ACT 1998
(1998, c 37)

96 Offences racially aggravated

(1) The provisions of this section shall apply where it is—

(a) libelled in an indictment; or

(b) specified in a complaint,

and, in either case, proved that an offence has been racially aggravated.

(2) An offence is racially aggravated for the purposes of this section if—

(a) at the time of committing the offence, or immediately before or after doing so, the offender evinces towards the victim (if any) of the offence malice and ill-will based on the victim's membership (or presumed membership) of a racial group; or

(b) the offence is motivated (wholly or partly) by malice and ill-will towards members of a racial group based on their membership of that group,

and evidence from a single source shall be sufficient evidence to establish, for the purposes of this subsection, that an offence is racially aggravated.

(3) In subsection (2)(a) above—

'membership', in relation to a racial group, includes association with members of that group;

'presumed' means presumed by the offender.

(4) It is immaterial for the purposes of paragraph (a) or (b) of subsection (2) above whether or not the offender's malice and ill-will is also based, to any extent, on—

(a) the fact or presumption that any person or group of persons belongs to any religious group; or

(b) any other factor not mentioned in that paragraph.

[(5) The court must—

(a) state on conviction that the offence was racially aggravated,

(b) record the conviction in a way that shows that the offence was so aggravated,

(c) take the aggravation into account in determining the appropriate sentence, and

(d) state—

(i) where the sentence in respect of the offence is different from that which the court would have imposed if the offence were not so aggravated, the extent of and the reasons for that difference, or

(ii) otherwise, the reasons for there being no such difference.]

(6) In this section 'racial group' means a group of persons defined by reference to race, colour, nationality (including citizenship) or ethnic or national origins.

HUMAN RIGHTS ACT 1998
(1998, c 42)

Introduction

1 The Convention Rights

(1) In this Act 'the Convention rights' means the rights and fundamental freedoms set out in—

(a) Articles 2 to 12 and 14 of the Convention,

(b) Articles 1 to 3 of the First Protocol, and

(c) [Article 1 of the Thirteenth Protocol],

as read with Articles 16 to 18 of the Convention.

(2) Those Articles are to have effect for the purposes of this Act subject to any designated derogation or reservation (as to which see sections 14 and 15).

(3) The Articles are set out in Schedule 1.

(4) The [Secretary of State] may by order make such amendments to this Act as he considers appropriate to reflect the effect, in relation to the United Kingdom, of a protocol.

(5) In subsection (4) 'protocol' means a protocol to the Convention—

(a) which the United Kingdom has ratified; or

(b) which the United Kingdom has signed with a view to ratification.

(6) No amendment may be made by an order under subsection (4) so as to come into force before the protocol concerned is in force in relation to the United Kingdom.

2 Interpretation of Convention rights

(1) A court or tribunal determining a question which has arisen in connection with a Convention right must take into account any—

(a) judgment, decision, declaration or advisory opinion of the European Court of Human Rights,

(b) opinion of the Commission given in a report adopted under Article 31 of the Convention,

(c) decision of the Commission in connection with Article 26 or 27(2) of the Convention, or

(d) decision of the Committee of Ministers taken under Article 46 of the Convention, whenever made or given, so far as, in the opinion of the court or tribunal, it is relevant to the proceedings in which that question has arisen.

(2) Evidence of any judgment, decision, declaration or opinion of which account may have to be taken under this section is to be given in proceedings before any court or tribunal in such manner as may be provided by rules.

(3) In this section 'rules' means rules of court or, in the case of proceedings before a tribunal, rules made for the purposes of this section—

(a) by [. . .] [the Lord Chancellor or] the Secretary of State, in relation to any proceedings outside Scotland;

(b) by the Secretary of State, in relation to proceedings in Scotland; or

(c) by a Northern Ireland department, in relation to proceedings before a tribunal in Northern Ireland—

(i) which deals with transferred matters; and

(ii) for which no rules made under paragraph (a) are in force.

Legislation

3 Interpretation of legislation

(1) So far as it is possible to do so, primary legislation and subordinate legislation must be read and given effect in a way which is compatible with the Convention rights.

(2) This section—

(a) applies to primary legislation and subordinate legislation whenever enacted;

(b) does not affect the validity, continuing operation or enforcement of any incompatible primary legislation; and

(c) does not affect the validity, continuing operation or enforcement of any incompatible subordinate legislation if (disregarding any possibility of revocation) primary legislation prevents removal of the incompatibility.

4 Declaration of incompatibility

(1) Subsection (2) applies in any proceedings in which a court determines whether a provision of primary legislation is compatible with a Convention right.

(2) If the court is satisfied that the provision is incompatible with a Convention right, it may make a declaration of that incompatibility.

(3) Subsection (4) applies in any proceedings in which a court determines whether a provision of subordinate legislation, made in the exercise of a power conferred by primary legislation, is compatible with a Convention right.

(4) If the court is satisfied—

(a) that the provision is incompatible with a Convention right, and

(b) that (disregarding any possibility of revocation) the primary legislation concerned prevents removal of the incompatibility,

it may make a declaration of that incompatibility.

(5) In this section 'court' means—

[(a) the Supreme Court;]

(b) the Judicial Committee of the Privy Council;

(c) the [Court Martial Appeal Court];

(d) in Scotland, the High Court of Justiciary sitting otherwise than as a trial court or the Court of Session;

(e) in England and Wales or Northern Ireland, the High Court or the Court of Appeal.

[(f) the Court of Protection, in any matter being dealt with by the President of the Family Division, the [Chancellor of the High Court] or a puisne judge of the High Court.]

(6) A declaration under this section ('a declaration of incompatibility')—

(a) does not affect the validity, continuing operation or enforcement of the provision in respect of which it is given; and

(b) is not binding on the parties to the proceedings in which it is made.

5 Right of Crown to intervene

(1) Where a court is considering whether to make a declaration of incompatibility, the Crown is entitled to notice in accordance with rules of court.

(2) In any case to which subsection (1) applies—

(a) a Minister of the Crown (or a person nominated by him),

(b) a member of the Scottish Executive,

(c) a Northern Ireland Minister,

(d) a Northern Ireland department,

is entitled, on giving notice in accordance with rules of court, to be joined as a party to the proceedings.

(3) Notice under subsection (2) may be given at any time during the proceedings.

(4) A person who has been made a party to criminal proceedings (other than in Scotland) as the result of a notice under subsection (2) may, with leave, appeal to the [Supreme Court] against any declaration of incompatibility made in the proceedings.

(5) In subsection (4)—

'criminal proceedings' includes all proceedings before the [Court Martial Appeal Court]; and

'leave' means leave granted by the court making the declaration of incompatibility or by the [Supreme Court].

Public authorities

6 Acts of public authorities

(1) It is unlawful for a public authority to act in a way which is incompatible with a Convention right.

(2) Subsection (1) does not apply to an act if—

(a) as the result of one or more provisions of primary legislation, the authority could not have acted differently; or

(b) in the case of one or more provisions of, or made under, primary legislation which cannot be read or given effect in a way which is compatible with the Convention rights, the authority was acting so as to give effect to or enforce those provisions.

(3) In this section 'public authority' includes—

(a) a court or tribunal, and

(b) any person certain of whose functions are functions of a public nature,

but does not include either House of Parliament or a person exercising functions in connection with proceedings in Parliament.

[. . .]

(5) In relation to a particular act, a person is not a public authority by virtue only of subsection (3)(b) if the nature of the act is private.

(6) 'An act' includes a failure to act but does not include a failure to—

(a) introduce in, or lay before, Parliament a proposal for legislation; or

(b) make any primary legislation or remedial order.

7 Proceedings

(1) A person who claims that a public authority has acted (or proposes to act) in a way which is made unlawful by section 6(1) may—

(a) bring proceedings against the authority under this Act in the appropriate court or tribunal, or

(b) rely on the Convention right or rights concerned in any legal proceedings,

but only if he is (or would be) a victim of the unlawful act.

(2) In subsection (1)(a) 'appropriate court or tribunal' means such court or

tribunal as may be determined in accordance with rules; and proceedings against an authority include a counterclaim or similar proceeding.

(3) If the proceedings are brought on an application for judicial review, the applicant is to be taken to have a sufficient interest in relation to the unlawful act only if he is, or would be, a victim of that act.

(4) If the proceedings are made by way of a petition for judicial review in Scotland, the applicant shall be taken to have title and interest to sue in relation to the unlawful act only if he is, or would be, a victim of that act.

(5) Proceedings under subsection (1)(a) must be brought before the end of—

(a) the period of one year beginning with the date on which the act complained of took place; or

(b) such longer period as the court or tribunal considers equitable having regard to all the circumstances,

but that is subject to any rule imposing a stricter time limit in relation to the procedure in question.

(6) In subsection (1)(b) 'legal proceedings' includes—

(a) proceedings brought by or at the instigation of a public authority; and

(b) an appeal against the decision of a court or tribunal.

(7) For the purposes of this section, a person is a victim of an unlawful act only if he would be a victim for the purposes of Article 34 of the Convention if proceedings were brought in the European Court of Human Rights in respect of that act.

(8) Nothing in this Act creates a criminal offence.

(9) In this section 'rules' means—

(a) in relation to proceedings before a court or tribunal outside Scotland, rules made by [. . .] [the Lord Chancellor or] the Secretary of State for the purposes of this section or rules of court,

(b) in relation to proceedings before a court or tribunal in Scotland, rules made by the Secretary of State for those purposes,

(c) in relation to proceedings before a tribunal in Northern Ireland—

(i) which deals with transferred matters; and

(ii) for which no rules made under paragraph (a) are in force,

rules made by a Northern Ireland department for those purposes, and includes provision made by order under section 1 of the Courts and Legal Services Act 1990.

(10) In making rules, regard must be had to section 9.

(11) The Minister who has power to make rules in relation to a particular tribunal may, to the extent he considers it necessary to ensure that the tribunal can provide an appropriate remedy in relation to an act (or proposed act) of a public authority which is (or would be) unlawful as a result of section 6(1), by order add to—

(a) the relief or remedies which the tribunal may grant; or

(b) the grounds on which it may grant any of them.

(12) An order made under subsection (11) may contain such incidental, supplemental, consequential or transitional provision as the Minister making it considers appropriate.

(13) 'The Minister' includes the Northern Ireland department concerned.

8 Judicial remedies

(1) In relation to any act (or proposed act) of a public authority which the court finds is (or would be) unlawful, it may grant such relief or remedy, or make such order, within its powers as it considers just and appropriate.

(2) But damages may be awarded only by a court which has power to award damages, or to order the payment of compensation, in civil proceedings.

(3) No award of damages is to be made unless, taking account of all the circumstances of the case, including—

(a) any other relief or remedy granted, or order made, in relation to the act in question (by that or any other court), and

(b) the consequences of any decision (of that or any other court) in respect of that act,

the court is satisfied that the award is necessary to afford just satisfaction to the person in whose favour it is made.

(4) In determining—

(a) whether to award damages, or

(b) the amount of an award,

the court must take into account the principles applied by the European Court of Human Rights in relation to the award of compensation under Article 41 of the Convention.

(5) A public authority against which damages are awarded is to be treated—

(a) in Scotland, for the purposes of section 3 of the Law Reform (Miscellaneous Provisions) (Scotland) Act 1940 as if the award were made in an action of damages in which the authority has been found liable in respect of loss or damage to the person to whom the award is made;

(b) for the purposes of the Civil Liability (Contribution) Act 1978 as liable in respect of damage suffered by the person to whom the award is made.

(6) In this section—

'court' includes a tribunal;

'damages' means damages for an unlawful act of a public authority; and

'unlawful' means unlawful under section 6(1).

9 Judicial acts

(1) Proceedings under section 7(1)(a) in respect of a judicial act may be brought only—

(a) by exercising a right of appeal;

(b) on an application (in Scotland a petition) for judicial review; or

(c) in such other forum as may be prescribed by rules.

(2) That does not affect any rule of law which prevents a court from being the subject of judicial review.

(3) In proceedings under this Act in respect of a judicial act done in good faith, damages may not be awarded otherwise than to compensate a person to the extent required by Article 5(5) of the Convention.

(4) An award of damages permitted by subsection (3) is to be made against the Crown; but no award may be made unless the appropriate person if not a party to the proceedings, is joined.

(5) In this section—

'appropriate person' means the Minister responsible for the court concerned, or a person or government department nominated by him;

'court' includes a tribunal;

'judge' includes a member of a tribunal, a justice of the peace [(or, in Northern Ireland, a lay magistrate)] and a clerk or other officer entitled to exercise the jurisdiction of a court;

'judicial act' means a judicial act of a court and includes an act done on the instructions, or on behalf, of a judge; and

'rules' has the same meaning as in section 7(9).

Remedial action

10 Power to take remedial action

(1) This section applies if—

(a) a provision of legislation has been declared under section 4 to be incompatible with a Convention right and, if an appeal lies—

(i) all persons who may appeal have stated in writing that they do not intend to do so;

(ii) the time for bringing an appeal has expired and no appeal has been brought within that time; or

(iii) an appeal brought within that time has been determined or abandoned; or

(b) it appears to a Minister of the Crown or Her Majesty in Council that, having regard to a finding of the European Court of Human Rights made after the coming into force of this section in proceedings against the United Kingdom, a provision of legislation is incompatible with an obligation of the United Kingdom arising from the Convention.

(2) If a Minister of the Crown considers that there are compelling reasons for proceeding under this section, he may by order make such amendments to the legislation as he considers necessary to remove the incompatibility.

(3) If, in the case of subordinate legislation, a Minister of the Crown considers—

(a) that it is necessary to amend the primary legislation under which the subordinate legislation in question was made, in order to enable the incompatibility to be removed, and

(b) that there are compelling reasons for proceeding under this section,

he may by order make such amendments to the primary legislation as he considers necessary.

(4) This section also applies where the provision in question is in subordinate legislation and has been quashed, or declared invalid, by reason of incompatibility with a Convention right and the Minister proposes to proceed under paragraph 2 (b) of Schedule 2.

(5) If the legislation is an Order in Council, the power conferred by subsection (2) or (3) is exercisable by Her Majesty in Council.

(6) In this section 'legislation' does not include a Measure of the Church Assembly or of the General Synod of the Church of England.

(7) Schedule 2 makes further provision about remedial orders.

Other rights and proceedings

11 Safeguard for existing human rights

(1) A person's reliance on a Convention right does not restrict—

(a) any other right or freedom conferred on him by or under any law having effect in any part of the United Kingdom; or

(b) his right to make any claim or bring any proceedings which he could make or bring apart from sections 7 to 9.

12 Freedom of expression

(1) This section applies if a court is considering whether to grant any relief which, if granted, might affect the exercise of the Convention right to freedom of expression.

(2) If the person against whom the application for relief is made ('the respondent') is neither present nor represented, no such relief is to be granted unless the court is satisfied—

(a) that the applicant has taken all practicable steps to notify the respondent; or

(b) that there are compelling reasons why the respondent should not be notified.

(3) No such relief is to be granted so as to restrain publication before trial unless the court is satisfied that the applicant is likely to establish that publication should not be allowed.

(4) The court must have particular regard to the importance of the Convention right to freedom of expression and, where the proceedings relate to material which the respondent claims, or which appears to the court, to be journalistic, literary or artistic material (or to conduct connected with such material), to—

(a) the extent to which—

(i) the material has, or is about to, become available to the public; or

(ii) it is, or would be, in the public interest for the material to be published;

(b) any relevant privacy code.

(5) In this section—
'court' includes a tribunal; and
'relief' includes any remedy or order (other than in criminal proceedings).

13 Freedom of thought, conscience and religion

(1) If a court's determination of any question arising under this Act might affect the exercise by a religious organisation (itself or its members collectively) of the Convention right to freedom of thought, conscience and religion, it must have particular regard to the importance of that right.

(2) In this section 'court' includes a tribunal.

Derogations and reservations

14 Derogations

(1) In this Act 'designated derogation' means—

[. . .]

any derogation by the United Kingdom from an Article of the Convention, or of any protocol to the Convention, which is designated for the purposes of this Act in an order made by the [Secretary of State].

[. . .]

(3) If a designated derogation is amended or replaced it ceases to be a designated derogation.

(4) But subsection (3) does not prevent the [Secretary of State] from exercising his power under subsection (1)[. . .] to make a fresh designation order in respect of the Article concerned.

(5) The [Secretary of State] must by order make such amendments to Schedule 3 as he considers appropriate to reflect—

(a) any designation order; or

(b) the effect of subsection (3).

(6) A designation order may be made in anticipation of the making by the United Kingdom of a proposed derogation.

15 Reservations

(1) In this Act 'designated reservation' means—

(a) the United Kingdom's reservation to Article 2 of the First Protocol to the Convention; and

(b) any other reservation by the United Kingdom to an Article of the Convention, or of any protocol to the Convention, which is designated for the purposes of this Act in an order made by the [Secretary of State].

(2) The text of the reservation referred to in subsection (1)(a) is set out in Part II of Schedule 3.

(3) If a designated reservation is withdrawn wholly or in part it ceases to be a designated reservation.

(4) But subsection (3) does not prevent the [Secretary of State] from exercising his power under subsection (1)(b) to make a fresh designation order in respect of the Article concerned.

(5) The [Secretary of State] must by order make such amendments to this Act as he considers appropriate to reflect—

(a) any designation order; or

(b) the effect of subsection (3).

16 Period for which designated derogations have effect

(1) If it has not already been withdrawn by the United Kingdom, a designated derogation ceases to have effect for the purposes of this Act—

[. . .] at the end of the period of five years beginning with the date on which the order designating it was made.

(2) At any time before the period—

(a) fixed by subsection (1) [. . .], or
(b) extended by an order under this subsection,

comes to an end, the [Secretary of State] may by order extend it by a further period of five years.

(3) An order under section 14(1) [. . .] ceases to have effect at the end of the period for consideration, unless a resolution has been passed by each House approving the order.

(4) Subsection (3) does not affect—
(a) anything done in reliance on the order; or
(b) the power to make a fresh order under section 14(1) [. . .].

(5) In subsection (3) 'period for consideration' means the period of forty days beginning with the day on which the order was made.

(6) In calculating the period for consideration, no account is to be taken of any time during which—
(a) Parliament is dissolved or prorogued; or
(b) both Houses are adjourned for more than four days.

(7) If a designated derogation is withdrawn by the United Kingdom, the [Secretary of State] must by order make such amendments to this Act as he considers are required to reflect that withdrawal.

17 Periodic review of designated reservations

(1) The appropriate Minister must review the designated reservation referred to in section 15(1)(a)—

(a) before the end of the period of five years beginning with the date on which section 1(2) came into force; and

(b) if that designation is still in force, before the end of the period of five years beginning with the date on which the last report relating to it was laid under subsection (3).

(2) The appropriate Minister must review each of the other designated reservations (if any)—

(a) before the end of the period of five years beginning with the date of which the order designating the reservation first came into force; and

(b) if the designation is still in force, before the end of the period of five years beginning with the date on which the last report relating to it was laid under subsection (3).

(3) The Minister conducting a review under this section must prepare a report on the result of the review and lay a copy of it before each House of Parliament.

. . .

Parliamentary procedure

19 Statements of compatibility

(1) A Minister of the Crown in charge of a Bill in either House of Parliament must, before Second Reading of the Bill—

(a) make a statement to the effect that in his view the provisions of the Bill are compatible with the Convention rights ('a statement of compatibility'); or

(b) make a statement to the effect that although he is unable to make a statement of compatibility the government nevertheless wishes the House to proceed with the Bill.

(2) The statement must be in writing and be published in such manner as the Minister making it considers appropriate.

. . .

SCHEDULES

Schedule 1 contains the European Convention on Human Rights which is reproduced in Part II on this volume.

SCHEDULE 2
REMEDIAL ORDERS

Orders

1—(1) A remedial order may—

(a) contain such incidental, supplemental, consequential or transitional provision as the person making it considers appropriate;

(b) be made so as to have effect from a date earlier than that on which it is made;

(c) make provision for the delegation of specific functions;

(d) make different provision for different cases.

(2) The power conferred by sub-paragraph (1)(a) includes—

(a) power to amend primary legislation (including primary legislation other than that which contains the incompatible provision); and

(b) power to amend or revoke subordinate legislation (including subordinate legislation other than that which contains the incompatible provision).

(3) A remedial order may be made so as to have the same extent as the legislation which it affects.

(4) No person is to be guilty of an offence solely as a result of the retrospective effect of a remedial order.

Procedure

2. No remedial order may be made unless—

(a) a draft of the order has been approved by a resolution of each House of Parliament made after the end of the period of 60 days beginning with the day on which the draft was laid; or

(b) it is declared in the order that it appears to the person making it that, because of the urgency of the matter, it is necessary to make the order without a draft being so approved.

Orders laid in draft

3—(1) No draft may be laid under paragraph 2(a) unless—

(a) the person proposing to make the order has laid before Parliament a document which contains a draft of the proposed order and the required information; and

(b) the period of 60 days, beginning with the day on which the document required by this sub-paragraph was laid, has ended.

(2) If representations have been made during that period, the draft laid under paragraph 2(a) must be accompanied by a statement containing—

(a) a summary of the representations; and

(b) if, as a result of the representations, the proposed order has been changed, details of the changes.

Urgent cases

4—(1) If a remedial order ('the original order') is made without being approved in draft, the person making it must lay it before Parliament, accompanied by the required information, after it is made.

(2) If representations have been made during the period of 60 days beginning with the day on which the original order was made, the person making it must (after the end of that period) lay before Parliament a statement containing—

(a) a summary of the representations; and

(b) if, as a result of the representations, he considers it appropriate to make changes to the original order, details of the changes.

(3) If sub-paragraph (2)(b) applies, the person making the statement must—

(a) make a further remedial order replacing the original order; and

(b) lay the replacement order before Parliament.

(4) If, at the end of the period of 120 days beginning with the day on which the original order was made, a resolution has not been passed by each House approving the original or replacement order, the order ceases to have effect (but without that affecting anything previously done under either order or the power to make a fresh remedial order).

Definitions

5. In this Schedule—

'representations' means representations about a remedial order (or proposed remedial order) made to the person making (or proposing to make) it and includes any relevant Parliamentary report or resolution; and

'required information' means—

(a) an explanation of the incompatibility which the order (or proposed order) seeks to remove, including particulars of the relevant declaration, finding or order; and

(b) a statement of the reasons for proceeding under section 10 and for making an order in those terms.

Calculating periods

6. In calculating any period for the purposes of this Schedule, no account is to be taken of any time during which—

(a) Parliament is dissolved or prorogued; or

(b) both Houses are adjourned for more than four days.

[7—(1) This paragraph applies in relation to—

(a) any remedial order made, and any draft of such an order proposed to be made—

(i) by the Scottish Ministers; or

(ii) within devolved competence (within the meaning of the Scotland Act 1998) by Her Majesty in Council; and

(b) any document or statement to be laid in connection with such an order (or proposed order).

(2) This Schedule has effect in relation to any such order (or proposed order), document or statement subject to the following modifications.

(3) Any reference to Parliament, each House of Parliament or both Houses of Parliament shall be construed as a reference to the Scottish Parliament.

(4) Paragraph 6 does not apply and instead, in calculating any period for the purposes of this Schedule, no account is to be taken of any time during which the Scottish Parliament is dissolved or is in recess for more than four days.]

SCHEDULE 3
DEROGATION AND RESERVATION

[. . .]

PART II
RESERVATION

At the time of signing the present (First) Protocol, I declare that, in view of certain provisions of the Education Acts in the United Kingdom, the principle affirmed in the second sentence of Article 2 is accepted by the United Kingdom only so far as is compatible with the provision of efficient instruction and training, and the avoidance of unreasonable public expenditure.

Dated 20 March 1952

Made by the United Kingdom Permanent Representative to the Council of Europe.

SCOTLAND ACT 1998
(1998, c 46)

PART I
THE SCOTTISH PARLIAMENT

The Scottish Parliament

1 The Scottish Parliament

(1) There shall be a Scottish Parliament.

(2) One member of the Parliament shall be returned for each constituency (under the simple majority system) at an election held in the constituency.

(3) Members of the Parliament for each region shall be returned at a general election under the additional member system of proportional representation provided for in this Part and vacancies among such members shall be filled in accordance with this Part.

(4) The validity of any proceedings of the Parliament is not affected by any vacancy in its membership.

(5) Schedule 1 (which makes provision for the constituencies and regions for the purposes of this Act and the number of regional members) shall have effect.

General elections

2 Ordinary general elections

(1) The day on which the poll at the first ordinary general election for membership of the Parliament shall be held, and the day, time and place for the meeting of the Parliament following that poll, shall be appointed by order made by the Secretary of State.

(2) The poll at subsequent ordinary general elections shall be held on the first Thursday in May in the fourth calendar year following that in which the previous ordinary general election was held, unless—

[(a) subsection (2A) prevents the poll being held on that day, or

(b) the day of the poll is determined by a proclamation under subsection (5).]

[(2A) The poll shall not be held on the same date as the date of the poll at—

(a) a parliamentary general election (other than an early parliamentary general election), or

(b) a European parliamentary general election.

(2B) Where subsection (2A) prevents the poll being held on the day specified in subsection (2), the poll shall be held on such day, subject to subsection (2A), as the Scottish Ministers may by order specify, unless the day of the poll is determined by a proclamation under subsection (5) as modified by subsection (5ZA).]

(3) If the poll is to be held on the first Thursday in May, [or on the day specified by an order under subsection (2B),] the Parliament—

(a) is dissolved by virtue of this section at the beginning of the minimum period which ends with that day, and

(b) shall meet within the period of seven days beginning immediately after the day of the poll.

(4) In subsection (3), 'the minimum period' means the period determined in accordance with an order under section 12(1).

(5) [Subject to subsection (2A),] if the Presiding Officer proposes a day for the holding of the poll which is not more than one month earlier, nor more than one month later, than the first Thursday in May, Her Majesty may by proclamation under the Scottish Seal—

(a) dissolve the Parliament,

(b) require the poll at the election to be held on the day proposed, and

(c) require the Parliament to meet within the period of seven days beginning immediately after the day of the poll.

[(5ZA) Where a day is specified by order under subsection (2B), subsection (5) applies as if the reference to the first Thursday in May were a reference to that day.]

(6) In this Act 'the Scottish Seal' means Her Majesty's Seal appointed by the Treaty of Union to be kept and used in Scotland in place of the Great Seal of Scotland.

3 Extraordinary general elections

(1) The Presiding Officer shall propose a day for the holding of a poll if—

(a) the Parliament resolves that it should be dissolved and, if the resolution is passed on a division, the number of members voting in favour of it is not less than two-thirds of the total number of seats for members of the Parliament, or

(b) any period during which the Parliament is required under section 46 to nominate one of its members for appointment as First Minister ends without such a nomination being made.

(2) If the Presiding Officer makes such a proposal, Her Majesty may by proclamation under the Scottish Seal—

(a) dissolve the Parliament and require an extraordinary general election to be held,

(b) require the poll at the election to be held on the day proposed, and

(c) require the Parliament to meet within the period of seven days beginning immediately after the day of the poll.

(3) If a poll is held under this section within the period of six months ending with the day on which the poll at the next ordinary general election would be held (disregarding section 2(5)), that ordinary general election shall not be held.

(4) Subsection (3) does not affect the year in which the subsequent ordinary general election is to be held.

5 Candidates

(1) At a general election, the candidates may stand for return as constituency members or regional members.

(2) A person may not be a candidate to be a constituency member for more than one constituency.

(3) The candidates to be regional members shall be those included in a list submitted under subsection (4) or individual candidates.

(4) Any registered political party may submit to the regional returning officer a list of candidates to be regional members for a particular region (referred to in this Act, in relation to the region, as the party's 'regional list').

(5) A registered political party's regional list has effect in relation to the general election and any vacancy occurring among the regional members after that election and before the next general election.

(6) Not more than twelve persons may be included in the list (but the list may include only one person).

(7) A registered political party's regional list must not include a person—

(a) who is included in any other list submitted under subsection (4) for the region or any list submitted under that subsection for another region,

(b) who is an individual candidate to be a regional member for the region or another region,

(c) who is a candidate to be a constituency member for a constituency not included in the region, or

(d) who is a candidate to be a constituency member for a constituency included in the region but is not a candidate of that party.

(8) A person may not be an individual candidate to be a regional member for a particular region if he is—

(a) included in a list submitted under subsection (4) for the region or another region,

(b) an individual candidate to be a regional member for another region,

(c) a candidate to be a constituency member for a constituency not included in the region, or

(d) a candidate of any registered political party to be a constituency member for a constituency included in the region.

(9) In this Act, 'registered political party' means a party registered under [Part II of the Political Parties, Elections and Referendums Act 2000].

6 Poll for regional members

(1) This section and sections 7 and 8 are about the return of regional members at a general election.

(2) In each of the constituencies for the Parliament, a poll shall be held at which each person entitled to vote as elector may give a vote (referred to in this Act as a 'regional vote') for—

(a) a registered political party which has submitted a regional list, or

(b) an individual candidate to be a regional member for the region.

(3) The right conferred on a person by subsection (2) is in addition to any right the person may have to vote in any poll for the return of a constituency member.

7 Calculation of regional figures

(1) The persons who are to be returned as constituency members for constituencies included in the region must be determined before the persons who are to be returned as the regional members for the region.

(2) For each registered political party which has submitted a regional list, the regional figure for the purposes of section 8 is—

(a) the total number of regional votes given for the party in all the constituencies included in the region, divided by

(b) the aggregate of one plus the number of candidates of the party returned as constituency members for any of those constituencies.

(3) Each time a seat is allocated to the party under section 8, that figure shall be recalculated by increasing (or further increasing) the aggregate in subsection (2)(b) by one.

(4) For each individual candidate to be a regional member for the region, the regional figure for the purposes of section 8 is the total number of regional votes given for him in all the constituencies included in the region.

8 Allocation of seats to regional members

(1) The first regional member seat shall be allocated to the registered political party or individual candidate with the highest regional figure.

(2) The second and subsequent regional member seats shall be allocated to the registered political party or individual candidate with the highest regional figure, after any recalculation required by section 7(3) has been carried out.

(3) An individual candidate already returned as a constituency or regional member shall be disregarded.

(4) Seats for the region which are allocated to a registered political party shall be filled by the persons in the party's regional list in the order in which they appear in the list.

(5) For the purposes of this section and section 10, a person in a registered political party's regional list who is returned as a member of the Parliament shall be treated as ceasing to be in the list (even if his return is void).

(6) Once a party's regional list has been exhausted (by the return of persons included in it as constituency members or by the previous application of subsection (1) or (2)) the party shall be disregarded.

(7) If (on the application of subsection (1) or any application of subsection (2)) the highest regional figure is the regional figure of two or more parties or individual candidates—

[(a) the subsection in question shall apply to each of them; or

(b) if paragraph (a) would result in more than the correct number of seats for the region being allocated, the subsection in question shall apply as if the regional figure for each of those parties or candidates had been adjusted in accordance with subsection (8).

(8) The regional figure for a party or candidate is adjusted in accordance with this subsection by—

(a) adding one vote to the total number of regional votes given for the party or candidate in all the constituencies included in the region; and

(b) (in the case of a party) recalculating the regional figure accordingly.

(9) If, on the application of the subsection in question in accordance with subsection (7)(b), seats would be allocated to two or more parties or individual candidates and that would result in more than the correct number of seats for the region being allocated, the regional returning officer shall decide between them by lot.]

Vacancies

9 Constituency vacancies

(1) Where the seat of a constituency member is vacant, an election shall be held to fill the vacancy (subject to subsection (4)).

(2) The date of the poll shall be fixed by the Presiding Officer.

(3) The date shall fall within the period of three months—

(a) beginning with the occurrence of the vacancy, or

(b) if the vacancy does not come to the notice of the Presiding Officer within the period of one month beginning with its occurrence, beginning when it does come to his notice.

(4) The election shall not be held if the latest date for holding the poll would fall within the period of three months ending with the day on which the poll at the next ordinary general election would be held (disregarding section 2(5)).

(5) For the purposes of this section, the date on which a vacancy is to be treated as occurring shall be determined under standing orders.

(6) A person may not be a candidate at such an election if he is a member of the Parliament or a candidate in another election to fill a vacancy.

10 Regional vacancies

(1) This section applies where the seat of a regional member is vacant.

(2) If the regional member was returned as an individual candidate, or the vacancy is not filled in accordance with the following provisions, the seat shall remain vacant until the next general election.

(3) If the regional member was returned (under section 8 or this section) from a registered political party's regional list, the regional returning officer shall notify the Presiding Officer of the name of the person who is to fill the vacancy.

(4) [The regional returning officer shall ascertain from that party's regional list the name and address of the person whose name appears highest on that list ('the first choice') and shall take such steps as appear to him to be reasonable to contact the first choice to ask whether he will—

(a) state in writing that he is willing and able to serve as a regional member for that region; and

(b) deliver a certificate signed by or on behalf of the nominating officer of the registered party which submitted that regional list stating that the first choice may be returned as a regional member from that list.]

[(4A) Where—

(a) within such period as the regional returning officer considers reasonable—

(i) he decides that the steps he has taken to contact the first choice have been unsuccessful; or

(ii) he has not received from that person the statement and certificate referred to in subsection (4); or

(b) the first choice has—

(i) stated in writing that he is not willing to serve as a regional member for that region; or

(ii) failed to deliver the certificate referred to in subsection (4)(b),

the regional returning officer shall repeat the procedure required by subsection (4) in respect of the person (if any) whose name and address appears next in that list ('the second choice') or, where sub-paragraph (a) or (b) of this subsection applies in respect of that person, in respect of the person (if any) whose name and address appear next highest after the second choice in that list; and the regional returning officer shall continue to repeat the procedure until the regional returning officer has notified the Presiding Officer of the name of the person who is to fill the vacancy or the names in the list are exhausted.

(5) Where a person whose name appears on that list provides the statement and certificate referred to in subsection (4), the regional returning officer shall notify to the Presiding Officer the name of that person.

(5A) Where—

(a) under subsection (4A), the regional returning officer has asked the second choice or a subsequent choice the questions referred to in subsection (4); and

(b) the person who was asked those questions on an earlier occasion then provides the statement and certificate referred to in that subsection,

that statement and certificate shall have no effect unless and until the circumstances described in sub-paragraph (a) or (b) of subsection (4A) apply in respect of the second choice or, as the case may be, of the subsequent choice.]

(6) Where a person's name has been notified under subsection (3), this Act shall apply as if he had been declared to be returned as a regional member for the region on the day on which notification of his name was received by the Presiding Officer.

(7) For the purposes of this section, the date on which a vacancy is to be treated as occurring shall be determined under standing orders.

Franchise and conduct of elections

11 Electors

(1) The persons entitled to vote as electors at an election for membership of the Parliament held in any constituency are those who on the day of the poll—

(a) would be entitled to vote as electors at a local government election in an electoral area falling wholly or partly within the constituency, and

(b) are registered in the register of local government electors at an address within the constituency.

(2) A person is not entitled to vote as elector in any constituency—

(a) more than once at a poll for the return of a constituency member, or

(b) more than once at a poll for the return of regional members,

or to vote as elector in more than one constituency at a general election.

[12 Power of the Scottish Ministers to make provision about elections

(1) The Scottish Ministers may by order make any provision that would be within the legislative competence of the Parliament, if included in an Act of the Scottish Parliament, as to—

(a) the conduct of elections for membership of the Parliament,

(b) the questioning of such an election and the consequences of irregularities, and

(c) the return of members of the Parliament otherwise than at an election.

(2) The provision that may be made under subsection (1)(a) includes, in particular, provision—

(a) about the registration of electors,

(b) for disregarding alterations in a register of electors,

(c) about the limitation of the election expenses of candidates,

(d) for the combination of polls,

(e) for modifying the application of section 7(1) where the poll at an election for the return of a constituency member is abandoned (or notice of it is countermanded), and

(f) for modifying section 8(7) to ensure the allocation of the correct number of seats for the region.

(3) The provision that may be made under subsection (1)(c) includes, in particular, provision modifying section 10(4) to (5A).

(4) An order under subsection (1) may—

(a) apply, with or without modifications or exceptions, any provision made by or under the Representation of the People Acts or the European Parliamentary Elections Act 2002 or by any other enactment relating to parliamentary elections, European Parliamentary elections or local government elections, and

(b) so far as may be necessary in consequence of any provision made by an order under subsection (1), modify any provision made by any enactment relating to the registration of parliamentary electors or local government electors.

(5) The return of a member of the Parliament at an election may be questioned only under Part 3 of the Representation of the People Act 1983 as applied by an order under subsection (1).

(6) For the purposes of this Act, the regional returning officer for any region is the person designated as such in accordance with an order made by the Scottish Ministers under this subsection.]

[12A Power of the Secretary of State to make provision about the combination of polls

(1) The Secretary of State may by regulations make provision for—

(a) the combination of polls at ordinary general elections for membership of the Parliament with polls at the elections listed in subsection (2), and

(b) the combination of polls at extraordinary general elections for membership of the Parliament, and by-elections for membership of the Parliament, with polls at the elections listed in subsections (2) and (3).

(2) The elections are—

(a) early parliamentary general elections,

(b) parliamentary by-elections, and

(c) European parliamentary by-elections.

(3) The elections are—

(a) parliamentary general elections, and

(b) European parliamentary general elections.

(4) The Secretary of State may not make regulations under this section without the agreement of the Scottish Ministers.

(5) Regulations under subsection (1) may—

(a) apply, with or without modifications or exceptions, any provision made by or under the Representation of the People Acts or the European Parliamentary Elections Act 2002 or by any other enactment relating to parliamentary elections, European Parliamentary elections or local government elections, and

(b) modify any form contained in, or in regulations or rules made under, the Representation of the People Acts so far as may be necessary to enable it to be used both for the original purpose and in relation to elections for membership of the Parliament.]

Disqualification

15 Disqualification from membership of the Parliament

(1) A person is disqualified from being a member of the Parliament (subject to section 16) if—

(a) he is disqualified from being a member of the House of Commons under paragraphs (a) to (e) of section 1(1) of the House of Commons Disqualification Act 1975 (judges, civil servants, members of the armed forces, members of police forces and members of foreign legislatures),

(b) he is disqualified otherwise than under that Act (either generally or in relation to a particular parliamentary constituency) from being a member of the House of Commons or from sitting and voting in it,

[. . .]

(d) he is an office-holder of a description specified in an Order in Council made by Her Majesty under this subsection.

(2) An office-holder of a description specified in an Order in Council made by Her Majesty under this subsection is disqualified from being a member of the Parliament for any constituency or region of a description specified in the Order in relation to the office-holder.

(3) In this section 'office-holder' includes employee or other post-holder.

16 Exceptions and relief from disqualification

(1) A person is not disqualified from being a member of the Parliament merely because—

(a) he is a peer (whether of the United Kingdom, Great Britain, England or Scotland), or

(b) [he is a Lord spiritual].

[. . .]

[(2A) A person is not disqualified from being a member of the Parliament merely because of section 3 of the Act of Settlement, provided the person—

(a) is resident in the United Kingdom, and

(b) meets one of the conditions mentioned in subsection (2B).

(2B) The conditions are that the person—

(a) is not a person who requires leave under the Immigration Act 1971 to enter or remain in the United Kingdom (excluding a person who does not require such leave by virtue only of section 8 of the Immigration Act 1971 (exceptions to requirement for leave in special cases)), or

(b) is such a person but for the time being—

(i) has (or is, by virtue of any enactment, to be treated as having) indefinite leave to remain within the meaning of that Act, or

(ii) has pre-settled status.

(2C) For the purposes of subsection (2B)(b)(ii), a person has pre-settled status if the person has limited leave to remain in the United Kingdom granted by virtue of residence scheme immigration rules (within the meaning of section 17(1) of the European Union (Withdrawal Agreement) Act 2020).]

(3) Subsection (4) applies where a person was, or is alleged to have been, disqualified from being a member of the Parliament (either generally or in relation to a particular constituency or region) on any ground other than one falling within section 15(1)(b).

(4) The Parliament may resolve to disregard any disqualification incurred by that person on the ground in question if it considers that—

(a) the ground has been removed, and

(b) it is proper to disregard any disqualification so incurred.

(5) A resolution under this section shall not—

(a) affect any proceedings under Part III of the Representation of the People Act 1983 as applied by an order under section 12, or

(b) enable the Parliament to disregard any disqualification which has been established in such proceedings or in proceedings under section 18.

17 Effect of disqualification

(1) If a person who is disqualified from being a member of the Parliament or from being a member for a particular constituency or region is returned as a member of the Parliament or (as the case may be) as a member for the constituency or region, his return shall be void and his seat vacant.

(2) If a member of the Parliament becomes disqualified from being a member of the Parliament or from being a member for the particular constituency or region for which he is sitting, he shall cease to be a member of the Parliament (so that his seat is vacant).

(3) Subsections (1) and (2) have effect subject to any resolution of the Parliament under section 16.

(4) Subsection (2) also has effect subject to [. . .] section 427 of the Insolvency Act 1986 (sequestration etc); and where, in consequence of [that section], the seat of a disqualified member of the Parliament is not vacant he shall not cease to be a member of the Parliament until his seat becomes vacant but—

(a) he shall not participate in any proceedings of the Parliament, and

(b) any of his other rights and privileges as a member of the Parliament may be withdrawn by a resolution of the Parliament.

(5) The validity of any proceedings of the Parliament is not affected by the disqualification of any person from being a member of the Parliament or from being a member for the constituency or region for which he purports to sit.

18 Judicial proceedings as to disqualification

(1) Any person who claims that a person purporting to be a member of the Parliament is disqualified or has been disqualified at any time since being returned may apply to the Court of Session for a declarator to that effect.

(2) An application in respect of any person may be made whether the grounds on which it is made are alleged to have subsisted when the person was returned or to have arisen subsequently.

(3) No declarator shall be made—

(a) on grounds which subsisted when the person was returned, if an election petition is pending or has been tried in which the disqualification on those grounds of the person concerned is or was in issue, or

(b) on any ground, if a resolution under section 16 requires that any disqualification incurred on that ground by the person concerned is to be disregarded.

(4) The person in respect of whom an application is made shall be the defender.

(5) The applicant shall give such caution for the expenses of the proceedings as the Court of Session may direct; but any such caution shall not exceed £5,000 or such other sum as the Scottish Ministers may by order specify.

(6) The decision of the court on an application under this section shall be final.

(7) In this section 'disqualified' means disqualified from being a member of the

Parliament or from being a member for the constituency or region for which the person concerned purports to sit.

Presiding Officer and administration

19 Presiding Officer

(1) The Parliament shall, [. . .] following a general election, elect from among its members a Presiding Officer and two deputies.

[(1A) The Parliament must do so—

(a) before it conducts any other proceedings, except the taking by its members of the oath of allegiance (see section 84), and

(b) in any event, within the period of 14 days beginning immediately after the day of the poll at the election.

(1B) The Parliament may, at any time, elect from among its members one or more additional deputies.]

(2) A person elected Presiding Officer or deputy shall hold office until the conclusion of the next election for Presiding Officer under subsection (1) unless he previously resigns, ceases to be a member of the Parliament otherwise than by virtue of a dissolution or is removed from office by resolution of the Parliament.

[(2A) But standing orders may make provision for additional deputies to hold office for a shorter time than provided by subsection (2).]

(3) If the Presiding Officer or a deputy [elected under subsection (1)] ceases to hold office before the Parliament is dissolved, the Parliament shall elect another from among its members to fill his place.

(4) The Presiding Officer's functions may be exercised by a deputy if the office of Presiding Officer is vacant or the Presiding Officer is for any reason unable to act.

(5) The Presiding Officer may (subject to standing orders) authorise any deputy to exercise functions on his behalf.

(6) Standing orders may include provision as to the participation (including voting) of the Presiding Officer and deputies in the proceedings of the Parliament.

(7) The validity of any act of the Presiding Officer or a deputy is not affected by any defect in his election.

20 Clerk of the Parliament

(1) There shall be a Clerk of the Parliament.

(2) The Clerk shall be appointed by the Scottish Parliamentary Corporate Body (established under section 21).

(3) The Clerk's functions may be exercised by any Assistant Clerk if the office of Clerk is vacant or the Clerk is for any reason unable to act.

(4) The Clerk may authorise any Assistant Clerk or other member of the staff of the Parliament to exercise functions on his behalf.

21 Scottish Parliamentary Corporate Body

(1) There shall be a body corporate to be known as 'The Scottish Parliamentary Corporate Body' (referred to in this Act as the Parliamentary corporation) to perform the functions conferred on the corporation by virtue of this Act or any other enactment.

(2) The members of the corporation shall be—

(a) the Presiding Officer, and

(b) four [at least] members of the Parliament appointed in accordance with standing orders.

(3) The corporation shall provide the Parliament, or ensure that the Parliament is provided, with the property, staff and services required for the Parliament's purposes.

(4) The Parliament may give special or general directions to the corporation for the purpose of or in connection with the exercise of the corporation's functions.

(5) Any property or liabilities acquired or incurred in relation to matters within the general responsibility of the corporation to which (apart from this subsection) the Parliament would be entitled or subject shall be treated for all purposes as property or (as the case may be) liabilities of the corporation.

(6) Any expenses of the corporation shall be payable out of the Scottish Consolidated Fund.

(7) Any sums received by the corporation shall be paid into that Fund, subject to any provision made by or under an Act of the Scottish Parliament for the disposal of or accounting for such sums.

(8) Schedule 2 (which makes further provision about the corporation) shall have effect.

Proceedings etc

22 Standing orders

(1) The proceedings of the Parliament shall be regulated by standing orders.

(2) Schedule 3 (which makes provision as to how certain matters are to be dealt with by standing orders) shall have effect.

Legislation

28 Acts of the Scottish Parliament

(1) Subject to section 29, the Parliament may make laws, to be known as Acts of the Scottish Parliament.

(2) Proposed Acts of the Scottish Parliament shall be known as Bills; and a Bill shall become an Act of the Scottish Parliament when it has been passed by the Parliament and has received Royal Assent.

(3) A Bill receives Royal Assent at the beginning of the day on which Letters Patent under the Scottish Seal signed with Her Majesty's own hand signifying Her Assent are recorded in the Register of the Great Seal.

(4) The date of Royal Assent shall be written on the Act of the Scottish Parliament by the Clerk, and shall form part of the Act.

(5) The validity of an Act of the Scottish Parliament is not affected by any invalidity in the proceedings of the Parliament leading to its enactment.

(6) Every Act of the Scottish Parliament shall be judicially noticed.

(7) This section does not affect the power of the Parliament of the United Kingdom to make laws for Scotland.

[(8) But it is recognised that the Parliament of the United Kingdom will not normally legislate with regard to devolved matters without the consent of the Scottish Parliament.]

29 Legislative competence

(1) An Act of the Scottish Parliament is not law so far as any provision of the Act is outside the legislative competence of the Parliament.

(2) A provision is outside that competence so far as any of the following paragraphs apply—

(a) it would form part of the law of a country or territory other than Scotland, or confer or remove functions exercisable otherwise than in or as regards Scotland,

(b) it relates to reserved matters,

(c) it is in breach of the restrictions in Schedule 4,

(d) it is incompatible with any of the Convention rights or [in breach of the restriction in section 30A(1)],

(e) it would remove the Lord Advocate from his position as head of the systems of criminal prosecution and investigation of deaths in Scotland.

(3) For the purposes of this section, the question whether a provision of an Act of the Scottish Parliament relates to a reserved matter is to be determined, subject

to subsection (4), by reference to the purpose of the provision, having regard (among other things) to its effect in all the circumstances.

(4) A provision which—

(a) would otherwise not relate to reserved matters, but

(b) makes modifications of Scots private law, or Scots criminal law, as it applies to reserved matters,

is to be treated as relating to reserved matters unless the purpose of the provision is to make the law in question apply consistently to reserved matters and otherwise.

[(5) Subsection (1) is subject to section 30(6).]

30 Legislative competence: supplementary

(1) Schedule 5 (which defines reserved matters) shall have effect.

(2) Her Majesty may by Order in Council make any modifications of Schedule 4 or 5 which She considers necessary or expedient.

(3) Her Majesty may by Order in Council specify functions which are to be treated, for such purposes of this Act as may be specified, as being, or as not being, functions which are exercisable in or as regards Scotland.

(4) An Order in Council under this section may also make such modifications of—

(a) any enactment or prerogative instrument (including any enactment comprised in or made under this Act), or

(b) any other instrument or document,

as Her Majesty considers necessary or expedient in connection with other provision made by the Order.

[(5) Subsection (6) applies where any alteration is made—

(a) to the matters which are reserved matters, or

(b) to Schedule 4,

(whether by virtue of the making, revocation or expiry of an Order in Council under this section or otherwise).

(6) Where the effect of the alteration is that a provision of an Act of the Scottish Parliament ceases to be within the legislative competence of the Parliament, the provision does not for that reason cease to have effect (unless an enactment provides otherwise).]

[30A Legislative competence: restriction relating to retained EU law

(1) An Act of the Scottish Parliament cannot modify, or confer power by subordinate legislation to modify, retained EU law so far as the modification is of a description specified in regulations made by a Minister of the Crown.

(2) But subsection (1) does not apply to any modification so far as it would, immediately before exit day, have been within the legislative competence of the Parliament.

(3) A Minister of the Crown must not lay for approval before each House of the Parliament of the United Kingdom a draft of a statutory instrument containing regulations under this section unless—

(a) the Scottish Parliament has made a consent decision in relation to the laying of the draft, or

(b) the 40 day period has ended without the Parliament having made such a decision.

(4) For the purposes of subsection (3) a consent decision is—

(a) a decision to agree a motion consenting to the laying of the draft,

(b) a decision not to agree a motion consenting to the laying of the draft, or

(c) a decision to agree a motion refusing to consent to the laying of the draft;

and a consent decision is made when the Parliament first makes a decision falling within any of paragraphs (a) to (c) (whether or not it subsequently makes another such decision).

(5) A Minister of the Crown who is proposing to lay a draft as mentioned in subsection (3) must—

(a) provide a copy of the draft to the Scottish Ministers, and

(b) inform the Presiding Officer that a copy has been so provided.

(6) See also paragraph 6 of Schedule 7 (duty to make explanatory statement about regulations under this section including a duty to explain any decision to lay a draft without the consent of the Parliament).

(7) No regulations may be made under this section after the end of the period of two years beginning with exit day.

(8) Subsection (7) does not affect the continuation in force of regulations made under this section at or before the end of the period mentioned in that subsection.

(9) Any regulations under this section which are in force at the end of the period of five years beginning with the time at which they came into force are revoked in their application to any Act of the Scottish Parliament which receives Royal Assent after the end of that period.

(10) Subsections (3) to (8) do not apply in relation to regulations which only relate to a revocation of a specification.

(11) In this section—

'the 40 day period' means the period of 40 days beginning with the day on which a copy of the draft instrument is provided to the Scottish Ministers, and, in calculating that period, no account is to be taken of any time during which the Parliament is dissolved or during which it is in recess for more than four days.]

31 Scrutiny of Bills [for legislative competence and protected subject-matter]

(1) [A person] in charge of a Bill shall, on or before introduction of the Bill in the Parliament, state that in his view the provisions of the Bill would be within the legislative competence of the Parliament.

(2) The Presiding Officer shall, on or before the introduction of a Bill in the Parliament, decide whether or not in his view the provisions of the Bill would be within the legislative competence of the Parliament and state his decision.

[(2A) The Presiding Officer shall, after the last time when a Bill may be amended but before the decision whether to pass or reject it, decide whether or not in his view any provision of the Bill relates to a protected subject-matter and state his decision.]

(3) The form of any statement, and the manner in which it is to be made, shall be determined under standing orders, and standing orders may provide for any statement to be published.

[(4) For the purposes of this Part a provision of a Bill relates to a protected subject-matter if it would modify, or confer power to modify, any of the matters listed in subsection (5) (but not if the provision is incidental to or consequential on another provision of the Bill).

(5) The matters are—

(a) the persons entitled to vote as electors at an election for membership of the Parliament,

(b) the system by which members of the Parliament are returned,

(c) the number of constituencies, regions or any equivalent electoral area, and

(d) the number of members to be returned for each constituency, region or equivalent electoral area.

[31A Two-thirds majority for Bills relating to a protected subject-matter

If the Presiding Officer states under section 31(2A) that in his view any provision of a Bill relates to a protected subject-matter, the Bill is not passed unless the number of members voting in favour of it at the final stage is at least two-thirds of the total number of seats for members of the Parliament.]

32 Submission of Bills for Royal Assent

(1) It is for the Presiding Officer to submit Bills for Royal Assent.

(2) The Presiding Officer shall not submit a Bill for Royal Assent at any time when—

(a) the Advocate General, the Lord Advocate or the Attorney General is entitled to make a reference in relation to the Bill under section [32A or] 33,

(b) any such reference has been made but has not been decided or otherwise disposed of by the [Supreme Court], or

(c) an order may be made in relation to the Bill under section 35.

[(2A) The Presiding Officer shall not submit a Bill for Royal Assent if the Supreme Court has decided on a reference made in relation to the Bill under section 32A(2)(b) that any provision of the Bill relates to a protected subject-matter, unless since the decision the Bill has been approved in accordance with standing orders made by virtue of section 36(5).]

(3) The Presiding Officer shall not submit a Bill in its unamended form for Royal Assent if—

(a) the [Supreme Court has] have decided that the Bill or any provision of it would not be within the legislative competence of the Parliament, or

(b) a reference made in relation to the Bill under section 33 has been withdrawn following a request for withdrawal of the reference under section 34(2)(b).

(4) In this Act—

'Advocate General' means the Advocate General for Scotland,

[. . .]

[32A Scrutiny of Bills by the Supreme Court (protected subject-matter)

(1) The Advocate General, the Lord Advocate or the Attorney General may refer the question of whether a Bill or any provision of a Bill relates to a protected subject-matter to the Supreme Court for decision.

(2) Subject to subsection (3), he may make a reference in relation to a Bill—

(a) at any time during the period of four weeks beginning with the rejection of the Bill, if the Presiding Officer has made a statement under section 31(2A) that in his view any provision of the Bill relates to a protected subject-matter, and

(b) at any time during the period of four weeks beginning with the passing of the Bill, if the Presiding Officer has made a statement under section 31(2A) that in his view no provision of the Bill relates to a protected subject-matter, unless the number of members voting in favour of the Bill at its passing is at least two-thirds of the total number of seats for members of the Parliament.

(3) He shall not make a reference in relation to a Bill if he has notified the Presiding Officer that he does not intend to make a reference in relation to the Bill, unless since the notification the Bill has been approved or rejected in accordance with standing orders made by virtue of section 36(5).]

33 Scrutiny of Bills by the [Supreme Court] [(legislative competence)]

(1) The Advocate General, the Lord Advocate or the Attorney General may refer the question of whether a Bill or any provision of a Bill would be within the legislative competence of the Parliament to the [Supreme Court] for decision.

(2) Subject to subsection (3), he may make a reference in relation to a Bill at any time during—

(a) the period of four weeks beginning with the passing of the Bill, and

(b) any period of four weeks beginning with any [. . .] approval of the Bill in accordance with standing orders made by virtue of section 36(5).

(3) He shall not make a reference in relation to a Bill if he has notified the Presiding Officer that he does not intend to make a reference in relation to the Bill, unless the Bill has been approved as mentioned in subsection (2)(b) since the notification.

34 ECJ references

(1) This section applies where—

(a) a reference has been made in relation to a Bill under section 33,

(b) a reference for a preliminary ruling has been made by the [Supreme Court] in connection with that reference, and

(c) neither of those references has been decided or otherwise disposed of.

(2) If the Parliament resolves that it wishes to reconsider the Bill—

(a) the Presiding Officer shall notify the Advocate General, the Lord Advocate and the Attorney General of that fact, and

(b) the person who made the reference in relation to the Bill under section 33 shall request the withdrawal of the reference.

(3) In this section 'a reference for a preliminary ruling' means a reference of a question to the European Court under [Article 267 of the Treaty on the Functioning of the European Union] or Article 150 of the Treaty establishing the European Atomic Energy Community.

35 Power to intervene in certain cases

(1) If a Bill contains provisions—

(a) which the Secretary of State has reasonable grounds to believe would be incompatible with any international obligations or the interests of defence or national security, or

(b) which make modifications of the law as it applies to reserved matters and which the Secretary of State has reasonable grounds to believe would have an adverse effect on the operation of the law as it applies to reserved matters,

he may make an order prohibiting the Presiding Officer from submitting the Bill for Royal Assent.

(2) The order must identify the Bill and the provisions in question and state the reasons for making the order.

(3) The order may be made at any time during—

(a) the period of four weeks beginning with the passing of the Bill,

(b) any period of four weeks beginning with any [. . .] approval of the Bill in accordance with standing orders made by virtue of section 36(5),

(c) if a reference is made in relation to the Bill under section [32A(2)(b) or] 33,

the period of four weeks beginning with the reference being decided or otherwise disposed of by the [Supreme Court].

(4) The Secretary of State shall not make an order in relation to a Bill if he has notified the Presiding Officer that he does not intend to do so, unless the Bill has been approved as mentioned in subsection (3)(b) since the notification.

(5) An order in force under this section at a time when such approval is given shall cease to have effect.

Other provisions

37 Acts of Union

The Union with Scotland Act 1706 and the Union with England Act 1707 have effect subject to this Act.

39 Members' interests

(1) Provision shall be made for a register of interests of members of the Parliament and for the register to be published and made available for public inspection.

(2) Provision shall be made—

(a) requiring members of the Parliament to register in that register financial interests (including benefits in kind), as defined for the purposes of this paragraph,

(b) requiring that any member of the Parliament who has a financial interest (including benefits in kind), as defined for the purposes of this paragraph, in any matter declares that interest before taking part in any proceedings of the Parliament relating to that matter.

(3) Provision made in pursuance of subsection (2) shall include any provision which the Parliament considers appropriate for preventing or restricting the participation in proceedings of the Parliament of a member with an interest defined for the purposes of subsection (2)(a) or (b) in a matter to which the proceedings relate.

(4) Provision shall be made prohibiting a member of the Parliament from—

(a) advocating or initiating any cause or matter on behalf of any person, by any means specified in the provision, in consideration of any payment or benefit in kind of a description so specified, or

(b) urging, in consideration of any such payment or benefit in kind, any other member of the Parliament to advocate or initiate any cause or matter on behalf of any person by any such means.

[(4A) Any requirement or prohibition (however expressed) imposed by provision made in pursuance of subsections (2) to (4) may be subject to such exceptions as are specified in the provision.

(5) Provision may be made for—

(a) excluding a member from the proceedings of the Parliament,

(b) imposing on a member such other sanctions as the Parliament considers appropriate,

if the member fails to comply with, or contravenes, any provision made in pursuance of subsections (2) to (4) or this subsection.

(5A) Provision made under subsection (5) may include provision that a sanction is not to be imposed in such circumstances as are specified in the provision.

(6) Provision made under subsection (5) may include provision that the member is guilty of an offence.

(7) A person guilty of such an offence is liable on summary conviction to a fine not exceeding level 5 on the standard scale.]

(8) In this section—

(a) 'provision' means provision made by or under an Act of the Scottish Parliament,

(b) references to members of the Parliament include references to the Lord Advocate and the Solicitor General for Scotland, whether or not they are such members.

41 Defamatory statements

(1) For the purposes of the law of defamation—

(a) any statement made in proceedings of the Parliament, and

(b) the publication under the authority of the Parliament of any statement,

shall be absolutely privileged.

(2) In subsection (1), 'statement' has the same meaning as in the Defamation Act 1996.

42 Contempt of court

(1) The strict liability rule shall not apply in relation to any publication—

(a) made in proceedings of the Parliament in relation to a Bill or subordinate legislation, or

(b) to the extent that it consists of a fair and accurate report of such proceedings made in good faith.

(2) In subsection (1), 'the strict liability rule' and 'publication' have the same meanings as in the Contempt of Court Act 1981.

PART II
THE SCOTTISH ADMINISTRATION

Ministers and their staff

44 The [Scottish Government]

(1) There shall be a [Scottish Government], whose members shall be—

(a) the First Minister,

(b) such Ministers as the First Minister may appoint under section 47, and

(c) the Lord Advocate and the Solicitor General for Scotland.

(2) The members of the [Scottish Government] are referred to collectively as the Scottish Ministers.

(3) A person who holds a Ministerial office may not be appointed a member of the [Scottish Government]; and if a member of the [Scottish Government] is appointed to a Ministerial office he shall cease to hold office as a member of the [Scottish Government].

(4) In subsection (3), references to a member of the [Scottish Government] include a junior Scottish Minister and 'Ministerial office' has the same meaning as in section 2 of the House of Commons Disqualification Act 1975.

45 The First Minister

(1) The First Minister shall be appointed by Her Majesty from among the members of the Parliament and shall hold office at Her Majesty's pleasure.

(2) The First Minister may at any time tender his resignation to Her Majesty and shall do so if the Parliament resolves that the [Scottish Government] no longer enjoys the confidence of the Parliament.

(3) The First Minister shall cease to hold office if a person is appointed in his place.

(4) If the office of First Minister is vacant or he is for any reason unable to act, the functions exercisable by him shall be exercisable by a person designated by the Presiding Officer.

(5) A person shall be so designated only if—

(a) he is a member of the Parliament, or

(b) if the Parliament has been dissolved, he is a person who ceased to be a member by virtue of the dissolution.

(6) Functions exercisable by a person by virtue of subsection (5)(a) shall continue to be exercisable by him even if the Parliament is dissolved.

(7) The First Minister shall be the Keeper of the Scottish Seal.

46 Choice of the First Minister

(1) If one of the following events occurs, the Parliament shall within the period allowed nominate one of its members for appointment as First Minister.

(2) The events are—

(a) the holding of a poll at a general election,

(b) the First Minister tendering his resignation to Her Majesty,

(c) the office of First Minister becoming vacant (otherwise than in consequence of his so tendering his resignation),

(d) the First Minister ceasing to be a member of the Parliament otherwise than by virtue of a dissolution.

(3) The period allowed is the period of 28 days which begins with the day on which the event in question occurs; but—

(a) if another of those events occurs within the period allowed, that period shall be extended (subject to paragraph (b)) so that it ends with the period of 28 days beginning with the day on which that other event occurred, and

(b) the period shall end if the Parliament passes a resolution under section 3 (1)(a) or when Her Majesty appoints a person as First Minister.

(4) The Presiding Officer shall recommend to Her Majesty the appointment of any member of the Parliament who is nominated by the Parliament under this section.

47 Ministers

(1) The First Minister may, with the approval of Her Majesty, appoint Ministers from among the members of the Parliament.

(2) The First Minister shall not seek Her Majesty's approval for any appointment under this section without the agreement of the Parliament.

(3) A Minister appointed under this section—

(a) shall hold office at Her Majesty's pleasure,

(b) may be removed from office by the First Minister,

(c) may at any time resign and shall do so if the Parliament resolves that the [Scottish Government] no longer enjoys the confidence of the Parliament,

(d) if he resigns, shall cease to hold office immediately, and

(e) shall cease to hold office if he ceases to be a member of the Parliament otherwise than by virtue of a dissolution.

49 Junior Scottish Ministers

(1) The First Minister may, with the approval of Her Majesty, appoint persons from among the members of the Parliament to assist the Scottish Ministers in the exercise of their functions.

(2) They shall be known as junior Scottish Ministers.

(3) The First Minister shall not seek Her Majesty's approval for any appointment under this section without the agreement of the Parliament.

(4) A junior Scottish Minister—

(a) shall hold office at Her Majesty's pleasure,

(b) may be removed from office by the First Minister,

(c) may at any time resign and shall do so if the Parliament resolves that the [Scottish Government] no longer enjoys the confidence of the Parliament,

(d) if he resigns, shall cease to hold office immediately, and

(e) shall cease to hold office if he ceases to be a member of the Parliament otherwise than by virtue of a dissolution.

50 Validity of acts of Scottish Ministers etc

The validity of any act of a member of the [Scottish Government] or junior Scottish Minister is not affected by any defect in his nomination by the Parliament or (as the case may be) in the Parliament's agreement to his appointment.

51 The Civil Service

(1) The Scottish Ministers may appoint persons to be members of the staff of the Scottish Administration.

(2) Service as—

(a) the holder of any office in the Scottish Administration which is not a ministerial office, or

(b) a member of the staff of the Scottish Administration,

shall be service in the civil service of the state.

[(3) See Part 1 of the Constitutional Reform and Governance Act 2010 (in particular, sections 3 and 4) for provision affecting—

(a) subsection (1), and

(b) any other enactment about the appointment of persons mentioned in subsection (2).]

[(4) See also section 1 of the Civil Service (Management Functions) Act 1992 under which functions conferred on the Minister for the Civil Service by section 3 of the Constitutional Reform and Governance Act 2010 may be delegated to the Scottish Ministers etc.]

(5) Any salary or allowances payable to or in respect of the persons mentioned

in subsection (2) (including contributions to any pension scheme) shall be payable out of the Scottish Consolidated Fund.

(6) Section 1(2) and (3) of the Superannuation Act 1972 (delegation of functions relating to civil service superannuation schemes etc) shall have effect as if references to a Minister of the Crown (other than the Minister for the Civil Service) included the Scottish Ministers.

(7) The Scottish Ministers shall make payments to the Minister for the Civil Service, at such times as he may determine, of such amounts as he may determine in respect of—

(a) the provision of pensions, allowances or gratuities by virtue of section 1 of the Superannuation Act 1972 to or in respect of persons who are or have been in such service as is mentioned in subsection (2), and

(b) any expenses to be incurred in administering those pensions, allowances or gratuities.

(8) Amounts required for payments under subsection (7) shall be charged on the Scottish Consolidated Fund.

[. . .]

Ministerial functions

52 Exercise of functions

(1) Statutory functions may be conferred on the Scottish Ministers by that name.

(2) Statutory functions of the Scottish Ministers, the First Minister or the Lord Advocate shall be exercisable on behalf of Her Majesty.

(3) Statutory functions of the Scottish Ministers shall be exercisable by any member of the [Scottish Government].

(4) Any act or omission of, or in relation to, any member of the [Scottish Government] shall be treated as an act or omission of, or in relation to, each of them; and any property acquired, or liability incurred, by any member of the [Scottish Government] shall be treated accordingly.

(5) Subsection (4) does not apply in relation to the exercise of—

(a) functions conferred on the First Minister alone, or

(b) retained functions of the Lord Advocate.

(6) In this Act, 'retained functions' in relation to the Lord Advocate means—

(a) any functions exercisable by him immediately before he ceases to be a Minister of the Crown, and

(b) other statutory functions conferred on him alone after he ceases to be a Minister of the Crown.

(7) In this section, 'statutory functions' means functions conferred by virtue of any enactment.

53 General transfer of functions

(1) The functions mentioned in subsection (2) shall, so far as they are exercisable within devolved competence, be exercisable by the Scottish Ministers instead of by a Minister of the Crown.

(2) Those functions are—

(a) those of Her Majesty's prerogative and other executive functions which are exercisable on behalf of Her Majesty by a Minister of the Crown,

(b) other functions conferred on a Minister of the Crown by a prerogative instrument, and

(c) functions conferred on a Minister of the Crown by any pre-commencement enactment,

but do not include any retained functions of the Lord Advocate.

(3) In this Act, 'pre-commencement enactment' means—

(a) an Act passed before or in the same session as this Act and any other enactment made before the passing of this Act,

(b) an enactment made, before the commencement of this section, under such an Act or such other enactment,

(c) subordinate legislation under section 106, to the extent that the legislation states that it is to be treated as a pre-commencement enactment.

[(3A) But see sections 9, 32 and 51 of the Scotland Act 2016 (which give 'pre-commencement enactment' a different meaning for functions exercisable within devolved competence by virtue of certain provisions of that Act.)]

(4) This section and section 54 are modified by Part III of Schedule 4.

54 Devolved competence

(1) References in this Act to the exercise of a function being within or outside devolved competence are to be read in accordance with this section.

(2) It is outside devolved competence—

(a) to make any provision by subordinate legislation which would be outside the legislative competence of the Parliament if it were included in an Act of the Scottish Parliament, or

(b) to confirm or approve any subordinate legislation containing such provision.

(3) In the case of any function other than a function of making, confirming or approving subordinate legislation, it is outside devolved competence to exercise the function (or exercise it in any way) so far as a provision of an Act of the Scottish Parliament conferring the function (or, as the case may be, conferring it so as to be exercisable in that way) would be outside the legislative competence of the Parliament.

56 Shared powers

(1) Despite the transfer by virtue of section 53 of any function under—

(a) section 17(1) of the Ministry of Transport Act 1919 (power to make advances for certain purposes),

(b) any Order in Council under section 1 of the United Nations Act 1946 (measures to give effect to Security Council decisions),

(c) section 9 of the Industrial Organisation and Development Act 1947 (levies for scientific research, promotion of exports, etc),

(d) section 5 of the Science and Technology Act 1965 (funding of scientific research),

(e) section 1 of the Mineral Exploration and Investment Grants Act 1972 (contributions in respect of mineral exploration),

(f) sections 10 to 12 of the Industry Act 1972 (credits and grants for construction of ships and offshore installations),

(g) sections 2, 11(3) and 12(4) of the Employment and Training Act 1973 (power to make arrangements for employment and training etc. and to make certain payments),

(h) sections 7 to 9 and 11 to 13 of the Industrial Development Act 1982 (financial and other assistance for industry), and

(i) sections 39 and 40 of the Road Traffic Act 1988 (road safety information and training),

the function shall be exercisable by a Minister of the Crown as well as by the Scottish Ministers.

(2) Despite the transfer of any other function by virtue of section 53, the function shall, if subordinate legislation so provides, be exercisable (or be exercisable so far as the legislation provides) by a Minister of the Crown as well as by the Scottish Ministers.

(3) Subordinate legislation under subsection (2) may not be made so as to come

into force at any time after the function in question has become exercisable by the Scottish Ministers.

(4) Any power referred to in section 53(2)(a) to establish, maintain or abolish a body, office or office-holder having functions which include both—

(a) functions which are exercisable in or as regards Scotland and do not relate to reserved matters, and

(b) other functions,

shall, despite that section, be exercisable jointly by the Minister of the Crown and the Scottish Ministers.

(5) In subsection (4), 'office-holder' includes employee or other post-holder.

57 [EU] law and Convention rights

(1) Despite the transfer to the Scottish Ministers by virtue of section 53 of functions in relation to observing and implementing obligations under [EU] law, any function of a Minister of the Crown in relation to any matter shall continue to be exercisable by him as regards Scotland for the purposes specified in section 2(2) of the European Communities Act 1972.

(2) A member of the [Scottish Government] has no power to make any subordinate legislation, or to do any other act, so far as the legislation or act is incompatible with any of the Convention rights [. . .].

(3) Subsection (2) does not apply to an act of the Lord Advocate—

(a) in prosecuting any offence, or

(b) in his capacity as head of the systems of criminal prosecution and investigation of deaths in Scotland,

[. . .]

[(4) A member of the Scottish Government has no power to make, confirm or approve any subordinate legislation so far as the legislation modifies retained EU law and the modification is of a description specified in regulations made by a Minister of the Crown.

(5) But subsection (4) does not apply—

(a) so far as the modification would be within the legislative competence of the Parliament if it were included in an Act of the Scottish Parliament, or

(b) to the making of regulations under Schedule 2 or 4 to the European Union (Withdrawal) Act 2018.

(6) A Minister of the Crown must not lay for approval before each House of the Parliament of the United Kingdom a draft of a statutory instrument containing regulations under subsection (4) unless—

(a) the Scottish Parliament has made a consent decision in relation to the laying of the draft, or

(b) the 40 day period has ended without the Parliament having made such a decision.

(7) For the purposes of subsection (6) a consent decision is—

(a) a decision to agree a motion consenting to the laying of the draft,

(b) a decision not to agree a motion consenting to the laying of the draft, or

(c) a decision to agree a motion refusing to consent to the laying of the draft;

and a consent decision is made when the Parliament first makes a decision falling within any of paragraphs (a) to (c) (whether or not it subsequently makes another such decision).

(8) A Minister of the Crown who is proposing to lay a draft as mentioned in subsection (6) must—

(a) provide a copy of the draft to the Scottish Ministers, and

(b) inform the Presiding Officer that a copy has been so provided.

(9) See also paragraph 6 of Schedule 7 (duty to make explanatory statement about regulations under subsection (4) including a duty to explain any decision to lay a draft without the consent of the Parliament).

(10) No regulations may be made under subsection (4) after the end of the period of two years beginning with exit day.

(11) Subsection (10) does not affect the continuation in force of regulations made under subsection (4) at or before the end of the period mentioned in subsection (10).

(12) Any regulations under subsection (4) which are in force at the end of the period of five years beginning with the time at which they came into force are revoked in their application to the making, confirming or approving of subordinate legislation after the end of that period.

(13) Subsections (6) to (11) do not apply in relation to regulations which only relate to a revocation of a specification.

(14) The restriction in subsection (4) is in addition to any restriction in section 7 of the European Union (Withdrawal) Act 2018 or elsewhere on the power of a member of the Scottish Government to make, confirm or approve any subordinate legislation so far as the legislation modifies retained EU law.

(15) In this section—

'the 40 day period' means the period of 40 days beginning with the day on which a copy of the draft instrument is provided to the Scottish Ministers, and, in calculating that period, no account is to be taken of any time during which the Parliament is dissolved or during which it is in recess for more than four days.]

58 Power to prevent or require action

(1) If the Secretary of State has reasonable grounds to believe that any action proposed to be taken by a member of the [Scottish Government] would be incompatible with any international obligations, he may by order direct that the proposed action shall not be taken.

(2) If the Secretary of State has reasonable grounds to believe that any action capable of being taken by a member of the [Scottish Government] is required for the purpose of giving effect to any such obligations, he may by order direct that the action shall be taken.

(3) In subsections (1) and (2), 'action' includes making, confirming or approving subordinate legislation and, in subsection (2), includes introducing a Bill in the Parliament.

(4) If any subordinate legislation made or which could be revoked by a member of the [Scottish Government] contains provisions—

(a) which the Secretary of State has reasonable grounds to believe to be incompatible with any international obligations or the interests of defence or national security, or

(b) which make modifications of the law as it applies to reserved matters and which the Secretary of State has reasonable grounds to believe to have an adverse effect on the operation of the law as it applies to reserved matters,

the Secretary of State may by order revoke the legislation.

(5) An order under this section must state the reasons for making the order.

Transfer of additional functions

63 Power to transfer functions

(1) Her Majesty may by Order in Council provide for any functions, so far as they are exercisable by a Minister of the Crown in or as regards Scotland, to be exercisable—

(a) by the Scottish Ministers instead of by the Minister of the Crown,

(b) by the Scottish Ministers concurrently with the Minister of the Crown, or

(c) by the Minister of the Crown only with the agreement of, or after consultation with, the Scottish Ministers.

(2) Where an Order is made under subsection (1)(a) or (b) in relation to a function of a Minister of the Crown which is exercisable only with the agreement of, or

after consultation with, another Minister of the Crown, the function shall, unless the Order provides otherwise, be exercisable by the Scottish Ministers free from any such requirement.

(3) An Order under this section may, in particular, provide for any function exercisable by the Scottish Ministers by virtue of an Order under subsection (1)(a) or (b) to be exercisable subject to a requirement for the function to be exercised with the agreement of, or after consultation with, a Minister of the Crown or other person.

[PART 2A
PERMANENCE OF THE SCOTTISH PARLIAMENT AND SCOTTISH GOVERNMENT

63A Permanence of the Scottish Parliament and Scottish Government

(1) The Scottish Parliament and the Scottish Government are a permanent part of the United Kingdom's constitutional arrangements.

(2) The purpose of this section is, with due regard to the other provisions of this Act, to signify the commitment of the Parliament and Government of the United Kingdom to the Scottish Parliament and the Scottish Government.

(3) In view of that commitment it is declared that the Scottish Parliament and the Scottish Government are not to be abolished except on the basis of a decision of the people of Scotland voting in a referendum.]

PART V
MISCELLANEOUS AND GENERAL

87 The Advocate General for Scotland

(1) In Schedule 2 to the House of Commons Disqualification Act 1975 (Ministerial offices) and Part III of Schedule 1 to the Ministerial and other Salaries Act 1975 (salaries of the Law Officers), after the entry for the Solicitor General there is inserted—

'Advocate General for Scotland'.

(2) The validity of anything done in relation to the Advocate General is not affected by a vacancy in that office.

(3) If that office is vacant or the Advocate General is for any reason unable to act, his functions shall be exercisable by such other Minister of the Crown as the Prime Minister may determine in writing.

91 Maladministration

(1) The Parliament shall make provision for the investigation of relevant complaints made to its members in respect of any action taken by or on behalf of—

(a) a member of the [Scottish Government] in the exercise of functions conferred on the Scottish Ministers, or

(b) any other office-holder in the Scottish Administration.

(2) For the purposes of subsection (1), a complaint is a relevant complaint if it is a complaint of a kind which could be investigated under the Parliamentary Commissioner Act 1967 if it were made to a member of the House of Commons in respect of a government department or other authority to which that Act applies.

(3) The Parliament may make provision for the investigation of complaints in respect of—

(a) any action taken by or on behalf of an office-holder in the Scottish Administration,

(b) any action taken by or on behalf of the Parliamentary corporation,

(c) any action taken by or on behalf of a Scottish public authority with mixed functions or no reserved functions, or

(d) any action concerning Scotland and not relating to reserved matters which is taken by or on behalf of a cross-border public authority.

(4) In making provision of the kind required by subsection (1), the Parliament shall have regard (among other things) to the Act of 1967.

(5) Sections 53 and 117 to 121 shall not apply in relation to functions conferred by or under the Act of 1967.

(6) In this section—

'action' includes failure to act (and related expressions shall be read accordingly),

'provision' means provision by an Act of the Scottish Parliament; and the references to the Act of 1967 are to that Act as it has effect on the commencement of this section.

95 Appointment and removal of judges

(1) It shall continue to be for the Prime Minister to recommend to Her Majesty the appointment of a person as Lord President of the Court of Session or Lord Justice Clerk.

(2) The Prime Minister shall not recommend to Her Majesty the appointment of any person who has not been nominated by the First Minister for such appointment.

(3) Before nominating persons for such appointment the First Minister shall consult the Lord President and the Lord Justice Clerk (unless, in either case, the office is vacant).

(4) It is for the First Minister, after consulting the Lord President, to recommend to Her Majesty the appointment of a person as—

(a) a judge of the Court of Session (other than the Lord President or the Lord Justice Clerk), or

(b) a sheriff principal or a sheriff.

(5) The First Minister shall comply with any requirement in relation to—

(a) a nomination under subsection (2), or

(b) a recommendation under subsection (4),

imposed by virtue of any enactment.

(6) A judge of the Court of Session and the Chairman of the Scottish Land Court may be removed from office only by Her Majesty; and any recommendation to Her Majesty for such removal shall be made by the First Minister.

(7) The First Minister shall make such a recommendation if (and only if) the Parliament, on a motion made by the First Minister, resolves that such a recommendation should be made.

(8) Provision shall be made for a tribunal constituted by the First Minister to investigate and report on whether a judge of the Court of Session or the Chairman of the Scottish Land Court is unfit for office by reason of inability, neglect of duty or misbehaviour and for the report to be laid before the Parliament.

(9) Such provision shall include provision—

(a) for the constitution of the tribunal by the First Minister when requested by the Lord President to do so and in such other circumstances as the First Minister thinks fit, and

[(b) for the appointment to chair the tribunal of a member of the Judicial Committee of the Privy Council who holds or has held high judicial office.]

(10) The First Minister may make a motion under subsection (7) only if—

(a) he has received from a tribunal constituted in pursuance of subsection (8) a written report concluding that the person in question is unfit for office by reason of inability, neglect of duty or misbehaviour and giving reasons for that conclusion,

(b) where the person in question is the Lord President or the Lord Justice Clerk, he has consulted the Prime Minister, and

(c) he has complied with any other requirement imposed by virtue of any enactment.

(11) In subsections (8) to (10)—

['high judicial office' has the meaning given by section 60 of the Constitutional Reform Act 2005,]

'provision' means provision by or under an Act of the Scottish Parliament,

'tribunal' means a tribunal of at least three persons.

Juridical

98 Devolution issues

Schedule 6 (which makes provision in relation to devolution issues) shall have effect.

99 Rights and liabilities of the Crown in different capacities

(1) Rights and liabilities may arise between the Crown in right of Her Majesty's Government in the United Kingdom and the Crown in right of the Scottish Administration by virtue of a contract, by operation of law or by virtue of an enactment as they may arise between subjects.

(2) Property and liabilities may be transferred between the Crown in one of those capacities and the Crown in the other capacity as they may be transferred between subjects; and they may together create, vary or extinguish any property or liability as subjects may.

(3) Proceedings in respect of—

(a) any property or liabilities to which the Crown in one of those capacities is entitled or subject under subsection (1) or (2), or

(b) the exercise of, or failure to exercise, any function exercisable by an office-holder of the Crown in one of those capacities,

may be instituted by the Crown in either capacity; and the Crown in the other capacity may be a separate party in the proceedings.

(4) This section applies to a unilateral obligation as it applies to a contract.

(5) In this section—

'office-holder', in relation to the Crown in right of Her Majesty's Government in the United Kingdom, means any Minister of the Crown or other office-holder under the Crown in that capacity and, in relation to the Crown in right of the Scottish Administration, means any office-holder in the Scottish Administration,

'subject' means a person not acting on behalf of the Crown.

100 Human rights

(1) This Act does not enable a person—

(a) to bring any proceedings in a court or tribunal on the ground that an act is incompatible with the Convention rights, or

(b) to rely on any of the Convention rights in any such proceedings,

unless he would be a victim for the purposes of Article 34 of the Convention (within the meaning of the Human Rights Act 1998) if proceedings in respect of the act were brought in the European Court of Human Rights.

(2) Subsection (1) does not apply to the Lord Advocate, the Advocate General, the Attorney General [, the Advocate General for Northern Ireland] or the Attorney General for Northern Ireland.

(3) This Act does not enable a court or tribunal to award any damages in respect of an act which is incompatible with any of the Convention rights which it could not award if section 8(3) and (4) of the Human Rights Act 1998 applied.

[(3A) Subsection (3B) applies to any proceedings brought by virtue of this Act against the Scottish Ministers or a member of the Scottish Government in a court or tribunal on the ground that an act of the Scottish Ministers or a member of the Scottish Government is incompatible with the Convention rights.

(3B) Proceedings to which this subsection applies must be brought before the end of—

(a) the period of one year beginning with the date on which the act complained of took place, or

(b) such longer period as the court or tribunal considers equitable having regard to all the circumstances,

but that is subject to any rule imposing a stricter time limit in relation to the procedure in question.

(3C) Subsection (3B) does not apply to proceedings brought by the Lord Advocate, the Advocate General, the Attorney General, the Attorney General for Northern Ireland or the Advocate General for Northern Ireland.

(3D) In subsections (3A) and (3B) 'act' does not include the making of any legislation but it does include any other act or failure to act (including a failure to make legislation).

(3E) In subsection (3B) 'rule' has the same meaning as it has in section 7(5) of the Human Rights Act 1998.]

(4) [Subject to subsection (3D),] in this section 'act' means—

(a) making any legislation,

(b) any other act or failure to act, if it is the act or failure of a member of the [Scottish Government].

101 Interpretation of Acts of the Scottish Parliament etc

(1) This section applies to—

(a) any provision of an Act of the Scottish Parliament, or of a Bill for such an Act, and

(b) any provision of subordinate legislation made, confirmed or approved, or purporting to be made, confirmed or approved, by a member of the [Scottish Government],

which could be read in such a way as to be outside competence.

(2) Such a provision is to be read as narrowly as is required for it to be within competence, if such a reading is possible, and is to have effect accordingly.

(3) In this section 'competence'—

(a) in relation to an Act of the Scottish Parliament, or a Bill for such an Act, means the legislative competence of the Parliament, and

(b) in relation to subordinate legislation, means the powers conferred by virtue of this Act.

102 Powers of courts or tribunals to vary retrospective decisions

(1) This section applies where any court or tribunal decides that—

(a) an Act of the Scottish Parliament or any provision of such an Act is not within the legislative competence of the Parliament, or

(b) a member of the[Scottish Government] does not have the power to make, confirm or approve a provision of subordinate legislation that he has purported to make, confirm or approve [, or

(c) any other purported exercise of a function by a member of the Scottish Government was outside devolved competence.]

(2) The court or tribunal may make an order—

(a) removing or limiting any retrospective effect of the decision, or

(b) suspending the effect of the decision for any period and on any conditions to allow the defect to be corrected.

(3) In deciding whether to make an order under this section, the court or tribunal shall (among other things) have regard to the extent to which persons who are not parties to the proceedings would otherwise be adversely affected.

(4) Where a court or tribunal is considering whether to make an order under this section, it shall order intimation of that fact to be given to—

(a) the Lord Advocate, and

(b) the appropriate law officer, where the decision mentioned in subsection

(1) relates to a devolution issue (within the meaning of Schedule 6) [or to a compatibility issue],

unless the person to whom the intimation would be given is a party to the proceedings.

(5) A person to whom intimation is given under subsection (4) may take part as a party in the proceedings so far as they relate to the making of the order.

[(5A) Where the decision mentioned in subsection (1) is a decision of the Supreme Court on a compatibility issue, the power to make an order under this section is exercisable by the High Court of Justiciary instead of the Supreme Court.]

(6) Paragraphs 36 and 37 of Schedule 6 apply with necessary modifications for the purposes of subsections (4) and (5) as they apply for the purposes of that Schedule.

(7) In this section—

['compatibility issue' has the meaning given by section 288ZA of the criminal Procedure (Scotland) Act 1995,]

'intimation' includes notice,

'the appropriate law officer' means—

(a) in relation to proceedings in Scotland, the Advocate General,

(b) in relation to proceedings in England and Wales, the Attorney General,

(c) in relation to proceedings in Northern Ireland, the [Advocate General for Northern Ireland].

PART VI
SUPPLEMENTARY

129 Transitional provisions etc

(1) Subordinate legislation may make such provision as the person making the legislation considers necessary or expedient for transitory or transitional purposes in connection with the coming into force of any provision of this Act.

(2) If any of the following provisions come into force before the Human Rights Act 1998 has come into force (or come fully into force), the provision shall have effect until the time when that Act is fully in force as it will have effect after that time: sections 29(2)(d), 57(2) and (3), 100 and 126(1) and Schedule 6.

SCHEDULES

[SCHEDULE 1
CONSTITUENCIES, REGIONS AND REGIONAL MEMBERS

General

1—(1) There are to be 73 constituencies for the purposes of this Act.

(2) The constituencies are—

(a) the Orkney Islands,

(b) the Shetland Islands, and

[(c) the constituencies provided for by an Order in Council under paragraph 6.]

[. . .]

2—(1) There are to be eight regions for the purposes of this Act.

[(2) The regions are the regions provided for by an Order in Council under paragraph 6.]

(3) Seven regional members are to be returned for each region.

Reports of the [Local Government Boundary Commission for Scotland]

3—(1) The [Local Government Boundary Commission for Scotland] must keep under review the boundaries of the constituencies (other than those mentioned in paragraph 1(2)(a) and (b)).

(2) The review must be conducted in accordance with the constituency rules.

(3) The [Local Government Boundary Commission for Scotland] must submit to the [Scottish Ministers] a report—

(a) showing the alterations they propose to the boundaries, or

(b) stating that in their opinion no alteration should be made.

(4) The first report of the [Local Government Boundary Commission for Scotland] [to the Scottish Ministers] under this paragraph must be submitted to the [Scottish Ministers] [no earlier than 1 May 2018 and no later than 1 May 2022].

(5) Subsequent reports must be submitted not less than eight nor more than twelve years after the date of the submission of the last report.

(6) The [Local Government Boundary Commission for Scotland] may also from time to time [. . .] submit to the [Scottish Ministers] reports with respect to the area comprised in any two or more constituencies showing the constituencies into which they recommend the area should be divided in order to give effect to the constituency rules.

(7) A report under sub-paragraph (6) must recommend the same number of constituencies as that in which the area is comprised.

(8) A report of the [Local Government Boundary Commission for Scotland] which recommends an alteration to the boundaries of constituencies must state as respects each constituency—

(a) the name by which they recommend it is to be known;

(b) whether they recommend that it is to be a county or a burgh constituency.

(9) As soon as practicable after the [Local Government Boundary Commission for Scotland] have submitted a report to the [Scottish Ministers] under this paragraph [they] must lay before [the Parliament]—

(a) the report, and

(b) the draft of an Order in Council for giving effect to the recommendations contained in the report.

(10) Sub-paragraph (9)(b) does not apply if the report states that no alteration is required to be made to the boundaries of the constituencies.

[. . .]

4—(1) This paragraph applies if the [Local Government Boundary Commission for Scotland] submit a report to the [Scottish Ministers] recommending an alteration in a constituency.

(2) In the report the [Local Government Boundary Commission for Scotland] must recommend any alteration in any of the regions which they think is necessary to give effect to the regional rules.

(3) A report making a recommendation for an alteration in a region must recommend the name by which the [Local Government Boundary Commission for Scotland] think the region should be known.

[. . .]

Orders in Council

6—(1) The draft of an Order in Council laid before [the Parliament] by the [Scottish Ministers] for giving effect to the recommendations contained in a report by the [Local Government Boundary Commission for Scotland] under paragraph 3 may make provision for any matters which [they] think are incidental to or consequential on the recommendations.

(2) If the draft is approved by resolution of [the Parliament] the [Scottish Ministers] must submit it to Her Majesty in Council.

(3) If a motion for the approval of the draft is rejected by [the Parliament] or withdrawn by leave of [the Parliament] the [Scottish Ministers] may amend the draft and lay the amended draft before [the Parliament].

(4) If the draft as so amended is approved by resolution of [the Parliament] the [Scottish Ministers] must submit it to Her Majesty in Council.

(5) If a draft of an Order in Council is submitted to Her Majesty in Council under this Schedule, Her Majesty in Council may make an order in terms of the draft.

(6) An Order in Council made as mentioned in sub-paragraph (5) comes into force on the date specified in the Order.

(7) The coming into force of the Order does not affect the return of any member to the Parliament or its constitution until the Parliament is dissolved.

(8) The validity of an Order in Council purporting to be made under this Schedule and reciting that a draft of the Order has been approved by a resolution of [the Parliament] must not be called in question in any legal proceedings whatsoever.

Notice of proposed report or recommendations

7—(1) If the [Local Government Boundary Commission for Scotland] intend to consider making a report under this Schedule—

(a) they must inform the [Scottish Ministers] by notice in writing;

(b) they must publish a copy of the notice in the Edinburgh Gazette.

[(2) If [the Local Government Boundary Commission for Scotland] have provisionally determined to make recommendations affecting a constituency they must publish in at least one newspaper circulating in the constituency a notice stating—

(a) the effect of the proposed recommendations and (except if the effect is that no alteration should be made in respect of the constituency) that a copy of the recommendations is open to inspection at a specified place in the constituency, and

(b) that representations with respect to the proposed recommendations may be made to the Commission before the end of the period of one month starting the day after the notice is published.]

(3) The [Local Government Boundary Commission for Scotland] must take into account any representations made in accordance with the notice.

(4) If the [Local Government Boundary Commission for Scotland] revise any proposed recommendations after publishing notice of them under sub-paragraph (2) they must comply again with sub-paragraphs (2) and (3) in relation to the revised recommendations as if no earlier notice had been published.

[. . .]

8—[(1) This paragraph applies if the [Local Government Boundary Commission for Scotland] provisionally determine to make recommendations which would involve any alteration in a constituency.]

(2) The [Local Government Boundary Commission for Scotland] must consider whether any alteration within paragraph 4(2) would be required in order to give effect to the regional rules.

(3) [. . .]

(4) Paragraph 7 applies for the purposes of the proposed recommendations as if for any reference to a constituency there is substituted a reference to a region.

Local inquiries

9—(1) The [Local Government Boundary Commission for Scotland] may if they think fit cause a local inquiry to be held in respect of any constituency or constituencies.

(2) If the [Local Government Boundary Commission for Scotland] receive any relevant representations objecting to a proposed recommendation for the alteration of a constituency they must not make the recommendation unless since the publication of the notice under paragraph 7(2) a local inquiry has been held in respect of the constituency.

(3) If a local inquiry was held in respect of the constituency before the publication of the notice under paragraph 7(2), sub-paragraph (2) above does not apply if the [Local Government Boundary Commission for Scotland] after considering—

(a) the matters discussed at the inquiry,

(b) the nature of the relevant representations received, and

(c) any other relevant circumstances, think that a further local inquiry is not justified.

(4) A relevant representation is a representation made in accordance with paragraph 7(2)(b)—

(a) by the council for an area which is wholly or partly comprised in the constituency;

(b) by a body of not less than 100 persons entitled to vote as electors at an election for membership of the Parliament held in the constituency.

10—(1) The [Local Government Boundary Commission for Scotland] may if they think fit cause a local inquiry to be held in respect of any region or regions.

(2) If the [Local Government Boundary Commission for Scotland] receive any relevant representations objecting to a proposed recommendation for the alteration of a region they must not make the recommendation unless since the publication of the notice under paragraph 7(2) a local inquiry has been held in respect of the region.

(3) If a local inquiry was held in respect of the region before the publication of the notice under paragraph 7(2), sub-paragraph (2) above does not apply if the [Local Government Boundary Commission for Scotland] after considering—

(a) the matters discussed at the inquiry,

(b) the nature of the relevant representations received, and

(c) any other relevant circumstances,

think that a further local inquiry is not justified.

(4) A relevant representation is a representation made in accordance with paragraph 7(2)(b)—

(a) by the council for an area which is wholly or partly included in the region;

(b) by a body of not less than 500 persons entitled to vote as electors at an election for membership of the Parliament held in any one or more of the constituencies included in the region.

11—Section 210(4) and (5) of the Local Government (Scotland) Act 1973 (c 69) (attendance of witnesses at inquiries) applies in relation to a local inquiry held under paragraph 9 or 10.

The constituency rules

12—These are the constituency rules.

Rule 1

(1) So far as is practicable, regard must be had to the boundaries of [the local government areas having effect from time to time under section 1 of the Local Government etc (Scotland) Act 1994].

[. . .]

Rule 2

(1) The electorate of a constituency must be as near the electoral quota as is practicable, having regard to Rule 1.

(2) [The Local Government Boundary Commission for Scotland] may depart from the strict application of Rule 1 if they think that it is desirable to do so to avoid an excessive disparity between the electorate of a constituency and the electoral quota or between the electorate of a constituency and that of neighbouring constituencies.

(3) The electoral quota is the number obtained by dividing the total electorate by 71.

(4) The electorate of a constituency is the aggregate of the persons falling within paragraphs (5) and (6) below.

(5) A person falls within this paragraph if his name appears on the register of local government electors in force on the enumeration date under the Representation of the People Acts for a local government area which is situated wholly in the constituency.

(6) A person falls within this paragraph if his name appears on the register of local government electors in force on the enumeration date under the Representation of the People Acts for a local government area which is situated partly in the constituency and his qualifying address is situated in the constituency.

(7) The total electorate is the total number of persons whose names appear on the registers of local government electors in force on the enumeration date under the Representation of the People Acts for all of the local government areas in Scotland (except the local government areas of Orkney and Shetland).

(8) The enumeration date is, in relation to a report of [the Local Government Boundary Commission for Scotland], the date on which notice with respect to the report is published in the Edinburgh Gazette in accordance with paragraph 7(1) above.

(9) 'Qualifying address' and 'local government area' have the same meanings as in the Representation of the People Act 1983 (c 2).

Rule 3

[The Local Government Boundary Commission for Scotland] may depart from the strict application of Rules 1 and 2 if they think that special geographical considerations (including in particular the size, shape and accessibility of a constituency) render it desirable to do so.

Rule 4

[The Local Government Boundary Commission for Scotland] need not aim at giving full effect in all circumstances to Rules 1 to 3 but they must take account (so far as they reasonably can)—

(a) of the inconveniences attendant on alterations of constituencies other than alterations made for the purposes of Rule 1, and

(b) of any local ties which would be broken by such alterations.

The regional rules

13—These are the regional rules.

Rule 1

A constituency must fall wholly within a region.

Rule 2

The regional electorate of a region must be as near the regional electorate of each of the other regions as is practicable, having regard (where appropriate) to special geographical considerations.

14—(1) This paragraph applies for the purposes of the regional rules.

(2) For the purposes of a report of [the Local Government Boundary Commission for Scotland] in relation to a region, the regional electorate is the number of persons—

(a) whose names appear on the enumeration date on the registers of local government electors in the region, and

(b) who are registered at addresses within a constituency included in the region.

(3) The enumeration date is the date on which notice with respect to the report is published in the Edinburgh Gazette in accordance with paragraph 7(1) above.]

(4) [. . .]

SCHEDULE 4
ENACTMENTS ETC PROTECTED FROM MODIFICATION

PART I
THE PROTECTED PROVISIONS

Particular enactments

1—(1) An Act of the Scottish Parliament cannot modify, or confer power by subordinate legislation to modify, any of the following provisions.

(2) The provisions are—

(a) Articles 4 and 6 of the Union with Scotland Act 1706 and of the Union with England Act 1707 so far as they relate to freedom of trade,

(b) the Private Legislation Procedure (Scotland) Act 1936,

[. . .]

(d) paragraphs 5(3)(b) and 15(4)(b) of Schedule 32 to the Local Government, Planning and Land Act 1980 (designation of enterprise zones),

(e) sections 140A to 140G of the Social Security Administration Act 1992 (rent rebate and rent allowance subsidy and council tax benefit),

(f) the Human Rights Act 1998.

[(g) the European Union (Withdrawal) Act 2018 (other than paragraphs 31 to 35 of Schedule 8 to that Act and any regulations made under that Act)].

The law on reserved matters

2—(1) An Act of the Scottish Parliament cannot modify, or confer power by subordinate legislation to modify, the law on reserved matters.

(2) In this paragraph, 'the law on reserved matters' means—

(a) any enactment the subject-matter of which is a reserved matter and which is comprised in an Act of Parliament or subordinate legislation under an Act of Parliament, and

(b) any rule of law which is not contained in an enactment and the subject-matter of which is a reserved matter,

and in this sub-paragraph 'Act of Parliament' does not include this Act.

(3) Sub-paragraph (1) applies in relation to a rule of Scots private law or Scots criminal law (whether or not contained in an enactment) only to the extent that the rule in question is special to a reserved matter or the subject-matter of the rule is—

(a) interest on sums due in respect of taxes or excise duties and refunds of such taxes or duties, or

(b) the obligations, in relation to occupational or personal pension schemes, of the trustees or managers.

[(c) the obligations under an order made by virtue of section 12A(2) or (3) of the Family Law (Scotland) Act 1985 (orders relating to pensions lump sums) of the person responsible for a pension arrangement other than an occupational or personal pension scheme; or

(d) the obligations under Chapter I of Part IV of the Welfare Reform and Pensions Act 1999 (sharing of rights under pension arrangements) of the person responsible for such a pension arrangement; or

(e) the effect of Chapter II of Part IV of that Act of 1999 (sharing of rights in state pension schemes) as read with Part II of the Social Security Contributions and Benefits Act 1992 (contributory benefits) [and Part 1 of the Pensions Act 2014 (state pension)].]

[(4) In sub-paragraph (3)(c) 'pension arrangement' and 'person responsible for a pension arrangement' have the same meaning as in section 27(1) of the Family Law (Scotland) Act 1985.]

[(5) Sub-paragraph (3) does not affect sub-paragraph (1) as it applies to an Act of the Scottish Parliament so far as any matter to which a provision of the Act relates falls within exception 10 of Section of Part 2 of Schedule 5.]

3—(1) Paragraph 2 does not apply to modifications which—

(a) are incidental to, or consequential on, provision made (whether by virtue of the Act in question or another enactment) which does not relate to reserved matters, and

(b) do not have a greater effect on reserved matters than is necessary to give effect to the purpose of the provision.

(2) In determining for the purposes of sub-paragraph (1)(b) what is necessary to give effect to the purpose of a provision, any power to make laws other than the power of the Parliament is to be disregarded.

[(3) Sub-paragraph (1) does not affect the application of paragraph 2 to modifications which are incidental to, or consequential on, any provision, if it is only by virtue of exception 10 of Section F1 of Part 2 of Schedule 5 that the provision does not relate to reserved matters.]

This Act

4—(1) An Act of the Scottish Parliament cannot modify, or confer power by subordinate legislation to modify, this Act.

[(2) This paragraph does not apply to modifying—

(a) the following sections in Part 1 (the Scottish Parliament)—

(i) section 1(2) to (5),

(ii) section 2(1), (2), (2B) and (3) to (6),

(iii) sections 3 to 12,

(iv) sections 13 to 22,

(v) sections 24 to 26,

(vi) section 27(1) and (2),

(vii) section 28(4) and (5),

(viii) section 31(3),

(ix) section 36(1)(a) and (b), and (2) and (3), and

(x) sections 38 to 42,

(b) the following sections in Part 2 (the Scottish Administration)—

(i) section 44(1)(a) to (c) and (2),

(ii) section 45(3) to (7),

(iii) section 46(1) to (3),

(iv) section 47(2) and (3)(b) to (e),

(v) section 48(2) to (4),

(vi) section 49(2), (3) and (4)(b) to (e), and

(vii) section 50,

(c) in Part 3 (financial provisions)—

(i) section 69(2) to (5), and

(ii) section 70(1) to (5) and (7) to (9),

(d) in Part 5 (miscellaneous and general), sections 81 to 83, 85, 91, 92(1), (2) and (4) to (6), 93, 94 and 97,

(e) the following provisions in Part 6 (supplementary)—

(i) section 112(1) and (3) to (5), section 113 (except the application of subsection (9)), section 115 and Schedule 7 (so far as those sections and that

Schedule apply to any power exercisable within devolved competence to make subordinate legislation),

(ii) sections 118, 120 and 121, and

(iii) section 124 (so far as that section applies to any power exercisable within devolved competence to make subordinate legislation),

(f) Schedule 1 (constituencies, regions and regional members),

(g) paragraphs 1, 2(1) and 3 to 6 of Schedule 2 (Scottish Parliamentary corporate body), and

(h) paragraphs 1 to 6 of Schedule 3 (standing orders–further provision).]

(3) This paragraph does not apply to modifying any provision of this Act (other than sections 64(7), 66(2), 71(7), [. . .] and 119) which—

(a) charges any sum on the Scottish Consolidated Fund,

(b) requires any sum to be paid out of that Fund without further approval,

[(c) requires any sum to be payable out of that Fund. [or

(d)] requires or authorises the payment of any sum into that Fund.

(4) This paragraph does not apply to any modifications of Part III which are necessary or expedient for the purpose or in consequence of the establishment of a new fund, in addition to the Scottish Consolidated Fund, out of which loans may be made by the Scottish Ministers.

(5) This paragraph does not apply to—

(a) modifying so much of any enactment as is modified by this Act,

(b) repealing so much of any provision of this Act as amends any enactment, if the provision ceases to have effect in consequence of any enactment comprised in or made under an Act of the Scottish Parliament.

Enactments modified by this Act

5—An Act of the Scottish Parliament cannot modify, or confer power by subordinate legislation to modify—

(a) the effect of section 119(3) in relation to any provision of an Act of Parliament relating to judicial salaries,

(b) so much of any enactment as—

(i) is amended by paragraph 2, 7 or 32 of Schedule 8, and

(ii) relates to the Advocate General,

(c) so much of any enactment as is amended by paragraph 9(b) or 29 of Schedule 8.

Shared powers

6—An Act of the Scottish Parliament cannot modify, or confer power by subordinate legislation to modify, any enactment so far as the enactment relates to powers exercisable by a Minister of the Crown by virtue of section 56.

PART II
GENERAL EXCEPTIONS

Restatement, etc

7—(1) Part I of this Schedule does not prevent an Act of the Scottish Parliament—

(a) restating the law (or restating it with such modifications as are not prevented by that Part), or

(b) repealing any spent enactment,

or conferring power by subordinate legislation to do so.

(2) For the purposes of paragraph 2, the law on reserved matters includes any restatement in an Act of the Scottish Parliament, or subordinate legislation under

such an Act, of the law on reserved matters if the subject-matter of the restatement is a reserved matter.

Effect of Interpretation Act 1978

8—Part I of this Schedule does not prevent the operation of any provision of the Interpretation Act 1978.

Change of title etc

9—(1) Part I of this Schedule does not prevent an Act of the Scottish Parliament amending, or conferring power by subordinate legislation to amend, any enactment by changing—

(a) any of the titles referred to in sub-paragraph (2), or

(b) any reference to a declarator,

in consequence of any provision made by or under an Act of the Scottish Parliament.

(2) The titles are those of—

(a) any court or tribunal or any judge, chairman or officer of a court or tribunal,

(b) any holder of an office in the Scottish Administration which is not a ministerial office or any member of the staff of the Scottish Administration,

(c) any register.

Accounts and audit and maladministration

10—Part I of this Schedule does not prevent an Act of the Scottish Parliament modifying, or conferring power by subordinate legislation to modify, any enactment for or in connection with the purposes of section 70 or 91.

Subordinate legislation

11—(1) Part I of this Schedule does not prevent an Act of the Scottish Parliament modifying, or conferring power by subordinate legislation to modify, any enactment for or in connection with any of the following purposes.

(2) Those purposes are—

(a) making different provision in respect of the document by which a power to make subordinate legislation within sub-paragraph (3) is to be exercised,

(b) making different provision (or no provision) for the procedure, in relation to the Parliament, to which legislation made in the exercise of such a power (or the instrument or other document in which it is contained) is to be subject,

(c) applying any enactment comprised in or made under an Act of the Scottish Parliament relating to the documents by which such powers may be exercised.

(3) The power to make the subordinate legislation, or a power to confirm or approve the legislation, must be exercisable by—

(a) a member of the Scottish Executive,

(b) any Scottish public authority with mixed functions or no reserved functions,

(c) any other person (not being a Minister of the Crown) within devolved competence.

[. . .]

PART III
CONSEQUENTIAL MODIFICATION OF SECTIONS 53 AND 54

12—(1) This paragraph applies to a function which (apart from this Schedule) would be transferred to the Scottish Ministers by virtue of section 53(2)(c).

(2) If, because of anything in Part I of this Schedule, a provision of an Act of the Scottish Parliament modifying an enactment so as to provide for the function to be exercisable by a different person would be outside the legislative competence of the Parliament, the function is not so transferred.

13—(1) Paragraph 12 does not apply to any function conferred by any provision of—

(a) the European Communities Act 1972,

(b) the Human Rights Act 1998, except sections 1, 5, 14 to 17 and 22 of that Act,

(c) the law on reserved matters (for the purposes of paragraph 2) so far as contained in an enactment.

(2) For the purpose of determining—

(a) whether any function under any of the provisions referred to in sub-paragraph (1) is transferred to the Scottish Ministers by virtue of section 53, and

(b) the extent to which any such function (other than a function of making, confirming or approving subordinate legislation) is exercisable by them,

the references in section 54 to the legislative competence of the Parliament are to be read as if section 29(2)(c) were omitted.

(3) Part I of this Schedule does not prevent an Act of the Scottish Parliament modifying, or conferring power by subordinate legislation to modify, any of the provisions mentioned in sub-paragraph (1) so as to provide for a function transferred to the Scottish Ministers by virtue of section 53 to be exercisable by a different person.

14—If any pre-commencement enactment or prerogative instrument is modified by subordinate legislation under section 105 [or under section 71 of the Scotland Act 2016], a function under that enactment or instrument (whether as it has effect before or after the modification) is not transferred by virtue of section 53 if the subordinate legislation provides that it is not to be so transferred.

SCHEDULE 5
RESERVED MATTERS

PART I
GENERAL RESERVATIONS

The Constitution

1—The following aspects of the constitution are reserved matters, that is—

(a) the Crown, including succession to the Crown and a regency,

(b) the Union of the Kingdoms of Scotland and England,

(c) the Parliament of the United Kingdom,

(d) the continued existence of the High Court of Justiciary as a criminal court of first instance and of appeal,

(e) the continued existence of the Court of Session as a civil court of first instance and of appeal.

2—(1) Paragraph 1 does not reserve—

(a) Her Majesty's prerogative and other executive functions,

(b) functions exercisable by any person acting on behalf of the Crown, or

(c) any office in the Scottish Administration.

(2) Sub-paragraph (1) does not affect the reservation by paragraph 1 of honours and dignities or the functions of the Lord Lyon King of Arms so far as relating to the granting of arms; but this sub-paragraph does not apply to the Lord Lyon King of Arms in his judicial capacity.

(3) Sub-paragraph (1) does not affect the reservation by paragraph 1 of the

management (in accordance with any enactment regulating the use of land) of the Crown Estate [(that is, the property, rights and interests under the management of the Crown Estate Commissioners)].

[(3A) Sub-paragraph (1) does not affect the reservation by paragraph 1 of the requirements of section 90B(5) to (8).]

(4) Sub-paragraph (1) does not affect the reservation by paragraph 1 of the functions of the Security Service, the Secret Intelligence Service and the Government Communications Headquarters.

[(5) Sub-paragraph (1) does not affect the reservation by paragraph 1 of the functions exercisable through the Export Credits Guarantee Department.]

3—(1) Paragraph 1 does not reserve property belonging to Her Majesty in right of the Crown or belonging to any person acting on behalf of the Crown or held in trust for Her Majesty for the purposes of any person acting on behalf of the Crown.

(2) Paragraph 1 does not reserve the ultimate superiority of the Crown or the superiority of the Prince and Steward of Scotland.

(3) Sub-paragraph (1) does not affect the reservation by paragraph 1 of—

(a) the hereditary revenues of the Crown, other than revenues from bona vacantia, ultimus haeres and treasure trove,

(b) the royal arms and standard,

(c) the compulsory acquisition of property held or used by a Minister of the Crown or government department.

4—(1) Paragraph 1 does not reserve property held by Her Majesty in Her private capacity.

(2) Sub-paragraph (1) does not affect the reservation by paragraph 1 of the subject-matter of the Crown Private Estates Acts 1800 to 1873.

5—Paragraph 1 does not reserve the use of the Scottish Seal.

Political parties

6—The registration and funding of political parties is a reserved matter [but this paragraph does not reserve making payments to any political party for the purpose of assisting members of the Parliament who are connected with the party to perform their Parliamentary duties].

Foreign affairs etc

7—(1) International relations, including relations with territories outside the United Kingdom, the [European Union] (and their institutions) and other international organisations, regulation of international trade, and international development assistance and co-operation are reserved matters.

(2) Sub-paragraph (1) does not reserve—

(a) observing and implementing international obligations, obligations under the Human Rights Convention and obligations under [EU] law,

(b) assisting Ministers of the Crown in relation to any matter to which that sub-paragraph applies.

Public service

8—(1) The Civil Service of the State is a reserved matter.

(2) Sub-paragraph (1) does not reserve the subject-matter of—

(a) Part I of the Sheriff Courts and Legal Officers (Scotland) Act 1927 (appointment of sheriff clerks and procurators fiscal etc),

(b) Part III of the Administration of Justice (Scotland) Act 1933 (officers of the High Court of Justiciary and of the Court of Session).

Defence

9—(1) The following are reserved matters—

(a) the defence of the realm,

(b) the naval, military or air forces of the Crown, including reserve forces,

(c) visiting forces,

(d) international headquarters and defence organisations,

(e) trading with the enemy and enemy property.

(2) Sub-paragraph (1) does not reserve—

(a) the exercise of civil defence functions by any person otherwise than as a member of any force or organisation referred to in sub-paragraph (1)(b) to (d) or any other force or organisation reserved by virtue of sub-paragraph (1)(a),

(b) the conferral of enforcement powers in relation to sea fishing.

Treason

10—Treason (including constructive treason), treason felony and misprision of treason are reserved matters.

PART II
SPECIFIC RESERVATIONS

Preliminary

1 The matters to which any of the Sections in this Part apply are reserved matters for the purposes of this Act.

2 A Section applies to any matter described or referred to in it when read with any illustrations, exceptions or interpretation provisions in that Section.

3 Any illustrations, exceptions or interpretation provisions in a Section relate only to that Section (so that an entry under the heading 'exceptions' does not affect any other Section).

Reservations

Head A – Financial and Economic Matters

A1. Fiscal, economic and monetary policy
Fiscal, economic and monetary policy, including the issue and circulation of money, taxes and excise duties, government borrowing and lending, control over United Kingdom public expenditure, the exchange rate and the Bank of England.

[*Exceptions*
Devolved taxes, including their collection and management.]

Local taxes to fund local authority expenditure (for example, council tax and non-domestic rates).

A2. The currency
Coinage, legal tender and bank notes.

A3. Financial services
Financial services, including investment business, banking and deposit-taking, collective investment schemes and insurance.

Exception
The subject-matter of section 1 of the Banking and Financial Dealings Act 1971 (bank holidays).

A4. Financial markets
Financial markets, including listing and public offers of securities and investments, transfer of securities and insider dealing.

A5. Money laundering
The subject-matter of the Money Laundering Regulations 1993, but in relation to any type of business.

Head B – Home Affairs

B1. Misuse of drugs
The subject-matter of—

(a) the Misuse of Drugs Act 1971,

(b) sections 12 to 14 of the Criminal Justice (International Co-operation) Act 1990 (substances useful for manufacture of controlled drugs), and

(c) Part V of the Criminal Law (Consolidation) (Scotland) Act 1995 (drug trafficking) and, so far as relating to drug trafficking, the Proceeds of Crime (Scotland) Act 1995.

B2. Data protection
The subject-matter of—

(a) the Data Protection Act 1998, and

(b) Council Directive 95/46/EC (protection of individuals with regard to the processing of personal data and on the free movement of such data).

Interpretation
If any provision of the Data Protection Act 1998 is not in force on the principal appointed day, it is to be treated for the purposes of this reservation as if it were.

B3. Elections
[*(A) Elections for membership of the House of Commons and the European Parliament*]

Elections for membership of the House of Commons [and the European Parliament], including the subject-matter of—

(a) [the European Parliamentary Elections Act 2002,]

(b) the Representation of the People Act 1983 and the Representation of the People Act 1985, and

(c) the Parliamentary Constituencies Act 1986,

so far as those enactments apply, or may be applied, in respect of such membership.

[*(B) Elections for membership of the Parliament and local government elections in Scotland*

The subject-matter of sections 2(2A) and 12A of this Act.

The subject-matter of section 43(1AA) of the Representation of the People Act 1983.

The combination of—

(a) polls at elections or referendums that are outside the legislative competence of the Parliament with polls at—

(i) elections for membership of the Parliament, or

(ii) local government elections in Scotland, and

(b) polls at ordinary general elections for membership of the Parliament with polls at ordinary local government elections in Scotland.

Any digital service provided by a Minister of the Crown for the registration of electors.

The subject matter of—

(a) Parts 5 and 6 of the Political Parties, Elections and Referendums Act 2000 (expenditure in connection with elections) where a limit applies to expenditure in relation to a period determined by reference both to the date of the poll for an election within the legislative competence of the Parliament and to the date of the poll at an election for membership of the House of Commons or the European Parliament, and

(b) sections 145 to 148 and 150 to 154 of that Act (enforcement) as they apply for the purposes of Part 5 or 6, so far as the subject-matter of that Part is reserved by paragraph (a).

The subject matter of—

(a) sections 155 and 156 of the Political Parties, Elections and Referendums Act 2000, except in relation to Parts 5 and 6 of that Act so far as those Parts relate to elections for membership of the Parliament, and

(b) sections 145 to 148 and 150 to 154 of that Act as they apply for the purposes of section 155 or 156, so far as the subject-matter of that section is reserved by paragraph (a).

The subject-matter of the following sections of the Political Parties, Elections and Referendums Act 2000 in relation to elections for membership of the Parliament—

(a) section 1, except in relation to—

(i) financing the Electoral Commission,

(ii) preparation, laying and publication by the Commission of reports about the performance of its functions, and

(iii) provision by the Commission of copies of regulations made by it or notice of the alteration or revocation of such regulations,

(b) sections 2 to 4, 6(1)(e) and (f) (and (g) to the extent that it relates to the law mentioned in those paragraphs),

(c) sections 12, 21 to 33, 35 to 37, 39 to 57, 58 to 67, 69, 71, 71F, 71G, 71H to 71Y and 140A,

(d) section 149 (except in relation to the register kept under section 89),

(e) sections 157 and 159 to 163, and

(f) sections 145 to 148 and 150 to 154 as they apply for the purposes of a provision mentioned in paragraphs (a) to (e), so far as the subject matter of that provision is reserved by those paragraphs.]

Interpretation

[Paragraph 5(1) of Part 3 of this Schedule does not apply to the subject-matter of the Political Parties, Elections and Referendums Act 2000, and references to the subject-matter of that Act are to be read as at the day on which the Scotland Act 2016 received Royal Assent.]

B4. Firearms

The subject-matter of the Firearms Acts 1968 to 1997.

[*Exception*

The regulation of air weapons within the meaning given by section 1(3)(b) of the Firearms Act 1968 (which is subject to the following which remain powers of the Secretary of State—

(a) the power to make rules under section 53 of that Act for the purposes of that provision (specially dangerous weapons requiring firearms certificate), and

(b) the power to make an order under section 1(4) of the Firearms (Amendment) Act 1988 (specially dangerous weapons to be prohibited)).]

B5. Entertainment

The subject-matter of—

(a) the Video Recordings Act 1984, and

(b) sections 1 to 3 and 5 to 16 of the Cinemas Act 1985 (control of exhibitions).

The classification of films for public exhibition by reference to their suitability for viewing by persons generally or above a particular age, with or without any advice as to the desirability of parental guidance.

B6. Immigration and nationality

Nationality; immigration, including asylum and the status and capacity of persons in the United Kingdom who are not British citizens; free movement of persons within the European Economic Area; issue of travel documents.

B7. Scientific procedures on live animals
The subject-matter of the Animals (Scientific Procedures) Act 1986.

B8. National security, interception of communications, official secrets and terrorism
National security.

The interception of communications; but not

(a) [the interception of any communication made to or by a person detained at a place of detention, if the communication—

(i) is a written communication and is intercepted there, or

(ii) is intercepted in the course of its transmission by means of a private telecommunication system running there,]

(b) the subject matter of Part III of the Police Act 1997 (authorisation to interfere with property etc) or surveillance not involving interference with property.

The subject-matter of—

(a) the Official Secrets Acts 1911 and 1920, and

(b) the Official Secrets Act 1989, except so far as relating to any information, document or other article protected against disclosure by section 4(2) (crime) and not by any other provision of sections 1 to 4.

Special powers, and other special provisions, for dealing with terrorism.

[*Interpretation*
'Place of detention' means a prison, young offenders institution, remand centre or legalised police cell (as those expressions are defined for the purposes of the Prisons (Scotland) Act 1989 or a hospital (within the meaning of the [given in section 329(1) of the Mental Health (Care and Treatment) (Scotland) Act 2003]; and 'person detained', in relation to a hospital, means a person detained there [under—

(a) section 24, 25 or 70 of the Mental Health (Scotland) Act 1984;

(b) Part 6 of the Criminal Procedure (Scotland) Act 1995;

(c) the Mental Health (Care and Treatment) (Scotland) Act 2003; or

(d) regulations under—

(i) subsection (3) of section 116B of the Army Act 1955;

(ii) subsection (3) of section 116B of the Air Force Act 1955; or

(iii) section 63B of the Naval Discipline Act 1957.]

['Private telecommunication system' has the meaning given in section 2(1) of the Regulation of Investigatory Powers Act 2000.]]

B9. Betting, gaming and lotteries
Betting, gaming and lotteries.

[*Exception*
In the case of a betting premises licence under the Gambling Act 2005, other than one in respect of a track, the number of gaming machines authorised for which the maximum charge for use is more than £10 (or whether such machines are authorised).]

B10. Emergency powers
Emergency powers.

B11. Extradition
Extradition.

B12. Lieutenancies
The subject-matter of the Lieutenancies Act 1997.

[B13. Access to information
Public access to information held by public bodies or holders of public offices (including government departments and persons acting on behalf of the Crown).

Exception
Information held by—
(a) the Parliament,
(b) any part of the Scottish Administration,
(c) the Parliamentary corporation,
(d) any Scottish public authority with mixed functions or no reserved functions,
unless supplied by a Minister of the Crown or government department and held in confidence.]

Head C – Trade and Industry

C1. Business associations
The creation, operation, regulation and dissolution of types of business association.

Exceptions
The creation, operation, regulation and dissolution of—
(a) particular public bodies, or public bodies of a particular type, established by or under any enactment, and
(b) charities.

Interpretation
'Business association' means any person (other than an individual) established for the purpose of carrying on any kind of business, whether or not for profit; and 'business' includes the provision of benefits to the members of an association.

C2. Insolvency
In relation to business associations—
(a) the modes of, the grounds for and the general legal effect of winding up, and the persons who may initiate winding up,
(b) liability to contribute to assets on winding up,
(c) powers of courts in relation to proceedings for winding up, other than the power to sist proceedings,
(d) arrangements with creditors, and
(e) procedures giving protection from creditors.
Preferred or preferential debts for the purposes of the Bankruptcy (Scotland) Act 1985, the Insolvency Act 1986, and any other enactment relating to the sequestration of the estate of any person or to the winding up of business associations, the preference of such debts against other such debts and the extent of their preference over other types of debt.
Regulation of insolvency practitioners.
Co-operation of insolvency courts.

Exceptions
In relation to business associations—
(a) the process of winding up, including the person having responsibility for the conduct of a winding up or any part of it, and his conduct of it or of that part,
(b) the effect of winding up on diligence, and
(c) avoidance and adjustment of prior transactions on winding up.
[In relation to business associations which are social landlords, the following additional exceptions—
(a) the general legal effect of winding up,
(b) procedures for the initiation of winding up,
(c) powers of courts in relation to proceedings for winding up, and
(d) procedures giving protection from creditors,

but only in so far as they relate to a moratorium on the disposal of property held by a social landlord and the management and disposal of such property.]

Floating charges and receivers, except in relation to preferential debts, regulation of insolvency practitioners and co-operation of insolvency courts.

Interpretation

'Business association' has the meaning given in Section C1 of this Part of this Schedule, but does not include any person whose estate may be sequestrated under the Bankruptcy (Scotland) Act 1985 or any public body established by or under an enactment.

['Social landlord' means a body which is—

(a) [a registered society within the meaning of the Co-operative and Community Benefit Societies Act 2014] which has its registered office for the purposes of that Act in Scotland and satisfies the relevant conditions, or

(b) a company registered under the Companies Act 1985 which has its registered office for the purposes of that Act in Scotland and satisfies the relevant conditions.

'The relevant conditions' are that the body does not trade for profit and is established for the purpose of, or has among its objects and powers, the provision, construction, improvement or management of—

(a) houses to be kept available for letting,

(b) houses for occupation by members of the body, where the rules of the body restrict membership to persons entitled or prospectively entitled (as tenants or otherwise) to occupy a house provided or managed by the body, or

(c) hostels, 'house' and 'hostel' having the meanings given in section 338(1) of the Housing (Scotland) Act 1987.]

'Winding up', in relation to business associations, includes winding up of solvent, as well as insolvent, business associations.

C3. Competition

Regulation of anti-competitive practices and agreements; abuse of dominant position; monopolies and mergers.

Exception

Regulation of particular practices in the legal profession for the purpose of regulating that profession or the provision of legal services.

Interpretation

'The legal profession' means advocates, solicitors and qualified conveyancers and executry practitioners within the meaning of Part II of the Law Reform (Miscellaneous Provisions) (Scotland) Act 1990.

C4. Intellectual property

Intellectual property.

Exception

The subject-matter of Parts I and II of the Plant Varieties Act 1997 (plant varieties and the Plant Varieties and Seeds Tribunal).

C5. Import and export control

The subject-matter of the Import, Export and Customs Powers (Defence) Act 1939.

Prohibition and regulation of the import and export of endangered species of animals and plants.

Exceptions

Prohibition and regulation of movement into and out of Scotland of—

(a) food, animals, animal products, plants and plant products for the purposes of protecting human, animal or plant health, animal welfare or the environment or observing or implementing obligations under the Common Agricultural Policy, and

(b) animal feeding stuffs, fertilisers and pesticides [(including anything treated as if it were a pesticide by virtue of section 16(16) of the Food and Environment Protection Act 1985)] for the purposes of protecting human, animal or plant health or the environment.

[*Interpretation*

'Food' has the same meaning as it has in Regulation (EC) No 178/2002 of the European Parliament and of the Council laying down the general principles and requirements of food law, establishing the European Food Safety Authority and laying down procedures in matters of food safety (as at 7th December 2004).]

C6. Sea fishing

Regulation of sea fishing outside the Scottish zone (except in relation to Scottish fishing boats).

Interpretation

'Scottish fishing boat' means a fishing vessel which is registered in the register maintained under section 8 of the Merchant Shipping Act 1995 and whose entry in the register specifies a port in Scotland as the port to which the vessel is to be treated as belonging.

C7. Consumer protection

Regulation of—

(a) the sale and supply of goods and services to consumers,

(b) guarantees in relation to such goods and services,

(c) hire-purchase, including the subject-matter of Part III of the Hire-Purchase Act 1964,

(d) trade descriptions, except in relation to food,

(e) misleading and comparative advertising, except regulation specifically in relation to food, tobacco and tobacco products,

(f) price indications,

(g) trading stamps,

(h) auctions and mock auctions of goods and services, and

(i) hallmarking and gun barrel proofing.

Safety of, and liability for, services supplied to consumers.

The subject-matter of—

(a) the Hearing Aid Council Act 1968,

(b) the Unsolicited Goods and Services Acts 1971 and 1975,

(c) Parts I to III and XI of the Fair Trading Act 1973,

(d) the Consumer Credit Act 1974,

(e) the Estate Agents Act 1979,

(f) the Timeshare Act 1992,

(g) the Package Travel, Package Holidays and Package Tours Regulations 1992, and

(h) the Commercial Agents (Council Directive) Regulations 1993.

[*Exceptions*]

[The provision of consumer advocacy and advice by, or by agreement with, a public body or the holder of a public office.]

The subject-matter of section 16 of the Food Safety Act 1990 (food safety and consumer protection).

Interpretation

['Food' has the same meaning as it has in Regulation (EC) No 178/2002 of the European Parliament and of the Council laying down the general principles and requirements of food law, establishing the European Food Safety Authority and laying down procedures in matters of food safety (as at 7th December 2004).

The reference to the subject-matter of section 16 of the Food Safety Act 1990 is to be construed as a reference to it as at 7th December 2004 (and, accordingly, paragraph 5(1) of Part 3 of this Schedule does not apply to that reference).]

C8. Product standards, safety and liability

Technical standards and requirements in relation to products in pursuance of an obligation under [EU] law.

[The national accreditation body and the accreditation of bodies which certify or assess conformity to technical standards in relation to products or environmental management systems.]

Product safety and liability.

Product labelling.

Exceptions

[The provision of consumer advocacy and advice by, or by agreement with, a public body or the holder of a public office.]

Food, agricultural and horticultural produce, fish and fish products, seeds, animal feeding stuffs, fertilisers and pesticides [(including anything treated as if it were a pesticide by virtue of section 16(16) of the Food and Environment Protection Act 1985)].

In relation to food safety, materials which come into contact with food.

[*Interpretation*

'Food' has the same meaning as it has in Regulation (EC) No 178/2002 of the European Parliament and of the Council laying down the general principles and requirements of food law, establishing the European Food Safety Authority and laying down procedures in matters of food safety (as at 7th December 2004).]

C9. Weights and measures

Units and standards of weight and measurement.

Regulation of trade so far as involving weighing, measuring and quantities.

[*Exceptions*

The provision of consumer advocacy and advice by, or by agreement with, a public body or the holder of a public office.]

C10. Telecommunications and wireless telegraphy

Telecommunications and wireless telegraphy.

Internet services.

Electronic encryption.

The subject-matter of Part II of the Wireless Telegraphy Act 1949 (electromagnetic disturbance).

Exception

The subject-matter of Part III of the Police Act 1997 (authorisation to interfere with property etc).

[C11. Posts

The subject matter of the Postal Services Act 2000.

[*Exceptions*]

[The provision of consumer advocacy and advice by, or by agreement with, a public body or the holder of a public office, but not any related compulsory levy on postal operators.]

Financial assistance for the provision of services (other than postal services and services relating to money or postal orders) to be provided from public post offices.

Interpretation

Paragraph 5(1) of Part III of this Schedule does not apply to this Section.

The reference to the subject matter of the Postal Services Act 2000 is to be read as a reference to the subject matter of that Act as at the date when it received Royal Assent.

['postal operator',] 'postal services' and 'public post offices' have the same meaning as in the Postal Services Act 2000.]

C12. Research Councils
Research Councils within the meaning of the Science and Technology Act 1965.
The subject-matter of section 5 of that Act (funding of scientific research) so far as relating to Research Councils.
[The Arts and Humanities Research Council within the meaning of Part 1 of the Higher Education Act 2004.
The subject-matter of section 10 of that Act (research in arts and humanities) so far as relating to that Council.
Interpretation
Paragraph 5(1) of Part 3 of this Schedule does not apply to the subject-matter of section 10 of the Higher Education Act 2004; and the reference to the subject-matter of that section is to be construed as a reference to it as at the date that Act received Royal Assent.]

C13. Designation of assisted areas
The subject-matter of section 1 of the Industrial Development Act 1982.

C14. Industrial Development Advisory Board
The Industrial Development Advisory Board.

C15. Protection of trading and economic interests
The subject-matter of—
(a) section 2 of the Emergency Laws (Re-enactments and Repeals) Act 1964 (Treasury power in relation to action damaging to economic position of United Kingdom),
(b) Part II of the Industry Act 1975 (powers in relation to transfer of control of important manufacturing undertakings), and
(c) the Protection of Trading Interests Act 1980.

Head D – Energy

D1. Electricity
Generation, transmission, distribution and supply of electricity.
The subject-matter of Part II of the Electricity Act 1989.
[*Exceptions*]
The subject-matter of Part I of the Environmental Protection Act 1990.
[The provision of consumer advocacy and advice by, or by agreement with, a public body or the holder of a public office, but not any related compulsory levy on persons supplying, generating, transmitting or distributing electricity.]

D2. Oil and gas
Oil and gas, including—
(a) the ownership of, exploration for and exploitation of deposits of oil and natural gas,
(b) the subject-matter of section 1 of the Mineral Exploration and Investment Grants Act 1972 (contributions in connection with mineral exploration) so far as relating to exploration for oil and gas,
(c) offshore installations and pipelines,
(d) the subject-matter of the Pipe-lines Act 1962 (including section 5 (deemed planning permission)) so far as relating to pipelines within the meaning of section 65 of that Act,
(e) the application of Scots law and the jurisdiction of the Scottish courts in relation to offshore activities,
(f) pollution relating to oil and gas exploration and exploitation, but only outside controlled waters (within the meaning of section 30A(1) of the Control of Pollution Act 1974),

(g) the subject-matter of Part II of the Food and Environment Protection Act 1985 so far as relating to oil and gas exploration and exploitation, but only in relation to activities outside such controlled waters,

(h) restrictions on navigation, fishing and other activities in connection with offshore activities,

(i) liquefaction of natural gas, and

(j) the conveyance, shipping and supply of gas through pipes.

Exceptions

The subject-matter of—

(a) sections 10 to 12 of the Industry Act 1972 (credits and grants for construction of ships and offshore installations),

(b) the Offshore Petroleum Development (Scotland) Act 1975, other than sections 3 to 7, and

(c) Part I of the Environmental Protection Act 1990.

The manufacture of gas.

The conveyance, shipping and supply of gas other than through pipes.

[The provision in relation to gas of consumer advocacy and advice by, or by agreement with, a public body or the holder of a public office, but not any related compulsory levy on persons supplying gas to premises or conveying gas through pipes.]

D3. Coal

Coal, including its ownership and exploitation, deep and opencast coal mining and coal mining subsidence.

Exceptions

The subject-matter of—

(a) Part I of the Environmental Protection Act 1990, and

(b) sections 53 (environmental duties in connection with planning) and 54 (obligation to restore land affected by coal-mining operations) of the Coal Industry Act 1994.

D4. Nuclear energy

Nuclear energy and nuclear installations, including—

(a) nuclear safety, security and safeguards, and

(b) liability for nuclear occurrences.

[The Office for Nuclear Regulation.]

Exceptions

The subject-matter of—

(a) Part I of the Environmental Protection Act 1990, and

(b) the Radioactive Substances Act 1993.

D5. Energy conservation

The subject-matter of the Energy Act 1976, other than section 9.

Exception

The encouragement of energy efficiency other than by prohibition or regulation.

Head E – Transport

E1. Road transport

The subject-matter of—

(a) the Motor Vehicles (International Circulation) Act 1952,

(b) the Public Passenger Vehicles Act 1981 and the Transport Act 1985, so far as relating to public service vehicle operator licensing,

(c) [section 17 of the Road Traffic Regulation Act 1984 (traffic regulation on special roads) except so far as relating to the speed of vehicles on special roads, and section 87 of that Act (exemption of emergency vehicles from speed limits) so far as relating to the training of drivers of vehicles,]

(d) the Road Traffic Act 1988 [, except so far as relating to the parking of vehicles on roads,] and the Road Traffic Offenders Act 1988,

(e) the Vehicle Excise and Registration Act 1994,

(f) the Road Traffic (New Drivers) Act 1995, and

(g) the Goods Vehicles (Licensing of Operators) Act 1995.

Regulation of proper hours or periods of work by persons engaged in the carriage of passengers or goods by road.

The conditions under which international road transport services for passengers or goods may be undertaken.

Regulation of the instruction of drivers of motor vehicles.

Exceptions

The subject-matter of sections [36 (offence of failing to comply with traffic sign),] 39 and 40 (road safety information and training) and 157 to 159 (payments for treatment of traffic casualties) of the Road Traffic Act 1988.

[The subject-matter of the Road Traffic Act 1988 so far as relating to the regulation of the description, by reference to their construction and equipment, of motor vehicles and trailers which may be used under arrangements for persons to travel to and from the places where they receive education or training, but not the setting of technical standards for the construction or equipment of such motor vehicles or trailers different from the standards that might otherwise apply to them.]

[Interpretation

The reference to the subject-matter of section 87 of the Road Traffic Regulation Act 1984 is to be construed as a reference to it as substituted by section 19 of the Road Safety Act 2006 as at the date when section 40 of the Scotland Act 2016 comes into force, treating section 19 and any amendment affecting it at that date as if they were in force (and, accordingly, paragraph 5(1) of Part 3 of this Schedule does not apply to that reference).]

E2. Rail transport

Provision and regulation of railway services.

Rail transport security.

The subject-matter of the Channel Tunnel Act 1987.

The subject-matter of the Railway Heritage Act 1996.

Exceptions

Grants so far as relating to railway services; but this exception does not apply in relation to—

(a) the subject-matter of section 63 of the Railways Act 1993 (government financial assistance where railway administration orders made),

(b) 'railway services' as defined in section 82(1)(b) of the Railways Act 1993 (carriage of goods by railway), or

(c) the subject-matter of section 136 of the Railways Act 1993 (grants and subsidies).

[Imposing requirements about the preparation and submission of strategies relating to the provision of rail services on Scottish public authorities with mixed functions relating to such services.]

[The transfer of functions of passenger transport executives or passenger transport authorities relating to the provision and regulation of rail services conferred by Part II of the Transport Act 1968 and sections 32 to 36 of the Railways Act 1993 to, and the allocation of such functions among, [relevant authorities].]

[The promotion and construction of railways which start, end and remain in Scotland.]

[Policing of railways and railway property.]

Interpretation

['railway' has the meaning given by section 67(1) of the Transport and Works Act 1992.]

['Railway property' has the meaning given by section 75(3) of the Railways and Transport Safety Act 2003.]

'Railway services' has the meaning given by section 82 of the Railways Act 1993 (excluding the wider meaning of 'railway' given by section 81(2) of that Act).

['relevant authority' means—

(a) the Scottish Ministers; or

(b) any Scottish public authority (not being a cross-border public authority or an authority exercising functions solely in relation to a reserved matter) which is set up wholly or mainly to exercise functions relating to transport.]

E3. Marine transport

The subject-matter of—

(a) the Coastguard Act 1925,

(b) the Hovercraft Act 1968, except so far as relating to the regulation of noise and vibration caused by hovercraft,

(c) the Carriage of Goods by Sea Act 1971,

(d) section 2 of the Protection of Wrecks Act 1973 (prohibition on approaching dangerous wrecks),

(e) the Merchant Shipping (Liner Conferences) Act 1982,

(f) the Dangerous Vessels Act 1985,

(g) the Aviation and Maritime Security Act 1990, other than Part I (aviation security),

(h) the Carriage of Goods by Sea Act 1992,

(i) the Merchant Shipping Act 1995,

(j) the Shipping and Trading Interests (Protection) Act 1995, and

(k) sections 24 (implementation of international agreements relating to protection of wrecks), 26 (piracy) and 27 and 28 (international bodies concerned with maritime matters) of the Merchant Shipping and Maritime Security Act 1997.

Navigational rights and freedoms.

Financial assistance for shipping services which start or finish or both outside Scotland.

Exceptions

Ports, harbours, piers and boatslips, except in relation to the matters reserved by virtue of paragraph (d), (f), (g) or (i).

Regulation of works which may obstruct or endanger navigation.

The subject-matter of the Highlands and Islands Shipping Services Act 1960 in relation to financial assistance for bulk freight services.

E4. Air transport

Regulation of aviation and air transport, including the subject-matter of—

(a) the Carriage by Air Act 1961,

(b) the Carriage by Air (Supplementary Provisions) Act 1962,

(c) the Carriage by Air and Road Act 1979 so far as relating to carriage by air,

(d) the Civil Aviation Act 1982,

(e) the Aviation Security Act 1982,

(f) the Airports Act 1986, and

(g) sections 1 (endangering safety at aerodromes) and 48 (powers in relation to certain aircraft) of the Aviation and Maritime Security Act 1990,

and arrangements to compensate or repatriate passengers in the event of an air transport operator's insolvency.

Exceptions

The subject-matter of the following sections of the Civil Aviation Act 1982—

(a) section 25 (Secretary of State's power to provide aerodromes),

(b) section 30 (provision of aerodromes and facilities at aerodromes by local authorities),

(c) section 31 (power to carry on ancillary business in connection with local authority aerodromes),

(d) section 34 (financial assistance for certain aerodromes),

(e) section 35 (facilities for consultation at certain aerodromes),

(f) section 36 (health control at Secretary of State's aerodromes and aerodromes of Civil Aviation Authority), and

(g) sections 41 to 43 and 50 (powers in relation to land exercisable in connection with civil aviation) where land is to be or was acquired for the purpose of airport development or expansion.

The subject-matter of Part II (transfer of airport undertakings of local authorities), sections 63 and 64 (airport byelaws) and 66 (functions of operators of designated airports as respects abandoned vehicles) of the Airports Act 1986.

The subject-matter of sections 59 (acquisition of land and rights over land) and 60 (disposal of compulsorily acquired land) of the Airports Act 1986 where land is to be or was acquired for the purpose of airport development or expansion.

[Imposing requirements about the preparation and submission of strategies relating to the provision of air services on Scottish public authorities with mixed functions relating to such services.]

E5. Other matters

Transport of radioactive material.

Technical specifications for public passenger transport for disabled persons, including the subject-matter of—

(a) section 125(7) and (8) of the Transport Act 1985 (Secretary of State's guidance and consultation with the Disabled Persons Transport Advisory Committee), and

(b) Part V of the Disability Discrimination Act 1995 (public transport).

Regulation of the carriage of dangerous goods.

Interpretation

'Radioactive material' has the same meaning as in section 1(1) of the Radioactive Material (Road Transport) Act 1991.

Head F – Social Security

F1. Social security schemes

Schemes supported from central or local funds which provide assistance for social security purposes to or in respect of individuals by way of benefits.

Requiring persons to—

(a) establish and administer schemes providing assistance for social security purposes to or in respect of individuals, or

(b) make payments to or in respect of such schemes,

and to keep records and supply information in connection with such schemes.

The circumstances in which a person is liable to maintain himself or another for the purposes of the enactments relating to social security and the Child Support Acts 1991 and 1995.

The subject-matter of the Vaccine Damage Payment Scheme.

Illustrations

National Insurance; Social Fund; [. . .] recovery of benefits for accident, injury or disease from persons paying damages; deductions from benefits for the purpose of meeting an individual's debts; sharing information between government departments for the purposes of the enactments relating to social security; making decisions for the purposes of schemes mentioned in the reservation and appeals against such decisions.

Exceptions

[*Exception 1*

Any of the following benefits—

(a) disability benefits, other than severe disablement benefit or industrial injuries benefits,

(b) severe disablement benefit, so far as payable in respect of a relevant person, and

(c) industrial injuries benefits, so far as relating to relevant employment or to participation in training for relevant employment;

but this exception does not except a benefit which is, or which is an element of, an excluded benefit.

Exception 2

Carer's benefits, other than a benefit which is, or which is an element of, an excluded benefit.'

[*Exception 3*]

The subject-matter of Part II of the Social Work (Scotland) Act 1968 (social welfare services), section 2 of the Chronically Sick and Disabled Persons Act 1970 (provision of welfare services), section 50 of the Children Act 1975 (payments towards maintenance of children), section 15 of the Enterprise and New Towns (Scotland) Act 1990 (industrial injuries benefit), and sections 22 (promotion of welfare of children in need), 29 and 30 (advice and assistance for young persons formerly looked after by local authorities) of the Children (Scotland) Act 1995.

[*Exception 4*

Providing financial or other assistance for the purposes of meeting or reducing—

(a) maternity expenses,

(b) funeral expenses, or

(c) expenses for heating in cold weather.]

[*Exception 5*

Providing financial assistance to an individual who—

(a) is entitled to a reserved benefit, and

(b) appears to require financial assistance, in addition to any amount the individual receives by way of reserved benefit, for the purpose, or one of the purposes, for which the benefit is being provided.

This exception does not except discretionary financial assistance in a reserved benefit.

This exception also does not except providing financial assistance to meet or help to meet housing costs (as to which, see exception 6).

This exception also does not except providing financial assistance where the requirement for it arises from reduction, non-payability or suspension of a reserved benefit as a result of an individual's conduct (for example, non-compliance with work-related requirements relating to the benefit) unless—

(a) the requirement for it also arises from some exceptional event or exceptional circumstances, and

(b) the requirement for it is immediate.

For the purposes of this exception 'reserved benefit' means a benefit which is to any extent a reserved matter.]

[*Exception 6*

Providing financial assistance to an individual who—

(a) is entitled to—

(i) housing benefit, or

(ii) any other reserved benefit payable in respect of a liability to make rent payments, and

(b) appears to require financial assistance, in addition to any amount the individual receives by way of housing benefit or such other reserved benefit, to meet or help to meet housing costs.

This exception does not except discretionary financial assistance in a reserved benefit.

This exception also does not except providing financial assistance where the requirement for it arises from reduction, non-payability or suspension of a reserved benefit as a result of an individual's conduct (for example, non-compliance with work-related requirements relating to the benefit) unless—

(a) the requirement for it also arises from some exceptional event or exceptional circumstances, and

(b) the requirement for it is immediate.

For the purposes of this exception—

'rent payments'—

(a) has the meaning given from time to time by paragraph 2 of Schedule 1 to the Universal Credit Regulations 2013 (SI 2013/376) or any re-enactment of that paragraph, or

(b) if at any time universal credit ceases to be payable to anyone, has the meaning given by that paragraph or any re-enactment of that paragraph immediately before that time;

'reserved benefit' means a benefit which is to any extent a reserved matter.]

[*Exception 7*

Providing financial or other assistance to or in respect of individuals who appear to require it for the purposes of meeting, or helping to meet, a short-term need that requires to be met to avoid a risk to the well-being of an individual.

This exception does not except providing assistance where the requirement for it arises from reduction, non-payability or suspension of a benefit as a result of an individual's conduct (for example, non-compliance with work-related requirements relating to the benefit) unless—

(a) the requirement for it also arises from some exceptional event or exceptional circumstances, and

(b) the need is immediate as well as short-term.

Exception 8

Providing occasional financial or other assistance to or in respect of individuals who have been or might otherwise be—

(a) in prison, hospital, a residential care establishment or other institution, or

(b) homeless or otherwise living an unsettled way of life,

and who appear to require the assistance to establish or maintain a settled home.]

[*Exception 9*

The subject-matter of section 13 of the Social Security Act 1988 (benefits under schemes for improving nutrition: pregnant women, mothers and children).]

[*Exception 10*

Schemes which provide assistance for social security purposes to or in respect of individuals by way of benefits and which—

(a) are supported from sums paid out of the Scottish Consolidated Fund,

(b) do not fall within exceptions 1 to 9, and

(c) are not connected with reserved matters (other than matters reserved only by virtue of this Section).

This exception does not except providing assistance by way of pensions to or in respect of individuals who qualify by reason of old age.

This exception does not except providing assistance where the requirement for it arises from reduction, non-payability or suspension of a reserved benefit as a result of an individual's conduct (for example, non-compliance with work-related requirements relating to the benefit) unless—

(a) the requirement for it also arises from some exceptional event or exceptional circumstances, and

(b) the requirement for it is immediate.

For the purposes of this exception 'reserved benefit' means a benefit which is to any extent a reserved matter.

In this exception the reference to schemes supported from sums paid out of the Scottish Consolidated Fund does not include schemes—

(a) in respect of which sums are at some time paid out of the Scottish Consolidated Fund, but

(b) which are directly supported from payments out of the Consolidated Fund, the National Insurance Fund or the Social Fund, or out of money provided by Parliament.]

[*Exclusions from exceptions 1 to 10*

Nothing in exceptions 1 to 10 is to be read as excepting—

(a) the National Insurance Fund,

(b) the Social Fund, or

(c) the provision by a Minister of the Crown of assistance by way of loan for the purpose of meeting, or helping to meet, an intermittent expense.

Interpretation

'Benefits' includes pensions, allowances, grants, loans and any other form of financial assistance.

Providing assistance for social security purposes to or in respect of individuals includes (among other things) providing assistance to or in respect of individuals—

(a) who qualify by reason of old age, survivorship, disability, sickness, incapacity, injury, unemployment, maternity or the care of children or others needing care,

(b) who qualify by reason of low income, or

(c) in relation to their housing costs or liabilities for local taxes.

[Paragraph 5(1) of Part 3 of this Schedule does not apply to the subject-matter of—

(a) section 138 of the Social Security Contributions and Benefits Act 1992, or

(b) section 69 of the Child Support, Pensions and Social Security Act 2000.

['Disability benefit' means a benefit which is normally payable in respect of—

(a) a significant adverse effect that impairment to a person's physical or mental condition has on his or her ability to carry out day-to-day activities (for example, looking after yourself, moving around or communicating), or

(b) a significant need (for example, for attention or for supervision to avoid substantial danger to anyone) arising from impairment to a person's physical or mental condition;

and for this purpose the adverse effect or need must not be short-term.

'Severe disablement benefit' means a benefit which is normally payable in respect of—

(a) a person's being incapable of work for a period of at least 28 weeks beginning not later than the person's 20th birthday, or

(b) a person's being incapable of work and disabled for a period of at least 28 weeks;

and 'relevant person', in relation to severe disablement benefit, means a person who is entitled to severe disablement allowance under section 68 of the Social Security Contributions and Benefits Act 1992 on the date on which section 22 of the Scotland Act 2016 comes into force as respects severe disablement benefit.

'Industrial injuries benefit' means a benefit which is normally payable in respect of—

(a) a person's having suffered personal injury caused by accident arising out of and in the course of his or her employment, or

(b) a person's having developed a disease or personal injury due to the nature of his or her employment;

and for this purpose 'employment' includes participation in training for employment.

'Relevant employment', in relation to industrial injuries benefit, means employment which—

(a) is employed earner's employment for the purposes of section 94 of the

Social Security Contributions and Benefits Act 1992 as at 28 May 2015 (the date of introduction into Parliament of the Bill for the Scotland Act 2016), or

(b) would be such employment but for—

(i) the contract purporting to govern the employment being void, or

(ii) the person concerned not being lawfully employed,

as a result of a contravention of, or non-compliance with, provision in or made by virtue of an enactment passed to protect employees.

'Carer's benefit' means a benefit which is normally payable in respect of the regular and substantial provision of care by a person to a disabled person; and for this purpose 'disabled person' means a person to whom a disability benefit is normally payable.

'Excluded benefit' means—

(a) a benefit, entitlement to which, or the amount of which, is normally determined to any extent by reference to a person's income or capital (for example, universal credit under Part 1 of the Welfare Reform Act 2012),

(b) a benefit which is payable out of the National Insurance Fund (for example, employment and support allowance under section 1(2)(a) of the Welfare Reform Act 2007), or

(c) a benefit payable by way of lump sum in respect of a person's having, or having had—

(i) pneumoconiosis,

(ii) byssinosis,

(iii) diffuse mesothelioma,

(iv) bilateral diffuse pleural thickening, or

(v) primary carcinoma of the lung where there is accompanying evidence of one or both of asbestosis and bilateral diffuse pleural thickening.

'Employment' includes any trade, business, profession, office or vocation (and 'employed' is to be read accordingly).'

[The reference to the subject-matter of section 13 of the Social Security Act 1988 is to be construed as a reference to it as at the day on which section 27 of the Scotland Act 2016 comes into force (and, accordingly, paragraph 5(1) of Part 3 of this Schedule does not apply to that reference).]

F2. Child support

The subject-matter of the Child Support Acts 1991 and 1995.

Exception

The subject-matter of sections 1 to 7 of the Family Law (Scotland) Act 1985 (aliment).

Interpretation

If section 30(2) of the Child Support Act 1991 (collection of payments other than child support maintenance) is not in force on the principal appointed day, it is to be treated for the purposes of this reservation as if it were.

F3. Occupational and personal pensions

The regulation of occupational pension schemes and personal pension schemes, including the obligations of the trustees or managers of such schemes.

Provision about pensions payable to, or in respect of, any persons, except—

(a) the persons referred to in section 81(3),

(b) in relation to a Scottish public authority with mixed functions or no reserved functions, persons who are or have been a member of the public body, the holder of the public office, or a member of the staff of the body, holder or office.

The subject-matter of the Pensions (Increase) Act 1971.

Schemes for the payment of pensions which are listed in Schedule 2 to that Act, except those mentioned in paragraphs 38A and 38AB.

Where pension payable to or in respect of any class of persons under a public service pension scheme is covered by this reservation, so is making provision in their case—

(a) for compensation for loss of office or employment, for their office or employment being affected by constitutional changes, or circumstances arising from such changes, in any territory or territories or for loss or diminution of emoluments, or

(b) for benefits in respect of death or incapacity resulting from injury or disease.

Interpretation

'Pension' includes gratuities and allowances.

F4. War pensions

Schemes for the payment of pensions for or in respect of persons who have a disablement or have died in consequence of service as members of the armed forces of the Crown.

The subject-matter of any scheme under the Personal Injuries (Emergency Provisions) Act 1939, sections 3 to 5 and 7 of the Pensions (Navy, Army, Air Force and Mercantile Marine) Act 1939 or section 1 of the Polish Resettlement Act 1947.

Illustration

The provision of pensions under the Naval, Military and Air Forces Etc (Disablement and Death) Service Pensions Order 1983.

Interpretation

'Pension' includes grants, allowances, supplements and gratuities.

Head G – Regulation of the Professions

G1. Architects

Regulation of the profession of architect.

G2. Health professions

Regulation of the health professions.

Exceptions

The subject-matter of—

(a) section 21 of the National Health Service (Scotland) Act 1978 (requirement of suitable experience for medical practitioners), and

(b) section 25 of that Act (arrangements for the provision of general dental services), so far as it relates to vocational training and disciplinary proceedings.

Interpretation

'The health professions' means the professions regulated by—

(a) the Pharmacy Act 1954,
(b) the Professions Supplementary to Medicine Act 1960,
(c) the Veterinary Surgeons Act 1966,
(d) the Medical Act 1983,
(e) the Dentists Act 1984,
(f) the Opticians Act 1989,
(g) the Osteopaths Act 1993,
(h) the Chiropractors Act 1994, and
(i) the Nurses, Midwives and Health Visitors Act 1997.

G3. Auditors

Regulation of the profession of auditor.

Head H – Employment

H1. Employment and industrial relations

Employment rights and duties and industrial relations, including the subject-matter of—

(a) the Employers' Liability (Compulsory Insurance) Act 1969,
(b) the Employment Agencies Act 1973,
(c) the Pneumoconiosis etc (Workers' Compensation) Act 1979,
(d) the Transfer of Undertakings (Protection of Employment) Regulations 1981,
(e) the Trade Union and Labour Relations (Consolidation) Act 1992,
(f) [the Employment Tribunals Act 1996],
(g) the Employment Rights Act 1996, and
(h) the National Minimum Wage Act 1998.

Exception

The subject-matter of the Agricultural Wages (Scotland) Act 1949.

H2. Health and safety

The subject-matter of [Part I of the Health and Safety at Work etc Act 1974

The Health and Safety Commission, the Health and Safety Executive and the Employment Medical Advisory Service

Interpretation

For the purposes of the reservation of the subject-matter of Part I of the Health and Safety at Work etc Act 1974—

(a) 'work' and 'at work' in that Part are to be taken to have the meaning they have on the principal appointed day;
(b) that subject-matter includes—
(i) process fire precautions;
(ii) fire precautions in relation to petroleum and petroleum spirit; [F71 and]
(iii) fire safety on [. . .] ships and hovercraft, in mines and on offshore installations;
[. . .]

but does not include any other aspect of fire safety.]

H3. Job search and support

The subject-matter of—

(a) the Disabled Persons (Employment) Act 1944, and
(b) the Employment and Training Act 1973, except so far as relating to training for employment.

[*Exceptions*]

[*Exception 1*

The making by a person of arrangements for, or arrangements for the purposes of or in connection with a scheme for, any of the following purposes—

(a) assisting disabled persons to select, obtain and retain employment;
(b) assisting persons claiming reserved benefits who are at risk of long-term unemployment to select, obtain and retain employment, where the assistance is for at least a year;
(c) assisting employers to obtain suitable employees who are persons referred to in paragraph (a) or (b).

The arrangements referred to in this exception include—

(a) The arrangements referred to in this exception include—
(b) providing or arranging for the provision of facilities, support or services to any person;
(c) the making of payments to any person.

The assistance referred to in this exception includes—

(a) work search support,
(b) skills training, and
(c) work placements for the benefit of the community.

In this exception—

(a) 'disabled person' has the same meaning as it has in the Equality Act 2010 as at 28 May 2015 (the date of introduction into Parliament of the Bill for the Scotland Act 2016);

(b) 'reserved benefit' means a benefit which is to any extent a reserved matter.]

[*Exception* 2]

The subject-matter of—

(a) sections 8 to 10A of the Employment and Training Act 1973 (careers services), and

(b) the following sections of Part I of the Enterprise and New Towns (Scotland) Act 1990 (Scottish Enterprise and Highlands and Islands Enterprise)—

(i) section 2(3)(c) (arrangements for the purpose of assisting persons to establish themselves as self-employed persons), and

(ii) section 12 (disclosure of information).

Head J – Health and Medicines

J1. Abortion

[. . .]

J2. Xenotransplantation

Xenotransplantation.

J3. Embryology, surrogacy and genetics

Surrogacy arrangements, within the meaning of the Surrogacy Arrangements Act 1985, including the subject-matter of that Act.

The subject-matter of the Human Fertilisation and Embryology Act 1990.

Human genetics.

J4. Medicines, medical supplies and poisons

The subject-matter of—

(a) [the Medicines Act 1968, except so far as it applies in relation to—

(i) medicinal products which are for use in relation to animals, and

(ii) animal feeding stuffs,

(aa) the Medicines for Human Use (Marketing Authorisations Etc) Regulations 1994,]

(b) the Poisons Act 1972, and

(c) the Biological Standards Act 1975.

Regulation of prices charged for medical supplies or medicinal products which (in either case) are supplied for the purposes of the health service established under section 1 of the National Health Service (Scotland) Act 1978.

[Regulation of—

(a) veterinary medicinal products,

(b) specified feed additives, and

(c) animal feeding stuffs, in relation to—

(i) the incorporation in them of veterinary medicinal products or specified feed additives,

(ii) matters arising in consequence of such incorporation.]

Interpretation

'Medical supplies' has the same meaning as in section 49(3) of the National Health Service (Scotland) Act 1978.

'Medicinal products' has [, in relation to the reservation of the regulation of prices charged for medical supplies or medicinal products supplied for the purposes of the health service,] the same meaning as in section 130(1) of the Medicines Act 1968.

['Specified feed additives' has the same meaning as in Schedule 5 to the Veterinary Medicines Regulations 2013 (as at 1st October 2013).

'Veterinary medicinal products' has the same meaning as in regulation 2(1) of the Veterinary Medicines Regulations 2013 (as at 1st October 2013).]

J5. Welfare foods

Schemes made by regulations under section 13 of the Social Security Act 1988 (schemes for distribution of welfare foods).

Head K – Media and Culture

K1. Broadcasting

The subject-matter of the Broadcasting Act 1990 and the Broadcasting Act 1996.

The British Broadcasting Corporation.

K2. Public lending right

The subject-matter of the Public Lending Right Act 1979.

K3. Government Indemnity Scheme

The subject-matter of sections 16 and 16A of the National Heritage Act 1980 (public indemnities for objects on loan to museums, art galleries, etc).

K4. Property accepted in satisfaction of tax

The subject-matter of sections 8 and 9 of the National Heritage Act 1980 (payments to Inland Revenue in respect of property accepted in satisfaction of tax, and disposal of such property).

Head L – Miscellaneous

L1. Judicial remuneration

Determination of the remuneration of—

(a) judges of the Court of Session,
(b) sheriffs principal and sheriffs,
(c) members of the Lands Tribunal for Scotland, and
(d) the Chairman of the Scottish Land Court.

L2. Equal opportunities

Equal opportunities [. . .]

Exceptions

The encouragement (other than by prohibition or regulation) of equal opportunities, and in particular of the observance of the equal opportunity requirements.

Imposing duties on—

(a) any office-holder in the Scottish Administration, or any Scottish public authority with mixed functions or no reserved functions, to make arrangements with a view to securing that the functions of the office-holder or authority are carried out with due regard to the need to meet the equal opportunity requirements, or

(b) any cross-border public authority to make arrangements with a view to securing that its Scottish functions are carried out with due regard to the need to meet the equal opportunity requirements.

[Equal opportunities so far as relating to the inclusion of persons with protected characteristics in non-executive posts on boards of Scottish public authorities with mixed functions or no reserved functions.

Equal opportunities in relation to the Scottish functions of any Scottish public authority or cross-border public authority, other than any function that relates to the inclusion of persons in non-executive posts on boards of Scottish public authorities with mixed functions or no reserved functions. The provision falling within this exception does not include any modification of the Equality Act 2010, or of any subordinate legislation made under that Act, but does include—

(a) provision that supplements or is otherwise additional to provision made by that Act;

(b) in particular, provision imposing a requirement to take action that that Act does not prohibit;

(c) provision that reproduces or applies an enactment contained in that Act, with or without modification, without affecting the enactment as it applies for the purposes of that Act.]

Interpretation

['Board' includes any other equivalent management body.]

'Equal opportunities' means the prevention, elimination or regulation of discrimination between persons on grounds of sex or marital status, on racial grounds, or on grounds of disability, age, sexual orientation, language or social origin, or of other personal attributes, including beliefs or opinions, such as religious beliefs or political opinions.

'Equal opportunity requirements' means the requirements of the law for the time being relating to equal opportunities.

['Non-executive post' in relation to an authority means any position the holder of which is not an employee of the authority.]

['Protected characteristic' has the same meaning as in the Equality Act 2010.]

'Scottish functions' means functions which are exercisable in or as regards Scotland and which do not relate to reserved matters.

[The references to the Equality Act 2010 and any subordinate legislation made under that Act are to be read as references to those enactments, as at the day on which section 37 of the Scotland Act 2016 comes into force, but treating any provision of them that is not yet in force on that day as if it were in force.]

L3. Control of weapons

Control of nuclear, biological and chemical weapons and other weapons of mass destruction.

L4. Ordnance survey

The subject-matter of the Ordnance Survey Act 1841.

L5. Time

Timescales, time zones and the subject-matter of the Summer Time Act 1972.

The calendar; units of time; the date of Easter.

Exceptions

The computation of periods of time.

The subject-matter of—

(a) section 1 of the Banking and Financial Dealings Act 1971 (bank holidays), and

(b) the Term and Quarter Days (Scotland) Act 1990.

L6. Outer space

Regulation of activities in outer space.

[L7. Antarctica

Regulation of activities in Antarctica.

Interpretation

'Antarctica' has the meaning given by section 1 of the Antarctic Act 1994.]

PART III
GENERAL PROVISIONS

Scottish public authorities

1 (1) This Schedule does not reserve any Scottish public authority if some of its functions relate to reserved matters and some do not, unless it is a cross-border public authority.

(2) Sub-paragraph (1) has effect as regards—

(a) the constitution of the authority, including its establishment and dissolution, its assets and liabilities and its funding and receipts,

(b) conferring or removing any functions specifically exercisable in relation to the authority.

(3) Sub-paragraph (2)(b) does not apply to any function which is specifically exercisable in relation to a particular function of the authority if the particular function relates to reserved matters.

(4) An authority to which this paragraph applies is referred to in this Act as a Scottish public authority with mixed functions.

2 Paragraph 1 of Part I of this Schedule does not reserve any Scottish public authority with functions none of which relate to reserved matters (referred to in this Act as a Scottish public authority with no reserved functions).

[Tribunals

2A (1) This Schedule does not reserve the transfer to a Scottish tribunal of functions of a tribunal that relate to reserved matters, so far as those functions are exercisable in relation to Scottish cases.

(2) 'Scottish cases' has the meaning given by an Order in Council made by Her Majesty under this sub-paragraph.

(3) Sub-paragraph (1) does not apply where a function is excluded from transfer.

(4) Where a function is not excluded from transfer but is subject to qualified transfer, sub-paragraph (1) applies only if the transfer of the function is in accordance with provision made by Her Majesty by Order in Council.

(5) An Order in Council under sub-paragraph (4)—

(a) must specify the function to which it relates,

(b) must specify the Scottish tribunal to which the function may be transferred, and

(c) may make any other provision which Her Majesty considers necessary or expedient for the purposes of or in consequence of the transfer of the function and its exercise by the Scottish tribunal.

(6) The functions that are subject to qualified transfer are the functions of the following tribunals—

(a) the First-tier Tribunal or the Upper Tribunal that are established under section 3 of the Tribunals, Courts and Enforcement Act 2007;

(b) an employment tribunal or the Employment Appeal Tribunal;

(c) a tribunal listed in Schedule 1 to the Tribunals and Inquiries Act 1992;

(d) a tribunal listed in Schedule 6 to the Tribunals, Courts and Enforcement Act 2007.

(7) Sub-paragraph (6)(c) and (d) include a tribunal added to the Schedule concerned after this paragraph comes into force.

(8) Provision made by virtue of sub-paragraph (5)(c) may—

(a) include provision that—

(i) modifies the function;

(ii) imposes conditions or restrictions (including conditions or restrictions relating to the composition or rules of procedure of the Scottish tribunal, or to its staff or accommodation);

(b) be made with a view to purposes including—

(i) securing consistency in any respect in practice or procedure or otherwise between the Scottish tribunal and other tribunals;

(ii) promoting judicial co-operation in the interests of consistency.

(9) Sub-paragraph (8) does not limit the provision that may be made by virtue of sub-paragraph (5)(c).

(10) The following functions are excluded from transfer—

(a) functions of a national security tribunal;

(b) functions of a regulator, or of a person or body that exercises functions on behalf of a regulator;

(c) functions of the Comptroller-General of Patents, Designs and Trade Marks.

(11) In this paragraph—

a 'national security tribunal' means—

(a) the Pathogens Access Appeal Commission;

(b) the Proscribed Organisations Appeal Commission;

(c) the Special Immigration Appeals Commission;

(d) the tribunal established by section 65(1) of the Regulation of Investigatory Powers Act 2000 (investigatory powers tribunal);

(e) any other tribunal that has functions relating to matters falling within Section B8 of Part 2 of this Schedule, except a tribunal mentioned in sub-paragraph (6);

a 'regulator' means a person or body that has regulatory functions (within the meaning given by section 32 of the Legislative and Regulatory Reform Act 2006);

a 'Scottish tribunal' means a tribunal in Scotland—

(a) that does not have functions in or as regards any other country or territory, except for purposes ancillary to its functions in or as regards Scotland, and

(b) that is not, and does not have as a member, a member of the Scottish Government.

(12) The powers conferred by this paragraph do not affect the powers conferred by section 30 or section 113.]

Reserved bodies

3 (1) The reservation of any body to which this paragraph applies has effect to reserve—

(a) its constitution, including its establishment and dissolution, its assets and liabilities and its funding and receipts,

(b) conferring functions on it or removing functions from it,

(c) conferring or removing any functions specifically exercisable in relation to it.

(2) This paragraph applies to—

(a) a body reserved by name by Part II of this Schedule,

(b) each of the councils reserved by Section C12 of that Part,

(c) the Commission for Racial Equality, the Equal Opportunities Commission and [the Disability Rights Commission],

[(d) the Commission for Equality and Human Rights.]

[(e) the Office of Communications,

(f) the Gas and Electricity Markets Authority.]

Financial assistance to industry

4 (1) This Schedule does not reserve giving financial assistance to commercial activities for the purpose of promoting or sustaining economic development or employment.

(2) Sub-paragraph (1)—

(a) does not apply to giving financial assistance to any activities in pursuance of a power exercisable only in relation to activities which are reserved,

(b) does not apply to Part I of this Schedule, except paragraph 9, or to a body to which paragraph 3 of this Part of this Schedule applies,

(c) is without prejudice to the exceptions from the reservations in Sections [C11,] E2 and E3 of Part II of this Schedule.

(3) Sub-paragraph (1) does not affect the question whether any matter other than financial assistance to which that sub-paragraph applies is reserved.

Interpretation

5 (1) References in this Schedule to the subject-matter of any enactment are to be read as references to the subject-matter of that enactment as it has effect on the principal appointed day or, if it ceased to have effect at any time within the period ending with that day and beginning with the day on which this Act is passed, as it had effect immediately before that time.

(2) Subordinate legislation under section 129(1) may, in relation to the operation of this Schedule at any time before the principal appointed day, modify the references to that day in sub-paragraph (1).

SCHEDULE 6
DEVOLUTION ISSUES

PART I
PRELIMINARY

1. In this Schedule 'devolution issue' means—

(a) a question whether an Act of the Scottish Parliament or any provision of an Act of the Scottish Parliament is within the legislative competence of the Parliament,

(b) a question whether any function (being a function which any person has purported, or is proposing, to exercise) is a function of the Scottish Ministers, the First Minister or the Lord Advocate,

(c) a question whether the purported or proposed exercise of a function by a member of the Scottish Executive is, or would be, within devolved competence,

(d) a question whether a purported or proposed exercise of a function by a member of the Scottish Executive is, or would be, incompatible with any of the Convention rights or with [EU] law,

(e) a question whether a failure to act by a member of the Scottish Executive is incompatible with any of the Convention rights or with [EU] law,

(f) any other question about whether a function is exercisable within devolved competence or in or as regards Scotland and any other question arising by virtue of this Act about reserved matters.

[But a question arising in criminal proceedings in Scotland that would, apart from this paragraph, be a devolution issue is not a devolution issue if (however formulated) it relates to the compatibility with any of the Convention rights or with EU law of—

(a) an Act of the Scottish Parliament or any provision of an Act of the Scottish Parliament,

(b) a function,

(c) the purported or proposed exercise of a function,

(d) a failure to act.]

PART II
PROCEEDINGS IN SCOTLAND

Application of Part II

3. This Part of this Schedule applies in relation to devolution issues in proceedings in Scotland.

Institution of proceedings

4 (1) Proceedings for the determination of a devolution issue may be instituted by the Advocate General or the Lord Advocate.

(2) The Lord Advocate may defend any such proceedings instituted by the Advocate General.

(3) This paragraph is without prejudice to any power to institute or defend proceedings exercisable apart from this paragraph by any person.

Intimation of devolution issue

5. Intimation of any devolution issue which arises in any proceedings before a court or tribunal shall be given to the Advocate General and the Lord Advocate (unless the person to whom the intimation would be given is a party to the proceedings).

6. A person to whom intimation is given in pursuance of paragraph 5 may take part as a party in the proceedings, so far as they relate to a devolution issue.

Reference of devolution issue to higher court

7. A court, other than the [Supreme Court] or any court consisting of three or more judges of the Court of Session, may refer any devolution issue which arises in proceedings (other than criminal proceedings) before it to the Inner House of the Court of Session.

8. A tribunal from which there is no appeal shall refer any devolution issue which arises in proceedings before it to the Inner House of the Court of Session; and any other tribunal may make such a reference.

9. A court, other than any court consisting of two or more judges of the High Court of Justiciary, may refer any devolution issue which arises in criminal proceedings before it to the High Court of Justiciary.

References from superior courts to [Supreme Court]

10. Any court consisting of three or more judges of the Court of Session may refer any devolution issue which arises in proceedings before it (otherwise than on a reference under paragraph 7 or 8) to the [Supreme Court].

11. Any court consisting of two or more judges of the High Court of Justiciary may refer any devolution issue which arises in proceedings before it (otherwise than on a reference under paragraph 9) to the [Supreme Court].

Appeals from superior courts to [Supreme Court]

12. An appeal against a determination of a devolution issue by the Inner House of the Court of Session on a reference under paragraph 7 or 8 shall lie to the [Supreme Court].

13. An appeal against a determination of a devolution issue by—

(a) a court of two or more judges of the High Court of Justiciary (whether in the ordinary course of proceedings or on a reference under paragraph 9), or

(b) a court of three or more judges of the Court of Session from which there is no appeal to the [Supreme Court apart from this paragraph],

shall lie to the [Supreme Court], but only with [permission] of the court [from which the appeal lies] or, failing such [permission], with [permission] of the [Supreme Court].

[13A In criminal proceedings, an application to the High Court for permission under paragraph 13 must be made—

(a) within 28 days of the date of the determination against which the appeal lies, or

(b) within such longer period as the High Court considers equitable having regard to all the circumstances.]

[13B In criminal proceedings, an application to the Supreme Court for permission under paragraph 13 must be made—

(a) within 28 days of the date on which the High Court refused permission under that paragraph, or

(b) within such longer period as the Supreme Court considers equitable having regard to all the circumstances.]

PART III
PROCEEDINGS IN ENGLAND AND WALES

Application of Part III

14. This Part of this Schedule applies in relation to devolution issues in proceedings in England and Wales.

Institution of proceedings

15 (1) Proceedings for the determination of a devolution issue may be instituted by the Attorney General.

(2) The Lord Advocate may defend any such proceedings.

(3) This paragraph is without prejudice to any power to institute or defend proceedings exercisable apart from this paragraph by any person.

Notice of devolution issue

16. A court or tribunal shall order notice of any devolution issue which arises in any proceedings before it to be given to the Attorney General and the Lord Advocate (unless the person to whom the notice would be given is a party to the proceedings).

17. A person to whom notice is given in pursuance of paragraph 16 may take part as a party in the proceedings, so far as they relate to a devolution issue.

Reference of devolution issue to High Court or Court of Appeal

18. A magistrates' court may refer any devolution issue which arises in proceedings (other than criminal proceedings) before it to the High Court.

19 (1) A court may refer any devolution issue which arises in proceedings (other than criminal proceedings) before it to the Court of Appeal.

(2) Sub-paragraph (1) does not apply to—

(a) a magistrates' court, the Court of Appeal or the [Supreme Court], or

(b) the High Court if the devolution issue arises in proceedings on a reference under paragraph 18.

20. A tribunal from which there is no appeal shall refer any devolution issue which arises in proceedings before it to the Court of Appeal; and any other tribunal may make such a reference.

21. A court, other than the [Supreme Court] or the Court of Appeal, may refer any devolution issue which arises in criminal proceedings before it to—

(a) the High Court (if the proceedings are summary proceedings), or

(b) the Court of Appeal (if the proceedings are proceedings on indictment).

References from Court of Appeal to [Supreme Court]

22. The Court of Appeal may refer any devolution issue which arises in proceedings before it (otherwise than on a reference under paragraph 19, 20 or 21) to the [Supreme Court].

Appeals from superior courts to [Supreme Court]
23. An appeal against a determination of a devolution issue by the High Court or the Court of Appeal on a reference under paragraph 18, 19, 20 or 21 shall lie to the [Supreme Court], but only with [permission] of the High Court or (as the case may be) the Court of Appeal or, failing such [permission], with special leave of the [Supreme Court].

PART IV
PROCEEDINGS IN NORTHERN IRELAND

Application of Part IV
24. This Part of this Schedule applies in relation to devolution issues in proceedings in Northern Ireland.

Institution of proceedings
25—(1) Proceedings for the determination of a devolution issue may be instituted by the [Advocate General for Northern Ireland].
(2) The Lord Advocate may defend any such proceedings.
(3) This paragraph is without prejudice to any power to institute or defend proceedings exercisable apart from this paragraph by any person.

Notice of devolution issue
26. A court or tribunal shall order notice of any devolution issue which arises in any proceedings before it to be given to the [Advocate General for Northern Ireland] and the Lord Advocate (unless the person to whom the notice would be given is a party to the proceedings).
27. A person to whom notice is given in pursuance of paragraph 26 may take part as a party in the proceedings, so far as they relate to a devolution issue.

Reference of devolution issue to Court of Appeal
28. A court, other than the [Supreme Court] or the Court of Appeal in Northern Ireland, may refer any devolution issue which arises in any proceedings before it to the Court of Appeal in Northern Ireland.
29. A tribunal from which there is no appeal shall refer any devolution issue which arises in any proceedings before it to the Court of Appeal in Northern Ireland; and any other tribunal may make such a reference.

References from Court of Appeal to [Supreme Court]
30. The Court of Appeal in Northern Ireland may refer any devolution issue which arises in proceedings before it (otherwise than on a reference under paragraph 28 or 29) to the [Supreme Court].

Appeals from Court of Appeal to [Supreme Court]
31. An appeal against a determination of a devolution issue by the Court of Appeal in Northern Ireland on a reference under paragraph 28 or 29 shall lie to the [Supreme Court], but only with [permission] of the Court of Appeal in Northern Ireland or, failing such [permission], with special leave of the [Supreme Court].

PART V
GENERAL

[. . .]

Direct references to [Supreme Court]
[. . .]
34. The Lord Advocate, the Attorney General, the Advocate General or the [Advocate General for Northern Ireland] may refer to the [Supreme Court] any devolution issue which is not the subject of proceedings.

35 (1) This paragraph applies where a reference is made under paragraph 34 in relation to a devolution issue which relates to the proposed exercise of a function by a member of the Scottish Executive.

(2) The person making the reference shall notify a member of the Scottish Executive of that fact.

(3) No member of the Scottish Executive shall exercise the function in the manner proposed during the period beginning with the receipt of the notification under sub-paragraph (2) and ending with the reference being decided or otherwise disposed of.

(4) Proceedings relating to any possible failure by a member of the Scottish Executive to comply with sub-paragraph (3) may be instituted by the Advocate General.

(5) Sub-paragraph (4) is without prejudice to any power to institute proceedings exercisable apart from that sub-paragraph by any person.

Expenses

36 (1) A court or tribunal before which any proceedings take place may take account of any additional expense of the kind mentioned in sub-paragraph (3) in deciding any question as to costs or expenses.

(2) In deciding any such question, the court or tribunal may award the whole or part of the additional expense as costs or (as the case may be) expenses to the party who incurred it (whatever the decision on the devolution issue).

(3) The additional expense is any additional expense which the court or tribunal considers that any party to the proceedings has incurred as a result of the participation of any person in pursuance of paragraph 6, 17 or 27.

Procedure of courts and tribunals

37. Any power to make provision for regulating the procedure before any court or tribunal shall include power to make provision for the purposes of this Schedule including, in particular, provision—

(a) for prescribing the stage in the proceedings at which a devolution issue is to be raised or referred,

(b) for the sisting or staying of proceedings for the purpose of any proceedings under this Schedule, and

(c) for determining the manner in which and the time within which any intimation or notice is to be given.

Interpretation

38. Any duty or power conferred by this Schedule to refer a devolution issue to a court shall be construed as a duty or (as the case may be) power to refer the issue to the court for decision.

HOUSE OF LORDS ACT 1999
(1999, c 34)

1 Exclusion of hereditary peers

No-one shall be a member of the House of Lords by virtue of a hereditary peerage.

2 Exception from section 1

(1) Section 1 shall not apply in relation to anyone excepted from it by or in accordance with Standing Orders of the House.

(2) At any one time 90 people shall be excepted from section 1; but anyone excepted as holder of the office of Earl Marshal, or as performing the office of Lord Great Chamberlain, shall not count towards that limit.

(3) Once excepted from section 1, a person shall continue to be so throughout his life (until an Act of Parliament provides to the contrary).

(4) Standing Orders shall make provision for filling vacancies among the people excepted from section 1; and in any case where—

(a) the vacancy arises on a death occurring after the end of the first Session of the next Parliament after that in which this Act is passed, and

(b) the deceased person was excepted in consequence of an election, that provision shall require the holding of a by-election.

(5) A person may be excepted from section 1 by or in accordance with Standing Orders made in anticipation of the enactment or commencement of this section.

(6) Any question whether a person is excepted from section 1 shall be decided by the Clerk of the Parliaments, whose certificate shall be conclusive.

3 Removal of disqualifications in relation to the House of Commons

(1) The holder of a hereditary peerage shall not be disqualified by virtue of that peerage for—

(a) voting at elections to the House of Commons, or

(b) being, or being elected as, a member of that House.

(2) Subsection (1) shall not apply in relation to anyone excepted from section 1 by virtue of section 2.

5 Commencement and transitional provision

(1) Sections 1 to 4 (including Schedules 1 and 2) shall come into force at the end of the Session of Parliament in which this Act is passed.

(2) Accordingly, any writ of summons issued for the present Parliament in right of a hereditary peerage shall not have effect after that Session unless it has been issued to a person who, at the end of the Session, is excepted from section 1 by virtue of section 2.

(3) The Secretary of State may by order make such transitional provision about the entitlement of holders of hereditary peerages to vote at elections to the House of Commons or the European Parliament as he considers appropriate.

(4) An order under this section—

(a) may modify the effect of any enactment or any provision made under an enactment, and

(b) shall be made by statutory instrument which shall be subject to annulment in pursuance of a resolution of either House of Parliament.

6 Interpretation and short title

(1) In this Act 'hereditary peerage' includes the principality of Wales and the earldom of Chester.

(2) This Act may be cited as the House of Lords Act 1999.

REGULATION OF INVESTIGATORY POWERS (SCOTLAND) ACT 2000 (2000, asp 11)

1 Conduct to which this Act applies

(1) This Act applies to the following conduct—

(a) directed surveillance;

(b) intrusive surveillance; and

(c) the conduct and use of covert human intelligence sources.

(2) For the purposes of this Act surveillance is directed if it is covert but not intrusive and is undertaken—

(a) for the purposes of a specific investigation or a specific operation;

(b) in such a manner as is likely to result in the obtaining of private information about a person (whether or not one specifically identified for the purposes of the investigation or operation); and

(c) otherwise than by way of an immediate response to events or circumstances the nature of which is such that it would not be reasonably practicable for an authorisation under this Act to be sought for the carrying out of the surveillance.

(3) Subject to subsections (4) and (5) below, surveillance is intrusive for the purposes of this Act if, and only if, it is covert surveillance that—

(a) is carried out in relation to anything taking place on any residential premises or in any private vehicle; and

(b) involves the presence of an individual on the premises or in the vehicle or is carried out by means of a surveillance device.

(4) For the purposes of this Act surveillance is not intrusive to the extent that it is carried out by means only of a surveillance device designed or adapted principally for the purpose of providing information about the location of a vehicle.

(5) For the purposes of this Act surveillance which—

(a) is carried out by means of a surveillance device in relation to anything taking place on any residential premises or in any private vehicle; but

(b) is carried out without that device being present on the premises or in the vehicle,

is not intrusive unless the device is such that it consistently provides information of the same quality and detail as might be expected to be obtained from a device actually present on the premises or in the vehicle.

(6) In this Act—

(a) references to the conduct of a covert human intelligence source are references to any conduct of such a source which falls within any of paragraphs (a) to (c) of subsection (7) below, or is incidental to anything falling within any of those paragraphs; and

(b) references to the use of a covert human intelligence source are references to inducing, asking or assisting a person to engage in the conduct of such a source, or to obtain information by means of the conduct of such a source.

(7) For the purposes of this Act a person is a covert human intelligence source if the person—

(a) establishes or maintains a personal or other relationship with another person for the covert purpose of facilitating the doing of anything falling within paragraph (b) or (c) below;

(b) covertly uses such a relationship to obtain information or to provide access to any information to another person; or

(c) covertly discloses information obtained by the use of such a relationship or as a consequence of the existence of such a relationship.

(8) For the purposes of this section—

(a) surveillance is covert if, and only if, it is carried out in a manner that is calculated to ensure that persons who are subject to the surveillance are unaware that it is or may be taking place;

(b) a purpose is covert, in relation to the establishment or maintenance of a personal or other relationship, if and only if the relationship is conducted in a manner that is calculated to ensure that one of the parties to the relationship is unaware of the purpose; and

(c) a relationship is used covertly, and information obtained as mentioned in subsection (7)(c) above is disclosed covertly, if and only if it is used or, as the case may be, disclosed in a manner that is calculated to ensure that one of the parties to the relationship is unaware of the use or disclosure in question.

(9) In this section 'private information', in relation to a person, includes any information relating to the person's private or family life.

(10) References in this section, in relation to a vehicle, to the presence of a surveillance device in the vehicle include references to its being located on or under the vehicle and also include references to its being attached to it.

7 Authorisation of covert human intelligence sources

(1) Subject to the following provisions of this Act, the persons designated for

the purposes of this section shall each have power to grant authorisations for the conduct or the use of a covert human intelligence source.

(2) A person shall not grant an authorisation for the conduct or the use of a covert human intelligence source unless that person is satisfied—

(a) that the authorisation is necessary on grounds falling within subsection (3) below;

(b) that the authorised conduct or use is proportionate to what is sought to be achieved by that conduct or use; and

(c) that arrangements exist for the source's case that satisfy the requirements of subsection (6) below and such other requirements as may be imposed by order made by the Scottish Ministers.

(3) An authorisation is necessary on grounds falling within this subsection if it is necessary—

(a) for the purpose of preventing or detecting crime or of preventing disorder;

(b) in the interests of public safety; or

(c) for the purpose of protecting public health.

(4) The Scottish Ministers may by order—

(a) prohibit the authorisation under this section of any such conduct or uses of covert human intelligence sources as may be described in the order; and

(b) impose requirements, in addition to those provided for by subsection (2) above, that must be satisfied before an authorisation is granted under this section for any such conduct or uses of covert human intelligence sources as may be described.

(5) The conduct that is authorised by an authorisation for the conduct or the use of a covert human intelligence source is any conduct that—

(a) is comprised in any such activities involving conduct of a covert human intelligence source, or the use of a covert human intelligence source, as are specified or described in the authorisation;

(b) consists in conduct by or in relation to the person who is so specified or described as the person to whose actions as a covert human intelligence source the authorisation relates; and

(c) is carried out for the purposes of, or in connection with, the investigation or operation so specified or described.

(6) For the purposes of this Act there are arrangements for the source's case that satisfy the requirements of this subsection if such arrangements are in force as are necessary for ensuring—

(a) that there will at all times be a person holding an office, rank or position with the relevant investigating authority who will have day-to-day responsibility for dealing with the source on behalf of that authority, and for the source's security and welfare;

(b) that there will at all times be another person holding an office, rank or position with the relevant investigating authority who will have general oversight of the use made of the source;

(c) that there will at all times be a person holding an office, rank or position with the relevant investigating authority who will have responsibility for maintaining a record of the use made of the source;

(d) that the records relating to the source that are maintained by the relevant investigating authority will always contain particulars of all such matters (if any) as may be specified for the purposes of this paragraph in regulations made by the Scottish Ministers; and

(e) that records maintained by the relevant investigating authority that disclose the identity of the source will not be available to persons except to the extent that there is a need for access to them to be made available to those persons.

(7) In this section 'relevant investigating authority', in relation to an authorisation for the conduct or the use of an individual as a covert human intelligence

source, means (subject to subsection (8) below) the public authority for whose benefit the activities of that individual as such a source are to take place.

(8) In the case of any authorisation for the conduct or the use of a covert human intelligence source whose activities are to be for the benefit of more than one public authority, the references in subsection (6) above to the relevant investigating authority are references to one of them (whether or not the same one in the case of each reference).

8 Persons entitled to grant authorisations under sections 6 and 7

(1) Subject to subsection (2) below, the persons designated for the purposes of sections 6 and 7 above are the individuals holding such offices, ranks or positions with relevant public authorities as are prescribed for the purposes of this subsection by order made by the Scottish Ministers.

(2) The Scottish Ministers may by order impose restrictions—

(a) on the authorisations under sections 6 and 7 above that may be granted by any individual holding an office, rank or position with a specified public authority; and

(b) on the circumstances in which, or the purposes for which, such authorisations may be granted by any such individual.

(3) A public authority is a relevant public authority for the purposes of this section in relation to sections 6 and 7 above if it is—

[(aa) the Police Service;]

(b) the Scottish Administration;

(c) a council constituted under section 2 of the Local Government etc (Scotland) Act 1994;

[(ca) the Police Investigations and Review Commissioner;]

(d)–(g) [. . .]

(h) the Scottish Environment Protection Agency;

[(i) the Common Services Agency for the Scottish Health Service.]

(4) The Scottish Ministers may by order amend subsection (3) above by—

(a) adding a public authority to those enumerated in that subsection;

(b) removing a public authority therefrom;

(c) making any change consequential on any change in the name of a public authority enumerated therein

(5) No order shall be made under subsection (4)(a) above unless it has been laid in draft before and approved by resolution of the Scottish Parliament.

14 Approval required for authorisations to take effect

(1) Subject to subsection (2) below, an authorisation for the carrying out of intrusive surveillance shall not take effect until such time (if any) as—

(a) the grant of the authorisation has been approved by [a Judicial Commissioner]; and

(b) written notice of the decision of that approval by that Commissioner has been given, in accordance with subsection (3) below, to the person who granted the authorisation.

(2) Where the person who grants the authorisation—

(a) is satisfied that the case is one of urgency; and

(b) gives notice in accordance with section 13(3)(b) above,

subsection (1) above shall not apply to the authorisation, and the authorisation shall have effect from the time of its grant.

(3) Where subsection (1) above applies to the authorisation—

(a) a [Judicial Commissioner] shall give approval under this section to the authorisation if, and only if, satisfied that there are reasonable grounds for being satisfied that the requirements of section 10(2)(a) and (b) above are satisfied in the case of the authorisation; and

(b) a [Judicial Commissioner] who makes a decision as to whether or not the authorisation should be approved shall, as soon as reasonably practicable after making that decision, give written notice of that decision to the person who granted the authorisation.

(4) If [a Judicial Commissioner] decides not to approve an authorisation to which subsection (1) above applies, the Commissioner shall make a report of that decision and the Commissioner's findings to the most senior relevant person.

(5) In this section 'the most senior relevant person' means—

(a) in relation to an authorisation granted on the application of a [constable of the Police Service, the chief constable of the Police Service; and

(aa) in relation to an authorisation granted on an application by a staff officer of the Police Investigations and Review Commissioner, the Police Investigations and Review Commissioner.]

[. . .]

(6) Any notice that is required by any provision of this section to be given in writing may be given, instead, by being transmitted by electronic means.

[. . .]

24 Issue and revision of codes of practice

(1) The Scottish Ministers shall issue one or more codes of practice relating to the exercise and performance of the powers and duties mentioned in subsection (2) below.

(2) Those powers and duties are those (excluding any power to make subordinate legislation) that are conferred or imposed, by or under—

(a) this Act;

[(aa) Part 5 of the Investigatory Powers Act 2016 (equipment interference) so far as relating to the police service;] and

(b) Part III of the Police Act 1997 (authorisation of interference with property or wireless telegraphy) insofar as relating to [the Police Service] [or to the Police Investigations and Review Commissioner],

otherwise than on [the Judicial Commissioners].

(3) Before issuing a code of practice under subsection (1) above, the Scottish Ministers shall—

(a) prepare and publish a draft of that code; and

(b) consider any representations made to them about the draft,

and the Scottish Ministers may incorporate in the code finally issued any modifications made by them to the draft after its publication.

(4) The Scottish Ministers shall lay before the Scottish Parliament every draft code of practice prepared and published by them under this section.

(5) A code of practice issued by the Scottish Ministers under this section shall not be brought into force except in accordance with an order made by them.

(6) An order under subsection (5) above may contain such transitional provisions and savings as appear to the Scottish Ministers to be necessary or expedient in connection with the bringing into force of the code brought into force by that order.

(7) The Scottish Ministers may from time to time—

(a) revise the whole or any part of a code issued under this section; and

(b) issue the revised code.

(8) Subsections (3) to (6) above shall apply (with appropriate modifications) in relation to the issue of any revised code under this section as they apply in relation to the first issue of such a code.

(9) The Scottish Ministers shall not make an order containing provision for any of the purposes of this section unless a draft of the order has been laid before, and approved by a resolution of the Parliament.

25 Interim codes of practice

(1) The Scottish Ministers may, notwithstanding the provisions of section 24

above, issue one or more interim codes of practice relating to the exercise and performance of the powers and duties mentioned in subsection (2) of that section.

(2) An interim code issued under subsection (1) above shall have effect from its date of issue as if it were a code issued under subsection (1) of section 24 above which had been brought into force by an order under subsection (5) of that section.

(3) An interim notice issued under subsection (1) above shall cease to have effect insofar as it is superseded by a code issued and brought into force under section 24 above.

26 Effect of codes of practice

(1) A person exercising or performing any power or duty in relation to which provision may be made by a code of practice under section 24 or 25 above shall, in doing so, have regard to the provisions (so far as they are applicable) of every code of practice for the time being in force under that section.

(2) A failure on the part of any person to comply with any provision of a code of practice for the time being in force under section 24 or 25 above shall not of itself render the person liable to any criminal or civil proceedings.

(3) A code of practice in force at any time under section 24 or 25 above shall be admissible in evidence in any criminal or civil proceedings.

(4) If any provision of a code of practice issued under section 24 or 25 or revised under section 24(7) above appears to—

(a) the court or tribunal conducting any civil or criminal proceedings;

(b) the [Investigatory Powers Commissioner] carrying out any of the functions of that Commissioner under this Act; or

(c) [a Judicial Commissioner (other than the Investigatory Powers Commissioner)] carrying out the functions of that Commissioner under this Act insofar as relating to [the Police Service] [or the Police Investigations and Review Commissioner],

to be relevant to any question arising in the proceedings, or in connection with the exercise of that jurisdiction or the carrying out of those functions, in relation to a time when it was in force, that provision of the code shall be taken into account in determining that question.

TERRORISM ACT 2000
(2000, c 11)

PART I
INTRODUCTORY

1 Terrorism: interpretation

(1) In this Act 'terrorism' means the use or threat of action where—

(a) the action falls within subsection (2),

(b) the use or threat is designed to influence the government [or an international governmental organisation] or to intimidate the public or a section of the public, and

(c) the use or threat is made for the purpose of advancing a political, religious [, racial] or ideological cause.

(2) Action falls within this subsection if it—

(a) involves serious violence against a person,

(b) involves serious damage to property,

(c) endangers a person's life, other than that of the person committing the action,

(d) creates a serious risk to the health or safety of the public or a section of the public, or

(e) is designed seriously to interfere with or seriously to disrupt an electronic system.

(3) The use or threat of action falling within subsection (2) which involves the use of firearms or explosives is terrorism whether or not subsection (1)(b) is satisfied.

(4) In this section—

(a) 'action' includes action outside the United Kingdom,

(b) a reference to any person or to property is a reference to any person, or to property, wherever situated,

(c) a reference to the public includes a reference to the public of a country other than the United Kingdom, and

(d) 'the government' means the government of the United Kingdom, of a Part of the United Kingdom or of a country other than the United Kingdom.

(5) In this Act a reference to action taken for the purposes of terrorism includes a reference to action taken for the benefit of a proscribed organisation.

PART II
PROSCRIBED ORGANISATIONS

Procedure

3 Proscription

(1) For the purposes of this Act an organisation is proscribed if—

(a) it is listed in Schedule 2, or

(b) it operates under the same name as an organisation listed in that Schedule.

(2) Subsection (1)(b) shall not apply in relation to an organisation listed in Schedule 2 if its entry is the subject of a note in that Schedule.

(3) The Secretary of State may by order—

(a) add an organisation to Schedule 2;

(b) remove an organisation from that Schedule;

(c) amend that Schedule in some other way.

(4) The Secretary of State may exercise his power under subsection (3)(a) in respect of an organisation only if he believes that it is concerned in terrorism.

(5) For the purposes of subsection (4) an organisation is concerned in terrorism if it—

(a) commits or participates in acts of terrorism,

(b) prepares for terrorism,

(c) promotes or encourages terrorism, or

(d) is otherwise concerned in terrorism.

[(5A) The cases in which an organisation promotes or encourages terrorism for the purposes of subsection (5)(c) include any case in which activities of the organisation—

(a) include the unlawful glorification of the commission or preparation (whether in the past, in the future or generally) of acts of terrorism; or

(b) are carried out in a manner that ensures that the organisation is associated with statements containing any such glorification.

(5B) The glorification of any conduct is unlawful for the purposes of subsection (5A) if there are persons who may become aware of it who could reasonably be expected to infer that what is being glorified, is being glorified as—

(a) conduct that should be emulated in existing circumstances, or

(b) conduct that is illustrative of a type of conduct that should be so emulated.

(5C) In this section—

'glorification' includes any form of praise or celebration, and cognate expressions are to be construed accordingly;

'statement' includes a communication without words consisting of sounds or images or both.

[(6) Where the Secretary of State believes—

(a) that an organisation listed in Schedule 2 is operating wholly or partly under a name that is not specified in that Schedule (whether as well as or instead of under the specified name), or

(b) that an organisation that is operating under a name that is not so specified is otherwise for all practical purposes the same as an organisation so listed,

he may, by order, provide that the name that is not specified in that Schedule is to be treated as another name for the listed organisation.

(7) Where an order under subsection (6) provides for a name to be treated as another name for an organisation, this Act shall have effect in relation to acts occurring while—

(a) the order is in force, and

(b) the organisation continues to be listed in Schedule 2,

as if the organisation were listed in that Schedule under the other name, as well as under the name specified in the Schedule.

(8) The Secretary of State may at any time by order revoke an order under subsection (6) or otherwise provide for a name specified in such an order to cease to be treated as a name for a particular organisation.

(9) Nothing in subsections (6) to (8) prevents any liability from being established in any proceedings by proof that an organisation is the same as an organisation listed in Schedule 2, even though it is or was operating under a name specified neither in Schedule 2 nor in an order under subsection (6).]

4 Deproscription: application

[(1) An application may be made to the Secretary of State for an order under section 3(3) or (8)—

(a) removing an organisation from Schedule 2, or

(b) providing for a name to cease to be treated as a name for an organisation listed in that Schedule.]

(2) An application may be made by—

(a) the organisation, or

(b) any person affected by the organisation's proscription [or by the treatment of the name as a name for the organisation].

(3) The Secretary of State shall make regulations prescribing the procedure for applications under this section.

(4) The regulations shall, in particular—

(a) require the Secretary of State to determine an application within a specified period of time, and

(b) require an application to state the grounds on which it is made.

5 Deproscription: appeal

(1) There shall be a commission, to be known as the Proscribed Organisations Appeal Commission.

(2) Where an application under section 4 has been refused, the applicant may appeal to the Commission.

(3) The Commission shall allow an appeal against a refusal to deproscribe an organisation [or to provide for a name to cease to be treated as a name for an organisation] if it considers that the decision to refuse was flawed when considered in the light of the principles applicable on an application for judicial review.

(4) Where the Commission allows an appeal under this section [. . .], it may make an order under this subsection.

(5) Where an order is made under subsection (4) [in respect of an appeal against a refusal to deproscribe an organisation,] the Secretary of State shall as soon as is reasonably practicable—

(a) lay before Parliament, in accordance with section 123(4), the draft of an order under section 3(3)(b) removing the organisation from the list in Schedule 2, or

(b) make an order removing the organisation from the list in Schedule 2 in pursuance of section 123(5).

[(5A) Where an order is made under subsection (4) in respect of an appeal against a refusal to provide for a name to cease to be treated as a name for an organisation, the Secretary of State shall, as soon as is reasonably practicable, make an order under section 3(8) providing that the name in question is to cease to be so treated in relation to that organisation.]

(6) Schedule 3 (constitution of the Commission and procedure) shall have effect.

6 Further appeal

(1) A party to an appeal under section 5 which the Proscribed Organisations Appeal Commission has determined may bring a further appeal on a question of law to—

(a) the Court of Appeal, if the first appeal was heard in England and Wales,

(b) the Court of Session, if the first appeal was heard in Scotland, or

(c) the Court of Appeal in Northern Ireland, if the first appeal was heard in Northern Ireland.

(2) An appeal under subsection (1) may be brought only with the permission—

(a) of the Commission, or

(b) where the Commission refuses permission, of the court to which the appeal would be brought.

(3) An order under section 5(4) shall not require the Secretary of State to take any action until the final determination or disposal of an appeal under this section (including any appeal to the [Supreme Court]).

10 Immunity

(1) The following shall not be admissible as evidence in proceedings for an offence under any of sections 11 to 13, 15 to 19 and 56—

(a) evidence of anything done in relation to an application to the Secretary of State under section 4,

(b) evidence of anything done in relation to proceedings before the Proscribed Organisations Appeal Commission under section 5 above or section 7(1) of the Human Rights Act 1998,

(c) evidence of anything done in relation to proceedings under section 6 (including that section as applied by section 9(2)), and

(d) any document submitted for the purposes of proceedings mentioned in any of paragraphs (a) to (c).

(2) But subsection (1) does not prevent evidence from being adduced on behalf of the accused.

Offences

11 Membership

(1) A person commits an offence if he belongs or professes to belong to a proscribed organisation.

(2) It is a defence for a person charged with an offence under subsection (1) to prove—

(a) that the organisation was not proscribed on the last (or only) occasion on which he became a member or began to profess to be a member, and

(b) that he has not taken part in the activities of the organisation at any time while it was proscribed.

(3) A person guilty of an offence under this section shall be liable—

(a) on conviction on indictment, to imprisonment for a term not exceeding ten years, to a fine or to both, or

(b) on summary conviction, to imprisonment for a term not exceeding six months, to a fine not exceeding the statutory maximum or to both.

(4) In subsection (2) 'proscribed' means proscribed for the purposes of any of the following—

(a) this Act;
(b) the Northern Ireland (Emergency Provisions) Act 1996;
(c) the Northern Ireland (Emergency Provisions) Act 1991;
(d) the Prevention of Terrorism (Temporary Provisions) Act 1989;
(e) the Prevention of Terrorism (Temporary Provisions) Act 1984;
(f) the Northern Ireland (Emergency Provisions) Act 1978;
(g) the Prevention of Terrorism (Temporary Provisions) Act 1976;
(h) the Prevention of Terrorism (Temporary Provisions) Act 1974;
(i) the Northern Ireland (Emergency Provisions) Act 1973.

12 Support

(1) A person commits an offence if—

(a) he invites support for a proscribed organisation, and

(b) the support is not, or is not restricted to, the provision of money or other property (within the meaning of section 15).

(2) A person commits an offence if he arranges, manages or assists in arranging or managing a meeting which he knows is—

(a) to support a proscribed organisation,

(b) to further the activities of a proscribed organisation, or

(c) to be addressed by a person who belongs or professes to belong to a proscribed organisation.

(3) A person commits an offence if he addresses a meeting and the purpose of his address is to encourage support for a proscribed organisation or to further its activities.

(4) Where a person is charged with an offence under subsection (2)(c) in respect of a private meeting it is a defence for him to prove that he had no reasonable cause to believe that the address mentioned in subsection (2)(c) would support a proscribed organisation or further its activities.

(5) In subsections (2) to (4)—

(a) 'meeting' means a meeting of three or more persons, whether or not the public are admitted, and

(b) a meeting is private if the public are not admitted.

(6) A person guilty of an offence under this section shall be liable—

(a) on conviction on indictment, to imprisonment for a term not exceeding ten years, to a fine or to both, or

(b) on summary conviction, to imprisonment for a term not exceeding six months, to a fine not exceeding the statutory maximum or to both.

13 Uniform

(1) A person in a public place commits an offence if he—

(a) wears an item of clothing, or

(b) wears, carries or displays an article,

in such a way or in such circumstances as to arouse reasonable suspicion that he is a member or supporter of a proscribed organisation.

(2) A constable in Scotland may arrest a person without a warrant if he has reasonable grounds to suspect that the person is guilty of an offence under this section.

(3) A person guilty of an offence under this section shall be liable on summary conviction to—

(a) imprisonment for a term not exceeding six months,
(b) a fine not exceeding level 5 on the standard scale, or
(c) both.

PART III
TERRORIST PROPERTY

Offences

15 Fund-raising

(1) A person commits an offence if he—

(a) invites another to provide money or other property, and

(b) intends that it should be used, or has reasonable cause to suspect that it may be used, for the purposes of terrorism.

(2) A person commits an offence if he—

(a) receives money or other property, and

(b) intends that it should be used, or has reasonable cause to suspect that it may be used, for the purposes of terrorism.

(3) A person commits an offence if he—

(a) provides money or other property, and

(b) knows or has reasonable cause to suspect that it will or may be used for the purposes of terrorism.

(4) In this section a reference to the provision of money or other property is a reference to its being given, lent or otherwise made available, whether or not for consideration.

19 Disclosure of information: duty

(1) This section applies where a person—

(a) believes or suspects that another person has committed an offence under any of sections 15 to 18, and

(b) bases his belief or suspicion on information which [comes to his attention—

(i) in the course of a trade, profession, business, or

(ii) in the course of his employment (whether or not in the course of a trade, profession or business).]

[(1A) But this section does not apply if the information came to the person in the course of a business in the regulated sector.]

(2) The person commits an offence if he does not disclose to a constable as soon as is reasonably practicable—

(a) his belief or suspicion, and

(b) the information on which it is based.

(3) It is a defence for a person charged with an offence under subsection (2) to prove that he had a reasonable excuse for not making the disclosure.

(4) Where—

(a) a person is in employment,

(b) his employer has established a procedure for the making of disclosures of the matters specified in subsection (2), and

(c) he is charged with an offence under that subsection,

it is a defence for him to prove that he disclosed the matters specified in that subsection in accordance with the procedure.

(5) Subsection (2) does not require disclosure by a professional legal adviser of—

(a) information which he obtains in privileged circumstances, or

(b) a belief or suspicion based on information which he obtains in privileged circumstances.

(6) For the purpose of subsection (5) information is obtained by an adviser in privileged circumstances if it comes to him, otherwise than with a view to furthering a criminal purpose—

(a) from a client or a client's representative, in connection with the provision of legal advice by the adviser to the client,

(b) from a person seeking legal advice from the adviser, or from the person's representative, or

(c) from any person, for the purpose of actual or contemplated legal proceedings.

(7) For the purposes of subsection (1)(a) a person shall be treated as having committed an offence under one of sections 15 to 18 if—

(a) he has taken an action or been in possession of a thing, and

(b) he would have committed an offence under one of those sections if he had been in the United Kingdom at the time when he took the action or was in possession of the thing.

[(7A) The reference to a business in the regulated sector must be construed in accordance with Schedule 3A.

(7B) The reference to a constable includes a reference to a [National Crime Agency officer] authorised for the purposes of this section by the Director General of [that Agency].]

(8) A person guilty of an offence under this section shall be liable—

(a) on conviction on indictment, to imprisonment for a term not exceeding five years, to a fine or to both, or

(b) on summary conviction, to imprisonment for a term not exceeding six months, or to a fine not exceeding the statutory maximum or to both.

PART V
COUNTER-TERRORIST POWERS

Suspected terrorists [etc]

40 Terrorist: interpretation

(1) In this Part 'terrorist' means a person who—

(a) has committed an offence under any of sections 11, 12, 15 to 18, 54 and 56 to 63, or

(b) is or has been concerned in the commission, preparation or instigation of acts of terrorism.

(2) The reference in subsection (1)(b) to a person who has been concerned in the commission, preparation or instigation of acts of terrorism includes a reference to a person who has been, whether before or after the passing of this Act, concerned in the commission, preparation or instigation of acts of terrorism within the meaning given by section 1.

41 Arrest without warrant

(1) A constable may arrest without a warrant a person whom he reasonably suspects to be a terrorist.

(2) Where a person is arrested under this section the provisions of Schedule 8 (detention: treatment, review and extension) shall apply.

(3) Subject to subsections (4) to (7), a person detained under this section shall (unless detained under any other power) be released not later than the end of the period of 48 hours beginning—

(a) with the time of his arrest under this section, or

(b) if he was being detained under Schedule 7 [*or under Part I of Schedule 3 to the Counter-Terrorism and Border Security Act 2019, or information derived from such samples*] when he was arrested under this section, with the time when his examination under that Schedule began.

(4) If on a review of a person's detention under Part II of Schedule 8 the review officer does not authorise continued detention, the person shall (unless detained in accordance with subsection (5) or (6) or under any other power) be released.

(5) Where a police officer intends to make an application for a warrant under paragraph 29 of Schedule 8 extending a person's detention, the person may be detained pending the making of the application.

(6) Where an application has been made under paragraph 29 or 36 of

Schedule 8 in respect of a person's detention, he may be detained pending the conclusion of proceedings on the application.

(7) Where an application under paragraph 29 or 36 of Schedule 8 is granted in respect of a person's detention, he may be detained, subject to paragraph 37 of that Schedule, during the period specified in the warrant.

(8) The refusal of an application in respect of a person's detention under paragraph 29 or 36 of Schedule 8 shall not prevent his continued detention in accordance with this section.

[(8A) If a person detained under this section, including by virtue of a warrant under Part 3 of Schedule 8, is removed to hospital because the person needs medical treatment—

(a) any time during which the person is being questioned in hospital or on the way there or back for the purpose of obtaining relevant evidence is to be included in calculating any period which falls to be calculated for the purposes of this section or Part 3 of Schedule 8, but

(b) any other time when the person is in hospital or on the way there or back is not to be included.

(8B) In subsection (8A), 'relevant evidence' means, in relation to the detained person, evidence which—

(a) relates to the person's commission of an offence under any of the provisions mentioned in section 40(1)(a), or

(b) indicates that the person is a person falling within section 40(1)(b).]

(9) A person who has the powers of a constable in one Part of the United Kingdom may exercise the power under subsection (1) in any Part of the United Kingdom.

42 Search of premises

(1) A justice of the peace may on the application of a constable issue a warrant in relation to specified premises if he is satisfied that there are reasonable grounds for suspecting that a person whom the constable reasonably suspects to be a person falling within section 40(1)(b) is to be found there.

(2) A warrant under this section shall authorise any constable to enter and search the specified premises for the purpose of arresting the person referred to in subsection (1) under section 41.

(3) In the application of subsection (1) to Scotland—

(a) 'justice of the peace' includes the sheriff, and

(b) the justice of the peace or sheriff can be satisfied as mentioned in that subsection only by having heard evidence on oath.

43 Search of persons

(1) A constable may stop and search a person whom he reasonably suspects to be a terrorist to discover whether he has in his possession anything which may constitute evidence that he is a terrorist.

(2) A constable may search a person arrested under section 41 to discover whether he has in his possession anything which may constitute evidence that he is a terrorist.

(3) A search of a person under this section must be carried out by someone of the same sex.

(4) A constable may seize and retain anything which he discovers in the course of a search of a person under subsection (1) or (2) and which he reasonably suspects may constitute evidence that the person is a terrorist.

[(4A) Subsection (4B) applies if a constable, in exercising the power under subsection (1) to stop a person whom the constable reasonably suspects to be a terrorist, stops a vehicle (see section 116(2)).

(4B) The constable—

(a) may search the vehicle and anything in or on it to discover whether there is anything which may constitute evidence that the person concerned is a terrorist, and

(b) may seize and retain anything which the constable—

(i) discovers in the course of such a search, and

(ii) reasonably suspects may constitute evidence that the person is a terrorist.

(4C) Nothing in subsection (4B) confers a power to search any person but the power to search in that subsection is in addition to the power in subsection (1) to search a person whom the constable reasonably suspects to be a terrorist.]

(5) A person who has the powers of a constable in one Part of the United Kingdom may exercise a power under this section in any Part of the United Kingdom.

[43A Search of vehicles

(1) Subsection (2) applies if a constable reasonably suspects that a vehicle is being used for the purposes of terrorism.

(2) The constable may stop and search—

(a) the vehicle;

(b) the driver of the vehicle;

(c) a passenger in the vehicle;

(d) anything in or on the vehicle or carried by the driver or a passenger;

to discover whether there is anything which may constitute evidence that the vehicle is being used for the purposes of terrorism.

(3) A constable may seize and retain anything which the constable—

(a) discovers in the course of a search under this section, and

(b) reasonably suspects may constitute evidence that the vehicle is being used for the purposes of terrorism.

(4) A person who has the powers of a constable in one Part of the United Kingdom may exercise a power under this section in any Part of the United Kingdom.

(5) In this section 'driver', in relation to an aircraft, hovercraft or vessel, means the captain, pilot or other person with control of the aircraft, hovercraft or vessel or any member of its crew and, in relation to a train, includes any member of its crew.]

PART VI
MISCELLANEOUS

Inciting terrorism overseas

61 Scotland

(1) A person commits an offence if—

(a) he incites another person to commit an act of terrorism wholly or partly outside the United Kingdom, and

(b) the act would, if committed in Scotland, constitute one of the offences listed in subsection (2).

(2) Those offences are—

(a) murder,

(b) assault to severe injury, and

(c) reckless conduct which causes actual injury.

(3) A person guilty of an offence under this section shall be liable to any penalty to which he would be liable on conviction of the offence listed in subsection (2) which corresponds to the act which he incites.

(4) For the purposes of subsection (1) it is immaterial whether or not the person incited is in the United Kingdom at the time of the incitement.

(5) Nothing in this section imposes criminal liability on any person acting on behalf of, or holding office under, the Crown.

Terrorist bombing and finance offences

62 Terrorist bombing: jurisdiction

(1) If—

(a) a person does anything outside the United Kingdom as an act of terrorism or for the purposes of terrorism, and

(b) his action would have constituted the commission of one of the offences listed in subsection (2) if it had been done in the United Kingdom,

he shall be guilty of the offence.

(2) The offences referred to in subsection (1)(b) are—

(a) an offence under section 2, 3 or 5 of the Explosive Substances Act 1883 (causing explosions, &c),

(b) an offence under section 1 of the Biological Weapons Act 1974 (biological weapons), and

(c) an offence under section 2 of the Chemical Weapons Act 1996 (chemical weapons).

63 Terrorist finance: jurisdiction

(1) If—

(a) a person does anything outside the United Kingdom, and

(b) his action would have constituted the commission of an offence under any of sections 15 to 18 if it had been done in the United Kingdom,

he shall be guilty of the offence.

(2) For the purposes of subsection (1)(b), section 18(1)(b) shall be read as if for 'the jurisdiction' there were substituted 'a jurisdiction'.

PART VIII
GENERAL

114 Police powers

(1) A power conferred by virtue of this Act on a constable—

(a) is additional to powers which he has at common law or by virtue of any other enactment, and

(b) shall not be taken to affect those powers.

(2) A constable may if necessary use reasonable force for the purpose of exercising a power conferred on him by virtue of this Act (apart from paragraphs 2 and 3 of Schedule 7).

(3) Where anything is seized by a constable under a power conferred by virtue of this Act, it may (unless the contrary intention appears) be retained for so long as is necessary in all the circumstances.

SCHEDULES

SCHEDULE 2
PROSCRIBED ORGANISATIONS

section 3

The Irish Republican Army
Cumann na mBan
Fianna na hEireann
The Red Hand Commando
Saor Eire
The Ulster Freedom Fighters
The Ulster Volunteer Force

The Irish National Liberation Army
The Irish People's Liberation Organisation
The Ulster Defence Association
The Loyalist Volunteer Force
The Continuity Army Council
The Orange Volunteers
The Red Hand Defenders
[Al-Qa'ida
Egyptian Islamic Jihad
Al-Gama'at al Islamiya
Armed Islamic Group (Groupe Islamique Armee) (GIA)
Salafist Group for Call and Combat (Groupe Salafiste pour la Predication et le Combat) (GSPC)
Babbar Khalsa
[. . .]
Harakat Mujahideen
Jaish e Mohammed
Lashkar e Tayyaba
Liberation Tigers of Tamil Eelam (LTTE)
[The military wing of Hizballah, including the Jihad Council and all units reporting to it (including the Hizballah External Security Organisation]
Hamas-Izz al-Din al-Qassem Brigades
Palestinian Islamic Jihad–Shaqaqi
Abu Nidal Organisation
Islamic Army of Aden
[. . .]
Kurdistan Workers' Party (Partiya Karkeren Kurdistan) (PKK)
Revolutionary People's Liberation Party–Front (Devrimci Halk Kurtulus Partisi-Cephesi) (DHKP-C)
Basque Homeland and Liberty (Euskadi ta Askatasuna) (ETA)
17 November Revolutionary Organisation (N17)]
[Abu Sayyaf Group
Asbat Al-Ansar
Islamic Movement of Uzbekistan
Jemaah Islamiyah]
[Al Ittihad Al Islamia
Ansar Al Islam
Ansar Al Sunna
Groupe Islamique Combattant Marocain
Harakat-ul-Jihad-ul-Islami
Harakat-ul-Jihad-ul-Islami (Bangladesh)
Harakat-ul-Mujahideen/Alami
[. . .]
Islamic Jihad Union
Jamaat ul-Furquan
Jundallah
Khuddam ul-Islam
Lashkar-e Jhangvi
Libyan Islamic Fighting Group
Sipah-e Sahaba Pakistan]
[Al-Ghurabaa
The Saved Sect
Baluchistan Liberation Army
Teyrebaz Azadiye Kurdistan]
[Jammat-ul Mujahideen Bangladesh
Tehrik Nefaz-e Shari'at Muhammadi]

[Al Shabaab]
[Tehrik-e Taliban Pakistan]
[Indian Mujahideen]
[Ansarul Muslimina Fi Biladis Sudan (Vanguard for the protection of Muslims in Black Africa) (Ansaru)]
[Jama'atu Ahli Sunna Lidda Awati Wal Jihad (Boko Haram)
Minbar Ansar Deen (Ansar Al Sharia UK)]
[Imarat Kavkaz (Caucasus Emirate)]
[Ansar Bayt al-Maqdis (Ansar Jerusalem)
Al Murabitun
Ansar al Sharia – Tunisia]
[Islamic State of Iraq and the Levant (Islamic State of Iraq and al-Sham) (Dawat al Islamiya fi Iraq wa al Sham (DAISh))
Turkiye Halk Kurtulus Partisi-Cephesi (Turkish People's Liberation Party) (The Hasty Ones) (Mukavamet Suriye)
Kateeba al-Kawthar (Ajnad al-sham) (Junud ar-Rahman al Muhajireen)
Abdallah Azzam Brigades, including the Ziyad al-Jarrah Battalions
Popular Front for the Liberation of Palestine – General Command]
[Ansar al-Sharia-Benghazi (Partisans of Islamic Law)
Ajnad Misr (Soldiers of Egypt)
Jaysh al Khalifatu Islamiya (Army of the Islamic Caliphate) (Majahideen of the Caucasus and the Levant)]
[Jund Al-Aqsa (Soldiers of Al-Aqsa)
Jund al Khalifa–Algeria (Soldiers of the Caliphate in Algeria)]
[Jamaat ul-Ahrar
The Haqqani Network]
[Global Islamic Media Front (including GIMF Bangla Team (Ansarullah Bangla Team) (Ansar-al Islam))]
[Mujahedeen Indonesia Timur (East Indonesia Mujahedeen)
Turkestan Islamic Party (East Turkestan Islamic Party) (East Turkestan Islamic Movement) (East Turkestan Jihadist Movement) (Hizb al-Islami al-Turkistani)
Jamaah Anshorut Daulah]
[National Action]
[al-Ashtar Brigades (Saraya al-Ashtar) (The Wa'ad Allah Brigades) (Islamic Allah Brigades) (Imam al-Mahdi Brigades) (al-Haydariyah Brigades)
al-Mukhtar Brigades (Saraya al-Mukhtar)
Hasam (Harakat Sawa'd Misr) (Harakat Hasm) (Hasm)
Liwa al-Thawra]

Notes The entry for The Orange Volunteers refers to the organisation which uses that name and in the name of which a statement described as a press release was published on 14th October 1998.

[The entry for Jemaah Islamiyah refers to the organisation using that name that is based in south-east Asia, members of which were arrested by the Singapore authorities in December 2001 in connection with a plot to attack US and other Western targets in Singapore.]

SCHEDULE 3
THE PROSCRIBED ORGANISATIONS APPEAL COMMISSION

section 5

Constitution and administration

1.—(1) The Commission shall consist of members appointed by the Lord Chancellor.

(2) The Lord Chancellor shall appoint one of the members as chairman.

(3) A member shall hold and vacate office in accordance with the terms of his appointment.

(4) A member may resign at any time by notice in writing to the Lord Chancellor.

2. The Lord Chancellor may appoint officers and servants for the Commission.

3. The Lord Chancellor—

(a) may pay sums by way of remuneration, allowances, pensions and gratuities to or in respect of members, officers and servants,

(b) may pay compensation to a person who ceases to be a member of the Commission if the Lord Chancellor thinks it appropriate because of special circumstances, and

(c) may pay sums in respect of expenses of the Commission.

Procedure

4.—(1) The Commission shall sit at such times and in such places as the Lord Chancellor may direct [after consulting the following—

(a) the Lord Chief Justice of England and Wales;

(b) the Lord President of the Court of Session;

(c) the Lord Chief Justice of Northern Ireland].

(2) The Commission may sit in two or more divisions.

(3) At each sitting of the Commission—

(a) three members shall attend,

(b) one of the members shall be a person who holds or has held high judicial office (within the meaning of [Part 3 of the Constitutional Reform Act 2005) or is or has been a member of the Judicial Committee of the Privy Council], and

(c) the chairman or another member nominated by him shall preside and report the Commission's decision.

(4) [*Applies to England and Wales.*]

[(5) The Lord President of the Court of Session may nominate a judge of the Court of Session who is a member of the First or Second Division of the Inner House of that Court to exercise his functions under this paragraph.]

(6) [*Applies to Northern Ireland.*]

5.—(1) The Lord Chancellor may make rules—

(a) regulating the exercise of the right of appeal to the Commission;

(b) prescribing practice and procedure to be followed in relation to proceedings before the Commission;

(c) providing for proceedings before the Commission to be determined without an oral hearing in specified circumstances

(d) making provision about evidence in proceedings before the Commission (including provision about the burden of proof and admissibility of evidence);

(e) making provision about proof of the Commission's decisions.

(2) In making the rules the Lord Chancellor shall, in particular, have regard to the need to secure—

(a) that decisions which are the subject of appeals are properly reviewed, and

(b) that information is not disclosed contrary to the public interest.

(3) The rules shall make provision permitting organisations to be legally represented in proceedings before the Commission.

(4) The rules may, in particular—

(a) provide for full particulars of the reasons for proscription or refusal to deproscribe to be withheld from the organisation or applicant concerned and from any person representing it or him;

[(aa) provide for full particulars of the reasons for—

(i) the making of an order under section 3(6), or

(ii) a refusal to provide for a name to cease to be treated as a name for an organisation, to be withheld from the organisation or applicant concerned and from any person representing it or him;]

(b) enable the Commission to exclude persons (including representatives) from all or part of proceedings;

(c) enable the Commission to provide a summary of evidence taken in the absence of a person excluded by virtue of paragraph (b);

(d) permit preliminary or incidental functions to be discharged by a single member;

(e) permit proceedings for permission to appeal under section 6 to be determined by a single member;

(f) make provision about the functions of persons appointed under paragraph 7;

(g) make different provision for different parties or descriptions of party.

(5) Rules under this paragraph—

(a) shall be made by statutory instrument, and

(b) shall not be made unless a draft has been laid before and approved by resolution of each House of Parliament.

(6) In this paragraph a reference to proceedings before the Commission includes a reference to proceedings arising out of proceedings before the Commission.

6.—(1) This paragraph applies to—

(a) proceedings brought by an organisation before the Commission, and

(b) proceedings arising out of proceedings to which paragraph (a) applies.

(2) Proceedings shall be conducted on behalf of the organisation by a person designated by the Commission (with such legal representation as he may choose to obtain).

(3) In [paragraph 5] of this Schedule a reference to an organisation includes a reference to a person designated under this paragraph.

7.—(1) The relevant law officer may appoint a person to represent the interests of an organisation or other applicant in proceedings in relation to which an order has been made by virtue of paragraph 5(4)(b).

(2) The relevant law officer is—

(a) in relation to proceedings in England and Wales, the Attorney General,

(b) in relation to proceedings in Scotland, the Advocate General for Scotland, and

(c) in relation to proceedings in Northern Ireland, the [Advocate General for Northern Ireland].

(3) A person appointed under this paragraph must—

(a) have a general qualification for the purposes of section 71 of the Courts and Legal Services Act 1990 (qualification for legal appointments),

(b) be an advocate or a solicitor who has rights of audience in the Court of Session or the High Court of Justiciary by virtue of section 25A of the Solicitors (Scotland) Act 1980, or

(c) be a member of the Bar of Northern Ireland.

(4) A person appointed under this paragraph shall not be responsible to the organisation or other applicant whose interests he is appointed to represent.

(5) In [paragraph 5] of this Schedule a reference to a representative does not include a reference to a person appointed under this paragraph.

REGULATION OF INVESTIGATORY POWERS ACT 2000
(2000, c 23)

65 The Tribunal

(1) There shall, for the purpose of exercising the jurisdiction conferred on them by this section, be a tribunal consisting of such number of members as Her Majesty may by Letters Patent appoint.

(2) The jurisdiction of the Tribunal shall be—

(a) to be the only appropriate tribunal for the purposes of section 7 of the Human Rights Act 1998 in relation to any proceedings under subsection (1)(a) of that section (proceedings for actions incompatible with Convention rights) which fall within subsection (3) of this section;

(b) to consider and determine any complaints made to them which, in accordance with subsection (4) [. . .], are complaints for which the Tribunal is the appropriate forum;

(c) to consider and determine any reference to them by any person that he has suffered detriment as a consequence of any prohibition or restriction, by virtue of [section 56 of the Investigatory Powers Act 2016], on his relying in, or for the purposes of, any civil proceedings on any matter; and

(d) to hear and determine any other such proceedings falling within subsection (3) as may be allocated to them in accordance with provision made by the Secretary of State by order.

(3) Proceedings fall within this subsection if—

(a) they are proceedings against any of the intelligence services;

(b) they are proceedings against any other person in respect of any conduct, or proposed conduct, by or on behalf of any of those services;

(c) they are proceedings brought by virtue of section 55(4); or

(d) they are proceedings relating to the taking place in any challengeable circumstances of any conduct falling within subsection (5).

(4) The Tribunal is the appropriate forum for any complaint if it is a complaint by a person who is aggrieved by any conduct falling within subsection (5) which he believes—

(a) to have taken place in relation to him, to any of his property, to any communications sent by or to him, or intended for him, or to his use of any postal service, telecommunications service or telecommunication system; and

(b) to have taken place in challengeable circumstances or to have been carried out by or on behalf of any of the intelligence services.

(5) Subject to subsection (6), conduct falls within this subsection if (whenever it occurred) it is—

(a) conduct by or on behalf of any of the intelligence services;

(b) conduct for or in connection with the interception of communications in the course of their transmission by means of a postal service or telecommunication system;

[(ba) conduct for or in connection with the obtaining of secondary data from communications transmitted by means of such a service or system;

(bb) the issue, modification, renewal or service of a warrant under Part 2 or Chapter 1 of Part 6 of the Investigatory Powers Act 2016 (interception of communications);]

[(c) conduct of a kind which may be permitted or required by an authorisation or notice under Part 3 of that Act or a warrant under Chapter 2 of Part 6 of that Act (acquisition of communications data);

(cza) the giving of an authorisation or notice under Part 3 of that Act or the issue, modification, renewal or service of a warrant under Chapter 2 of Part 6 of that Act;

(czb) conduct of a kind which may be required or permitted by a retention notice under Part 4 of that Act (retention of communications data) but excluding any conduct which is subject to review by the Information Commissioner;

(czc) the giving or varying of a retention notice under that Part of that Act;

(czd) conduct of a kind which may be required or permitted by a warrant under Part 5 or Chapter 3 of Part 6 of that Act (equipment interference);

(cze) the issue, modification, renewal or service of a warrant under Part 5 or Chapter 3 of Part 6 of that Act;

(czf) the issue, modification, renewal or service of a warrant under Part 7 of that Act (bulk personal dataset warrants);

(czg) the giving of an authorisation under section 219(3)(b) (authorisation for the retention, or retention and examination, of material following expiry of bulk personal dataset warrant);

(czh) the giving or varying of a direction under section 225 of that Act (directions where no bulk personal dataset warrant required);

(czi) conduct of a kind which may be required by a notice under section 252 or 253 of that Act (national security or technical capability notices);

(czj) the giving or varying of such a notice;

(czk) the giving of an authorisation under section 152(5)(c) or 193(5)(c) of that Act (certain authorisations to examine intercepted content or protected material);

(czl) any failure to—

(i) cancel a warrant under Part 2, 5, 6 or 7 of that Act or an authorisation under Part 3 of that Act;

(ii) cancel a notice under Part 3 of that Act;

(iii) revoke a notice under Part 4, or section 252 or 253, of that Act; or

(iv) revoke a direction under section 225 of that Act;

(czm) any conduct in connection with any conduct falling within paragraph (c), (czb), (czd) or (czi);]

[(ca) the carrying out of surveillance by a foreign police or customs officer (within the meaning of section 76A);]

(d) [other] conduct to which Part II applies;

(e) the giving of a notice under section 49 or any disclosure or use of a key to protected information;

(f) any entry on or interference with property or any interference with wireless telegraphy.

(6) For the purposes only of subsection (3), nothing mentioned in paragraph (d) or (f) of subsection (5) shall be treated as falling within that subsection unless it is conducted by or on behalf of [an immigration officer or] a person holding any office, rank or position with—

(a) any of the intelligence services;

(b) any of Her Majesty's forces;

(c) any police force;

[(ca) the Police Investigations and Review Commissioner;]

[(d) the National Crime Agency;]

[(dza) the Competition and Markets Authority;]

[. . .]

[(f) the Commissioners for Her Majesty's Revenue and Customs];

and section 48(5) applies for the purposes of this subsection as it applies for the purposes of Part II.

[(6A) Subsection (6) does not apply to anything mentioned in paragraph (d) or (f) of subsection (5) which also falls within paragraph (czd) of that subsection.]

(7) For the purposes of this section conduct takes place in challengeable circumstances if [it is conduct of a public authority and]—

(a) it takes place with the authority, or purported authority, of anything falling within subsection (8); or

(b) the circumstances are such that (whether or not there is such authority) it would not have been appropriate for the conduct to take place without it, or at least without proper consideration having been given to whether such authority should be sought;

but [, subject to subsection (7ZA),] conduct does not take place in challengeable circumstances to the extent that it is authorised by, or takes place with the permission of, a judicial authority.

[(7ZA) The exception in subsection (7) so far as conduct is authorised by, or takes place with the permission of, a judicial authority does not include conduct authorised by an approval given [by a Judicial Commissioner or under section 32A of this Act or section 75 of the Investigatory Powers Act 2016]

[(7ZB) For the purposes of this section conduct also takes place in challengeable circumstances if it is, or purports to be, conduct falling within subsection (5)(bb), (cza), (czc), (cze), (czf), (czg), (czh), (czj), (czk) or (czl) or (so far as the conduct is, or purports to be, the giving of a notice under section 49) subsection (5)(e).]

[(7A) For the purposes of this section conduct also takes place in challengeable circumstances if it takes place, or purports to take place, under section 76A.]

(8) The following fall within this subsection—

[(a) a warrant under Part 2, 5, 6 or 7 of the Investigatory Powers Act 2016;

(b) an authorisation or notice under Part 3 of that Act;

(ba) a retention notice under Part 4 of that Act;

(bb) a direction under section 225 of that Act;

(bc) a notice under section 252 or 253 of that Act;]

(c) an authorisation under Part II of this Act or under any enactment contained in or made under an Act of the Scottish Parliament which makes provision equivalent to that made by that Part;

(d) a permission for the purposes of Schedule 2 to this Act;

(e) a notice under section 49 of this Act; or

(f) an authorisation under section 93 of the Police Act 1997.

(9) Schedule 3 (which makes further provision in relation to the Tribunal) shall have effect.

[(9A) In subsection (5)(ba) the reference to obtaining secondary data from communications transmitted by means of a postal service or telecommunication system is to be read in accordance with section 16 of the Investigatory Powers Act 2016.]

(10) In this section—

(a) references to a key and to protected information shall be construed in accordance with section 56;

(b) references to the disclosure or use of a key to protected information taking place in relation to a person are references to such a disclosure or use taking place in a case in which that person has had possession of the key or of the protected information; and

(c) references to the disclosure of a key to protected information include references to the making of any disclosure in an intelligible form (within the meaning of section 56) of protected information by a person who is or has been in possession of the key to that information;

and the reference in paragraph (b) to a person's having possession of a key or of protected information shall be construed in accordance with section 56.

(11) In this section 'judicial authority' means—

(a) any judge of the High Court or of the Crown Court or any Circuit Judge;

(b) any judge of the High Court of Justiciary or any sheriff;

(c) any justice of the peace;

(d) any county court judge or resident magistrate in Northern Ireland;

(e) any person holding any such judicial office as entitles him to exercise the jurisdiction of a judge of the Crown Court or of a justice of the peace.

67 Exercise of the Tribunal's jurisdiction

(1) Subject to subsections (4) and (5), it shall be the duty of the Tribunal—

(a) to hear and determine any proceedings brought before them by virtue of section 65(2)(a) or (d); and

(b) to consider and determine any complaint or reference made to them by virtue of section 65(2)(b) or (c).

(2) Where the Tribunal hear any proceedings by virtue of section 65(2)(a), they shall apply the same principles for making their determination in those proceedings as would be applied by a court on an application for judicial review.

(3) Where the Tribunal consider a complaint made to them by virtue of section 65(2)(b), it shall be the duty of the Tribunal—

(a) to investigate whether the persons against whom any allegations are made in the complaint have engaged in relation to—

(i) the complainant,

(ii) any of his property,

(iii) any communications sent by or to him, or intended for him, or

(iv) his use of any postal service, telecommunications service or telecommunication system,

in any conduct falling within section 65(5);

(b) to investigate the authority (if any) for any conduct falling within section 65(5) which they find has been so engaged in; and

(c) in relation to the Tribunal's findings from their investigations, to determine the complaint by applying the same principles as would be applied by a court on an application for judicial review.

(4) The Tribunal shall not be under any duty to hear, consider or determine any proceedings, complaint or reference if it appears to them that the bringing of the proceedings or the making of the complaint or reference is frivolous or vexatious.

(5) Except where the Tribunal, having regard to all the circumstances, are satisfied that it is equitable to do so, they shall not consider or determine any complaint made by virtue of section 65(2)(b) if it is made more than one year after the taking place of the conduct to which it relates.

(6) Subject to any provision made by rules under section 69, where any proceedings have been brought before the Tribunal or any reference made to the Tribunal, they shall have power to make such interim orders, pending their final determination, as they think fit.

(7) Subject to any provision made by rules under section 69, the Tribunal on determining any proceedings, complaint or reference shall have power to make any such award of compensation or other order as they think fit; and, without prejudice to the power to make rules under section 69(2)(h), the other orders that may be made by the Tribunal include—

(a) an order quashing or cancelling any warrant or authorisation;

[(aza) an order quashing or cancelling a notice under Part 3 of the Investigatory Powers Act 2016 or a retention notice under Part 4 of that Act;

(azb) an order quashing or revoking a direction under section 225 of that Act;

(azc) an order quashing or revoking a notice under section 252 or 253 of that Act;]

[(aa) an order quashing an order under [section 23A or 32A, section 75 of the Investigatory Powers Act 2016 or section 32A of this Act] by the relevant judicial authority (within the meaning of that section);] and

(b) an order requiring the destruction of any records of information which—

(i) has been obtained in exercise of any power conferred by a warrant or authorisation [or by a notice under Part 3 of the Investigatory Powers Act 2016]; or

(ii) is held by any public authority in relation to any person.

(8) [Except as provided by virtue of section 67A,] determinations, awards, orders and other decisions of the Tribunal (including decisions as to whether they have jurisdiction) shall not be subject to appeal or be liable to be questioned in any court.

[. . .]

[67A Appeals from the Tribunal

(1) A relevant person may appeal on a point of law against any determination of the Tribunal of a kind mentioned in section 68(4) or any decision of the Tribunal of a kind mentioned in section 68(4C).

(2) Before making a determination or decision which might be the subject of an appeal under this section, the Tribunal must specify the court which is to have jurisdiction to hear the appeal (the 'relevant appellate court').

(3) This court is whichever of the following courts appears to the Tribunal to be the most appropriate—

(a) the Court of Appeal in England and Wales,

(b) the Court of Session.

(4) The Secretary of State may by regulations, with the consent of the Northern Ireland Assembly, amend subsection (3) so as to add the Court of Appeal in Northern Ireland to the list of courts mentioned there.

(5) The Secretary of State may by regulations specify criteria to be applied by the Tribunal in making decisions under subsection (2) as to the identity of the relevant appellate court.

(6) An appeal under this section—

(a) is to be heard by the relevant appellate court, but

(b) may not be made without the leave of the Tribunal or, if that is refused, of the relevant appellate court.

(7) The Tribunal or relevant appellate court must not grant leave to appeal unless it considers that—

(a) the appeal would raise an important point of principle or practice, or

(b) there is another compelling reason for granting leave.

(8) In this section—

'relevant appellate court' has the meaning given by subsection (2),

'relevant person', in relation to any proceedings, complaint or reference, means the complainant or—

(a) in the case of proceedings, the respondent,

(b) in the case of a complaint, the person complained against, and

(c) in the case of a reference, any public authority to whom the reference relates.]

68 Tribunal procedure

(1) Subject to any rules made under section 69, the Tribunal shall be entitled to determine their own procedure in relation to any proceedings, complaint or reference brought before or made to them.

(2) The Tribunal shall have power—

(a) in connection with the investigation of any matter, or

(b) otherwise for the purposes of the Tribunal's consideration or determination of any matter,

to require a relevant Commissioner appearing to the Tribunal to have functions in relation to the matter in question to provide the Tribunal with all such assistance (including that Commissioner's opinion as to any issue falling to be determined by the Tribunal) as the Tribunal think fit.

(3) Where the Tribunal hear or consider any proceedings, complaint or reference relating to any matter, they shall secure that every relevant Commissioner appearing to them to have functions in relation to that matter—

(a) is aware that the matter is the subject of proceedings, a complaint or a reference brought before or made to the Tribunal; and

(b) is kept informed of any determination, award, order or other decision made by the Tribunal with respect to that matter.

(4) Where the Tribunal determine any proceedings, complaint or reference brought before or made to them, they shall give notice to the complainant which (subject to any rules made by virtue of section 69(2)(i)) shall be confined, as the case may be, to either—

(a) a statement that they have made a determination in his favour; or

(b) a statement that no determination has been made in his favour.

[(4A) Where the Tribunal make any determination of a kind mentioned in subsection (4), they must also give notice to—

(a) in the case of proceedings, the respondent,

(b) in the case of a complaint, the person complained against, and

(c) in the case of a reference, any public authority to whom the reference relates.

(4B) A notice under subsection (4A) is (subject to any rules made by virtue of section 69(2)(j)) to be confined, as the case may be, to either—

(a) a statement that they have made a determination in the complainant's favour, or

(b) a statement that no determination has been made in the complainant's favour.

(4C) Where the Tribunal make any decision which—

(a) is a final decision of a preliminary issue in relation to any proceedings, complaint or reference brought before or made to them, and

(b) is neither a determination of a kind mentioned in subsection (4) nor a decision relating to a procedural matter,

they must give notice of that decision to every person who would be entitled to receive notice of the determination under subsection (4) or (4A).

(4D) A notice under subsection (4C) is (subject to any rules made by virtue of section 69(2)(i) or (j)) to be confined to a statement as to what the decision is.

(4E) Subsections (4C) and (4D) do not apply so far as—

(a) the Tribunal are prevented from giving notice of a decision to a person by rules made by virtue of section 69(4) or decide under such rules not to give such a notice, or

(b) the giving of such a notice is inconsistent with such rules.]

(5) Where—

(a) the Tribunal make a determination in favour of any person by whom any proceedings have been brought before the Tribunal or by whom any complaint or reference has been made to the Tribunal, and

(b) the determination relates to any act or omission by or on behalf of the Secretary of State or to conduct for which any warrant, authorisation or permission [, or notice under Part 4 of the Investigatory Powers Act 2016 or under section 252 or 253 of that Act or direction under section 225 of that Act,] was issued, granted or given by the Secretary of State,

they shall make a report of their findings to the Prime Minister.

(6) It shall be the duty of the persons specified in subsection (7) to disclose or provide to the Tribunal all such documents and information as the Tribunal may require for the purpose of enabling them—

(a) to exercise the jurisdiction conferred on them by or under section 65; or

(b) otherwise to exercise or perform any power or duty conferred or imposed on them by or under this Act [or the Investigatory Powers Act 2016].

(7) Those persons are—

(a) every person holding office under the Crown;

[. . .]

(d) every person employed by or for the purposes of a police force;

[(da) the Police Investigations and Review Commissioner and every member of the Commissioner's staff;]

(e) every person required for the purposes of [section 41, 126, 149, 168 or 190 of the Investigatory Powers Act 2016] to provide assistance with giving effect to [a warrant];

(f) every person on whom an obligation to take any steps has been imposed under [section 252 or 253 of that Act];

[(g) every person by or to whom an authorisation under Part 3 of that Act has been granted;

(h) every person to whom a notice under Part 3 of that Act has been given;

(ha) every person to whom a retention notice under Part 4 of that Act or a notice under section 252 or 253 of that Act has been given;]

(i) every person by whom, or on whose application, there has been granted or given any authorisation under Part II of this Act or under Part III of the Police Act 1997;

(j) every person who holds or has held any office, rank or position with the same public authority as a person falling within paragraph (i);

(k) every person who has engaged in any conduct with the authority of [—

(i) an authorisation under Part 3 of the Investigatory Powers Act 2016, Part 2 of this Act or Part 3 of the Police Act 1997, or

(ii) a warrant under Chapter 2 of Part 6 of the Investigatory Powers Act 2016;]

(l) every person who holds or has held any office, rank or position with a public authority for whose benefit any such authorisation [or warrant] has been or may be given;

(m) every person to whom a notice under section 49 has been given; and

(n) every person who is or has been employed for the purposes of any business of a person falling within paragraph (e), (f), (h) [, (ha)] or (m).

(8) In this section 'relevant Commissioner' means the [Investigatory Powers Commissioner or any other Judicial Commissioner or the Investigatory Powers Commissioner for Northern Ireland].

FREEDOM OF INFORMATION ACT 2000
(2000, c 36)

PART I
ACCESS TO INFORMATION HELD BY PUBLIC AUTHORITIES

Right to information

1 General right of access to information held by public authorities

(1) Any person making a request for information to a public authority is entitled—

(a) to be informed in writing by the public authority whether it holds information of the description specified in the request, and

(b) if that is the case, to have that information communicated to him.

(2) Subsection (1) has effect subject to the following provisions of this section and to the provisions of sections 2, 9, 12 and 14.

(3) Where a public authority—

(a) reasonably requires further information in order to identify and locate the information requested, and

(b) has informed the applicant of that requirement,

the authority is not obliged to comply with subsection (1) unless it is supplied with that further information.

(4) The information—

(a) in respect of which the applicant is to be informed under subsection (1)(a), or

(b) which is to be communicated under subsection (1)(b),

is the information in question held at the time when the request is received, except that account may be taken of any amendment or deletion made between that time and the time when the information is to be communicated under subsection (1)(b), being an amendment or deletion that would have been made regardless of the receipt of the request.

(5) A public authority is to be taken to have complied with subsection (1)(a) in

relation to any information if it has communicated the information to the applicant in accordance with subsection (1)(b).

(6) In this Act, the duty of a public authority to comply with subsection (1)(a) is referred to as 'the duty to confirm or deny'.

2 Effect of the exemptions in Part II

(1) Where any provision of Part II states that the duty to confirm or deny does not arise in relation to any information, the effect of the provision is that where either—

(a) the provision confers absolute exemption, or

(b) in all the circumstances of the case, the public interest in maintaining the exclusion of the duty to confirm or deny outweighs the public interest in disclosing whether the public authority holds the information,

section 1(1)(a) does not apply.

(2) In respect of any information which is exempt information by virtue of any provision of Part II, section 1(1)(b) does not apply if or to the extent that—

(a) the information is exempt information by virtue of a provision conferring absolute exemption, or

(b) in all the circumstances of the case, the public interest in maintaining the exemption outweighs the public interest in disclosing the information.

(3) For the purposes of this section, the following provisions of Part II (and no others) are to be regarded as conferring absolute exemption—

(a) section 21,

(b) section 23,

(c) section 32,

(d) section 34,

(e) section 36 so far as relating to information held by the House of Commons or the House of Lords,

[(ea) in section 37, paragraphs (a) to (ab) of subsection (1), and subsection (2) so far as relating to those paragraphs.]

[(f) section 40(1),]

[(fa) section 40(2) so far as relating to cases where the first condition referred to in that subsection is satisfied,]

(g) section 41, and

(h) section 44.

3 Public authorities

(1) In this Act 'public authority' means—

(a) subject to section 4(4), any body which, any other person who, or the holder of any office which—

(i) is listed in Schedule 1, or

(ii) is designated by order under section 5, or

(b) a publicly-owned company as defined by section 6.

(2) For the purposes of this Act, information is held by a public authority if—

(a) it is held by the authority, otherwise than on behalf of another person, or

(b) it is held by another person on behalf of the authority.

6 Publicly-owned companies

(1) A company is a 'publicly-owned company' for the purposes of section 3(1)(b) if—

(a) it is wholly owned by the Crown,

(b) it is wholly owned by [the wider public sector] [, or

(c) it is wholly owned by the Crown and the wider public sector.]

[(2) For the purposes of this section—

(a) a company is wholly owned by the Crown if, and only if, every member is a person falling within sub-paragraph (i) or (ii)—

(i) a Minister of the Crown, government department or company wholly owned by the Crown, or

(ii) a person acting on behalf of a Minister of the Crown, government department or company wholly owned by the Crown,

(b) a company is wholly owned by the wider public sector if, and only if, every member is a person falling within sub-paragraph (i) or (ii)—

(i) a relevant public authority or a company wholly owned by the wider public sector, or

(ii) a person acting on behalf of a relevant public authority or of a company wholly owned by the wider public sector, and

(c) a company is wholly owned by the Crown and the wider public sector if, and only if, condition A, B or C is met.]

[(2A) In subsection (2)(c)—

(a) condition A is met if—

(i) at least one member is a person falling within subsection (2)(a)(i) or (ii),

(ii) at least one member is a person falling within subsection (2)(b)(i) or (ii), and

(iii) every member is a person falling within subsection (2)(a)(i) or (ii) or (b)(i) or (ii),

(b) condition B is met if—

(i) at least one member is a person falling within subsection (2)(a)(i) or (ii) or (b)(i) or (ii),

(ii) at least one member is a company wholly owned by the Crown and the wider public sector, and

(iii) every member is a person falling within subsection (2)(a)(i) or (ii) or (b)(i) or (ii) or a company wholly owned by the Crown and the wider public sector, and

(c) condition C is met if every member is a company wholly owned by the Crown and the wider public sector.]

(3) In this section—

'company' includes any body corporate;

'Minister of the Crown' includes a Northern Ireland Minister;

['relevant public authority' means any public authority listed in Schedule 1 other than—

a government department, or

any authority which is listed only in relation to particular information.]

8 Request for information

(1) In this Act any reference to a 'request for information' is a reference to such a request which—

(a) is in writing,

(b) states the name of the applicant and an address for correspondence, and

(c) describes the information requested.

(2) For the purposes of subsection (1)(a), a request is to be treated as made in writing where the text of the request—

(a) is transmitted by electronic means,

(b) is received in legible form, and

(c) is capable of being used for subsequent reference.

9 Fees

(1) A public authority to whom a request for information is made may, within the period for complying with section 1(1), give the applicant a notice in writing (in this Act referred to as a 'fees notice') stating that a fee of an amount specified in the notice is to be charged by the authority for complying with section 1(1).

(2) Where a fees notice has been given to the applicant, the public authority is

not obliged to comply with section 1(1) unless the fee is paid within the period of three months beginning with the day on which the fees notice is given to the applicant.

(3) Subject to subsection (5), any fee under this section must be determined by the public authority in accordance with regulations made by the [Minister for the Cabinet Office].

(4) Regulations under subsection (3) may, in particular, provide—

(a) that no fee is to be payable in prescribed cases,

(b) that any fee is not to exceed such maximum as may be specified in, or determined in accordance with, the regulations, and

(c) that any fee is to be calculated in such manner as may be prescribed by the regulations.

(5) Subsection (3) does not apply where provision is made by or under any enactment as to the fee that may be charged by the public authority for the disclosure of the information.

10 Time for compliance with request

(1) Subject to subsections (2) and (3), a public authority must comply with section 1(1) promptly and in any event not later than the twentieth working day following the date of receipt.

(2) Where the authority has given a fees notice to the applicant and the fee is paid in accordance with section 9(2), the working days in the period beginning with the day on which the fees notice is given to the applicant and ending with the day on which the fee is received by the authority are to be disregarded in calculating for the purposes of subsection (1) the twentieth working day following the date of receipt.

(3) If, and to the extent that—

(a) section 1(1)(a) would not apply if the condition in section 2(1)(b) were satisfied, or

(b) section 1(1)(b) would not apply if the condition in section 2(2)(b) were satisfied,

the public authority need not comply with section 1(1)(a) or (b) until such time as is reasonable in the circumstances; but this subsection does not affect the time by which any notice under section 17(1) must be given.

(4) The [Minister for the Cabinet Office] may by regulations provide that subsections (1) and (2) are to have effect as if any reference to the twentieth working day following the date of receipt were a reference to such other day, not later than the sixtieth working day following the date of receipt, as may be specified in, or determined in accordance with, the regulations.

(5) Regulations under subsection (4) may—

(a) prescribe different days in relation to different cases, and

(b) confer a discretion on the Commissioner.

(6) In this section—

'the date of receipt' means—

(a) the day on which the public authority receives the request for information, or

(b) if later, the day on which it receives the information referred to in section 1(3);

'working day' means any day other than a Saturday, a Sunday, Christmas Day, Good Friday or a day which is a bank holiday under the Banking and Financial Dealings Act 1971 in any part of the United Kingdom.

11 Means by which communication to be made

(1) Where, on making his request for information, the applicant expresses a preference for communication by any one or more of the following means, namely—

(a) the provision to the applicant of a copy of the information in permanent form or in another form acceptable to the applicant,

(b) the provision to the applicant of a reasonable opportunity to inspect a record containing the information, and

(c) the provision to the applicant of a digest or summary of the information in permanent form or in another form acceptable to the applicant,

the public authority shall so far as reasonably practicable give effect to that preference.

[(1A) Where—

(a) an applicant makes a request for information to a public authority in respect of information that is, or forms part of, a dataset held by the public authority, and

(b) on making the request for information, the applicant expresses a preference for communication by means of the provision to the applicant of a copy of the information in electronic form,

the public authority must, so far as reasonably practicable, provide the information to the applicant in an electronic form which is capable of re-use.]

(2) In determining for the purposes of this section whether it is reasonably practicable to communicate information by particular means, the public authority may have regard to all the circumstances, including the cost of doing so.

(3) Where the public authority determines that it is not reasonably practicable to comply with any preference expressed by the applicant in making his request, the authority shall notify the applicant of the reasons for its determination.

(4) Subject to [subsections (1) and (1A)], a public authority may comply with a request by communicating information by any means which are reasonable in the circumstances.

[(5) In this Act 'dataset' means information comprising a collection of information held in electronic form where all or most of the information in the collection—

(a) has been obtained or recorded for the purpose of providing a public authority with information in connection with the provision of a service by the authority or the carrying out of any other function of the authority,

(b) is factual information which—

(i) is not the product of analysis or interpretation other than calculation, and

(ii) is not an official statistic (within the meaning given by section 6(1) of the Statistics and Registration Service Act 2007), and

(c) remains presented in a way that (except for the purpose of forming part of the collection) has not been organised, adapted or otherwise materially altered since it was obtained or recorded.]

12 Exemption where cost of compliance exceeds appropriate limit

(1) Section 1(1) does not oblige a public authority to comply with a request for information if the authority estimates that the cost of complying with the request would exceed the appropriate limit.

(2) Subsection (1) does not exempt the public authority from its obligation to comply with paragraph (a) of section 1(1) unless the estimated cost of complying with that paragraph alone would exceed the appropriate limit.

(3) In subsections (1) and (2) 'the appropriate limit' means such amount as may be prescribed, and different amounts may be prescribed in relation to different cases.

(4) The [Minister for the Cabinet Office] may by regulations provide that, in such circumstances as may be prescribed, where two or more requests for information are made to a public authority—

(a) by one person, or

(b) by different persons who appear to the public authority to be acting in concert or in pursuance of a campaign,

the estimated cost of complying with any of the requests is to be taken to be the estimated total cost of complying with all of them.

(5) The [Minister for the Cabinet Office] may by regulations make provision for

the purposes of this section as to the costs to be estimated and as to the manner in which they are to be estimated.

14 Vexatious or repeated requests

(1) Section 1(1) does not oblige a public authority to comply with a request for information if the request is vexatious.

(2) Where a public authority has previously complied with a request for information which was made by any person, it is not obliged to comply with a subsequent identical or substantially similar request from that person unless a reasonable interval has elapsed between compliance with the previous request and the making of the current request.

15 Special provisions relating to public records transferred to Public Record Office, etc

(1) Where—

(a) the appropriate records authority receives a request for information which relates to information which is, or if it existed would be, contained in a transferred public record, and

(b) either of the conditions in subsection (2) is satisfied in relation to any of that information,

that authority shall, within the period for complying with section 1(1), send a copy of the request to the responsible authority.

(2) The conditions referred to in subsection (1)(b) are—

(a) that the duty to confirm or deny is expressed to be excluded only by a provision of Part II not specified in subsection (3) of section 2, and

(b) that the information is exempt information only by virtue of a provision of Part II not specified in that subsection.

(3) On receiving the copy, the responsible authority shall, within such time as is reasonable in all the circumstances, inform the appropriate records authority of the determination required by virtue of subsection (3) or (4) of section 66.

(4) In this Act 'transferred public record' means a public record which has been transferred—

(a) to the Public Record Office,

(b) to another place of deposit appointed by the [Secretary of State] under the Public Records Act 1958, or

(c) to the Public Record Office of Northern Ireland.

(5) In this Act—

'appropriate records authority', in relation to a transferred public record, means—

(a) in a case falling within subsection (4)(a), the Public Record Office,

(b) in a case falling within subsection (4)(b), the [Secretary of State], and

(c) in a case falling within subsection (4)(c), the Public Record Office of Northern Ireland;

'responsible authority', in relation to a transferred public record, means—

(a) in the case of a record transferred as mentioned in subsection (4)(a) or (b) from a government department in the charge of a Minister of the Crown, the Minister of the Crown who appears to the [Secretary of State] to be primarily concerned,

(b) in the case of a record transferred as mentioned in subsection (4)(a) or (b) from any other person, the person who appears to the [Secretary of State] to be primarily concerned,

(c) in the case of a record transferred to the Public Record Office of Northern Ireland from a government department in the charge of a Minister of the Crown, the Minister of the Crown who appears to the appropriate Northern Ireland Minister to be primarily concerned,

(d) in the case of a record transferred to the Public Record Office of Northern Ireland from a Northern Ireland department, the Northern Ireland Minister who appears to the appropriate Northern Ireland Minister to be primarily concerned, or

(e) in the case of a record transferred to the Public Record Office of Northern Ireland from any other person, the person who appears to the appropriate Northern Ireland Minister to be primarily concerned.

16 Duty to provide advice and assistance

(1) It shall be the duty of a public authority to provide advice and assistance, so far as it would be reasonable to expect the authority to do so, to persons who propose to make, or have made, requests for information to it.

(2) Any public authority which, in relation to the provision of advice or assistance in any case, conforms with the code of practice under section 45 is to be taken to comply with the duty imposed by subsection (1) in relation to that case.

Refusal of request

17 Refusal of request

(1) A public authority which, in relation to any request for information, is to any extent relying on a claim that any provision of Part II relating to the duty to confirm or deny is relevant to the request or on a claim that information is exempt information must, within the time for complying with section 1(1), give the applicant a notice which—

(a) states that fact,

(b) specifies the exemption in question, and

(c) states (if that would not otherwise be apparent) why the exemption applies.

(2) Where—

(a) in relation to any request for information, a public authority is, as respects any information, relying on a claim—

(i) that any provision of Part II which relates to the duty to confirm or deny and is not specified in section 2(3) is relevant to the request, or

(ii) that the information is exempt information only by virtue of a provision not specified in section 2(3), and

(b) at the time when the notice under subsection (1) is given to the applicant, the public authority (or, in a case falling within section 66(3) or (4), the responsible authority) has not yet reached a decision as to the application of subsection (1)(b) or (2)(b) of section 2,

the notice under subsection (1) must indicate that no decision as to the application of that provision has yet been reached and must contain an estimate of the date by which the authority expects that such a decision will have been reached.

(3) A public authority which, in relation to any request for information, is to any extent relying on a claim that subsection (1)(b) or (2)(b) of section 2 applies must, either in the notice under subsection (1) or in a separate notice given within such time as is reasonable in the circumstances, state the reasons for claiming—

(a) that, in all the circumstances of the case, the public interest in maintaining the exclusion of the duty to confirm or deny outweighs the public interest in disclosing whether the authority holds the information, or

(b) that, in all the circumstances of the case, the public interest in maintaining the exemption outweighs the public interest in disclosing the information.

(4) A public authority is not obliged to make a statement under subsection (1)(c) or (3) if, or to the extent that, the statement would involve the disclosure of information which would itself be exempt information.

(5) A public authority which, in relation to any request for information, is relying on a claim that section 12 or 14 applies must, within the time for complying with section 1(1), give the applicant a notice stating that fact.

(6) Subsection (5) does not apply where—

(a) the public authority is relying on a claim that section 14 applies,

(b) the authority has given the applicant a notice, in relation to a previous request for information, stating that it is relying on such a claim, and

(c) it would in all the circumstances be unreasonable to expect the authority to serve a further notice under subsection (5) in relation to the current request.

(7) A notice under subsection (1), (3) or (5) must—

(a) contain particulars of any procedure provided by the public authority for dealing with complaints about the handling of requests for information or state that the authority does not provide such a procedure, and

(b) contain particulars of the right conferred by section 50.

The Information Commissioner [. . .]

18 The Information Commissioner [. . .]

[. . .]

(3) In this Act—

(a) the Information Commissioner is referred to as 'the Commissioner',

[. . .]

(4) Schedule 2 (which makes provision consequential on subsections (1) and (2) and amendments of the Data Protection Act 1998 relating to the extension by this Act of the functions of the Commissioner and the Tribunal) has effect.

[. . .]

Publication schemes

19 Publication schemes

(1) It shall be the duty of every public authority—

(a) to adopt and maintain a scheme which relates to the publication of information by the authority and is approved by the Commissioner (in this Act referred to as a 'publication scheme'),

(b) to publish information in accordance with its publication scheme, and

(c) from time to time to review its publication scheme.

(2) A publication scheme must—

(a) specify classes of information which the public authority publishes or intends to publish,

(b) specify the manner in which information of each class is, or is intended to be, published, and

(c) specify whether the material is, or is intended to be, available to the public free of charge or on payment.

[(2A) A publication scheme must, in particular, include a requirement for the public authority concerned—

(a) to publish—

(i) any dataset held by the authority in relation to which a person makes a request for information to the authority, and

(ii) any up-dated version held by the authority of such a dataset,

unless the authority is satisfied that it is not appropriate for the dataset to be published,

(b) where reasonably practicable, to publish any dataset the authority publishes by virtue of paragraph (a) in an electronic form which is capable of re-use,

(c) where [subject to subsections (2AA) and (2AB)] any information in a dataset published by virtue of paragraph (a) is a relevant copyright work in relation to which the authority is the only owner, to make the information available for re-use in accordance with the terms of the specified licence.

[(2AA) If the whole of the relevant copyright work is a document to which the Re-use of Public Sector Information Regulations 2015 apply, subsections (2A)(c) and (2B) to (2F) do not apply to the relevant copyright work.

(2AB) If part of the relevant copyright work is a document to which those Regulations apply—

(a) subsections (2A)(c) and (2B) to (2F) do not apply to that part, but

(b) those provisions do apply to the part to which the Regulations do not apply (and references in the following provisions of this section to the relevant copyright work are to be read as references to that part).]

(2B) The public authority may exercise any power that it has by virtue of regulations under section 11B to charge a fee in connection with making the relevant copyright work available for re-use in accordance with a requirement imposed by virtue of subsection (2A)(c).

(2C) Nothing in this section or section 11B prevents a public authority which is subject to such a requirement from exercising any power that it has by or under an enactment other than this Act to charge a fee in connection with making the relevant copyright work available for re-use.

(2D) Where a public authority intends to charge a fee (whether in accordance with regulations under section 11B or as mentioned in subsection (2C)) in connection with making a relevant copyright work available for re-use by an applicant, the authority must give the applicant a notice in writing (in this section referred to as a 're-use fee notice') stating that a fee of an amount specified in, or determined in accordance with, the notice is to be charged by the authority in connection with complying with the requirement imposed by virtue of subsection (2A)(c).

(2E) Where a re-use fee notice has been given to the applicant, the public authority is not obliged to comply with the requirement imposed by virtue of subsection (2A)(c) while any part of the fee which is required to be paid is unpaid.

(2F) Where a public authority intends to charge a fee as mentioned in subsection (2C), the re-use fee notice may be combined with any other notice which is to be given under the power which enables the fee to be charged.]

(3) In adopting or reviewing a publication scheme, a public authority shall have regard to the public interest—

(a) in allowing public access to information held by the authority, and

(b) in the publication of reasons for decisions made by the authority.

(4) A public authority shall publish its publication scheme in such manner as it thinks fit.

(5) The Commissioner may, when approving a scheme, provide that his approval is to expire at the end of a specified period.

(6) Where the Commissioner has approved the publication scheme of any public authority, he may at any time give notice to the public authority revoking his approval of the scheme as from the end of the period of six months beginning with the day on which the notice is given.

(7) Where the Commissioner—

(a) refuses to approve a proposed publication scheme, or

(b) revokes his approval of a publication scheme,

he must give the public authority a statement of his reasons for doing so.

[(8) In this section—

'copyright owner' has the meaning given by Part 1 of the Copyright, Designs and Patents Act 1988 (see section 173 of that Act);

'copyright work' has the meaning given by Part 1 of the Act of 1988 (see section 1(2) of that Act);

'database' has the meaning given by section 3A of the Act of 1988;

'database right' has the same meaning as in Part 3 of the Copyright and Rights in Databases Regulations 1997 (SI 1997/3032);

'owner', in relation to a relevant copyright work, means—

(a) the copyright owner, or

(b) the owner of the database right in the database;

'relevant copyright work' means—
(a) a copyright work, or
(b) a database subject to a database right,
but excludes a relevant Crown work or a relevant Parliamentary work;
'relevant Crown work' means—
(a) a copyright work in relation to which the Crown is the copyright owner, or
(b) a database in relation to which the Crown is the owner of the database right;
'relevant Parliamentary work' means—
(a) a copyright work in relation to which the House of Commons or the House of Lords is the copyright owner, or
(b) a database in relation to which the House of Commons or the House of Lords is the owner of the database right;
'the specified licence' has the meaning given by section 11A(8).]

20 Model publication schemes

(1) The Commissioner may from time to time approve, in relation to public authorities falling within particular classes, model publication schemes prepared by him or by other persons.

(2) Where a public authority falling within the class to which an approved model scheme relates adopts such a scheme without modification, no further approval of the Commissioner is required so long as the model scheme remains approved; and where such an authority adopts such a scheme with modifications, the approval of the Commissioner is required only in relation to the modifications.

(3) The Commissioner may, when approving a model publication scheme, provide that his approval is to expire at the end of a specified period.

(4) Where the Commissioner has approved a model publication scheme, he may at any time publish, in such manner as he thinks fit, a notice revoking his approval of the scheme as from the end of the period of six months beginning with the day on which the notice is published.

(5) Where the Commissioner refuses to approve a proposed model publication scheme on the application of any person, he must give the person who applied for approval of the scheme a statement of the reasons for his refusal.

(6) Where the Commissioner refuses to approve any modifications under subsection (2), he must give the public authority a statement of the reasons for his refusal.

(7) Where the Commissioner revokes his approval of a model publication scheme, he must include in the notice under subsection (4) a statement of his reasons for doing so.

PART II
EXEMPT INFORMATION

21 Information accessible to applicant by other means

(1) Information which is reasonably accessible to the applicant otherwise than under section 1 is exempt information.

(2) For the purposes of subsection (1)—
(a) information may be reasonably accessible to the applicant even though it is accessible only on payment, and
(b) information is to be taken to be reasonably accessible to the applicant if it is information which the public authority or any other person is obliged by or under any enactment to communicate (otherwise than by making the information available for inspection) to members of the public on request, whether free of charge or on payment.

(3) For the purposes of subsection (1), information which is held by a public authority and does not fall within subsection (2)(b) is not to be regarded as

reasonably accessible to the applicant merely because the information is available from the public authority itself on request, unless the information is made available in accordance with the authority's publication scheme and any payment required is specified in, or determined in accordance with, the scheme.

22 Information intended for future publication

(1) Information is exempt information if—

(a) the information is held by the public authority with a view to its publication, by the authority or any other person, at some future date (whether determined or not),

(b) the information was already held with a view to such publication at the time when the request for information was made, and

(c) it is reasonable in all the circumstances that the information should be withheld from disclosure until the date referred to in paragraph (a).

(2) The duty to confirm or deny does not arise if, or to the extent that, compliance with section 1(1)(a) would involve the disclosure of any information (whether or not already recorded) which falls within subsection (1).

[22A Research

(1) Information obtained in the course of, or derived from, a programme of research is exempt information if—

(a) the programme is continuing with a view to the publication, by a public authority or any other person, of a report of the research (whether or not including a statement of that information), and

(b) disclosure of the information under this Act before the date of publication would, or would be likely to, prejudice—

(i) the programme,

(ii) the interests of any individual participating in the programme,

(iii) the interests of the authority which holds the information, or

(iv) the interests of the authority mentioned in paragraph (a) (if it is a different authority from that which holds the information).

(2) The duty to confirm or deny does not arise in relation to information which is (or if it were held by the public authority would be) exempt information by virtue of subsection (1) if, or to the extent that, compliance with section 1(1)(a) would, or would be likely to, prejudice any of the matters mentioned in subsection (1)(b).]

23 Information supplied by, or relating to, bodies dealing with security matters

(1) Information held by a public authority is exempt information if it was directly or indirectly supplied to the public authority by, or relates to, any of the bodies specified in subsection (3).

(2) A certificate signed by a Minister of the Crown certifying that the information to which it applies was directly or indirectly supplied by, or relates to, any of the bodies specified in subsection (3) shall, subject to section 60, be conclusive evidence of that fact.

(3) The bodies referred to in subsections (1) and (2) are—

(a) the Security Service,

(b) the Secret Intelligence Service,

(c) the Government Communications Headquarters,

(d) the special forces,

(e) the Tribunal established under section 65 of the Regulation of Investigatory Powers Act 2000,

(f) the Tribunal established under section 7 of the Interception of Communications Act 1985,

(g) the Tribunal established under section 5 of the Security Service Act 1989,

(h) the Tribunal established under section 9 of the Intelligence Services Act 1994,
(i) the Security Vetting Appeals Panel,
(j) the Security Commission,
(k) the National Criminal Intelligence Service,
(l) the Service Authority for the National Criminal Intelligence Service,
[(m) the Serious Organised Crime Agency],
[(n) the National Crime Agency,]
[(o) the Intelligence and Security Committee of Parliament.]

(4) In subsection (3)(c) 'the Government Communications Headquarters' includes any unit or part of a unit of the armed forces of the Crown which is for the time being required by the Secretary of State to assist the Government Communications Headquarters in carrying out its functions.

(5) The duty to confirm or deny does not arise if, or to the extent that, compliance with section 1(1)(a) would involve the disclosure of any information (whether or not already recorded) which was directly or indirectly supplied to the public authority by, or relates to, any of the bodies specified in subsection (3).

24 National security

(1) Information which does not fall within section 23(1) is exempt information if exemption from section 1(1)(b) is required for the purpose of safeguarding national security.

(2) The duty to confirm or deny does not arise if, or to the extent that, exemption from section 1(1)(a) is required for the purpose of safeguarding national security.

(3) A certificate signed by a Minister of the Crown certifying that exemption from section 1(1)(b), or from section 1(1)(a) and (b), is, or at any time was, required for the purpose of safeguarding national security shall, subject to section 60, be conclusive evidence of that fact.

(4) A certificate under subsection (3) may identify the information to which it applies by means of a general description and may be expressed to have prospective effect.

25 Certificates under ss 23 and 24: supplementary provisions

(1) A document purporting to be a certificate under section 23(2) or 24(3) shall be received in evidence and deemed to be such a certificate unless the contrary is proved.

(2) A document which purports to be certified by or on behalf of a Minister of the Crown as a true copy of a certificate issued by that Minister under section 23 (2) or 24(3) shall in any legal proceedings be evidence (or, in Scotland, sufficient evidence) of that certificate.

(3) The power conferred by section 23(2) or 24(3) on a Minister of the Crown shall not be exercisable except by a Minister who is a member of the Cabinet or by the Attorney General, the Advocate General for Scotland or the Attorney General for Northern Ireland.

26 Defence

(1) Information is exempt information if its disclosure under this Act would, or would be likely to, prejudice—
(a) the defence of the British Islands or of any colony, or
(b) the capability, effectiveness or security of any relevant forces.

(2) In subsection (1)(b) 'relevant forces' means—
(a) the armed forces of the Crown, and
(b) any forces co-operating with those forces,
or any part of any of those forces.

(3) The duty to confirm or deny does not arise if, or to the extent that,

compliance with section 1(1)(a) would, or would be likely to, prejudice any of the matters mentioned in subsection (1).

27 International relations

(1) Information is exempt information if its disclosure under this Act would, or would be likely to, prejudice—

(a) relations between the United Kingdom and any other State,

(b) relations between the United Kingdom and any international organisation or international court,

(c) the interests of the United Kingdom abroad, or

(d) the promotion or protection by the United Kingdom of its interests abroad.

(2) Information is also exempt information if it is confidential information obtained from a State other than the United Kingdom or from an international organisation or international court.

(3) For the purposes of this section, any information obtained from a State, organisation or court is confidential at any time while the terms on which it was obtained require it to be held in confidence or while the circumstances in which it was obtained make it reasonable for the State, organisation or court to expect that it will be so held.

(4) The duty to confirm or deny does not arise if, or to the extent that, compliance with section 1(1)(a)—

(a) would, or would be likely to, prejudice any of the matters mentioned in subsection (1), or

(b) would involve the disclosure of any information (whether or not already recorded) which is confidential information obtained from a State other than the United Kingdom or from an international organisation or international court.

(5) In this section—

'international court' means any international court which is not an international organisation and which is established—

(a) by a resolution of an international organisation of which the United Kingdom is a member, or

(b) by an international agreement to which the United Kingdom is a party;

'international organisation' means any international organisation whose members include any two or more States, or any organ of such an organisation;

'State' includes the government of any State and any organ of its government, and references to a State other than the United Kingdom include references to any territory outside the United Kingdom.

28 Relations within the United Kingdom

(1) Information is exempt information if its disclosure under this Act would, or would be likely to, prejudice relations between any administration in the United Kingdom and any other such administration.

(2) In subsection (1) 'administration in the United Kingdom' means—

(a) the government of the United Kingdom,

(b) the Scottish Administration,

(c) the Executive Committee of the Northern Ireland Assembly, or

(d) [the Welsh Assembly Government].

(3) The duty to confirm or deny does not arise if, or to the extent that, compliance with section 1(1)(a) would, or would be likely to, prejudice any of the matters mentioned in subsection (1).

29 The economy

(1) Information is exempt information if its disclosure under this Act would, or would be likely to, prejudice—

(a) the economic interests of the United Kingdom or of any part of the United Kingdom, or

(b) the financial interests of any administration in the United Kingdom, as defined by section 28(2).

(2) The duty to confirm or deny does not arise if, or to the extent that, compliance with section 1(1)(a) would, or would be likely to, prejudice any of the matters mentioned in subsection (1).

30 Investigations and proceedings conducted by public authorities

(1) Information held by a public authority is exempt information if it has at any time been held by the authority for the purposes of—

(a) any investigation which the public authority has a duty to conduct with a view to it being ascertained—

(i) whether a person should be charged with an offence, or

(ii) whether a person charged with an offence is guilty of it,

(b) any investigation which is conducted by the authority and in the circumstances may lead to a decision by the authority to institute criminal proceedings which the authority has power to conduct, or

(c) any criminal proceedings which the authority has power to conduct.

(2) Information held by a public authority is exempt information if—

(a) it was obtained or recorded by the authority for the purposes of its functions relating to—

(i) investigations falling within subsection (1)(a) or (b),

(ii) criminal proceedings which the authority has power to conduct,

(iii) investigations (other than investigations falling within subsection (1)(a) or (b)) which are conducted by the authority for any of the purposes specified in section 31(2) and either by virtue of Her Majesty's prerogative or by virtue of powers conferred by or under any enactment, or

(iv) civil proceedings which are brought by or on behalf of the authority and arise out of such investigations, and

(b) it relates to the obtaining of information from confidential sources.

(3) The duty to confirm or deny does not arise in relation to information which is (or if it were held by the public authority would be) exempt information by virtue of subsection (1) or (2).

(4) In relation to the institution or conduct of criminal proceedings or the power to conduct them, references in subsection (1)(b) or (c) and subsection (2)(a) to the public authority include references—

(a) to any officer of the authority,

(b) in the case of a government department other than a Northern Ireland department, to the Minister of the Crown in charge of the department, and

(c) in the case of a Northern Ireland department, to the Northern Ireland Minister in charge of the department.

[(5) In this section—

'criminal proceedings' includes service law proceedings (as defined by section 324(5) of the Armed Forces Act 2006);

'offence' includes a service offence (as defined by section 50 of that Act).]

(6) In the application of this section to Scotland—

(a) in subsection (1)(b), for the words from 'a decision' to the end there is substituted 'a decision by the authority to make a report to the procurator fiscal for the purpose of enabling him to determine whether criminal proceedings should be instituted',

(b) in subsections (1)(c) and (2)(a)(ii) for 'which the authority has power to conduct' there is substituted 'which have been instituted in consequence of a report made by the authority to the procurator fiscal', and

(c) for any reference to a person being charged with an offence there is substituted a reference to the person being prosecuted for the offence.

31 Law enforcement

(1) Information which is not exempt information by virtue of section 30 is

exempt information if its disclosure under this Act would, or would be likely to, prejudice—

(a) the prevention or detection of crime,

(b) the apprehension or prosecution of offenders,

(c) the administration of justice,

(d) the assessment or collection of any tax or duty or of any imposition of a similar nature,

(e) the operation of the immigration controls,

(f) the maintenance of security and good order in prisons or in other institutions where persons are lawfully detained,

(g) the exercise by any public authority of its functions for any of the purposes specified in subsection (2),

(h) any civil proceedings which are brought by or on behalf of a public authority and arise out of an investigation conducted, for any of the purposes specified in subsection (2), by or on behalf of the authority by virtue of Her Majesty's prerogative or by virtue of powers conferred by or under an enactment, or

(i) any inquiry held under the [Inquiries into Fatal Accidents and Sudden Deaths etc (Scotland) Act 2016] to the extent that the inquiry arises out of an investigation conducted, for any of the purposes specified in subsection (2), by or on behalf of the authority by virtue of Her Majesty's prerogative or by virtue of powers conferred by or under an enactment.

(2) The purposes referred to in subsection (1)(g) to (i) are—

(a) the purpose of ascertaining whether any person has failed to comply with the law,

(b) the purpose of ascertaining whether any person is responsible for any conduct which is improper,

(c) the purpose of ascertaining whether circumstances which would justify regulatory action in pursuance of any enactment exist or may arise,

(d) the purpose of ascertaining a person's fitness or competence in relation to the management of bodies corporate or in relation to any profession or other activity which he is, or seeks to become, authorised to carry on,

(e) the purpose of ascertaining the cause of an accident,

(f) the purpose of protecting charities against misconduct or mismanagement (whether by trustees or other persons) in their administration,

(g) the purpose of protecting the property of charities from loss or misapplication,

(h) the purpose of recovering the property of charities,

(i) the purpose of securing the health, safety and welfare of persons at work, and

(j) the purpose of protecting persons other than persons at work against risk to health or safety arising out of or in connection with the actions of persons at work.

(3) The duty to confirm or deny does not arise if, or to the extent that, compliance with section 1(1)(a) would, or would be likely to, prejudice any of the matters mentioned in subsection (1).

33 Audit functions

(1) This section applies to any public authority which has functions in relation to—

(a) the audit of the accounts of other public authorities, or

(b) the examination of the economy, efficiency and effectiveness with which other public authorities use their resources in discharging their functions.

(2) Information held by a public authority to which this section applies is exempt information if its disclosure would, or would be likely to, prejudice the exercise of any of the authority's functions in relation to any of the matters referred to in subsection (1).

(3) The duty to confirm or deny does not arise in relation to a public authority

to which this section applies if, or to the extent that, compliance with section 1(1)(a) would, or would be likely to, prejudice the exercise of any of the authority's functions in relation to any of the matters referred to in subsection (1).

34 Parliamentary privilege

(1) Information is exempt information if exemption from section 1(1)(b) is required for the purpose of avoiding an infringement of the privileges of either House of Parliament.

(2) The duty to confirm or deny does not apply if, or to the extent that, exemption from section 1(1)(a) is required for the purpose of avoiding an infringement of the privileges of either House of Parliament.

(3) A certificate signed by the appropriate authority certifying that exemption from section 1(1)(b), or from section 1(1)(a) and (b), is, or at any time was, required for the purpose of avoiding an infringement of the privileges of either House of Parliament shall be conclusive evidence of that fact.

(4) In subsection (3) 'the appropriate authority' means—

(a) in relation to the House of Commons, the Speaker of that House, and

(b) in relation to the House of Lords, the Clerk of the Parliaments.

35 Formulation of government policy, etc

(1) Information held by a government department or by [the Welsh Assembly Government] is exempt information if it relates to—

(a) the formulation or development of government policy,

(b) Ministerial communications,

(c) the provision of advice by any of the Law Officers or any request for the provision of such advice, or

(d) the operation of any Ministerial private office.

(2) Once a decision as to government policy has been taken, any statistical information used to provide an informed background to the taking of the decision is not to be regarded—

(a) for the purposes of subsection (1)(a), as relating to the formulation or development of government policy, or

(b) for the purposes of subsection (1)(b), as relating to Ministerial communications.

(3) The duty to confirm or deny does not arise in relation to information which is (or if it were held by the public authority would be) exempt information by virtue of subsection (1).

(4) In making any determination required by section 2(1)(b) or (2)(b) in relation to information which is exempt information by virtue of subsection (1)(a), regard shall be had to the particular public interest in the disclosure of factual information which has been used, or is intended to be used, to provide an informed background to decision-taking.

(5) In this section—

'government policy' includes the policy of the Executive Committee of the Northern Ireland Assembly and the policy of [the Welsh Assembly Government];

'the Law Officers' means the Attorney General, the Solicitor General, the Advocate General for Scotland, the Lord Advocate, the Solicitor General for Scotland [, the Counsel General to the Welsh Assembly Government] and the Attorney General for Northern Ireland;

'Ministerial communications' means any communications—

(a) between Ministers of the Crown,

(b) between Northern Ireland Ministers, including Northern Ireland junior Ministers, or

(c) [between members of the Welsh Assembly Government],

and includes, in particular, proceedings of the Cabinet or of any committee of the Cabinet, proceedings of the Executive Committee of the Northern Ireland

Assembly, and proceedings of [the Cabinet or any committee of the Welsh Assembly Government];

'Ministerial private office' means any part of a government department which provides personal administrative support to a Minister of the Crown, to a Northern Ireland Minister or a Northern Ireland junior Minister or [any part of the administration of the Welsh Assembly Government providing personal administrative support to the members of the Welsh Assembly Government];

'Northern Ireland junior Minister' means a member of the Northern Ireland Assembly appointed as a junior Minister under section 19 of the Northern Ireland Act 1998.

36 Prejudice to effective conduct of public affairs

(1) This section applies to—

(a) information which is held by a government department or by [the Welsh Assembly Government] and is not exempt information by virtue of section 35, and

(b) information which is held by any other public authority.

(2) Information to which this section applies is exempt information if, in the reasonable opinion of a qualified person, disclosure of the information under this Act—

(a) would, or would be likely to, prejudice—

(i) the maintenance of the convention of the collective responsibility of Ministers of the Crown, or

(ii) the work of the Executive Committee of the Northern Ireland Assembly, or

(iii) [the work of the Cabinet of the Welsh Assembly Government],

(b) would, or would be likely to, inhibit—

(i) the free and frank provision of advice, or

(ii) the free and frank exchange of views for the purposes of deliberation, or

(c) would otherwise prejudice, or would be likely otherwise to prejudice, the effective conduct of public affairs.

(3) The duty to confirm or deny does not arise in relation to information to which this section applies (or would apply if held by the public authority) if, or to the extent that, in the reasonable opinion of a qualified person, compliance with section 1(1)(a) would, or would be likely to, have any of the effects mentioned in subsection (2).

(4) In relation to statistical information, subsections (2) and (3) shall have effect with the omission of the words 'in the reasonable opinion of a qualified person'.

(5) In subsections (2) and (3) 'qualified person'—

(a) in relation to information held by a government department in the charge of a Minister of the Crown, means any Minister of the Crown,

(b) in relation to information held by a Northern Ireland department, means the Northern Ireland Minister in charge of the department,

(c) in relation to information held by any other government department, means the commissioners or other person in charge of that department,

(d) in relation to information held by the House of Commons, means the Speaker of that House,

(e) in relation to information held by the House of Lords, means the Clerk of the Parliaments,

(f) in relation to information held by the Northern Ireland Assembly, means the Presiding Officer,

[(g) in relation to information held by the Welsh Assembly Government, means the Welsh Ministers or the Counsel General to the Welsh Assembly Government,

(ga) in relation to information held by the National Assembly for Wales, means the Presiding Officer of the National Assembly for Wales, (gb) in relation to information held by any Welsh public authority (other than one referred to in section 83(1)(b)(ii)(subsidiary of the Assembly Commission), the Auditor General for Wales [, the Wales Audit Office] or the Public Services Ombudsman for Wales), means—

(i) the public authority, or

(ii) any officer or employee of the authority authorised by the Welsh Ministers or the Counsel General to the Welsh Assembly Government,

(gc) in relation to information held by a Welsh public authority referred to in section 83(1)(b)(ii), means—

(i) the public authority, or

(ii) any officer or employee of the authority authorised by the Presiding Officer of the National Assembly for Wales,]

(i) in relation to information held by the National Audit Office [or the Comptroller and Auditor General], means the Comptroller and Auditor General,

(j) in relation to information held by the Northern Ireland Audit Office, means the Comptroller and Auditor General for Northern Ireland,

(k) in relation to information held by the Auditor General for Wales, [or the Wales Audit Office] means the Auditor General for Wales,

[(ka) in relation to information held by the Public Services Ombudsman for Wales, means the Public Services Ombudsman for Wales,]

(l) in relation to information held by any Northern Ireland public authority other than the Northern Ireland Audit Office, means—

(i) the public authority, or

(ii) any officer or employee of the authority authorised by the First Minister and deputy First Minister in Northern Ireland acting jointly,

(m) in relation to information held by the Greater London Authority, means the Mayor of London,

(n) in relation to information held by a functional body within the meaning of the Greater London Authority Act 1999, means the chairman of that functional body, and

(o) in relation to information held by any public authority not falling within any of paragraphs (a) to (n), means—

(i) a Minister of the Crown,

(ii) the public authority, if authorised for the purposes of this section by a Minister of the Crown, or

(iii) any officer or employee of the public authority who is authorised for the purposes of this section by a Minister of the Crown.

(6) Any authorisation for the purposes of this section—

(a) may relate to a specified person or to persons falling within a specified class,

(b) may be general or limited to particular classes of case, and

(c) may be granted subject to conditions.

(7) A certificate signed by the qualified person referred to in subsection (5)(d) or (e) above certifying that in his reasonable opinion—

(a) disclosure of information held by either House of Parliament, or

(b) compliance with section 1(1)(a) by either House,

would, or would be likely to, have any of the effects mentioned in subsection (2) shall be conclusive evidence of that fact.

37 Communications with Her Majesty, etc and honours

(1) Information is exempt information if it relates to—

[(a) communications with the Sovereign,

(aa) communications with the heir to, or the person who is for the time being second in line of succession to, the Throne,

(ab) communications with a person who has subsequently acceded to the Throne or become heir to, or second in line to, the Throne, (ac) communications with other members of the Royal Family (other than communications which fall within any of paragraphs (a) to (ab) because they are made or received on behalf of a person falling within any of those paragraphs), and

(ad) communications with the Royal Household (other than communications which fall within any of paragraphs (a) to (ac) because they are made or received on behalf of a person falling within any of those paragraphs), or]

(b) the conferring by the Crown of any honour or dignity.

(2) The duty to confirm or deny does not arise in relation to information which is (or if it were held by the public authority would be) exempt information by virtue of subsection (1).

42 Legal professional privilege

(1) Information in respect of which a claim to legal professional privilege or, in Scotland, to confidentiality of communications could be maintained in legal proceedings is exempt information.

(2) The duty to confirm or deny does not arise if, or to the extent that, compliance with section 1(1)(a) would involve the disclosure of any information (whether or not already recorded) in respect of which such a claim could be maintained in legal proceedings.

43 Commercial interests

(1) Information is exempt information if it constitutes a trade secret.

(2) Information is exempt information if its disclosure under this Act would, or would be likely to, prejudice the commercial interests of any person (including the public authority holding it).

(3) The duty to confirm or deny does not arise if, or to the extent that, compliance with section 1(1)(a) would, or would be likely to, prejudice the interests mentioned in subsection (2).

44 Prohibitions on disclosure

(1) Information is exempt information if its disclosure (otherwise than under this Act) by the public authority holding it—

(a) is prohibited by or under any enactment,

(b) is incompatible with any [EU] obligation, or

(c) would constitute or be punishable as a contempt of court.

(2) The duty to confirm or deny does not arise if the confirmation or denial that would have to be given to comply with section 1(1)(a) would (apart from this Act) fall within any of paragraphs (a) to (c) of subsection (1).

PART IV
ENFORCEMENT

50 Application for decision by Commissioner

(1) Any person (in this section referred to as 'the complainant') may apply to the Commissioner for a decision whether, in any specified respect, a request for information made by the complainant to a public authority has been dealt with in accordance with the requirements of Part I.

(2) On receiving an application under this section, the Commissioner shall make a decision unless it appears to him—

(a) that the complainant has not exhausted any complaints procedure which is provided by the public authority in conformity with the code of practice under section 45,

(b) that there has been undue delay in making the application,

(c) that the application is frivolous or vexatious, or

(d) that the application has been withdrawn or abandoned.

(3) Where the Commissioner has received an application under this section, he shall either—

(a) notify the complainant that he has not made any decision under this section as a result of the application and of his grounds for not doing so, or

(b) serve notice of his decision (in this Act referred to as a 'decision notice') on the complainant and the public authority.

(4) Where the Commissioner decides that a public authority—

(a) has failed to communicate information, or to provide confirmation or denial, in a case where it is required to do so by section 1(1), or

(b) has failed to comply with any of the requirements of sections 11 and 17,

the decision notice must specify the steps which must be taken by the authority for complying with that requirement and the period within which they must be taken.

(5) A decision notice must contain particulars of the right of appeal conferred by section 57.

(6) Where a decision notice requires steps to be taken by the public authority within a specified period, the time specified in the notice must not expire before the end of the period within which an appeal can be brought against the notice and, if such an appeal is brought, no step which is affected by the appeal need be taken pending the determination or withdrawal of the appeal.

(7) This section has effect subject to section 53.

51 Information notices

(1) If the Commissioner—

(a) has received an application under section 50, or

(b) reasonably requires any information—

(i) for the purpose of determining whether a public authority has complied or is complying with any of the requirements of Part I, or

(ii) for the purpose of determining whether the practice of a public authority in relation to the exercise of its functions under this Act conforms with that proposed in the codes of practice under sections 45 and 46,

he may serve the authority with a notice (in this Act referred to as 'an information notice') requiring it, within such time as is specified in the notice, to furnish the Commissioner, in such form as may be so specified, with such information relating to the application, to compliance with Part I or to conformity with the code of practice as is so specified.

(2) An information notice must contain—

(a) in a case falling within subsection (1)(a), a statement that the Commissioner has received an application under section 50, or

(b) in a case falling within subsection (1)(b), a statement—

(i) that the Commissioner regards the specified information as relevant for either of the purposes referred to in subsection (1)(b), and

(ii) of his reasons for regarding that information as relevant for that purpose.

(3) An information notice must also contain particulars of the right of appeal conferred by section 57.

(4) The time specified in an information notice must not expire before the end of the period within which an appeal can be brought against the notice and, if such an appeal is brought, the information need not be furnished pending the determination or withdrawal of the appeal.

(5) An authority shall not be required by virtue of this section to furnish the Commissioner with any information in respect of—

(a) any communication between a professional legal adviser and his client in connection with the giving of legal advice to the client with respect to his obligations, liabilities or rights under this Act, or

(b) any communication between a professional legal adviser and his client, or between such an adviser or his client and any other person, made in connection with or in contemplation of proceedings under or arising out of this Act (including proceedings before the Tribunal) and for the purposes of such proceedings.

(6) In subsection (5) references to the client of a professional legal adviser include references to any person representing such a client.

(7) The Commissioner may cancel an information notice by written notice to the authority on which it was served.

(8) In this section 'information' includes unrecorded information.

52 Enforcement notices

(1) If the Commissioner is satisfied that a public authority has failed to comply with any of the requirements of Part I, the Commissioner may serve the authority with a notice (in this Act referred to as 'an enforcement notice') requiring the authority to take, within such time as may be specified in the notice, such steps as may be so specified for complying with those requirements.

(2) An enforcement notice must contain—

(a) a statement of the requirement or requirements of Part I with which the Commissioner is satisfied that the public authority has failed to comply and his reasons for reaching that conclusion, and

(b) particulars of the right of appeal conferred by section 57.

(3) An enforcement notice must not require any of the provisions of the notice to be complied with before the end of the period within which an appeal can be brought against the notice and, if such an appeal is brought, the notice need not be complied with pending the determination or withdrawal of the appeal.

(4) The Commissioner may cancel an enforcement notice by written notice to the authority on which it was served.

(5) This section has effect subject to section 53.

53 Exception from duty to comply with decision notice or enforcement notice

(1) This section applies to a decision notice or enforcement notice which—

(a) is served on—

(i) a government department,

(ii) [the Welsh Assembly Government, or]

(iii) any public authority designated for the purposes of this section by an order made by the [Minister for the Cabinet Office], and

(b) relates to a failure, in respect of one or more requests for information—

(i) to comply with section 1(1)(a) in respect of information which falls within any provision of Part II stating that the duty to confirm or deny does not arise, or

(ii) to comply with section 1(1)(b) in respect of exempt information.

(2) A decision notice or enforcement notice to which this section applies shall cease to have effect if, not later than the twentieth working day following the effective date, the accountable person in relation to that authority gives the Commissioner a certificate signed by him stating that he has on reasonable grounds formed the opinion that, in respect of the request or requests concerned, there was no failure falling within subsection (1)(b).

(3) Where the accountable person gives a certificate to the Commissioner under subsection (2) he shall as soon as practicable thereafter lay a copy of the certificate before—

(a) each House of Parliament,

(b) the Northern Ireland Assembly, in any case where the certificate relates to a decision notice or enforcement notice which has been served on a Northern Ireland department or any Northern Ireland public authority, or

(c) [the National Assembly for Wales, in any case where the certificate relates to a decision notice or enforcement notice which has been served on—

(i) the Welsh Assembly Government,

(ii) the National Assembly for Wales, or

(iii) any Welsh public authority.]

(4) In subsection (2) 'the effective date', in relation to a decision notice or enforcement notice, means—

(a) the day on which the notice was given to the public authority, or

(b) where an appeal under section 57 is brought, the day on which that appeal (or any further appeal arising out of it) is determined or withdrawn.

(5) Before making an order under subsection (1)(a)(iii), the [Minister for the Cabinet Office] shall—

(a) if the order relates to a Welsh public authority, consult [the Welsh Ministers],

[(aa) if the order relates to the National Assembly for Wales, consult the Presiding Officer of that Assembly,]

(b) if the order relates to the Northern Ireland Assembly, consult the Presiding Officer of that Assembly, and

(c) if the order relates to a Northern Ireland public authority, consult the First Minister and deputy First Minister in Northern Ireland.

(6) Where the accountable person gives a certificate to the Commissioner under subsection (2) in relation to a decision notice, the accountable person shall, on doing so or as soon as reasonably practicable after doing so, inform the person who is the complainant for the purposes of section 50 of the reasons for his opinion.

(7) The accountable person is not obliged to provide information under subsection (6) if, or to the extent that, compliance with that subsection would involve the disclosure of exempt information.

(8) In this section 'the accountable person'—

(a) in relation to a Northern Ireland department or any Northern Ireland public authority, means the First Minister and deputy First Minister in Northern Ireland acting jointly,

(b) [in relation to the Welsh Assembly Government, the National Assembly for Wales or any Welsh public authority, means the First Minister for Wales, and]

(c) in relation to any other public authority, means—

(i) a Minister of the Crown who is a member of the Cabinet, or

(ii) the Attorney General, the Advocate General for Scotland or the Attorney General for Northern Ireland.

(9) In this section 'working day' has the same meaning as in section 10.

54 Failure to comply with notice

(1) If a public authority has failed to comply with—

(a) so much of a decision notice as requires steps to be taken,

(b) an information notice, or

(c) an enforcement notice,

the Commissioner may certify in writing to the court that the public authority has failed to comply with that notice.

(2) For the purposes of this section, a public authority which, in purported compliance with an information notice—

(a) makes a statement which it knows to be false in a material respect, or

(b) recklessly makes a statement which is false in a material respect,

is to be taken to have failed to comply with the notice.

(3) Where a failure to comply is certified under subsection (1), the court may inquire into the matter and, after hearing any witness who may be produced against or on behalf of the public authority, and after hearing any statement that may be offered in defence, deal with the authority as if it had committed a contempt of court.

(4) In this section 'the court' means the High Court or, in Scotland, the Court of Session.

PART V
APPEALS

57 Appeal against notices served under Part IV

(1) Where a decision notice has been served, the complainant or the public authority may appeal to the Tribunal against the notice.

(2) A public authority on which an information notice or an enforcement notice has been served by the Commissioner may appeal to the Tribunal against the notice.

(3) In relation to a decision notice or enforcement notice which relates—

(a) to information to which section 66 applies, and

(b) to a matter which by virtue of subsection (3) or (4) of that section falls to be determined by the responsible authority instead of the appropriate records authority,

subsections (1) and (2) shall have effect as if the reference to the public authority were a reference to the public authority or the responsible authority.

58 Determination of appeals

(1) If on an appeal under section 57 the Tribunal considers—

(a) that the notice against which the appeal is brought is not in accordance with the law, or

(b) to the extent that the notice involved an exercise of discretion by the Commissioner, that he ought to have exercised his discretion differently,

the Tribunal shall allow the appeal or substitute such other notice as could have been served by the Commissioner; and in any other case the Tribunal shall dismiss the appeal.

(2) On such an appeal, the Tribunal may review any finding of fact on which the notice in question was based.

[. . .]

PART VIII
MISCELLANEOUS AND SUPPLEMENTAL

77 Offence of altering etc records with intent to prevent disclosure

(1) Where—

(a) a request for information has been made to a public authority, and

(b) under section 1 of this Act [. . .], the applicant would have been entitled (subject to payment of any fee) to communication of any information in accordance with that section,

any person to whom this subsection applies is guilty of an offence if he alters, defaces, blocks, erases, destroys or conceals any record held by the public authority, with the intention of preventing the disclosure by that authority of all, or any part, of the information to the communication of which the applicant would have been entitled.

(2) Subsection (1) applies to the public authority and to any person who is employed by, is an officer of, or is subject to the direction of, the public authority.

(3) A person guilty of an offence under this section is liable on summary conviction to a fine not exceeding level 5 on the standard scale.

(4) No proceedings for an offence under this section shall be instituted—

(a) in England or Wales, except by the Commissioner or by or with the consent of the Director of Public Prosecutions;

(b) in Northern Ireland, except by the Commissioner or by or with the consent of the Director of Public Prosecutions for Northern Ireland.

POLITICAL PARTIES, ELECTIONS AND REFERENDUMS ACT 2000
(2000, c 41)

1 Establishment of the Electoral Commission

(1) There shall be a body corporate to be known as the Electoral Commission or, in Welsh, Comisiwn Etholiadol (in this Act referred to as 'the Commission').

(2) The Commission shall consist of members to be known as Electoral Commissioners.

(3) There shall be [nine or ten] Electoral Commissioners.

(4) The Electoral Commissioners shall be appointed by Her Majesty (in accordance with section 3).

(5) Her Majesty shall (in accordance with section 3) [but subject to section 3A (6)] appoint one of the Electoral Commissioners to be the chairman of the Commission.

(6) Schedule 1, which makes further provision in relation to the Commission, shall have effect.

2 Speaker's Committee

(1) There shall be a Committee (to be known as 'the Speaker's Committee') to perform the functions conferred on the Committee by this Act.

(2) The Speaker's Committee shall consist of the Speaker of the House of Commons, who shall be the chairman of the Committee, and the following other members, namely—

(a) the Member of the House of Commons who is for the time being the Chairman of the Home Affairs Select Committee of the House of Commons;

(b) [Minister for the Cabinet Office;]

(c) a Member of the House of Commons who is a Minister of the Crown with responsibilities in relation to local government; and

(d) five Members of the House of Commons who are not Ministers of the Crown.

(3) The member of the Committee mentioned in subsection (2)(c) shall be appointed to membership of the Committee by the Prime Minister.

(4) The members of the Committee mentioned in subsection (2)(d) shall be appointed to membership of the Committee by the Speaker of the House of Commons.

(5) Schedule 2, which makes further provision in relation to the Speaker's Committee, shall have effect.

(6) In this section and that Schedule, references to the Home Affairs Select Committee shall—

(a) if the name of that Committee is changed, be taken (subject to paragraph (b)) to be references to the Committee by its new name;

(b) if the functions of that Committee at the passing of this Act with respect to electoral matters (or functions substantially corresponding thereto) become functions of a different committee of the House of Commons, be taken to be references to the committee by whom the functions are for the time being exercisable.

22 Parties to be registered in order to field candidates at elections

(1) Subject to subsection (4), no nomination may be made in relation to a relevant election unless the nomination is in respect of—

(a) a person who stands for election in the name of a qualifying registered party; or

(b) a person who does not purport to represent any party; or

(c) a qualifying registered party, where the election is one for which registered parties may be nominated.

(2) For the purposes of subsection (1) a party (other than a minor party) is a 'qualifying registered party' in relation to a relevant election if—

(a) the constituency, [police area,] local government area or electoral region in which the election is held—

(i) is in England, Scotland or Wales, or

(ii) is the electoral region of Scotland or Wales,

and the party was, [on the day ('the relevant day') which is two days before the last day for the delivery of nomination papers at that election], registered in respect of that part of Great Britain in the Great Britain register maintained by the Commission under section 23, or

(b) the constituency, district electoral area or electoral region in which the election is held—

(i) is in Northern Ireland, or

(ii) is the electoral region of Northern Ireland,

and the party was, [on the relevant day], registered in the Northern Ireland register maintained by the Commission under that section.

[(2A) For the purposes of subsection (2) any day falling within rule 2(1) of the parliamentary elections rule in Schedule 1 to the Representation of the People Act 1983 [(subject to rule 2(2A))] shall be disregarded.]

(3) For the purposes of subsection (1) a person does not purport to represent any party if either—

(a) the description of the candidate given in his nomination paper, is—

(i) 'Independent', or

(ii) where the candidate is the Speaker of the House of Commons seeking re-election, 'The Speaker seeking re-election'; or

(b) no description of the candidate is given in his nomination paper.

(4) Subsection (1) does not apply in relation to any parish or community election.

(5) The following elections are relevant elections for the purposes of this Part—

(a) parliamentary elections,

(b) elections to the European Parliament,

(c) elections to the Scottish Parliament,

(d) elections to the National Assembly for Wales,

(e) elections to the Northern Ireland Assembly,

[(ea) elections of police and crime commissioners,]

(f) local government elections, and

(g) local elections in Northern Ireland.

(6) For the purposes of this Act a person stands for election in the name of a registered party if his nomination paper includes a description authorised by a certificate issued by or on behalf of the registered nominating officer of the party.

37 Party political broadcasts

(1) A broadcaster shall not include in its broadcasting services any party political broadcast made on behalf of a party which is not a registered party.

(2) In this Act 'broadcaster' means—

(a) the holder of a licence under the Broadcasting Act 1990 or 1996,

(b) the British Broadcasting Corporation, or

(c) Sianel Pedwar Cymru.

[(3) The reference in subsection (1) to a broadcaster includes a reference to the Gibraltar Broadcasting Corporation, but only as respects party political broadcasts relating to elections to the European Parliament.]

54 Permissible donors

(1) A donation received by a registered party must not be accepted by the party if—

(a) the person by whom the donation would be made is not, at the time of its receipt by the party, a permissible donor; or

(b) the party is (whether because the donation is given anonymously or by reason of any deception or concealment or otherwise) unable to ascertain the identity of that person.

(2) For the purposes of this Part the following are permissible donors—

(a) an individual registered in an electoral register;

(b) a company—

(i) [registered under the Companies Act 2006], and

(ii) incorporated within the United Kingdom or another member State,

which carries on business in the United Kingdom;

(c) a registered party [other than a Gibraltar party whose entry in the register includes a statement that it intends to contest one or more elections to the European Parliament in the combined region;]

(d) a trade union entered in the list kept under the Trade Union and Labour Relations (Consolidation) Act 1992 or the Industrial Relations (Northern Ireland) Order 1992;

(e) a building society (within the meaning of the Building Societies Act 1986);

(f) a limited liability partnership registered under the Limited Liability Partnerships Act 2000, or any corresponding enactment in force in Northern Ireland, which carries on business in the United Kingdom;

(g) a friendly society registered under the Friendly Societies Act 1974 [a registered society within the meaning of the Co-operative and Community Benefit Societies Act 2014 or a society registered or deemed to be registered] under the Industrial and Provident Societies Act (Northern Ireland) 1969; and

(h) any unincorporated association of two or more persons which does not fall within any of the preceding paragraphs but which carries on business or other activities wholly or mainly in the United Kingdom and whose main office is there.

[(2A) As respects a registered party whose entry in the register includes a statement that it intends to contest one or more elections to the European Parliament in the combined region, the following are also permissible donors for the purposes of this Part—

(a) a Gibraltar elector;

[(b) a company—

(i) registered under the Companies Act or the Companies Act 2014 (see section 160(b) below); and

(ii) incorporated within Gibraltar, the United Kingdom or another member State,

which carries on business in Gibraltar;]

(c) a Gibraltar party whose entry in the register includes a statement that it intends to contest one or more elections to the European Parliament in the combined region;

(d) a trade union within the meaning of the [Trade Unions and Trade Disputes Act];

[. . .]

[(f) a limited partnership registered under the Limited Partnerships Act, which carries on business in Gibraltar;] and

(g) any unincorporated association of two or more persons which does not fall within any of the preceding paragraphs but which carries on business or other activities wholly or mainly in Gibraltar and whose main office is there,

but, in the case of a party other than a Gibraltar party, only where the donation is received by the party within the period of four months ending with the date of the poll for an election to the European Parliament in the combined region.]

(3) In relation to a donation in the form of a bequest subsection (2)(a) shall be read as referring to an individual who was, at any time within the period of five years ending with the date of his death, registered in an electoral register.

[(3A) In relation to a donation in the form of a bequest subsection (2A)(a) shall be read as referring to an individual who was, at any time within the period of five years ending with the date of his death, a Gibraltar elector.]

(4) Where any person ('the principal donor') causes an amount ('the principal donation') to be received by a registered party by way of a donation—

(a) on behalf of himself and one or more other persons, or

(b) on behalf of two or more other persons,

then for the purposes of this Part each individual contribution by a person falling within paragraph (a) or (b) of more than [£500] shall be treated as if it were a separate donation received from that person.

(5) In relation to each such separate donation, the principal donor must ensure that, at the time when the principal donation is received by the party, the party is given—

(a) (except in the case of a donation which the principal donor is treated as making) all such details in respect of the person treated as making the donation as are required by virtue of paragraph 2 [or 2A] of Schedule 6 to be given in respect of the donor of a recordable donation; and

(b) (in any case) all such details in respect of the donation as are required by virtue of paragraph 4 of Schedule 6 to be given in respect of a recordable donation.

(6) Where—

(a) any person ('the agent') causes an amount to be received by a registered party by way of a donation on behalf of another person ('the donor'), and

(b) the amount of that donation is more than [£500],

the agent must ensure that, at the time when the donation is received by the party, the party is given all such details in respect of the donor as are required by virtue of paragraph 2 [or 2A] of Schedule 6 to be given in respect of the donor of a recordable donation.

(7) A person commits an offence if, without reasonable excuse, he fails to comply with subsection (5) or (6).

(8) In this section 'electoral register' means any of the following—

(a) a register of parliamentary or local government electors maintained under section 9 of the Representation of the People Act 1983;

(b) a register of relevant citizens of the European Union prepared under [the European Parliamentary Elections (Franchise of Relevant Citizens of the Union) Regulations 2001]; or

(c) a register of peers prepared under regulations under section 3 of the Representation of the People Act 1985.

56 Acceptance or return of donations: general

(1) Where—

(a) a donation is received by a registered party, and

(b) it is not immediately decided that the party should (for whatever reason) refuse the donation,

all reasonable steps must be taken forthwith by or on behalf of the party to verify (or, so far as any of the following is not apparent, ascertain) the identity of the donor, whether he is a permissible donor, and (if that appears to be the case) all such details in respect of him as are required by virtue of paragraph 2 [or 2A] of Schedule 6 to be given in respect of the donor of a recordable donation.

(2) If a registered party receives a donation which it is prohibited from accepting by virtue of section 54(1), or which it is decided that the party should for any other reason refuse, then—

(a) unless the donation falls within section 54(1)(b), the donation, or a payment of an equivalent amount, must be sent back to the person who made the donation or any person appearing to be acting on his behalf,

(b) if the donation falls within that provision, the required steps (as defined by section 57(1)) must be taken in relation to the donation,

within the period of 30 days beginning with the date when the donation is received by the party.

(3) Where—

(a) subsection (2)(a) applies in relation to a donation, and

(b) the donation is not dealt with in accordance with that provision,

the party and the treasurer of the party are each guilty of an offence.

[(3A) Where a party or its treasurer is charged with an offence under subsection (3), it shall be a deference to prove that—

(a) all reasonable steps were taken by or on behalf of the party to verify (or ascertain) whether the donor was a permissible donor, and

(b) as a result, the treasurer believed the donor to be a permissible donor.]

(4) Where—

(a) subsection (2)(b) applies in relation to a donation, and

(b) the donation is not dealt with in accordance with that provision,

the treasurer of the party is guilty of an offence.

(5) For the purposes of this Part a donation received by a registered party shall be taken to have been accepted by the party unless—

(a) the steps mentioned in paragraph (a) or (b) of subsection (2) are taken in relation to the donation within the period of 30 days mentioned in that subsection; and

(b) a record can be produced of the receipt of the donation and—

(i) of the return of the donation, or the equivalent amount, as mentioned in subsection (2)(a), or

(ii) of the required steps being taken in relation to the donation as mentioned in subsection (2)(b),

as the case may be.

(6) Where a donation is received by a registered party in the form of an amount paid into any account held by the party with a financial institution, it shall be taken for the purposes of this Part to have been received by the party at the time when the party is notified in the usual way of the payment into the account.

57 Return of donations where donor unidentifiable

(1) For the purposes of section 56(2)(b) the required steps are as follows—

(a) if the donation mentioned in that provision was transmitted by a person other than the donor, and the identity of that person is apparent, to return the donation to that person;

(b) if paragraph (a) does not apply but it is apparent that the donor has, in connection with the donation, used any facility provided by an identifiable financial institution, to return the donation to that institution; and

(c) in any other case, to send the donation to the Commission.

(2) In subsection (1) any reference to returning or sending a donation to any person or body includes a reference to sending a payment of an equivalent amount to that person or body.

(3) Any amount sent to the Commission in pursuance of subsection (1)(c) shall be paid by them into the Consolidated Fund.

58 Forfeiture of donations made by impermissible or unidentifiable donors

(1) This section applies to any donation received by a registered party—

(a) which, by virtue of section 54(1)(a) or (b), the party are prohibited from accepting, but

(b) which has been accepted by the party.

(2) The court may, on an application made by the Commission, order the forfeiture by the party of an amount equal to the value of the donation.

(3) The standard of proof in proceedings on an application under this section shall be that applicable to civil proceedings.

(4) An order may be made under this section whether or not proceedings are brought against any person for an offence connected with the donation.

(5) In this section 'the court' means—

(a) in relation to England and Wales, a magistrates' court;

(b) in relation to Scotland, the sheriff; [. . .]
(c) in relation to Northern Ireland, a court of summary jurisdiction; [and]
[(d) in relation to Gibraltar, the Gibraltar court;]
and proceedings on an application under this section to the sheriff shall be civil proceedings.

101 Referendums to which this Part applies

(1) Subject to the following provisions of this section, this Part applies to any referendum held throughout—

(a) the United Kingdom;

(b) one or more of England, Scotland, Wales and Northern Ireland; or

(c) any region in England specified in Schedule 1 to the Regional Development Agencies Act 1998.

(2) In this Part—

(a) 'referendum' means a referendum or other poll held, in pursuance of any provision made by or under an Act of Parliament, on one or more questions specified in or in accordance with any such provision;

(b) 'question' includes proposition (and 'answer' accordingly includes response).

(3) A poll held under [section 64 of the Government of Wales Act 2006] is not, however, to be taken to be a referendum falling within subsection (2).

(4) If the Secretary of State by order so provides—

(a) subsection (2) shall apply to any specified Bill which has been introduced into Parliament before the making of the order as if it were an Act; and

(b) any specified provisions of this Part shall apply, subject to any specified modifications, in relation to any specified referendum for which provision is made by the Bill.

(5) In subsection (4) 'specified' means specified in the order under that subsection.

104 Referendum questions

(1) Subsection (2) applies where a Bill is introduced into Parliament which—

(a) provides for the holding of a poll that would be a referendum to which this Part applies, and

(b) specifies the wording of the referendum question.

(2) The Commission shall consider the wording of the referendum question, and shall publish a statement of any views of the Commission as to the intelligibility of that question—

(a) as soon as reasonably practicable after the Bill is introduced, and

(b) in such manner as they may determine.

(3) Subsections (4) and (5) apply where the wording of the referendum question in the case of any poll that would be a referendum to which this Part applies falls to be specified in subordinate legislation within the meaning of the Interpretation Act 1978.

(4) If a draft of the instrument in question is to be laid before Parliament for approval by each House, the Secretary of State—

(a) shall consult the Commission on the wording of the referendum question before any such draft is so laid, and

(b) shall, at the time when any such draft is so laid, lay before each House a report stating any views as to the intelligibility of that question which the Commission have expressed in response to that consultation.

(5) If the instrument in question is to be subject to annulment in pursuance of a resolution of either House of Parliament, the Secretary of State—

(a) shall consult the Commission on the wording of the referendum question before making the instrument; and

(b) shall, at the time when the instrument is laid before Parliament, lay before each House a report stating any views as to the intelligibility of that question which the Commission have expressed in response to that consultation.

(6) Where any Bill, draft instrument or instrument to which subsection (2), (4) or (5) applies specifies not only the referendum question but also any statement which is to precede that question on the ballot paper at the referendum, any reference in that subsection to the referendum question shall be read as a reference to that question and that statement taken together.

(7) In this section 'the referendum question' means the question or questions to be included in the ballot paper at the referendum.

105 Permitted participants

(1) In this Part 'permitted participant', in relation to a particular referendum to which this Part applies, means—

(a) a registered party by whom a declaration has been made under section 106 in relation to the referendum; or

(b) any of the following by whom a notification has been given under section 106 in relation to the referendum, namely—

(i) any individual resident in the United Kingdom or registered in an electoral register (as defined by section 54(8)), or

(ii) any body falling within any of paragraphs (b) and (d) to (h) of section 54(2).

(2) In this Part 'responsible person' means—

(a) if the permitted participant is a registered party—

(i) the treasurer of the party, or

(ii) in the case of a minor party, the person for the time being notified to the Commission by the party in accordance with section 106(2)(b);

(b) if the permitted participant is an individual, that individual; and

(c) otherwise, the person or officer for the time being notified to the Commission by the permitted participant in accordance with section 106(4)(b)(ii).

108 Designation of organisations to whom assistance is available

(1) The Commission may, in respect of any referendum to which this Part applies, designate permitted participants as organisations to whom assistance is available in accordance with section 110.

(2) Where there are only two possible outcomes in the case of a referendum to which this Part applies, the Commission—

(a) may, in relation to each of those outcomes, designate one permitted participant as representing those campaigning for the outcome in question; but

(b) otherwise shall not make any designation in respect of the referendum.

(3) Where there are more than two possible outcomes in the case of a referendum to which this Part applies, the Secretary of State may, after consulting the Commission, by order specify the possible outcomes in relation to which permitted participants may be designated in accordance with subsection (4).

(4) In such a case the Commission—

(a) may, in relation to each of two or more outcomes specified in any such order, designate one permitted participant as representing those campaigning for the outcome in question; but

(b) otherwise shall not make any designation in respect of the referendum.

110 Assistance available to designated organisations

(1) Where the Commission have made any designations under section 108 in respect of a referendum, assistance shall be available to the designated organisations in accordance with this section.

(2) The Commission shall make to each designated organisation a grant of the same amount, which shall be an amount not exceeding £600,000 determined by the Commission.

(3) A grant under subsection (2) may be made subject to such conditions as the Commission consider appropriate.

(4) Each designated organisation (or, as the case may be, persons authorised by the organisation) shall have the rights conferred by or by virtue of Schedule 12, which makes provision as to—

(a) the sending of referendum addresses free of charge;

(b) the use of rooms free of charge for holding public meetings; and

(c) referendum campaign broadcasts.

(5) In this section and Schedule 12 'designated organisation', in relation to a referendum, means a person or body designated by the Commission under section 108 in respect of that referendum.

113 Restriction on incurring referendum expenses

(1) No amount of referendum expenses shall be incurred by or on behalf of a permitted participant unless it is incurred with the authority of—

(a) the responsible person; or

(b) a person authorised in writing by the responsible person.

(2) A person commits an offence if, without reasonable excuse, he incurs any expenses in contravention of subsection (1).

(3) Where, in the case of a permitted participant that is a registered party, any expenses are incurred in contravention of subsection (1), the expenses shall not count for the purposes of sections 117 to 123 or Schedule 14 as referendum expenses incurred by or on behalf of the permitted participant.

117 General restriction on referendum expenses

(1) The total referendum expenses incurred by or on behalf of any individual or body during the referendum period in the case of a particular referendum to which this Part applies must not exceed £10,000 unless the individual or body is a permitted participant.

(2) Where—

(a) during the referendum period any referendum expenses are incurred by or on behalf of any individual in excess of the limit imposed by subsection (1), and

(b) he is not a permitted participant,

he is guilty of an offence if he knew, or ought reasonably to have known, that the expenses were being incurred in excess of that limit.

(3) Where—

(a) during the referendum period any referendum expenses are incurred by or on behalf of any body in excess of the limit imposed by subsection (1), and

(b) the body is not a permitted participant,

any person who authorised the expenses to be incurred by or on behalf of the body is guilty of an offence if he knew, or ought reasonably to have known, that the expenses would be incurred in excess of that limit.

(4) Where subsection (3)(a) and (b) apply, the body in question is also guilty of an offence.

(5) Where—

(a) at any time before the beginning of any referendum period, any expenses within section 111(2) are incurred by or on behalf of an individual or body in respect of any property, services or facilities, but

(b) the property, services or facilities is or are made use of by or on behalf of the individual or body during the referendum period in circumstances such that, had any expenses been incurred in respect of that use during that period, they would by virtue of section 111(2) have constituted referendum expenses incurred by or on behalf of the individual or body during that period,

the appropriate proportion of the expenses mentioned in paragraph (a) shall be treated for the purposes of this section as referendum expenses incurred by or on behalf of the individual or body during that period.

(6) For the purposes of subsection (5) the appropriate proportion of the expenses mentioned in paragraph (a) of that subsection is such proportion of those expenses as is reasonably attributable to the use made of the property, services or facilities as mentioned in paragraph (b).

127 Referendum campaign broadcasts

(1) A broadcaster shall not include in its broadcasting services any referendum campaign broadcast made on behalf of any person or body other than one designated in respect of the referendum in question under section 108.

(2) In this section 'referendum campaign broadcast' means any broadcast whose purpose (or main purpose) is or may reasonably be assumed to be—

(a) to further any campaign conducted with a view to promoting or procuring a particular outcome in relation to any question asked in a referendum to which this Part applies, or

(b) otherwise to promote or procure any such outcome.

CONVENTION RIGHTS (COMPLIANCE) (SCOTLAND) ACT 2001 (2001, asp 7)

12 Remedial orders

(1) In the circumstances set out in subsection (2) below, the Scottish Ministers may, by order (in this Part of this Act, a 'remedial order'), make such provision as they consider necessary or expedient in consequence of—

(a) an Act of Parliament or an Act of the Scottish Parliament;

(b) any subordinate legislation made under any such Act;

(c) any provision of any such Act or subordinate legislation; or

(d) any exercise or purported exercise of functions by a member of the Scottish Executive,

which is or may be incompatible with any of the Convention rights.

(2) Those circumstances are that the Scottish Ministers are of the opinion that there are compelling reasons for making a remedial order as distinct from taking any other action.

(3) A remedial order may—

(a) make different provision for different purposes;

(b) relate to—

(i) all cases to which the power to make it extends;

(ii) those cases subject to specified exceptions; or

(iii) any particular case or class of case;

(c) make—

(i) any supplementary, incidental or consequential provision; or

(ii) any transitory, transitional or saving provision,

which the Scottish Ministers consider necessary or expedient;

(d) modify any enactment or prerogative instrument or any other instrument or document relating to the exercise or purported exercise of functions by the Scottish Ministers;

(e) make provision (other than provision creating criminal offences or increasing the punishment for criminal offences) which has retrospective effect;

(f) provide for the delegation of functions.

(4) A remedial order shall not, however, create any criminal offence punishable—

(a) on summary conviction, with imprisonment for a period exceeding three months or with a fine exceeding the amount specified as level 5 on the standard scale;

(b) on conviction on indictment, with a period of imprisonment exceeding two years.

(5) The conferring by subsection (1) above of the power to make remedial orders does not prejudice the extent of any other power.

13 Procedure for remedial orders: general

(1) A remedial order shall be made by statutory instrument.

(2) No remedial order shall be made unless laid in draft before and approved by resolution of the Scottish Parliament.

(3) Before laying a draft remedial order for the purposes of subsection (2) above, the Scottish Ministers shall—

(a) lay a copy of the proposed draft order, together with a statement of their reasons for proposing to make the order, before the Scottish Parliament;

(b) give such public notice of the contents of the proposed draft order as they consider appropriate and invite persons wishing to make observations on the draft order to do so, in writing, within the period of 60 days beginning with the day on which that public notice was given or the day on which the draft order was laid under this subsection, whichever is earlier, or, if both those actions occurred on the same day, that day;

(c) have regard to any written observations submitted within that period.

(4) When laying a draft remedial order for the purposes of subsection (2) above, the Scottish Ministers shall lay before the Scottish Parliament a statement—

(a) summarising all the observations to which they had to have regard under subsection (3)(c) above; and

(b) specifying the changes (if any) which they have made in the draft order and the reasons for them.

(5) In reckoning, for the purposes of subsection (3)(b) above, any period of 60 days no account shall be taken of any time during which the Scottish Parliament is dissolved or is in recess for more than four days.

ANTI-TERRORISM, CRIME AND SECURITY ACT 2001
(2001, c 24)

4 Power to make order

(1) The Treasury may make a freezing order if the following two conditions are satisfied.

(2) The first condition is that the Treasury reasonably believe that—

(a) action to the detriment of the United Kingdom's economy (or part of it) has been or is likely to be taken by a person or persons, or

(b) action constituting a threat to the life or property of one or more nationals of the United Kingdom or residents of the United Kingdom has been or is likely to be taken by a person or persons.

(3) If one person is believed to have taken or to be likely to take the action the second condition is that the person is—

(a) the government of a country or territory outside the United Kingdom, or

(b) a resident of a country or territory outside the United Kingdom.

(4) If two or more persons are believed to have taken or to be likely to take the action the second condition is that each of them falls within paragraph (a) or (b) of subsection (3); and different persons may fall within different paragraphs.

5 Contents of order

(1) A freezing order is an order which prohibits persons from making funds available to or for the benefit of a person or persons specified in the order.

(2) The order must provide that these are the persons who are prohibited—

(a) all persons in the United Kingdom, and

(b) all persons elsewhere who are nationals of the United Kingdom or are bodies incorporated under the law of any part of the United Kingdom or are Scottish partnerships.

(3) The order may specify the following (and only the following) as the person or persons to whom or for whose benefit funds are not to be made available—

(a) the person or persons reasonably believed by the Treasury to have taken or to be likely to take the action referred to in section 4;

(b) any person the Treasury reasonably believe has provided or is likely to provide assistance (directly or indirectly) to that person or any of those persons.

(4) A person may be specified under subsection (3) by—

(a) being named in the order, or

(b) falling within a description of persons set out in the order.

(5) The description must be such that a reasonable person would know whether he fell within it.

(6) Funds are financial assets and economic benefits of any kind.

19 Disclosure of information held by revenue departments

(1) This section applies to information which is held by or on behalf of the Commissioners of Inland Revenue or by or on behalf of the Commissioners of Customs and Excise, including information obtained before the coming into force of this section.

(2) No obligation of secrecy imposed by statute or otherwise prevents the disclosure, in accordance with the following provisions of this section, of information to which this section applies if the disclosure is made—

[. . .]

(b) for the purposes of any criminal investigation whatever which is being or may be carried out, whether in the United Kingdom or elsewhere;

(c) for the purposes of any criminal proceedings whatever which have been or may be initiated, whether in the United Kingdom or elsewhere;

(d) for the purposes of the initiation or bringing to an end of any such investigation or proceedings; or

(e) for the purpose of facilitating a determination of whether any such investigation or proceedings should be initiated or brought to an end.

(3) No disclosure of information to which this section applies shall be made by virtue of this section unless the person by whom the disclosure is made is satisfied that the making of the disclosure is proportionate to what is sought to be achieved by it.

(4) Information to which this section applies shall not be disclosed by virtue of this section except by the Commissioners by or on whose behalf it is held or with their authority.

(5) Information obtained by means of a disclosure authorised by subsection (2) shall not be further disclosed except—

(a) for a purpose mentioned in that subsection; and

(b) with the consent of the Commissioners by whom or with whose authority it was initially disclosed;

and information so obtained otherwise than by or on behalf of any of the intelligence services shall not be further disclosed (with or without such consent) to any of those services, or to any person acting on behalf of any of those services, except for a purpose mentioned in paragraphs (b) to (e) of that subsection.

(6) A consent for the purposes of subsection (5) may be given either in relation to a particular disclosure or in relation to disclosures made in such circumstances as may be specified or described in the consent.

(7) Nothing in this section authorises the making of any disclosure which is prohibited by any provision of [the data protection legislation].

(8) References in this section to information which is held on behalf of the Commissioners of Inland Revenue or of the Commissioners of Customs and Excise include references to information which—

(a) is held by a person who provides services to the Commissioners of Inland Revenue or, as the case may be, to the Commissioners of Customs and Excise; and

(b) is held by that person in connection with the provision of those services.

(9) In this section—

['the data protection legislation' has the same meaning as in the Data Protection Act 2018 (see section 3 of that Act),]

'intelligence service' has the same meaning as in the Regulation of Investigatory Powers Act 2000 (c 23).

(10) Nothing in this section shall be taken to prejudice any power to disclose information which exists apart from this section.

SCHEDULE 1
FORFEITURE OF TERRORIST [PROPERTY]

PART 2
SEIZURE AND DETENTION [OF TERRORIST CASH]

Seizure of cash

2 (1) An authorised officer may seize any cash if he has reasonable grounds for suspecting that it is terrorist cash.

(2) An authorised officer may also seize cash part of which he has reasonable grounds for suspecting to be terrorist cash if it is not reasonably practicable to seize only that part.

Detention of seized cash

3 (1) While the authorised officer continues to have reasonable grounds for his suspicion, cash seized under this Schedule may be detained initially for a period of 48 hours.

[(1A) In determining the period of 48 hours specified in sub-paragraph (1) there shall be disregarded—

(a) any Saturday or Sunday;

(b) Christmas Day;

(c) Good Friday;

(d) any day that is a bank holiday under the Banking and Financial Dealings Act 1971 in the part of the United Kingdom in which the cash is seized;

(e) any day prescribed under section 8(2) of the Criminal Procedure (Scotland) Act 1995 as a court holiday in the sheriff court district in which the cash is seized.]

(2) The period for which the cash or any part of it may be detained may be extended by an order made by a magistrates' court or (in Scotland) the sheriff; but the order may not authorise the detention of any of the cash—

(a) beyond the end of the period of [6] months beginning with the date of the order, and

(b) in the case of any further order under this paragraph, beyond the end of the period of two years beginning with the date of the first order.

. . .

(4) An order under sub-paragraph (2) must provide for notice to be given to persons affected by it.

(5) An application for an order under sub-paragraph (2)—

(a) [*does not apply to Scotland*]

(b) in relation to Scotland, may be made by a procurator fiscal, and the court, sheriff or justice may make the order if satisfied, in relation to any cash to be further detained, that one of the following conditions is met.

(6) The first condition is that there are reasonable grounds for suspecting that the cash is intended to be used for the purposes of terrorism and that either—

(a) its continued detention is justified while its intended use is further investigated or consideration is given to bringing (in the United Kingdom or elsewhere) proceedings against any person for an offence with which the cash is connected, or

(b) proceedings against any person for an offence with which the cash is connected have been started and have not been concluded.

(7) The second condition is that there are reasonable grounds for suspecting that the cash consists of resources of an organisation which is a proscribed organisation and that either—

(a) its continued detention is justified while investigation is made into whether or not it consists of such resources or consideration is given to bringing (in the United Kingdom or elsewhere) proceedings against any person for an offence with which the cash is connected, or

(b) proceedings against any person for an offence with which the cash is connected have been started and have not been concluded.

(8) The third condition is that there are reasonable grounds for suspecting that the cash is property earmarked as terrorist property and that either—

(a) its continued detention is justified while its derivation is further investigated or consideration is given to bringing (in the United Kingdom or elsewhere) proceedings against any person for an offence with which the cash is connected, or

(b) proceedings against any person for an offence with which the cash is connected have been started and have not been concluded.

[(9) Where an application for an order under sub-paragraph (2) relates to cash seized under paragraph 2(2), the court, sheriff or justice may make the order if satisfied that—

(a) the condition in sub-paragraph (6), (7) or (8) is met in respect of part of the cash, and

(b) it is not reasonably practicable to detain only that part.]

Payment of detained cash into an account

4 (1) If cash is detained under this Schedule for more than 48 hours [(determined in accordance with paragraph 3(1A))], it is to be held in an interest-bearing account and the interest accruing on it is to be added to it on its forfeiture or release.

. . .

Release of detained cash

5 (1) This paragraph applies while any cash is detained under [any provision of this Schedule other than Part 2A].

(2) A magistrates' court or (in Scotland) the sheriff may direct the release of the whole or any part of the cash if satisfied, on an application by the person from whom it was seized, that the conditions in paragraph 3 for the detention of cash are no longer met in relation to the cash to be released.

(3) A authorised officer or (in Scotland) a procurator fiscal may, after notifying the magistrates' court, sheriff or justice under whose order cash is being detained, release the whole or any part of it if satisfied that the detention of the cash to be released is no longer justified.

[. . .]

PART 3
FORFEITURE [OF TERRORIST CASH]

Forfeiture

6 (1) While cash is detained under this Schedule, an application for the forfeiture of the whole or any part of it may be made—

(a) to a magistrates' court by the Commissioners of Customs and Excise or an authorised officer,

(b) (in Scotland) to the sheriff by the Scottish Ministers.

(2) The court or sheriff may order the forfeiture of the cash or any part of it if satisfied that the cash or part is terrorist cash.

(3) In the case of property earmarked as terrorist property which belongs to joint tenants one of whom is an excepted joint owner, the order may not apply to so much of it as the court or sheriff thinks is attributable to the excepted joint owner's share.

(4) An excepted joint owner is a joint tenant who obtained the property in circumstances in which it would not (as against him) be earmarked; and references to his share of the earmarked property are to so much of the property as would have been his if the joint tenancy had been severed.

[Appeal against decision in forfeiture proceedings]

[7 (1) A party to proceedings for an order under paragraph 6 ('a forfeiture order') who is aggrieved by a forfeiture order made in the proceedings or by the decision of the court or sheriff not to make a forfeiture order may appeal—

(a) in England and Wales, to the Crown Court;

(b) in Scotland, to the sheriff principal;

(c) in Northern Ireland, to a county court.

(2) The appeal must be brought before the end of the period of 30 days beginning with the date on which the order is made or, as the case may be, the decision is given. This is subject to paragraph 7A (extended time for appealing in certain cases of deproscription).

(3) The court or sheriff principal hearing the appeal may make any order that appears to the court or sheriff principal to be appropriate.

(4) If an appeal against a forfeiture order is upheld, the court or sheriff principal may order the release of [the whole or any part of] the cash.]

[Extended time for appealing in certain cases where deproscription order made]

[7A (1) This paragraph applies where—

(a) a successful application for a forfeiture order relies (wholly or partly) on the fact that an organisation is proscribed,

(b) an application under section 4 of the Terrorism Act 2000 for a deproscription order in respect of the organisation is refused by the Secretary of State,

(c) the forfeited cash is seized under this Schedule on or after the date of the refusal of that application,

(d) an appeal against that refusal is allowed under section 5 of that Act,

(e) a deproscription order is made accordingly, and

(f) if the order is made in reliance on section 123(5) of that Act, a resolution is passed by each House of Parliament under section 123(5)(b).

(2) Where this paragraph applies, an appeal under paragraph 7 above against the forfeiture order may be brought at any time before the end of the period of 30 days beginning with the date on which the deproscription order comes into force.

(3) In this paragraph a 'deproscription order' means an order under section 3 (3)(b) or (8) of the Terrorism Act 2000.]

Application of forfeited cash

8 (1) Cash forfeited under [paragraph 6], and any accrued interest on it—

(a) if forfeited by a magistrates' court in England and Wales or Northern Ireland, is to be paid into the Consolidated Fund,

(b) if forfeited by the sheriff, is to be paid into the Scottish Consolidated Fund.

(2) But it is not to be paid in—

(a) before the end of the period within which an appeal under paragraph 7 may be made, or

(b) if a person appeals under that paragraph, before the appeal is determined or otherwise disposed of.

PART 4
MISCELLANEOUS [: TERRORIST CASH]

Victims

9 (1) A person who claims that any cash detained under this Schedule, or any part of it, belongs to him may apply to a magistrates' court or (in Scotland) the sheriff for the cash or part to be released to him.

(2) The application may be made in the course of proceedings under paragraph 3 or 6 or at any other time.

(3) If it appears to the court or sheriff concerned that—

(a) the applicant was deprived of the cash claimed, or of property which it represents, by criminal conduct,

(b) the property he was deprived of was not, immediately before he was deprived of it, property obtained by or in return for criminal conduct and nor did it then represent such property, and

(c) the cash claimed belongs to him,

the court or sheriff may order the cash to be released to the applicant.

[(4) If sub-paragraph (5) applies, the court or sheriff may order the cash to be released to the applicant or to the person from whom it was seized.

(5) This sub-paragraph applies where—

(a) the applicant is not the person from whom the cash claimed was seized,

(b) it appears to the court or sheriff that the cash belongs to the applicant,

(c) the court or sheriff is satisfied that the release condition is met in relation to the cash, and

(d) no objection to the making of an order under sub-paragraph (4) has been made by the person from whom the cash was seized.

(6) The release condition is met—

(a) in relation to cash detained under paragraph 3, if the conditions in that paragraph for the detention of the cash are no longer met,

(b) in relation to cash detained under paragraph 5B or 5C, if the cash is not terrorist cash, and

(c) in relation to cash detained pending the conclusion of proceedings in pursuance of an application under paragraph 6, if the court or sheriff decides not to make an order under that paragraph in relation to the cash.]

[*Restrictions on release*]

[9A Cash is not to be released under any power or duty conferred or imposed by this Schedule (and so is to continue to be detained)—

(a) if an application for its forfeiture under paragraph 6, or for its release under paragraph 9, is made, until any proceedings in pursuance of the application (including any proceedings on appeal) are concluded;

(b) if (in the United Kingdom or elsewhere) proceedings are started against any person for an offence with which the cash is connected, until the proceedings are concluded.]

Compensation

10 (1) If no forfeiture order is made in respect of any cash detained under this Schedule, [and the cash is not otherwise forfeited in pursuance of a cash forfeiture notice,] the person to whom the cash belongs or from whom it was seized may make an application to the magistrates' court or (in Scotland) the sheriff for compensation.

(2) If, for any period after the initial detention of the cash for 48 hours [(determined in accordance with paragraph 3(1A))], the cash was not held in an interest-bearing account while detained, the court or sheriff may order an amount of compensation to be paid to the applicant.

(3) The amount of compensation to be paid under sub-paragraph (2) is the amount the court or sheriff thinks would have been earned in interest in the period in question if the cash had been held in an interest-bearing account.

(4) If the court or sheriff is satisfied that, taking account of any interest to be paid under this Schedule or any amount to be paid under sub-paragraph (2), the applicant has suffered loss as a result of the detention of the cash and that the circumstances are exceptional, the court or sheriff may order compensation (or additional compensation) to be paid to him.

(5) The amount of compensation to be paid under sub-paragraph (4) is the amount the court or sheriff thinks reasonable, having regard to the loss suffered and any other relevant circumstances.

(6) If the cash was seized by a customs officer, the compensation is to be paid by the Commissioners of Customs and Excise.

(7) If the cash was seized by a constable, the compensation is to be paid as follows—

(a) in the case of a constable of a police force in England and Wales, it is to be paid out of the police fund from which the expenses of the police force are met,

(b) in the case of [the Police Service of Scotland, is to be paid by the Scottish Police Authority],

(c) in the case of a police officer within the meaning of the Police (Northern Ireland) Act 2000 (c 32), it is to be paid out of money provided by the Chief Constable.

[(7A) If the cash was seized by a counter-terrorism financial investigator, the compensation is to be paid as follows—

(a) in the case of a counter-terrorism financial investigator who was—

(i) a member of the civilian staff of a police force (including the metropolitan police force), within the meaning of Part 1 of the Police Reform and Social Responsibility Act 2011, or

(ii) a member of staff of the City of London police force, it is to be paid out of the police fund from which the expenses of the police force are met,

(b) in the case of a counter-terrorism financial investigator who was a member of staff of the Police Service of Northern Ireland, it is to be paid out of money provided by the Chief Constable of the Police Service of Northern Ireland.]

(8) If the cash was seized by an immigration officer, the compensation is to be paid by the Secretary of State.

[(8A) If any cash is detained under this Schedule and part only of the cash is forfeited in pursuance of a cash forfeiture notice, this paragraph has effect in relation to the other part.]

(9) If a forfeiture order is made in respect only of a part of any cash detained under this Schedule, this paragraph has effect in relation to the other part.

(10) This paragraph does not apply if the court or sheriff makes an order under paragraph 9.

FREEDOM OF INFORMATION (SCOTLAND) ACT 2002
(2002, asp 13)

PART 1
ACCESS TO INFORMATION HELD BY SCOTTISH PUBLIC AUTHORITIES

Right to information

1 General entitlement

(1) A person who requests information from a Scottish public authority which holds it is entitled to be given it by the authority.

(2) The person who makes such a request is in this Part and in Parts 2 and 7 referred to as the 'applicant'.

(3) If the authority—

(a) requires further information in order to identify and locate the requested information; and

(b) has told the applicant so (specifying what the requirement for further information is),

then, provided that the requirement is reasonable, the authority is not obliged to give the requested information until it has the further information.

(4) The information to be given by the authority is that held by it at the time the request is received, except that, subject to subsection (5), any amendment or deletion which would have been made, regardless of the receipt of the request, between that time and the time it gives the information may be made before the information is given.

(5) The requested information is not, by virtue of subsection (4), to be destroyed before it can be given (unless the circumstances are such that it is not reasonably practicable to prevent such destruction from occurring).

(6) This section is subject to sections 2, 9, 12 and 14.

2 Effect of exemptions

(1) To information which is exempt information by virtue of any provision of Part 2, section 1 applies only to the extent that—

(a) the provision does not confer absolute exemption; and

(b) in all the circumstances of the case, the public interest in disclosing the information is not outweighed by that in maintaining the exemption.

(2) For the purposes of paragraph (a) of subsection (1), the following provisions of Part 2 (and no others) are to be regarded as conferring absolute exemption—

(a) section 25;

(b) section 26;

(c) section 36(2);

(d) section 37; and

(e) in subsection (1) of section 38—

(i) paragraphs (a), (c) and (d); and

(ii) paragraph (b) where the first condition referred to in that paragraph is satisfied [. . .].

3 Scottish public authorities

(1) In this Act, 'Scottish public authority' means—

(a) any body which, any other person who, or the holder of any office which—

(i) is listed in schedule 1; or

(ii) is designated by order under section 5(1); or

(b) a publicly-owned company, as defined by section 6.

(2) For the purposes of this Act but subject to subsection (4), information is held by an authority if it is held—

(a) by the authority otherwise than—

(i) on behalf of another person; or

(ii) in confidence, having been supplied by a Minister of the Crown or by a department of the Government of the United Kingdom; or

(b) by a person other than the authority, on behalf of the authority.

(3) Subsection (1)(a)(i) is subject to any qualification set out in schedule 1.

(4) Information is not held by the Keeper of the Records of Scotland if it is contained in a record transferred to the Keeper by a public authority within the meaning of the Freedom of Information Act 2000 (c 36) unless it is information—

(a) to which subsections (2) to (5) of section 22 apply by virtue of subsection (6) of that section;

(b) designated by that authority as open information for the purposes of this subsection.

(5) Where the public authority mentioned in subsection (4) is the Secretary of State for Scotland and the information is contained in a record transferred as is mentioned in subsection (6) of section 22 the reference in subsection (4)(b) to 'that authority' is to be construed as a reference to the Scottish Ministers.

4 Amendment of schedule 1

(1) The Scottish Ministers may by order amend schedule 1 by—

(a) adding to that schedule a reference to—

(i) any body which; or

(ii) the holder of any office which,

is not for the time being listed there and is either a part of the Scottish Administration or a Scottish public authority with mixed functions or no reserved functions; or

(b) removing from that schedule an entry for the time being listed there.

(2) The reference in paragraph (a) of subsection (1) to an authority with mixed functions or no reserved functions is to be construed in accordance with paragraphs 1(4) and 2 of Part III of Schedule 5 to the Scotland Act 1998.

(3) An order under subsection (1) may relate to a specified person or office or to persons or offices falling within a specified description.

5 Further power to designate Scottish public authorities

(1) The Scottish Ministers may by order designate as a Scottish public authority for the purposes of this Act any person mentioned in subsection (2) who—

(a) is neither for the time being listed in schedule 1 nor capable of being added to that schedule by order under section 4(1); and

(b) is neither a public body nor the holder of any public office.

(2) The persons are those who either—

(a) appear to the Scottish Ministers to exercise functions of a public nature; or

(b) are providing, under a contract made with a Scottish public authority, any service whose provision is a function of that authority.

(3) An order under subsection (1) may designate a specified person or persons falling within a specified description.

(4) An order under subsection (1) made by virtue of—

(a) subsection (2)(a) must specify the functions of a public nature which appear to be exercised;

(b) subsection (2)(b) must specify the service being provided.

(5) [Before making an order under subsection (1), the Scottish Ministers must—

(a) consult—

(i) every person to whom the order relates, or

(ii) persons appearing to them to represent such persons, and

(b) also consult such other persons as they consider appropriate.]

6 Publicly-owned companies

(1) A company is a 'publicly-owned company' for the purposes of section 3(1)(b) if it is wholly owned—

(a) by the Scottish Ministers; or

(b) by any other Scottish public authority listed in schedule 1, other than an authority so listed only in relation to information of a specified description.

(2) For the purposes of subsection (1), a company is wholly owned—

(a) by the Scottish Ministers if it has no members except—

(i) the Scottish Ministers or companies wholly owned by the Scottish Ministers; or

(ii) persons acting on behalf of the Scottish Ministers or of such companies; and

(b) by any other Scottish public authority if it has no members except—

(i) the authority or companies wholly owned by the authority; or

(ii) persons acting on behalf of the authority or of such companies.

(3) In subsections (1) and (2), 'company' includes any body corporate.

7 Public authorities to which Act has limited application

(1) An order under section 4(1)(a) may, in adding an entry to schedule 1, list the authority only in relation to information of a specified description; and where an authority is so listed nothing in this Act applies to any other information held by the authority.

(2) The Scottish Ministers may by order amend that schedule—

(a) by limiting the entry relating to an authority to information of a specified description; or

(b) by removing or amending any such limitation for the time being contained in an entry so relating.

(3) Nothing in this Act applies to information held by a person designated as a Scottish public authority by order under subsection (1) of section 5 if the order is made by virtue of—

(a) subsection (2)(a) of that section and the information does not relate to the functions; or

(b) subsection (2)(b) of that section and the information does not relate to the service,

specified in the order.

(4) Nothing in this Act applies in relation to information—

(a) held by a publicly-owned company; and

(b) of a description specified in relation to that company in an order made for the purposes of this subsection by the Scottish Ministers.

[7A Reports on section 5 power

(1) In accordance with this section, the Scottish Ministers must lay before the Parliament reports about the exercise of the section 5 power.

(2) The first report is to be laid on or before 31 October 2015.

(3) Each subsequent report is to be laid no later than 2 years after the date on which the previous report is laid.

(4) A report must—

(a) state whether the section 5 power has been exercised during the reporting period, and

(b) as the case may be—

(i) explain how the power has been exercised during the reporting period (and why), or

(ii) give the reason for leaving the power unexercised during the reporting period.

(5) A report may—

(a) summarise any response to a consultation carried out during the reporting period as regards the exercise of the section 5 power,

(b) indicate any intention to exercise the power in the future,

(c) include such additional information as the Scottish Ministers consider appropriate.

(6) In this section—

'reporting period' means—

(a) in the case of the first report, period of time from the date on which section 1 of the Freedom of Information (Amendment) (Scotland) Act 2013 comes into force until the date on which the first report is laid,

(b) in the case of a subsequent report, period of time from the date on which the previous report is laid until the date on which the subsequent report is laid,

'section 5 power' means order-making power conferred by section 5(1).]

8 Requesting information

(1) Any reference in this Act to 'requesting' information is a reference to making a request which—

(a) is in writing or in another form which, by reason of its having some permanency, is capable of being used for subsequent reference (as, for example, a recording made on audio or video tape);

(b) states the name of the applicant and an address for correspondence; and

(c) describes the information requested.

(2) For the purposes of paragraph (a) of subsection (1) (and without prejudice to the generality of that paragraph), a request is to be treated as made in writing where the text of the request is—

(a) transmitted by electronic means;

(b) received in legible form; and

(c) capable of being used for subsequent reference.

9 Fees

(1) A Scottish public authority receiving a request which requires it to comply with section 1(1) may, within the time allowed by section 10 for so complying, give the applicant a notice in writing (in this Act referred to as a 'fees notice') stating that a fee of an amount specified in the notice is to be charged by the authority for so complying.

(2) Subsection (1) is subject to section 19.

(3) If a fees notice is given to the applicant, the authority is not obliged to give the requested information unless the fee is duly paid; and for the purposes of this subsection and section 10(2) due payment is payment within the period of three months beginning with the day on which the notice is given.

(4) Subject to subsection (7), a fee charged under subsection (1) is to be determined by the authority in accordance with regulations made by the Scottish Ministers.

(5) Without prejudice to the generality of subsection (4), the regulations may in particular provide that—

(a) a fee is not to exceed such amount as may be specified in, or determined in accordance with, the regulations;

(b) a fee is to be calculated in such manner as may be so specified; and

(c) no fee is payable in a case so specified.

(6) Before making the regulations, the Scottish Ministers are to consult the Commissioner.

(7) Subsection (4) does not apply where provision is made, by or under any enactment, as to the fee that may be charged by the authority for the disclosure of the information.

10 Time for compliance

(1) Subject to subsections (2) and (3), a Scottish public authority receiving a request which requires it to comply with section 1(1) must comply promptly; and in any event by not later than the twentieth working day after—

(a) in a case other than that mentioned in paragraph (b), the receipt by the authority of the request; or

(b) in a case where section 1(3) applies, the receipt by it of the further information.

(2) If—

(a) the authority is the Keeper of the Records of Scotland; and

(b) the information is information to which section 22(2) to (5) applies,

subsection (1) applies with the substitution, for the reference to the twentieth working day, of a reference to the thirtieth working day.

(3) Where the authority gives a fees notice to the applicant and the fee is duly paid, the working days in the period—

(a) beginning with the day on which that notice is given; and

(b) ending with the day on which the fee is received by the authority,

are to be disregarded in calculating, for the purposes of subsection (1), the twentieth (or as the case may be the thirtieth) working day mentioned in that subsection.

(4) The Scottish Ministers may by regulations provide that subsections (1) and (3) are to have effect as if references to the twentieth (or as the case may be the thirtieth) working day were references to such other working day, not later than the sixtieth, after receipt by the authority of the request as is specified in, or determined in accordance with, the regulations.

(5) Regulations under subsection (4) may—

(a) prescribe different days in relation to different cases; and

(b) confer a discretion on the Scottish Information Commissioner,

exercisable both at the request of the authority and where no such request has been made.

11 Means of providing information

(1) Where, in requesting information from a Scottish public authority, the applicant expresses a preference for receiving it by any one or more of the means mentioned in subsection (2), the authority must, so far as is reasonably practicable, give effect to that preference.

(2) The means are—

(a) the provision to the applicant, in permanent form or in another form acceptable to the applicant, of a copy of the information;

(b) such provision to the applicant of a digest or summary of the information; and

(c) the provision to the applicant of a reasonable opportunity to inspect a record containing the information.

(3) In determining, for the purposes of subsection (1), what is reasonably practicable, the authority may have regard to all the circumstances, including cost; and where it determines that it is not reasonably practicable to give effect to the preference it must notify the applicant of the reasons for that determination.

(4) Subject to subsection (1), information given in compliance with section 1(1) may be given by any means which are reasonable in the circumstances.

(5) Such tests of reasonable practicability as are imposed by this section are not to be construed as detracting from any duty which a provider of services has

under or by virtue of section 21 of the Disability Discrimination Act 1995 (duty to make adjustments to practices, policies, procedures or physical features so that use of services by disabled persons is facilitated or made possible).

12 Excessive cost of compliance

(1) Section 1(1) does not oblige a Scottish public authority to comply with a request for information if the authority estimates that the cost of complying with the request would exceed such amount as may be prescribed in regulations made by the Scottish Ministers; and different amounts may be so prescribed in relation to different cases.

(2) The regulations may provide that, in such circumstances as they may specify, where two or more requests for information are made to the authority—

(a) by one person;

(b) by different persons who appear to it to be acting in concert or whose requests appear to have been instigated wholly or mainly for a purpose other than the obtaining of the information itself; or

(c) by different persons in circumstances where the authority considers it would be reasonable to make the information available to the public at large and elects to do so,

then if the authority estimates that the total cost of complying with both (or all) of the requests exceeds the amount prescribed, in relation to complying with either (or any) of those requests, under subsection (1), section 1(1) does not oblige the authority to comply with either (or any) of those requests.

(3) The regulations may, in respect of an election made as mentioned in subsection (2)(c), make provision as to the means by which and the time within which the information is to be made available to the public at large.

(4) The regulations may make provision as to—

(a) the costs to be estimated; and

(b) the manner in which those costs are to be estimated.

(5) Before making the regulations, the Scottish Ministers are to consult the Commissioner.

(6) References in this section to the cost of complying with a request are not to be construed as including any reference to costs incurred in fulfilling any such duty under or by virtue of the [Equality Act 2010] as is mentioned in section 11(5).

13 Fees for disclosure in certain circumstances

(1) A Scottish public authority may charge for the communication of any information—

(a) which by virtue of section 12(1) or (2) it is not obliged to communicate; and

(b) which it is not otherwise required by law to communicate,

such fee as may be determined by it in accordance with regulations made by the Scottish Ministers.

(2) Without prejudice to the generality of subsection (1), the regulations may in particular provide that a fee—

(a) is not to exceed such amount as may be specified in, or determined in accordance with, the regulations; and

(b) is to be calculated in such manner as may be so specified.

(3) Before making the regulations, the Scottish Ministers are to consult the Commissioner.

(4) Subsection (1) does not apply where provision is made, by or under any enactment, as to the fee that may be charged by the authority for the disclosure of the information.

14 Vexatious or repeated requests

(1) Section 1(1) does not oblige a Scottish public authority to comply with a request for information if the request is vexatious.

(2) Where a Scottish public authority has complied with a request from a person for information, it is not obliged to comply with a subsequent request from that person which is identical or substantially similar unless there has been a reasonable period of time between the making of the request complied with and the making of the subsequent request.

15 Duty to provide advice and assistance

(1) A Scottish public authority must, so far as it is reasonable to expect it to do so, provide advice and assistance to a person who proposes to make, or has made, a request for information to it.

(2) A Scottish public authority which, in relation to the provision of advice or assistance in any case, conforms with the code of practice issued under section 60 is, as respects that case, to be taken to comply with the duty imposed by subsection (1).

Responses to request

16 Refusal of request

(1) Subject to section 18, a Scottish public authority which, in relation to a request for information which it holds, to any extent claims that, by virtue of any provision of Part 2, the information is exempt information must, within the time allowed by or by virtue of section 10 for complying with the request, give the applicant a notice in writing (in this Act referred to as a 'refusal notice') which—

(a) discloses that it holds the information;
(b) states that it so claims;
(c) specifies the exemption in question; and
(d) states (if not otherwise apparent) why the exemption applies.

(2) Where the authority's claim is made only by virtue of a provision of Part 2 which does not confer absolute exemption, the notice must state the authority's reason for claiming that, in all the circumstances of the case, the public interest in maintaining the exemption outweighs that in disclosure of the information.

(3) The authority is not obliged to make a statement under subsection (1)(d) in so far as the statement would disclose information which would itself be exempt information.

(4) A Scottish public authority which, in relation to a request for information, claims that section 12(1) applies must, within the time allowed by or by virtue of section 10 for complying with the request, give the applicant a notice which states that it so claims.

(5) A Scottish public authority which, in relation to such a request, claims that section 14 applies must, within that time, give the applicant a notice which states that it so claims; except that the notice need not be given if—

(a) the authority has, in relation to a previous identical or substantially similar such request, given the applicant a notice under this subsection; and

(b) it would in all the circumstances be unreasonable to expect it to serve a further such notice in relation to the current request.

(6) Subsections (1), (4) and (5) are subject to section 19.

17 Notice that information is not held

(1) Where—

(a) a Scottish public authority receives a request which would require it either—

(i) to comply with section 1(1); or

(ii) to determine any question arising by virtue of paragraph (a) or (b) of section 2(1),

if it held the information to which the request relates; but

(b) the authority does not hold that information,

it must, within the time allowed by or by virtue of section 10 for complying with the request, give the applicant notice in writing that it does not hold it.

(2) Subsection (1) is subject to section 19.

(3) Subsection (1) does not apply if, by virtue of section 18, the authority instead gives the applicant a refusal notice.

18 Further provision as respects responses to request

(1) Where, if information existed and was held by a Scottish public authority, the authority could give a refusal notice under section 16(1) on the basis that the information was exempt information by virtue of any of sections 28 to 35, [38,] 39 (1) or 41 but the authority considers that to reveal whether the information exists or is so held would be contrary to the public interest, it may (whether or not the information does exist and is held by it) give the applicant a refusal notice by virtue of this section.

(2) Neither paragraph (a) of subsection (1) of section 16 nor subsection (2) of that section applies as respects a refusal notice given by virtue of this section.

Content of certain notices

19 Content of certain notices

A notice under section 9(1) or 16(1), (4) or (5) (including a refusal notice given by virtue of section 18(1)) or 17(1) must contain particulars—

(a) of the procedure provided by the authority for dealing with complaints about the handling by it of requests for information; and

(b) about the rights of application to the authority and the Commissioner conferred by sections 20(1) and 47(1).

Review of refusal, etc

20 Requirement for review of refusal etc

(1) An applicant who is dissatisfied with the way in which a Scottish public authority has dealt with a request for information made under this Part of this Act may require the authority to review its actions and decisions in relation to that request.

(2) A requirement under subsection (1) is referred to in this Act as a 'requirement for review'.

(3) A requirement for review must—

(a) be in writing or in another form which, by reason of its having some permanency, is capable of being used for subsequent reference (as, for example, a recording made on audio or video tape);

(b) state the name of the applicant and an address for correspondence; and

(c) specify—

(i) the request for information to which the requirement for review relates; and

(ii) the matter which gives rise to the applicant's dissatisfaction mentioned in subsection (1).

(4) For the purposes of paragraph (a) of subsection (3) (and without prejudice to the generality of that paragraph), a requirement for review is treated as made in writing where the text of the requirement is as mentioned in paragraphs (a) to (c) of section 8(2).

(5) Subject to subsection (6), a requirement for review must be made by not later than the fortieth working day after—

(a) the expiry of the time allowed by or by virtue of section 10 for complying with the request; or

(b) in a case where the authority purports under this Act—

(i) to comply with a request for information; or

(ii) to give the applicant a fees notice, a refusal notice or a notice under section 17(1) that information is not held,

but does so outwith that time, the receipt by the applicant of the information provided or, as the case may be, the notice.

(6) A Scottish public authority may comply with a requirement for review made after the expiry of the time allowed by subsection (5) for making such a requirement if it considers it appropriate to do so.

(7) The Scottish Ministers may by regulations provide that subsections (5) and (6) are to have effect as if the reference in subsection (5) to the fortieth working day were a reference to such other working day as is specified in (or determined in accordance with) the regulations.

(8) Regulations under subsection (7) may—

(a) prescribe different days in relation to different cases; and

(b) confer a discretion on the Scottish Information Commissioner.

(9) In subsection (1), the reference to 'actions' and 'decisions' includes inaction and failure to reach a decision.

21 Review by Scottish public authority

(1) Subject to subsection (2), a Scottish public authority receiving a requirement for review must (unless that requirement is withdrawn or is as mentioned in subsection (8)) comply promptly; and in any event by not later than the twentieth working day after receipt by it of the requirement.

(2) If—

(a) the authority is the Keeper of the Records of Scotland; and

(b) a different authority is, by virtue of section 22(4), to review a decision to which the requirement relates,

subsection (1) applies with the substitution, for the reference to the twentieth working day, of a reference to the thirtieth working day.

(3) A requirement for review may be withdrawn by the applicant who made it, by notice in writing to the authority, at any time before the authority makes its decision on the requirement.

(4) The authority may, as respects the request for information to which the requirement relates—

(a) confirm a decision complained of, with or without such modifications as it considers appropriate;

(b) substitute for any such decision a different decision; or

(c) reach a decision, where the complaint is that no decision had been reached.

(5) Within the time allowed by subsection (1) for complying with the requirement for review, the authority must give the applicant notice in writing of what it has done under subsection (4) and a statement of its reasons for so doing.

(6) The Scottish Ministers may by regulations provide that subsections (1) and (5) and section 47(4)(b) are to have effect as if the reference in subsection (1) to the twentieth (or as the case may be the thirtieth) working day were a reference to such other working day as is specified in (or determined in accordance with) the regulations.

(7) Regulations under subsection (6) may—

(a) prescribe different days in relation to different cases; and

(b) confer a discretion on the Scottish Information Commissioner.

(8) Subsection (1) does not oblige a Scottish public authority to comply with a requirement for review if—

(a) the requirement is vexatious; or

(b) the request for information to which the requirement for review relates was one with which, by virtue of section 14, the authority was not obliged to comply.

(9) Where the authority considers that paragraph (a) or (b) of subsection (8) applies, it must give the applicant who made the requirement for review notice in writing, within the time allowed by subsection (1) for complying with that requirement, that it so claims.

(10) A notice under subsection (5) or (9) must contain particulars about the rights of application to the Commissioner and of appeal conferred by sections 47 (1) and 56.

Publication schemes

23 Publication schemes

(1) A Scottish public authority must—

(a) adopt and maintain a scheme (in this Act referred to as a 'publication scheme') which relates to the publication of information by the authority and is approved by the Commissioner;

(b) publish information in accordance with that scheme; and

(c) from time to time review that scheme.

(2) A publication scheme must specify—

(a) classes of information which the authority publishes or intends to publish;

(b) the manner in which information of each class is, or is intended to be, published; and

(c) whether the published information is, or is intended to be, available to the public free of charge or on payment.

(3) In adopting or reviewing its publication scheme the authority must have regard to the public interest in—

(a) allowing public access to information held by it and in particular to information which—

(i) relates to the provision of services by it, the cost to it of providing them or the standards attained by services so provided; or

(ii) consists of facts, or analyses, on the basis of which decisions of importance to the public have been made by it;

(b) the publication of reasons for decisions made by it.

(4) The authority must publish its publication scheme but may do so in such manner as it thinks fit.

(5) The Commissioner may—

(a) when approving a publication scheme, provide that the approval expires at the end of a specified period; and

(b) at any time give notice to an authority revoking, as from the end of the period of six months beginning at that time, approval of its publication scheme.

(6) The Commissioner, when—

(a) refusing to approve a proposed publication scheme; or

(b) revoking approval of a publication scheme,

must state the reason for doing so.

PART 2
EXEMPT INFORMATION

25 Information otherwise accessible

(1) Information which the applicant can reasonably obtain other than by requesting it under section 1(1) is exempt information.

(2) For the purposes of subsection (1), information—

(a) may be reasonably obtainable even if payment is required for access to it;

(b) is to be taken to be reasonably obtainable if—

(i) the Scottish public authority which holds it, or any other person, is obliged by or under any enactment to communicate it (otherwise than by making it available for inspection) to; or

(ii) the Keeper of the Records of Scotland holds it and makes it available for inspection and (in so far as practicable) copying by, members of the public on request, whether free of charge or on payment.

[(3) For the purposes of subsection (1), information is to be taken to be reasonably obtainable if—

(a) it is available—

(i) on request from the Scottish public authority which holds it, and

(ii) in accordance with the authority's publication scheme, and

(b) any associated payment required by the authority is specified in or determined under the scheme.]

26 Prohibitions on disclosure

Information is exempt information if its disclosure by a Scottish public authority (otherwise than under this Act)—

(a) is prohibited by or under an enactment;

(b) is incompatible with [an EU] obligation; or

(c) would constitute, or be punishable as, a contempt of court.

27 Information intended for future publication

(1) Information is exempt information if—

(a) it is held with a view to its being published by—

(i) a Scottish public authority; or

(ii) any other person,

at a date not later than twelve weeks after that on which the request for the information is made;

(b) when that request is made the information is already being held with that view; and

(c) it is reasonable in all the circumstances that the information be withheld from disclosure until such date as is mentioned in paragraph (a).

(2) Information obtained in the course of, or derived from, a programme of research is exempt information if—

(a) the programme is continuing with a view to a report of the research (whether or not including a statement of that information) being published by—

(i) a Scottish public authority; or

(ii) any other person; and

(b) disclosure of the information before the date of publication would, or would be likely to, prejudice substantially—

(i) the programme;

(ii) the interests of any individual participating in the programme;

(iii) the interests of the authority which holds the information; or

(iv) the interests of the authority mentioned in sub-paragraph (i) of paragraph (a) (if it is a different authority from that which holds the information).

28 Relations within the United Kingdom

(1) Information is exempt information if its disclosure under this Act would, or would be likely to, prejudice substantially relations between any administration in the United Kingdom and any other such administration.

(2) In subsection (1), 'administration in the United Kingdom' means—

(a) the Government of the United Kingdom;

(b) the Scottish Administration;

(c) the Executive Committee of the Northern Ireland Assembly; or

(d) the National Assembly for Wales.

29 Formulation of Scottish Administration policy etc

(1) Information held by the Scottish Administration is exempt information if it relates to—

(a) the formulation or development of government policy;

(b) Ministerial communications;

(c) the provision of advice by any of the Law Officers or any request for the provision of such advice; or

(d) the operation of any Ministerial private office.

(2) Once a decision as to policy has been taken, any statistical information used to provide an informed background to the taking of the decision is not to be regarded, for the purposes of—

(a) paragraph (a) of subsection (1), as relating to the formulation or development of the policy in question; or

(b) paragraph (b) of that subsection, as relating to Ministerial communications.

(3) In determining any question under section 2(1)(b) as respects information which is exempt information by virtue of subsection (1)(a), the Scottish Administration must have regard to the public interest in the disclosure of factual information which has been used, or is intended to be used, to provide an informed background to the taking of a decision.

(4) In this section—

'government policy' means—

(a) the policy of the Scottish Administration; and

(b) in relation to information created before 1st July 1999, the policy of the Government of the United Kingdom;

'the Law Officers' means the Lord Advocate, the Solicitor General for Scotland, the Advocate General for Scotland, the Attorney General, the Solicitor General and the Attorney General for Northern Ireland;

'Ministerial communications' means any communications between Ministers and includes, in particular, communications relating to proceedings of the Scottish Cabinet (or of any committee of that Cabinet); and

'Ministerial private office' means any part of the Scottish Administration which provides personal administrative support to a Minister.

(5) In the definitions of 'Ministerial communications' and 'Ministerial private office' in subsection (4), 'Minister' means a member of the Scottish Executive or a junior Scottish Minister.

30 Prejudice to effective conduct of public affairs

Information is exempt information if its disclosure under this Act—

(a) would, or would be likely to, prejudice substantially the maintenance of the convention of the collective responsibility of the Scottish Ministers;

(b) would, or would be likely to, inhibit substantially—

(i) the free and frank provision of advice; or

(ii) the free and frank exchange of views for the purposes of deliberation; or

(c) would otherwise prejudice substantially, or be likely to prejudice substantially, the effective conduct of public affairs.

31 National security and defence

(1) Information is exempt information if exemption from section 1(1) is required for the purpose of safeguarding national security.

(2) A certificate signed by a member of the Scottish Executive certifying that such exemption is, or at any time was, required for the purpose of safeguarding national security is conclusive of that fact.

(3) Without prejudice to the generality of subsection (2), a certificate under that subsection may identify the information to which it applies by means of a general description and may be expressed to have prospective effect.

(4) Information is exempt information if its disclosure under this Act would, or would be likely to, prejudice substantially—

(a) the defence of the British Islands or of any colony; or

(b) the capability, effectiveness or security of any relevant forces.

(5) In subsection (4)—

(a) in paragraph (a), 'British Islands' and 'colony' are to be construed in accordance with Schedule 1 to the Interpretation Act 1978 (c 30); and

(b) in paragraph (b), 'relevant forces' means—

(i) the armed forces of the Crown; and

(ii) any forces co-operating with those forces,

or any part of the armed forces of the Crown or of any such co-operating forces.

32 International relations

(1) Information is exempt information if—

(a) its disclosure under this Act would, or would be likely to, prejudice substantially—

(i) relations between the United Kingdom and any other State;

(ii) relations between the United Kingdom and any international organisation or international court;

(iii) the interests of the United Kingdom abroad; or

(iv) the promotion or protection by the United Kingdom of its interests abroad; or

(b) it is confidential information obtained from—

(i) a State other than the United Kingdom; or

(ii) an international organisation or international court.

(2) For the purposes of subsection (1), information obtained from a State, organisation or court is confidential at any time while—

(a) the terms on which that information was obtained require it to be held in confidence; or

(b) the circumstances in which it was obtained make it reasonable for the State, organisation or court to expect that it will be so held.

(3) In subsection (1)—

'international court' means an international court which—

(a) is not an international organisation; and

(b) is established—

(i) by a resolution of an international organisation of which the United Kingdom is a member; or

(ii) by an international agreement to which the United Kingdom is a party;

'international organisation' means—

(a) an international organisation whose members include any two or more States; or

(b) an organ of such an international organisation;

'State' includes—

(a) the government of any State; and

(b) any organ of such a government,

and references to a State other than the United Kingdom include references to any territory outwith the United Kingdom.

33 Commercial interests and the economy

(1) Information is exempt information if—

(a) it constitutes a trade secret; or

(b) its disclosure under this Act would, or would be likely to, prejudice substantially the commercial interests of any person (including, without prejudice to that generality, a Scottish public authority).

(2) Information is exempt information if its disclosure under this Act would, or would be likely to, prejudice substantially—

(a) the economic interests of the whole or part of the United Kingdom; or

(b) the financial interests of an administration in the United Kingdom.

(3) In subsection (2), 'administration in the United Kingdom' has the same meaning as in section 28(2).

34 Investigations by Scottish public authorities and proceedings arising out of such investigations

(1) Information is exempt information if it has at any time been held by a Scottish public authority for the purposes of—

(a) an investigation which the authority has a duty to conduct to ascertain whether a person—

(i) should be prosecuted for an offence; or

(ii) prosecuted for an offence is guilty of it;

(b) an investigation, conducted by the authority, which in the circumstances may lead to a decision by the authority to make a report to the procurator fiscal to enable it to be determined whether criminal proceedings should be instituted; or

(c) criminal proceedings instituted in consequence of a report made by the authority to the procurator fiscal.

(2) Information is exempt information if—

(a) held by a Scottish public authority for the purposes of an inquiry instituted under the [Inquiries into Fatal Accidents and Sudden Deaths etc (Scotland) Act 2016] but not for the time being concluded; or

(b) held at any time by a Scottish public authority for the purposes of any other investigation being carried out—

(i) by virtue of a duty to ascertain; or

(ii) for the purpose of making a report to the procurator fiscal as respects,

the cause of death of a person.

(3) Information held by a Scottish public authority is exempt information if—

(a) it was obtained or recorded by the authority for the purposes of investigations (other than such investigations as are mentioned in subsection (1)) which are, by virtue either of Her Majesty's prerogative or of powers conferred by or under any enactment, conducted by the authority for any purpose specified in section 35(2); and

(b) it relates to the obtaining of information from confidential sources.

(4) Information is exempt information if obtained or recorded by a Scottish public authority for the purposes of civil proceedings, brought by or on behalf of the authority, which arise out of such investigations as are mentioned in subsection (1) or (3).

35 Law enforcement

(1) Information is exempt information if its disclosure under this Act would, or would be likely to, prejudice substantially—

(a) the prevention or detection of crime;

(b) the apprehension or prosecution of offenders;

(c) the administration of justice;

(d) the assessment or collection of any tax or duty (or of any imposition of a similar nature);

(e) the operation of the immigration controls;

(f) the maintenance of security and good order in prisons or in other institutions where persons are lawfully detained;

(g) the exercise by any public authority (within the meaning of the Freedom of Information Act 2000) or Scottish public authority of its functions for any of the purposes mentioned in subsection (2);

(h) any civil proceedings—

(i) brought; and

(ii) arising out of an investigation conducted, for any such purpose,

by or on behalf of any such authority, by virtue either of Her Majesty's prerogative or of powers conferred by or under any enactment.

(2) The purposes are—

(a) to ascertain whether a person has failed to comply with the law;

(b) to ascertain whether a person is responsible for conduct which is improper;

(c) to ascertain whether circumstances which would justify regulatory action in pursuance of any enactment exist or may arise;

(d) to ascertain a person's fitness or competence in relation to—

(i) the management of bodies corporate; or

(ii) any profession or other activity which the person is, or seeks to become, authorised to carry on;

(e) to ascertain the cause of an accident;

(f) to protect a charity against misconduct or mismanagement (whether by trustees or other persons) in its administration;

(g) to protect the property of a charity from loss or mismanagement;

(h) to recover the property of a charity;

(i) to secure the health, safety and welfare of persons at work; and

(j) to protect persons, other than persons at work, against risk to health or safety where that risk arises out of, or in connection with, the actions of persons at work.

36 Confidentiality

(1) Information in respect of which a claim to confidentiality of communications could be maintained in legal proceedings is exempt information.

(2) Information is exempt information if—

(a) it was obtained by a Scottish public authority from another person (including another such authority); and

(b) its disclosure by the authority so obtaining it to the public (otherwise than under this Act) would constitute a breach of confidence actionable by that person or any other person.

37 Court records, etc

(1) Information is exempt information if it is contained in—

(a) a document—

(i) lodged with, or otherwise placed in the custody of, a court for the purposes of proceedings in a cause or matter;

(ii) served on, or by, a Scottish public authority for the purposes of such proceedings; or

(iii) created by a court or a member of its administrative staff for the purposes of, or in the course of, such proceedings; or

(b) a document—

(i) lodged with, or otherwise placed in the custody of, a person conducting an inquiry or arbitration, for the purposes of that inquiry or arbitration; or

(ii) created by such a person for such purposes,

and a Scottish public authority holds the information solely because it is contained in such a document.

(2) In this section—

'court' includes a tribunal or body exercising the judicial power of the State; and

'inquiry' means an inquiry or hearing held under a provision contained in, or made under, an enactment.

(3) This section does not apply to information held by a Scottish public authority for the purposes of an inquiry instituted under the [Inquiries into Fatal Accidents and Sudden Deaths etc (Scotland) Act 2016].

38 Personal information

(1) Information is exempt information if it constitutes—

(a) personal data of which the applicant is the data subject;

[(b) personal data and [the first, second or third condition is satisfied (see subsections (2A) to (3A));]].

(c) personal census information; or

(d) a deceased person's health record.

[. . .]

[(2A) The first condition is that the disclosure of the information to a member of the public otherwise than under this Act—

(a) would contravene any of the data protection principles, or

(b) would do so if the exemptions in section 24(1) of the Data Protection Act 2018 (manual unstructured data held by public authorities) were disregarded.

(2B) The second condition is that the disclosure of the information to a member of the public otherwise than under this Act would contravene Article 21 of the GDPR (general processing: right to object to processing).]

[. . .]

[(3A) The third condition is that—

(a) on a request under Article 15(1) of the GDPR (general processing: right of access by the data subject) for access to personal data, the information would be withheld in reliance on provision made by or under section 15, 16 or 26 of, or Schedule 2, 3 or 4 to, the Data Protection Act 2018, or

(b) on a request under section 45(1)(b) of that Act (law enforcement processing: right of access by the data subject), the information would be withheld in reliance on subsection (4) of that section.]

[. . .]

(5) In this section—

['the data protection principles' means the principles set out in—

(a) Article 5(1) of the GDPR, and

(b) section 34(1) of the Data Protection Act 2018;

'data subject' has the same meaning as in the Data Protection Act 2018 (see section 3 of that Act);

'the GDPR', 'personal data', 'processing' and references to a provision of Chapter 2 of Part 2 of the Data Protection Act 2018 have the same meaning as in Parts 5 to 7 of that Act (see section 3(2), (4), (10), (11) and (14) of that Act);]

'health record' has the meaning assigned to that term by section 1(1) of the Access to Health Records Act 1990; and

'personal census information' means any census information—

(a) as defined in section 8(7) of the Census Act 1920; or

(b) acquired or derived by virtue of sections 1 to 9 of the Census (Great Britain) Act 1910,

which relates to an identifiable person or household.

[(5A) In determining for the purposes of this section whether the lawfulness principle in Article 5(1)(a) of the GDPR would be contravened by the disclosure of information, Article 6(1) of the GDPR (lawfulness) is to be read as if the second sub-paragraph (disapplying the legitimate interests gateway in relation to public authorities) were omitted.]

(6) In section 8(7) of the Census Act 1920 (penalties), in the definition of 'personal census information', at the end there is added 'but does not include information which, by virtue of section 58(2)(b) of the Freedom of Information (Scotland) Act 2002 (falling away of exemptions with time), is not exempt information within the meaning of that Act'.

39 Health, safety and the environment

(1) Information is exempt information if its disclosure under this Act would, or would be likely to, endanger the physical or mental health or the safety of an individual.

(2) Information is exempt information if a Scottish public authority—

(a) is obliged by regulations under section 62 to make it available to the public in accordance with the regulations; or

(b) would be so obliged but for any exemption contained in the regulations.

(3) Subsection (2)(a) is without prejudice to the generality of section 25(1).

40 Audit functions

Information is exempt information if its disclosure under this Act would, or would be likely to, prejudice substantially the exercise of a Scottish public authority's functions in relation to—

(a) the audit of the accounts of other Scottish public authorities; or

(b) the examination of the economy, efficiency and effectiveness with which such authorities use their resources in discharging their functions.

41 Communications with Her Majesty etc and honours

Information is exempt information if it relates to—

(a) communications with Her Majesty, with other members of the Royal Family or with the Royal Household; or

(b) the exercise by Her Majesty of Her prerogative of honour.

PART 3
THE SCOTTISH INFORMATION COMMISSIONER

42 The Scottish Information Commissioner

(1) For the purposes of this Act there is to be an officer known as the Scottish Information Commissioner (in this Act referred to as the 'Commissioner') who is to be an individual appointed by Her Majesty on the nomination of the Parliament.

[(1A) A person is disqualified from appointment as the Commissioner if the person is, or holds office in, or is an employee or appointee of, another Scottish public authority.

(1B) The Commissioner may not, without the approval of the Parliamentary corporation, also be, or hold office in, or be an employee or appointee of, another Scottish public authority.]

(2) The Commissioner is entitled to—

(a) a salary of such amount; and

(b) such allowances,

as the Parliamentary corporation may determine.

(3) Subject to subsection (4), the Commissioner is to hold office for such period not exceeding [eight] years as the Parliamentary corporation, at the time of appointment, may determine.

[(3A) The Commissioner is to hold office otherwise on such terms and conditions as the Parliamentary corporation may determine.

(3B) Those terms and conditions may, without prejudice to subsection (1A)—

(a) prohibit the Commissioner from holding any other specified office, employment or appointment or engaging in any other specified occupation,

(b) provide that the Commissioner's holding of any such office, employment or appointment or engagement in any such occupation is subject to the approval of the Parliamentary corporation.

(3C) In subsection (3B), 'specified' means specified in the terms and conditions of office or within a description so specified.]

(4) The Commissioner—

(a) may be relieved of office by Her Majesty at that officer's request;

[. . .]

(c) may be removed from office by Her Majesty [if subsection (4A) applies];

[. . .]

[(4A) This subsection applies if—

(a) the Parliamentary corporation is satisfied that the Commissioner has breached the terms and conditions of office and the Parliament resolves that the Commissioner should be removed from office for that breach, or

(b) the Parliament resolves that it has lost confidence in the Commissioner's willingness, suitability or ability to perform the functions of the Commissioner, and, in either case, the resolution is voted for by a number of members not fewer than two thirds of the total number of seats for members of the Parliament.]

(5) [A person who has held office as Commissioner is ineligible for reappointment at any time.]

(6) The validity of any actings of the Commissioner is not affected by a defect in the nomination by the Parliament for that officer's appointment.

(7) The Commissioner, in the exercise of that officer's functions (except the function of preparing accounts), is not subject to the direction or control of the Parliamentary corporation, of any member of the Scottish Executive or of the Parliament; but this subsection is without prejudice to [sections 42(9C), 46(2A) and paragraphs 3(4), 4A, 6(2), 7 and 8] of schedule 2.

(8) Where the office of Commissioner is vacant, the Parliamentary corporation may appoint a person (who may or may not be a member of the Commissioner's staff) to discharge the functions of that office until a new Commissioner is appointed.

(9) A person appointed under subsection (8)—

(a) may be relieved of that appointment at that person's request;

(b) may be removed from office by the Parliamentary corporation by notice in writing given by it;

(c) in other respects, holds office on such terms and conditions as the Parliamentary corporation may determine; and

(d) while holding that appointment, is to be treated for all purposes, except those of subsections (1) to (6) and those of paragraph 2 of schedule 2, as the Commissioner.

[(9A) The Commissioner may obtain advice, assistance or any other service from any person who, in the opinion of the Commissioner, is qualified to give it.

(9B) The Commissioner may pay to that person such fees and allowances as the Commissioner determines.

(9C) Any payment under subsection (9B) is subject to the approval of the Parliamentary corporation.]

(10) Any function of the Commissioner may be exercised on behalf of that officer by any person (whether or not a member of that officer's staff) authorised by the Commissioner to do so (and to the extent so authorised).

(11) The Parliamentary corporation is to pay—

(a) the salary and allowances of the Commissioner;

(b) any expenses [properly] incurred by that officer in the exercise of functions under this Act [so far as those expenses are not met out of sums received and applied by that officer under section 43(6)]; and

(c) any sums payable by virtue of subsection (9)(a) to (c) to, or in respect of, a person who—

(i) is appointed under subsection (8); or

(ii) has ceased to hold office by virtue of having been so appointed.

[(11A) Subsection (11)(b) does not require the Parliamentary corporation to pay any expenses incurred by the Commissioner which exceed or are otherwise not covered by a budget or, as the case may be, revised budget approved under paragraph 4A of schedule 2.

(11B) However, the Parliamentary corporation may pay those expenses.

(11C) The Parliamentary corporation is to indemnify the Commissioner in respect of any liabilities incurred by the Commissioner in the exercise of the Commissioner's functions under this Act.]

(12) Schedule 2 to this Act has effect with respect to the Commissioner.

43 General functions of Commissioner

(1) The Commissioner, with a view in particular to promoting the observance by Scottish public authorities of the provisions of—

(a) this Act; and

(b) the codes of practice issued under sections 60 and 61,

is to promote the following of good practice by those authorities.

(2) The Commissioner—

(a) must determine what information it is expedient to give the public concerning the following matters—

(i) the operation of this Act;

(ii) good practice;

(iii) other matters within the scope of that officer's functions,

and must secure the dissemination of that information in an appropriate form and manner; and

(b) may give advice to any person as to any of those matters.

(3) The Commissioner may assess whether a Scottish public authority is following good practice.

(4) The Commissioner may from time to time make proposals to the Scottish Ministers for the exercise by them of their functions under sections 4 and 5 of this Act.

(5) The Commissioner may determine and charge [reasonable sums for anything done or provided by the Commissioner in the performance of, or in connection with the Commissioner's functions].

(6) Any sum received by the Commissioner by virtue of subsection (5) is to be retained by that officer and applied to meet expenditure incurred in [doing or providing whatever is charged for].

(7) The Commissioner must from time to time consult the Keeper of the Records of Scotland about the promotion under subsection (1) of the observance by Scottish public authorities of the provisions of the code of practice issued under section 61.

(8) In this section 'good practice', in relation to a Scottish public authority, means such practice in the discharge of its functions under this Act as appears to the Commissioner to be desirable, and includes (but is not limited to) compliance with the requirements of this Act and the provisions of the codes of practice issued under sections 60 and 61.

44 Recommendations as to good practice

(1) If it appears to the Commissioner that the practice of a Scottish public authority in relation to the exercise of its functions under this Act does not conform with the code of practice issued under section 60 or 61, the Commissioner may give the authority a recommendation (in this Act referred to as a 'practice recommendation').

(2) A practice recommendation must—

(a) be in writing and specify the code and the provisions of that code with which, in the Commissioner's opinion, the authority's practice does not conform; and

(b) specify the steps which that officer considers the authority ought to take in order to conform.

(3) The Commissioner must consult the Keeper of the Records of Scotland before giving a practice recommendation to a Scottish public authority (other than the Keeper) in relation to conformity with the code of practice issued under section 61.

45 Confidentiality of information obtained by or furnished to Commissioner

(1) A person who is or has been the Commissioner, a member of the Commissioner's staff or an agent of the Commissioner must not disclose any information which—

(a) has been obtained by, or furnished to, the Commissioner under or for the purposes of this Act; and

(b) is not at the time of the disclosure, and has not previously been, available to the public from another source, unless the disclosure is made with lawful authority.

(2) For the purposes of subsection (1), disclosure is made with lawful authority only if, and to the extent that—

(a) the disclosure is made with the consent of the person from whom the information was so obtained or by whom it was so furnished;

(b) the information was provided for the purpose of its being made available to the public (in whatever manner) under a provision of this Act;

(c) the disclosure is made for the purpose of, and is necessary for, the discharge of—

(i) a function under this Act; or

(ii) [an EU] obligation;

(d) the disclosure is made for the purpose of proceedings, whether criminal or civil and whether arising under, or by virtue of, this Act or otherwise; or

(e) either—

(i) in a case where the person mentioned in paragraph (a) is a Scottish public authority, had that person received on the day of disclosure a request for the information that person; or

(ii) in any other case, had the Commissioner received on that day such a request the Commissioner, would, by virtue of section 1(1), have been under an obligation to give it.

(3) A person who knowingly or recklessly discloses information in contravention of subsection (1) is guilty of an offence.

(4) A person guilty of an offence under subsection (3) is liable—

(a) on summary conviction, to a fine not exceeding the statutory maximum; or

(b) on conviction on indictment, to a fine.

46 [Laying and publication of reports]

(1) The Commissioner must lay annually before the Parliament a general report on the exercise [during the reporting year] of the functions conferred on that officer under this Act.

[(1A) Each report must be so laid within 7 months after the end of the reporting year.

(1B) In this section, 'reporting year' means the year beginning on 1 April.]

(2) The report mentioned in subsection (1) (without prejudice to the generality of that subsection) must record the number of occasions, during the period covered by the report, on which the Commissioner failed to reach a decision on an application under section 47(1) (being an application on which a decision fell to be made) within the period of four months specified in section 49(3)(b).

[(2A) In preparing a report under subsection (1), the Commissioner must comply with any direction given by the Parliamentary corporation as to the form and content of the report.]

(3) The Commissioner may from time to time lay before the Parliament such other reports with respect to the functions conferred on that officer under this Act as that officer thinks fit.

[(3A) The Commissioner must arrange for the publication of each report laid before the Parliament under this section.]

[46A Strategic plans

(1) The Commissioner must, in respect of each 4 year period, lay before the Parliament a plan (referred to in this section as a 'strategic plan') setting out how the Commissioner proposes to perform the Commissioner's functions during the 4 year period.

(2) A strategic plan must, in particular, set out—

(a) the Commissioner's objectives and priorities during the 4 year period,

(b) how the Commissioner proposes to achieve them,

(c) a timetable for doing so, and
(d) estimates of the costs of doing so.

(3) Before laying a strategic plan before the Parliament, the Commissioner must provide a draft of it to and invite, and (if any are given) consider, comments on it from—

(a) the Parliamentary corporation,
(b) the Keeper of the Records of Scotland, and
(c) such other persons as the Commissioner thinks appropriate.

(4) The reference in subsection (3)(c) to other persons includes a committee of the Parliament.

(5) The Commissioner must lay each strategic plan before the Parliament not later than the beginning of the 4 year period to which the plan relates.

(6) The Commissioner must arrange for the publication of each strategic plan laid before the Parliament.

(7) The Commissioner may, at any time during a 4 year period, review the strategic plan for the period and lay a revised strategic plan before the Parliament.

(8) Subsections (2) to (7) apply to a revised strategic plan as they apply to a strategic plan.

(9) In that application, the reference in subsection (5) to the 4 year period is a reference to the period to which the revised strategic plan relates.

(10) In this section, '4 year period' means the period of 4 years beginning on 1 April next following the coming into force of this section and each subsequent period of 4 years.]

PART 4
ENFORCEMENT

47 Application for decision by Commissioner

(1) A person who is dissatisfied with—

(a) a notice given under section 21(5) or (9); or

(b) the failure of a Scottish public authority to which a requirement for review was made to give such a notice,

may make application to the Commissioner for a decision whether, in any respect specified in that application, the request for information to which the requirement relates has been dealt with in accordance with Part 1 of this Act.

(2) An application under subsection (1) must—

(a) be in writing or in another form which, by reason of its having some permanency, is capable of being used for subsequent reference (as, for example, a recording made on audio or video tape);

(b) state the name of the applicant and an address for correspondence; and

(c) specify—

(i) the request for information to which the requirement for review relates;

(ii) the matter which was specified under sub-paragraph (ii) of section 20 (3)(c); and

(iii) the matter which gives rise to the dissatisfaction mentioned in subsection (1).

(3) For the purposes of paragraph (a) of subsection (2) (and without prejudice to the generality of that paragraph), an application under that subsection is treated as made in writing where the text of the application is as mentioned in paragraphs (a) to (c) of section 8(2).

(4) Subject to subsection (5), an application to the Commissioner under subsection (1) must be made—

(a) where the application concerns a matter mentioned in paragraph (a) of subsection (1), before the expiry of six months after the date of receipt by the applicant of the notice complained of; or

(b) where the application concerns a matter mentioned in paragraph (b) of that subsection, before the expiry of six months after the period allowed in section 21(1) for complying with a requirement for review has elapsed.

(5) The Commissioner may consider an application under subsection (1) made after the expiry of the time allowed by subsection (4) for the making of that application if, in the opinion of the Commissioner, it is appropriate to do so.

(6) The Scottish Ministers may by regulations provide—

(a) that a paragraph of subsection (4) is to have effect as if the reference in that paragraph to six months were a reference to such other period of months (being a period of not less than six months) as is specified in (or determined in accordance with) the regulations; and

(b) that subsection (5) is to have effect accordingly.

(7) Regulations under subsection (6) may—

(a) prescribe different periods of months in relation to different cases; and

(b) confer a discretion on the Commissioner.

(8) This section is subject to section 48.

48 When application excluded

No application may be made to the Commissioner for a decision under section 47 (1) as respects a request for review made to—

(a) the Commissioner;

(b) a procurator fiscal; or

(c) the Lord Advocate, to the extent that the information requested is held by the Lord Advocate as head of the systems of criminal prosecution and investigation of deaths in Scotland.

49 Commissioner's decision

(1) The Commissioner must make a decision in relation to an application made in accordance with section 47(1)which is not excluded by section 48 unless—

(a) in the opinion of the Commissioner, the application is frivolous or vexatious; or

(b) in the opinion of the Commissioner, the application appears to have been withdrawn or abandoned.

(2) In a case where the Commissioner determines that subsection (1) does not require a decision to be made, that officer must give the applicant and the Scottish public authority in question notice in writing within one month of receipt of the application, or within such other period as is reasonable in the circumstances, specifying—

(a) that no decision falls to be made in relation to the application; and

(b) the reasons why that is the case.

(3) In any other case, the Commissioner must—

(a) give that authority notice in writing of the application and invite its comments; and

(b) if no settlement has in the meantime been effected, reach a decision on the application before the expiry of four months after receiving it, or before the expiry of such other period as is reasonable in the circumstances.

(4) The Commissioner may endeavour to effect a settlement between the applicant and that authority before the expiry of the period allowed by subsection (3) for reaching a decision on the application.

(5) The Commissioner must give the applicant and that authority, within the time allowed by subsection (3), notice in writing (referred to in this Act as a 'decision notice') of any decision under paragraph (b) of that subsection.

(6) Where the Commissioner decides that that authority has not dealt with a request for information in accordance with Part 1 of this Act, the notice under subsection (5) must specify—

(a) the provision of that Part with which the authority has failed to comply and the respect in which it has so failed;

(b) the steps which, in the opinion of the Commissioner, the authority must take to comply with the provision; and

(c) the time within which those steps must be taken.

(7) The time specified under subsection (6)(c) must not expire before the end of the period within which an appeal may be brought under section 56 against the decision of the Commissioner and, if such an appeal is brought, no step which is affected by the appeal need be taken before the cause is finally determined.

(8) A notice under subsection (2) or (5) must contain particulars of the right of appeal conferred by section 56.

(9) This section is subject to section 52.

50 Information notices

(1) Where the Commissioner—

(a) has received an application under section 47(1); or

(b) reasonably requires information—

(i) for the purpose of determining whether a Scottish public authority has complied or is complying with the provisions of this Act; or

(ii) for the purpose of determining whether the practice of a Scottish public authority conforms with the code of practice issued under section 60 or 61,

that officer may give the authority notice in writing (referred to in this Act as 'an information notice') requiring it, within such time as is specified in the notice, to give the officer, in such form as may be so specified, such information relating to the application, to compliance with this Act or to conformity with the code of practice as is so specified.

(2) An information notice must contain—

(a) in a case mentioned in paragraph (a) of subsection (1) a statement that the Commissioner has received an application under section 47(1); or

(b) in a case mentioned in paragraph (b) of that subsection, a statement of—

(i) the purpose mentioned in that paragraph for which that officer regards the specified information as relevant;

(ii) the officer's reasons for so regarding the information; and

(iii) the time within which the information is to be given.

(3) An information notice must contain also particulars of the right of appeal conferred by section 56.

(4) The time specified under subsection (2)(b)(iii) in an information notice must not expire before the end of the period within which an appeal may be brought under section 56 against the notice; and, if such an appeal is brought, the information need not be given pending the determination or withdrawal of the appeal.

(5) A Scottish public authority is not obliged by virtue of this section to give the Commissioner information in respect of—

(a) a communication between professional legal adviser and client in connection with the giving of legal advice to the client with respect to that client's obligations under this Act; or

(b) a communication between professional legal adviser and client, or between such adviser or client and another person, made in connection with or in contemplation of proceedings under or arising out of this Act and for the purpose of such proceedings.

(6) In subsection (5), references to the client of a professional legal adviser include references to a person representing such client.

(7) Subject to subsection (5), neither—

(a) an obligation to maintain secrecy; nor

(b) any other restriction on disclosure,

however arising or imposed, affects the duty to comply with an information notice.

(8) The Commissioner may cancel an information notice by notice in writing given to the authority.

(9) In this section, 'information' includes unrecorded information.

51 Enforcement notices

(1) If the Commissioner is satisfied that a Scottish public authority has failed to comply with a provision of Part 1 of this Act, the Commissioner may give the authority a notice (referred to in this Act as 'an enforcement notice') requiring the authority to take, within such time as is specified in the notice, such steps as are so specified for so complying.

(2) An enforcement notice must contain—

(a) a statement of the provision with which the Commissioner is satisfied that the authority has failed to comply and the respect in which it has not done so; and

(b) particulars of the right of appeal conferred by section 56.

(3) The time specified under subsection (1) must not expire before the end of the period within which an appeal may be brought under section 56 against the notice and, if such an appeal is brought, the notice need not be complied with before the cause is finally determined.

(4) The Commissioner may cancel an enforcement notice by notice in writing given to the authority.

(5) This section is subject to section 52.

52 Exception from duty to comply with certain notices

(1) This section applies to a decision notice or enforcement notice which—

(a) is given to the Scottish Administration; and

(b) relates to a perceived failure, in respect of one or more requests for information, to comply with section 1(1) in respect of information which, by virtue of section 29, 31(1), 32(1)(b), 34, 36(1) or 41(b), is exempt information.

(2) A decision notice or enforcement notice to which this section applies ceases to have effect, in so far as it relates to the perceived failure, if, not later than the thirtieth working day following the effective date, the First Minister of the Scottish Executive, after consulting the other members of that Executive, signs and gives the Commissioner a certificate stating that the First Minister has on reasonable grounds formed, after such consultation, the opinion both that—

(a) there was no such failure; and

(b) the information requested is of exceptional sensitivity.

(3) The First Minister is, by not later than the tenth working day after such a certificate—

(a) is given, to lay a copy of it before the Parliament; and

(b) is given in relation to a decision notice, to inform the person to whose application the notice relates of the reasons for the opinion formed,

except that the First Minister is not obliged to provide information under paragraph (b) if, or to the extent that, compliance with that paragraph would necessitate the disclosure of exempt information.

(4) In subsection (2), 'the effective date', in relation to a notice, means—

(a) the day on which the notice was given to the Scottish Administration; or

(b) where an appeal under section 56 is brought, the day on which the cause is finally determined.

53 Failure to comply with notice

(1) If a Scottish public authority has failed to comply with—

(a) so much of a notice given to it by the Commissioner under subsection (5) of section 49 as, by virtue of subsection (6)(b) of that section, requires steps to be taken by the authority;

(b) an information notice; or

(c) an enforcement notice,

the Commissioner may certify in writing to the court that the authority has failed to comply with the notice.

(2) For the purposes of this section, a Scottish public authority which, in purported compliance with an information notice—

(a) makes a statement which it knows to be false in a material respect; or

(b) recklessly makes a statement which is false in a material respect,

is to be taken to have failed to comply with the notice.

(3) Where a failure to comply is certified under subsection (1), the court may inquire into the matter and, after hearing any witness who may be produced against or on behalf of the authority, and after hearing any statement that may be offered in defence, may deal with the authority as if it had committed a contempt of court.

(4) In this section, 'the court' means the Court of Session.

54 Powers of entry and inspection

Schedule 3, which makes provision as to powers of entry and inspection, has effect.

55 No civil right of action against Scottish public authority

(1) This Act does not confer a right of action in civil proceedings in respect of failure by a Scottish public authority to comply with a duty imposed by, under or by virtue of this Act.

(2) Subsection (1) does not affect the powers of the Commissioner under section 53(1).

56 Appeal against notices under Part 4

An appeal, on a point of law, to the Court of Session may be made—

(a) against a decision by the Commissioner under subsection (2) of section 49, by the person who applied for that decision;

(b) against a decision by the Commissioner under subsection (3)(b) of that section—

(i) by that person; or

(ii) by the Scottish public authority in respect of which the decision was made; or

(c) against the decision which resulted in the giving of—

(i) an information notice; or

(ii) an enforcement notice,

to a Scottish public authority, by that authority.

PART 7
MISCELLANEOUS AND SUPPLEMENTAL

62 Power to make provision relating to environmental information

(1) In this section 'the Aarhus Convention' means the Convention on Access to Information, Public Participation in Decision making and Access to Justice in Environmental Matters signed at Aarhus on 25th June 1998.

(2) For the purposes of this section, 'the information provisions' of the Aarhus Convention are Article 4, together with Articles 3 and 9 so far as relating to that Article.

(3) The Scottish Ministers may, in relation to information held by or requested from any Scottish public authority, by regulations make such provision as they consider appropriate—

(a) for the purpose of implementing the information provisions of the Aarhus Convention or any amendment of those provisions made in accordance with Article 14 of the Convention; and

(b) for the purpose of dealing with matters arising out of, or related to, the implementation of those provisions or of any such amendment.

(4) Regulations under subsection (3) may in particular—

(a) enable charges to be made for making information available in accordance with the regulations;

(b) provide that any obligation imposed by the regulations in relation to the disclosure of information is to have effect notwithstanding any enactment or rule of law;

(c) make provision for the issue by the Scottish Ministers of a code of practice;

(d) provide for sections 43 and 44 to apply in relation to such a code with such modifications as may be specified in the regulations;

(e) provide for all or any of the provisions of Part 4 to apply, with such modifications as may be so specified, in relation to compliance with any requirement of the regulations; and

(f) contain such transitional or consequential provision (including provision modifying any enactment) as the Scottish Ministers consider appropriate.

63 Disclosure of information to Scottish Public Services Ombudsman or to Information Commissioner

The Commissioner may disclose to—

(a) the Scottish Public Services Ombudsman any information obtained by, or furnished to, the Commissioner under or for the purposes of this Act if it appears to the Commissioner that the information relates to a matter which is, or could be, the subject of an investigation by the Ombudsman under the Scottish Public Services Ombudsman Act 2002; or

(b) the Information Commissioner any information so obtained or furnished if it appears to the Commissioner that the information so relates as is mentioned in paragraph (a) or (b) of section 11AA(1) of the Parliamentary Commissioner Act 1967 (disclosure of information by Parliamentary Commissioner to Information Commissioner).

64 Power to amend or repeal enactments prohibiting disclosure of information

(1) If it appears to the Scottish Ministers that by virtue of section 26(a) a relevant enactment is capable of preventing the disclosure of information under section 1, they may by order repeal or amend that enactment, in so far as it relates to any Scottish public authority, so as to remove or relax the prohibition.

(2) In subsection (1)—

'relevant enactment' means an Act of Parliament, or Act of the Scottish Parliament, which receives Royal Assent before the end of the calendar year in which this Act receives Royal Assent or any subordinate legislation made before the date on which this Act receives Royal Assent; and

'information' includes unrecorded information.

(3) An order under subsection (1) may do all or any of the following—

(a) make such modifications of enactments as, in the opinion of the Scottish Ministers, are consequential upon, or incidental to, the repeal or amendment of the relevant enactment;

(b) contain such transitional provisions and savings as appear to them to be appropriate;

(c) make different provision in relation to different cases.

65 Offence of altering etc records with intent to prevent disclosure

(1) Where—

(a) a request for information is made to a Scottish public authority; and

(b) the applicant is, under section 1, entitled to be given the information or any part of it, a person to whom this subsection applies who, with the intention of preventing the disclosure by the authority of the information, or part, to which the entitlement relates, alters, defaces, blocks, erases, destroys or conceals a record held by the authority, is guilty of an offence.

(2) Subsection (1) applies to the authority and to any person who is employed by, is an officer of, or is subject to the direction of, the authority.

(3) A person guilty of an offence under subsection (1) is liable, on summary conviction, to a fine not exceeding level 5 on the standard scale.

[65A Time limit for proceedings

(1) Proceedings for an offence under section 65(1) may be commenced within the period of 6 months beginning with the date on which evidence that the prosecutor believes is sufficient to justify the proceedings came to the prosecutor's knowledge.

(2) No such proceedings may be commenced more than 3 years—

(a) after the commission of the offence, or

(b) in the case of a continuous contravention, after the last date on which the offence was committed.

(3) In the case of a continuous contravention, the complaint may specify the entire period during which the offence was committed.

(4) A certificate signed by or on behalf of the prosecutor stating the date on which the evidence referred to in subsection (1) came to the prosecutor's knowledge is conclusive as to that fact (and such a certificate purporting to be so signed is to be regarded as being so signed unless the contrary is proved).

(5) Section 136(3) of the Criminal Procedure (Scotland) Act 1995 applies for the purposes of this section as it does for those of that section.]

66 Saving for existing powers of disclosure

Nothing in this Act is to be taken to limit the powers of a Scottish public authority to disclose information held by it.

67 Protection from actions for defamation

Where, in compliance with a request for information, information supplied to a Scottish public authority by a third party is communicated by the authority, under section 1, to the applicant, the publication to the applicant of any defamatory matter contained in the information so supplied is privileged unless that publication is shown to have been made with malice.

68 Scottish Parliament and Scottish Administration

Section 65 and paragraph 10 of schedule 3 apply to—

(a) a member of the staff of, or a person acting on behalf of, the Parliament or the Parliamentary corporation; or

(b) a member of the staff of the Scottish Administration,

as they apply to any other person; but none of those bodies is liable to prosecution under this Act.

69 Exercise of rights by children

(1) Where a question falls to be determined as to the legal capacity of a person who has not attained the age of sixteen years to exercise any right conferred by any provision of this Act, any such person is to be taken to have that capacity who has a general understanding of what it means to exercise the right.

(2) Without prejudice to the generality of subsection (1), a person who has attained the age of twelve years is to be presumed to be of sufficient age and maturity to have such understanding as is mentioned in that subsection.

73 Interpretation

In this Act, unless the context requires a different interpretation—

'the Commissioner' means the Scottish Information Commissioner;

'body' includes an unincorporated association;

'decision notice' has the meaning given by section 49(5);
'enactment' includes an enactment comprised in, or in an instrument made under, an Act of the Scottish Parliament;
'enforcement notice' has the meaning given by section 51(1);
'exempt information' means information which is so described in any provision of Part 2;
'fees notice' has the meaning given by section 9(1);
'information' (subject to sections 50(9) and 64(2)) means information recorded in any form;
'information notice' has the meaning given by section 50(1);
'Minister of the Crown' has the same meaning as in the Ministers of the Crown Act 1975 (c 26);
'the Parliamentary corporation' means the Scottish Parliamentary Corporate Body;
'publication scheme' has the meaning given by section 23(1)(a);
'refusal notice' has the meaning given by section 16(1) (including that section as read with section 18(2));
'requirement for review' has the meaning given by section 20(2);
'Scottish public authority' has the meaning given by section 3(1);
'subordinate legislation' has the same meaning as in the Interpretation Act 1978 (c 30) but includes an instrument made under an Act of the Scottish Parliament; and
'working day' means any day other than a Saturday, a Sunday, Christmas Day or a day which, under the Banking and Financial Dealings Act 1971 (c 80), is a bank holiday in Scotland.

SCOTTISH PARLIAMENTARY STANDARDS COMMISSIONER ACT 2002
(2002, asp 16)

The Scottish Parliamentary Standards Commissioner

[. . .]

3 Functions of the Commissioner

(1) Subject to the provisions of this Act, where a complaint has been made to the [Commissioner for Ethical Standards in Public Life in Scotland ('the Commissioner')] about the conduct of a member of the Parliament, it shall be the function of the Commissioner to—

(a) investigate whether the member has committed the conduct complained about and has, as a result of that conduct, breached a relevant provision; and
(b) report upon the outcome of that investigation to the Parliament.

(2) However, subject to section 12, the Commissioner shall not investigate any complaint which falls within a class of complaint which is excluded from the jurisdiction of the Commissioner by any provision in the standing orders or in the Code of Conduct; and any such complaint is referred to in this Act as an 'excluded complaint'.

(3) A 'relevant provision' is any provision in force at the relevant time—

(a) in the standing orders;
(b) in the Code of Conduct;
(c) in the Scotland Act 1998 (Transitory and Transitional Provisions) (Members' Interests) Order 1999; or
(d) made by or under an Act of the Scottish Parliament in pursuance of section 39 (members' interests) of the Scotland Act.

(4) The 'relevant time' is the time when the conduct in question is alleged to have taken place, whether before or after this section comes into force.

(5) The Commissioner may give advice to a member of the Parliament or to a

member of the public about the procedures for making a complaint to the Commissioner and the procedures following upon the making of such a complaint.

(6) However, the Commissioner shall not—

(a) give advice to a member of the Parliament or to a member of the public as to whether any conduct which has been, or is proposed to be, committed by a member of the Parliament (whether or not the member seeking such advice) would constitute a breach of a relevant provision; or

(b) otherwise express any view upon any of the relevant provisions except in the context of an investigation in any particular case or in a report upon the outcome of that investigation or in such other circumstances as may be specified in any direction given to the Commissioner by the Parliament.

(7) In addition to the functions mentioned in subsections (1) and (5), the Commissioner also has the functions which are conferred or imposed upon the Commissioner by virtue of any other provision in this Act or in any other enactment or in the standing orders.

4 Directions to the Commissioner

(1) The Commissioner shall, in carrying out the functions of that office, comply with any directions given by the Parliament.

(2) Any direction to the Commissioner by the Parliament under this section may, in particular—

(a) make provision as to the procedure to be followed by the Commissioner when conducting—

(i) investigations generally into any complaint about the conduct of a member of the Parliament; or

(ii) investigations into complaints falling within such class or classes as may be specified in the direction (and different provision may be made in relation to different classes of complaint); or

(b) require the Commissioner to make a report to the Parliament upon such matter relating to the exercise of the functions of the Commissioner as may be specified in the direction.

(3) However, any direction to the Commissioner by the Parliament under this section shall not direct the Commissioner as to whether or how any particular investigation is to be carried out.

Investigation of complaints

5 General provisions relating to an investigation into a complaint

(1) There are two possible stages to any investigation by the Commissioner into a complaint, namely—

(a) Stage 1 which consists of investigating and determining whether a complaint is admissible; and

(b) if the complaint is admissible, Stage 2 which consists of further investigating the complaint and reporting upon it to the Parliament, and any reference in this Act to 'the stage of an investigation' or to 'Stage 1' or 'Stage 2' shall be construed accordingly.

(2) Each stage of an investigation into a complaint shall be conducted in private.

(3) The Commissioner may at any time make a report to the Parliament as to the progress of an investigation into a complaint.

(4) Subject to the provisions of this Act, it is for the Commissioner to decide when and how to carry out any investigation at each stage.

6 Stage 1: Admissibility of complaints

(1) At Stage 1, the Commissioner shall investigate and determine whether a complaint is admissible.

(2) A complaint is admissible if it appears to the Commissioner that the following three tests are satisfied, namely—

(a) that the complaint is relevant;

(b) that the complaint meets all the requirements specified in subsection (5) ('the specified requirements') or that the Parliament has, as under section 7(7)(b), directed the Commissioner to treat the complaint as if it had met all of those requirements; and

(c) that the complaint warrants further investigation.

(3) The three tests mentioned in paragraphs (a), (b) and (c) of subsection (2) are referred to as the first, second and third tests respectively.

(4) For the purposes of the first test, a complaint is relevant if—

(a) it is about the conduct of a member of the Parliament;

(b) it is not an excluded complaint or, if it is, that the Commissioner has been directed under section 12 to investigate it; and

(c) it appears at first sight that, if all or part of the conduct complained about is established to have been committed by that member, it might amount to a breach of a relevant provision or provisions identified by the Commissioner.

(5) For the purposes of the second test, the specified requirements are that the complaint—

(a) is made in writing to the Commissioner;

(b) is made by an individual person, is signed by that person and states that person's name and address;

(c) names the member of the Parliament concerned;

(d) sets out the facts relevant to the conduct complained about and is accompanied by any supporting evidence which the complainer wishes to submit; and

(e) is made within one year from the date when the complainer could reasonably have become aware of the conduct complained about.

(6) For the purposes of the third test, a complaint warrants further investigation if it appears after an initial investigation that the evidence is sufficient to suggest that the conduct complained about may have taken place.

7 Procedures at Stage 1

(1) When the Commissioner receives a complaint about the conduct of a member of the Parliament, the Commissioner shall—

(a) notify that member that a complaint has been made;

(b) inform that member of the nature of the complaint; and

(c) except where the Commissioner considers that it would be inappropriate to do so, inform that member of the name of the complainer.

(2) If the Commissioner considers that the complaint is admissible, the Commissioner shall proceed to Stage 2 of the investigation into the complaint and shall—

(a) make a report to the Parliament informing it of that fact and of the relevant provision or provisions identified by the Commissioner for the purposes of the first test; and

(b) inform the complainer and the member of the Parliament concerned accordingly.

(3) If the Commissioner considers that the complaint is inadmissible for failing to satisfy the first or the third test, the Commissioner shall dismiss the complaint and shall inform the complainer and the member of the Parliament concerned accordingly, together with the reasons for that view.

(4) Subject to subsection (6), where the Commissioner considers that a complaint satisfies the first test but fails to meet one or more of the specified requirements, the Commissioner shall not dismiss the complaint as inadmissible for failing to satisfy the second test without making a report upon the matter to the Parliament and receiving a direction under subsection (7)(a).

(5) The report under subsection (4) shall set out—

(a) the reasons as to why the Commissioner considers that the complaint fails to meet one or more of the specified requirements;

(b) the reasons (if known) for that failure;

(c) any other matters which the Commissioner considers relevant; and

(d) the recommendation of the Commissioner as to whether, having regard to all the circumstances of the case, the complaint should be dismissed as inadmissible for failing to satisfy the second test or should be treated as if it had met all of those requirements.

(6) Except in the case of a complaint falling within such class or classes of case as may be specified in any direction by the Parliament under this section, the Commissioner shall, before making the report to the Parliament under subsection (4), investigate whether the complaint satisfies the third test and, if it does, the report shall contain a statement to that effect; but, if the Commissioner considers that the complaint fails to satisfy that test, the Commissioner shall dismiss the complaint accordingly and no report requires to be made under that subsection.

(7) After receiving a report under subsection (4), the Parliament shall give the Commissioner a direction under this section either—

(a) to dismiss the complaint as inadmissible for failing to satisfy the second test; or

(b) to treat the complaint as if it had met all of the specified requirements.

(8) Where the Commissioner is directed by the Parliament to dismiss the complaint under subsection (7)(a), the Commissioner shall dismiss the complaint and shall inform the complainer and the member of the Parliament concerned accordingly.

(9) In any case where the member of the Parliament concerned has not been named in the complaint or the complainer is anonymous, subsections (1), (2), (3) and (8) shall apply only to the extent that they are capable of applying.

(10) The Commissioner may make a report to the Parliament informing it of any complaint which the Commissioner has dismissed as being inadmissible and of the reasons for the dismissal.

(11) If the Commissioner has not completed the investigation and determined the admissibility of a complaint within two months of the complaint being received, the Commissioner shall, as soon as possible thereafter, make a report to the Parliament upon the progress of any investigation into the complaint at Stage 1.

8 Stage 2: Investigation of an admissible complaint

(1) At Stage 2, the Commissioner shall investigate an admissible complaint with a view to—

(a) making findings of fact in relation to whether the member of the Parliament concerned (whether or not named in the complaint) has committed the conduct complained about; and

(b) reaching a conclusion as to whether that member has, as a result of that conduct, breached the relevant provision or provisions identified by the Commissioner for the purposes of the first test.

(2) The Commissioner may make a finding of fact if satisfied on a balance of probabilities that the fact is established.

(3) If the Commissioner has not completed the investigation under this section within the period of six months beginning with the date on which the Commissioner found that complaint to be admissible, the Commissioner shall, as soon as possible thereafter, make a report to the Parliament upon the progress of any such investigation.

9 Report

(1) At the conclusion of an investigation into a complaint at Stage 2, the Commissioner shall make a report to the Parliament upon the outcome of the investigation.

(2) The report shall include—

(a) details of the complaint;

(b) details of the investigation carried out by the Commissioner;

(c) the facts found by the Commissioner in relation to whether the member of the Parliament concerned (whether or not named in the complaint) has committed the conduct complained about;

(d) the conclusion reached by the Commissioner as to whether that member has, as a result of that conduct, breached the relevant provision or provisions identified by the Commissioner for the purposes of the first test and the reasons for that view,

but shall not express any view upon what sanction would be appropriate for any breach.

(3) No report concluding that a member of the Parliament, who is named in the report, has breached a relevant provision shall be made to the Parliament unless the member concerned has been given a copy of the draft report and an opportunity to make representations on the alleged breach and on the draft report; and there shall be annexed to the report made to the Parliament any representations made by that member which are not given effect to in that report.

10 Action on receipt of a report

(1) The Parliament is not bound by the facts found, or the conclusions reached, by the Commissioner in a report made under section 9.

(2) The Parliament may direct the Commissioner to carry out such further investigations as may be specified in the direction and to report on the outcome of these investigations to it.

(3) Subject to any such direction, the provisions of this Act and of any other direction given under this Act shall apply, subject to any necessary modifications, in relation to any investigation and report by virtue of subsection (2) as they apply in relation to an investigation and report into a complaint made to the Commissioner.

11 Withdrawal of a complaint

(1) At any time after a complaint has been made to the Commissioner and before a report is made to the Parliament under section 9, the complaint may be withdrawn by the complainer by notice in writing to the Commissioner which is signed by the complainer.

(2) When a complaint has been withdrawn as mentioned in subsection (1) during Stage 1, the Commissioner shall—

(a) cease to investigate that complaint; and

(b) inform the member of the Parliament concerned that the complaint has been withdrawn, that the investigation into the complaint has ceased and of the reasons given by the complainer for withdrawing the complaint.

(3) When a complaint has been withdrawn as mentioned in subsection (1) during Stage 2, the Commissioner shall—

(a) inform the member of the Parliament concerned that the complaint has been withdrawn and of the reasons given by the complainer for withdrawing the complaint;

(b) invite that member to give the Commissioner any views upon whether the investigation should nevertheless continue; and

(c) after taking into account any relevant information, including any reasons given by the complainer for withdrawing the complaint and any views expressed by that member, determine whether to recommend to the Parliament that the investigation into the complaint should nevertheless continue.

(4) If the Commissioner determines not to make any such recommendation as is mentioned in subsection (3), the Commissioner shall—

(a) cease to investigate that complaint;

(b) inform the complainer and the member of the Parliament concerned the investigation into the complaint has ceased; and

(c) report to the Parliament that the complaint has been withdrawn,

that the investigation into the complaint has ceased and the reasons given by the complainer for withdrawing the complaint.

(5) If the Commissioner determines to make any such recommendation as is mentioned in subsection (3), the Commissioner shall report to the Parliament—

(a) that the complaint has been withdrawn, the reasons given by the complainer for withdrawing the complaint and the views, if any, expressed by the member concerned as mentioned in subsection (3)(b); and

(b) that the Commissioner recommends that the complaint should nevertheless continue to be investigated, together with the reasons for that view.

(6) After receiving a report under subsection (5), the Parliament shall give the Commissioner a direction under this section either to continue the investigation into the complaint or to cease that investigation; and the Commissioner shall comply with that direction and inform the member of the Parliament concerned and the complainer accordingly.

(7) Where the Commissioner is required under this section to inform the member of the Parliament concerned of, or to report to the Parliament, the reasons given by the complainer for withdrawing the complaint, the Commissioner may do so by providing a summary of those reasons.

(8) In any case where the member of the Parliament concerned has not been named in the complaint or the complainer has not given any reasons for withdrawing the complaint, subsections (2) to (7) shall apply only to the extent that they are capable of applying.

12 Investigation into excluded complaints

(1) The Parliament may direct the Commissioner to undertake an investigation into any excluded complaint specified in the direction.

(2) Any such direction may direct the Commissioner to take into account any information in connection with the excluded complaint which is specified in the direction.

(3) Any such direction may direct the Commissioner to treat an excluded complaint as being admissible and, if so, shall specify the relevant provision or provisions which is or are to be treated as having been identified by the Commissioner for the purposes of the first test.

(4) Subject to any such direction, any excluded complaint which the Commissioner is directed to investigate shall be treated in the same way as any other complaint made to the Commissioner.

(5) Subject to any such direction, the provisions of this Act and of any other direction given under this Act shall apply, subject to any necessary modifications, in relation to any investigation and report by virtue of this section as they apply in relation to a complaint made to the Commissioner.

. . .

LOCAL GOVERNMENT IN SCOTLAND ACT 2003
(2003, asp 1)

PART 1
BEST VALUE AND ACCOUNTABILITY

Duty to secure best value

1 Local authorities' duty to secure best value

(1) It is the duty of a local authority to make arrangements which secure best value.

(2) Best value is continuous improvement in the performance of the authority's functions.

(3) In securing best value, the local authority shall maintain an appropriate balance among—

(a) the quality of its performance of its functions;

(b) the cost to the authority of that performance; and

(c) the cost to persons of any service provided by it for them on a wholly or partly rechargeable basis.

(4) In maintaining that balance, the local authority shall have regard to—

(a) efficiency;

(b) effectiveness;

(c) economy; and

(d) the need to meet the equal opportunity requirements.

(5) The local authority shall discharge its duties under this section in a way which contributes to the achievement of sustainable development.

(6) In measuring the improvement of the performance of a local authority's functions for the purposes of this section, regard shall be had to the extent to which the outcomes of that performance have improved.

(7) In this section, 'equal opportunity requirements' has the same meaning as in Section L2 of Part II of Schedule 5 to the Scotland Act 1998.

2 Considerations bearing on performance of duty under section 1

(1) In the performance of its duties under section 1 above, a local authority shall have regard—

(a) to any guidance provided by the Scottish Ministers for local authorities on the performance of those duties; and such guidance may include guidance on—

(i) how to make and what is to be included in the arrangements referred to in subsection (1) of that section;

(ii) how to implement the duty imposed by that subsection; and

(b) to what are, whether by reference to any generally recognised, published code or otherwise, regarded as proper arrangements for the purposes of section 1(1) above (or purposes which include those purposes).

(2) Before providing guidance under this section, the Scottish Ministers shall consult such associations of local authorities and such other persons as they think appropriate.

(3) In the event of a conflict in any respect between the considerations to which a local authority is to have regard under paragraph (a) of subsection (1) above and those to which it has to have regard under paragraph (b) of that subsection, it shall in that respect have regard only to those within paragraph (a).

PART 3
POWER TO ADVANCE WELL-BEING

20 Power to advance well-being

(1) A local authority has power to do anything which it considers is likely to promote or improve the well-being of—

(a) its area and persons within that area; or

(b) either of those.

(2) The power under subsection (1) above includes power to—

(a) incur expenditure,

(b) give financial assistance to any person,

(c) enter into arrangements or agreements with any person,

(d) co-operate with, or facilitate or co-ordinate the activities of, any person,

(e) exercise on behalf of any person any functions of that person, and

(f) provide staff, goods, materials, facilities, services or property to any person.

(3) The power under subsection (1) above may be exercised in relation to, or for the benefit of—

(a) the whole or any part of the area of the local authority;

(b) all or some of the persons within that area.

(4) The power under subsection (1) above includes power to do anything—

(a) in relation to, or for the benefit of, any persons or place outwith the area of the local authority; or

(b) in any such place,

if the authority considers that doing so is likely to achieve the purpose set out in that subsection.

(5) The Scottish Ministers may, by order, extend the meaning of 'well-being' for the purposes of this section.

(6) Such an order shall be made by statutory instrument but not unless a draft of it has been laid before and approved by resolution of the Scottish Parliament.

(7) Before laying such a statutory instrument, the Scottish Ministers shall consult such associations of local authorities as they think fit.

21 Guidance on exercise of power under section 20

(1) Before exercising the power under section 20 above, a local authority shall have regard to any guidance provided by the Scottish Ministers about the exercise of the power.

(2) Before providing any such guidance, the Scottish Ministers shall consult such associations of local authorities and other persons as they think fit.

22 Limits on power under section 20

(1) The power under section 20 above does not enable a local authority to do anything which it is, by virtue of a limiting provision, unable to do.

(2) In subsection (1) above, a 'limiting provision' is one which—

(a) prohibits or prevents the local authority from doing anything or limits its powers in that respect; and

(b) is expressed in an enactment (whenever passed or made).

(3) The absence from any enactment of provision conferring any power does not of itself make that enactment a limiting provision.

(4) The power under section 20 above shall not be exercised in a way which unreasonably duplicates anything which may or must be done in pursuance of a function, under any enactment (whenever passed or made), of a person other than the local authority.

(5) Subsection (4) above does not prevent the exercise of the power under section 20 in a way which duplicates anything of the kind mentioned in that subsection if the person there mentioned consents to that exercise of the power.

(6) The power under section 20 above does not enable the doing of anything which may be done under the Local Authorities (Goods and Services) Act 1970.

(7) The power under section 20 above does not enable a local authority to do anything for the purposes of enabling the authority to raise money by levying or imposing any form of tax or charge, by borrowing or otherwise.

(8) Nothing in subsection (7) above prevents a local authority from—

(a) setting and determining amounts of council tax; or

(b) subject to subsection (9) below, imposing reasonable charges for anything done by the authority under section 20 above.

(9) [. . .] the saving in subsection (8)(b) above does not enable a local authority to impose charges in respect of anything done by it in pursuance of any of the following functions—

(a) functions relating to education in schools;

(b) functions relating to the provision of a public library service;

[. . .]

(d) functions relating to the registration of elections;

(e) functions relating to the conduct of elections;

(f) such other functions as may by order be prescribed for the purposes of this subsection by the Scottish Ministers.

(10) Before making an order under subsection (9)(f) above, the Scottish Ministers shall consult such associations of local authorities and such other persons as they think fit.

(11) Where, under section 20 above, a local authority imposes any charge, it shall publish its reason for doing so and an explanation of how it arrived at the amount of the charge.

(12) Any order under subsection (9)(f) above shall be made by statutory instrument which shall be subject to annulment in pursuance of a resolution of the Scottish Parliament.

(13) A local authority shall not, without the prior consent of the Scottish Ministers, do anything under section 20 above outside the United Kingdom for the purpose of promoting or improving the economic development of its area.

(14) Nothing in section 20 above affects section 92(5) of the Housing (Scotland) Act 2001 (by which it is provided that certain assistance, including financial assistance, provided by a local authority for certain housing purposes requires the consent of the Scottish Ministers).

PART 4
ENFORCEMENT AND SCRUTINY

23 Enforcement: preliminary notice

(1) Where, on a recommendation having been made to them under section 103D of the 1973 Act as applied by section 4 above, it appears to the Scottish Ministers—

(a) that a local authority is not complying or has not complied with its duties under section 1, 13, 15 or, as the case may be, 17 above; and

(b) that an enforcement notice is justified,

they may service a preliminary notice on the authority.

(2) Where, without a recommendation having been so made to them, it appears to Scottish Ministers—

(a) that a local authority is not complying or has not complied with section 1; and

(b) that giving the local authority an enforcement direction is justified in order to protect the public interest from substantial harm,

they may serve a preliminary notice on the authority.

(3) A preliminary notice is a written notice which—

(a) informs the authority of its apparent failure to comply with its duties under sections 1, 13, 15 or, as the case may be, 17 above; and

(b) requires the authority to submit to the Scottish Ministers, within such time as is specified in the notice, a written response which—

(i) states that it has not failed to comply with its duties under section 1, 13, 15 or, as the case may be, 17 above in the respects described in the notice and justifies the statement; or

(ii) states it has so failed but gives reasons why they should not give it an enforcement direction.

24 Enforcement directions

(1) Where, following the service of a preliminary notice and the expiry of the time specified in it under section 23(3)(b) above, it still appears to the Scottish Ministers that the local authority is not complying with its duties under section 1, 13, 15 or, as the case may be, 17 above and that action by them under this section is justified they may give the authority an enforcement direction.

(2) An enforcement direction is a direction by the Scottish Ministers requiring the local authority to which it is given to take such action as is specified in the direction being action calculated to remedy or prevent the recurrence of its failure to comply with its duties under section 1, 13, 15 or, as the case may be, 17 above.

(3) An enforcement direction may place such conditions as the Scottish Ministers may specify in it upon the carrying out of such functions of the local authority as are so specified.

(4) The action referred to in subsection (2) above may include rectification of accounts.

(5) The Scottish Ministers may vary an enforcement direction by giving a further such direction.

(6) A further such direction need not proceed upon a further preliminary notice under section 23 above.

(7) An enforcement direction may be revoked by the Scottish Ministers.

(8) It is the duty of the local authority to which an enforcement direction is given to comply with it.

(9) The Scottish Ministers may, instead of or as well as giving an enforcement direction, make such recommendations to such persons as they think appropriate.

(10) If the Scottish Ministers exercise their power to give, vary or revoke an enforcement direction they shall—

(a) prepare a report on their exercise of that power; and

(b) lay that report before the Scottish Parliament.

PART 7
FINANCE

35 Capital expenditure limits

(1) It is the duty of a local authority to determine and keep under review the maximum amount which it can afford to allocate to capital expenditure.

(2) In discharging that duty, the local authority shall comply with regulations made by the Scottish Ministers for the purposes of this section.

. . .

36 Imposition of capital expenditure limits

(1) The Scottish Ministers may—

(a) by order, set the maximum amounts which local authorities may allocate to capital expenditure;

(b) by direction, set the maximum amounts which a particular local authority may allocate to capital expenditure.

(2) A maximum amount set under subsection (1) above supersedes any corresponding amount determined under section 35 above.

(3) Different amounts may be set under subsection (1) above in relation to different kinds of capital expenditure.

(4) As soon as practicable after the making of an order or direction under subsection (1) above, the Scottish Ministers shall lay before the Scottish Parliament a report containing information about the effect of the order or, as the case may be, direction and the reasons for making it.

37 Capital grants

(1) The Scottish Ministers may make grants to local authorities in respect of their capital expenditure.

(2) Grants made under this section shall be of such amount and may be made subject to such conditions (including conditions requiring their repayment in specified circumstances) as the Scottish Ministers may determine.

38 Scottish Ministers' power to pay off loans made to local authorities

(1) The Scottish Ministers may make to the Public Works Loan Commissioners or to any other person payment reducing or extinguishing a local authority's liability to the Commissioners or, as the case may be, that other person in respect of a loan made by the Commissioners or that other person to the authority for the purposes of capital expenditure.

(2) If the Scottish Ministers make a payment in pursuance of subsection (1) above they shall—

(a) prepare a report on their reasons for making that payment; and

(b) lay that report before the Scottish Parliament.

40 Power of local authorities to invest money

(1) A local authority may, in accordance with regulations made under this section, invest money.

(2) The Scottish Ministers may make regulations—

(a) specifying (by reference or otherwise) the investments or kinds of investments which a local authority may, or may not, make;

(b) providing that any code or other document containing guidance or advice specified or referred to in the regulations is to have effect for the purpose of regulating the investments or kinds of investments which a local authority may, or may not, make;

(c) providing for the amendment, disapplication or repeal of any enactment relating to the subject matter of the regulations.

(3) Those regulations may make different provision—

(a) for investments for different purposes;

(b) for different local authorities or classes of local authority.

CRIMINAL JUSTICE (SCOTLAND) ACT 2003
(2003, asp 7)

3 The Risk Management Authority

(1) There is established an authority (to be known as the 'Risk Management Authority') whose functions under this Act and any other enactment are to be exercised for the purpose of ensuring the effective assessment and minimisation of risk.

(2) For the purposes of subsection (1) and sections 4 to 6, 'risk' means, as regards—

(a) a person convicted of an offence; or

(b) a person who is subject to a disposal under section 57 (disposal of case where accused found [not criminally responsible or unfit for trial]) of the 1995 Act,

the risk the person's being at liberty presents to the safety of the public at large.

(3) Schedule 2 has effect with respect to the Authority.

4 Policy and research

In, or as the case may be in relation to, the assessment and minimisation of risk—

(a) the Risk Management Authority is to—

(i) compile and keep under review information about the provision of services in Scotland;

(ii) compile and keep under review research and development;

(iii) promote effective practice; and

(iv) give such advice and make such recommendations to the Scottish Ministers as it considers appropriate; and

(b) the Authority may—

(i) carry out, commission or co-ordinate research and publish the results of such research; and

(ii) undertake pilot schemes for the purposes of developing and improving methods.

5 Guidelines and standards

(1) The Risk Management Authority is to—

(a) prepare and issue guidelines as to the assessment and minimisation of risk; and

(b) set and publish standards according to which measures taken in respect of the assessment and minimisation of risk are to be judged.

(2) Any person having functions in relation to the assessment and minimisation of risk is to have regard to such guidelines and standards in the exercise of those functions.

40 Remote monitoring of released prisoners

(1) This section applies where a person is released on licence under—

(a) section 22 of the 1989 Act (persons sentenced before 1st October 1993); or

(b) Part I of the 1993 Act (persons sentenced on or after that date).

[. . .]

(2) Conditions which may be specified in the licence include conditions for securing the remote monitoring of the person's—

(a) compliance with any other condition so specified;

(b) whereabouts (other than for the purposes of paragraph (a)).

(3) Where the Scottish Ministers specify such conditions in the licence they must designate in it a person who is to be responsible for the monitoring and must, as soon as practicable after they do so, send that person a copy of the conditions so specified together with such information as they consider requisite to the fulfilment of the responsibility.

(4) Subject to subsection (5), the designated person's responsibility—

(a) commences on that person's receipt of the copy so sent;

(b) is suspended during any period in which the conditions for securing the monitoring are suspended; and

(c) ends when those conditions are cancelled or the licence is revoked or otherwise ceases to be in force.

(5) The Scottish Ministers may from time to time designate a person who, in place of the person designated under subsection (3) (or last designated under this subsection), is to be responsible for the monitoring; and on the Scottish Ministers amending the licence in respect of the new designation, that subsection and subsection (4) apply in relation to the person designated under this subsection as they apply in relation to the person replaced.

(6) If a designation under subsection (5) is made, the Scottish Ministers must, in so far as it is practicable to do so, notify the person replaced accordingly.

(7) Section 245C of the 1995 Act (contractual and other arrangements for, and devices which may be used for the purposes of, remote monitoring) applies in relation to the imposition of, and compliance with, conditions specified by virtue of subsection (2) as that section applies in relation to the making of, and compliance with, a restriction of liberty order.

(8) A designation under this section is not a licence condition for the purposes of—

(a) section 22(7) of the 1989 Act (requirement for recommendation of Parole Board); or

(b) section 12(3)(b) of the 1993 Act (requirement for recommendation of, or consultation with, Parole Board).

42 Drugs courts

(1) It may be prescribed that a court, or class of court, is designated as a 'drugs court'; that is to say, as a court especially appropriate to deal with cases involving persons dependent on, or with a propensity to misuse, drugs.

(2) [It may be prescribed that there is to be a drugs court within a sheriffdom or sheriff court district, in which case the sheriff principal is, subject to subsection (1), to nominate a court within that sheriffdom or, as the case may be, sheriff court district to be a drugs court.]

(3) Any designation under subsection (1) or nomination under subsection (2) is

without prejudice to the powers and jurisdiction of any court; but only a drugs court is to have the powers provided for in subsection (4), being powers—

(a) additional to any other powers the court may have; and

(b) exercisable only as respects such persons as the court is satisfied are persons such as are mentioned in subsection (1).

(4) The powers are, that where an offender has failed to comply with the requirements of a drug treatment and testing order or a [community payback order], the court may, subject to subsections (6) and (7), on one, or more than one, occasion—

(a) sentence that person to imprisonment, or as the case may be detention, so however that the total of all periods so imposed in respect of the order is not to exceed twenty-eight days (and accordingly any one such period may be less than any minimum sentence which, but for this paragraph, would fall to be imposed); or

(b) [in the case of a failure to comply with the requirements of a drug treatment and testing order, make a community payback order imposing a level 1 unpaid work or other activity requirement, so however that the total hours of unpaid work or other activity] thus required in respect of the order is not to exceed forty hours (and accordingly any one such requirement will be for a period less than that which, but for this paragraph, would fall to be specified),

but the imposition of a sentence under paragraph (a) or making of an order under paragraph (b) does not of itself affect the drug treatment and testing order or [community payback order].

51 Physical punishment of children

(1) Where a person claims that something done to a child was a physical punishment carried out in exercise of a parental right or of a right derived from having charge or care of the child, then in determining any question as to whether what was done was, by virtue of being in such exercise, a justifiable assault a court must have regard to the following factors—

(a) the nature of what was done, the reason for it and the circumstances in which it took place;

(b) its duration and frequency;

(c) any effect (whether physical or mental) which it has been shown to have had on the child;

(d) the child's age; and

(e) the child's personal characteristics (including, without prejudice to the generality of this paragraph, sex and state of health) at the time the thing was done.

(2) The court may also have regard to such other factors as it considers appropriate in the circumstances of the case.

(3) If what was done included or consisted of—

(a) a blow to the head;

(b) shaking; or

(c) the use of an implement,

the court must determine that it was not something which, by virtue of being in exercise of a parental right or of a right derived as is mentioned in subsection (1), was a justifiable assault; but this subsection is without prejudice to the power of the court so to determine on whatever other grounds it thinks fit.

(4) In subsection (1), 'child' means a person who had not, at the time the thing was done, attained the age of sixteen years.

(5) *[Amends Children and Young Persons (Scotland) Act 1937.]*

74 Offences aggravated by religious prejudice

(1) This section applies where it is—

(a) libelled in an indictment; or

(b) specified in a complaint,

and, in either case, proved that an offence has been aggravated by religious prejudice.

(2) For the purposes of this section, an offence is aggravated by religious prejudice if—

(a) at the time of committing the offence or immediately before or after doing so, the offender evinces towards the victim (if any) of the offence malice and ill-will based on the victim's membership (or presumed membership) of a religious group, or of a social or cultural group with a perceived religious affiliation; or

(b) the offence is motivated (wholly or partly) by malice and ill-will towards members of a religious group, or of a social or cultural group with a perceived religious affiliation, based on their membership of that group.

[(2A) It is immaterial whether or not the offender's malice and ill-will is also based (to any extent) on any other factor.]

[. . .]

[(4A) The court must—

(a) state on conviction that the offence was aggravated by religious prejudice,

(b) record the conviction in a way that shows that the offence was so aggravated,

(c) take the aggravation into account in determining the appropriate sentence, and

(d) state—

(i) where the sentence in respect of the offence is different from that which the court would have imposed if the offence were not so aggravated, the extent of and the reasons for that difference, or

(ii) otherwise, the reasons for there being no such difference.]

(5) For the purposes of this section, evidence from a single source is sufficient to prove that an offence is aggravated by religious prejudice.

(6) In subsection (2)(a)—

'membership' in relation to a group includes association with members of that group; and

'presumed' means presumed by the offender.

(7) In this section, 'religious group' means a group of persons defined by reference to their—

(a) religious belief or lack of religious belief;

(b) membership of or adherence to a church or religious organisation;

(c) support for the culture and traditions of a church or religious organisation; or

(d) participation in activities associated with such a culture or such traditions.

EXTRADITION ACT 2003
(2003, c 41)

1 Extradition to category 1 territories

(1) This Part deals with extradition from the United Kingdom to the territories designated for the purposes of this Part by order made by the Secretary of State.

(2) In this Act references to category 1 territories are to the territories designated for the purposes of this Part.

(3) A territory may not be designated for the purposes of this Part if a person found guilty in the territory of a criminal offence may be sentenced to death for the offence under the general criminal law of the territory.

4 Person arrested under Part 1 warrant

(1) This section applies if a person is arrested under a Part 1 warrant.

(2) A copy of the warrant must be given to the person as soon as practicable after his arrest.

(3) The person must be brought as soon as practicable before the appropriate judge.

(4) If subsection (2) is not complied with and the person applies to the judge to be discharged, the judge may order his discharge.

(5) If subsection (3) is not complied with and the person applies to the judge to be discharged, the judge must order his discharge.

(6) A person arrested under the warrant must be treated as continuing in legal custody until he is brought before the appropriate judge under subsection (3) or he is discharged under subsection (4) or (5).

5 Provisional arrest

(1) A constable, a customs officer or a service policeman may arrest a person without a warrant if he has reasonable grounds for believing—

(a) that a Part 1 warrant has been or will be issued in respect of the person by an authority of a category 1 territory, and

(b) that the authority has the function of issuing arrest warrants in the category 1 territory.

(2) A constable or a customs officer may arrest a person under subsection (1) in any part of the United Kingdom.

(3) [A service policeman may arrest a person under subsection (1) only if the person is subject to service law or is a civilian subject to service discipline.

(4) If a service policeman has power to arrest a person under subsection (1) he may exercise the power anywhere.]

9 Judge's powers at extradition hearing

(1) [*Applies to England and Wales.*]

(2) In Scotland, at the extradition hearing the appropriate judge has the same powers (as nearly as may be) as if the proceedings were summary proceedings in respect of an offence alleged to have been committed by the person in respect of whom the Part 1 warrant was issued.

(3) [*Applies to Northern Ireland.*]

(4) If the judge adjourns the extradition hearing he must remand the person in custody or on bail.

(5) [If the person is remanded in custody, the appropriate judge may] later grant bail.

10 Initial stage of extradition hearing

(1) This section applies if a person in respect of whom a Part 1 warrant is issued appears or is brought before the appropriate judge for the extradition hearing.

(2) The judge must decide whether the offence specified in the Part 1 warrant is an extradition offence.

(3) If the judge decides the question in subsection (2) in the negative he must order the person's discharge.

(4) If the judge decides that question in the affirmative he must proceed under section 11.

11 Bars to extradition

(1) If the judge is required to proceed under this section he must decide whether the person's extradition to the category 1 territory is barred by reason of—

(a) the rule against double jeopardy;

[(aa) absence of prosecution decision;]

(b) extraneous considerations;

(c) the passage of time;

(d) the person's age;

[. . .]

(f) speciality;
(g) the person's earlier extradition to the United Kingdom from another category 1 territory;
(h) the person's earlier extradition to the United Kingdom from a non-category 1 territory;
[(i) the person's earlier transfer to the United Kingdom by the International Criminal Court.]

(2) Sections [12 to 19B apply] for the interpretation of subsection (1).

(3) If the judge decides any of the questions in subsection (1) in the affirmative he must order the person's discharge.

(4) If the judge decides those questions in the negative and the person is alleged to be unlawfully at large after conviction of the extradition offence, the judge must proceed under section 20.

(5) If the judge decides those questions in the negative and the person is accused of the commission of the extradition offence but is not alleged to be unlawfully at large after conviction of it, the judge must proceed under section [21A].

12 Rule against double jeopardy

A person's extradition to a category 1 territory is barred by reason of the rule against double jeopardy if (and only if) it appears that he would be entitled to be discharged under any rule of law relating to previous acquittal or conviction on the assumption—

(a) that the conduct constituting the extradition offence constituted an offence in the part of the United Kingdom where the judge exercises jurisdiction;
(b) that the person were charged with the extradition offence in that part of the United Kingdom.

[12A Absence of prosecution decision

(1) A person's extradition to a category 1 territory is barred by reason of absence of prosecution decision if (and only if)—

(a) it appears to the appropriate judge that there are reasonable grounds for believing that—
(i) the competent authorities in the category 1 territory have not made a decision to charge or have not made a decision to try (or have made neither of those decisions), and
(ii) the person's absence from the category 1 territory is not the sole reason for that failure, and
(b) those representing the category 1 territory do not prove that—
(i) the competent authorities in the category 1 territory have made a decision to charge and a decision to try, or
(ii) in a case where one of those decisions has not been made (or neither of them has been made), the person's absence from the category 1 territory is the sole reason for that failure.

(2) In this section 'to charge' and 'to try', in relation to a person and an extradition offence, mean—

(a) to charge the person with the offence in the category 1 territory, and
(b) to try the person for the offence in the category 1 territory.]

13 Extraneous considerations

A person's extradition to a category 1 territory is barred by reason of extraneous considerations if (and only if) it appears that—

(a) the Part 1 warrant issued in respect of him (though purporting to be issued on account of the extradition offence) is in fact issued for the purpose of prosecuting or punishing him on account of his race, religion, nationality, gender, sexual orientation or political opinions, or
(b) if extradited he might be prejudiced at his trial or punished, detained or

restricted in his personal liberty by reason of his race, religion, nationality, gender, sexual orientation or political opinions.

14 Passage of time

A person's extradition to a category 1 territory is barred by reason of the passage of time if (and only if) it appears that it would be unjust or oppressive to extradite him by reason of the passage of time [since he is alleged to have—

(a) committed the extradition offence (where he is accused of its commission), or

(b) become unlawfully at large (where he is alleged to have been convicted of it).]

15 Age

A person's extradition to a category 1 territory is barred by reason of his age if (and only if) it would be conclusively presumed because of his age that he could not be guilty of the extradition offence on the assumption—

(a) that the conduct constituting the extradition offence constituted an offence in the part of the United Kingdom where the judge exercises jurisdiction;

(b) that the person carried out the conduct when the extradition offence was committed (or alleged to be committed);

(c) that the person carried out the conduct in the part of the United Kingdom where the judge exercises jurisdiction.

[59 Return of person to serve remainder of sentence

(1) This section applies if—

(a) a person who is serving a sentence of imprisonment or another form of detention in the United Kingdom is extradited to a category 1 territory in accordance with this Part;

(b) the person is returned to the United Kingdom to serve the remainder of the sentence or the person otherwise returns to the United Kingdom.

(2) Time during which the person was outside the United Kingdom as a result of the extradition does not count as time served by the person as part of the sentence.

(3) But subsection (2) does not apply if—

(a) the person was extradited for the purpose of being prosecuted for an offence, and

(b) the person has not been convicted of the offence or of any other offence in respect of which the person was permitted to be dealt with in the category 1 territory.

(4) In a case falling within subsection (3), time during which the person was outside the United Kingdom as a result of the extradition counts as time served by the person as part of the sentence if (and only if) it was spent in custody in connection with the offence or any other offence in respect of which the person was permitted to be dealt with in the territory.

(5) In a case where the person is not entitled to be released from detention pursuant to the sentence—

(a) the person is liable to be detained in pursuance of the sentence, and

(b) if at large, the person must be treated as being unlawfully at large.

(6) In a case where the person is entitled to be released from detention on licence pursuant to the sentence—

(a) if the person was released on licence at the time of extradition, the licence is suspended until the person's return;

(b) if the person was not released on licence at that time, subsections (7) to (10) apply in relation to the person ('the offender').

(7) The offender is liable to be detained, on return, in any place in which the offender could have been detained pursuant to the sentence before the time of extradition.

(8) A constable or immigration officer may—
(a) take the offender into custody, and
(b) convey the offender to the place mentioned in subsection (7).
(9) The offender must be released on licence within the period of 5 days beginning when the offender is taken (or retaken) into custody under this section.
(10) In calculating a period of 5 days for the purposes of subsection (9) no account is to be taken of—
(a) any Saturday or Sunday,
(b) Christmas Day,
(c) Good Friday, or
(d) in any part of the United Kingdom, any day that is a bank holiday under the Banking and Financial Dealings Act 1971 in that part of the United Kingdom.
(11) A person is entitled to be released from detention if there is—
[. . .]
(b) a duty to release the person under [Chapter 6 of Part 12] of the Criminal Justice Act 2003 [. . .],
(c) a duty to release the person under section 1, 1AA or 7(1) of the Prisoners and Criminal Proceedings (Scotland) Act 1993 or section 5, 11(2), 13, 19 or 23 of the Custodial Sentences and Weapons (Scotland) Act 2007, or
(d) a duty to release the person under section 1 of the Northern Ireland (Remission of Sentences) Act 1995, Article 26 of the Criminal Justice (Northern Ireland) Order 1996 or Article 17 or 18(8) of the Criminal Justice (Northern Ireland) Order 2008.
(12) The powers conferred on a constable by subsection (8) are exercisable in any part of the United Kingdom.
(13) An immigration officer is a person who is an immigration officer within the meaning of the Immigration Act 1971.]

67 The appropriate judge

(1) The appropriate judge is—
(a) in England and Wales, a District Judge (Magistrates' Courts) designated for the purposes of this Part [by the Lord Chief Justice of England and Wales after consulting the Lord Chancellor];
(b) in Scotland, the sheriff of Lothian and Borders;
(c) in Northern Ireland, such county court judge or resident magistrate as is designated for the purposes of this Part [by the Lord Chief Justice of Northern Ireland after consulting the [Department of Justice in Northern Ireland].]
(2) A designation under subsection (1) may be made for all cases or for such cases (or cases of such description) as the designation stipulates.
(3) More than one designation may be made under subsection (1).
[(3A) The use of the expression 'the judge' in a section containing a previous reference to 'the appropriate judge' or 'the judge' does not in itself require both references to be read as referring to the same individual.]
(4) This section applies for the purposes of this Part.
. . .

94 Death penalty

(1) The Secretary of State must not order a person's extradition to a category 2 territory if he could be, will be or has been sentenced to death for the offence concerned in the category 2 territory.
(2) Subsection (1) does not apply if the Secretary of State receives a written assurance which he considers adequate that a sentence of death—
(a) will not be imposed, or
(b) will not be carried out (if imposed).

CONSTITUTIONAL REFORM ACT 2005
(2005, c 4)

PART 1
THE RULE OF LAW

1 The rule of law

This Act does not adversely affect—

(a) the existing constitutional principle of the rule of law, or

(b) the Lord Chancellor's existing constitutional role in relation to that principle.

PART 2
ARRANGEMENTS TO MODIFY THE OFFICE OF LORD CHANCELLOR

Qualifications for office of Lord Chancellor

2 Lord Chancellor to be qualified by experience

(1) A person may not be recommended for appointment as Lord Chancellor unless he appears to the Prime Minister to be qualified by experience.

(2) The Prime Minister may take into account any of these—

(a) experience as a Minister of the Crown;

(b) experience as a member of either House of Parliament;

(c) experience as a qualifying practitioner;

(d) experience as a teacher of law in a university;

(e) other experience that the Prime Minister considers relevant.

(3) In this section 'qualifying practitioner' means any of these—

(a) a person who has a Senior Courts qualification, within the meaning of section 71 of the Courts and Legal Services Act 1990,

(b) an advocate in Scotland or a solicitor entitled to appear in the Court of Session and the High Court of Justiciary;

(c) a member of the Bar of Northern Ireland or a solicitor of the Court of Judicature of Northern Ireland.

Continued judicial independence

3 Guarantee of continued judicial independence

(1) The Lord Chancellor, other Ministers of the Crown and all with responsibility for matters relating to the judiciary or otherwise to the administration of justice must uphold the continued independence of the judiciary.

(2) Subsection (1) does not impose any duty which it would be within the legislative competence of the Scottish Parliament to impose.

(3) A person is not subject to the duty imposed by subsection (1) if he is subject to the duty imposed by section 1(1) of the Justice (Northern Ireland) Act 2002.

(4) The following particular duties are imposed for the purpose of upholding that independence.

(5) The Lord Chancellor and other Ministers of the Crown must not seek to influence particular judicial decisions through any special access to the judiciary.

(6) The Lord Chancellor must have regard to—

(a) the need to defend that independence;

(b) the need for the judiciary to have the support necessary to enable them to exercise their functions;

(c) the need for the public interest in regard to matters relating to the judiciary or otherwise to the administration of justice to be properly represented in decisions affecting those matters.

(7) In this section 'the judiciary' includes the judiciary of any of the following—

(a) the Supreme Court;

(b) any other court established under the law of any part of the United Kingdom;

(c) any international court.

[(7A) In this section 'the judiciary' also includes every person who—

(a) holds an office listed in Schedule 14 or holds an office listed in subsection (7B), and

(b) but for this subsection would not be a member of the judiciary for the purposes of this section.

(7B) The offices are those of—

(a) Senior President of Tribunals;

(b) President of Employment Tribunals (Scotland);

(c) Vice President of Employment Tribunals (Scotland);

(d) member of a panel of [Employment Judges] (Scotland);

(e) member of a panel of members of employment tribunals that is not a panel of [Employment Judges];

[. . .]

(8) In subsection (7) 'international court' means the International Court of Justice or any other court or tribunal which exercises jurisdiction, or performs functions of a judicial nature, in pursuance of—

(a) an agreement to which the United Kingdom or Her Majesty's Government in the United Kingdom is a party, or

(b) a resolution of the Security Council or General Assembly of the United Nations.

4 ***[Applies to Northern Ireland.]***

Representations by senior judges

5 Representations to Parliament

[(A1) The President of the Supreme Court may lay before Parliament written representations on matters that appear to the President to be matters of importance relating to the Supreme Court or to the jurisdiction it exercises.]

(1) The chief justice of any part of the United Kingdom may lay before Parliament written representations on matters that appear to him to be matters of importance relating to the judiciary, or otherwise to the administration of justice, in that part of the United Kingdom.

(2) In relation to Scotland [the matters mentioned in subsections (A1) and (1)] do not include matters within the legislative competence of the Scottish Parliament, unless they are matters to which a Bill for an Act of Parliament relates.

(3) In relation to Northern Ireland [the matters mentioned in subsections (A1) and (1)] do not include transferred matters within the legislative competence of the Northern Ireland Assembly, unless they are matters to which a Bill for an Act of Parliament relates.

(4) In subsection (3) the reference to transferred matters has the meaning given by section 4(1) of the Northern Ireland Act 1998.

(5) In this section 'chief justice' means—

(a) in relation to England and Wales or Northern Ireland, the Lord Chief Justice of that part of the United Kingdom;

(b) in relation to Scotland, the Lord President of the Court of Session.

6 *[Applies to Northern Ireland.]*

Judiciary and courts in England and Wales

7 President of the Courts of England and Wales

(1) The Lord Chief Justice holds the office of President of the Courts of England and Wales and is Head of the Judiciary of England and Wales.

(2) As President of the Courts of England and Wales he is responsible—

(a) for representing the views of the judiciary of England and Wales to Parliament, to the Lord Chancellor and to Ministers of the Crown generally;

(b) for the maintenance of appropriate arrangements for the welfare, training and guidance of the judiciary of England and Wales within the resources made available by the Lord Chancellor;

(c) for the maintenance of appropriate arrangements for the deployment of the judiciary of England and Wales and the allocation of work within courts.

(3) The President of the Courts of England and Wales is president of the courts listed in subsection (4) and is entitled to sit in any of those courts.

(4) The courts are—

the Court of Appeal
the High Court
the Crown Court
[the family court]
the [county court]
the magistrates' courts.

(5) In section 1 of the Supreme Court Act 1981, subsection (2) (Lord Chancellor to be president of the Supreme Court of England and Wales) ceases to have effect.

Other provisions about the judiciary and courts

12 Powers to make rules

(1) Part 1 of Schedule 1 sets out a process for the exercise of rule-making powers.

(2) Part 2 of the Schedule contains amendments of Acts that contain rule-making powers.

(3) Those amendments—

(a) provide for those powers to be exercised in accordance with the process set out in Part 1 of the Schedule, and

(b) make consequential provision.

13 Powers to give directions

(1) Part 1 of Schedule 2 sets out a process for the exercise of powers to give directions.

(2) Part 2 of the Schedule contains amendments of Acts that contain powers to give directions.

(3) Those amendments—

(a) provide for those powers to be exercised in accordance with the process set out in Part 1 of the Schedule, and

(b) make consequential provision.

14 Transfer of appointment functions to Her Majesty

Schedule 3 provides for—

(a) Her Majesty instead of the Lord Chancellor to make appointments to certain offices, and

(b) the modification of enactments relating to those offices.

Functions subject to transfer, modification or abolition

19 Transfer, modification or abolition of functions by order

(1) The Lord Chancellor may by order make provision for any of these purposes—

(a) to transfer an existing function of the Lord Chancellor to another person;

(b) to direct that an existing function of the Lord Chancellor is to be exercisable concurrently with another person;

(c) to direct that an existing function of the Lord Chancellor exercisable concurrently with another person is to cease to be exercisable by the Lord Chancellor;

(d) to modify an existing function of the Lord Chancellor;

(e) to abolish an existing function of the Lord Chancellor.

. . .

PART 3
THE SUPREME COURT

The Supreme Court

23 The Supreme Court

(1) There is to be a Supreme Court of the United Kingdom.

(2) The Court consists of [the persons appointed as its judges] by Her Majesty by letters patent [, but no appointment may cause the full-time equivalent number of judges of the Court at any time to be more than 12].

(3) Her Majesty may from time to time by Order in Council amend subsection (2) so as to increase or further increase the [maximum full-time equivalent] number of judges of the Court.

(4) No recommendation may be made to Her Majesty in Council to make an Order under subsection (3) unless a draft of the Order has been laid before and approved by resolution of each House of Parliament.

(5) Her Majesty may by letters patent appoint one of the judges to be President and one to be Deputy President of the Court.

(6) The judges other than the President and Deputy President are to be styled 'Justices of the Supreme Court'.

(7) The Court is to be taken to be duly constituted despite any vacancy [. . .] in the office of President or Deputy President.

[(8) For the purposes of this section, the full-time equivalent number of judges of the Court is to be calculated by taking the number of full-time judges and adding, for each judge who is not a full-time judge, such fraction as is reasonable.]

24 First members of the Court

On the commencement of section 23—

(a) the persons who immediately before that commencement are Lords of Appeal in Ordinary become judges of the Supreme Court,

(b) the person who immediately before that commencement is the senior Lord of Appeal in Ordinary becomes the President of the Court, and

(c) the person who immediately before that commencement is the second senior Lord of Appeal in Ordinary becomes the Deputy President of the Court.

Appointment of judges

25 Qualification for appointment

(1) A person is not qualified to be appointed a judge of the Supreme Court unless he has (at any time)—

(a) held high judicial office for a period of at least 2 years,

(b) [satisfied the judicial-appointment eligibility condition on a 15-year basis, or

(c) been a qualifying practitioner for a period of at least 15 years.]

(2) A person is a qualifying practitioner for the purposes of this section at any time when—

[. . .]

(b) he is an advocate in Scotland or a solicitor entitled to appear in the Court of Session and the High Court of Justiciary, or

(c) he is a member of the Bar of Northern Ireland or a solicitor of the Court of Judicature of Northern Ireland.

26 Selection of members of the Court

(1) This section applies to a recommendation for an appointment to one of the following offices—

(a) judge of the Supreme Court;

(b) President of the Court;

(c) Deputy President of the Court.

(2) A recommendation may be made only by the Prime Minister.

(3) The Prime Minister—

(a) must recommend any person [who is selected as a result of the convening of a selection commission under this section];

(b) may not recommend any other person.

(4) [Where a person who is not a judge of the Court is recommended for appointment as President or Deputy President, the recommendation must also recommend the person for appointment as a judge.]

(5) If there is a vacancy in [the office of President of the Court or in the office of Deputy President of the Court] or it appears to him that there will soon be such a vacancy, the Lord Chancellor must convene a selection commission for the selection of a person to be recommended.

[(5A) If—

(a) the full-time equivalent number of judges of the Court is less than the maximum specified in section 23(2), or it appears to the Lord Chancellor that the full-time equivalent number of judges of the Court will soon be less than that maximum, and

(b) the Lord Chancellor, or the senior judge of the Court, after consulting the other considers it desirable that a recommendation be made for an appointment to the office of judge of the Court,

the Lord Chancellor must convene a selection commission for the selection of a person to be recommended.

(5B) In subsection (5A)(b) 'the senior judge of the Court' means—

(a) the President of the Court, or

(b) if there is no President, the Deputy President, or

(c) if there is no President and no Deputy President, the senior ordinary judge.]

(6) Schedule 8 is about selection commissions.

(7) [Subsections (5) and (5A) are subject to Schedule 8 (cases where duty to convene a selection commission are suspended).]

[(7A) For the purposes of this section and Schedule 8, a person is selected as a result of the convening of a selection commission if the person's selection is the final outcome of—

(a) the selection process mentioned in section 27(1) being applied by the commission, and

(b) any process provided for by regulations under section 27A being applied in the particular case.]

(8) [Section 27 applies] where a selection commission is convened under this section.

27 Selection process

(1) The commission must—

(a) determine the selection process to be applied [by it],

(b) apply the selection process, and

(c) make a selection accordingly.

[(1A) The commission must have an odd number of members not less than five.

(1B) The members of the commission must include—

(a) at least one who is non-legally-qualified,

(b) at least one judge of the Court,

(c) at least one member of the Judicial Appointments Commission,

(d) at least one member of the Judicial Appointments Board for Scotland, and

(e) at least one member of the Northern Ireland Judicial Appointments Commission,

and more than one of the requirements may be met by the same person's membership of the commission.

(1C) If the commission is convened for the selection of a person to be recommended for appointment as President of the Court—

(a) its members may not include the President of the Court, and

(b) it is to be chaired by one of its non-legally-qualified members.

(1D) If the commission is convened for the selection of a person to be recommended for appointment as Deputy President of the Court, its members may not include the Deputy President of the Court.]

[. . .]

(4) Subsections (5) to (10) apply to any selection under this section or [regulations under section 27A].

(5) Selection must be on merit.

[(5A) Where two persons are of equal merit—

(a) section 159 of the Equality Act 2010 (positive action: recruitment etc) does not apply in relation to choosing between them, but

(b) Part 5 of that Act (public appointments etc) does not prevent the commission from preferring one of them over the other for the purpose of increasing diversity within the group of persons who are the judges of the Court.]

(6) A person may be selected only if he meets the requirements of section 25.

(7) A person may not be selected if he is a member of the commission.

(8) In making selections for the appointment of judges of the Court the commission must ensure that between them the judges will have knowledge of, and experience of practice in, the law of each part of the United Kingdom.

(9) The commission must have regard to any guidance given by the Lord Chancellor as to matters to be taken into account (subject to any other provision of this Act) in making a selection.

(10) Any selection must be of one person only.

[(11) For the purposes of this section a person is non-legally-qualified if the person—

(a) does not hold, and has never held, any of the offices listed in Schedule 1 to the House of Commons Disqualification Act 1975 (judicial offices disqualifying for membership of the House of Commons), and

(b) is not practising or employed as a lawyer, and never has practised or been employed as a lawyer.]

33 Tenure

A judge of the Supreme Court holds that office during good behaviour, but may be removed from it on the address of both Houses of Parliament.

Jurisdiction, relation to other courts etc

40 Jurisdiction

(1) The Supreme Court is a superior court of record.

(2) An appeal lies to the Court from any order or judgment of the Court of Appeal in England and Wales in civil proceedings.

[. . .]

(4) Schedule 9—

(a) transfers other jurisdiction from the House of Lords to the Court,

(b) transfers devolution jurisdiction from the Judicial Committee of the Privy Council to the Court, and

(c) makes other amendments relating to jurisdiction.

(5) The Court has power to determine any question necessary to be determined for the purposes of doing justice in an appeal to it under any enactment.

(6) An appeal under subsection (2) lies only with the permission of the Court of Appeal or the Supreme Court; but this is subject to provision under any other enactment restricting such an appeal.

41 Relation to other courts etc

(1) Nothing in this Part is to affect the distinctions between the separate legal systems of the parts of the United Kingdom.

(2) A decision of the Supreme Court on appeal from a court of any part of the United Kingdom, other than a decision on a devolution matter, is to be regarded as the decision of a court of that part of the United Kingdom.

(3) A decision of the Supreme Court on a devolution matter—

(a) is not binding on that Court when making such a decision;

(b) otherwise, is binding in all legal proceedings.

(4) In this section 'devolution matter' means—

(a) a question referred to the Supreme Court under [section 99 or 112 of the Government of Wales Act 2006] section 33 of the Scotland Act 1998 or section 11 of the Northern Ireland Act 1998;

(b) a devolution issue as defined in [Schedule 9 to the Government of Wales Act 2006], Schedule 6 to the Scotland Act 1998 or Schedule 10 to the Northern Ireland Act 1998.

Composition for proceedings

42 Composition

(1) The Supreme Court is duly constituted in any proceedings only if all of the following conditions are met—

(a) the Court consists of an uneven number of judges;

(b) the Court consists of at least three judges;

(c) more than half of those judges are permanent judges.

(2) Paragraphs and of subsection are subject to any directions that in specified proceedings the Court is to consist of a specified number of judges that is both uneven and greater than three.

(3) Paragraph of subsection is subject to any directions that in specified descriptions of proceedings the Court is to consist of a specified minimum number of judges that is greater than three.

(4) This section is subject to section 43.

(5) In this section—

(a) 'directions' means directions given by the President of the Court;

(b) 'specified', in relation to directions, means specified in those directions;

(c) references to permanent judges are references to those judges of the Court who are not acting judges under section 38.

(6) This section and section 43 apply to the constitution of the Court in any proceedings from the time judges are designated to hear the proceedings.

INQUIRIES ACT 2005
(2005, c 12)

Constitution of inquiry

1 Power to establish inquiry

(1) A Minister may cause an inquiry to be held under this Act in relation to a case where it appears to him that—

(a) particular events have caused, or are capable of causing, public concern, or

(b) there is public concern that particular events may have occurred.

(2) In this Act 'Minister' means—

(a) a United Kingdom Minister;

(b) the Scottish Ministers;

[(ba) the Welsh Ministers;]

(c) a Northern Ireland Minister.

[. . .]

(3) References in this Act to an inquiry, except where the context requires otherwise, are to an inquiry under this Act.

2 No determination of liability

(1) An inquiry panel is not to rule on, and has no power to determine, any person's civil or criminal liability.

(2) But an inquiry panel is not to be inhibited in the discharge of its functions by any likelihood of liability being inferred from facts that it determines or recommendations that it makes.

3 The inquiry panel

(1) An inquiry is to be undertaken either—

(a) by a chairman alone, or

(b) by a chairman with one or more other members.

(2) References in this Act to an inquiry panel are to the chairman and any other member or members.

4 Appointment of inquiry panel

(1) Each member of an inquiry panel is to be appointed by the Minister by an instrument in writing.

(2) The instrument appointing the chairman must state that the inquiry is to be held under this Act.

(3) Before appointing a member to the inquiry panel (otherwise than as chairman) the Minister must consult the person he has appointed, or proposes to appoint, as chairman.

5 Setting-up date and terms of reference

(1) In the instrument under section 4 appointing the chairman, or by a notice given to him within a reasonable time afterwards, the Minister must—

(a) specify the date that is to be the setting-up date for the purposes of this Act; and

(b) before that date—

(i) set out the terms of reference of the inquiry;

(ii) state whether or not the Minister proposes to appoint other members to the inquiry panel, and if so how many.

(2) An inquiry must not begin considering evidence before the setting-up date.

(3) The Minister may at any time after setting out the terms of reference under this section amend them if he considers that the public interest so requires.

(4) Before setting out or amending the terms of reference the Minister must consult the person he proposes to appoint, or has appointed, as chairman.

(5) Functions conferred by this Act on an inquiry panel, or a member of an inquiry panel, are exercisable only within the inquiry's terms of reference.

(6) In this Act 'terms of reference', in relation to an inquiry under this Act, means—

(a) the matters to which the inquiry relates;

(b) any particular matters as to which the inquiry panel is to determine the facts;

(c) whether the inquiry panel is to make recommendations;

(d) any other matters relating to the scope of the inquiry that the Minister may specify.

6 Minister's duty to inform Parliament or Assembly

(1) A Minister who proposes to cause an inquiry to be held, or who has already done so without making a statement under this section, must as soon as is reasonably practicable make a statement to that effect to the relevant Parliament or Assembly.

(2) A statement under subsection (1) must state—

(a) who is to be, or has been, appointed as chairman of the inquiry;

(b) whether the Minister has appointed, or proposes to appoint, any other members to the inquiry panel, and if so how many;

(c) what are to be, or are, the inquiry's terms of reference.

(3) Where the terms of reference of an inquiry are amended under section 5(3), the Minister must, as soon as is reasonably practicable, make a statement to the relevant Parliament or Assembly setting out the amended terms of reference.

(4) A statement under this section may be oral or written.

7 Further appointments to inquiry panel

(1) The Minister may at any time (whether before the setting-up date or during the course of the inquiry) appoint a member to the inquiry panel—

(a) to fill a vacancy that has arisen in the panel (including a vacancy in the position of chairman), or

(b) to increase the number of members of the panel.

(2) The power to appoint a member under subsection (1)(b) is exercisable only—

(a) in accordance with a proposal under section 5(1)(b)(ii), or

(b) with the consent of the chairman.

(3) The power to appoint a replacement chairman may be exercised by appointing a person who is already a member of the inquiry panel.

8 Suitability of inquiry panel

(1) In appointing a member of the inquiry panel, the Minister must have regard—

(a) to the need to ensure that the inquiry panel (considered as a whole) has the necessary expertise to undertake the inquiry;

(b) in the case of an inquiry panel consisting of a chairman and one or more other members, to the need for balance (considered against the background of the terms of reference) in the composition of the panel.

(2) For the purposes of subsection (1)(a) the Minister may have regard to the assistance that may be provided to the inquiry panel by any assessor whom the Minister proposes to appoint, or has appointed, under section 11.

9 Requirement of impartiality

(1) The Minister must not appoint a person as a member of the inquiry panel if it appears to the Minister that the person has—

(a) a direct interest in the matters to which the inquiry relates, or

(b) a close association with an interested party,

unless, despite the person's interest or association, his appointment could not reasonably be regarded as affecting the impartiality of the inquiry panel.

(2) Before a person is appointed as a member of an inquiry panel he must notify the Minister of any matters that, having regard to subsection (1), could affect his eligibility for appointment.

(3) If at any time (whether before the setting-up date or during the course of the inquiry) a member of the inquiry panel becomes aware that he has an interest or association falling within paragraph (a) or (b) of subsection (1), he must notify the Minister.

(4) A member of the inquiry panel must not, during the course of the inquiry, undertake any activity that could reasonably be regarded as affecting his suitability to serve as such.

10 Appointment of judge as panel member

(1) If the Minister proposes to appoint as a member of an inquiry panel a particular person who is a judge of a description specified in the first column of the following table, he must first consult the person specified in the second column.

Description of judge	*Person to be consulted*
Lord of Appeal in Ordinary	The senior Lord of Appeal in Ordinary
Judge of the Supreme Court of England and Wales, or Circuit judge	The Lord Chief Justice of England and Wales
Judge of the Court of Session, sheriff principal [, sheriff or summary sheriff]	The Lord President of the Court of Session
Judge of the Supreme Court of Northern Ireland, or county court judge in Northern Ireland	The Lord Chief Justice of Northern Ireland

[. . .]

11 Assessors

(1) One or more persons may be appointed to act as assessors to assist the inquiry panel.

(2) The power to appoint assessors is exercisable—

(a) before the setting-up date, by the Minister;

(b) during the course of the inquiry, by the chairman (whether or not the Minister has appointed assessors).

(3) Before exercising his powers under subsection (2)(a) the Minister must consult the person he proposes to appoint, or has appointed, as chairman.

(4) A person may be appointed as an assessor only if it appears to the Minister or the chairman (as the case requires) that he has expertise that makes him a suitable person to provide assistance to the inquiry panel.

(5) The chairman may at any time terminate the appointment of an assessor, but only with the consent of the Minister in the case of an assessor appointed by the Minister.

13 Power to suspend inquiry

(1) The Minister may at any time, by notice to the chairman, suspend an inquiry for such period as appears to him to be necessary to allow for—

(a) the completion of any other investigation relating to any of the matters to which the inquiry relates, or

(b) the determination of any civil or criminal proceedings (including proceedings before a disciplinary tribunal) arising out of any of those matters.

(2) The power conferred by subsection (1) may be exercised whether or not the investigation or proceedings have begun.

(3) Before exercising that power the Minister must consult the chairman.

(4) A notice under subsection (1) may suspend the inquiry until a specified day, until the happening of a specified event or until the giving by the Minister of a further notice to the chairman.

(5) Where the Minister gives a notice under subsection (1) he must—

(a) set out in the notice his reasons for suspending the inquiry;

(b) lay a copy of the notice, as soon as is reasonably practicable, before the relevant Parliament or Assembly.

(6) A member of an inquiry panel may not exercise the powers conferred by this Act during any period of suspension; but the duties imposed on a member of an inquiry panel by section 9(3) and (4) continue during any such period.

(7) In this section 'period of suspension' means the period beginning with the receipt by the chairman of the notice under subsection (1) and ending with whichever of the following is applicable—

(a) the day referred to in subsection (4);

(b) the happening of the event referred to in that subsection;

(c) the receipt by the chairman of the further notice under that subsection.

14 End of inquiry

(1) For the purposes of this Act an inquiry comes to an end—

(a) on the date, after the delivery of the report of the inquiry, on which the chairman notifies the Minister that the inquiry has fulfilled its terms of reference, or

(b) on any earlier date specified in a notice given to the chairman by the Minister.

(2) The date specified in a notice under subsection (1)(b) may not be earlier than the date on which the notice is sent.

(3) Before exercising his power under subsection (1)(b) the Minister must consult the chairman.

(4) Where the Minister gives a notice under subsection (1)(b) he must—

(a) set out in the notice his reasons for bringing the inquiry to an end;

(b) lay a copy of the notice, as soon as is reasonably practicable, before the relevant Parliament or Assembly.

Conversion of inquiries

15 Power to convert other inquiry into inquiry under this Act

(1) Where—

(a) an inquiry ('the original inquiry') is being held, or is due to be held, by one or more persons appointed otherwise than under this Act,

(b) a Minister gives a notice under this section to those persons, and

(c) the person who caused the original inquiry to be held consents,

the original inquiry becomes an inquiry under this Act as from the date of the notice or such later date as may be specified in the notice (the 'date of conversion').

(2) The power conferred by this section is exercisable only if the original inquiry relates to a case where it appears to the Minister that—

(a) particular events have caused, or are capable of causing, public concern, or

(b) there is public concern that particular events may have occurred.

(3) Before exercising that power the Minister must consult the chairman.

(4) A notice under this section must—

(a) state that, as from the date of conversion, the inquiry is to be held under this Act;

(b) in the case of an inquiry panel consisting of more than one member, identify who is to be chairman of the panel;

(c) set out what are to be the terms of reference of the inquiry.

(5) The terms of reference set out under subsection (4) may be different from those of the original inquiry.

(6) The Minister may at any time after setting out the terms of reference under this section amend them if he considers that the public interest so requires.

(7) The Minister must consult the chairman before—

(a) setting out terms of reference that are different from those of the original inquiry, or

(b) amending the terms of reference under subsection (6).

(8) Section 6 applies, with any necessary modifications, in relation to—

(a) converting an inquiry under this section, or

(b) amending an inquiry's terms of reference under subsection (6),

as it applies in relation to causing an inquiry to be held, or amending an inquiry's terms of reference under section 5(3).

16 Inquiries converted under section 15

(1) This section applies where an inquiry (the 'original inquiry') is converted under section 15 into an inquiry under this Act.

(2) The appointment of a person who at the date of conversion is—

(a) one of the persons holding, or due to hold, the original inquiry (an 'original member'),

(b) an assessor, counsel or solicitor to the inquiry, or

(c) a person engaged to provide assistance to the inquiry, continues as if made under this Act, and for the purposes of section 12(5) is treated as made by the Minister on the date of conversion.

(3) Any obligation arising under an order of the original inquiry, or otherwise in connection with that inquiry, is enforceable only as it would be if the original inquiry had not been converted.

(4) No rights or obligations arise under or by virtue of this Act before the date of conversion.

Inquiry proceedings

17 Evidence and procedure

(1) Subject to any provision of this Act or of rules under section 41, the procedure and conduct of an inquiry are to be such as the chairman of the inquiry may direct.

(2) In particular, the chairman may take evidence on oath, and for that purpose may administer oaths.

(3) In making any decision as to the procedure or conduct of an inquiry, the chairman must act with fairness and with regard also to the need to avoid any unnecessary cost (whether to public funds or to witnesses or others).

18 Public access to inquiry proceedings and information

(1) Subject to any restrictions imposed by a notice or order under section 19, the chairman must take such steps as he considers reasonable to secure that members of the public (including reporters) are able—

(a) to attend the inquiry or to see and hear a simultaneous transmission of proceedings at the inquiry;

(b) to obtain or to view a record of evidence and documents given, produced or provided to the inquiry or inquiry panel.

(2) No recording or broadcast of proceedings at an inquiry may be made except—

(a) at the request of the chairman, or

(b) with the permission of the chairman and in accordance with any terms on which permission is given.

Any such request or permission must be framed so as not to enable a person to see or hear by means of a recording or broadcast anything that he is prohibited by a notice under section 19 from seeing or hearing.

(3) Section 32(2) of the Freedom of Information Act 2000 (certain inquiry records etc exempt from obligations under that Act) does not apply in relation to information contained in documents that, in pursuance of rules under section 41(1)(b) below, have been passed to and are held by a public authority.

(4) Section 37(1)(b) of the Freedom of Information (Scotland) Act 2002 (certain inquiry records etc exempt from obligations under that Act) does not apply in relation to information contained in documents that, in pursuance of rules under section 41(1)(b) below, have been passed to and are held by a Scottish public authority.

19 Restrictions on public access etc

(1) Restrictions may, in accordance with this section, be imposed on—

(a) attendance at an inquiry, or at any particular part of an inquiry;

(b) disclosure or publication of any evidence or documents given, produced or provided to an inquiry.

. . .

21 Powers of chairman to require production of evidence etc

(1) The chairman of an inquiry may by notice require a person to attend at a time and place stated in the notice—

(a) to give evidence;

(b) to produce any documents in his custody or under his control that relate to a matter in question at the inquiry;

(c) to produce any other thing in his custody or under his control for inspection, examination or testing by or on behalf of the inquiry panel.

(2) The chairman may by notice require a person, within such period as appears to the inquiry panel to be reasonable—

(a) to provide evidence to the inquiry panel in the form of a written statement;

(b) to provide any documents in his custody or under his control that relate to a matter in question at the inquiry;

(c) to produce any other thing in his custody or under his control for inspection, examination or testing by or on behalf of the inquiry panel.

(3) A notice under subsection (1) or (2) must—

(a) explain the possible consequences of not complying with the notice;

(b) indicate what the recipient of the notice should do if he wishes to make a claim within subsection (4).

(4) A claim by a person that—

(a) he is unable to comply with a notice under this section, or

(b) it is not reasonable in all the circumstances to require him to comply with such a notice,

is to be determined by the chairman of the inquiry, who may revoke or vary the notice on that ground.

(5) In deciding whether to revoke or vary a notice on the ground mentioned in subsection (4)(b), the chairman must consider the public interest in the information in question being obtained by the inquiry, having regard to the likely importance of the information.

(6) For the purposes of this section a thing is under a person's control if it is in his possession or if he has a right to possession of it.

22 Privileged information etc

(1) A person may not under section 21 be required to give, produce or provide any evidence or document if—

(a) he could not be required to do so if the proceedings of the inquiry were civil proceedings in a court in the relevant part of the United Kingdom, or

(b) the requirement would be incompatible with an [EU] obligation.

(2) The rules of law under which evidence or documents are permitted or required to be withheld on grounds of public interest immunity apply in relation to an inquiry as they apply in relation to civil proceedings in a court in the relevant part of the United Kingdom.

23 Risk of damage to the economy

(1) This section applies where it is submitted to an inquiry panel, on behalf of the Crown, the [Financial Conduct Authority, the Prudential Regulation Authority] or the Bank of England, that there is information held by any person which, in order to avoid a risk of damage to the economy, ought not to be revealed.

(2) The panel must not permit or require the information to be revealed, or cause it to be revealed, unless satisfied that the public interest in the information being revealed outweighs the public interest in avoiding a risk of damage to the economy.

(3) In making a decision under this section the panel must take account of any restriction notice given under section 19 or any restriction order that the chairman has made or proposes to make under that section.

(4) In this section—

'damage to the economy' means damage to the economic interests of the United Kingdom or of any part of the United Kingdom;

'revealed' means revealed to anyone who is not a member of the inquiry panel.

(5) This section does not prevent the inquiry panel from communicating any information in confidence to the Minister.

(6) This section does not affect the rules of law referred to in section 22(2).

Inquiry reports

24 Submission of reports

(1) The chairman of an inquiry must deliver a report to the Minister setting out—

(a) the facts determined by the inquiry panel;

(b) the recommendations of the panel (where the terms of reference required it to make recommendations).

The report may also contain anything else that the panel considers to be relevant to the terms of reference (including any recommendations the panel sees fit to make despite not being required to do so by the terms of reference).

(2) In relation to an inquiry that is brought to an end under section 14(1)(b), the duty imposed by subsection (1) to deliver a report is to be read as a power to do so.

(3) Before making a report under subsection (1) the chairman may deliver to the Minister a report under this subsection (an 'interim report') containing anything that a report under subsection (1) may contain.

(4) A report of an inquiry must be signed by each member of the inquiry panel.

(5) If the inquiry panel is unable to produce a unanimous report, the report must reasonably reflect the points of disagreement.

(6) In subsections (4) and (5) 'report' includes an interim report.

25 Publication of reports

(1) It is the duty of the Minister, or the chairman if subsection (2) applies, to arrange for reports of an inquiry to be published.

(2) This subsection applies if—

(a) the Minister notifies the chairman before the setting-up date that the chairman is to have responsibility for arranging publication, or

(b) at any time after that date the chairman, on being invited to do so by the Minister, accepts responsibility for arranging publication.

(3) Subject to subsection (4), a report of an inquiry must be published in full.

(4) The person whose duty it is to arrange for a report to be published may withhold material in the report from publication to such extent—

(a) as is required by any statutory provision, enforceable [EU] obligation or rule of law, or

(b) as the person considers to be necessary in the public interest, having regard in particular to the matters mentioned in subsection (5).

(5) Those matters are—

(a) the extent to which withholding material might inhibit the allaying of public concern;

(b) any risk of harm or damage that could be avoided or reduced by withholding any material;

(c) any conditions as to confidentiality subject to which a person acquired information that he has given to the inquiry.

(6) In subsection (5)(b) 'harm or damage' includes in particular—

(a) death or injury;

(b) damage to national security or international relations;

(c) damage to the economic interests of the United Kingdom or of any part of the United Kingdom;

(d) damage caused by disclosure of commercially sensitive information.

(7) Subsection (4)(b) does not affect any obligation of the Minister, or any other public authority or Scottish public authority, that may arise under the Freedom of Information Act 2000 or the Freedom of Information (Scotland) Act 2002.

(8) In this section 'report' includes an interim report.

26 Laying of reports before Parliament or Assembly

Whatever is required to be published under section 25 must be laid by the Minister, either at the time of publication or as soon afterwards as is reasonably practicable, before the relevant Parliament or Assembly.

Scotland, Wales and Northern Ireland

27 United Kingdom inquiries

(1) This section applies to an inquiry for which a United Kingdom Minister is responsible.

(2) The Minister may not, without first consulting the relevant administration, include in the terms of reference anything that would require the inquiry—

(a) to determine any fact that is wholly or primarily concerned with a Scottish matter or a Welsh matter;

(b) to determine any fact that is wholly or primarily concerned with a matter which is, and was at the relevant time, a transferred Northern Ireland matter;

(c) to make any recommendation that is wholly or primarily concerned with a Scottish matter, a Welsh matter or a transferred Northern Ireland matter.

(3) Unless the Minister gives written permission to the chairman, the powers conferred by section 21 are not exercisable—

(a) in respect of evidence, documents or other things that are wholly or primarily concerned with—

(i) a Scottish matter or a Welsh matter, or

(ii) a matter which is, and was at the relevant time, a Northern Ireland matter;

(b) so as to require any evidence, document or other thing to be given, produced or provided by or on behalf of the Scottish Ministers, the [Welsh Ministers] or a Northern Ireland Minister.

(4) Before granting permission under subsection (3) the Minister must consult the relevant administration.

(5) Permission under subsection (3) may be granted subject to such conditions or qualifications as the Minister may specify.

(6) Permission under subsection (3) is not required for the exercise of powers in circumstances in which subsection (6) of section 30 would prevent the powers from being exercised in the case of an inquiry to which that section applies.

(7) In this section—

'Northern Ireland matter' means—

(a) a transferred Northern Ireland matter, or

(b) a matter falling within section 44(2)(b) of the Northern Ireland Act 1998 (matters in relation to which statutory functions are exercisable by Northern Ireland Ministers etc);

'the relevant administration' means whichever of the following the case requires—

(a) the Scottish Ministers;

(b) [the Welsh Ministers;]

(c) such one or more Northern Ireland Ministers as appear to the Minister to be appropriate;

'the relevant time' means the time when the fact or event in question occurred (or is alleged to have occurred);

'Scottish matter' means a matter that relates to Scotland and is not a reserved matter within the meaning of the Scotland Act 1998;

'transferred Northern Ireland matter' means a matter that relates to Northern Ireland and is a transferred matter within the meaning of the Northern Ireland Act 1998 (or, in relation to any time when Part 1 of the Northern Ireland Constitution Act 1973 was in force, within the meaning of that Act);

'Welsh matter' means a matter in relation to which the [Welsh Ministers have] functions.

28 Scottish inquiries

(1) This section applies to an inquiry for which the Scottish Ministers are responsible.

(2) The terms of reference of the inquiry must not require it to determine any fact or to make any recommendation that is not wholly or primarily concerned with a Scottish matter.

(3) The powers conferred by section 21 are exercisable only—

(a) in respect of evidence, documents or other things that are wholly or primarily concerned with a Scottish matter, or

(b) for the purpose of inquiring into something that is wholly or primarily a Scottish matter.

(4) Those powers are not exercisable so as to require any evidence, document or other thing to be given, produced or provided by or on behalf of Her Majesty's Government in the United Kingdom, the [Welsh Ministers] or a Northern Ireland Minister.

(5) In this section 'Scottish matter' means a matter that relates to Scotland and is not a reserved matter (within the meaning of the Scotland Act 1998).

29, 30 *[Welsh and Northern Ireland inquiries]*

31 The relevant part of the United Kingdom and the applicable rules

(1) The Minister responsible for an inquiry must specify whether the relevant part of the United Kingdom in relation to the inquiry is—

(a) England and Wales,

(b) Scotland, or

(c) Northern Ireland.

(2) The Ministers responsible for an inquiry that—

(a) is one to which section 33 applies, and

(b) would (but for this subsection) be subject to more than one set of rules, must specify which of those sets, or what combination of rules from more than one of those sets, is to apply.

(3) In subsection (2) 'set of rules' means the rules made by virtue of a particular paragraph of section 41(3).

(4) If in the case of an inquiry (other than one to which section 33 applies) for which a United Kingdom Minister is responsible—

(a) the Minister specifies that the relevant part of the United Kingdom is Scotland,

(b) the Minister specifies that the relevant part of the United Kingdom is England and Wales, and the inquiry is expected to be held wholly or partly in Wales, or

(c) the Minister specifies that the relevant part of the United Kingdom is Northern Ireland,

he may if he thinks fit specify that some or all of the rules that are to apply are rules made by virtue of paragraph (b), (c) or (d) (as appropriate) of section 41(3).

(5) The relevant part of the United Kingdom and, where subsection (2) or (4) applies, the applicable rules must be specified no later than the setting-up date or, as the case may be, the date of conversion.

Inquiries for which more than one Minister responsible

32 Joint inquiries

(1) The power under section 1 to cause an inquiry to be held, or to convert an inquiry under section 15, is exercisable by two or more Ministers acting jointly.

(2) In this Act 'joint inquiry' means an inquiry for which by virtue of this section, or section 34, two or more Ministers are responsible.

(3) In the case of a joint inquiry—

(a) powers conferred on a Minister by any provision of this Act (except section 41) are exercisable by the Ministers in question acting jointly;

(b) duties imposed by this Act on a Minister are joint duties of those Ministers.

(4) Subsection (3)(b), so far as relating to obligations under section 39, is subject to any different arrangements that may be agreed by the Ministers in question.

33 Inquiries involving more than one administration

(1) This section applies to a joint inquiry for which the Ministers responsible ('the relevant Ministers') are not all United Kingdom Ministers and are not all Northern Ireland Ministers.

(2) A limitation imposed by section 27(2), 28(2), 29(2) or 30(2) or (3) on the terms of reference of an inquiry for which a particular Minister is responsible has effect only to the extent that it applies in relation to all of the relevant Ministers.

(3) A limitation imposed by section 27(3), 28(3) or (4), 29(3) or (4) or 30(4) or (5) on the powers conferred on the chairman of an inquiry for which a particular Minister is responsible has effect only to the extent that it applies in relation to all of the relevant Ministers.

(4) Subsections (6) and (7) of section 30 do not apply if at least one of the relevant Ministers is a United Kingdom Minister.

34 Change of responsibility for inquiry

(1) Each of the Ministers concerned may agree in writing that, as from a date specified in the agreement ('the specified date'), one or more Ministers should become, or cease to be, responsible for an inquiry.

(2) Where an agreement is made under this section—

(a) in relation to any time on or after the specified date, references in this Act to the Minister responsible for the inquiry are to be read in accordance with the agreement;

(b) each of the Ministers concerned has obligations under section 39 only in relation to the period when that Minister was or is responsible for the inquiry.

(3) Subsection (2)(b) is subject to any different arrangements that may be specified in the agreement under this section.

(4) Where as a result of an agreement under this section the terms of reference of the inquiry fail to comply with an applicable limitation imposed by section 27 (2), 28(2), 29(2) or 30(2) or (3), they are to be read subject to such modifications as are necessary to make them comply with the limitation.

(5) In this section 'the Ministers concerned' means the Ministers responsible for the inquiry before the specified date together with any who, under the agreement, are to become responsible for it as from that date.

Supplementary

. . .

36 Enforcement by High Court or Court of Session

(1) Where a person—

(a) fails to comply with, or acts in breach of, a notice under section 19 or 21 or an order made by an inquiry, or

(b) threatens to do so,

the chairman of the inquiry, or after the end of the inquiry the Minister, may certify the matter to the appropriate court.

(2) The court, after hearing any evidence or representations on a matter certified to it under subsection (1), may make such order by way of enforcement or otherwise as it could make if the matter had arisen in proceedings before the court.

(3) In this section 'the appropriate court' means the High Court or, in the case of an inquiry in relation to which the relevant part of the United Kingdom is Scotland, the Court of Session.

37 Immunity from suit

(1) No action lies against—

(a) a member of an inquiry panel,

(b) an assessor, counsel or solicitor to an inquiry, or

(c) a person engaged to provide assistance to an inquiry,

in respect of any act done or omission made in the execution of his duty as such, or any act done or omission made in good faith in the purported execution of his duty as such.

(2) Subsection (1) applies only to acts done or omissions made during the course of the inquiry, otherwise than during any period of suspension (within the meaning of section 13).

(3) For the purposes of the law of defamation, the same privilege attaches to—

(a) any statement made in or for the purposes of proceedings before an inquiry (including the report and any interim report of the inquiry), and

(b) reports of proceedings before an inquiry,

as would be the case if those proceedings were proceedings before a court in the relevant part of the United Kingdom.

Final provisions

50 Crown application

This Act and any provisions made under it bind the Crown (but do not affect Her Majesty in her personal capacity or in right of Her Duchy of Lancaster or the Duke of Cornwall).

SERIOUS ORGANISED CRIME AND POLICE ACT 2005
(2005, c 15)

Trespass on designated site

129 Corresponding Scottish offence

(1) A person commits an offence if he enters, or is on, any [protected] Scottish site without lawful authority.

[(1A) In this section 'protected Scottish site' means—

(a) a nuclear site in Scotland; or

(b) a designated Scottish site.

(1B) In this section 'nuclear site' means—

(a) so much of any premises in respect of which a nuclear site licence (within the meaning of the Nuclear Installations Act 1965) is for the time being in force as lies within the outer perimeter of the protection provided for those premises; and

(b) so much of any other premises of which premises falling within paragraph (a) form a part as lies within that outer perimeter.

(1C) For this purpose—

(a) the outer perimeter of the protection provided for any premises is the line of the outermost fences, walls or other obstacles provided or relied on for protecting those premises from intruders; and

(b) that line shall be determined on the assumption that every gate, door or other barrier across a way through a fence, wall or other obstacle is closed.]

(2) A 'designated Scottish site' means a site in Scotland—

(a) specified or described (in any way) in an order made by the Secretary of State, and

(b) designated for the purposes of this section by the order.

(3) The Secretary of State may only designate a site for the purposes of this section if it appears to him that it is appropriate to designate the site in the interests of national security.

(4) It is a defence for a person charged with an offence under this section to prove that he did not know, and had no reasonable cause to suspect, that the site in relation to which the offence is alleged to have been committed was a [protected] Scottish site.

(5) A person guilty of an offence under this section is liable on summary conviction

(a) to imprisonment for a term not exceeding 12 months, or

(b) to a fine not exceeding level 5 on the standard scale,

or to both.

(6) For the purposes of subsection (1), a person who is on any [protected] Scottish site without lawful authority does not acquire lawful authority by virtue of being allowed time to leave the site.

(7) In this section 'site' means the whole or part of any building or buildings, or any land, or both.

POLICE, PUBLIC ORDER AND CRIMINAL JUSTICE (SCOTLAND) ACT 2006
(2006, asp 10)

33 [The Police Investigations and Review Commissioner]

(1) There is to be an officer known as the [Police Investigations and Review Commissioner] Scotland ('the Commissioner').

(2) The Commissioner is to be an individual appointed by the Scottish Ministers.

(3) Schedule 4 (which makes further provision about the Commissioner) has effect.

[33A General functions of the Commissioner

The Commissioner's general functions are—

(a) to maintain, and to secure the maintenance by the Authority and the chief constable of, suitable arrangements for—

(i) the handling of relevant complaints; and

(ii) the examination of the handling of relevant complaints and the reconsideration of such complaints in accordance with sections 34 to 41;

(b) where directed to do so by the appropriate prosecutor—

(i) to investigate any circumstances in which there is an indication that a person serving with the police may have committed an offence;

(ii) to investigate, on behalf of the relevant procurator fiscal, the circumstances of any death involving a person serving with the police which that procurator fiscal is required to investigate under section 1 of the [Inquiries into Fatal Accidents and Sudden Deaths etc (Scotland) Act 2016];

(c) where requested to do so by the Authority or the chief constable, to investigate and report on certain serious incidents involving the police (see section 41B); and

(d) to investigate other matters relating to the Authority or the Police Service where the Commissioner considers that it would be in the public interest to do so (see section 41C).]

35 Examination of manner of handling of complaint

(1) The Commissioner may, at the request of—

(a) the person who made the complaint ('the complainer'); or

(b) the appropriate authority in relation to the complaint,

examine the manner in which a relevant complaint has been dealt with (such an examination being a 'complaint handling review').

(2) The Commissioner may carry out a complaint handling review under subsection (1)(b) only if satisfied that the appropriate authority in relation to the complaint has taken reasonable steps to deal with the complaint.

(3) On completion of a complaint handling review, the Commissioner must—

(a) inform the persons mentioned in subsection (4) about—

(i) the conclusions the Commissioner has drawn from the complaint handling review and the reasons for them;

(ii) what action (if any) the Commissioner proposes to take in consequence of those conclusions;

(b) draw up a report of the complaint handling review and the conclusions, reasons and proposed action referred to in paragraph (a) and send it to the appropriate authority in relation to the complaint [; and

(c) if the Commissioner considers it appropriate to do so, publish the report drawn up under paragraph (b) in such manner as the Commissioner considers appropriate.]

(4) Those persons are—

(a) the complainer; and

(b) where the complaint is in respect of an act or omission by a person mentioned in section 34(2)(f) and identifies the person who is the subject of it, that person.

(5) The duties imposed by subsection (3)(a) are subject to such exceptions as may be prescribed by regulations made by the Scottish Ministers; but they are to make regulations under this subsection only to the extent that they consider it necessary for the purpose of any of the following—

(a) preventing the premature or inappropriate disclosure of information that is relevant to, or may be used in, any criminal proceedings or prospective criminal proceedings;

(b) preventing the disclosure of information in any circumstances in which it has been determined in accordance with the regulations that its non-disclosure—

(i) is in the interests of national security;

(ii) is for the purposes of the prevention or detection of crime or the apprehension or prosecution of offenders;

(iii) is justified on proportionality grounds; or

(iv) is otherwise necessary in the public interest.

(6) The non-disclosure of information is justified on proportionality grounds only if its disclosure would cause, directly or indirectly, an adverse effect which would be disproportionate to the benefits arising from its disclosure.

(7) If, having completed a complaint handling review, the Commissioner is of the opinion that the complaint should be reconsidered, the Commissioner may give a direction requiring the reconsideration of the complaint (a 'reconsideration direction').

(8) A reconsideration direction may be given—

(a) to the appropriate authority in relation to the complaint; or

(b) if the Commissioner thinks it more appropriate to do so, to [the Authority where the appropriate authority is the chief constable],

(the person to whom the direction is given being 'the reconsidering authority').

(9) A reconsideration direction given under subsection (8)(b) must be accompanied by a copy of the report sent to the appropriate authority in relation to the complaint under subsection (3)(b).

(10) A reconsideration direction may be given as respects so much of the complaint as has been, or is, the subject of [procedures made by regulations made under section 48 of the Police and Fire Reform (Scotland) Act 2012 (asp 8) for dealing with constables whose standard of behaviour or performance is unsatisfactory] only in so far as it relates to the extent of compliance with the procedures established by virtue of that provision.

(11) A reconsideration direction may (either or both)—

(a) instruct that the reconsideration of the complaint is to have regard to such further information as may have become available (whether or not as a result of the complaint handling review) after the complaint was dealt with;

(b) contain a requirement that reconsideration of the complaint is to take place under the supervision of the Commissioner (a 'supervision requirement').

(12) In deciding whether a reconsideration direction should contain a supervision requirement, the Commissioner must have regard to—

(a) the seriousness of the case; and

(b) the public interest.

(13) The Commissioner may at any time issue a direction varying a reconsideration direction by inserting or, as the case may be, deleting a supervision requirement.

(14) Where a reconsideration direction is varied under subsection (13), the Commissioner may give—

(a) the reconsidering authority; or

(b) any person previously appointed to carry out the reconsideration,

such directions as the Commissioner considers appropriate for the purpose of giving effect to the variation.

36 Duty of Commissioner not to proceed with certain complaint handling reviews

(1) If it appears to the Commissioner (whether on an application by the appropriate authority in relation to the complaint or otherwise) that a complaint handling review is or would, if it took place, be one to which subsection [(1A) or] (2)

applies, the Commissioner must discontinue or, as the case may be, not proceed with the review.

[(1A) This subsection applies to a complaint handling review if—

(a) it relates or, if it took place, would relate to a relevant complaint in respect of which the appropriate authority in relation to the complaint—

(i) has concluded its consideration of the complaint; and

(ii) has communicated its findings to the complainer;

(b) a period of 3 months or longer has elapsed between the date on which those findings were so communicated and the date on which the Commissioner was requested to carry out the complaint handling review; and

(c) the Commissioner is not satisfied that there are exceptional circumstances which justified the delay in requesting the review.]

(2) This subsection applies to a complaint handling review which relates or, if it took place, would relate to a relevant complaint of a specified description.

(3) In subsection (2), 'specified' means specified in regulations made by the Scottish Ministers.

(4) Where a complaint handling review is, under this section, discontinued or not proceeded with—

(a) the Commissioner must notify the appropriate authority in relation to the complaint and the persons mentioned in section 35(4) of that fact;

(b) the Commissioner may give the appropriate authority in relation to the complaint directions to do any such things as the Commissioner is authorised to direct by regulations made by the Scottish Ministers;

(c) the Commissioner may himself or herself take any steps of a description specified in regulations so made as the Commissioner considers appropriate for purposes connected with the discontinuance of the complaint handling review or the fact that it is not to take place; and

(d) subject to paragraphs (b) and (c), the Commissioner is to take no further action in accordance with this Chapter in relation to the review or the complaint to which it relates.

37 Appointment of person to reconsider complaint

(1) The reconsidering authority must appoint a person to reconsider the complaint to which the reconsideration direction relates.

(2) But where the reconsideration direction contains a supervision requirement, the reconsidering authority must not appoint a person unless the Commissioner has given notice to the authority that the Commissioner approves the person whom the authority proposes to appoint.

(3) Where the reconsidering authority is the appropriate authority in relation to the complaint, the person appointed must be one who was not previously involved in the consideration of the complaint.

(4) Where the reconsideration of a complaint is subject to a supervision requirement, the person appointed under this section to reconsider the complaint must comply with all such requirements in relation to the carrying out of that reconsideration as may be imposed by the Commissioner in relation to that reconsideration.

38 Reconsideration of complaint: duties to keep persons informed

(1) This section applies where there is a reconsideration of a complaint in accordance with section 35.

(2) The reconsidering authority or, where the reconsideration of a complaint is subject to a supervision requirement, the Commissioner must provide the persons mentioned in subsection (3) with all such information as will keep those persons properly informed, while the reconsideration is being carried out and subsequently, of—

(a) the action (if any) which is taken in respect of the matters dealt with in any report under section 40; and

(b) the outcome of any such action.

(3) Those persons are—

(a) the complainer;

(b) the appropriate authority in relation to the complaint (except where that authority is the reconsidering authority); and

(c) where the complaint is in respect of an act or omission by a person mentioned in section 34(2)(f) and identifies the person who is the subject of it, that person.

(4) Subsections (5) and (6) of section 35 apply in relation to the duties imposed by subsection (2) as they apply to the duties imposed by subsection (3)(a) of that section.

(5) A person appointed under section 37 to reconsider a complaint must provide the Commissioner with all such information as is reasonably required by the Commissioner for the purposes of the Commissioner's functions.

(6) Where the reconsideration of a complaint is not subject to a supervision requirement the reconsidering authority must comply with any direction or guidance given by the Commissioner as to how the authority is to perform its functions under this section.

51 Making of order on conviction of a football-related offence

(1) This section applies where—

(a) a person is convicted of an offence; and

(b) the person was aged 16 or over at the time the offence was committed.

(2) Instead of or in addition to any sentence which it could impose, the court which deals with the person in respect of the offence may, if satisfied as to the matters mentioned in subsection (3), make a football banning order against the person.

(3) Those matters are—

(a) that the offence was one to which subsection (4) applies; and

(b) that there are reasonable grounds to believe that making the football banning order would help to prevent violence or disorder at or in connection with any football matches.

(4) This subsection applies to an offence if—

(a) the offence involved the person who committed it engaging in violence or disorder; and

(b) the offence related to a football match.

(5) Where the court does not make a football banning order, but is nevertheless satisfied that the offence was one to which subsection (4) applies, it may declare that to be the case.

(6) For the purpose of subsection (4)(b), an offence relates to a football match if it is committed—

(a) at a football match or while the person committing it is entering or leaving (or trying to enter or leave) the ground;

(b) on a journey to or from a football match; or

(c) otherwise, where it appears to the court from all the circumstances that the offence is motivated (wholly or partly) by a football match.

(7) The references in subsection (6)(a) and (b) to a football match include a reference to any place (other than domestic premises) at which a football match is being televised; and, in the case of such a place, the reference in subsection (6)(a) to the ground is to be taken to be a reference to that place.

(8) For the purpose of subsection (6)(b)—

(a) a person may be regarded as having been on a journey to or from a football match whether or not the person attended or intended to attend the match; and

(b) a person's journey includes breaks (including overnight breaks).

(9) On making a football banning order, or a declaration, under this section, a

court must explain to the person in ordinary language the effect of the order or declaration.

(10) But failure to comply with subsection (9) does not affect the order's (or declaration's) validity.

52 Making of order on application to the sheriff

(1) The chief constable of [the Police Service of Scotland] may apply for a football banning order against any person.

[. . .]

(2) An application under subsection (1) may be made to any sheriff—

(a) in whose sheriffdom the person against whom the order is sought resides;

(b) in whose sheriffdom that person is believed by the applicant to be; or

(c) to whose sheriffdom that person is believed by the applicant to be intending to come.

(3) An application under subsection (1) is to be made by summary application.

(4) A sheriff may make a football banning order if satisfied that—

(a) the person against whom the order is sought has at any time contributed to any violence or disorder in the United Kingdom or elsewhere; and

(b) there are reasonable grounds to believe that making the order would help to prevent violence or disorder at or in connection with any football matches.

(5) Subsections (6) and (8) apply where a sheriff is determining whether to make a football banning order against a person.

(6) The sheriff may take into account the matters mentioned in subsection (7) (amongst others), so far as considering it appropriate to do so.

(7) Those matters are—

(a) any decision of a court or tribunal outside the United Kingdom in respect of the person;

(b) the person's deportation or exclusion from a country or territory outside the United Kingdom;

(c) the person's removal or exclusion from premises used for playing football matches, whether in the United Kingdom or elsewhere;

(d) the person's conduct recorded on video or by any other means.

(8) The sheriff may not take into account anything done by the person before the beginning of the relevant period, except circumstances ancillary to a conviction.

(9) In subsection (8)—

'the relevant period' means the period of 10 years ending with the day on which the application for the order was made; and

'circumstances ancillary to a conviction' has the same meaning as it has for the purposes of section 4 of the Rehabilitation of Offenders Act 1974 (c.53).

(10) Subsection (8) does not prejudice anything in the Rehabilitation of Offenders Act 1974.

(11) On making a football banning order, the sheriff must explain to the person (if present in court) in ordinary language the effect of the order.

(12) But failure to comply with subsection (11) does not affect the order's validity.

53 Content of order

(1) A football banning order is an order which—

(a) prohibits the person against whom it is made from entering any premises for the purposes of attending any regulated football matches in the United Kingdom; and

(b) requires the person against whom it is made to report at a police station in accordance with this Chapter, in connection with regulated football matches outside the United Kingdom.

(2) A football banning order must require the person against whom it is made—

(a) to report initially at a police station [. . .] specified in the order within 5 days beginning with the day on which the order is made; and

(b) where a relevant event occurs, to notify the football banning orders authority of the prescribed information in relation to the event within 7 days beginning with the day on which the event occurs.

(3) A football banning order must, unless it appears to the court making it that there are exceptional circumstances, impose a requirement as to the surrender in accordance with this Chapter, in connection with regulated football matches outside the United Kingdom, of the person's passport.

(4) A football banning order may, if the court making it considers it would help to prevent violence or disorder at or in connection with any football matches, impose on the person additional requirements.

(5) Such requirements may include prohibiting the person from entering any premises (including premises to be entered for the purposes of attending football matches which are not regulated football matches).

(6) A football banning order must specify the period for which it is to have effect.

(7) That period is not to exceed—

(a) 10 years, in the case of an order made under section 51 made in addition to a sentence of imprisonment;

(b) 5 years, in the case of an order made under section 51 other than one mentioned in paragraph (a);

(c) 3 years, in the case of an order made under section 52.

61 Foreign matches: reporting and other requirements

(1) The constable responsible for the police station at which a person subject to a football banning order reports initially may make such requirements of the person as are determined by the football banning orders authority to be necessary or expedient for giving effect to the football banning order, so far as relating to regulated football matches outside the United Kingdom.

(2) Subject to section 64, if, in connection with any regulated football match outside the United Kingdom, the football banning orders authority is of the opinion mentioned in subsection (3) in relation to a person subject to a football banning order, the authority must cause the person to be served with a notice in writing under subsection (4).

(3) That opinion is that requiring the person to report in accordance with a notice under subsection (4) is necessary or expedient in order to reduce the likelihood of violence or disorder at or in connection with the match.

(4) A notice under this subsection is a notice requiring the person—

(a) to report at a specified police station at the time, or between the times, specified; and

(b) if the order imposes a requirement as to the surrender of the person's passport, to attend at a specified police station at the time, or between the times, specified and—

(i) if the person has a passport, to surrender it; or

(ii) if the person does not have a passport, to make a declaration to that effect.

(5) In subsection (4), 'specified' means specified in the notice.

(6) The football banning orders authority may establish criteria for determining whether a notice under subsection (4) ought to be imposed on any person or on persons of a particular description.

INTERESTS OF MEMBERS OF THE SCOTTISH PARLIAMENT ACT 2006 (2006 asp 12)

1 The register

(1) There shall be a Register of Interests of Members of the Scottish Parliament (in this Act referred to as 'the register').

(2) The register shall be kept by the Clerk at the office of the Clerk.

(3) In the register, there shall be an entry for each member which shall contain—

(a) the information required by or under this Act; and

(b) any other matter which the Parliament may determine should be included in each entry.

(4) The register shall be kept in such form (which need not be in documentary form) as the Clerk considers appropriate but, if it is kept otherwise than in documentary form, it shall be in such form that, when printed or displayed, it shows what the register contains.

2 Registrable interests

(1) In this Act, a 'registrable interest' means a registrable financial interest.

(2) The schedule sets out the circumstances in which a member has, or had, a registrable financial interest.

(3) A financial interest is defined for the purposes of paragraph (a) of section 39(2) of the 1998 Act as a registrable financial interest.

5 Registration of registrable interests acquired after date of return

(1) This section applies where a member acquires a registrable interest after the date on which the member was returned.

(2) Within 30 days [beginning with] the date on which the member acquired that interest, that member shall register that interest by lodging a written statement with the Clerk.

. . .

[17 Offences

(1) Any member who—

(a) takes part in any proceedings of the Parliament without having complied with, or in contravention of, section 3, 5, 6, 8A(4) and (5) or 13 or a measure taken by the Parliament under section 15 or 16; or

(b) contravenes section 14,

is guilty of an offence.

(2) A person guilty of an offence is liable on summary conviction to a fine not exceeding level 5 on the standard scale.]

SCOTTISH COMMISSION FOR HUMAN RIGHTS ACT 2006 (2006 asp 16)

Scottish Commission for Human Rights

1 Scottish Commission for Human Rights

(1) There is established a body corporate to be known as the Scottish Commission for Human Rights (and referred to in this Act as the 'Commission').

(2) Schedule 1 makes further provision about the Commission.

General functions

2 General duty to promote human rights

(1) The Commission's general duty is, through the exercise of its functions under this Act, to promote human rights and, in particular, to encourage best practice in relation to human rights.

(2) In this Act, 'human rights' means—

(a) the Convention rights within the meaning of section 1 of the Human Rights Act 1998, and

(b) other human rights contained in any international convention, treaty or other international instrument ratified by the United Kingdom.

(3) In this section, 'promote', in relation to human rights, means promote awareness and understanding of, and respect for, those rights.

(4) In deciding what action to take under this Act in pursuance of its general duty, the Commission must have regard, in particular, to the importance of exercising its functions under this Act in relation to—

(a) the Convention rights, and

(b) human rights of those groups in society whose human rights are not, in the Commission's opinion, otherwise being sufficiently promoted.

3 Information, guidance, education etc

(1) For the purposes of its general duty, the Commission may—

(a) publish or otherwise disseminate information or ideas,

(b) provide advice or guidance,

(c) conduct research,

(d) provide education or training.

(2) The Commission may charge reasonable fees in connection with anything done by it or on its behalf under subsection (1).

(3) Sums paid to the Commission in respect of fees charged under subsection (2) are to be retained by it and applied to meet expenses incurred by it in doing anything under subsection (1).

4 Monitoring of law, policies and practices

(1) For the purposes of its general duty, the Commission may review and recommend changes to—

(a) any area of the law of Scotland, or

(b) any policies or practices of any Scottish public authorities.

(2) The Commission must consult the Scottish Law Commission before undertaking a review of any area of the law under subsection (1)(a).

5 Power to co-operate etc with others

(1) The Commission may, in the exercise of any of its functions—

(a) consult,

(b) act jointly with,

(c) co-operate with, or

(d) assist, any other person.

(2) The Commission must seek to ensure, so far as practicable, that any activity undertaken by it under this Act does not duplicate unnecessarily any activity undertaken by any other person under any other enactment.

6 No power to assist in claims or legal proceedings

(1) The Commission may not provide assistance to or in respect of any person in connection with any claim or legal proceedings to which that person is or may become a party.

(2) In subsection (1), 'assistance' includes advice, guidance and grants.

[6A Subsequent appointments

(1) A person who has ceased to be a member of the Commission may not, without the approval of the Parliamentary corporation—

(a) be employed or appointed in any other capacity by the Commission,

(b) hold office in or be an employee or appointee of any Scottish public authority in relation to which the Commission conducted an inquiry under section 8(1)(a) while that person was a member of the Commission, or

(c) hold any other office, employment or appointment or engage in any other occupation, being an office, employment, appointment or occupation which, by virtue of paragraph 5(9)(a), that person could not have held or, as the case may be, engaged in when a member of the Commission.

(2) The restriction in sub-paragraph (1)—

(a) starts when the person ceases to be a member of the Commission, and

(b) ends on the expiry of the financial year next following the one in which it started.]

SCHEDULE 1
SCOTTISH COMMISSION FOR HUMAN RIGHTS

(introduced by section 1(2))

Membership

1.—(1) The Commission consists of the following members—

(a) a member appointed to chair the Commission, and

(b) not more than 4 other members.

(2) The member appointed to chair the Commission is to be an individual appointed by Her Majesty on the nomination of the Scottish Parliament.

(3) The other members are to be individuals appointed by the Parliamentary corporation.

Status

2. The Commission—

(a) is not a servant or agent of the Crown, and

(b) has no status, immunity or privilege of the Crown.

Independence

3.—(1) The Commission, in the exercise of its functions, is not to be subject to the direction or control of—

(a) any member of the Parliament,

(b) any member of the Scottish Executive, or

(c) the Parliamentary corporation.

(2) Sub-paragraph (1) is subject to section 15(3), paragraphs [8(3)], 10, 11 [, 11A, 12(3), 13A] and 15(1) of this schedule and paragraph 5 of schedule 2.

Disqualification

4.—(1) A person is disqualified from appointment, and from holding office, as a member of the Commission if that person is—

(a) a member of the House of Commons,

(b) a member of the Scottish Parliament, or

(c) a member of the European Parliament.

(2) A person is also disqualified from such appointment if that person has, in the relevant period, held any of the offices set out in sub-paragraph (1)(a) to (c).

(3) The relevant period is—

(a) in relation to the appointment of a member to chair the Commission, the year preceding the date of nomination,

(b) in relation to the appointment of any other member of the Commission, the year preceding the proposed date of appointment.

Terms of office and remuneration

5 (1) Each member of the Commission—

(a) holds office for such period not exceeding [eight] years as the Parliamentary corporation, at the time of appointment, may determine, [but]

[(b) is ineligible for reappointment at any time.]

(2) The member appointed to chair the Commission may be—

(a) relieved of office by Her Majesty at the member's request, or

(b) removed from office by Her Majesty if condition A or B is satisfied.

(3) Any other member of the Commission may be—

(a) relieved of office by the Parliamentary corporation at the member's request, or

(b) removed from office by the Parliamentary corporation if condition A or B is satisfied.

(4) Condition A is that—

(a) the Parliamentary corporation is satisfied that the member has breached the member's terms of appointment, and

(b) the Parliament resolves that the member should be removed from office for that reason

(5) Condition B is that the Parliament resolves that it has lost confidence in the [member's willingness, suitability or ability to perform that member's functions]

(6) A resolution under sub-paragraph (4)(b) or (5), [must be voted for by a number of members not fewer than two thirds of the total number of seats for members of the Parliament].

(7) Each member of the Commission is entitled to—

(a) such remuneration, and

(b) such allowances,

as the Parliamentary corporation may determine.

(8) In other respects, each member of the Commission holds office on such terms and conditions as the Parliamentary corporation may determine.

[(9) Those terms and conditions may, without prejudice to paragraph 4—

(a) prohibit the member from holding any other specified office, employment or appointment or engaging in any other specified occupation,

(b) provide that a member's holding of any such office, employment or appointment or engagement in any such occupation is subject to the approval of the Parliamentary corporation,

(c) for the purposes of this sub-paragraph, provide differently for the member appointed to chair the Commission and the other members.

(10) In sub-paragraph (9), 'specified' means specified in the terms and conditions or within a description so specified.]

Pensions etc

6 (1) The Commission may, with the approval of the Parliamentary corporation, make arrangements for the payment of pensions, allowances or gratuities to, or in respect of, any person who has ceased to be a member of the Commission and such arrangements may include, in particular—

(a) the making of contributions or payments towards provision for such pensions, allowances, or gratuities, and

(b) the establishing and administering of one or more pension schemes.

(2) References in sub-paragraph (1) to pensions, allowances and gratuities include references to, as the case may be, pensions, allowances or gratuities by way of compensation for loss of office.

Proceedings etc

7 (1) The Commission may regulate its own procedure (including any quorum).

(2) Where the member appointed to chair the Commission is not present at a

meeting of the Commission, any other member of the Commission may chair the meeting.

(3) The validity of any acts of the Commission is not affected by any—

(a) defect in the appointment of a member of the Commission,

(b) disqualification from appointment as a member of the Commission, or

(c) vacancy in the membership of the Commission.

General powers

8 (1) The Commission may do anything which appears necessary or expedient for the purpose of, or in connection with, or which appears conducive to, the exercise of its functions.

(2) In particular, the Commission may—

(a) enter into contracts, and

[(b) acquire and dispose of land and other property,]

[(3) The exercise of the power to acquire or dispose of land is subject to the approval of the Parliamentary corporation.]

Delegation

9 (1) Any function of the Commission may be exercised on its behalf—

(a) by any person (whether or not a member of the Commission or its staff) authorised by the Commission to do so, and

(b) to the extent so authorised.

(2) Sub-paragraph (1) does not affect the Commission's responsibility for the exercise of its functions.

[Location of office]

[10 The Commission must comply with any direction given by the Parliamentary corporation as to the location of the Commission's office.]

Staff

11 (1) The Commission may, with the consent of the Parliamentary corporation as to numbers, appoint staff.

(2) The appointment of staff is to be on such terms and conditions as the Commission may, with the approval of the Parliamentary corporation, determine.

(3) The Commission may, with the approval of the Parliamentary corporation, make arrangements for the payment of pensions, allowances or gratuities to, or in respect of, any person who has ceased to be a member of staff.

(4) References in sub-paragraph (3) to pensions, allowances and gratuities include references to, as the case may be, pensions, allowances or gratuities by way of compensation for loss of employment.

Sharing of premises, staff, services and other resources

12 (1) The Commission may enter into arrangements with any other public body or office-holder for the sharing of premises, staff, services or other resources.

(2) In considering its requirements as to premises, staff, services and other resources, the Commission must have regard, with a view to ensuring the economic, efficient and effective use of resources, to the desirability of entering into arrangements under sub-paragraph (1).

[(3) The exercise of the power in sub-paragraph (1) is subject to the approval of the Parliamentary corporation.]

Accountable officer

13 (1) The Parliamentary corporation must designate a member of the Commission or of the Commission's staff as the accountable officer for the purposes of this paragraph.

(2) The functions of the accountable officer are—

(a) signing the accounts of the expenditure and receipts of the Commission,

(b) ensuring the propriety and regularity of the finances of the Commission,

(c) ensuring that the resources of the Commission are used economically, efficiently and effectively, and

(d) the duty set out in sub-paragraph (3),

and the accountable officer is answerable to the Parliament for the exercise of those functions.

(3) Where the accountable officer is required to act in some way but considers that to do so would be inconsistent with the proper performance of the functions specified in sub-paragraph (2)(a) to (c), the accountable officer must—

(a) obtain written authority from the Commission before taking the action, and

(b) send a copy of the authority as soon as possible to the Auditor General for Scotland.

Finance

14 [(1) The Parliamentary corporation is to—

(a) pay the remuneration and allowances of each member of the Commission,

(b) pay any expenses properly incurred by the Commission in the exercise of its functions, so far as those expenses are not met out of sums retained and applied by it under section 3(3), and

(c) indemnify the Commission in respect of any liabilities incurred by it in the exercise of its functions.]

(2) The Commission must, before the start of each financial year, prepare proposals for its use of resources and expenditure during the year and send the proposals to the Parliamentary corporation for approval by such date as the Parliamentary corporation may determine.

(3) The Commission may, in the course of a financial year, prepare revised proposals for its use of resources and expenditure during the remainder of the year and send the proposals to the Parliamentary corporation for approval.

(4) The proposals or, as the case may be, revised proposals must include a statement that the Commission has complied with the duty in paragraph 12(2) in preparing the proposals.

(5) Sub-paragraph (1)(b) does not require the Parliamentary corporation to pay any expenses incurred by the Commission which exceed, or are otherwise not covered by, any proposals approved under sub-paragraph (2) or (3).

(6) However, the Parliamentary corporation may pay those expenses.

(7) The financial year of the Commission is—

(a) the period beginning with the date on which the Commission is established and ending with 31st March next following that date, and

(b) each successive period of 12 months ending with 31st March.

Accounts and audit

15 (1) The Commission must, in accordance with such directions as the Scottish Ministers may give—

(a) keep proper accounts and accounting records,

(b) prepare annual accounts in respect of each financial year, and

(c) send a copy of the annual accounts to the Auditor General for Scotland for auditing.

(2) If requested by any person, the Commission must make available at any reasonable time, and without charge, in printed or electronic form, the audited accounts, so that they may be inspected by that person.

TERRORISM ACT 2006
(2006, c 11)

17 Commission of offences abroad

(1) If—

(a) a person does anything outside the United Kingdom, and

(b) his action, if done in a part of the United Kingdom, would constitute an offence falling within subsection (2),

he shall be guilty in that part of the United Kingdom of the offence.

(2) The offences falling within this subsection are—

(a) an offence under section 1 [. . .] of this Act so far as it is committed in relation to any statement [. . .] in relation to which that section has effect by reason of its relevance to the commission, preparation or instigation of one or more Convention offences;

(b) an offence under [section 5 or 6 or] any of sections 8 to 11 of this Act;

(c) an offence under section 11(1) of the Terrorism Act 2000 (c 11) (membership of proscribed organisations);

(d) an offence under section 54 of that Act (weapons training);

(e) conspiracy to commit an offence falling within this subsection;

(f) inciting a person to commit such an offence;

(g) attempting to commit such an offence;

(h) aiding, abetting, counselling or procuring the commission of such an offence.

(3) Subsection (1) applies irrespective of whether the person is a British citizen or, in the case of a company, a company incorporated in a part of the United Kingdom.

(4) In the case of an offence falling within subsection (2) which is committed wholly or partly outside the United Kingdom—

(a) proceedings for the offence may be taken at any place in the United Kingdom; and

(b) the offence may for all incidental purposes be treated as having been committed at any such place.

(5) In section 3(1)(a) and (b) of the Explosive Substances Act 1883 (c 3) (offences committed in preparation for use of explosives with intent to endanger life or property in the United Kingdom or the Republic of Ireland), in each place, for 'the Republic of Ireland' substitute 'elsewhere'.

(6) Subsection (5) does not extend to Scotland except in relation to—

(a) the doing of an act as an act of terrorism or for the purposes of terrorism; or

(b) the possession or control of a substance for the purposes of terrorism.

LEGISLATIVE AND REGULATORY REFORM ACT 2006
(2006 c 51)

PART I
ORDER-MAKING POWERS

Powers

1 Power to remove or reduce burdens

(1) A Minister of the Crown may by order under this section make any provision which he considers would serve the purpose in subsection (2).

(2) That purpose is removing or reducing any burden, or the overall burdens, resulting directly or indirectly for any person from any legislation.

(3) In this section 'burden' means any of the following—

(a) a financial cost;

(b) an administrative inconvenience;

(c) an obstacle to efficiency, productivity or profitability; or

(d) a sanction, criminal or otherwise, which affects the carrying on of any lawful activity.

(4) Provision may not be made under subsection (1) in relation to any burden which affects only a Minister of the Crown or government department, unless it affects the Minister or department in the exercise of a regulatory function.

(5) For the purposes of subsection (2), a financial cost or administrative inconvenience may result from the form of any legislation (for example, where the legislation is hard to understand).

(6) In this section 'legislation' means any of the following or a provision of any of the following—

(a) a public general Act or local Act (whether passed before or after the commencement of this section),

[(aa) a Measure or Act of the Assembly, or]

(b) any Order in Council, order, rules, regulations, scheme, warrant, byelaw or other subordinate instrument made at any time [under—

(i) an Act referred to in paragraph (a), or

(ii) a Measure or Act of the Assembly,]

but does not include any instrument which is, or is made under, Northern Ireland legislation.

(7) Subject to this Part, the provision that may be made under subsection (1) includes—

(a) provision abolishing, conferring or transferring, or providing for the delegation of, functions of any description,

(b) provision creating or abolishing a body or office,

and provision made by amending or repealing any enactment.

(8) An order under this section may contain such consequential, supplementary, incidental or transitional provision (including provision made by amending or repealing any enactment or other provision) as the Minister making it considers appropriate.

(9) An order under this section may bind the Crown.

(10) An order under this section must be made in accordance with this Part.

2 Power to promote regulatory principles

(1) A Minister of the Crown may by order under this section make any provision which he considers would serve the purpose in subsection (2).

(2) That purpose is securing that regulatory functions are exercised so as to comply with the principles in subsection (3).

(3) Those principles are that—

(a) regulatory activities should be carried out in a way which is transparent, accountable, proportionate and consistent;

(b) regulatory activities should be targeted only at cases in which action is needed.

(4) Subject to this Part, the provision that may be made under subsection (1) for the purpose in subsection (2) includes—

(a) provision modifying the way in which a regulatory function is exercised by any person,

(b) provision amending the constitution of a body exercising regulatory functions which is established by or under an enactment,

(c) provision transferring, or providing for the delegation of, the regulatory functions conferred on any person, and provision made by amending or repealing any enactment.

(5) The provision referred to in subsection (4)(c) includes provision—

(a) to create a new body to which, or a new office to the holder of which, regulatory functions are transferred;

(b) to abolish a body from which, or office from the holder of which, regulatory functions are transferred.

(6) The provision that may be made under subsection (1) does not include provision conferring any new regulatory function or abolishing any regulatory function.

(7) An order under this section may contain such consequential, supplementary, incidental or transitional provision (including provision made by amending or repealing any enactment or other provision) as the Minister making it considers appropriate.

(8) An order under this section may bind the Crown. (9) An order under this section must be made in accordance with this Part.

Restrictions

3 Preconditions

(1) A Minister may not make provision under section 1(1) or 2(1), other than provision which merely restates an enactment, unless he considers that the conditions in subsection (2), where relevant, are satisfied in relation to that provision.

(2) Those conditions are that—

(a) the policy objective intended to be secured by the provision could not be satisfactorily secured by non-legislative means;

(b) the effect of the provision is proportionate to the policy objective;

(c) the provision, taken as a whole, strikes a fair balance between the public interest and the interests of any person adversely affected by it;

(d) the provision does not remove any necessary protection;

(e) the provision does not prevent any person from continuing to exercise any right or freedom which that person might reasonably expect to continue to exercise;

(f) the provision is not of constitutional significance.

(3) A Minister may not make provision under section 1(1) or 2(1) which merely restates an enactment unless he considers that the condition in subsection (4) is satisfied in relation to that provision.

(4) That condition is that the provision made would make the law more accessible or more easily understood.

(5) In this section and sections 4 to 7, to 'restate' an enactment means to replace it with alterations only of form or arrangement (and for these purposes to remove an ambiguity is to make an alteration other than one of form or arrangement).

4 Subordinate legislation

(1) An order under this Part may only confer or transfer a function of legislating on or to—

(a) a Minister of the Crown;

(b) any person on or to whom functions are conferred or have been transferred by an enactment; or

(c) a body which, or the holder of an office which, is created by the order.

(2) An order under this Part may not make provision for the delegation of any function of legislating.

(3) An order under this Part may not make provision to confer a function of legislating on a Minister of the Crown (alone or otherwise) unless the conditions in subsections (4) and (5) are satisfied.

[(3A) An order under this Part may not make provision to confer a function of legislating on the Welsh Ministers, the First Minister for Wales or the Counsel General to the Welsh Assembly Government (alone or otherwise) unless the conditions in subsections (4) and (5A) are satisfied.]

(4) The condition in this subsection is that the function is exercisable by statutory instrument.

(5) The condition in this subsection is that such a statutory instrument—

(a) is an instrument to which section 5(1) of the Statutory Instruments Act 1946 applies (instruments subject to annulment by resolution of either House of Parliament); or

(b) is not to be made unless a draft of the statutory instrument has been laid before and approved by a resolution of each House of Parliament.

[(5A) The condition in this subsection is that such a statutory instrument—

(a) is an instrument to which section 5(1) of the Statutory Instruments Act 1946 applied (instruments subject to annulment); or

(b) is not to be made unless a draft of the statutory instrument has been laid before and approved by a resolution of the Assembly.]

(6) [Subsections (1) to (3A)] do not apply to provision which merely restates an enactment.

(7) For the purposes of this section a 'function of legislating' is a function of legislating by order, rules, regulations or other subordinate instrument.

5 Taxation

(1) An order under this Part may not make provision to impose, abolish or vary any tax.

(2) The Treasury may by regulations make provision for varying the way in which a relevant tax has effect in relation to—

(a) any property, rights or liabilities transferred by or under an order under this Part; or

(b) anything done for the purposes of, or in relation to, the transfer of any property, rights or liabilities by or under an order under this Part.

(3) The provision which may be made under subsection (2)(a) includes in particular provision for—

(a) a tax provision not to apply, or to apply with modifications, in relation to any property, rights or liabilities transferred;

(b) any property, rights or liabilities transferred to be treated in a specified way for the purposes of a tax provision;

(c) the Minister of the Crown making the order to be required or permitted, with the consent of the Treasury, to determine, or specify the method for determining, anything which needs to be determined for the purposes of any tax provision so far as relating to any property, rights or liabilities transferred.

(4) The provision which may be made under subsection (2)(b) includes in particular provision for—

(a) a tax provision not to apply, or to apply with modifications, in relation to anything done for the purposes of or in relation to the transfer;

(b) anything done for the purposes of or in relation to the transfer to have or not have a specified consequence or be treated in a specified way;

(c) the Minister of the Crown making the order to be required or permitted, with the consent of the Treasury, to determine, or specify the method for determining, anything which needs to be determined for the purposes of any tax provision so far as relating to anything done for the purposes of or in relation to the transfer.

(5) Regulations under subsection (2) are to be made by statutory instrument.

(6) A statutory instrument containing regulations under subsection (2) is subject to annulment in pursuance of a resolution of the House of Commons.

(7) In this section—

'relevant tax' means income tax, corporation tax, capital gains tax, stamp duty or stamp duty reserve tax;

'tax provision' means a provision of an enactment about a relevant tax.

6 Criminal penalties

(1) An order under this Part may not make provision to create a new offence that is punishable, or increase the penalty for an existing offence so that it is punishable—

(a) on indictment, with imprisonment for a term exceeding two years; or

(b) on summary conviction, with—

(i) imprisonment for a term exceeding the normal maximum term; or

(ii) a fine exceeding level 5 on the standard scale.

(2) In subsection (1)(b)(i), 'the normal maximum term' means—

(a) in relation to England and Wales—

(i) in the case of a summary offence, 51 weeks; and

(ii) in the case of an offence triable either way, twelve months; and

(b) in relation to Scotland or Northern Ireland, six months.

(3) In the case of an offence which, if committed by an adult, is triable either on indictment or summarily and is not an offence triable on indictment only by virtue of—

(a) Part 5 of the Criminal Justice Act 1988 (c 33), or

(b) section 292(6) and (7) of the Criminal Procedure (Scotland) Act 1995 (c 46),

the reference in subsection (1)(b)(ii) to a fine exceeding level 5 on the standard scale is to be construed as a reference to the statutory maximum.

(4) If an order under this Part making provision creating an offence, or altering the penalty for an offence, is made before the date on which section 281(5) of the Criminal Justice Act 2003 (c. 44) comes into force, the order must provide that, in relation to a summary offence committed before that date, any reference to a term of imprisonment of 51 weeks is to be read as a reference to six months.

(5) If an order under this Part making provision creating an offence, or altering the penalty for an offence, is made before the date on which section 154(1) of the Criminal Justice Act 2003 (c. 44) comes into force, the order must provide that, in relation to an offence triable either way committed before that date, any reference to a term of imprisonment of twelve months is to be read as a reference to six months.

(6) Subsection (1) does not apply to provision which merely restates an enactment.

7 Forcible entry etc

(1) An order under this Part may not make provision to—

(a) authorise any forcible entry, search or seizure; or

(b) compel the giving of evidence.

(2) Subsection (1) does not prevent an order under this Part from extending any power for purposes similar to those to which the power applied before the order was made.

(3) Subsection (1) does not apply to provision which merely restates an enactment.

8 Excepted enactments

An order under this Part may not make provision amending or repealing any provision of—

(a) this Part; or

(b) the Human Rights Act 1998.

9 Scotland

An order under this Part may not, except by virtue of section 1(8) or 2(7), make provision which would be within the legislative competence of the Scottish Parliament if it were contained in an Act of that Parliament.

10, 11 [*Apply to Wales and Northern Ireland*]

Procedure

12 Procedure: introductory

(1) An order under this Part must be made by statutory instrument.

(2) A Minister may not make an order under this Part unless—

(a) he has consulted in accordance with section 13;

(b) following that consultation, he has laid a draft order and explanatory document before Parliament in accordance with section 14; and

(c) the order is made, as determined under section 15, in accordance with—

(i) the negative resolution procedure (see section 16);

(ii) the affirmative resolution procedure (see section 17); or

(iii) the super-affirmative resolution procedure (see section 18).

13 Consultation

(1) If a Minister proposes to make an order under this Part he must—

(a) consult such organisations as appear to him to be representative of interests substantially affected by the proposals;

(b) where the proposals relate to the functions of one or more statutory bodies, consult those bodies, or persons appearing to him to be representative of those bodies;

(c) [consult the Welsh Ministers where the proposals, so far as applying in or as regards Wales, relate to any matters in relation to which the Welsh Ministers, the First Minister for Wales or the Counsel General to the Welsh Assembly Government exercise functions (and where the agreement of the Welsh Ministers in not required under section 11);]

(d) in such cases as he considers appropriate, consult the Law Commission, the Scottish Law Commission or the Northern Ireland Law Commission; and

(e) consult such other persons as he considers appropriate.

(2) If, as a result of any consultation required by subsection (1), it appears to the Minister that it is appropriate to change the whole or any part of his proposals, he must undertake such further consultation with respect to the changes as he considers appropriate.

(3) If, before the day on which this section comes into force, any consultation was undertaken which, had it been undertaken after that day, would to any extent have satisfied the requirements of this section, those requirements shall to that extent be taken to have been satisfied.

(4) Where—

(a) proposals for an order under this Part are the same as proposals for an order under section 1 of the Regulatory Reform Act 2001,

(b) consultation has at any time been undertaken in relation to the proposals under section 5 of that Act, and

(c) that consultation satisfied the requirements of that section in relation to the proposals,

the requirements of this section shall be taken to have been satisfied in relation to the proposals.

(5) In subsection (1)(b) 'statutory body' means—

(a) a body established by or under any enactment; or

(b) the holder of any office so established.

14 Draft order and explanatory document laid before Parliament

(1) If, after the conclusion of the consultation required by section 13, the Minister considers it appropriate to proceed with the making of an order under this Part, he must lay before Parliament—

(a) a draft of the order, together with
(b) an explanatory document.

(2) The explanatory document must—

(a) explain under which power or powers in this Part the provision contained in the order is made;
(b) introduce and give reasons for the provision;
(c) explain why the Minister considers that—
(i) the conditions in section 3(2) are satisfied (where relevant); or
(ii) the condition in section 3(4) is satisfied;
(d) in the case of an order under section 1, include, so far as appropriate, an assessment of the extent to which the provision made by the order would remove or reduce any burden or burdens (within the meaning of subsection (2) of that section);
(e) identify and give reasons for—
(i) any functions of legislating conferred by the order; and
(ii) the procedural requirements attaching to the exercise of those functions; and
(f) give details of—
(i) any consultation undertaken under section 13;
(ii) any representations received as a result of the consultation;
(iii) the changes (if any) made as a result of those representations.

(3) Where a person making representations in response to consultation under section 13 has requested the Minister not to disclose them, the Minister must not disclose them under subsection (2)(f)(ii) if or to the extent that to do so would (disregarding any connection with proceedings in Parliament) constitute a breach of confidence actionable by any person.

(4) If information in representations made by a person in response to consultation under section 13 relates to another person, the Minister need not disclose the information under subsection (2)(f)(ii) if or to the extent that—

(a) it appears to the Minister that the disclosure of that information could adversely affect the interests of that other person; and
(b) the Minister has been unable to obtain the consent of that other person to the disclosure.

(5) Subsections (3) and (4) do not affect any disclosure that is requested by, and made to, a committee of either House of Parliament charged with reporting on the draft order.

(6) In subsection (2)(e) 'function of legislating' has the same meaning as in section 4.

15 Determination of Parliamentary procedure

(1) The explanatory document laid with a draft order under section 14 must contain a recommendation by the Minister as to which of the following should apply in relation to the making of an order pursuant to the draft order—

(a) the negative resolution procedure (see section 16);
(b) the affirmative resolution procedure (see section 17); or
(c) the super-affirmative resolution procedure (see section 18).

(2) The explanatory document must give reasons for the Minister's recommendation.

(3) Where the Minister's recommendation is that the negative resolution procedure should apply, that procedure shall apply unless, within the 30-day period—

(a) either House of Parliament requires that the super-affirmative resolution procedure shall apply, in which case that procedure shall apply; or
(b) in a case not falling within paragraph (a), either House of Parliament requires that the affirmative resolution procedure shall apply, in which case that procedure shall apply.

(4) Where the Minister's recommendation is that the affirmative resolution

procedure should apply, that procedure shall apply unless, within the 30-day period, either House of Parliament requires that the super-affirmative resolution procedure shall apply, in which case the super-affirmative resolution procedure shall apply.

(5) Where the Minister's recommendation is that the super-affirmative resolution procedure should apply, that procedure shall apply.

(6) For the purposes of this section a House of Parliament shall be taken to have required a procedure within the 30-day period if—

(a) that House resolves within that period that that procedure shall apply; or

(b) in a case not falling within paragraph (a), a committee of that House charged with reporting on the draft order has recommended within that period that that procedure should apply and the House has not by resolution rejected that recommendation within that period.

(7) In this section the '30-day period' means the period of 30 days beginning with the day on which the draft order was laid before Parliament under section 14.

16 Negative resolution procedure

(1) For the purposes of this Part, the 'negative resolution procedure' in relation to the making of an order pursuant to a draft order laid under section 14 is as follows.

(2) The Minister may make an order in the terms of the draft order subject to the following provisions of this section.

(3) The Minister may not make an order in the terms of the draft order if either House of Parliament so resolves within the 40-day period.

(4) A committee of either House charged with reporting on the draft order may, at any time after the expiry of the 30-day period and before the expiry of the 40-day period, recommend under this subsection that the Minister not make an order in the terms of the draft order.

(5) Where a recommendation is made by a committee of either House under subsection (4) in relation to a draft order, the Minister may not make an order in the terms of the draft order unless the recommendation is, in the same Session, rejected by resolution of that House.

(6) For the purposes of this section an order is made in the terms of a draft order if it contains no material changes to the provisions of the draft order.

(7) In this section—

(a) the '30-day period' has the meaning given by section 15(7); and

(b) the '40-day period' means the period of 40 days beginning with the day on which the draft order was laid before Parliament under section 14.

(8) For the purpose of calculating the 40-day period in a case where a recommendation is made under subsection (4) by a committee of either House but the recommendation is rejected by that House under subsection (5), no account shall be taken of any day between the day on which the recommendation was made and the day on which the recommendation was rejected.

17 Affirmative resolution procedure

(1) For the purposes of this Part the 'affirmative resolution procedure' in relation to the making of an order pursuant to a draft order laid under section 14 is as follows.

(2) If after the expiry of the 40-day period the draft order is approved by a resolution of each House of Parliament, the Minister may make an order in the terms of the draft.

(3) However, a committee of either House charged with reporting on the draft order may, at any time after the expiry of the 30-day period and before the expiry of the 40-day period, recommend under this subsection that no further proceedings be taken in relation to the draft order.

(4) Where a recommendation is made by a committee of either House under

subsection (3) in relation to a draft order, no proceedings may be taken in relation to the draft order in that House under subsection (2) unless the recommendation is, in the same Session, rejected by resolution of that House.

(5) For the purposes of subsection (2) an order is made in the terms of a draft order if it contains no material changes to the provisions of the draft order.

(6) In this section—

(a) the '30-day period' has the meaning given by section 15(7); and

(b) the '40-day period' has the meaning given by section 16(7).

(7) For the purpose of calculating the 40-day period in a case where a recommendation is made under subsection (3) by a committee of either House but the recommendation is rejected by that House under subsection (4), no account shall be taken of any day between the day on which the recommendation was made and the day on which the recommendation was rejected.

18 Super-affirmative resolution procedure

(1) For the purposes of this Part the 'super-affirmative resolution procedure' in relation to the making of an order pursuant to a draft order laid under section 14 is as follows.

(2) The Minister must have regard to—

(a) any representations,

(b) any resolution of either House of Parliament, and

(c) any recommendations of a committee of either House of Parliament charged with reporting on the draft order, made during the 60-day period with regard to the draft order.

(3) If, after the expiry of the 60-day period, the Minister wishes to make an order in the terms of the draft, he must lay before Parliament a statement—

(a) stating whether any representations were made under subsection (2)(a); and

(b) if any representations were so made, giving details of them.

(4) The Minister may after the laying of such a statement make an order in the terms of the draft if it is approved by a resolution of each House of Parliament.

(5) However, a committee of either House charged with reporting on the draft order may, at any time after the laying of a statement under subsection (3) and before the draft order is approved by that House under subsection (4), recommend under this subsection that no further proceedings be taken in relation to the draft order.

(6) Where a recommendation is made by a committee of either House under subsection (5) in relation to a draft order, no proceedings may be taken in relation to the draft order in that House under subsection (4) unless the recommendation is, in the same Session, rejected by resolution of that House.

(7) If, after the expiry of the 60-day period, the Minister wishes to make an order consisting of a version of the draft order with material changes, he must lay before Parliament—

(a) a revised draft order; and

(b) a statement giving details of—

(i) any representations made under subsection (2)(a); and

(ii) the revisions proposed.

(8) The Minister may after laying a revised draft order and statement under subsection (7) make an order in the terms of the revised draft if it is approved by a resolution of each House of Parliament.

(9) However, a committee of either House charged with reporting on the revised draft order may, at any time after the revised draft order is laid under subsection (7) and before it is approved by that House under subsection (8), recommend under this subsection that no further proceedings be taken in relation to the revised draft order.

(10) Where a recommendation is made by a committee of either House under

subsection (9) in relation to a revised draft order, no proceedings may be taken in relation to the revised draft order in that House under subsection (8) unless the recommendation is, in the same Session, rejected by resolution of that House.

(11) Subsections (3) to (5) of section 14 shall apply in relation to the disclosure of representations under subsections (3)(b) and (7)(b)(i) of this section as they apply in relation to the disclosure of representations under subsection (2)(f)(ii) of that section.

(12) For the purposes of subsections (4) and (8) an order is made in the terms of a draft order if it contains no material changes to the provisions of the draft order. (13) In this section the '60-day period' means the period of 60 days beginning with the day on which the draft order was laid before Parliament under section 14.

General

19 Calculation of time periods

In calculating any period of days for the purposes of sections 15 to 18, no account shall be taken of any time during which Parliament is dissolved or prorogued or during which either House is adjourned for more than four days.

20 Combination with powers under European Communities Act 1972

(1) The power to make an order under this Part may be exercised together with, and by the same instrument as, the power to make an order under section 2 (2) of the European Communities Act 1972 (c 68).

(2) Where the powers referred to in subsection (1) are so exercised—

(a) sections 12(2) to 18 above apply to the order under section 2(2) of the European Communities Act 1972 as to the order under this Part; and

(b) paragraph 2(2) of Schedule 2 to the European Communities Act 1972 does not apply.

TRIBUNALS, COURTS AND ENFORCEMENT ACT 2007
(2007 c 15)

PART I
TRIBUNALS AND INQUIRIES

Chapter 1
Tribunal judiciary: independence and Senior President

1 [*Amends Constitutional Reform Act 2005*]

2 Senior President of Tribunals

(1) Her Majesty may, on the recommendation of the Lord Chancellor, appoint a person to the office of Senior President of Tribunals.

(2) Schedule 1 makes further provision about the Senior President of Tribunals and about recommendations for appointment under subsection (1).

(3) A holder of the office of Senior President of Tribunals must, in carrying out the functions of that office, have regard to—

(a) the need for tribunals to be accessible,

(b) the need for proceedings before tribunals—

(i) to be fair, and

(ii) to be handled quickly and efficiently,

(c) the need for members of tribunals to be experts in the subject-matter of, or the law to be applied in, cases in which they decide matters, and

(d) the need to develop innovative methods of resolving disputes that are of a type that may be brought before tribunals.

(4) In subsection (3) 'tribunals' means—
(a) the First-tier Tribunal,
(b) the Upper Tribunal,
(c) employment tribunals, and
(d) the Employment Appeal Tribunal
[. . .]

Chapter 2
First-tier Tribunal and Upper Tribunal

Establishment

3 The First-tier Tribunal and the Upper Tribunal

(1) There is to be a tribunal, known as the First-tier Tribunal, for the purpose of exercising the functions conferred on it under or by virtue of this Act or any other Act.

(2) There is to be a tribunal, known as the Upper Tribunal, for the purpose of exercising the functions conferred on it under or by virtue of this Act or any other Act.

(3) Each of the First-tier Tribunal, and the Upper Tribunal, is to consist of its judges and other members.

(4) The Senior President of Tribunals is to preside over both of the First-tier Tribunal and the Upper Tribunal.

(5) The Upper Tribunal is to be a superior court of record.

Members and composition of tribunals

[. . .]

5 Judges and other members of the Upper Tribunal

(1) A person is a judge of the Upper Tribunal if the person—

(a) is the Senior President of Tribunals,

(b) is a judge of the Upper Tribunal by virtue of appointment under paragraph 1(1) of Schedule 3,

(c) is a transferred-in judge of the Upper Tribunal (see section 31(2)),

(d) [. . .]

(e) is the Chief Social Security Commissioner, or any other Social Security Commissioner, appointed under section 50(1) of the Social Security Administration (Northern Ireland) Act 1992,

(f) is a Social Security Commissioner appointed under section 50(2) of that Act (deputy Commissioners),

(g) is within section 6(1),

(h) is a deputy judge of the Upper Tribunal (whether under paragraph 7 of Schedule 3 or under section 31(2)), or

(i) is a Chamber President or a Deputy Chamber President, whether of a chamber of the Upper Tribunal or of a chamber of the First-tier Tribunal, and does not fall within any of paragraphs (a) to (h).

Review of decisions and appeals

9 Review of decision of First-tier Tribunal

(1) The First-tier Tribunal may review a decision made by it on a matter in a case, other than a decision that is an excluded decision for the purposes of section 11(1) (but see subsection (9)).

(2) The First-tier Tribunal's power under subsection (1) in relation to a decision is exercisable—

(a) of its own initiative, or

(b) on application by a person who for the purposes of section 11(2) has a right of appeal in respect of the decision.

(3) Tribunal Procedure Rules may—

(a) provide that the First-tier Tribunal may not under subsection (1) review (whether of its own initiative or on application under subsection (2)(b)) a decision of a description specified for the purposes of this paragraph in Tribunal Procedure Rules;

(b) provide that the First-tier Tribunal's power under subsection (1) to review a decision of a description specified for the purposes of this paragraph in Tribunal Procedure Rules is exercisable only of the tribunal's own initiative;

(c) provide that an application under subsection (2)(b) that is of a description specified for the purposes of this paragraph in Tribunal Procedure Rules may be made only on grounds specified for the purposes of this paragraph in Tribunal Procedure Rules;

(d) provide, in relation to a decision of a description specified for the purposes of this paragraph in Tribunal Procedure Rules, that the First-tier Tribunal's power under subsection (1) to review the decision of its own initiative is exercisable only on grounds specified for the purposes of this paragraph in Tribunal Procedure Rules.

(4) Where the First-tier Tribunal has under subsection (1) reviewed a decision, the First-tier Tribunal may in the light of the review do any of the following—

(a) correct accidental errors in the decision or in a record of the decision;

(b) amend reasons given for the decision;

(c) set the decision aside.

(5) Where under subsection (4)(c) the First-tier Tribunal sets a decision aside, the First-tier Tribunal must either—

(a) re-decide the matter concerned, or

(b) refer that matter to the Upper Tribunal.

(6) Where a matter is referred to the Upper Tribunal under subsection (5)(b), the Upper Tribunal must re-decide the matter.

(7) Where the Upper Tribunal is under subsection (6) re-deciding a matter, it may make any decision which the First-tier Tribunal could make if the First-tier Tribunal were re-deciding the matter.

(8) Where a tribunal is acting under subsection (5)(a) or (6), it may make such findings of fact as it considers appropriate.

(9) This section has effect as if a decision under subsection (4)(c) to set aside an earlier decision were not an excluded decision for the purposes of section 11(1), but the First-tier Tribunal's only power in the light of a review under subsection (1) of a decision under subsection (4)(c) is the power under subsection (4)(a).

(10) A decision of the First-tier Tribunal may not be reviewed under subsection (1) more than once, and once the First-tier Tribunal has decided that an earlier decision should not be reviewed under subsection (1) it may not then decide to review that earlier decision under that subsection.

(11) Where under this section a decision is set aside and the matter concerned is then re-decided, the decision set aside and the decision made in re-deciding the matter are for the purposes of subsection (10) to be taken to be different decisions.

10 Review of decision of Upper Tribunal

(1) The Upper Tribunal may review a decision made by it on a matter in a case, other than a decision that is an excluded decision for the purposes of section 13(1) (but see subsection (7)).

(2) The Upper Tribunal's power under subsection (1) in relation to a decision is exercisable—

(a) of its own initiative, or

(b) on application by a person who for the purposes of section 13(2) has a right of appeal in respect of the decision.

(3) Tribunal Procedure Rules may—

(a) provide that the Upper Tribunal may not under subsection (1) review (whether of its own initiative or on application under subsection (2)(b)) a decision of a description specified for the purposes of this paragraph in Tribunal Procedure Rules;

(b) provide that the Upper Tribunal's power under subsection (1) to review a decision of a description specified for the purposes of this paragraph in Tribunal Procedure Rules is exercisable only of the tribunal's own initiative;

(c) provide that an application under subsection (2)(b) that is of a description specified for the purposes of this paragraph in Tribunal Procedure Rules may be made only on grounds specified for the purposes of this paragraph in Tribunal Procedure Rules;

(d) provide, in relation to a decision of a description specified for the purposes of this paragraph in Tribunal Procedure Rules, that the Upper Tribunal's power under subsection (1) to review the decision of its own initiative is exercisable only on grounds specified for the purposes of this paragraph in Tribunal Procedure Rules.

(4) Where the Upper Tribunal has under subsection (1) reviewed a decision, the Upper Tribunal may in the light of the review do any of the following—

(a) correct accidental errors in the decision or in a record of the decision;

(b) amend reasons given for the decision;

(c) set the decision aside.

(5) Where under subsection (4)(c) the Upper Tribunal sets a decision aside, the Upper Tribunal must re-decide the matter concerned.

(6) Where the Upper Tribunal is acting under subsection (5), it may make such findings of fact as it considers appropriate.

(7) This section has effect as if a decision under subsection (4)(c) to set aside an earlier decision were not an excluded decision for the purposes of section 13(1), but the Upper Tribunal's only power in the light of a review under subsection (1) of a decision under subsection (4)(c) is the power under subsection (4)(a).

(8) A decision of the Upper Tribunal may not be reviewed under subsection (1) more than once, and once the Upper Tribunal has decided that an earlier decision should not be reviewed under subsection (1) it may not then decide to review that earlier decision under that subsection.

(9) Where under this section a decision is set aside and the matter concerned is then re-decided, the decision set aside and the decision made in re-deciding the matter are for the purposes of subsection (8) to be taken to be different decisions.

11 Right to appeal to Upper Tribunal

(1) For the purposes of subsection (2), the reference to a right of appeal is to a right to appeal to the Upper Tribunal on any point of law arising from a decision made by the First-tier Tribunal other than an excluded decision.

(2) Any party to a case has a right of appeal, subject to subsection (8).

(3) That right may be exercised only with permission (or, in Northern Ireland, leave).

(4) Permission (or leave) may be given by—

(a) the First-tier Tribunal, or

(b) the Upper Tribunal, on an application by the party.

(5) For the purposes of subsection (1), an 'excluded decision' is—

(a) any decision of the First-tier Tribunal on an appeal made in exercise of a right conferred by the Criminal Injuries Compensation Scheme in compliance with section 5(1)(a) of the Criminal Injuries Compensation Act 1995 (appeals against decisions on reviews),

[(aa) any decision of the First-tier Tribunal on an appeal made in exercise of a right conferred by the Criminal Injuries Compensation Scheme in compliance with section 5(1)(a) of the Criminal Injuries Compensation Act 1995 (c 55) (appeals against decisions on reviews)],

(b) any decision of the First-tier Tribunal on an appeal under [section 27(3) or (5), 79(5) or (7) or 111(3) or (5) of the Data Protection Act 2018] (appeals against national security certificate),

(c) any decision of the First-tier Tribunal on an appeal under section 60(1) or (4) of the Freedom of Information Act 2000 (appeals against national security certificate),

(d) a decision of the First-tier Tribunal under section 9—

(i) to review, or not to review, an earlier decision of the tribunal,

(ii) to take no action, or not to take any particular action, in the light of a review of an earlier decision of the tribunal,

(iii) to set aside an earlier decision of the tribunal, or

(iv) to refer, or not to refer, a matter to the Upper Tribunal,

(e) a decision of the First-tier Tribunal that is set aside under section 9 (including a decision set aside after proceedings on an appeal under this section have been begun), or

(f) any decision of the First-tier Tribunal that is of a description specified in an order made by the Lord Chancellor.

(6) A description may be specified under subsection (5)(f) only if—

(a) in the case of a decision of that description, there is a right to appeal to a court, the Upper Tribunal or any other tribunal from the decision and that right is, or includes, something other than a right (however expressed) to appeal on any point of law arising from the decision, or

(b) decisions of that description are made in carrying out a function transferred under section 30 and prior to the transfer of the function under section 30 (1) there was no right to appeal from decisions of that description.

(7) Where—

(a) an order under subsection (5)(f) specifies a description of decisions, and

(b) decisions of that description are made in carrying out a function transferred under section 30,

the order must be framed so as to come into force no later than the time when the transfer under section 30 of the function takes effect (but power to revoke the order continues to be exercisable after that time, and power to amend the order continues to be exercisable after that time for the purpose of narrowing the description for the time being specified).

(8) The Lord Chancellor may by order make provision for a person to be treated as being, or to be treated as not being, a party to a case for the purposes of subsection (2).

12 Proceedings on appeal to Upper Tribunal

(1) Subsection (2) applies if the Upper Tribunal, in deciding an appeal under section 11, finds that the making of the decision concerned involved the making of an error on a point of law.

(2) The Upper Tribunal—

(a) may (but need not) set aside the decision of the First-tier Tribunal, and

(b) if it does, must either—

(i) remit the case to the First-tier Tribunal with directions for its reconsideration, or

(ii) re-make the decision.

(3) In acting under subsection (2)(b)(i), the Upper Tribunal may also—

(a) direct that the members of the First-tier Tribunal who are chosen to reconsider the case are not to be the same as those who made the decision that has been set aside;

(b) give procedural directions in connection with the reconsideration of the case by the First-tier Tribunal.

(4) In acting under subsection (2)(b)(ii), the Upper Tribunal—

(a) may make any decision which the First-tier Tribunal could make if the First-tier Tribunal were re-making the decision, and

(b) may make such findings of fact as it considers appropriate.

13 Right to appeal to Court of Appeal etc

(1) For the purposes of subsection (2), the reference to a right of appeal is to a right to appeal to the relevant appellate court on any point of law arising from a decision made by the Upper Tribunal other than an excluded decision.

(2) Any party to a case has a right of appeal, subject to subsection (14).

(3) That right may be exercised only with permission (or, in Northern Ireland, leave).

(4) Permission (or leave) may be given by—

(a) the Upper Tribunal, or

(b) the relevant appellate court, on an application by the party.

(5) An application may be made under subsection (4) to the relevant appellate court only if permission (or leave) has been refused by the Upper Tribunal.

(6) The Lord Chancellor may, as respects an application under subsection (4) that falls within subsection (7) and for which the relevant appellate court is the Court of Appeal in England and Wales or the Court of Appeal in Northern Ireland, by order make provision for permission (or leave) not to be granted on the application unless the Upper Tribunal or (as the case may be) the relevant appellate court considers—

(a) that the proposed appeal would raise some important point of principle or practice, or

(b) that there is some other compelling reason for the relevant appellate court to hear the appeal.

[(6A) Rules of court may make provision for permission not to be granted on an application under subsection (4) to the Court of Session that falls within subsection (7) unless the court considers—

(a) that the proposed appeal would raise some important point of principle [or practice], or

(b) that there is some other compelling reason for the court to hear the appeal.]

(7) An application falls within this subsection if the application is for permission (or leave) to appeal from any decision of the Upper Tribunal on an appeal under section 11.

(8) For the purposes of subsection (1), an 'excluded decision' is—

(a) any decision of the Upper Tribunal on an appeal under [section 27(3) or (5), 79(5) or (7) or 111(3) or (5) of the Data Protection Act 2018] (appeals against national security certificate),

(b) any decision of the Upper Tribunal on an appeal under section 60(1) or (4) of the Freedom of Information Act 2000 (appeals against national security certificate),

(c) any decision of the Upper Tribunal on an application under section 11(4)(b) (application for permission or leave to appeal),

(d) a decision of the Upper Tribunal under section 10—

(i) to review, or not to review, an earlier decision of the tribunal,

(ii) to take no action, or not to take any particular action, in the light of a review of an earlier decision of the tribunal, or

(iii) to set aside an earlier decision of the tribunal,

(e) a decision of the Upper Tribunal that is set aside under section 10 (including a decision set aside after proceedings on an appeal under this section have been begun), or

(f) any decision of the Upper Tribunal that is of a description specified in an order made by the Lord Chancellor.

(9) A description may be specified under subsection (8)(f) only if—

(a) in the case of a decision of that description, there is a right to appeal to a court from the decision and that right is, or includes, something other than a right (however expressed) to appeal on any point of law arising from the decision, or

(b) decisions of that description are made in carrying out a function transferred under section 30 and prior to the transfer of the function under section 30 (1) there was no right to appeal from decisions of that description.

(10) Where—

(a) an order under subsection (8)(f) specifies a description of decisions, and

(b) decisions of that description are made in carrying out a function transferred under section 30,

the order must be framed so as to come into force no later than the time when the transfer under section 30 of the function takes effect (but power to revoke the order continues to be exercisable after that time, and power to amend the order continues to be exercisable after that time for the purpose of narrowing the description for the time being specified).

(11) Before the Upper Tribunal decides an application made to it under subsection (4), the Upper Tribunal must specify the court that is to be the relevant appellate court as respects the proposed appeal.

(12) The court to be specified under subsection (11) in relation to a proposed appeal is whichever of the following courts appears to the Upper Tribunal to be the most appropriate—

(a) the Court of Appeal in England and Wales;

(b) the Court of Session;

(c) the Court of Appeal in Northern Ireland.

(13) In this section except subsection (11), 'the relevant appellate court', as respects an appeal, means the court specified as respects that appeal by the Upper Tribunal under subsection (11).

(14) The Lord Chancellor may by order make provision for a person to be treated as being, or to be treated as not being, a party to a case for the purposes of subsection (2).

(15) Rules of court may make provision as to the time within which an application under subsection (4) to the relevant appellate court must be made.

14 Proceedings on appeal to Court of Appeal etc

(1) Subsection (2) applies if the relevant appellate court, in deciding an appeal under section 13, finds that the making of the decision concerned involved the making of an error on a point of law.

(2) The relevant appellate court—

(a) may (but need not) set aside the decision of the Upper Tribunal, and

(b) if it does, must either—

(i) remit the case to the Upper Tribunal or, where the decision of the Upper Tribunal was on an appeal or reference from another tribunal or some other person, to the Upper Tribunal or that other tribunal or person, with directions for its reconsideration, or

(ii) re-make the decision.

(3) In acting under subsection (2)(b)(i), the relevant appellate court may also—

(a) direct that the persons who are chosen to reconsider the case are not to be the same as those who—

(i) where the case is remitted to the Upper Tribunal, made the decision of the Upper Tribunal that has been set aside, or

(ii) where the case is remitted to another tribunal or person, made the decision in respect of which the appeal or reference to the Upper Tribunal was made;

(b) give procedural directions in connection with the reconsideration of the case by the Upper Tribunal or other tribunal or person.

(4) In acting under subsection (2)(b)(ii), the relevant appellate court—

(a) may make any decision which the Upper Tribunal could make if the Upper Tribunal were re-making the decision or (as the case may be) which the other tribunal or person could make if that other tribunal or person were re-making the decision, and

(b) may make such findings of fact as it considers appropriate.

(5) Where—

(a) under subsection (2)(b)(i) the relevant appellate court remits a case to the Upper Tribunal, and

(b) the decision set aside under subsection (2)(a) was made by the Upper Tribunal on an appeal or reference from another tribunal or some other person,

the Upper Tribunal may (instead of reconsidering the case itself) remit the case to that other tribunal or person, with the directions given by the relevant appellate court for its reconsideration.

(6) In acting under subsection (5), the Upper Tribunal may also—

(a) direct that the persons who are chosen to reconsider the case are not to be the same as those who made the decision in respect of which the appeal or reference to the Upper Tribunal was made;

(b) give procedural directions in connection with the reconsideration of the case by the other tribunal or person.

(7) In this section 'the relevant appellate court', as respects an appeal under section 13, means the court specified as respects that appeal by the Upper Tribunal under section 13(11).

[14A Appeal to Supreme Court: grant of certificate by Upper Tribunal

(1) If the Upper Tribunal is satisfied that—

(a) the conditions in subsection (4) or (5) are fulfilled in relation to the Upper Tribunal's decision in any proceedings, and

(b) as regards that decision, a sufficient case for an appeal to the Supreme Court has been made out to justify an application under section 14B,

the Upper Tribunal may grant a certificate to that effect.

(2) The Upper Tribunal may grant a certificate under this section only on an application made by a party to the proceedings.

(3) The Upper Tribunal may grant a certificate under this section only if the relevant appellate court as regards the proceedings is—

(a) the Court of Appeal in England and Wales, or

(b) the Court of Appeal in Northern Ireland.

(4) The conditions in this subsection are that a point of law of general public importance is involved in the decision of the Upper Tribunal and that point of law is—

(a) a point of law that—

(i) relates wholly or mainly to the construction of an enactment or statutory instrument, and

(ii) has been fully argued in the proceedings and fully considered in the judgment of the Upper Tribunal in the proceedings, or

(b) a point of law—

(i) in respect of which the Upper Tribunal is bound by a decision of the relevant appellate court or the Supreme Court in previous proceedings, and

(ii) that was fully considered in the judgments given by the relevant appellate court or, as the case may be, the Supreme Court in those previous proceedings.

(5) The conditions in this subsection are that a point of law of general public importance is involved in the decision of the Upper Tribunal and that—

(a) the proceedings entail a decision relating to a matter of national importance or consideration of such a matter,

(b) the result of the proceedings is so significant (whether considered on its own or together with other proceedings or likely proceedings) that, in the opinion of the Upper Tribunal, a hearing by the Supreme Court is justified, or

(c) the Upper Tribunal is satisfied that the benefits of earlier consideration by the Supreme Court outweigh the benefits of consideration by the Court of Appeal.

(6) Before the Upper Tribunal decides an application made to it under this section, the Upper Tribunal must specify the court that would be the relevant appellate court if the application were an application for permission (or leave) under section 13.

(7) In this section except subsection (6) and in sections 14B and 14C, 'the relevant appellate court', as respects an application, means the court specified as respects that application by the Upper Tribunal under subsection (6).

(8) No appeal lies against the grant or refusal of a certificate under subsection (1).]

[14B Appeal to Supreme Court: permission to appeal

(1) If the Upper Tribunal grants a certificate under section 14A in relation to any proceedings, a party to those proceedings may apply to the Supreme Court for permission to appeal directly to the Supreme Court.

(2) An application under subsection (1) must be made—

(a) within one month from the date on which that certificate is granted, or

(b) within such time as the Supreme Court may allow in a particular case.

(3) If on such an application it appears to the Supreme Court to be expedient to do so, the Supreme Court may grant permission for such an appeal.

(4) If permission is granted under this section—

(a) no appeal from the decision to which the certificate relates lies to the relevant appellate court, but

(b) an appeal lies from that decision to the Supreme Court.

(5) An application under subsection (1) is to be determined without a hearing.

(6) Subject to subsection (4), no appeal lies to the relevant appellate court from a decision of the Upper Tribunal in respect of which a certificate is granted under section 14A until—

(a) the time within which an application can be made under subsection (1) has expired, and

(b) where such an application is made, that application has been determined in accordance with this section.]

[14C Appeal to Supreme Court: exclusions

(1) No certificate may be granted under section 14A in respect of a decision of the Upper Tribunal in any proceedings where, by virtue of any enactment (other than sections 14A and 14B), no appeal would lie from that decision of the Upper Tribunal to the relevant appellate court, with or without the permission (or leave) of the Upper Tribunal or the relevant appellate court.

(2) No certificate may be granted under section 14A in respect of a decision of the Upper Tribunal in any proceedings where, by virtue of any enactment, no appeal would lie from a decision of the relevant appellate court on that decision of the Upper Tribunal to the Supreme Court, with or without the permission (or leave) of the relevant appellate court or the Supreme Court.

(3) Where no appeal would lie to the relevant appellate court from the decision of the Upper Tribunal except with the permission (or leave) of the Upper Tribunal or the relevant appellate court, no certificate may be granted under section 14A in respect of a decision of the Upper Tribunal unless it appears to the Upper Tribunal

that it would be a proper case for giving permission (or leave) to appeal to the relevant appellate court.

(4) No certificate may be granted under section 14A in respect of a decision or order of the Upper Tribunal made by it in the exercise of its jurisdiction to punish for contempt.]

Judicial review

15 Upper Tribunal's 'judicial review' jurisdiction

(1) The Upper Tribunal has power, in cases arising under the law of England and Wales or under the law of Northern Ireland, to grant the following kinds of relief—

(a) a mandatory order;
(b) a prohibiting order;
(c) a quashing order;
(d) a declaration;
(e) an injunction.

(2) The power under subsection (1) may be exercised by the Upper Tribunal if—

(a) certain conditions are met (see section 18), or

(b) the tribunal is authorised to proceed even though not all of those conditions are met (see section 19(3) and (4)).

(3) Relief under subsection (1) granted by the Upper Tribunal—

(a) has the same effect as the corresponding relief granted by the High Court on an application for judicial review, and

(b) is enforceable as if it were relief granted by the High Court on an application for judicial review.

(4) In deciding whether to grant relief under subsection (1)(a), (b) or (c), the Upper Tribunal must apply the principles that the High Court would apply in deciding whether to grant that relief on an application for judicial review.

(5) In deciding whether to grant relief under subsection (1)(d) or (e), the Upper Tribunal must—

(a) in cases arising under the law of England and Wales apply the principles that the High Court would apply in deciding whether to grant that relief under section 31(2) of the Supreme Court Act 1981 (c 54) on an application for judicial review, and

(b) in cases arising under the law of Northern Ireland apply the principles that the High Court would apply in deciding whether to grant that relief on an application for judicial review.

[(5A) In cases arising under the law of England and Wales, subsections (2A) and (2B) of section 31 of the Senior Courts Act 1981 apply to the Upper Tribunal when deciding whether to grant relief under subsection (1) as they apply to the High Court when deciding whether to grant relief on an application for judicial review.

(5B) If the tribunal grants relief in reliance on section 31(2B) of the Senior Courts Act 1981 as applied by subsection (5A), the tribunal must certify that the condition in section 31(2B) as so applied is satisfied.]

(6) For the purposes of the application of subsection (3)(a) in relation to cases arising under the law of Northern Ireland—

(a) a mandatory order under subsection (1)(a) shall be taken to correspond to an order of mandamus,

(b) a prohibiting order under subsection (1)(b) shall be taken to correspond to an order of prohibition, and

(c) a quashing order under subsection (1)(c) shall be taken to correspond to an order of certiorari.

18 Limits of jurisdiction under section 15(1)

(1) This section applies where an application made to the Upper Tribunal seeks (whether or not alone)—

(a) relief under section 15(1), or

(b) permission (or, in a case arising under the law of Northern Ireland, leave) to apply for relief under section 15(1).

(2) If Conditions 1 to 4 are met, the tribunal has the function of deciding the application.

(3) If the tribunal does not have the function of deciding the application, it must by order transfer the application to the High Court.

(4) Condition 1 is that the application does not seek anything other than—

(a) relief under section 15(1);

(b) permission (or, in a case arising under the law of Northern Ireland, leave) to apply for relief under section 15(1);

(c) an award under section 16(6);

(d) interest;

(e) costs.

(5) Condition 2 is that the application does not call into question anything done by the Crown Court.

(6) Condition 3 is that the application falls within a class specified for the purposes of this subsection in a direction given in accordance with Part 1 of Schedule 2 to the Constitutional Reform Act 2005 (c 4).

(7) The power to give directions under subsection (6) includes—

(a) power to vary or revoke directions made in exercise of the power, and

(b) power to make different provision for different purposes.

(8) Condition 4 is that the judge presiding at the hearing of the application is either—

(a) a judge of the High Court or the Court of Appeal in England and Wales or Northern Ireland, or a judge of the Court of Session, or

(b) such other persons as may be agreed from time to time between the Lord Chief Justice, the Lord President, or the Lord Chief Justice of Northern Ireland, as the case may be, and the Senior President of Tribunals.

(9) Where the application is transferred to the High Court under subsection (3)—

(a) the application is to be treated for all purposes as if it—

(i) had been made to the High Court, and

(ii) sought things corresponding to those sought from the tribunal, and

(b) any steps taken, permission (or leave) given or orders made by the tribunal in relation to the application are to be treated as taken, given or made by the High Court.

(10) Rules of court may make provision for the purpose of supplementing subsection (9).

(11) The provision that may be made by Tribunal Procedure Rules about amendment of an application for relief under section 15(1) includes, in particular, provision about amendments that would cause the application to become transferrable under subsection (3).

(12) For the purposes of subsection (9)(a)(ii), in relation to an application transferred to the High Court in Northern Ireland—

(a) an order of mandamus shall be taken to correspond to a mandatory order under section 15(1)(a),

(b) an order of prohibition shall be taken to correspond to a prohibiting order under section 15(1)(b), and

(c) an order of certiorari shall be taken to correspond to a quashing order under section 15(1)(c).

20 Transfer of judicial review applications from the Court of Session

(1) Where an application is made to the supervisory jurisdiction of the Court of Session, the Court—

(a) must, if Conditions 1 [and 2 are met], and

(b) may, if Conditions 1 [and 3 are met], but Condition 2 is not,

by order transfer the application to the Upper Tribunal.

(2) Condition 1 is that the application does not seek anything other than an exercise of the supervisory jurisdiction of the Court of Session.

(3) Condition 2 is that the application falls within a class specified for the purposes of this subsection by act of sederunt made with the consent of the Lord Chancellor.

(4) Condition 3 is that the subject matter of the application is not a devolved Scottish matter.

[. . .]

(6) There may not be specified under subsection (3) any class of application which includes an application the subject matter of which is a devolved Scottish matter.

(7) For the purposes of this section, the subject matter of an application is a devolved Scottish matter if it—

(a) concerns the exercise of functions in or as regards Scotland, and

(b) does not relate to a reserved matter within the meaning of the Scotland Act 1998.

(8) In subsection (2), the reference to the exercise of the supervisory jurisdiction of the Court of Session includes a reference to the making of any order in connection with or in consequence of the exercise of that jurisdiction.

21 Upper Tribunal's 'judicial review' jurisdiction: Scotland

(1) The Upper Tribunal has the function of deciding applications transferred to it from the Court of Session under section 20(1).

(2) The powers of review of the Upper Tribunal in relation to such applications are the same as the powers of review of the Court of Session in an application to the supervisory jurisdiction of that Court.

(3) In deciding an application by virtue of subsection (1), the Upper Tribunal must apply principles that the Court of Session would apply in deciding an application to the supervisory jurisdiction of that Court.

(4) An order of the Upper Tribunal by virtue of subsection (1)—

(a) has the same effect as the corresponding order granted by the Court of Session on an application to the supervisory jurisdiction of that Court, and

(b) is enforceable as if it were an order so granted by that Court.

(5) Where an application is transferred to the Upper Tribunal by virtue of section 20(1), any steps taken or orders made by the Court of Session in relation to the application (other than the order to transfer the application under section 20 (1)) are to be treated as taken or made by the tribunal.

(6) Tribunal Procedure Rules may make further provision for the purposes of supplementing subsection (5).

Miscellaneous

22 Tribunal Procedure Rules

(1) There are to be rules, to be called 'Tribunal Procedure Rules', governing—

(a) the practice and procedure to be followed in the First-tier Tribunal, and

(b) the practice and procedure to be followed in the Upper Tribunal.

. . .

(4) Power to make Tribunal Procedure Rules is to be exercised with a view to securing—

(a) that, in proceedings before the First-tier Tribunal and Upper Tribunal, justice is done,

(b) that the tribunal system is accessible and fair,

(c) that proceedings before the First-tier Tribunal or Upper Tribunal are handled quickly and efficiently,

(d) that the rules are both simple and simply expressed, and

(e) that the rules where appropriate confer on members of the First-tier Tribunal, or Upper Tribunal,

responsibility for ensuring that proceedings before the tribunal are handled quickly and efficiently.

(5) In subsection (4)(b) 'the tribunal system' means the system for deciding matters within the jurisdiction of the First-tier Tribunal or the Upper Tribunal.

37 Power to amend lists of tribunals in Schedule 6

(1) The Lord Chancellor may by order amend Schedule 6—

(a) for the purpose of adding a tribunal to a list in the Schedule;

(b) for the purpose of removing a tribunal from a list in the Schedule;

(c) for the purpose of removing a list from the Schedule;

(d) for the purpose of adding to the Schedule a list of tribunals that has effect for the purposes of any one or more of sections 30, 32(3), 35 and 36.

(2) The following rules apply to the exercise of power under subsection (1)—

(a) a tribunal may not be added to a list, or be in an added list, if the tribunal is established otherwise than by or under an enactment;

(b) a tribunal established by an enactment passed or made after the last day of the Session in which this Act is passed must not be added to a list, or be in an added list, that has effect for the purposes of section 30;

(c) if any relevant function is exercisable in relation to a tribunal by the Welsh Ministers (whether by the Welsh Ministers alone, or by the Welsh Ministers jointly or concurrently with any other person), the tribunal may be added to a list, or be in an added list, only with the consent of the Welsh Ministers;

(d) a tribunal may be in more than one list.

(3) In subsection (2)(c) 'relevant function', in relation to a tribunal, means a function which relates—

(a) to the operation of the tribunal (including, in particular, its membership, administration, staff, accommodation and funding, and payments to its members or staff), or

(b) to the provision of expenses and allowances to persons attending the tribunal or attending elsewhere in connection with proceedings before the tribunal.

(4) In subsection (1) 'tribunal' does not include an ordinary court of law.

(5) In this section 'enactment' means any enactment whenever passed or made, including an enactment comprised in subordinate legislation (within the meaning of the Interpretation Act 1978 (c 30)).

39 The general duty

(1) The Lord Chancellor is under a duty to ensure that there is an efficient and effective system to support the carrying on of the business of—

(a) the First-tier Tribunal,

(b) the Upper Tribunal,

(c) employment tribunals, [and]

(d) the Employment Appeal Tribunal,

(e) [. . .]

and that appropriate services are provided for those tribunals (referred to in this section and in sections 40 and 41 as 'the tribunals').

43 Report by Senior President of Tribunals

(1) Each year the Senior President of Tribunals must give the Lord Chancellor a report covering, in relation to relevant tribunal cases—

(a) matters that the Senior President of Tribunals wishes to bring to the attention of the Lord Chancellor, and

(b) matters that the Lord Chancellor has asked the Senior President of Tribunals to cover in the report.

(2) The Lord Chancellor must publish each report given to him under subsection (1).

(3) In this section 'relevant tribunal cases' means—

(a) cases coming before the First-tier Tribunal,

(b) cases coming before the Upper Tribunal,

(c) cases coming before the Employment Appeal Tribunal, [. . .] [and]

(d) cases coming before employment tribunals,

(e) [. . .]

50 Judicial appointments: 'judicial-appointment eligibility condition'

(1) Subsection (2) applies for the purposes of any statutory provision that—

(a) relates to an office or other position, and

(b) refers to a person who satisfies the judicial-appointment eligibility condition on an N-year basis (where N is the number stated in the provision).

(2) A person satisfies that condition on an N-year basis if—

(a) the person has a relevant qualification, and

(b) the total length of the person's qualifying periods is at least N years.

(3) In subsection (2) 'qualifying period', in relation to a person, means a period during which the person—

(a) has a relevant qualification, and

(b) gains experience in law (see section 52).

(4) For the purposes of subsections (2) and (3), a person has a relevant qualification if the person—

(a) is a solicitor or a barrister (but see section 51), or

(b) holds a qualification that under section 51(1) is a relevant qualification in relation to the office, or other position, concerned.

(5) In this section—

'barrister' means barrister in England and Wales;

'solicitor' means solicitor of the Senior Courts of England and Wales;

'statutory provision' means—

(a) a provision of an Act, or

(b) a provision of subordinate legislation (within the meaning given by section 21(1) of the Interpretation Act 1978 (c 30)).

(6) Schedule 10, which makes amendments—

for the purpose of substituting references to satisfying the judicial-appointment eligibility condition in place of references to having a qualification mentioned in section 71 of the Courts and Legal Services Act 1990 (c 41),

for the purpose of reducing qualifying periods for eligibility for appointment to certain judicial offices from ten and seven years to seven and five years respectively, and

for connected purposes,

has effect.

(7) At any time before the coming into force of section 59(1) of the Constitutional Reform Act 2005 (c 4) (renaming of Supreme Court), the reference to the Senior Courts in subsection (5) is to be read as a reference to the Supreme Court.

SCHEDULE 2
JUDGES AND OTHER MEMBERS OF THE FIRST-TIER TRIBUNAL

Appointed and transferred-in judges and other members: removal from office

3 (1) This paragraph applies to any power by which—

(a) a person appointed under paragraph 1(1) or 2(1),

(b) a transferred-in judge of the First-tier Tribunal, or

(c) a transferred-in other member of the First-tier Tribunal,
may be removed from office.

(2) If the person exercises functions wholly or mainly in Scotland, the power may be exercised only with the concurrence of the Lord President of the Court of Session.

(3) If the person exercises functions wholly or mainly in Northern Ireland, the power may be exercised only with the concurrence of the Lord Chief Justice of Northern Ireland.

(4) If neither of sub-paragraphs (2) and (3) applies, the power may be exercised only with the concurrence of the Lord Chief Justice of England and Wales.

Terms of appointment

4 (1) This paragraph applies—
(a) to a person appointed under paragraph 1(1) or 2(1),
(b) to a transferred-in judge of the First-tier Tribunal, and
(c) to a transferred-in other member of the First-tier Tribunal.

(2) If the terms of the person's appointment provide that he is appointed on a salaried (as opposed to fee-paid) basis, the person may be removed from office—
(a) only by the Lord Chancellor (and in accordance with paragraph 3), and
(b) only on the ground of inability or misbehaviour.

[(2A) If the terms of the person's appointment provide that the person is appointed on a fee-paid basis, the person may be removed from office—
(a) only by the Lord Chancellor (and in accordance with paragraph 3), and
(b) only on—
(i) the ground of inability or misbehaviour, or
(ii) a ground specified in the person's terms of appointment.

(2B) If the period (or extended period) for which the person is appointed ends before—
(a) the day on which the person attains the age of 70, or
(b) if different, the day that for the purposes of section 26 of the Judicial Pensions and Retirement Act 1993 is the compulsory retirement date for the office concerned in the person's case,
then, subject to sub-paragraph (2C), the Lord Chancellor must extend the period of the person's appointment (including a period already extended under this sub-paragraph) before it ends.

(2C) Extension under sub-paragraph (2B)—
(a) requires the person's agreement,
(b) is to be for such period as the Lord Chancellor considers appropriate, and
(c) may be refused on—
(i) the ground of inability or misbehaviour, or
(ii) a ground specified in the person's terms of appointment,
but only with any agreement of a senior judge (see section 46(7)), or a nominee of a senior judge, that may be required by those terms.]

(3) Subject to [the preceding provisions of this paragraph (but subject in the first place] to the Judicial Pensions and Retirement Act 1993 (c 8)), the person is to hold and vacate office in accordance with the terms of his appointment[, which are to be such as the Lord Chancellor may determine].

SCHEDULE 3
JUDGES AND OTHER MEMBERS OF THE UPPER TRIBUNAL

Appointed and transferred-in judges and other members: removal from office

3 (1) This paragraph applies to any power by which—
(a) a person appointed under paragraph 1(1) or 2(1),

(b) a transferred-in judge of the Upper Tribunal,

[(ba) a person who is a deputy judge of the Upper Tribunal (whether by appointment under paragraph 7(1) or as a result of provision under section 31 (2)),] or

(c) a transferred-in other member of the Upper Tribunal,

may be removed from office.

(2) If the person exercises functions wholly or mainly in Scotland, the power may be exercised only with the concurrence of the Lord President of the Court of Session.

(3) If the person exercises functions wholly or mainly in Northern Ireland, the power may be exercised only with the concurrence of the Lord Chief Justice of Northern Ireland.

(4) If neither of sub-paragraphs (2) and (3) applies, the power may be exercised only with the concurrence of the Lord Chief Justice of England and Wales.

Terms of appointment

4 (1) This paragraph applies—

(a) to a person appointed under paragraph 1(1) or 2(1),

(b) to a transferred-in judge of the Upper Tribunal, and

(c) to a transferred-in other member of the Upper Tribunal.

(2) If the terms of the person's appointment provide that he is appointed on a salaried (as opposed to fee-paid) basis, the person may be removed from office—

(a) only by the Lord Chancellor (and in accordance with paragraph 3), and

(b) only on the ground of inability or misbehaviour.

[(2A) If the terms of the person's appointment provide that the person is appointed on a fee-paid basis, the person may be removed from office—

(a) only by the Lord Chancellor (and in accordance with paragraph 3), and

(b) only on—

(i) the ground of inability or misbehaviour, or

(ii) a ground specified in the person's terms of appointment.

(2B) If the period (or extended period) for which the person is appointed ends before—

(a) the day on which the person attains the age of 70, or

(b) if different, the day that for the purposes of section 26 of the Judicial Pensions and Retirement Act 1993 is the compulsory retirement date for the office concerned in the person's case,

then, subject to sub-paragraph (2C), the Lord Chancellor must extend the period of the person's appointment (including a period already extended under this sub-paragraph) before it ends.

(2C) Extension under sub-paragraph (2B)—

(a) requires the person's agreement,

(b) is to be for such period as the Lord Chancellor considers appropriate, and

(c) may be refused on—

(i) the ground of inability or misbehaviour, or

(ii) a ground specified in the person's terms of appointment,

but only with any agreement of a senior judge (see section 46(7)), or a nominee of a senior judge, that may be required by those terms.]

(3) Subject to [the preceding provisions of this paragraph (but subject in the first place] to the Judicial Pensions and Retirement Act 1993 (c 8)), the person is to hold and vacate office as a judge, or other member, of the Upper Tribunal in accordance with the terms of his appointment[, which are to be such as the Lord Chancellor may determine].

JUDICIARY AND COURTS (SCOTLAND) ACT 2008
(2008, asp 6)

1 Guarantee of continued judicial independence

(1) The following persons must uphold the continued independence of the judiciary—

(a) the First Minister,
(b) the Lord Advocate,
(c) the Scottish Ministers,
(d) members of the Scottish Parliament, and
(e) all other persons with responsibility for matters relating to—
(i) the judiciary, or
(ii) the administration of justice,

where that responsibility is to be discharged only in or as regards Scotland.

(2) In particular, the First Minister, the Lord Advocate and the Scottish Ministers—

(a) must not seek to influence particular judicial decisions through any special access to the judiciary, and

(b) must have regard to the need for the judiciary to have the support necessary to enable them to carry out their functions.

. . .

2 Head of the Scottish Judiciary

(1) The Lord President is the Head of the Scottish Judiciary.

. . .

4 Lord President

(1) This section applies during any period when—

(a) the office of Lord President is vacant,
(b) the Lord President is incapacitated, or
(c) the Lord President is suspended.

(2) During such a period—

(a) any function of the Lord President is exercisable instead by the Lord Justice Clerk,

(b) anything that falls to be done in relation to the Lord President falls to be done instead in relation to the Lord Justice Clerk,

(c) any function of the Lord Justice Clerk is exercisable instead by the senior judge of the Inner House, and

(d) anything that falls to be done in relation to the Lord Justice Clerk falls to be done instead in relation to the senior judge of the Inner House.

(3) For the purposes of this section—

(a) the Lord President is to be regarded as incapacitated only if the First Minister has received a declaration in writing signed by a majority of the total number of judges of the Inner House declaring that they are satisfied that the Lord President is incapacitated,

(b) in such a case, the Lord President is to be regarded as incapacitated until the First Minister has received a declaration in writing signed by a majority of the total number of judges of the Inner House declaring that they are satisfied that the Lord President is no longer incapacitated.

(4) The judges of the Inner House making a declaration for the purposes of subsection (3)(a) or (b) must include the Lord Justice Clerk.

(5) The requirement in subsection (4)—

(a) does not apply during any period when section 5 applies, and
(b) is subject to section 7(4).

(6) The First Minister must send a copy of a declaration received under subsection (3)(a) or (b) to the Presiding Officer of the Scottish Parliament.

(7) The reference in subsection (2)(a) to functions of the Lord President does not include the function of participating in a panel established under section 19(2) in connection with a vacancy, or an expected vacancy, in the office of Lord Justice Clerk.

5 Lord Justice Clerk

(1) This section applies during any period when—

(a) the office of Lord Justice Clerk is vacant,

(b) the Lord Justice Clerk is incapacitated, or

(c) the Lord Justice Clerk is suspended.

(2) During such a period—

(a) any function of the Lord Justice Clerk is exercisable instead by the senior judge of the Inner House, and

(b) anything that falls to be done in relation to the Lord Justice Clerk falls to be done instead in relation to the senior judge of the Inner House.

(3) For the purposes of this section—

(a) the Lord Justice Clerk is to be regarded as incapacitated only if the First Minister has received a declaration in writing signed by a majority of the total number of judges of the Inner House declaring that they are satisfied that the Lord Justice Clerk is incapacitated,

(b) in such a case, the Lord Justice Clerk is to be regarded as incapacitated until the First Minister has received a declaration in writing signed by a majority of the total number of judges in the Inner House declaring that they are satisfied that the Lord Justice Clerk is no longer incapacitated.

(4) The judges of the Inner House making a declaration for the purposes of subsection (3)(a) or (b) must include the Lord President.

(5) The requirement in subsection (4)—

(a) does not apply during any period when section 4 applies, and

(b) is subject to section 7(4).

(6) The First Minister must send a copy of a declaration received under subsection (3)(a) or (b) to the Presiding Officer of the Scottish Parliament.

6 Periods when both sections 4 and 5 apply

(1) Subsection (2) applies during any period when both sections 4 and 5 apply.

(2) During such a period, subsection (2) of each of those sections does not apply and instead—

(a) any function of the Lord President is exercisable instead by the senior judge of the Inner House,

(b) anything that falls to be done in relation to the Lord President falls to be done instead in relation to the senior judge of the Inner House,

(c) any function of the Lord Justice Clerk is exercisable instead by the second senior judge of the Inner House, and

(d) anything that falls to be done in relation to the Lord Justice Clerk falls to be done instead in relation to the second senior judge of the Inner House.

9 The Judicial Appointments Board for Scotland

(1) There is established a body to be known as the Judicial Appointments Board for Scotland (referred to in this Chapter as 'the Board').

(2) The functions of the Board are—

(a) to recommend to members of the Scottish Executive individuals for appointment to judicial offices within the Board's remit, and

(b) to provide advice to members of the Scottish Executive in connection with such appointments.

(3) In carrying out its functions, the Board is not to be subject to the direction or control of any member of the Scottish Executive or any other person.

(4) Schedule 1 makes further provision about the Board.

11 Recommendations of the Board

(1) The relevant Minister may—

(a) appoint an individual to a judicial office within the Board's remit, or

(b) nominate or recommend an individual for appointment to such an office, only if the Board has recommended the individual for appointment to the office.

. . .

12 Selection criteria

(1) This section applies where the Board is selecting an individual to be recommended by it for appointment.

(2) Selection must be solely on merit.

(3) The Board may select an individual only if it is satisfied that the individual is of good character.

14 Encouragement of diversity

(1) In carrying out its functions, the Board must have regard to the need to encourage diversity in the range of individuals available for selection to be recommended for appointment to a judicial office.

(2) Subsection (1) is subject to section 12.

19 Appointment

(1) This section applies where a vacancy arises, or is expected to arise, in the office of Lord President or the office of Lord Justice Clerk.

(2) The First Minister must establish a panel in accordance with schedule 2.

(3) The function of the panel is to recommend to the First Minister individuals who are suitable for appointment to fill the vacancy.

(4) For the purposes of section 95(2) of the Scotland Act 1998 (c 46), the First Minister must not nominate any individual for appointment to fill the vacancy until the panel has made its recommendation under subsection (3).

(5) In deciding whom to nominate for the purposes of that section, the First Minister must have regard to the panel's recommendation

20 Selection criteria

(1) This section applies where a panel established under section 19(2) is selecting an individual to be recommended by it as suitable for appointment.

(2) Selection must be solely on merit.

(3) The panel may select an individual only if it is satisfied that the individual is of good character.

34 Suspension

(1) If the Lord President considers that it is necessary for the purpose of maintaining public confidence in the judiciary, the Lord President may suspend a judicial office holder—

(a) from acting as a judge as mentioned in paragraph (b) or (c) of the definition of 'judicial office holder' in subsection (1) of section 43, or

(b) from any of the judicial offices mentioned in subsection (2) of that section.

(2) Such a suspension lasts for such period as the Lord President may specify when suspending the judicial office holder.

(3) Nothing in subsection (1) affects any remuneration payable to, or in respect of, the judicial office holder.

(4) The Lord President's functions under this section may be carried out—

(a) where the Lord President is unavailable, by the Lord Justice Clerk,

(b) where both the Lord President and the Lord Justice Clerk are unavailable, by the senior judge of the Inner House.

(5) In subsection (4)(b) the reference to the senior judge of the Inner House is to be construed by reference to seniority of appointment to a Division of the Inner House.

35 Tribunal to consider fitness for judicial office

(1) The First Minister—

(a) must, when requested to do so by the Lord President, and

(b) may, in such other circumstances as the First Minister thinks fit,

constitute a tribunal to investigate and report on whether a person holding a judicial office to which this section applies is unfit to hold the office by reason of inability, neglect of duty or misbehaviour.

. . .

(4) A tribunal constituted under this section is to consist of—

(a) two individuals who hold, or have held, high judicial office ('judicial members'),

(b) one individual who is, and has been for at least 10 years, an advocate or solicitor, and

(c) one individual who does not hold (and has never held) high judicial office and is not (and never has been) an advocate or solicitor.

. . .

(7) At least one of the judicial members must hold, or have held, office as a judge of the Court of Session.

(8) The selection of persons to be members of a tribunal under this section is to be made by the First Minister with the agreement of—

(a) where the tribunal is to be constituted for the purpose of considering the Lord President's fitness for office, the Lord Justice Clerk,

(b) where the tribunal is to be constituted for any other purpose, the Lord President.

. . .

36 Suspension during investigation

(1) Where the Lord President has requested that the First Minister constitute a tribunal under section 35, the Lord President may, at any time before the tribunal reports to the First Minister, suspend the person who is to be, or is, the subject of the investigation, from office.

. . .

(3) A tribunal constituted under section 35 may, at any time before the tribunal reports to the First Minister, recommend to the First Minister that the person who is the subject of the tribunal's investigation be suspended from office.

. . .

(5) The First Minister on receiving such a recommendation may suspend the person from office.

37 Further provision about tribunals

(1) A tribunal constituted under section 35 may require any person—

(a) to attend its proceedings for the purpose of giving evidence,

(b) to produce documents in the person's custody or under the person's control.

. . .

(5) The Court of Session may by act of sederunt make provision as to the procedure to be followed by and before tribunals constituted under section 35.

. . .

38 Report of tribunal

(1) The report of a tribunal constituted under section 35 must—

(a) be in writing,

(b) contain reasons for its conclusion, and
(c) be submitted to the First Minister.
(2) The First Minister must lay the report before the Scottish Parliament.

39 Temporary judges: removal from office
(1) Where subsection (2) applies, a person may be removed from office as a temporary judge by the First Minister.
(2) This subsection applies if—
(a) a tribunal constituted under section 35 has reported to the First Minister that the person is unfit to hold that office by reason of inability, neglect of duty or misbehaviour, and
(b) the First Minister has laid the report before the Scottish Parliament.

SCHEDULE 1
THE JUDICIAL APPOINTMENTS BOARD FOR SCOTLAND

The judicial and legal members

3 (1) The judicial members comprise—
(a) one person holding the office of judge of the Court of Session (other than the Lord President and the Lord Justice Clerk),
(b) one person holding the office of sheriff principal, [. . .]
(c) one person holding the office of sheriff [, and
(d) one person holding the position of Chamber President or of Vice-President within the Scottish Tribunals.]
(2) The legal members comprise—
(a) one advocate practising as such in Scotland, and
(b) one solicitor practising as such in Scotland.
(3) Each of the descriptions of members mentioned—
(a) in sub-paragraph (1) is referred to in this schedule as a 'judicial membership category', and
(b) in sub-paragraph (2) is referred to in this schedule as a 'legal membership category'.
(4) The Scottish Ministers may by order modify sub-paragraph (1) or (2).
(5) However, an order under sub-paragraph (4) may not remove any judicial or legal membership category other than one added by such an order.
[(6) For the purposes of sub-paragraph (1)(d)—
'Scottish Tribunals' is to be construed in accordance with the Tribunals (Scotland) Act 2014,
'Chamber President' means Chamber President in the First-tier Tribunal as referred to in that Act and 'Vice-President' means Vice-President of the Upper Tribunal as referred to in that Act.]

The lay members

4 (1) The number of lay members is to be equal to the total number of judicial and legal members.
(2) Each lay member is to be an individual who—
(a) is resident in Scotland,
(b) is not a solicitor or advocate practising as such in Scotland, and
(c) does not hold and has not held any judicial office within the Board's remit.

INTERPRETATION AND LEGISLATIVE REFORM (SCOTLAND) ACT 2010 (2010, asp 10)

PART 2
SCOTTISH STATUTORY INSTRUMENTS

Definition

27 Definition of 'Scottish statutory instrument'

(1) The document by which a function to which this section applies is exercised is to be known as a 'Scottish statutory instrument'.

(2) This section applies to—

(a) a function of the Scottish Ministers, the First Minister or the Lord Advocate of making, confirming or approving an order, regulations or rules under an enactment,

(b) a function of the Scottish Ministers, the First Minister or the Lord Advocate of making, confirming or approving other subordinate legislation under an enactment if the enactment conferring the function or any other enactment provides for the function to be exercisable by Scottish statutory instrument,

(c) a function of Her Majesty of making an Order in Council by virtue of—

(i) an Act of the Scottish Parliament,

(ii) a Scottish instrument, or

(iii) any other enactment, so far as the function is exercisable within devolved competence,

(d) a function of the High Court of Justiciary of making an act of adjournal under an enactment,

(e) a function of the Court of Session of making an act of sederunt under an enactment, and

(f) a function of any other person of making, confirming or approving subordinate legislation if the enactment conferring the function or any other enactment provides for the function to be exercisable by Scottish statutory instrument.

(3) Despite subsection (2), this section does not apply to—

(a) a function falling within subsection (2)(a), (c), (d) or (e) where the enactment conferring the function or any other enactment provides that the function is not to be exercisable by Scottish statutory instrument,

(b) a function of agreeing, consenting to or otherwise approving subordinate legislation made by a Minister of the Crown,

(c) a function which is exercised jointly with a Minister of the Crown, or

(d) a function of making an Order in Council which is, or a draft of which is, to be laid before each House of Parliament as well as the Scottish Parliament.

(4) The reference in subsection (2)(c)(iii) to a function's being exercisable within devolved competence is to be construed in accordance with section 54 of the Scotland Act 1998 (c 46).

(5) Section 10 of the Law Reform (Miscellaneous Provisions) (Scotland) Act 1966 (c 19) (acts of adjournal and acts of sederunt to be statutory instruments) is repealed.

(6) Schedule 2 makes transitional and consequential provision.

Parliamentary scrutiny

28 Instruments subject to the negative procedure

(1) This section applies where, by virtue of an enactment, devolved subordinate legislation is subject to the negative procedure.

(2) The Scottish statutory instrument containing the subordinate legislation must be laid before the Scottish Parliament as soon as practicable after the instrument is made (and in any event at least 28 days before the instrument comes into force).

(3) The Parliament may, before the expiry of the period of 40 days beginning with the date on which the instrument is laid before it, resolve that the instrument be annulled.

(4) Where the Parliament makes such a resolution in relation to an instrument—

(a) so far as the instrument is not in force on the date of the resolution, the instrument is not to come into force after that date (despite any provision in it for its coming into force),

(b) so far as the instrument is in force on that date, nothing further is to be done or continued under, or in reliance on, the instrument after that date.

(5) Where the Parliament makes such a resolution in relation to an instrument which contains an Order in Council or an Order of Council, Her Majesty may by Order in Council revoke the instrument.

(6) Where the Parliament makes such a resolution in relation to any other instrument, the responsible authority must by order revoke the instrument.

(7) Any such resolution or revocation does not affect—

(a) the validity of anything previously done under the instrument, or

(b) the making of a new Scottish statutory instrument.

(8) In calculating the period of 28 days mentioned in subsection (2), or the period of 40 days mentioned in subsection (3), no account is to be taken of any time during which the Scottish Parliament is dissolved or in recess for more than four days.

(9) In subsection (6), 'responsible authority', in relation to a Scottish statutory instrument, means—

(a) the Scottish Ministers in a case where the instrument is made, confirmed or approved by the Scottish Ministers, the First Minister or the Lord Advocate, and

(b) in any other case, the person who made, confirmed or approved the instrument.

(10) An order under subsection (5) or (6) is to be made by Scottish statutory instrument.

29 Instruments subject to the affirmative procedure

(1) This section applies where, by virtue of an enactment, devolved subordinate legislation is subject to the affirmative procedure.

(2) The subordinate legislation is not to be made unless a draft of the Scottish statutory instrument containing it is laid before, and approved by resolution of, the Scottish Parliament.

(3) If the requirements of subsection (2) are not complied with in relation to any subordinate legislation to which this section applies, the purported subordinate legislation has no effect.

(4) Subsection (3) is without prejudice to section 32(3).

30 Other instruments laid before the Parliament

(1) This section applies where devolved subordinate legislation is not, by virtue of an enactment, subject to the negative procedure or the affirmative procedure.

(2) The Scottish statutory instrument containing the subordinate legislation must be laid before the Scottish Parliament as soon as practicable after the legislation is made (and in any event before the legislation is due to come into force).

(3) References in subsections (1) and (2) to devolved subordinate legislation do not include references to subordinate legislation made under an enactment mentioned in subsection (4).

(4) Those enactments are—

(a) the Harbours Act 1964 (c 40),

(b) the Water (Scotland) Act 1980 (c 45),

(c) the Road Traffic Regulation Act 1984 (c 27),

(d) the Roads (Scotland) Act 1984 (c 54),
(e) section 1, 2 or 8 of the Salmon Act 1986 (c 62),
(f) the Natural Heritage (Scotland) Act 1991 (c 28),
[(fa) section 155(2)(a) of the Political Parties, Elections and Referendums Act 2000 (c 41),]
(g) section 33, 34 or 35 of the Salmon and Freshwater Fisheries (Consolidation) (Scotland) Act 2003 (asp 15),
(h) article 53 of the Scotland Act 1998 (River Tweed) Order 2006 (SI 2006/2913),
(i) the Transport and Works (Scotland) Act 2007 (asp 8),
[(j) section 216(4) of the Equality Act 2010 (c 15)].

(5) The Scottish Ministers may by order modify subsection (4).

(6) An order under this section is subject to the affirmative procedure.

[(7) This section does not apply in relation to any regulations made in accordance with paragraph 6 of Schedule 7 to the European Union (Withdrawal) Act 2018 [. . .].]

31 Failure to lay instruments in accordance with section 28(2) or 30(2)

(1) This section applies where section 28 or 30 applies in relation to devolved subordinate legislation.

(2) Failure to lay the Scottish statutory instrument containing the legislation in accordance with the laying requirements does not affect the validity of the instrument.

(3) Where the instrument is laid before the Scottish Parliament, but not in accordance with the laying requirements, the responsible authority must explain to the Presiding Officer why the laying requirements have not been complied with.

(4) The explanation is to be given in writing as soon as practicable after the instrument is laid before the Parliament.

(5) In this section, 'the laying requirements' are—
(a) in the case where section 28 applies, the requirements of subsection (2) of that section,
(b) in the case where section 30 applies, the requirements of subsection (2) of that section.

(6) In subsection (3), 'responsible authority', in relation to a Scottish statutory instrument, means—
(a) the Scottish Ministers in a case where the instrument is—
(i) made, confirmed or approved by the Scottish Ministers, the First Minister or the Lord Advocate,
(ii) an Order in Council, or
(iii) an Order of Council, and
(b) in any other case, the person who made, confirmed or approved the instrument.

32 Laying of Scottish statutory instruments before the Scottish Parliament

(1) This section applies where an enactment authorises or requires the laying of a Scottish statutory instrument, or a draft of such an instrument, before the Scottish Parliament.

(2) Unless the contrary intention appears, the reference to the laying of the instrument, or draft instrument, is to be construed as a reference to the taking of such action as is specified in standing orders of the Parliament as constituting the laying of a Scottish statutory instrument, or a draft of such an instrument, before the Parliament.

(3) Failure to lay an instrument, or draft instrument, in accordance with the enactment does not affect the validity of the instrument.

Combination of certain powers

33 Combination of certain powers

(1) This section applies where—

(a) a power of a person to make devolved subordinate legislation is subject to the affirmative procedure,

(b) a power of a person to make devolved subordinate legislation is subject to the negative procedure,

(c) section 30 applies to a power of a person to make devolved subordinate legislation, or

(d) a power of a person to make devolved subordinate legislation does not fall within any of paragraphs (a) to (c).

(2) If the person considers that it is desirable to exercise two or more of the powers together, the powers may be exercised together and by the same Scottish statutory instrument.

(3) If the powers exercised together include a power of the type mentioned in paragraph (a) of subsection (1), the devolved subordinate legislation contained in the instrument is subject to the affirmative procedure.

(4) If the powers exercised together do not include a power of the type mentioned in paragraph (a) of subsection (1) but include a power of the type mentioned in paragraph (b) of that subsection, the devolved subordinate legislation contained in the instrument is subject to the negative procedure.

(5) If the powers exercised together do not include a power of the type mentioned in paragraph (a) or (b) of subsection (1), section 30 applies to the devolved subordinate legislation contained in the instrument.

(6) Any other requirements relating to the exercise of one of the powers continue to apply only in relation to the exercise of that power.

(7) References in this section to devolved subordinate legislation do not include references to subordinate legislation in relation to which an enactment provides, or has the effect of providing, that the subordinate legislation, or the Scottish statutory instrument containing it, cannot remain in force unless it is approved by resolution of the Scottish Parliament.

Further provision about procedures

34 Power to change procedure to which subordinate legislation is subject

(1) Subsection (2) applies if—

(a) in relation to a function of making, confirming or approving devolved subordinate legislation which is subject to the negative procedure, the Scottish Parliament resolves that the subordinate legislation should instead be subject to the affirmative procedure,

(b) in relation to a function of making, confirming or approving devolved subordinate legislation which is subject to the affirmative procedure, the Parliament resolves that the subordinate legislation should instead be subject to the negative procedure, or

(c) in relation to a function of making, confirming or approving devolved subordinate legislation to which section 30 applies, the Scottish Parliament resolves that the subordinate legislation should instead be subject to the negative or the affirmative procedure.

(2) The Scottish Ministers may by order make such modifications of any enactment as are necessary for the purpose of giving effect to the resolution.

(3) An order under this section is subject to the affirmative procedure.

35 Procedures prescribed in pre-commencement enactments

Schedule 3 modifies procedures prescribed in pre-commencement enactments.

Statutory instruments subject to procedure in the Scottish Parliament

36 Statutory instruments subject to procedure in the Scottish Parliament
Schedule 4 makes provision for the application of certain provisions of this Part in relation to statutory instruments, and draft statutory instruments, which are subject to procedure in the Scottish Parliament.

Interpretation of Part 2

37 Interpretation of Part 2
In this Part—

'devolved subordinate legislation' means subordinate legislation (other than special procedure orders) which is to be made by Scottish statutory instrument,

'enactment' includes any enactment comprised in this Act [and any retained direct EU legislation],

['retained direct EU legislation' has the same meaning as in the European Union (Withdrawal) Act 2018 (see section 20(1) of that Act),]

'special procedure order' means an order in relation to which Part 4 applies,

['subordinate legislation includes an instrument made or to be made under any retained direct EU legislation on or after exit day (within the meaning of the European Union (Withdrawal) Act 2018 (see section 20(1) to (5) of that Act)).]

PART 4
ORDERS SUBJECT TO SPECIAL PARLIAMENTARY PROCEDURE

48 Application of Part 4

(1) This Part applies in relation to an order which—

(a) the Scottish Ministers have power to make, confirm or approve, and

(b) is, by virtue of an enactment, subject to special parliamentary procedure.

(2) Such an order is referred to in this Part as a 'special procedure order'.

(3) For the purposes of paragraph (b) of section 94(2) of the Scotland Act 1998 (c 46), this Part is to be taken to provide the special procedure referred to in that paragraph.

(4) In subsection (1), 'order' includes scheme, certificate or byelaw.

49 Notice of special procedure orders

(1) Before a special procedure order is made, confirmed or approved by the Scottish Ministers—

(a) the requirements of the empowering enactment with respect to the service of notices must be complied with, and

(b) notice in accordance with subsection (2) must be given by advertisement—

(i) in the Edinburgh Gazette, and

(ii) in the case of a special procedure order relating to a particular area, in at least one newspaper circulating in that area.

(2) That notice is—

(a) in the case of a special procedure order to be made by the Scottish Ministers on the application of any person, notice by the applicant of the purport of the application,

(b) in the case of a special procedure order to be confirmed or approved by the Scottish Ministers on the application of any person, notice by the applicant of the order as submitted for confirmation or approval (as the case may be),

(c) in the case of a special procedure order to be made by the Scottish Ministers otherwise than on the application of any person, notice by the Scottish Ministers of the order as proposed to be made.

(3) The notice must specify the time by which and the manner in which objections may be made to the application or, as the case may be, to the proposed order.

(4) For the purposes of this section, notice of a special procedure order is sufficient if it—

(a) sets out the purport of the order, and
(b) specifies a place where copies can be obtained free of charge at all reasonable hours.

50 Orders to which objections are made

(1) This section applies where, in relation to a special procedure order—
(a) a relevant objection is made, and
(b) the objection is not withdrawn.
(2) The order may not take effect unless it is confirmed, whether with or without amendments, by an Act of the Scottish Parliament.
(3) In subsection (1) and section 51(1), a 'relevant objection' is an objection which—
(a) if made in pursuance of a notice under section 49(1)(b), is made in accordance with the requirements of the notice,
(b) if made in pursuance of the empowering enactment, is made in accordance with the provisions of the enactment, and
(c) is not disregarded under subsection (4).
(4) An objection may be disregarded if—
(a) it is, in the opinion of the Scottish Ministers, frivolous or vexatious, or
(b) it relates to a matter that can be dealt with by an arbiter by whom compensation may be assessed.
(5) The Bill for an Act to confirm the order—
(a) may be introduced—
(i) by a member of the Scottish Executive, or
(ii) in the case of an order which is to be made, confirmed or approved by the Scottish Ministers on the application of any person, by the applicant,
(b) must set out the order, and
(c) in the absence of any special provision in standing orders of the Parliament concerning the procedure for such a Bill, is to be treated after introduction as a Private Bill for the purposes of those standing orders.

51 Orders to which no objections are made

(1) This section applies where, in relation to a special procedure order—
(a) no relevant objection is made, or
(b) a relevant objection is made and subsequently withdrawn.
(2) The Scottish Ministers may, after the order is made, confirmed or approved, lay the order before the Scottish Parliament.
(3) If, before the expiry of the period of 40 days beginning with the day on which a copy of the order is laid before it, the Scottish Parliament resolves that the order be annulled, the order becomes void and no further proceedings may be taken in respect of it.
(4) If no resolution is made, the order comes into operation—
(a) on the day on which the period of 40 days mentioned in subsection (3) expires, or
(b) on such later day as may be specified in the order.
(5) Subsection (3) is without prejudice to the laying before the Parliament of a new special procedure order.
(6) In calculating the period of 40 days mentioned in subsection (3), no account is to be taken of any time during which the Parliament is dissolved or in recess for more than 4 days.

52 Statement of objections

(1) Subsection (2) applies where—
(a) a Bill for an Act of the Scottish Parliament to confirm a special procedure order is introduced in the Scottish Parliament, or
(b) a special procedure order is laid before the Scottish Parliament.

(2) The Scottish Ministers must, at the same time as the Bill is introduced or, as the case may be, the order is laid, lay before the Parliament a statement specifying—

(a) any objections which were not withdrawn, and

(b) any objections which were disregarded under section 50(4).

53 Interpretation of Part 4

In this Part, 'empowering enactment', in relation to a special procedure order, includes any enactment other than this Act which has the effect of requiring the service of notices in connection with the order.

SCHEDULE 2

SCOTTISH STATUTORY INSTRUMENTS: TRANSITIONAL AND CONSEQUENTIAL PROVISION

(introduced by section 27(6))

Interpretation

1 (1) In this schedule—

'devolved Scottish public authority' means an authority to which paragraph 1 or 2 of Part 3 of Schedule 5 to the Scotland Act 1998 (c 46) applies (Scottish public authorities with mixed or no reserved functions), and

'pre-commencement enactment' means an enactment passed or made before Part 2 comes into force.

(2) A reference in this schedule to a function's being exercisable within devolved competence is to be construed in accordance with section 54 of the Scotland Act 1998 (c 46).

(3) For the purpose of the definition of 'pre-commencement enactment' in sub-paragraph (1), an Act of the Scottish Parliament is to be taken to have been passed on the date on which the Bill for the Act was passed by the Parliament.

Ministerial functions of making orders or regulations under pre-commencement enactments

2 (1) This paragraph applies in relation to any function of the Scottish Ministers, the First Minister or the Lord Advocate of making, confirming or approving orders, regulations or rules under a pre-commencement enactment.

(2) If a provision of any pre-commencement enactment provides for the function to be exercisable by statutory instrument, that provision ceases to have effect so far as it relates to the exercise of the function.

(3) If no provision is made in any pre-commencement enactment for the function to be exercisable by statutory instrument, then the function is not to be exercisable by Scottish statutory instrument.

Functions of making Orders in Council

3 (1) This paragraph applies in relation to any function of Her Majesty of making Orders in Council under a pre-commencement enactment, so far as the function is exercisable within devolved competence.

(2) Section 1 of the Statutory Instruments Act 1946 (c 36) (definition of 'statutory instrument') ceases to have effect in relation to the exercise of the function.

(3) If provision is made in any pre-commencement enactment which disapplies that section in relation to the function, then the function is not to be exercisable by Scottish statutory instrument.

Functions of making acts of adjournal or acts of sederunt

4 (1) This paragraph applies in relation to any function of the High Court of Justiciary of making acts of adjournal or the Court of Session of making acts of sederunt under a pre-commencement enactment.

(2) If provision is made in the pre-commencement enactment conferring the function for the function to be exercisable otherwise than by statutory instrument, then the function is not to be exercisable by Scottish statutory instrument.

Other functions of making etc subordinate legislation under pre-commencement enactments

5 (1) This paragraph applies in relation to—

(a) a function of the Scottish Ministers, the First Minister or the Lord Advocate of making, confirming or approving subordinate legislation under a pre-commencement enactment,

(b) a function of a devolved Scottish public authority of making, confirming or approving subordinate legislation under such an enactment, and

(c) a function of any other person (other than a Minister of the Crown) of making, confirming or approving subordinate legislation under such an enactment, so far as the function is exercisable within devolved competence.

(2) A provision of any pre-commencement enactment which provides for the function to be exercisable by statutory instrument has effect in relation to the exercise of the function as if it provided instead for the function to be exercisable by Scottish statutory instrument.

(3) This paragraph does not apply in relation to a function to which paragraph 2 or 3 applies.

Functions to which this schedule does not apply

6 Nothing in this schedule applies in relation to—

(a) a function of agreeing or consenting to, or otherwise approving, subordinate legislation made by a Minister of the Crown,

(b) a function which is exercised jointly with a Minister of the Crown, or

(c) a function of making an Order in Council which is, or a draft of which is, to be laid before each House of Parliament as well as the Scottish Parliament.

SCHEDULE 3
MODIFICATION OF PRE-COMMENCEMENT ENACTMENTS
(introduced by section 35)

Interpretation

1 (1) In this schedule, 'pre-commencement enactment' means an enactment passed or made before Part 2 comes into force.

(2) For the purposes of that definition, an Act of the Scottish Parliament is to be taken to have been passed on the date on which the Bill for the Act was passed by the Parliament.

Instruments subject to annulment in pursuance of a resolution of the Parliament

2 (1) Sub-paragraph (2) applies where, in relation to devolved subordinate legislation, a pre-commencement enactment provides, or has the effect of providing, that the legislation, or the Scottish statutory instrument containing the legislation, is subject to annulment in pursuance of a resolution of the Scottish Parliament.

(2) The enactment is to be read as if it instead provided for the legislation to be subject to the negative procedure.

Instruments laid in draft which cannot be made where the Parliament so resolves within 40 days

3 (1) Sub-paragraph (2) applies where, in relation to devolved subordinate legislation, a pre-commencement enactment provides, or has the effect of providing, that the legislation, or the Scottish statutory instrument containing the legislation, may be laid in draft but cannot be made if the Scottish Parliament so resolves within 40 days of the draft being laid.

(2) The enactment is to be read as if it instead provided for the legislation to be subject to the negative procedure.

Instruments required to be laid for a specified period before coming into force and subject to annulment by the Parliament

4 (1) Sub-paragraph (2) applies where, in relation to devolved subordinate legislation, a pre-commencement enactment provides, or has the effect of providing, that the legislation, or the Scottish statutory instrument containing the legislation—

(a) is to be laid before the Scottish Parliament for a specified period before it comes into force, and

(b) is subject to annulment in pursuance of a resolution of the Parliament.

(2) The enactment is to be read as if it instead provided for the legislation to be subject to the negative procedure.

Instruments which cannot be made unless a draft is laid before and approved by resolution of the Parliament

5 (1) Sub-paragraph (2) applies where, in relation to devolved subordinate legislation, a pre-commencement enactment provides, or has the effect of providing, that the legislation cannot be made unless a draft of the Scottish statutory instrument containing it is laid before and approved by resolution of the Scottish Parliament.

(2) The enactment is to be read as if it instead provided for the legislation to be subject to the affirmative procedure.

Instruments made but which cannot come into force unless laid before, and approved by resolution of, the Parliament

6 (1) Sub-paragraph (2) applies where, in relation to devolved subordinate legislation, a pre-commencement enactment provides, or has the effect of providing, that the legislation, or the Scottish statutory instrument containing the legislation, may be made, but cannot come into force, unless it is laid before and approved by resolution of the Scottish Parliament.

(2) The enactment is to be read as if it instead provided for the legislation to be subject to the affirmative procedure.

Instruments required to be laid for a specified period before coming into force

7 (1) Sub-paragraph (2) applies where, in relation to devolved subordinate legislation, a pre-commencement enactment provides, or has the effect of providing, that the legislation, or the Scottish statutory instrument containing the legislation, is to be laid before the Scottish Parliament for a specified period before it comes into force.

(2) The enactment is to be read as if it did not so provide, or have the effect of so providing, in relation to the legislation.

(3) Sub-paragraph (2) does not affect the operation of section 30 in relation to the legislation.

SCHEDULE 4
APPLICATION OF PART 2 TO STATUTORY INSTRUMENTS LAID BEFORE THE PARLIAMENT

(introduced by section 36)

Interpretation

1 In this schedule—

'pre-commencement enactment' means an enactment passed or made before Part 2 comes into force, and

'statutory instrument' means a statutory instrument within the meaning of section 1 of the Statutory Instruments Act 1946 (c 36).

Instruments subject to annulment in pursuance of a resolution of the Parliament

2 (1) This paragraph applies where, in relation to subordinate legislation which is to be made by statutory instrument, a pre-commencement enactment provides, or has the effect of providing, that the legislation, or the statutory instrument containing it, is subject to annulment in pursuance of a resolution of the Scottish Parliament.

(2) The enactment is to be read as if it instead provided for the subordinate legislation to be subject to the negative procedure in the Scottish Parliament.

(3) Sections 28 and 31 apply in relation to the subordinate legislation as they apply in relation to devolved subordinate legislation which is subject to the negative procedure, but as if the references in them to a Scottish statutory instrument were references to a statutory instrument.

Instruments which cannot be made unless a draft is laid before and approved by resolution of the Parliament

3 (1) This paragraph applies where, in relation to subordinate legislation which is to be made by statutory instrument, a pre-commencement enactment provides, or has the effect of providing, that the legislation cannot be made unless a draft of the statutory instrument containing it is laid before, and approved by resolution of, the Scottish Parliament.

(2) The enactment is to be read as if it instead provided for the subordinate legislation to be subject to the affirmative procedure in the Scottish Parliament.

(3) Section 29 applies in relation to the subordinate legislation as it applies in relation to devolved subordinate legislation which is subject to the affirmative procedure, but as if the reference in it to a draft of a Scottish statutory instrument were a reference to a draft of a statutory instrument.

Other instruments laid before the Parliament

4 (1) This paragraph applies where, in relation to subordinate legislation which is to be made by statutory instrument—

(a) a pre-commencement enactment provides, or has the effect of providing, that the legislation, or the statutory instrument containing it, must be laid before the Scottish Parliament, and

(b) paragraphs 2 and 3 do not apply.

(2) Sections 30 and 31 apply in relation to the subordinate legislation as they apply in relation to devolved subordinate legislation which is not subject to the negative procedure or the affirmative procedure, but as if the references in them to a Scottish statutory instrument were references to a statutory instrument.

Laying of statutory instruments before the Parliament

5 Section 32 applies in relation to the laying of a statutory instrument, or a draft of a statutory instrument, before the Scottish Parliament as it applies in relation to the laying of a Scottish statutory instrument or, as the case may be, a draft of a Scottish statutory instrument, before the Parliament.

CONSTITUTIONAL REFORM AND GOVERNANCE ACT 2010
(2010, c 25)

PART 1
THE CIVIL SERVICE

Chapter 1
Statutory Basis for Management of the Civil Service

Application

1 Application of Chapter

(1) Subject to subsections (2) and (3), this Chapter applies to the civil service of the State.

(2) This Chapter does not apply to the following parts of the civil service of the State—

(a) the Secret Intelligence Service;

(b) the Security Service;

(c) the Government Communications Headquarters;

(d) the Northern Ireland Civil Service;

[. . .]

(3) Further, this Chapter—

(a) does not apply in relation to the making, outside the United Kingdom, of selections of persons who are not members of the civil service of the State for appointment to that service for the purpose only of duties to be carried out wholly outside the United Kingdom;

(b) does not apply in relation to the appointment of a person to the civil service of the State who was selected for the appointment as mentioned in paragraph (a);

(c) does not apply to the civil service of the State so far as it consists of persons—

(i) who were appointed to the civil service of the State as mentioned in paragraph (b), and

(ii) all of whose duties are carried out wholly outside the United Kingdom.

(4) In this Chapter references to the civil service—

(a) are to the civil service of the State excluding the parts mentioned in subsections (2) and (3)(c);

(b) are to be read subject to subsection (3)(a) and (b); and references to civil servants are to be read accordingly.

Civil Service Commission

2 Establishment of the Civil Service Commission

(1) There is to be a body corporate called the Civil Service Commission ('the Commission').

(2) Schedule 1 (which is about the Commission) has effect.

(3) The Commission has the role in relation to selections for appointments to the civil service set out in sections 11 to 14.

(4) See also—

(a) section 9 (which sets out the Commission's role in dealing with conduct that conflicts with civil service codes of conduct);

(b) section 17 (under which the Commission may be given additional functions).

Power to manage the civil service

3 Management of the civil service

(1) The Minister for the Civil Service has the power to manage the civil service (excluding the diplomatic service).

(2) The Secretary of State has the power to manage the diplomatic service.

(3) The powers in subsections (1) and (2) include (among other things) power to make appointments.

(4) But they do not cover national security vetting (and, accordingly, subsections (1) and (2) do not affect any power relating to national security vetting).

(5) The agreement of the Minister for the Civil Service is required for any exercise of the power in subsection (2) in relation to—

(a) remuneration of civil servants (including compensation payable on leaving the civil service), or

(b) the conditions on which a civil servant may retire.

(6) In exercising his power to manage the civil service, the Minister for the Civil Service shall have regard to the need to ensure that civil servants who advise Ministers are aware of the constitutional significance of Parliament and of the conventions governing the relationship between Parliament and Her Majesty's Government.

. . .

Codes of conduct

5 Civil service code

(1) The Minister for the Civil Service must publish a code of conduct for the civil service (excluding the diplomatic service).

(2) For this purpose, the Minister may publish separate codes of conduct covering civil servants who serve the Scottish Executive or the Welsh Assembly Government.

(3) Before publishing a code (or any revision of a code) under subsection (2), the Minister must consult the First Minister for Scotland or the First Minister for Wales (as the case may be).

(4) In this Chapter 'civil service code' means a code of conduct published under this section as it is in force for the time being.

(5) The Minister for the Civil Service must lay any civil service code before Parliament.

(6) The First Minister for Scotland must lay before the Scottish Parliament any civil service code under subsection (2) that covers civil servants who serve the Scottish Executive.

(7) The First Minister for Wales must lay before the National Assembly for Wales any civil service code under subsection (2) that covers civil servants who serve the Welsh Assembly Government.

(8) A civil service code forms part of the terms and conditions of service of any civil servant covered by the code.

6 Diplomatic service code

(1) The Secretary of State must publish a code of conduct for the diplomatic service.

(2) In this Chapter 'diplomatic service code' means the code of conduct published under this section as it is in force for the time being.

(3) The Secretary of State must lay the diplomatic service code before Parliament.

(4) The diplomatic service code forms part of the terms and conditions of service of any civil servant covered by the code.

7 Minimum requirements for civil service and diplomatic service codes

. . .

(2) The code must require civil servants who serve an administration mentioned in subsection (3) to carry out their duties for the assistance of the administration as it is duly constituted for the time being, whatever its political complexion.

. . .

(4) The code must require civil servants to carry out their duties—

(a) with integrity and honesty, and

(b) with objectivity and impartiality.

(5) But the code need not require special advisers (see section 15) to carry out their duties with objectivity or impartiality.

8 Special advisers code

(1) The Minister for the Civil Service must publish a code of conduct for special advisers (see section 15).

(2) For this purpose, the Minister may publish separate codes of conduct covering special advisers who serve the Scottish Executive or the Welsh Assembly Government.

(3) Before publishing a code (or any revision of a code) under subsection (2), the Minister must consult the First Minister for Scotland or the First Minister for Wales (as the case may be).

(4) In this Chapter 'special advisers code' means a code of conduct published under this section as it is in force for the time being.

(5) Subject to subsection (6), a special advisers code must provide that a special adviser may not—

(a) authorise the expenditure of public funds;

(b) exercise any power in relation to the management of any part of the civil service of the State;

(c) otherwise exercise any power conferred by or under this or any other Act or any power under Her Majesty's prerogative.

(6) A special advisers code may permit a special adviser to exercise any power within subsection (5)(b) in relation to another special adviser.

(7) In subsection (5)(c) 'Act' includes—

(a) an Act of the Scottish Parliament;

(b) an Act or Measure of the National Assembly for Wales;

(c) Northern Ireland legislation.

(8) The Minister for the Civil Service must lay any special advisers code before Parliament.

(9) The First Minister for Scotland must lay before the Scottish Parliament any special advisers code under subsection (2) that covers special advisers who serve the Scottish Executive.

(10) The First Minister for Wales must lay before the National Assembly for

Wales any special advisers code under subsection (2) that covers special advisers who serve the Welsh Assembly Government.

(11) A special advisers code forms part of the terms and conditions of service of any special adviser covered by the code.

10 Selections for appointments to the civil service

(1) This section applies to the selection of persons who are not civil servants for appointment to the civil service.

(2) A person's selection must be on merit on the basis of fair and open competition.

(3) The following selections are excepted from this requirement—

(a) a person's selection for an appointment to the diplomatic service either as head of mission or in connection with the person's appointment (or selection for appointment) as Governor of an overseas territory;

(b) selection for an appointment as special adviser (see section 15);

(c) a selection excepted by the recruitment principles (see sections 11 and 12 (1)(b)).

(4) In determining for the purposes of subsection (1) whether or not a person is a civil servant, ignore any appointment for which the person was selected in reliance on subsection (3).

(5) But, in relation to persons selected in reliance on subsection (3)(c), the recruitment principles may disapply subsection (4) in specified cases.

11 Recruitment principles

(1) The Commission must publish a set of principles to be applied for the purposes of the requirement in section 10(2).

(2) Before publishing the set of principles (or any revision of it), the Commission must consult the Minister for the Civil Service.

(3) In this Chapter 'recruitment principles' means the set of principles published under this section as it is in force for the time being.

(4) Civil service management authorities must comply with the recruitment principles.

12 Approvals for selections and exceptions

(1) The recruitment principles may include provision—

(a) requiring the Commission's approval to be obtained for a selection which is subject to the requirement in section 10(2);

(b) excepting a selection from that requirement for the purposes of section 10(3)(c).

(2) The Commission may participate in the process for a selection for which its approval is required by provision within subsection (1)(a).

(3) It is up to the Commission to decide how it will participate.

(4) Provision within subsection (1)(b) may be included only if the Commission is satisfied—

(a) that the provision is justified by the needs of the civil service, or

(b) that the provision is needed to enable the civil service to participate in a government employment initiative that major employers in the United Kingdom (or a part of the United Kingdom) have been asked to participate in.

(5) Provision within subsection (1)(a) or (b) may be made in any way, including (for example) by reference to—

(a) particular appointments or descriptions of appointments;

(b) the circumstances in which a selection is made;

(c) the circumstances of the person to be selected;

(d) the purpose of the requirement to obtain approval or the purpose of the exception.

(6) Provision within subsection (1)(b) may also (for example)—

(a) deal with the way in which selections made in reliance on section 10(3)(c) are to be made;

(b) specify terms and conditions that must be included in the terms and conditions of an appointment resulting from a selection made in reliance on section 10(3)(c).

(7) Provision within subsection (1)(a) or (b) may confer discretions on the Commission or civil service management authorities.

13 Complaints about competitions

(1) Subsection (2) applies if a person has reason to believe that a selection for an appointment has been made in contravention of the requirement in section 10 (2).

(2) The person may complain to the Commission about the matter.

(3) The Commission—

(a) may determine steps that must be taken by a person before making a complaint (and those steps must be taken accordingly);

(b) must determine procedures for the making of complaints and for the investigation and consideration of complaints by the Commission;

(c) after considering a complaint, may make recommendations about how the matter should be resolved.

(4) For the purposes of the investigation or consideration of a complaint, the following must provide the Commission with any information it reasonably requires—

(a) civil service management authorities;

(b) the complainant.

14 Monitoring by the Commission

(1) The Commission must carry out whatever reviews of recruitment policies and practices it thinks are necessary to establish—

(a) that the principle of selection on merit on the basis of fair and open competition is being upheld in accordance with the requirement in section 10(2) and the recruitment principles, and

(b) that the requirement in section 10(2) and the recruitment principles are not being undermined in any way (apart from non-compliance).

(2) For this purpose, civil service management authorities must provide the Commission with any information it reasonably requires.

Special advisers

15 Definition of 'special adviser'

(1) In this Chapter 'special adviser' means a person ('P') who holds a position in the civil service serving an administration mentioned below and whose appointment to that position meets the applicable requirements set out below.

Her Majesty's Government in the United Kingdom

The requirements are—

(a) P is appointed to assist a Minister of the Crown after being selected for the appointment by that Minister personally;

(b) the appointment is approved by the Prime Minister;

(c) the terms and conditions of the appointment (apart from those by virtue of section 8(11)) are approved by the Minister for the Civil Service;

(d) those terms and conditions provide for the appointment to end not later than—

(i) when the person who selected P ceases to hold the ministerial office in relation to which P was appointed to assist that person, or

(ii) if earlier, the end of the day after the day of the poll at the first parliamentary general election following the appointment.

Scottish Executive

The requirements are—

(a) P is appointed to assist the Scottish Ministers (or one or more of the ministers mentioned in section 44(1)(a) and (b) of the Scotland Act 1998) after being selected for the appointment by the First Minister for Scotland personally;

(b) the terms and conditions of the appointment (apart from those by virtue of section 8(11)) are approved by the Minister for the Civil Service;

(c) those terms and conditions provide for the appointment to end not later than when the person who selected P ceases to hold office as First Minister.

The reference above to the Scottish Ministers excludes the Lord Advocate and the Solicitor General for Scotland.

Welsh Assembly Government

The requirements are—

(a) P is appointed to assist the Welsh Ministers (or one or more of the ministers mentioned in section 45(1)(a) and (b) of the Government of Wales Act 2006) after being selected for the appointment by the First Minister for Wales personally;

(b) the terms and conditions of the appointment (apart from those by virtue of section 8(11)) are approved by the Minister for the Civil Service;

(c) those terms and conditions provide for the appointment to end not later than when the person who selected P ceases to hold office as First Minister.

(2) In subsection (1), in relation to an appointment for which the selection is made personally by a person designated under section 45(4) of the Scotland Act 1998 or section 46(5) of the Government of Wales Act 2006, the reference to the person who selected P ceasing to hold office as First Minister for Scotland or Wales (as the case may be) is to be read as a reference to the designated person ceasing to be able to exercise the functions of the First Minister by virtue of the designation.

16 Annual reports about special advisers

. . .

(2) The First Minister for Scotland must—

(a) prepare an annual report about special advisers serving the Scottish Executive, and

(b) lay the report before the Scottish Parliament.

(3) The First Minister for Wales must—

(a) prepare an annual report about special advisers serving the Welsh Assembly Government, and

(b) lay the report before the National Assembly for Wales.

. . .

PART 2
RATIFICATION OF TREATIES

20 Treaties to be laid before Parliament before ratification

(1) Subject to what follows, a treaty is not to be ratified unless—

(a) a Minister of the Crown has laid before Parliament a copy of the treaty,

(b) the treaty has been published in a way that a Minister of the Crown thinks appropriate, and

(c) period A has expired without either House having resolved, within period A, that the treaty should not be ratified.

(2) Period A is the period of 21 sitting days beginning with the first sitting day after the date on which the requirement in subsection (1)(a) is met.

(3) Subsections (4) to (6) apply if the House of Commons resolved as mentioned in subsection (1)(c) (whether or not the House of Lords also did so).

(4) The treaty may be ratified if—

(a) a Minister of the Crown has laid before Parliament a statement indicating that the Minister is of the opinion that the treaty should nevertheless be ratified and explaining why, and

(b) period B has expired without the House of Commons having resolved, within period B, that the treaty should not be ratified.

(5) Period B is the period of 21 sitting days beginning with the first sitting day after the date on which the requirement in subsection (4)(a) is met.

(6) A statement may be laid under subsection (4)(a) in relation to the treaty on more than one occasion.

(7) Subsection (8) applies if—

(a) the House of Lords resolved as mentioned in subsection (1)(c), but

(b) the House of Commons did not.

(8) The treaty may be ratified if a Minister of the Crown has laid before Parliament a statement indicating that the Minister is of the opinion that the treaty should nevertheless be ratified and explaining why.

(9) 'Sitting day' means a day on which both Houses of Parliament sit.

EUROPEAN UNION ACT 2011
(2011, c 12)

Note: This Act will be repealed on IP completion day.

Restrictions relating to amendments of TEU or TFEU

2 Treaties amending or replacing TEU or TFEU

(1) A treaty which amends or replaces TEU or TFEU is not to be ratified unless—

(a) a statement relating to the treaty was laid before Parliament in accordance with section 5,

(b) the treaty is approved by Act of Parliament, and

(c) the referendum condition or the exemption condition is met.

(2) The referendum condition is that—

(a) the Act providing for the approval of the treaty provides that the provision approving the treaty is not to come into force until a referendum about whether the treaty should be ratified has been held throughout the United Kingdom or, where the treaty also affects Gibraltar, throughout the United Kingdom and Gibraltar,

(b) the referendum has been held, and

(c) the majority of those voting in the referendum are in favour of the ratification of the treaty.

(3) The exemption condition is that the Act providing for the approval of the treaty states that the treaty does not fall within section 4.

3 Amendment of TFEU under simplified revision procedure

(1) Where the European Council has adopted an Article 48(6) decision subject to its approval by the member States, a Minister of the Crown may not confirm the approval of the decision by the United Kingdom unless—

(a) a statement relating to the decision was laid before Parliament in accordance with section 5,

(b) the decision is approved by Act of Parliament, and

(c) the referendum condition, the exemption condition or the significance condition is met.

(2) The referendum condition is that—

(a) the Act providing for the approval of the decision provides that the provision approving the decision is not to come into force until a referendum about whether the decision should be approved has been held throughout the United Kingdom or, where the decision also affects Gibraltar, throughout the United Kingdom and Gibraltar,

(b) the referendum has been held, and

(c) the majority of those voting in the referendum are in favour of the approval of the decision.

(3) The exemption condition is that the Act providing for the approval of the decision states that the decision does not fall within section 4.

(4) The significance condition is that the Act providing for the approval of the decision states that—

(a) the decision falls within section 4 only because of provision of the kind mentioned in subsection (1)(i) or (j) of that section, and

(b) the effect of that provision in relation to the United Kingdom is not significant.

4 Cases where treaty or Article 48(6) decision attracts a referendum

(1) Subject to subsection (4), a treaty or an Article 48(6) decision falls within this section if it involves one or more of the following—

(a) the extension of the objectives of the EU as set out in Article 3 of TEU;

(b) the conferring on the EU of a new exclusive competence;

(c) the extension of an exclusive competence of the EU;

(d) the conferring on the EU of a new competence shared with the member States;

(e) the extension of any competence of the EU that is shared with the member States;

(f) the extension of the competence of the EU in relation to—

(i) the co-ordination of economic and employment policies, or

(ii) common foreign and security policy;

(g) the conferring on the EU of a new competence to carry out actions to support, co-ordinate or supplement the actions of member States;

(h) the extension of a supporting, co-ordinating or supplementing competence of the EU;

(i) the conferring on an EU institution or body of power to impose a requirement or obligation on the United Kingdom, or the removal of any limitation on any such power of an EU institution or body;

(j) the conferring on an EU institution or body of new or extended power to impose sanctions on the United Kingdom;

(k) any amendment of a provision listed in Schedule 1 that removes a requirement that anything should be done unanimously, by consensus or by common accord;

(l) any amendment of Article 31(2) of TEU (decisions relating to common foreign and security policy to which qualified majority voting applies) that removes or amends the provision enabling a member of the Council to oppose the adoption of a decision to be taken by qualified majority voting;

(m) any amendment of any of the provisions specified in subsection (3) that removes or amends the provision enabling a member of the Council, in relation to a draft legislative act, to ensure the suspension of the ordinary legislative procedure.

(2) Any reference in subsection (1) to the extension of a competence includes a reference to the removal of a limitation on a competence.

(3) The provisions referred to in subsection (1)(m) are—

(a) Article 48 of TFEU (social security),

(b) Article 82(3) of TFEU (judicial co-operation in criminal matters), and

(c) Article 83(3) of TFEU (particularly serious crime with a cross-border dimension).

(4) A treaty or Article 48(6) decision does not fall within this section merely because it involves one or more of the following—

(a) the codification of practice under TEU or TFEU in relation to the previous exercise of an existing competence;

(b) the making of any provision that applies only to member States other than the United Kingdom;

(c) in the case of a treaty, the accession of a new member State.

5 Statement to be laid before Parliament

(1) If a treaty amending TEU or TFEU is agreed in an inter-governmental conference, a Minister of the Crown must lay the required statement before Parliament before the end of the 2 months beginning with the date on which the treaty is agreed.

(2) If an Article 48(6) decision is adopted by the European Council subject to its approval by the member States, a Minister of the Crown must lay the required statement before Parliament before the end of the 2 months beginning with the date on which the decision is adopted.

(3) The required statement is a statement as to whether, in the Minister's opinion, the treaty or Article 48(6) decision falls within section 4.

(4) If the Minister is of the opinion that an Article 48(6) decision falls within section 4 only because of provision of the kind mentioned in subsection (1)(i) or (j) of that section, the statement must indicate whether in the Minister's opinion the effect of that provision in relation to the United Kingdom is significant.

(5) The statement must give reasons for the Minister's opinion under subsection (3) and, if relevant, subsection (4).

(6) In relation to an Article 48(6) decision adopted by the European Council before the day on which this section comes into force ('the commencement date'), the condition in section 3(1)(a) is to be taken to be complied with if a statement under this section is laid before Parliament before the end of the 2 months beginning with the commencement date.

Restrictions relating to other decisions under TEU or TFEU

6 Decisions requiring approval by Act and by referendum

(1) A Minister of the Crown may not vote in favour of or otherwise support a decision to which this subsection applies unless—

(a) the draft decision is approved by Act of Parliament, and

(b) the referendum condition is met.

(2) Where the European Council has recommended to the member States the adoption of a decision under Article 42(2) of TEU in relation to a common EU defence, a Minister of the Crown may not notify the European Council that the decision is adopted by the United Kingdom unless—

(a) the decision is approved by Act of Parliament, and

(b) the referendum condition is met.

(3) A Minister of the Crown may not give a notification under Article 4 of Protocol (No. 21) on the position of the United Kingdom and Ireland in respect of the area of freedom, security and justice annexed to TEU and TFEU which relates to participation by the United Kingdom in a European Public Prosecutor's Office or an extension of the powers of that Office unless—

(a) the notification has been approved by Act of Parliament, and

(b) the referendum condition is met.

(4) The referendum condition is that set out in section 3(2), with references to a decision being read for the purposes of subsection (1) as references to a draft decision and for the purposes of subsection (3) as references to a notification.

(5) The decisions to which subsection (1) applies are—

(a) a decision under the provision of Article 31(3) of TEU that permits the adoption of qualified majority voting;

(b) a decision under Article 48(7) of TEU which in relation to any provision listed in Schedule 1—

(i) adopts qualified majority voting, or

(ii) applies the ordinary legislative procedure in place of a special legislative procedure requiring the Council to act unanimously;

(c) a decision under Article 86(1) of TFEU involving participation by the United Kingdom in a European Public Prosecutor's Office;

(d) where the United Kingdom has become a participant in a European Public Prosecutor's Office, a decision under Article 86(4) of TFEU to extend the powers of that Office;

(e) a decision under Article 140(3) of TFEU which would make the euro the currency of the United Kingdom;

(f) a decision under the provision of Article 153(2) of TFEU (social policy) that permits the application of the ordinary legislative procedure in place of a special legislative procedure;

(g) a decision under the provision of Article 192(2) of TFEU (environment) that permits the application of the ordinary legislative procedure in place of a special legislative procedure;

(h) a decision under the provision of Article 312(2) of TFEU (EU finance) that permits the adoption of qualified majority voting;

(i) a decision under the provision of Article 333(1) of TFEU (enhanced co-operation) that permits the adoption of qualified majority voting, where the decision relates to a provision listed in Schedule 1 and the United Kingdom is a participant in the enhanced co-operation to which the decision relates;

(j) a decision under the provision of Article 333(2) of TFEU (enhanced co-operation) that permits the adoption of the ordinary legislative procedure in place of a special legislative procedure, where—

(i) the decision relates to a provision listed in Schedule 1,

(ii) the special legislative procedure requires the Council to act unanimously, and

(iii) the United Kingdom is a participant in the enhanced co-operation to which the decision relates;

(k) a decision under Article 4 of the Schengen Protocol that removes any border control of the United Kingdom.

(6) In subsection (5)(k) 'the Schengen Protocol' means the Protocol (No. 19) on the Schengen acquis integrated into the framework of the European Union, annexed to TEU and TFEU.

7 Decisions requiring approval by Act

(1) A Minister of the Crown may not confirm the approval by the United Kingdom of a decision to which this subsection applies unless the decision is approved by Act of Parliament.

(2) The decisions to which subsection (1) applies are—

(a) a decision under the provision of Article 25 of TFEU that permits the adoption of provisions to strengthen or add to the rights listed in Article 20(2) of that Treaty (rights of citizens of the European Union);

(b) a decision under the provision of Article 223(1) of TFEU that permits the laying down of the provisions necessary for the election of the members of the European Parliament in accordance with that Article;

(c) a decision under the provision of Article 262 of TFEU that permits the conferring of jurisdiction on the Court of Justice of the European Union in disputes relating to the application of acts adopted on the basis of the EU Treaties which create European intellectual property rights;

(d) a decision under the third paragraph of Article 311 of TFEU to adopt a decision laying down provisions relating to the system of own resources of the European Union.

(3) A Minister of the Crown may not vote in favour of or otherwise support a decision to which this subsection applies unless the draft decision is approved by Act of Parliament.

(4) The decisions to which subsection (3) applies are—

(a) a decision under the provision of Article 17(5) of TEU that permits the alteration of the number of members of the European Commission;

(b) a decision under Article 48(7) of TEU which in relation to any provision not listed in Schedule 1—

(i) adopts qualified majority voting, or

(ii) applies the ordinary legislative procedure in place of a special legislative procedure requiring the Council to act unanimously;

(c) a decision under the provision of Article 64(3) of TFEU that permits the adoption of measures which constitute a step backwards in European Union law as regards the liberalisation of the movement of capital to or from third countries;

(d) a decision under the provision of Article 126(14) of TFEU that permits the adoption of provisions to replace the Protocol (No. 12) on the excessive deficit procedure annexed to TEU and TFEU;

(e) a decision under the provision of Article 333(1) of TFEU (enhanced co-operation) that permits the adoption of qualified majority voting, where the decision relates to a provision not listed in Schedule 1 and the United Kingdom is a participant in the enhanced co-operation to which the decision relates;

(f) a decision under the provision of Article 333(2) of TFEU (enhanced co-operation) that permits the adoption of the ordinary legislative procedure in place of a special legislative procedure, where—

(i) the decision relates to a provision not listed in Schedule 1,

(ii) the special legislative procedure requires the Council to act unanimously, and

(iii) the United Kingdom is a participant in the enhanced co-operation to which the decision relates.

8 Decisions under Article 352 of TFEU

(1) A Minister of the Crown may not vote in favour of or otherwise support an Article 352 decision unless one of subsections (3) to (5) is complied with in relation to the draft decision.

(2) An Article 352 decision is a decision under the provision of Article 352 of TFEU that permits the adoption of measures to attain one of the objectives set out in the EU Treaties (but for which those Treaties have not provided the necessary powers).

(3) This subsection is complied with if a draft decision is approved by Act of Parliament.

(4) This subsection is complied with if—

(a) in each House of Parliament a Minister of the Crown moves a motion that the House approves Her Majesty's Government's intention to support a specified draft decision and is of the opinion that the measure to which it relates is required as a matter of urgency, and

(b) each House agrees to the motion without amendment.

(5) This subsection is complied with if a Minister of the Crown has laid before Parliament a statement specifying a draft decision and stating that in the opinion of the Minister the decision relates only to one or more exempt purposes.

(6) The exempt purposes are—

(a) to make provision equivalent to that made by a measure previously adopted under Article 352 of TFEU, other than an excepted measure;

(b) to prolong or renew a measure previously adopted under that Article, other than an excepted measure;

(c) to extend a measure previously adopted under that Article to another member State or other country;

(d) to repeal existing measures adopted under that Article;

(e) to consolidate existing measures adopted under that Article without any change of substance.

(7) In subsection (6)(a) and (b), 'excepted measure' means a measure adopted after the commencement of this section and resulting from a decision in relation to which a Minister of the Crown had relied on compliance with subsection (4).

9 Approval required in connection with Title V of Part 3 of TFEU

(1) A Minister of the Crown may not give a notification to which this subsection applies unless Parliamentary approval has been given in accordance with subsection (3).

(2) Subsection (1) applies in relation to a notification under Article 3 of Protocol (No 21) on the position of the United Kingdom and Ireland in respect of the area of freedom, security and justice annexed to TEU and TFEU (the 'AFSJ Protocol') that the United Kingdom wishes to take part in the adoption and application of a measure proposed under any of the following—

(a) the provision of Article 81(3) of TFEU (family law) that permits the application of the ordinary legislative procedure in place of a special legislative procedure;

(b) the provision of Article 82(2)(d) of TFEU (criminal procedure) that permits the identification of further specific aspects of criminal procedure to which directives adopted under the ordinary legislative procedure may relate;

(c) the provision of Article 83(1) of TFEU (particularly serious crime with a cross-border dimension) that permits the identification of further areas of crime to which directives adopted under the ordinary legislative procedure may relate.

(3) Parliamentary approval is given if—

(a) in each House of Parliament a Minister of the Crown moves a motion that the House approves Her Majesty's Government's intention to give a notification in respect of a specified measure, and

(b) each House agrees to the motion without amendment.

(4) Despite any Parliamentary approval given for the purposes of subsection (1), a Minister may not vote in favour of or otherwise support a decision under a provision falling within any of paragraphs (a) to (c) of subsection (2) unless the draft decision is approved by Act of Parliament.

(5) A Minister of the Crown may not give a notification under Article 4 of the AFSJ Protocol that the United Kingdom wishes to accept a measure to which this subsection applies unless the notification in respect of the measure has been approved by Act of Parliament.

(6) The measures to which subsection (5) applies are—

(a) a measure adopted under a provision described in any of paragraphs (a) to (c) of subsection (2), or

(b) a measure established under Article 81(3), 82(2)(d) or 83(1) of TFEU by virtue of a previous decision adopted, without the participation of the United Kingdom, under a provision falling within any of those paragraphs.

10 Parliamentary control of certain decisions not requiring approval by Act

(1) A Minister of the Crown may not vote in favour of or otherwise support a decision under any of the following unless Parliamentary approval has been given in accordance with this section—

(a) the provision of Article 56 of TFEU that permits the extension of the provisions of Chapter 3 of Title IV of Part 3 of that Treaty (free movement of services) to nationals of a third country;

(b) Article 129(3) of TFEU (amendment of provisions of the Statute of the European System of Central Banks or of the European Central Bank);

(c) the provision of Article 252 of TFEU that permits an increase in the number of Advocates-General;

(d) the provision of Article 257 of TFEU that permits the establishment of specialised courts attached to the General Court;

(e) the provision of Article 281 of TFEU that permits the amendment of the Statute of the Court of Justice of the European Union;

(f) the provision of Article 308 of TFEU that permits the amendment of the Statute of the European Investment Bank.

(2) A Minister of the Crown may not vote in favour of or otherwise support a

decision to which this subsection applies unless Parliamentary approval has been given in accordance with this section.

(3) Subsection (2) applies to a decision under Article 48(7) of TEU which in relation to a provision of TFEU applies the ordinary legislative procedure in place of a special legislative procedure not requiring the Council to act unanimously.

(4) A Minister of the Crown may not confirm the approval by the United Kingdom of a decision under Article 218(8) of TFEU for the accession of the European Union to the European Convention for the Protection of Human Rights and Fundamental Freedoms in accordance with Article 6(2) of TEU unless Parliamentary approval has been given in accordance with this section.

(5) Parliamentary approval is given if—

(a) in each House of Parliament a Minister of the Crown moves a motion that the House approves Her Majesty's Government's intention to support the adoption of a specified draft decision, and

(b) each House agrees to the motion without amendment.

Status of EU law

18 Status of EU law dependent on continuing statutory basis

Directly applicable or directly effective EU law (that is, the rights, powers, liabilities, obligations, restrictions, remedies and procedures referred to in section 2(1) of the European Communities Act 1972) falls to be recognised and available in law in the United Kingdom only by virtue of that Act or where it is required to be recognised and available in law by virtue of any other Act.

FIXED-TERM PARLIAMENTS ACT 2011
(2011, c 14)

1 Polling days for parliamentary general elections

(1) This section applies for the purposes of the Timetable in rule 1 in Schedule 1 to the Representation of the People Act 1983 and is subject to section 2.

(2) The polling day for the next parliamentary general election after the passing of this Act is to be 7 May 2015.

(3) The polling day for each subsequent parliamentary general election is to be the first Thursday in May in the fifth calendar year following that in which the polling day for the previous parliamentary general election fell.

(4) But, if the polling day for the previous parliamentary general election—

(a) was appointed under section 2(7), and

(b) in the calendar year in which it fell, fell before the first Thursday in May,

subsection (3) has effect as if for 'fifth' there were substituted ' fourth '.

(5) The Prime Minister may by order made by statutory instrument provide that the polling day for a parliamentary general election in a specified calendar year is to be later than the day determined under subsection (2) or (3), but not more than two months later.

(6) A statutory instrument containing an order under subsection (5) may not be made unless a draft has been laid before and approved by a resolution of each House of Parliament.

(7) The draft laid before Parliament must be accompanied by a statement setting out the Prime Minister's reasons for proposing the change in the polling day.

2 Early parliamentary general elections

(1) An early parliamentary general election is to take place if—

(a) the House of Commons passes a motion in the form set out in subsection (2), and

(b) if the motion is passed on a division, the number of members who vote in favour of the motion is a number equal to or greater than two thirds of the number of seats in the House (including vacant seats).

(2) The form of motion for the purposes of subsection (1)(a) is—

'That there shall be an early parliamentary general election.'

(3) An early parliamentary general election is also to take place if—

(a) the House of Commons passes a motion in the form set out in subsection (4), and

(b) the period of 14 days after the day on which that motion is passed ends without the House passing a motion in the form set out in subsection (5).

(4) The form of motion for the purposes of subsection (3)(a) is—

'That this House has no confidence in Her Majesty's Government.'

(5) The form of motion for the purposes of subsection (3)(b) is—

'That this House has confidence in Her Majesty's Government.'

(6) Subsection (7) applies for the purposes of the Timetable in rule 1 in Schedule 1 to the Representation of the People Act 1983.

(7) If a parliamentary general election is to take place as provided for by subsection (1) or (3), the polling day for the election is to be the day appointed by Her Majesty by proclamation on the recommendation of the Prime Minister (and, accordingly, the appointed day replaces the day which would otherwise have been the polling day for the next election determined under section 1).

3 Dissolution of Parliament

(1) The Parliament then in existence dissolves at the beginning of the [25th] working day before the polling day for the next parliamentary general election as determined under section 1 or appointed under section 2(7).

(2) Parliament cannot otherwise be dissolved.

(3) Once Parliament dissolves, the Lord Chancellor and, in relation to Northern Ireland, the Secretary of State have the authority to have the writs for the election sealed and issued (see rule 3 in Schedule 1 to the Representation of the People Act 1983).

(4) Once Parliament dissolves, Her Majesty may issue the proclamation summoning the new Parliament which may—

(a) appoint the day for the first meeting of the new Parliament;

(b) deal with any other matter which was normally dealt with before the passing of this Act by proclamations summoning new Parliaments (except a matter dealt with by subsection (1) or (3)).

(5) In this section 'working day' means any day other than—

(a) a Saturday or Sunday;

(b) a Christmas Eve, Christmas Day or Good Friday;

(c) a day which is a bank holiday under the Banking and Financial Dealings Act 1971 in any part of the United Kingdom;

(d) a day appointed for public thanksgiving or mourning.

(6) But, if—

(a) on a day ('the relevant day') one or more working days are fixed or appointed as bank holidays or days for public thanksgiving or mourning, and

(b) as a result, the day for the dissolution of a Parliament would (apart from this subsection) be brought forward from what it was immediately before the relevant day to a day that is earlier than 30 days after the relevant day,

the day or days in question are to continue to be treated as working days (even if the polling day is subsequently changed).

4 General election for Scottish Parliament not to fall on same date as parliamentary general election under section 1(2)

(1) This section applies in relation to the ordinary general election for membership of the Scottish Parliament the poll for which would, apart from this section

and disregarding sections 2(5) and 3(3) of the Scotland Act 1998, be held on 7 May 2015 (that is, the date specified in section 1(2) of this Act).

(2) Section 2(2) of the 1998 Act has effect as if, instead of providing for the poll for that election to be held on that date, it provided (subject to sections 2(5) and 3 (3) of that Act) for the poll to be held on 5 May 2016 (and section 2(2) has effect in relation to subsequent ordinary general elections accordingly).

5 *[Omitted by virtue of Wales Act 2014, ss 1(2), 29(2)(a).]*

6 Supplementary provisions

. . .

(2) This Act does not affect the way in which the sealing of a proclamation summoning a new Parliament may be authorised; and the sealing of a proclamation to be issued under section 2(7) may be authorised in the same way.

POLICE AND FIRE REFORM (SCOTLAND) ACT 2012
(2012, asp 8)

6 The Police Service of Scotland

There is to be a constabulary to be known as the Police Service of Scotland (or, in Gaelic, Seirbheis Phoilis na h-Alba) comprising—

(a) a constable holding the office of chief constable,

(b) one or more constables holding the office of deputy chief constable,

(c) one or more constables holding the office of assistant chief constable, and

(d) other individuals holding the office of constable

20 Constables: general duties

(1) It is the duty of a constable—

(a) to prevent and detect crime,

(b) to maintain order,

(c) to protect life and property,

(d) to take such lawful measures, and make such reports to the appropriate prosecutor, as may be needed to bring offenders with all due speed to justice,

(e) where required, to serve and execute a warrant, citation or deliverance issued, or process duly endorsed, by a Lord Commissioner of Justiciary, [sheriff, summary sheriff or justice of the peace] in relation to criminal proceedings, and

(f) to attend court to give evidence.

[. . .]

90 Assaulting or impeding police

(1) It is an offence for a person to assault—

(a) a person ('A') acting in a capacity mentioned in subsection (3), or

(b) a person assisting A while A is acting in such capacity.

(2) It is an offence for a person to resist, obstruct or hinder—

(a) a person ('A') acting in a capacity mentioned in subsection (3), or

(b) a person assisting A while A is acting in such capacity.

(3) The capacities are—

(a) that of a constable,

(b) that of a member of police staff,

(c) that of a member of a relevant police force when such memberis executing a warrant or is otherwise acting in Scotland by virtue of any enactment conferring powers on the member in Scotland,

(d) that of a person who—

(i) is a member of an international joint investigation team that is led by a person acting in a capacity mentioned in paragraph (a) or (c), and

(ii) is carrying out functions as a member of that team.

(4) A person who is guilty of an offence under subsection (1) or (2) is liable on summary conviction to imprisonment for a period not exceeding 12 months or to a fine not exceeding the statutory maximum, or to both.

(5) A complaint may include a charge that is framed so as to comprise (in a combined form) the specification of both an offence under subsection (1) and an offence under subsection (2).

(6) Where a charge in a complaint is so framed the charge is to be regarded as being a single yet cumulative charge.

(7) In this section and section 91, a reference to a member of a relevant police force is a reference to a member of—

(a) a police force maintained under section 2 of the Police Act 1996 (c 16),

(b) the metropolitan police force,

(c) the City of London police force, or

(d) the Police Service of Northern Ireland.

91 Escape from custody

(1) It is an offence for a person—

(a) to remove a person from custody, or

(b) to assist the escape of a person in custody.

(2) The reference in subsection (1) to a person in custody is to be construed as a reference to a person—

(a) who is in the lawful custody of a person ('A') acting in a capacity mentioned in subsection (3) or a person assisting A while A is acting in such capacity, or

(b) who is in the act of eluding or escaping from such custody, whether or not the person has actually been arrested.

(3) The capacities are—

(a) that of a constable,

(b) that of a police custody and security officer,

(c) that of a member of a relevant police force when such member is executing a warrant or is otherwise acting in Scotland by virtue of any enactment conferring powers on the member in Scotland,

(d) that of a person who—

(i) is a member of an international joint investigation team that is led by a person acting in a capacity mentioned in paragraph (a) or (c), and

(ii) is carrying out functions as a member of that team.

(4) A person who is guilty of an offence under subsection (1) is liable on summary conviction to imprisonment for a period not exceeding 12 months or to a fine not exceeding the statutory maximum, or to both.

SCOTLAND ACT 2012
(2012, c 11)

Note – Sections 34–37 make amendments to the Criminal Procedure (Scotland) Act 1995 in respect of Convention rights and EU compatibility issues, and devolution issues. These amendments have been included in the 1995 Act as reproduced in this volume.

38 Review and power to amend sections 34 to 37

(1) The Secretary of State must arrange—

(a) for a review of the provision made by sections 34 to 37,

(b) for a report of the conclusions of the review to be made to the Secretary of State, and

(c) for a copy of the report to be given to the Scottish Ministers.

(2) The review must be carried out as soon as practicable after the end of 3

years beginning with the day on which section 36(6) comes into force, or earlier if the Secretary of State considers it appropriate.

(3) The review must—

(a) consider whether changes should be made to the provision made by sections 34 to 37;

(b) consider whether further provision should be made in relation to any matter dealt with by those sections;

(c) consider (in particular) whether an appeal to the Supreme Court on a compatibility issue should lie only if the High Court of Justiciary certifies that the issue raises a point of law of general public importance.

(4) The Secretary of State may by order—

(a) amend the provision made by sections 34 to 37;

(b) make further provision in relation to any matter dealt with by those sections.

(5) Provision made by order under subsection (4) may—

(a) amend, repeal or revoke an enactment passed or made before the order is made;

(b) confer power on the Secretary of State or the Scottish Ministers to make an order or regulations;

(c) include consequential, transitional or saving provision.

(6) In this section 'enactment' includes an enactment contained in subordinate legislation (within the meaning of the Interpretation Act 1978) and an enactment contained in, or in an instrument made under, an Act of the Scottish Parliament.

(7) In making the first order under subsection (4) the Secretary of State must take into account the report made in accordance with subsection (1)(b).

(8) No order under subsection (4) may be made unless the Secretary of State has consulted the Scottish Ministers.

(9) A statutory instrument containing an order under subsection (4) may not be made unless a draft of the instrument has been laid before and approved by a resolution of each House of Parliament.

SCOTTISH INDEPENDENCE REFERENDUM ACT 2013
(2013, asp 14)

1 Referendum on Scottish independence

(1) A referendum is to be held in Scotland on a question about the independence of Scotland.

(2) The question is—

'Should Scotland be an independent country?'

(3) The ballot paper to be used for the purpose of the referendum is to be printed—

(a) in the form set out in schedule 1, and

(b) according to the directions set out in that schedule.

(4) The date on which the poll at the referendum is to be held is 18 September 2014, unless before then an order is made under subsection (6).

(5) Subsection (6) applies if the Scottish Ministers are satisfied—

(a) that it is impossible or impracticable for the poll at the referendum to be held on 18 September 2014, or

(b) that it cannot be conducted properly if held on that date.

(6) The Scottish Ministers may by order appoint a later day (being no later than 31 December 2014) as the day on which the poll at the referendum is to be held.

(7) An order under subsection (6)—

(a) may include supplementary or consequential provision,

(b) may modify any enactment (including this Act), and

(c) is subject to the affirmative procedure.

JUSTICE AND SECURITY ACT 2013
(2013, c 18)

1 The Intelligence and Security Committee of Parliament

(1) There is to be a body known as the Intelligence and Security Committee of Parliament (in this Part referred to as 'the ISC').

(2) The ISC is to consist of nine members who are to be drawn both from the members of the House of Commons and from the members of the House of Lords.

(3) Each member of the ISC is to be appointed by the House of Parliament from which the member is to be drawn.

(4) A person is not eligible to become a member of the ISC unless the person—

(a) is nominated for membership by the Prime Minister, and

(b) is not a Minister of the Crown.

(5) Before deciding whether to nominate a person for membership, the Prime Minister must consult the Leader of the Opposition.

(6) A member of the ISC is to be the Chair of the ISC chosen by its members.

(7) Schedule 1 (which makes further provision about the ISC) has effect.

2 Main functions of the ISC

(1) The ISC may examine or otherwise oversee the expenditure, administration, policy and operations of—

(a) the Security Service,

(b) the Secret Intelligence Service, and

(c) the Government Communications Headquarters.

(2) The ISC may examine or otherwise oversee such other activities of Her Majesty's Government in relation to intelligence or security matters as are set out in a memorandum of understanding.

(3) The ISC may, by virtue of subsection (1) or (2), consider any particular operational matter but only so far as—

(a) the ISC and the Prime Minister are satisfied that the matter—

(i) is not part of any ongoing intelligence or security operation, and

(ii) is of significant national interest,

(b) the Prime Minister has asked the ISC to consider the matter, or

(c) the ISC's consideration of the matter is limited to the consideration of information provided voluntarily to the ISC (whether or not in response to a request by the ISC) by—

(i) the Security Service,

(ii) the Secret Intelligence Service,

(iii) the Government Communications Headquarters, or

(iv) a government department.

(4) The ISC's consideration of a particular operational matter under subsection (3)(a) or (b) must, in the opinion of the ISC and the Prime Minister, be consistent with any principles set out in, or other provision made by, a memorandum of understanding.

(5) A memorandum of understanding under this section—

(a) may include other provision about the ISC or its functions which is not of the kind envisaged in subsection (2) or (4),

(b) must be agreed between the Prime Minister and the ISC, and

(c) may be altered (or replaced with another memorandum) with the agreement of the Prime Minister and the ISC.

(6) The ISC must publish a memorandum of understanding under this section and lay a copy of it before Parliament.

3 Reports of the ISC

(1) The ISC must make an annual report to Parliament on the discharge of its functions.

(2) The ISC may make such other reports to Parliament as it considers appropriate concerning any aspect of its functions.

(3) Before making a report to Parliament, the ISC must send it to the Prime Minister.

(4) The ISC must exclude any matter from any report to Parliament if the Prime Minister, after consultation with the ISC, considers that the matter would be prejudicial to the continued discharge of the functions of the Security Service, the Secret Intelligence Service, the Government Communications Headquarters or any person carrying out activities falling within section 2(2).

(5) A report by the ISC to Parliament must contain a statement as to whether any matter has been excluded from the report by virtue of subsection (4).

(6) The ISC must lay before Parliament any report made by it to Parliament.

(7) The ISC may make a report to the Prime Minister in relation to matters which would be excluded by virtue of subsection (4) if the report were made to Parliament.

SCHEDULE 1
THE INTELLIGENCE AND SECURITY COMMITTEE OF PARLIAMENT

4—(1) This paragraph applies to information requested by the ISC in the exercise of its functions that—

(a) does not relate to any particular operational matter, or

(b) relates to a particular operational matter that the ISC is considering under section 2(3)(a) or (b).

(2) If the Director-General of the Security Service, the Chief of the Secret Intelligence Service or the Director of the Government Communications Headquarters is asked by the ISC to disclose the information, then, as to the whole or any part of the information which is sought, that person must either—

(a) arrange for it to be made available to the ISC subject to and in accordance with a memorandum of understanding under section 2, or

(b) inform the ISC that the information cannot be disclosed because the Secretary of State has decided that it should not be disclosed.

CRIME AND COURTS ACT 2013
(2013, c 22)

PART 1
THE NATIONAL CRIME AGENCY

The NCA and its officers

1 The National Crime Agency

(1) A National Crime Agency, consisting of the NCA officers, is to be formed.

(2) The NCA is to be under the direction and control of one of the NCA officers, who is to be known as the Director General of the National Crime Agency.

(3) The NCA is to have—

(a) the functions conferred by this section;

(b) the functions conferred by the Proceeds of Crime Act 2002; and

(c) the other functions conferred by this Act and by other enactments.

(4) The NCA is to have the function (the 'crime-reduction function') of securing that efficient and effective activities to combat organised crime and serious crime are carried out (whether by the NCA, other law enforcement agencies, or other persons).

(5) The NCA is to have the function (the 'criminal intelligence function') of gathering, storing, processing, analysing, and disseminating information that is relevant to any of the following—

(a) activities to combat organised crime or serious crime;

(b) activities to combat any other kind of crime;

(c) exploitation proceeds investigations (within the meaning of section 341(5) of the Proceeds of Crime Act 2002), exploitation proceeds orders (within the meaning of Part 7 of the Coroners and Justice Act 2009), and applications for such orders.

(6) The NCA must discharge the crime-reduction function in the following ways (in particular).

(7) The first way is by the NCA itself—

(a) preventing and detecting organised crime and serious crime,

(b) investigating offences relating to organised crime or serious crime, and

(c) otherwise carrying out activities to combat organised crime and serious crime, including by instituting criminal proceedings in England and Wales and Northern Ireland.

(8) The second way is by the NCA securing that activities to combat organised crime or serious crime are carried out by persons other than the NCA.

(9) The third way is by the NCA securing improvements—

(a) in co-operation between persons who carry out activities to combat organised crime or serious crime, and

(b) in co-ordination of activities to combat organised crime or serious crime.

(10) The crime-reduction function does not include—

(a) the function of the NCA itself prosecuting offences; or

(b) the function of the NCA itself instituting criminal proceedings in Scotland.

(11) In this Part, a reference to activities to combat crime (or a particular kind of crime, such as organised crime or serious crime) is a reference to—

(a) the prevention and detection of crime (or that kind of crime),

(b) the investigation and prosecution of offences (or offences relating to that kind of crime),

(c) the reduction of crime (or that kind of crime) in other ways, and

(d) the mitigation of the consequences of crime (or that kind of crime);

and references to the carrying out of activities to combat crime (or a particular kind of crime) are to be construed accordingly.

(12) Schedule 1 (the NCA & NCA officers) has effect.

2 Modification of NCA functions

(1) The Secretary of State may, by order, make—

(a) provision about NCA counter-terrorism functions (and, in particular, may make provision conferring, removing, or otherwise modifying such functions); and

(b) other provision which the Secretary of State considers necessary in consequence of provision made under paragraph (a) (and, in particular, may make provision about the functions of any person other than the NCA, including provision conferring or otherwise modifying, but not removing, such functions).

(2) If an order under this section confers an NCA counter-terrorism function, an NCA officer may only carry out activities in Northern Ireland for the purpose of the discharge of the function if the NCA officer does so with the agreement of the Chief Constable of the Police Service of Northern Ireland.

(3) That includes cases where an order under this section confers an NCA counter-terrorism function by the modification of a function.

(4) An order under this section may amend or otherwise modify this Act or any other enactment.

(5) An order under this section is subject to the super-affirmative procedure (see section 58 and Schedule 23).

(6) In this section 'NCA counter-terrorism function' means an NCA function relating to terrorism (and for this purpose 'terrorism' has the same meaning as in the Terrorism Act 2000 — see section 1 of that Act).

3 Strategic priorities

(1) The Secretary of the State must determine strategic priorities for the NCA.

(2) In determining strategic priorities for the NCA (including deciding whether there should be such priorities), the Secretary of State must consult—

(a) the strategic partners,

(b) the Director General, and

(c) any other persons whom the Secretary of State considers it is appropriate to consult.

4 Operations

(1) The Director General has (by virtue of the function of direction and control of the NCA) the power to decide—

(a) which particular operations are to be mounted by NCA officers, and

(b) how such operations are to be conducted.

(2) In exercising functions, the Director General must have regard to—

(a) any strategic priorities for the NCA (see section 3);

(b) the annual plan (see below); and

(c) the framework document (see Part 1 of Schedule 2).

(3) Before the beginning of each financial year, the Director General must issue a document (the 'annual plan') setting out how the Director General intends that NCA functions are to be exercised during that year (including how they are to be exercised in Scotland and Northern Ireland).

(4) The annual plan for a financial year must include—

(a) a statement of any strategic priorities for the NCA,

(b) a statement of the operational priorities for the NCA, and

(c) in relation to each of the strategic and operational priorities, an explanation of how the Director General intends that the priority will be given effect to.

(5) The Director General must determine operational priorities for the NCA; and those priorities may relate—

(a) to matters to which current strategic priorities also relate, or

(b) to other matters;

but operational priorities must, in any event, be framed so as to be consistent with the current strategic priorities.

(6) In preparing any annual plan, the Director General must consult—

(a) the strategic partners [and the Northern Ireland Policing Board], and

(b) any other persons whom the Director General considers it is appropriate to consult.

(7) The Director General is required by subsection (6)(a)—

(a) to consult the Scottish Ministers about the annual plan only as it relates to activities in Scotland; and

(b) to consult the Department of Justice in Northern Ireland [and the Northern Ireland Policing Board] about the annual plan only as it relates to activities in Northern Ireland.

(8) Before issuing any annual plan, the Director General must obtain—

(a) the consent of the Secretary of State to the plan,

(b) the consent of the Scottish Ministers to the plan as it relates to activities in Scotland, and

(c) the consent of the Department of Justice in Northern Ireland [and the Northern Ireland Policing Board] as it relates to activities in Northern Ireland.

(9) The Director General must arrange for each annual plan to be published in the manner which the Director General considers appropriate.

(10) Schedule 2 (the framework document & annual report) has effect.

Other functions etc

5 Relationships between NCA and other agencies: tasking etc

(1) Any of the following persons may perform a task if the Director General requests the person to perform it—

(a) the chief officer of a UK police force;

(b) a UK law enforcement agency.

(2) A request under subsection (1)—

(a) may be made only if the Director General considers that performance of the task would assist the NCA to exercise functions;

(b) must explain how performance of the requested task would so assist the exercise of functions.

(3) The Director General may perform a task if any of the following persons requests the Director General to perform it—

(a) the chief officer of a UK police force;

(b) a UK law enforcement agency.

(4) A request under subsection (3)—

(a) may be made only if the person making it considers that performance of the task would assist that person — or, in a case where that person is the chief officer of a police force, would assist that person or police force — to exercise functions;

(b) must explain how performance of the requested task would so assist the exercise of functions.

(5) The Director General may direct any of the following persons to perform a task specified in the direction—

(a) the chief officer of an England and Wales police force;

(b) the Chief Constable of the British Transport Police.

(6) The Director General may give a direction under subsection (5) only if the Director General considers that—

(a) performance of the task would assist the NCA to exercise functions;

(b) it is expedient for the directed person to perform that task; and

(c) satisfactory arrangements cannot be made, or cannot be made in time, under subsection (1).

(7) A person given a direction under this section must comply with it.

(8) If a person is requested or directed under this section to perform a task, the person may comply with that request or direction by securing that the task is performed by another person.

(9) The Director General may give a direction under this section to the Chief Constable of the British Transport Police only if the Secretary of State consents.

(10) Schedule 3 (relationships between NCA and other agencies) has effect.

(11) This section has effect subject to Part 5 (payment for tasks etc) of Schedule 3.

(12) Paragraph 33 of Schedule 3 gives the Secretary of State power to amend this section.

6 Duty to publish information

(1) The Director General must—

(a) make arrangements for publishing information about the exercise of NCA functions and other matters relating to the NCA, and

(b) publish information in accordance with those arrangements.

(2) The framework document may impose on the Director General requirements in relation to performance of the duties imposed by subsection (1) (including requirements about what information is not to be published).

(3) The Director General must comply with any such requirements in the framework document (and accordingly the duty in section 4(2)(c) to have regard to that document does not apply in relation to such requirements).

(4) This section is subject to Schedule 7 (information: restrictions on disclosure).

7 Information gateways

(1) A person may disclose information to the NCA if the disclosure is made for the purposes of the exercise of any NCA function.

(2) Subsection (1) does not authorise any of the following to disclose information to the NCA—

(a) a person serving in the Security Service;

(b) a person serving in the Secret Intelligence Service;

(c) a person serving in GCHQ;

but this does not affect the disclosures which such a person may make to the NCA in accordance with intelligence service disclosure arrangements.

(3) Information obtained by the NCA in connection with the exercise of any NCA functions may be used by the NCA in connection with the exercise of any other NCA function.

(4) An NCA officer may disclose information obtained by the NCA in connection with the exercise of any NCA function if the disclosure is for any permitted purpose.

(5) Subsection (4) authorises an NCA officer to disclose information for the purpose of the exercise of—

(a) the functions of the Lord Advocate under Part 3 of the Proceeds of Crime Act 2002 ('PCA 2002'), or

(b) the functions of the Scottish Ministers under, or in relation to, Part 5 of PCA 2002,

only where the information has been obtained by the NCA in connection with the exercise of a function under PCA 2002 (other than a function under Part 6 of that Act).

(6) Where information has been obtained by the NCA in connection with the exercise of a function under Part 6 of PCA 2002 (revenue functions), subsection (4) does not authorise an NCA officer to disclose the information.

(7) But an NCA officer may disclose the information if the disclosure is—

(a) to the Commissioners for Her Majesty's Revenue and Customs,

(b) to the Lord Advocate for the purposes of the exercise by the Lord Advocate of the Lord Advocate's functions under Part 3 of PCA 2002 (confiscation: Scotland),

(c) to any person for purposes relating to civil proceedings (whether or not in the United Kingdom) which relate to a matter in respect of which the NCA has functions, or

(d) to any person for the purposes of compliance with an order of a court or tribunal (whether or not in the United Kingdom).

(8) A disclosure of information which is authorised or required by this Part does not breach—

(a) an obligation of confidence owed by the person making the disclosure, or

(b) any other restriction on the disclosure of information (however imposed).

(9) This section is subject to Schedule 7 (information: restrictions on disclosure).

(10) In this section—

'GCHQ' has the same meaning as in the Intelligence Services Act 1994;

'intelligence service disclosure arrangements' means—

(a) arrangements made by the Director-General of the Security Service under section 2(2)(a) of the Security Service Act 1989 about the disclosure of information by that Service,

(b) arrangements made by the Chief of the Intelligence Service under section 2(2)(a) of the Intelligence Services Act 1994 about the disclosure of information by that Service, or

(c) arrangements made by the Director of GCHQ under section 4(2)(a) of that Act about the disclosure of information by GCHQ.

8 [*Amends the Children Act 2004*]

9 Director General: customs powers of Commissioners & operational powers

(1) The Director General has, in relation to any customs matter, the same powers as the Commissioners for Her Majesty's Revenue and Customs would have.

(2) The Secretary of State may designate the Director General as a person having one or more of the following—

(a) the powers and privileges of a constable;

(b) the powers of an officer of Revenue and Customs;

[(ba) the powers of a general customs official;]

(c) the powers of an immigration officer.

(3) The Secretary of State may modify or withdraw a designation of the Director General by giving notice of the modification or withdrawal to the Director General.

(4) Schedule 5 (police, customs and immigration powers) has effect.

(5) If, in accordance with paragraph 4 of Schedule 5, recommendations are made to the Secretary of State as to the operational powers which the Director General should have, the Secretary of State must exercise the powers of designation to give effect to those recommendations (unless the recommendations are already given effect to by a previous exercise of the powers of designation).

(6) The Secretary of State may not exercise the powers of designation unless—

(a) required to do so by subsection (5); or

(b) required or otherwise authorised to do so by regulations under paragraph 5 of Schedule 5.

(7) In this section 'powers of designation' means the powers conferred by subsections (2) and (3).

(8) In this Part—

'customs matter' means any matter other than—

(a) a matter to which section 7 of the Commissioners for Revenue and Customs Act 2005 applies (former Inland Revenue matters), or

(b) any tax or duty not mentioned in Schedule 1 to that Act (which lists such matters);

'operational power' means any of the following—

(a) a power or privilege of a constable;

(b) a power of an officer of Revenue and Customs;

[(ba) a power of a general customs official;]

(c) a power of an immigration officer.

10 Operational powers of other NCA officers

(1) The Director General may designate any other NCA officer as a person having one or more of the following—

(a) the powers and privileges of a constable;

(b) the powers of an officer of Revenue and Customs;

[(ba) the powers of a general customs official;]

(c) the powers of an immigration officer.

(2) The Director General may not designate an NCA officer under this section as having particular operational powers unless the Director General is satisfied that the officer—

(a) is capable of effectively exercising those powers;

(b) has received adequate training in respect of the exercise of those powers; and

(c) is otherwise a suitable person to exercise those powers.

(3) The Director General may modify or withdraw a designation of an NCA officer by giving notice of the modification or withdrawal to the officer.

(4) For further provision about designations under this section, see Schedule 5.

General

11 Inspections and complaints

(1) Her Majesty's Inspectors of Constabulary ('HMIC') must carry out inspections of the NCA.

(2) HMIC must also carry out an inspection of the NCA if requested to do so by the Secretary of State either—

(a) generally, or

(b) in respect of a particular matter.

[(2A) The Secretary of State must consult the Department of Justice in Northern Ireland before requesting HMIC to carry out an inspection in respect of a particular matter which relates only to the exercise of NCA functions in Northern Ireland.

(2B) The Department of Justice may request that HMIC carry out an inspection in respect of a particular matter that relates only to the exercise of NCA functions in Northern Ireland, but only with the consent of the Secretary of State.]

(3) Following an inspection under this section, HMIC must report to the Secretary of State on the efficiency and effectiveness of the NCA either—

(a) generally, or

(b) in the case of an inspection under subsection (2)(b), in respect of the matter to which the inspection related.

(4) HMIC must carry out such other duties for the purpose of furthering the efficiency and effectiveness of the NCA as the Secretary of State may from time to time direct.

(5) Paragraphs 2 and 5 of Schedule 4A to the Police Act 1996 (inspection programmes and inspection frameworks) apply to functions of inspection and reporting under this section as they apply to other such functions.

(6), (7) [*Amending provisions*]

12 Information: restrictions on disclosure etc

(1) Schedule 7 (information: restrictions on disclosure) has effect.

(2) Schedule 7 applies to disclosures made for the purposes of the criminal intelligence function.

(3) Any duty to disclose information imposed on an NCA officer (including the duty of the Director General under paragraph 4 or 6 of Schedule 3 to disclose information by keeping other persons informed of information obtained by the NCA), and any power of an NCA officer to disclose information, has effect subject to Schedule 7.

(4) Subsections (2) and (3) do not limit Schedule 7.

13 NCA officers with operational powers: labour relations

(1) A person must not induce the Director General or any NCA officer designated under section 10 to withhold (or to continue to withhold) services as an NCA officer.

(2) The duty imposed by subsection (1) is a duty owed to the Secretary of State.

(3) A breach of that duty which causes the Secretary of State to sustain loss or damage is to be actionable, at the Secretary of State's suit or instance, against the person in breach.

(4) Subsection (3) is without prejudice to the right of the Secretary of State, by virtue of subsections (1) and (2), to bring civil proceedings in respect of any apprehended contravention of subsection (1).

(5) The no-strike provisions must be disregarded in determining for the purposes of any of the relevant employment legislation whether any trade union is an independent trade union.

(6) Nothing in the relevant employment legislation is to affect the rights of the Secretary of State by virtue of the no-strike provisions.

(7) The Secretary of State may, by order, suspend, or later revive, the operation of the no-strike provisions.

(8) In this section—

'no-strike provisions' means subsections (1) to (3) of this section;

'relevant employment legislation' means—

(a) the Trade Union and Labour Relations (Consolidation) Act 1992;

(b) the Employment Rights Act 1996;

(c) the Trade Union and Labour Relations (Northern Ireland) Order 1995;

(d) the Employment Rights (Northern Ireland) Order 1996.

14 NCA officers with operational powers: pay and allowances

(1) The Secretary of State may, by regulations, provide for the establishment, maintenance and operation of procedures for the determination from time to time of—

(a) the rates of pay and allowances to be applied to the Director General and to NCA officers designated under section 10; and

(b) other associated terms and conditions of employment as the Director General or as an NCA officer designated under section 10.

(2) Regulations under this section may—

(a) provide for determinations with respect to matters to which the regulations relate to be made wholly or partly by reference to such factors, and the opinion or recommendations of such persons, as may be specified or described in the regulations;

(b) authorise the matters considered and determined in pursuance of the regulations to include matters applicable to times and periods before they are considered or determined.

(3) In this section 'associated terms and conditions' means such terms and conditions as may appear to the Secretary of State to fall to be determined in association with the determination of rates of pay and allowances.

15 Abolition of SOCA and NPIA

(1) The Serious Organised Crime Agency is abolished.

(2) The National Policing Improvement Agency is abolished.

(3) Schedule 8 (abolition of SOCA and NPIA) has effect.

16 Interpretation of Part 1

(1) In this Part—

'chief officer' means—

(a) the chief constable of a police force maintained under section 2 of the Police Act 1996 (police forces in England and Wales outside London);

(b) the Commissioner of Police of the Metropolis;

(c) the Commissioner of Police for the City of London;

(d) the chief constable of the Police Service of Scotland;

(e) the Chief Constable of the Police Service of Northern Ireland;

(f) the chief constable of the British Transport Police;

(g) the chief constable of the Civil Nuclear Constabulary;

(h) the chief constable of the Ministry of Defence Police;

'customs revenue official' has the same meaning as in the Borders, Citizenship and Immigration Act 2009 (see section 11 of that Act);

'Director General' means the Director General of the National Crime Agency;

'Director of Border Revenue' means the person designated under section 6 of the Borders, Citizenship and Immigration Act 2009;

'enactment' means any enactment, whenever passed or made, contained in—

(a) an Act of Parliament;

(b) an Act of the Scottish Parliament;

(c) Northern Ireland legislation;
(d) a Measure or Act of the National Assembly for Wales;
(e) an instrument made under any such Act, legislation or Measure;
(f) any other subordinate legislation (within the meaning of the Interpretation Act 1978);

'England and Wales police force' means—
(a) a police force maintained under section 2 of the Police Act 1996 (police forces in England and Wales outside London);
(b) the metropolitan police force;
(c) the City of London police force;

'functions' means all functions of any description, including powers and duties, whether conferred by an enactment or arising otherwise;

'general customs official' has the same meaning as in Borders, Citizenship and Immigration Act 2009 (see section 3 of that Act);

'Island law enforcement agency' means any person charged with the duty of investigating or prosecuting offences who operates in any of the Channel Islands or in the Isle of Man (apart from an Island police force);

'Island police force' means—
(a) the States of Jersey Police Force;
(b) the salaried police force of the Island of Guernsey;
(c) the Isle of Man Constabulary;

'local policing body' means—
(a) a police and crime commissioner;
(b) the Mayor's Office for Policing and Crime;
(c) the Common Council of the City of London as police authority for the City of London police area;

'NCA' means the National Crime Agency;

'NCA functions' means—
(a) functions of the NCA,
(b) functions of the Director General, and
(c) functions of other NCA officers;

'NCA officers' means—
(a) the Director General,
(b) the other National Crime Agency officers appointed under paragraph 9 of Schedule 1,
(c) persons who have been seconded to the NCA to serve as National Crime Agency officers under paragraph 13 of Schedule 1 (unless the context otherwise requires), and
(d) NCA specials;

'permitted purpose' means any of the following purposes—
(a) the prevention or detection of crime, whether in the United Kingdom or elsewhere;
(b) the investigation or prosecution of offences, whether in the United Kingdom or elsewhere;
(c) the prevention, detection or investigation of conduct for which penalties other than criminal penalties are provided under the law of any part of the United Kingdom or the law of any country or territory outside the United Kingdom;
(d) the exercise of any NCA functions (so far as not falling within any of paragraphs (a) to (c));
(e) purposes relating to civil proceedings (whether or not in the United Kingdom) which relate to a matter in respect of which the NCA has functions;
(f) compliance with an order of a court or tribunal (whether or not in the United Kingdom);
(g) the exercise of any function relating to the provision or operation of the

system of accreditation of financial investigators under section 3 of the Proceeds of Crime Act 2002;

(h) the exercise of any function of the prosecutor under Parts 2, 3 and 4 of the Proceeds of Crime Act 2002;

(i) the exercise of any function of—

(i) the Director of Public Prosecutions,

(ii) the Director of the Serious Fraud Office,

(iii) the Director of Public Prosecutions for Northern Ireland, or

(iv) the Scottish Ministers,

under, or in relation, to Part 5 or 8 of the Proceeds of Crime Act 2002;

(j) the exercise of any function of—

(i) an officer of Revenue and Customs,

(ii) a general customs official,

(iii) a customs revenue official,

(iv) an immigration officer,

(v) an accredited financial investigator, or

(vi) a constable,

under Chapter 3 of Part 5 of the Proceeds of Crime Act 2002;

(k) investigations or proceedings outside the United Kingdom which have led, or may lead, to the making of an external order (within the meaning of section 447 of the Proceeds of Crime Act 2002);

(l) the exercise of any function of any intelligence service (within the meaning of the Regulation of Investigatory Powers Act 2000);

(m) the exercise of any function under—

(i) Part 2 of the Football Spectators Act 1989, or

(ii) sections 104 to 106 of the Policing and Crime Act 2009;

(n) the exercise of any function relating to public health;

(o) the exercise of any function of the Financial Services Authority;

(p) the exercise of any function designated by the Secretary of State by order;

but a function may be designated under paragraph (p) only if the function appears to the Secretary of State to be a function of a public nature;

'policing body' means—

(a) a police and crime commissioner;

(b) the Mayor's Office for Policing and Crime;

(c) the Common Council of the City of London as police authority for the City of London police area;

(d) the Scottish Police Authority;

(e) the Northern Ireland Policing Board;

(f) the British Transport Police Authority;

(g) the Civil Nuclear Police Authority;

(h) the Secretary of State, in relation to the Ministry of Defence Police;

'special police force' means—

(a) the British Transport Police;

(b) the Civil Nuclear Constabulary;

(c) the Ministry of Defence Police;

'strategic partners' means—

(a) the Scottish Ministers;

(b) the Department of Justice in Northern Ireland;

(c) such persons as appear to the Secretary of State to represent the views of local policing bodies;

(d) such persons as appear to the Secretary of State to represent the views of the chief officers of England and Wales police forces;

(e) the chief constable of the Police Service of Scotland;

(f) the Chief Constable of the Police Service of Northern Ireland;

(g) the Commissioners for Her Majesty's Revenue and Customs;

(h) the Director of the Serious Fraud Office;

'UK law enforcement agency' means—
(a) the Commissioners for Her Majesty's Revenue and Customs;
(b) the Director of the Serious Fraud Office;
(c) the Director of Border Revenue;
(d) the Scottish Administration;
(e) a Northern Ireland department;
(f) any other person operating in England, Scotland, Northern Ireland or Wales charged with the duty of investigating or prosecuting offences (apart from a UK police force);

'UK police force' means—
(a) an England and Wales police force;
(b) the Police Service of Scotland;
(c) the Police Service of Northern Ireland;
(d) a special police force.

(2) In this Part—
(a) a reference to the powers and privileges of a constable is a reference to any powers and privileges of the constable, whether arising under an enactment or otherwise;
(b) a reference to the Police Service of Northern Ireland includes a reference to the Police Service of Northern Ireland Reserve.

(3) In any enactment—
(a) a reference to a National Crime Agency officer is to be construed as a reference to an NCA officer within the meaning of this Part;
(b) a reference to a function of the National Crime Agency is to be construed as a reference to an NCA function within the meaning of this Part (unless the context otherwise requires).

(4) Definitions of the following terms used in this Part, or other provision relating to the meanings of such terms, are contained in the provisions (outside this section) which are indicated.

Term	**Provision containing definition etc**
activities to combat crime (or a particular kind of crime)	section 1(11)
annual plan	section 4(3)
annual report	Part 2 of Schedule 2
crime-reduction function	section 1(4)
criminal intelligence function	section 1(5)
customs matter	section 9(8)
framework document	Part 1 of Schedule 2
NCA special	paragraph 15 of Schedule 1
operational power	section 9(8)
strategic priorities	section 3

PART 2
COURTS AND JUSTICE

. . .

20 Judicial appointments

Schedule 13 has effect. In that Schedule—

Part 1 provides for there to be no more than the equivalent of 12 full-time judges of the Supreme Court, rather than exactly 12 judges, and makes provision about their selection,

Part 2 contains provisions to facilitate greater diversity among judges,

Part 3 amends provisions about membership of the Judicial Appointments Commission,

Part 4—

(a) makes provision about selection for certain judicial appointments, and

(b) provides for the transfer, from the Lord Chancellor to the Lord Chief Justice or the Senior President of Tribunals, of functions in connection with selection for and appointment to judicial offices,

Part 5 amends the selection procedure for certain senior judicial appointments until Part 4 of the Schedule is in force,

Part 6 makes provision for the exercise of certain functions where the Master of the Rolls, the President of the Queen's Bench Division, the President of the Family Division or the Chancellor of the High Court is incapable of exercising the functions or one of those offices is vacant, and

Part 7 abolishes the office of assistant Recorder.

SUCCESSION TO THE CROWN ACT 2013
(2013, c 20)

1 Succession to the Crown not to depend on gender

In determining the succession to the Crown, the gender of a person born after 28 October 2011 does not give that person, or that person's descendants, precedence over any other person (whenever born).

2 Removal of disqualification arising from marriage to a Roman Catholic

(1) A person is not disqualified from succeeding to the Crown or from possessing it as a result of marrying a person of the Roman Catholic faith.

(2) Subsection (1) applies in relation to marriages occurring before the time of the coming into force of this section where the person concerned is alive at that time (as well as in relation to marriages occurring after that time).

3 Consent of Sovereign required to certain Royal Marriages

(1) A person who (when the person marries) is one of the 6 persons next in the line of succession to the Crown must obtain the consent of Her Majesty before marrying.

(2) Where any such consent has been obtained, it must be—

(a) signified under the Great Seal of the United Kingdom,

(b) declared in Council, and

(c) recorded in the books of the Privy Council.

(3) The effect of a person's failure to comply with subsection (1) is that the person and the person's descendants from the marriage are disqualified from succeeding to the Crown.

(4) The Royal Marriages Act 1772 (which provides that, subject to certain exceptions, a descendant of King George II may marry only with the consent of the Sovereign) is repealed.

(5) A void marriage under that Act is to be treated as never having been void if—

(a) neither party to the marriage was one of the 6 persons next in the line of succession to the Crown at the time of the marriage,

(b) no consent was sought under section 1 of that Act, or notice given under section 2 of that Act, in respect of the marriage,

(c) in all the circumstances it was reasonable for the person concerned not to have been aware at the time of the marriage that the Act applied to it, and

(d) no person acted, before the coming into force of this section, on the basis that the marriage was void.

(6) Subsection (5) applies for all purposes except those relating to the succession to the Crown.

4 Consequential amendments etc

(1) The Schedule contains consequential amendments.

(2) References (however expressed) in any enactment to the provisions of the Bill of Rights or the Act of Settlement relating to the succession to, or possession of, the Crown are to be read as including references to the provisions of this Act.

(3) The following enactments (which relate to the succession to, and possession of, the Crown) are subject to the provision made by this Act—

Article II of the Union with Scotland Act 1706;

Article II of the Union with England Act 1707;

Article Second of the Union with Ireland Act 1800;

Article Second of the Act of Union (Ireland) 1800.

TRIBUNALS (SCOTLAND) ACT 2014
(2014, asp 10)

1 Establishment of the Tribunals

(1) There are established two tribunals to be known as—

(a) the First-tier Tribunal for Scotland,

(b) the Upper Tribunal for Scotland.

(2) The Tribunals mentioned in subsection (1) are referred to in this Act—

(a) respectively as—

(i) the First-tier Tribunal,

(ii) the Upper Tribunal,

(b) collectively as the Scottish Tribunals.

(3) The constitution, operation and administration of the Scottish Tribunals are as provided for by or under this Act or another Act.

(4) The jurisdiction, powers and other functions of the Scottish Tribunals are as conferred by or under this Act or another Act.

2 Head of the Tribunals

(1) The Lord President is the Head of the Scottish Tribunals.

(2) In that capacity, the Lord President has the functions exercisable by him or her by virtue of this Act.

3 Upholding independence

(1) The following persons must uphold the independence of the members of the Scottish Tribunals—

(a) the First Minister,

(b) the Lord Advocate,

(c) the Scottish Ministers,

(d) members of the Scottish Parliament,

(e) all other persons with responsibility for matters relating to—

(i) the members of the Scottish Tribunals, or

(ii) the administration of justice,

where that responsibility is to be discharged only in or as regards Scotland.

(2) In particular, the First Minister, the Lord Advocate and the Scottish Ministers—

(a) must not seek to influence particular decisions of the members of the Scottish Tribunals through any special access to the members, and

(b) must have regard to the need for the members to have the support necessary to enable them to carry out their functions.

4 Assignment to office

(1) There is established the office to be known as that of President of the Scottish Tribunals.

(2) It is for the Lord President to assign a person to that office.

(3) An assignment of a person to that office continues for as long as the Lord President considers appropriate.

(4) The Lord President may nominate a Vice-President of the Upper Tribunal to act temporarily in that office—

(a) if a person assigned to that office is for the time being unable to act in it, or

(b) pending an assignment of a person to that office.

(5) A person assigned to that office under subsection (2) or nominated to act in it under subsection (4) must be a judge of the Court of Session (but may not be a temporary judge).

17 Sheriffs and judges

(1) By reason of holding judicial office, a person is eligible to act as a member of the First-tier Tribunal if the person is a sheriff (including a part-time sheriff).

(2) By reason of holding judicial office, a person is eligible to act as a member of the Upper Tribunal if the person is—

(a) apart from the Lord President and the President of Tribunals, a judge of the Court of Session (including a temporary judge),

(b) the Chairman of the Scottish Land Court, or

(c) a sheriff (except a part-time sheriff).

(3) A sheriff may act as a member of—

(a) the First-tier Tribunal, or

(b) the Upper Tribunal, only if authorised to do so by the President of Tribunals.

(4) A judge of the Court of Session or the Chairman of the Scottish Land Court may act as a member of the Upper Tribunal only if authorised to do so by the President of Tribunals (but see next instead for the Lord President and the President of Tribunals).

(5) By reason of holding office within the Scottish Tribunals, each of the Lord President and the President of Tribunals is a member of the Upper Tribunal and needs no further authorisation to act as such.

(6) An authorisation for the purpose of subsection (3)(a) or (b) or (4)—

(a) requires—

(i) the Lord President's approval (including as to the person to be authorised), and

(ii) the agreement of the person concerned,

(b) in the case of a sheriff (apart from a sheriff principal), also requires the concurrence of the relevant sheriff principal.

(7) An authorisation for the purpose of subsection (3)(a) or (b) or (4) remains in effect until such time as the President of Tribunals may determine (with the same approval, agreement and concurrence as is referred to in subsection (6)).

20 Chambers in the Tribunal

(1) The First-tier Tribunal is to be organised into a number of chambers, having regard to—

(a) the different subject-matters falling within the Tribunal's jurisdiction, and

(b) any other factors relevant in relation to the exercise of the Tribunal's functions.

(2) Accordingly, the Scottish Ministers may by regulations make provision for and in connection with—

(a) the organisation of the Tribunal as required by subsection (1),

(b) the allocation of the Tribunal's functions between the chambers.

46 Appeal from the Tribunal

(1) A decision of the First-tier Tribunal in any matter in a case before the Tribunal may be appealed to the Upper Tribunal.

(2) An appeal under this section is to be made—

(a) by a party in the case,

(b) on a point of law only.

(3) An appeal under this section requires the permission of—

(a) the First-tier Tribunal, or

(b) if the First-tier Tribunal refuses its permission, the Upper Tribunal.

(4) Such permission may be given in relation to an appeal under this section only if the First-tier Tribunal or (as the case may be) the Upper Tribunal is satisfied that there are arguable grounds for the appeal.

(5) This section—

(a) is subject to sections 43(4) and 55(2),

(b) does not apply in relation to an excluded decision.

48 Appeal from the Tribunal

(1) A decision of the Upper Tribunal in any matter in a case before the Tribunal may be appealed to the Court of Session.

(2) An appeal under this section is to be made—

(a) by a party in the case,

(b) on a point of law only.

(3) An appeal under this section requires the permission of—

(a) the Upper Tribunal, or

(b) if the Upper Tribunal refuses its permission, the Court of Session.

(4) Such permission may be given in relation to an appeal under this section only if the Upper Tribunal or (as the case may be) the Court of Session is satisfied that there are arguable grounds for the appeal.

(5) This section—

(a) is subject to sections 43(4) and 55(2),

(b) does not apply in relation to an excluded decision.

57 Judicial review cases

(1) Subsection (2) applies where a petition is made to the Court of Session for judicial review.

(2) The Court may by order remit the petition to the Upper Tribunal if—

(a) both of Conditions A and B are met, and

(b) having regard to the functions and expertise of the Tribunal in relation to the subject-matter of the petition, the Court considers that it is appropriate to do so.

(3) Condition A is that the petition does not seek anything other than the exercise of the Court's judicial review function.

(4) Condition B is that the petition falls within a category specified by an act of sederunt made by the Court for the purpose of this subsection.

COURTS REFORM (SCOTLAND) ACT 2014
(2014, asp 18)

8 Part-time sheriffs

(1) The Scottish Ministers may appoint individuals to act as sheriffs; and individuals so appointed are to be known as 'part-time sheriffs'.

(2) The Scottish Ministers may appoint an individual only if—

(a) the individual is qualified for appointment (see section 14), and

(b) the Scottish Ministers have consulted the Lord President of the Court of Session before making the appointment.

(3) Subject to section 20, an appointment as a part-time sheriff lasts for 5 years.

(4) A part-time sheriff may exercise the jurisdiction and powers that attach to the office of sheriff in every sheriffdom, and does not need a commission for that purpose.

(5) A part-time sheriff is subject to such instructions, arrangements and other provisions as may be made under this Act by the sheriff principal of the sheriffdom in which the part-time sheriff is for the time being sitting.

9 Reappointment of part-time sheriffs

(1) A part-time sheriff whose appointment comes to an end by virtue of the expiry of the 5 year period mentioned in section 8(3) is to be reappointed unless—

(a) the part-time sheriff declines reappointment,

(b) a sheriff principal has made a recommendation to the Scottish Ministers against the reappointment, or

(c) the part-time sheriff has sat for fewer than 50 days in total in that 5 year period.

(2) Section 8 (apart from subsection (2)) applies to a reappointment under subsection (1) as it applies to an appointment.

(3) A part-time sheriff whose appointment comes to an end by resignation under section 20 may be reappointed.

(4) Section 8 applies to a reappointment under subsection (3) as it applies to an appointment.

16 Remuneration

(1) Each sheriff principal and sheriff is to be paid such salary as the Treasury may determine.

(2) Such salary is to be paid quarterly or otherwise in every year, as the Treasury may determine.

(3) Each summary sheriff is to be paid such remuneration as the Scottish Ministers may determine.

(4) The Scottish Ministers may determine different amounts of remuneration for—

(a) different summary sheriffs, or

(b) different descriptions of summary sheriff.

(5) Each judicial officer mentioned in subsection (7) is to be paid such remuneration as the Scottish Ministers may determine.

(6) The Scottish Ministers may determine different amounts of remuneration for—

(a) different judicial officers mentioned in subsection (7), or

(b) different descriptions of such judicial officers.

(7) The judicial officers are—

[(za) a temporary sheriff principal,]

(a) a part-time sheriff,

(b) a part-time summary sheriff,

(c) an individual appointed to act as a sheriff or summary sheriff under section 12(1).

(8) Subsection (9) applies in relation to—

(a) a sheriff principal of a sheriffdom authorised under section 30 to perform the functions of a sheriff principal in another sheriffdom, and

(b) a sheriff of a sheriffdom ('sheriffdom A') directed under section 31 to perform the functions of sheriff in another sheriffdom in addition to sheriffdom A.

(9) The sheriff principal or sheriff is to be paid, in respect of the additional functions, such remuneration as appears to the Secretary of State, with the consent of the Treasury, to be reasonable in all the circumstances.

(10) Subsection (11) applies in relation to a summary sheriff of a sheriffdom ('sheriffdom B') directed under section 31 to perform the functions of a summary sheriff in another sheriffdom in addition to sheriffdom B.

(11) The summary sheriff is to be paid, in respect of the additional functions, such remuneration as appears to the Scottish Ministers to be reasonable in all the circumstances.

(12) Salaries and remuneration under subsections (1) to (11) are to be paid by the Scottish Courts and Tribunals Service.

(13) Sums required by the Scottish Courts and Tribunals Service for the payment of a salary under subsection (1) or remuneration under subsection (3) are charged on the Scottish Consolidated Fund.

21 Tribunal to consider fitness for office

(1) The First Minister must, if requested to do so by the Lord President of the Court of Session, constitute a tribunal to investigate and report on whether an individual holding a judicial office mentioned in subsection (3) is unfit to hold the office by reason of inability, neglect of duty or misbehaviour.

(2) Subject to subsection (1), the First Minister may, in such circumstances as the First Minister thinks fit and after consulting the Lord President, constitute such a tribunal.

(3) The judicial offices are—

(a) sheriff principal,

(b) sheriff,

(c) summary sheriff,

(d) part-time sheriff, and

(e) part-time summary sheriff.

(4) A tribunal constituted under this section is to consist of—

(a) one individual who is a qualifying member of the Judicial Committee of the Privy Council,

(b) one individual who holds the relevant judicial office,

(c) one individual who is, and has been for at least 10 years—

(i) an advocate, or

(ii) a solicitor, and

(d) one individual who—

(i) is not and never has been a qualifying member of the Judicial Committee of the Privy Council,

(ii) does not hold and never has held a judicial office mentioned in subsection (3), and

(iii) is not and never has been an advocate or solicitor.

(5) In subsection (4)—

'a qualifying member of the Judicial Committee of the Privy Council' means someone who is a member of that Committee by virtue of section 1(2)(a) of the Judicial Committee Act 1833 (that is, someone who holds or has held high judicial office),

'the relevant judicial office' means—

(a) in respect of an investigation into whether an individual is fit to hold the office of sheriff principal, that office,

(b) in respect of an investigation into whether an individual is fit to hold the office of sheriff or part-time sheriff, the office of sheriff,

(c) in respect of an investigation into whether an individual is fit to hold the office of summary sheriff or part-time summary sheriff, the office of summary sheriff.

(6) It is for the First Minister, with the agreement of the Lord President, to select persons to be members of a tribunal constituted under this section.

(7) The person who is an individual mentioned in subsection (4)(a) is to chair the tribunal and has a casting vote.

22 Tribunal investigations: suspension from office

(1) Subsection (2) applies where the Lord President of the Court of Session has requested that the First Minister constitute a tribunal under section 21.

(2) The Lord President may, at any time before the tribunal reports to the First Minister, suspend from office the individual who is, or is to be, the subject of the tribunal's investigation.

(3) Such a suspension lasts until the Lord President orders otherwise.

(4) A tribunal constituted under section 21 may, at any time before the tribunal reports to the First Minister, recommend in writing to the First Minister that the individual who is the subject of the tribunal's investigation be suspended from office.

(5) On receiving such a recommendation, the First Minister may suspend the individual from office.

(6) Such a suspension lasts until the First Minister orders otherwise.

(7) Suspension of an individual from the office of sheriff principal, sheriff or summary sheriff under this section does not affect any remuneration payable to, or in respect of, the individual in respect of the period of suspension.

23 Further provision about tribunals

(1) A tribunal constituted under section 21 may require any person—

(a) to attend its proceedings for the purpose of giving evidence,

(b) to produce documents in the person's custody or under the person's control.

(2) A person on whom such a requirement is imposed is not obliged—

(a) to answer any question which the person would be entitled to refuse to answer in a court in Scotland,

(b) to produce any document which the person would be entitled to refuse to produce in such a court.

(3) Subsection (4) applies where a person on whom a requirement has been imposed under subsection (1)—

(a) refuses or fails, without reasonable excuse, to comply with the requirement,

(b) refuses or fails, without reasonable excuse, to answer any question while attending the tribunal proceedings to give evidence,

(c) deliberately alters, conceals or destroys any document that the person is required to produce.

(4) The Court of Session may, on an application made to it by the tribunal—

(a) make such order for enforcing compliance as it sees fit, or

(b) deal with the matter as if it were a contempt of the Court.

(5) The Court of Session may by act of sederunt make provision as to the procedure to be followed by and before a tribunal constituted under section 21.

(6) The Scottish Ministers—

(a) must pay such expenses as they consider are reasonably required to be incurred to enable a tribunal constituted under section 21 to carry out its functions, and

(b) may pay such remuneration to, and such expenses of, the members of such a tribunal as they think fit.

24 Tribunal report

(1) The report of a tribunal constituted under section 21 must—

(a) be in writing,

(b) contain reasons for its conclusion, and

(c) be submitted to the First Minister.

(2) The First Minister must lay the report before the Scottish Parliament.

25 Removal from office

(1) The First Minister may remove an individual from the office of sheriff principal, sheriff, part-time sheriff, summary sheriff or part-time summary sheriff—

(a) if a tribunal constituted under section 21 reports to the First Minister that the individual is unfit to hold that office by reason of inability, neglect of duty or misbehaviour, and

(b) only after the First Minister has laid the report before the Scottish Parliament under section 24(2).

(2) The First Minister may remove a sheriff principal, sheriff or summary sheriff under subsection (1) only by order.

(3) Such an order is subject to the negative procedure.

27 Sheriff principal's responsibility for efficient disposal of business in sheriff courts

(1) The sheriff principal of a sheriffdom is responsible for ensuring the efficient disposal of business in the sheriff courts of the sheriffdom.

(2) The sheriff principal must make such arrangements as appear necessary or expedient for the purpose of carrying out the responsibility imposed by subsection (1).

(3) In particular, the sheriff principal may—

(a) provide for the allocation of business among the judiciary of the sheriffdom,

(b) make special provision of a temporary nature for the disposal of any business by any member of the judiciary of the sheriffdom in addition to or in place of that member's own duties.

(4) If, in carrying out the responsibility imposed by subsection (1), the sheriff principal gives a direction of an administrative character to a person mentioned in subsection (5), the person must comply with the direction.

(5) Those persons are—

(a) any other member of the judiciary of the sheriffdom,

(b) a member of the staff of the Scottish Courts and Tribunals Service.

(6) Nothing in subsections (1) to (4) enables a member of the judiciary of the sheriffdom to dispose of any business which that member could not otherwise competently dispose of in the exercise of the jurisdiction and powers that attach to the member's office.

(7) Subsections (1) to (4) are subject to section 2(2)(a) and (3) of the Judiciary and Courts (Scotland) Act 2008 (the Head of the Scottish Judiciary's responsibility for efficient disposal of business in the Scottish courts).

28 Sheriff principal's power to fix sittings of sheriff courts

(1) The sheriff principal of a sheriffdom may by order prescribe—

(a) the number of sittings of sheriff courts to be held at each place designated for the holding of sheriff courts in the sheriffdom,

(b) the days on which, and the times at which, those sittings are to be held, and

(c) the descriptions of business to be disposed of at those sittings.

(2) The sheriff principal must publish notice of the matters prescribed by an order under subsection (1) in such manner as the sheriff principal thinks appropriate in order to bring those matters to the attention of persons having an interest in them.

(3) Subsection (1) is subject to section 2(2)(a) and (3) of the Judiciary and Courts (Scotland) Act 2008.

29 Lord President's power to exercise functions under sections 27 and 28

(1) Subsection (2) applies where in any case the Lord President of the Court of Session considers that the exercise by the sheriff principal of a sheriffdom of a function under section 27 or 28—

(a) is prejudicial to the efficient disposal of business in the sheriff courts of the sheriffdom,

(b) is prejudicial to the efficient organisation or administration of those courts, or

(c) is otherwise against the interest of the public.

(2) The Lord President may in that case—

(a) rescind the sheriff principal's exercise of the function, and

(b) exercise the function.

(3) Subsections (1) and (2) apply in relation to a failure to exercise a function mentioned in subsection (1) as they apply to the exercise of such a function, but as if paragraph (a) of subsection (2) were omitted.

(4) The exercise of a function by the Lord President by virtue of subsection (2)(b) is to be treated as if it were the exercise of the function by the sheriff principal.

41 Power to confer all-Scotland jurisdiction for specified cases

(1) The Scottish Ministers may by order provide that the jurisdiction of a sheriff of a specified sheriffdom sitting at a specified sheriff court extends territorially throughout Scotland for the purposes of dealing with specified types of civil proceedings.

(2) In subsection (1), 'specified' means specified in an order under that subsection.

(3) An order under subsection (1) may be made only with the consent of the Lord President of the Court of Session.

(4) An order under subsection (1) does not affect—

(a) in relation to the sheriffdom specified in the order, the jurisdiction or competence of a sheriff of any other sheriffdom to deal with proceedings of the type specified in the order, or

(b) in relation to the sheriff court specified in the order, the jurisdiction or competence of a sheriff sitting at any other sheriff court to deal with such proceedings.

(5) This section does not apply in relation to proceedings under the Children's Hearings (Scotland) Act 2011.

50 Appointment of sheriffs as Appeal Sheriffs

(1) The Lord President of the Court of Session may appoint persons holding the office of sheriff to hold office also as Appeal Sheriffs.

(2) The Lord President may appoint as many Appeal Sheriffs under subsection (1) as the Lord President considers necessary for the purposes of the Sheriff Appeal Court.

(3) A person may be appointed under subsection (1) only if the individual has held office as a sheriff for at least 5 years.

(4) The appointment of a sheriff as an Appeal Sheriff does not affect the sheriff's appointment as a sheriff and the sheriff may accordingly continue to act in that capacity.

(5) A person holding office as an Appeal Sheriff under this section ceases to hold that office if the person ceases to hold office as a sheriff.

(6) If a person holding office as an Appeal Sheriff under this section is suspended from the office of sheriff for any period, the person is also suspended from office as an Appeal Sheriff for the same period.

(7) The Lord President may, with the consent of a majority of the sheriffs principal, remove a sheriff from office as an Appeal Sheriff.

(8) Removal of a sheriff from the office of Appeal Sheriff under subsection (7) does not affect the sheriff's appointment as a sheriff.

128 Abolition of the office of stipendiary magistrate

(1) The office of stipendiary magistrate is abolished.

(2) Subsection (3) applies to a person who, immediately before this section comes into force, holds office as a full-time stipendiary magistrate.

(3) The person is to be appointed, by virtue of this subsection, as a summary sheriff unless the person declines the appointment.

(4) Subsection (3) applies regardless of whether the person is qualified for appointment as a summary sheriff.

(5) Subsection (6) applies to a person who, immediately before this section comes into force, holds office as a part-time stipendiary magistrate.

(6) The person is to be appointed, by virtue of this subsection, as a part-time summary sheriff unless the person declines the appointment.

(7) Subsection (6) applies regardless of whether the person is qualified for appointment as a part-time summary sheriff.

(8) A person appointed—

(a) as a summary sheriff by virtue of subsection (3) is to be treated for all purposes as if appointed as such under section 5(2),

(b) as a part-time summary sheriff by virtue of subsection (6) is to be treated for all purposes as if appointed as such under section 10(1).

HOUSE OF LORDS REFORM ACT 2014
(2014, c 24)

4 Effect of ceasing to be a member

(1) This section applies where a person ceases to be a member of the House of Lords in accordance with this Act.

(2) The person becomes disqualified from attending the proceedings of the House of Lords (including the proceedings of a Committee of the House).

(3) Accordingly, the person shall not be entitled to receive a writ to attend the House (whether under section 1 of the Life Peerages Act 1958, by virtue of the dignity conferred by virtue of appointment as a Lord of Appeal in Ordinary, by virtue of a hereditary peerage or as a Lord Spiritual) and may not attend the House in pursuance of a writ already received.

(4) If the person is a hereditary peer who is excepted from section 1 of the House of Lords Act 1999 by virtue of section 2 of that Act, the person ceases to be excepted from section 1 of that Act (and accordingly section 3 of that Act applies (removal of disqualification on voting in parliamentary elections or being an MP)).

(5) If the person is a peer other than a hereditary peer, the person is not, by virtue of that peerage, disqualified for—

(a) voting at elections to the House of Commons, or

(b) being, or being elected as, a member of that House.

(6) In relation to a peer who ceases to be a member of the House of Lords in accordance with this Act, any reference in section 1(3) or (4)(b) of the Representation of the People Act 1985 to a register of parliamentary electors is to be read as including—

(a) any register of local government electors in Great Britain, and

(b) any register of local electors in Northern Ireland,

which was required to be published on any date before the date on which the peer ceased to be a member.

(7) The Standing Orders of the House required by section 2(4) of the House of Lords Act 1999 (filling of vacancies) must make provision requiring the holding of a by-election to fill any vacancy which arises under this Act among the people excepted from section 1 of that Act in consequence of an election.

(8) Subject to section 3(7), a person who ceases to be a member of the House of Lords in accordance with this Act may not subsequently become a member of that House.

HOUSE OF LORDS (EXPULSION AND SUSPENSION) ACT 2015
(2015, c 14)

1 Expulsion and suspension of members of the House of Lords

(1) Standing Orders of the House of Lords may make provision under which the House of Lords may by resolution—

(a) expel a member of the House of Lords, or

(b) suspend a member of the House of Lords for the period specified in the resolution.

(2) A person expelled by virtue of this section ceases to be a member.

(3) A person suspended by virtue of this section remains a member during the period of suspension, but during that period the person—

(a) is not entitled to receive writs of summons to attend the House of Lords, and

(b) despite any writ of summons previously issued to the person, is disqualified from sitting or voting in the House of Lords or a committee of the House of Lords.

(4) A resolution passed by virtue of subsection (1) must state that, in the opinion of the House of Lords, the conduct giving rise to the resolution—

(a) occurred after the coming into force of this Act, or

(b) occurred before the coming into force of this Act and was not public knowledge before that time.

LORDS SPIRITUAL (WOMEN) ACT 2015
(2015, c 18)

1 Vacancies among the Lords Spiritual

(1) This section applies where—

(a) a vacancy arises among the Lords Spiritual in the House of Lords in the 10 years beginning with the day on which this Act comes into force,

(b) at the time the vacancy arises there is at least one eligible bishop who is a woman, and

(c) the person who would otherwise be entitled to fill the vacancy under section 5 of the Bishoprics Act 1878 is a man.

(2) If at the time the vacancy arises there is only one eligible bishop who is a woman, the vacancy is to be filled by the issue of writs of summons to her.

(3) If at the time the vacancy arises there are two or more eligible bishops who are women, the vacancy is to be filled by the issue of writs of summons to the one whose election as a bishop of a diocese in England was confirmed first.

(4) In this section 'eligible bishop' means a bishop of a diocese in England who is not yet entitled in that capacity to the issue of writs of summons.

(5) The reference in subsection (1) to a vacancy does not include a vacancy arising by the avoidance of the see of Canterbury, York, London, Durham or Winchester.

RECALL OF MPs ACT 2015
(2015, c 25)

1 How an MP becomes subject to a recall petition process

(1) An MP becomes subject to a recall petition process if—

(a) the first, second or third recall condition has been met in relation to the MP, and

(b) the Speaker gives notice of that fact under section 5.

(2) In this Act 'recall petition' means a petition calling—

(a) for an MP to lose his or her seat in the House of Commons, and

(b) for a by-election to be held to decide who should be the MP for the constituency in question.

(3) The first recall condition is that—

(a) the MP has, after becoming an MP, been convicted in the United Kingdom of an offence and sentenced or ordered to be imprisoned or detained, and

(b) the appeal period expires without the conviction, sentence or order having being overturned on appeal.

Sections 2 to 4 contain more about the first recall condition.

(4) The second recall condition is that, following on from a report from the Committee on Standards in relation to the MP, the House of Commons orders the suspension of the MP from the service of the House for a specified period of the requisite length.

(5) A specified period is 'of the requisite length' for the purposes of subsection (4) if—

(a) where the period is expressed as a number of sitting days, the period specified is of at least 10 sitting days, or

(b) in any other case, the period specified (however expressed) is a period of at least 14 days.

(6) For the purposes of subsection (4) it does not matter—

(a) when the period of suspension starts, and

(b) where that period is expressed as a number of sitting days, what provision (if any) is made by the House regarding what does, or does not, count as a sitting day for the purpose of calculating that period.

(7) The reference in subsection (4) to the Committee on Standards is to any committee of the House of Commons concerned with the standards of conduct of individual members of that House.

(8) Any question arising under subsection (7) is to be determined by the Speaker.

(9) The third recall condition is that—

(a) the MP has, after becoming an MP, been convicted of an offence under section 10 of the Parliamentary Standards Act 2009 (offence of providing false or misleading information for allowances claims), and

(b) the appeal period expires without the conviction having been overturned on appeal.

Sections 2 to 4 contain more about the third recall condition.

(10) The provision made by or under this Act does not affect other ways in which an MP's seat may be vacated, whether—

(a) by the MP's disqualification – for example, under the Representation of the People Act 1981 (disqualification of certain offenders), or

(b) by the MP's death or otherwise.

(11) The loss by an MP of his or her seat under this Act as a result of a recall petition does not prevent him or her standing in the resulting by-election.

2 The first and third recall conditions: further provision

(1) In section 1(3) and (9) (the first and third recall conditions)—

(a) the reference to an offence includes an offence committed before the MP became an MP and an offence committed before the day on which section 1 comes into force, but

(b) the reference to an MP being convicted of an offence is only to an MP being convicted of an offence on or after the day on which section 1 comes into force.

(2) The reference in section 1(3) to an offence does not include an offence mentioned in section 1(9).

(3) The reference in section 1(3) to an MP being sentenced or ordered—

(a) includes the MP being sentenced or ordered where the sentence or order is suspended,

(b) does not include the MP being remanded in custody, and

(c) does not include the MP being authorised to be detained under mental health legislation if there is no sentence or order for imprisonment or detention other than under that legislation.

(4) 'Mental health legislation' means—

(a) the Mental Health Act 1983,

(b) Part 6 or section 200(2)(b) of the Criminal Procedure (Scotland) Act 1995, or

(c) the Mental Health (Northern Ireland) Order 1986 (SI 1986/595 (NI 4)).

(5) For the purposes of this Act the time at which a person becomes an MP is the beginning of the day after—

(a) the polling day for the parliamentary election at which the person is elected as an MP, or

(b) where the person has been elected as an MP more than once, the polling day for the parliamentary election at which the person was last so elected.

. . .

4 The first and third recall conditions: courts to notify the Speaker

(1) This section applies if an MP, after becoming an MP—

(a) is convicted in the United Kingdom of an offence and sentenced or ordered to be imprisoned or detained within the meaning of section 1(3) (see section 2), or

(b) is convicted of an offence mentioned in section 1(9) within the meaning of that provision (see section 2).

(2) The court that imposes the sentence or order in relation to the conviction must notify the Speaker—

(a) of the conviction and of the sentence or order, and

(b) whether an appeal may be brought in respect of the conviction, sentence or order.

(3) Subsections (4) to (6) apply in a case in which an appeal is brought in respect of the conviction, sentence or order (including from a court that determines or otherwise disposes of such an appeal).

(4) The court to which the appeal is brought must notify the Speaker that an appeal has been brought in respect of the conviction, sentence or order.

(5) Where the appeal is determined or otherwise disposed of, the relevant court must notify the Speaker—

(a) that the appeal has been determined or otherwise disposed of,

(b) that—

(i) in a case within subsection (1)(a), the conviction, sentence or order has, or has not, been overturned on appeal;

(ii) in a case within subsection (1)(b), the conviction has, or has not, been overturned on appeal, and

(c) whether any further appeal may be brought in respect of the conviction, sentence or order.

(6) 'The relevant court' means—

(a) the court to which the appeal is brought, or

(b) if that court remits the matter to another court, that other court.

(7) Section 3(5) and (6) (interpretation of references to an appeal and to the determination of an appeal) apply in relation to this section as they apply in relation to section 3, except that references in this section to an appeal do include a petition to the nobile officium.

(8) A court is not required under this section to notify the Speaker if, at any time since the application of the section, the MP's seat has been vacated (whether by the MP's disqualification or death, or otherwise).

5 Speaker's notice that first, second or third recall condition has been met

(1) As soon as reasonably practicable after becoming aware that the first, second or third recall condition has been met in relation to an MP, the Speaker must give notice of that fact to the petition officer for the MP's constituency.

(2) But subsection (1) does not apply if it would require the Speaker to give notice at a time—

(a) within the period of 6 months ending with the polling day for the next parliamentary general election,

(b) when the MP is already subject to a recall petition process, or

(c) when the MP's seat has already been vacated (whether by the MP's disqualification or death, or otherwise).

(3) For the purposes of subsection (2)(a), the possibility that, after the time mentioned in that subsection, the polling day for a parliamentary general election will be altered by virtue of section 1(5) or 2(7) of the Fixed-term Parliaments Act 2011 is to be disregarded.

(4) For the purposes of subsection (2)(b), an MP is 'subject to a recall petition process' during the period beginning with the giving of a notice under this section in relation to the MP and ending with—

(a) the receipt by the petition officer of a notice under section 13(6) (early termination of recall petition process) in relation to the recall petition in question, or

(b) the giving by the petition officer of a notice under section 14(2)(b) (determination of whether recall petition successful) of the outcome of that recall petition.

(5) A notice under this section—

(a) must specify the day on which it is given,

(b) must specify which of the recall conditions has been met in relation to the MP, and

(c) in a case in which the first recall condition has been met, must specify the offence of which the MP has been convicted.

(6) For the purposes of this Act, a notice under this section—

(a) is to be treated as given on the day specified in it under subsection (5)(a), and

(b) is to be treated as received by the petition officer on the first working day after the day on which it is given.

(7) References in this Act to a 'Speaker's notice' are to a notice under this section.

EUROPEAN UNION REFERENDUM ACT 2015
(2015, c 36)

1 The referendum

(1) A referendum is to be held on whether the United Kingdom should remain a member of the European Union.

(2) The Secretary of State must, by regulations, appoint the day on which the referendum is to be held.

(3) The day appointed under subsection (2)—

(a) must be no later than 31 December 2017,

(b) must not be 5 May 2016, and

(c) must not be 4 May 2017.

(4) The question that is to appear on the ballot papers is—

'Should the United Kingdom remain a member of the European Union or leave the European Union?'

(5) The alternative answers to that question that are to appear on the ballot papers are—

'Remain a member of the European Union
Leave the European Union'.

(6) In Wales, there must also appear on the ballot papers—

(a) the following Welsh version of the question—

'A ddylai'r Deyrnas Unedig aros yn aelod o'r Undeb Ewropeaidd neu adael yr Undeb Ewropeaidd?', and

(b) the following Welsh versions of the alternative answers—

'Aros yn aelod o'r Undeb Ewropeaidd
Gadael yr Undeb Ewropeaidd'.

2 Entitlement to vote in the referendum

(1) Those entitled to vote in the referendum are—

(a) the persons who, on the date of the referendum, would be entitled to vote as electors at a parliamentary election in any constituency,

(b) the persons who, on that date, are disqualified by reason of being peers from voting as electors at parliamentary elections but—

(i) would be entitled to vote as electors at a local government election in any electoral area in Great Britain,

(ii) would be entitled to vote as electors at a local election in any district electoral area in Northern Ireland, or

(iii) would be entitled to vote as electors at a European Parliamentary election in any electoral region by virtue of section 3 of the Representation of the People Act 1985 (peers resident outside the United Kingdom), and

(c) the persons who, on the date of the referendum—

(i) would be entitled to vote in Gibraltar as electors at a European Parliamentary election in the combined electoral region in which Gibraltar is comprised, and

(ii) fall within subsection (2).

(2) A person falls within this subsection if the person is either—

(a) a Commonwealth citizen, or

(b) a citizen of the Republic of Ireland.

(3) In subsection (1)(b)(i) 'local government election' includes a municipal election in the City of London (that is, an election to the office of mayor, alderman, common councilman or sheriff and also the election of any officer elected by the mayor, aldermen and liverymen in common hall).

CRIMINAL JUSTICE (SCOTLAND) ACT 2016
(2016, asp 1)

1 Power of a constable

(1) A constable may arrest a person without a warrant if the constable has reasonable grounds for suspecting that the person has committed or is committing an offence.

(2) In relation to an offence not punishable by imprisonment, a constable may arrest a person under subsection (1) only if the constable is satisfied that it would not be in the interests of justice to delay the arrest in order to seek a warrant for the person's arrest.

(3) Without prejudice to the generality of subsection (2), it would not be in the interests of justice to delay an arrest in order to seek a warrant if the constable reasonably believes that unless the person is arrested without delay the person will—

(a) continue committing the offence, or

(b) obstruct the course of justice in any way, including by—

(i) seeking to avoid arrest, or

(ii) interfering with witnesses or evidence.

(4) For the avoidance of doubt, an offence is to be regarded as not punishable by imprisonment for the purpose of subsection (2) only if no person convicted of the offence can be sentenced to imprisonment in respect of it.

3 Information to be given on arrest

When a constable arrests a person (or as soon afterwards as is reasonably practicable), a constable must inform the person—

(a) that the person is under arrest,

(b) of the general nature of the offence in respect of which the person is arrested [if any],

(c) of the reason for the arrest,

(d) that the person is under no obligation to say anything, other than to give the information specified in section 34(4), and

(e) of the person's right to have—

(i) intimation sent to a solicitor under section 43, and

(ii) access to a solicitor under section 44.

38 Right to have intimation sent to other person

(1) A person in police custody has the right to have intimation sent to another person of—

(a) the fact that the person is in custody,

(b) the place where the person is in custody.

(2) Intimation under subsection (1) must be sent—

(a) where a constable believes that the person in custody is under 16 years of age, regardless of whether the person requests that it be sent,

(b) in any other case, if the person requests that it be sent.

(3) The person to whom intimation is to be sent under subsection (1) is—

(a) where a constable believes that the person in custody is under 16 years of age, a parent of the person,

(b) in any other case, an adult reasonably named by the person in custody.

(4) Intimation under subsection (1) must be sent—

(a) as soon as reasonably practicable, or

(b) if subsection (5) applies, with no more delay than is necessary.

(5) This subsection applies where an appropriate constable considers some delay to be necessary in the interests of—

(a) the investigation or prevention of crime,

(b) the apprehension of offenders, or

(c) safeguarding and promoting the wellbeing of the person in custody, where a constable believes that person to be under 18 years of age.

(6) In subsection (5), 'an appropriate constable' means a constable who—

(a) is of the rank of sergeant or above, and

(b) has not been involved in the investigation in connection with which the person is in custody.

(7) The sending of intimation may be delayed by virtue of subsection (5)(c) only for so long as is necessary to ascertain whether a local authority will arrange for someone to visit the person in custody under section 41(2).

(8) In this section and section 39—

'adult' means person who is at least 18 years of age,

'parent' includes guardian and any person who has the care of the person in custody.

43 Right to have intimation sent to solicitor

(1) A person who is in police custody has the right to have intimation sent to a solicitor of any or all of the following—

(a) the fact that the person is in custody,

(b) the place where the person is in custody,

(c) that the solicitor's professional assistance is required by the person,

(d) if the person has been officially accused of an offence—
(i) whether the person is to be released from custody, and
(ii) where the person is not to be released, the court before which the person is to be brought in accordance with section 21(2) and the date on which the person is to be brought before that court.

(2) Where the person requests that intimation be sent under subsection (1), the intimation must be sent as soon as reasonably practicable.

44 Right to consultation with solicitor

(1) A person who is in police custody has the right to have a private consultation with a solicitor at any time.

(2) In exceptional circumstances, the person's exercise of the right under subsection (1) may be delayed so far as that is necessary in the interests of—
(a) the investigation or the prevention of crime, or
(b) the apprehension of offenders.

(3) A decision to delay the person's exercise of the right under subsection (1) may be taken only by a constable who—
(a) is of the rank of sergeant or above, and
(b) has not been involved in the investigation in connection with which the person is in custody.

(4) In subsection (1), 'consultation' means consultation by such method as may be appropriate in the circumstances and includes (for example) consultation by telephone.

54 Abolition of pre-enactment powers of arrest

A constable has no power to arrest a person without a warrant in respect of an offence that has been or is being committed other than—
(a) the power of arrest conferred by section 1,
(b) the power of arrest conferred by section 41(1) of the Terrorism Act 2000.

INVESTIGATORY POWERS ACT 2016
(2016, c 25)

PART 6
BULK WARRANTS

Chapter 1
Bulk interception warrants

136 Bulk interception warrants

(1) For the purposes of this Act a 'bulk interception warrant' is a warrant issued under this Chapter which meets conditions A and B.

(2) Condition A is that the main purpose of the warrant is one or more of the following—
(a) the interception of overseas-related communications (see subsection (3));
(b) the obtaining of secondary data from such communications (see section 137).

(3) In this Chapter 'overseas-related communications' means—
(a) communications sent by individuals who are outside the British Islands, or
(b) communications received by individuals who are outside the British Islands.

(4) Condition B is that the warrant authorises or requires the person to whom it is addressed to secure, by any conduct described in the warrant, any one or more of the following activities—

(a) the interception, in the course of their transmission by means of a telecommunication system, of communications described in the warrant;

(b) the obtaining of secondary data from communications transmitted by means of such a system and described in the warrant;

(c) the selection for examination, in any manner described in the warrant, of intercepted content or secondary data obtained under the warrant;

(d) the disclosure, in any manner described in the warrant, of anything obtained under the warrant to the person to whom the warrant is addressed or to any person acting on that person's behalf.

(5) A bulk interception warrant also authorises the following conduct (in addition to the conduct described in the warrant)—

(a) any conduct which it is necessary to undertake in order to do what is expressly authorised or required by the warrant, including—

(i) the interception of communications not described in the warrant, and

(ii) conduct for obtaining secondary data from such communications;

(b) conduct by any person which is conduct in pursuance of a requirement imposed by or on behalf of the person to whom the warrant is addressed to be provided with assistance in giving effect to the warrant;

(c) any conduct for obtaining related systems data from any telecommunications operator.

(6) For the purposes of subsection (5)(c)—

'related systems data', in relation to a warrant, means systems data relating to a relevant communication or to the sender or recipient, or intended recipient, of a relevant communication (whether or not a person), and

'relevant communication', in relation to a warrant, means—

(a) any communication intercepted in accordance with the warrant in the course of its transmission by means of a telecommunication system, or

(b) any communication from which secondary data is obtained under the warrant.

137 Obtaining secondary data

(1) This section has effect for the purposes of this Chapter.

(2) References to obtaining secondary data from a communication transmitted by means of a telecommunication system are references to obtaining such data—

(a) while the communication is being transmitted, or

(b) at any time when the communication is stored in or by the system (whether before or after its transmission),

and references to secondary data obtained under a bulk interception warrant are to be read accordingly.

(3) 'Secondary data', in relation to a communication transmitted by means of a telecommunication system, means any data falling within subsection (4) or (5).

(4) The data falling within this subsection is systems data which is comprised in, included as part of, attached to or logically associated with the communication (whether by the sender or otherwise).

(5) The data falling within this subsection is identifying data which—

(a) is comprised in, included as part of, attached to or logically associated with the communication (whether by the sender or otherwise),

(b) is capable of being logically separated from the remainder of the communication, and

(c) if it were so separated, would not reveal anything of what might reasonably be considered to be the meaning (if any) of the communication, disregarding any meaning arising from the fact of the communication or from any data relating to the transmission of the communication.

(6) For the meaning of 'systems data' and 'identifying data', see section 263.

138 Power to issue bulk interception warrants

(1) The Secretary of State may, on an application made by or on behalf of the head of an intelligence service, issue a bulk interception warrant if—

(a) the Secretary of State considers that the main purpose of the warrant is one or more of the following—

(i) the interception of overseas-related communications, and

(ii) the obtaining of secondary data from such communications,

(b) the Secretary of State considers that the warrant is necessary—

(i) in the interests of national security, or

(ii) on that ground and on any other grounds falling within subsection (2),

(c) the Secretary of State considers that the conduct authorised by the warrant is proportionate to what is sought to be achieved by that conduct,

(d) the Secretary of State considers that—

(i) each of the specified operational purposes (see section 142) is a purpose for which the examination of intercepted content or secondary data obtained under the warrant is or may be necessary, and

(ii) the examination of intercepted content or secondary data for each such purpose is necessary on any of the grounds on which the Secretary of State considers the warrant to be necessary,

(e) the Secretary of State considers that satisfactory arrangements made for the purposes of sections 150 and 151 (safeguards relating to disclosure etc.) are in force in relation to the warrant,

(f) in a case where the Secretary of State considers that a telecommunications operator outside the United Kingdom is likely to be required to provide assistance in giving effect to the warrant if it is issued, the Secretary of State has complied with section 139, and

(g) the decision to issue the warrant has been approved by a Judicial Commissioner.

For the meaning of 'head of an intelligence service', see section 263.

(2) A warrant is necessary on grounds falling within this subsection if it is necessary—

(a) for the purpose of preventing or detecting serious crime, or

(b) in the interests of the economic well-being of the United Kingdom so far as those interests are also relevant to the interests of national security (but see subsection (3)).

(3) A warrant may be considered necessary on the ground falling within subsection (2)(b) only if the information which it is considered necessary to obtain is information relating to the acts or intentions of persons outside the British Islands.

(4) A warrant may not be considered necessary in the interests of national security or on any other grounds falling within subsection (2) if it is considered necessary only for the purpose of gathering evidence for use in any legal proceedings.

(5) An application for the issue of a bulk interception warrant may only be made on behalf of the head of an intelligence service by a person holding office under the Crown.

139 Additional requirements in respect of warrants affecting overseas operators

(1) This section applies where—

(a) an application for a bulk interception warrant has been made, and

(b) the Secretary of State considers that a telecommunications operator outside the United Kingdom is likely to be required to provide assistance in giving effect to the warrant if it is issued.

(2) Before issuing the warrant, the Secretary of State must consult the operator.

(3) Before issuing the warrant, the Secretary of State must, among other matters, take into account—

(a) the likely benefits of the warrant,
(b) the likely number of users (if known) of any telecommunications service which is provided by the operator and to which the warrant relates,
(c) the technical feasibility of complying with any requirement that may be imposed on the operator to provide assistance in giving effect to the warrant,
(d) the likely cost of complying with any such requirement, and
(e) any other effect of the warrant on the operator.

140 Approval of warrants by Judicial Commissioners

(1) In deciding whether to approve a decision to issue a warrant under section 138, a Judicial Commissioner must review the Secretary of State's conclusions as to the following matters—
(a) whether the warrant is necessary as mentioned in subsection (1)(b) of that section,
(b) whether the conduct that would be authorised by the warrant is proportionate to what is sought to be achieved by that conduct,
(c) whether—
(i) each of the specified operational purposes (see section 142) is a purpose for which the examination of intercepted content or secondary data obtained under the warrant is or may be necessary, and
(ii) the examination of intercepted content or secondary data for each such purpose is necessary as mentioned in section 138(1)(d)(ii), and
(d) any matters taken into account in accordance with section 139.

(2) In doing so, the Judicial Commissioner must—
(a) apply the same principles as would be applied by a court on an application for judicial review, and
(b) consider the matters referred to in subsection (1) with a sufficient degree of care as to ensure that the Judicial Commissioner complies with the duties imposed by section 2 (general duties in relation to privacy).

(3) Where a Judicial Commissioner refuses to approve a decision to issue a warrant under section 138, the Judicial Commissioner must give the Secretary of State written reasons for the refusal.

(4) Where a Judicial Commissioner, other than the Investigatory Powers Commissioner, refuses to approve a decision to issue a warrant under section 138, the Secretary of State may ask the Investigatory Powers Commissioner to decide whether to approve the decision to issue the warrant.

141 Decisions to issue warrants to be taken personally by Secretary of State

(1) The decision to issue a bulk interception warrant must be taken personally by the Secretary of State.

(2) Before a bulk interception warrant is issued, it must be signed by the Secretary of State.

142 Requirements that must be met by warrants

(1) A bulk interception warrant must contain a provision stating that it is a bulk interception warrant.

(2) A bulk interception warrant must be addressed to the head of the intelligence service by whom, or on whose behalf, the application for the warrant was made.

(3) A bulk interception warrant must specify the operational purposes for which any intercepted content or secondary data obtained under the warrant may be selected for examination.

(4) The operational purposes specified in the warrant must be ones specified, in a list maintained by the heads of the intelligence services ('the list of operational purposes'), as purposes which they consider are operational purposes for which intercepted content or secondary data obtained under bulk interception warrants may be selected for examination.

(5) The warrant may, in particular, specify all of the operational purposes which, at the time the warrant is issued, are specified in the list of operational purposes.

(6) An operational purpose may be specified in the list of operational purposes only with the approval of the Secretary of State.

(7) The Secretary of State may give such approval only if satisfied that the operational purpose is specified in a greater level of detail than the descriptions contained in section 138(1)(b) or (2).

(8) At the end of each relevant three-month period the Secretary of State must give a copy of the list of operational purposes to the Intelligence and Security Committee of Parliament.

(9) In subsection (8) 'relevant three-month period' means—

(a) the period of three months beginning with the day on which this section comes into force, and

(b) each successive period of three months.

(10) The Prime Minister must review the list of operational purposes at least once a year.

(11) In this Chapter 'the specified operational purposes', in relation to a bulk interception warrant, means the operational purposes specified in the warrant in accordance with this section.

Duration, modification and cancellation of warrants

143 Duration of warrants

(1) A bulk interception warrant (unless already cancelled) ceases to have effect at the end of the period of 6 months beginning with—

(a) the day on which the warrant was issued, or

(b) in the case of a warrant that has been renewed, the day after the day at the end of which the warrant would have ceased to have effect if it had not been renewed.

(2) For provision about the renewal of warrants, see section 144.

144 Renewal of warrants

(1) If the renewal conditions are met, a bulk interception warrant may be renewed, at any time during the renewal period, by an instrument issued by the Secretary of State.

This is subject to subsection (6).

(2) The renewal conditions are—

(a) that the Secretary of State considers that the warrant continues to be necessary—

(i) in the interests of national security, or

(ii) on that ground and on any other grounds falling within section 138(2),

(b) that the Secretary of State considers that the conduct that would be authorised by the renewed warrant continues to be proportionate to what is sought to be achieved by that conduct,

(c) that the Secretary of State considers that—

(i) each of the specified operational purposes (see section 142) is a purpose for which the examination of intercepted content or secondary data obtained under the warrant continues to be, or may be, necessary, and

(ii) the examination of intercepted content or secondary data for each such purpose continues to be necessary on any of the grounds on which the Secretary of State considers that the warrant continues to be necessary, and

(d) that the decision to renew the warrant has been approved by a Judicial Commissioner.

(3) 'The renewal period' means the period of 30 days ending with the day at the end of which the warrant would otherwise cease to have effect.

(4) The decision to renew a bulk interception warrant must be taken personally by the Secretary of State, and the instrument renewing the warrant must be signed by the Secretary of State.

(5) Section 140 (approval of warrants by Judicial Commissioners) applies in relation to a decision to renew a bulk interception warrant as it applies in relation to a decision to issue a bulk interception warrant, but with the omission of paragraph (d) of subsection (1).

This is subject to subsection (6).

(6) In the case of the renewal of a bulk interception warrant that has been modified so that it no longer authorises or requires the interception of communications or the obtaining of secondary data—

(a) the renewal condition in subsection (2)(a) is to be disregarded,

(b) the reference in subsection (2)(c)(ii) to the grounds on which the Secretary of State considers the warrant to be necessary is to be read as a reference to any grounds falling within section 138(1)(b) or (2), and

(c) section 140 has effect as if—

(i) paragraph (a) of subsection (1) were omitted, and

(ii) the reference in subsection (1)(c)(ii) to the grounds on which the Secretary of State considers the warrant to be necessary were a reference to any grounds falling within section 138(1)(b) or (2).

145 Modification of warrants

(1) The provisions of a bulk interception warrant may be modified at any time by an instrument issued by the person making the modification.

(2) The only modifications that may be made under this section are—

(a) adding, varying or removing any operational purpose specified in the warrant as a purpose for which any intercepted content or secondary data obtained under the warrant may be selected for examination, and

(b) providing that the warrant no longer authorises or requires (to the extent that it did so previously)—

(i) the interception of any communications in the course of their transmission by means of a telecommunication system, or

(ii) the obtaining of any secondary data from communications transmitted by means of such a system.

(3) In this section—

(a) a modification adding or varying any operational purpose as mentioned in paragraph (a) of subsection (2) is referred to as a 'major modification', and

(b) any other modification within that subsection is referred to as a 'minor modification'.

(4) A major modification—

(a) must be made by the Secretary of State, and

(b) may be made only if the Secretary of State considers that it is necessary on any of the grounds on which the Secretary of State considers the warrant to be necessary (see section 138(1)(b)).

(5) Except where the Secretary of State considers that there is an urgent need to make the modification, a major modification has effect only if the decision to make the modification is approved by a Judicial Commissioner.

(6) A minor modification may be made by—

(a) the Secretary of State, or

(b) a senior official acting on behalf of the Secretary of State.

(7) Where a minor modification is made by a senior official, the Secretary of State must be notified personally of the modification and the reasons for making it.

(8) If at any time a person mentioned in subsection (6) considers that any operational purpose specified in a warrant is no longer a purpose for which the examination of intercepted content or secondary data obtained under the warrant

is or may be necessary, the person must modify the warrant by removing that operational purpose.

(9) The decision to modify the provisions of a warrant must be taken personally by the person making the modification, and the instrument making the modification must be signed by that person.

This is subject to subsection (10).

(10) If it is not reasonably practicable for an instrument making a major modification to be signed by the Secretary of State, the instrument may be signed by a senior official designated by the Secretary of State for that purpose.

(11) In such a case, the instrument making the modification must contain a statement that—

(a) it is not reasonably practicable for the instrument to be signed by the Secretary of State, and

(b) the Secretary of State has personally and expressly authorised the making of the modification.

(12) Despite section 136(2), the modification of a bulk interception warrant as mentioned in subsection (2)(b) above does not prevent the warrant from being a bulk interception warrant.

(13) Nothing in this section applies in relation to modifying the provisions of a warrant in a way which does not affect the conduct authorised or required by it.

146 Approval of major modifications by Judicial Commissioners

(1) In deciding whether to approve a decision to make a major modification of a bulk interception warrant, a Judicial Commissioner must review the Secretary of State's conclusions as to whether the modification is necessary on any of the grounds on which the Secretary of State considers the warrant to be necessary.

(2) In doing so, the Judicial Commissioner must—

(a) apply the same principles as would be applied by a court on an application for judicial review, and

(b) consider the matter referred to in subsection (1) with a sufficient degree of care as to ensure that the Judicial Commissioner complies with the duties imposed by section 2 (general duties in relation to privacy).

(3) Where a Judicial Commissioner refuses to approve a decision to make a major modification under section 145, the Judicial Commissioner must give the Secretary of State written reasons for the refusal.

(4) Where a Judicial Commissioner, other than the Investigatory Powers Commissioner, refuses to approve a decision to make a major modification under section 145, the Secretary of State may ask the Investigatory Powers Commissioner to decide whether to approve the decision to make the modification.

147 Approval of major modifications made in urgent cases

(1) This section applies where—

(a) the Secretary of State makes a major modification of a bulk interception warrant without the approval of a Judicial Commissioner, and

(b) the Secretary of State considered that there was an urgent need to make the modification.

(2) The Secretary of State must inform a Judicial Commissioner that the modification has been made.

(3) The Judicial Commissioner must, before the end of the relevant period—

(a) decide whether to approve the decision to make the modification, and

(b) notify the Secretary of State of the Judicial Commissioner's decision.

'The relevant period' means the period ending with the third working day after the day on which the modification was made.

(4) If the Judicial Commissioner refuses to approve the decision to make the modification—

(a) the warrant (unless it no longer has effect) has effect as if the modification had not been made, and

(b) the person to whom the warrant is addressed must, so far as is reasonably practicable, secure that anything in the process of being done under the warrant by virtue of that modification stops as soon as possible,

and section 146(4) does not apply in relation to the refusal to approve the decision.

(5) Nothing in this section affects the lawfulness of—

(a) anything done under the warrant by virtue of the modification before the modification ceases to have effect;

(b) if anything is in the process of being done under the warrant by virtue of the modification when the modification ceases to have effect—

(i) anything done before that thing could be stopped, or

(ii) anything done which it is not reasonably practicable to stop.

148 Cancellation of warrants

(1) The Secretary of State, or a senior official acting on behalf of the Secretary of State, may cancel a bulk interception warrant at any time.

(2) If the Secretary of State, or a senior official acting on behalf of the Secretary of State, considers that any of the cancellation conditions are met in relation to a bulk interception warrant, the person must cancel the warrant.

(3) The cancellation conditions are—

(a) that the warrant is no longer necessary in the interests of national security;

(b) that the conduct authorised by the warrant is no longer proportionate to what is sought to be achieved by that conduct;

(c) that the examination of intercepted content or secondary data obtained under the warrant is no longer necessary for any of the specified operational purposes (see section 142).

(4) But the condition in subsection (3)(a) does not apply where the warrant has been modified so that it no longer authorises or requires the interception of communications or the obtaining of secondary data.

(5) Where a warrant is cancelled under this section, the person to whom the warrant was addressed must, so far as is reasonably practicable, secure that anything in the process of being done under the warrant stops as soon as possible.

(6) A warrant that has been cancelled under this section may not be renewed.

Implementation of warrants

149 Implementation of warrants

(1) In giving effect to a bulk interception warrant, the person to whom it is addressed ('the implementing authority') may (in addition to acting alone) act through, or together with, such other persons as the implementing authority may require (whether under subsection (2) or otherwise) to provide the authority with assistance in giving effect to the warrant.

(2) For the purpose of requiring any person to provide assistance in relation to a bulk interception warrant, the implementing authority may—

(a) serve a copy of the warrant on any person who the implementing authority considers may be able to provide such assistance, or

(b) make arrangements for the service of a copy of the warrant on any such person.

(3) A copy of a warrant may be served under subsection (2) on a person outside the United Kingdom for the purpose of requiring the person to provide such assistance in the form of conduct outside the United Kingdom.

(4) For the purposes of this Act, the provision of assistance in giving effect to a bulk interception warrant includes any disclosure to the implementing authority, or to persons acting on behalf of the implementing authority, of anything obtained under the warrant.

(5) Sections 42 (service of warrants) and 43 (duty of operators to assist with

implementation) apply in relation to a bulk interception warrant as they apply in relation to a targeted interception warrant.

(6) References in this section (and in sections 42 and 43 as they apply in relation to bulk interception warrants) to the service of a copy of a warrant include—

(a) the service of a copy of one or more schedules contained in the warrant with the omission of the remainder of the warrant, and

(b) the service of a copy of the warrant with the omission of any schedule contained in the warrant.

Restrictions on use or disclosure of material obtained under warrants etc.

150 Safeguards relating to retention and disclosure of material

(1) The Secretary of State must ensure, in relation to every bulk interception warrant, that arrangements are in force for securing—

(a) that the requirements of subsections (2) and (5) are met in relation to the material obtained under the warrant, and

(b) that the requirements of section 152 are met in relation to the intercepted content or secondary data obtained under the warrant.

This is subject to subsection (8).

(2) The requirements of this subsection are met in relation to the material obtained under a warrant if each of the following is limited to the minimum that is necessary for the authorised purposes (see subsection (3))—

(a) the number of persons to whom any of the material is disclosed or otherwise made available;

(b) the extent to which any of the material is disclosed or otherwise made available;

(c) the extent to which any of the material is copied;

(d) the number of copies that are made.

(3) For the purposes of subsection (2) something is necessary for the authorised purposes if, and only if—

(a) it is, or is likely to become, necessary in the interests of national security or on any other grounds falling within section 138(2),

(b) it is necessary for facilitating the carrying out of any functions under this Act of the Secretary of State, the Scottish Ministers or the head of the intelligence service to whom the warrant is or was addressed,

(c) it is necessary for facilitating the carrying out of any functions of the Judicial Commissioners or the Investigatory Powers Tribunal under or in relation to this Act,

(d) it is necessary to ensure that a person ('P') who is conducting a criminal prosecution has the information P needs to determine what is required of P by P's duty to secure the fairness of the prosecution, or

(e) it is necessary for the performance of any duty imposed on any person by the Public Records Act 1958 or the Public Records Act (Northern Ireland) 1923.

(4) The arrangements for the time being in force under this section for securing that the requirements of subsection (2) are met in relation to the material obtained under the warrant must include arrangements for securing that every copy made of any of that material is stored, for so long as it is retained, in a secure manner.

(5) The requirements of this subsection are met in relation to the material obtained under a warrant if every copy made of any of that material (if not destroyed earlier) is destroyed as soon as there are no longer any relevant grounds for retaining it (see subsection (6)).

(6) For the purposes of subsection (5), there are no longer any relevant grounds for retaining a copy of any material if, and only if—

(a) its retention is not necessary, or not likely to become necessary, in the interests of national security or on any other grounds falling within section 138 (2), and

(b) its retention is not necessary for any of the purposes mentioned in paragraphs (b) to (e) of subsection (3) above.

(7) Subsection (8) applies if—

(a) any material obtained under the warrant has been handed over to any overseas authorities, or

(b) a copy of any such material has been given to any overseas authorities.

(8) To the extent that the requirements of subsections (2) and (5) and section 152 relate to any of the material mentioned in subsection (7)(a), or to the copy mentioned in subsection (7)(b), the arrangements made for the purposes of this section are not required to secure that those requirements are met (see instead section 151).

(9) In this section—

'copy', in relation to material obtained under a warrant, means any of the following (whether or not in documentary form)—

(a) any copy, extract or summary of the material which identifies the material as having been obtained under the warrant, and

(b) any record which—

(i) refers to any interception or to the obtaining of any material, and

(ii) is a record of the identities of the persons to or by whom the material was sent, or to whom the material relates,

and 'copied' is to be read accordingly;

'overseas authorities' means authorities of a country or territory outside the United Kingdom.

151 Safeguards relating to disclosure of material overseas

(1) The Secretary of State must ensure, in relation to every bulk interception warrant, that arrangements are in force for securing that—

(a) any material obtained under the warrant is handed over to overseas authorities only if the requirements of subsection (2) are met, and

(b) copies of any such material are given to overseas authorities only if those requirements are met.

(2) The requirements of this subsection are met in the case of a warrant if it appears to the Secretary of State—

(a) that requirements corresponding to the requirements of section 150(2) and (5) and section 152 will apply, to such extent (if any) as the Secretary of State considers appropriate, in relation to any of the material which is handed over, or any copy of which is given, to the authorities in question, and

(b) that restrictions are in force which would prevent, to such extent (if any) as the Secretary of State considers appropriate, the doing of anything in, for the purposes of or in connection with any proceedings outside the United Kingdom which would result in a prohibited disclosure.

(3) In subsection (2)(b) 'prohibited disclosure' means a disclosure which, if made in the United Kingdom, would breach the prohibition in section 56(1) (see section 156).

(4) In this section—

'copy' has the same meaning as in section 150;

'overseas authorities' means authorities of a country or territory outside the United Kingdom.

152 Safeguards relating to examination of material

(1) For the purposes of section 150 the requirements of this section are met in relation to the intercepted content and secondary data obtained under a warrant if—

(a) the selection of any of the intercepted content or secondary data for examination is carried out only for the specified purposes (see subsection (2)),

(b) the selection of any of the intercepted content or secondary data for examination is necessary and proportionate in all the circumstances, and

(c) the selection of any of the intercepted content for examination meets any of the selection conditions (see subsection (3)).

(2) The selection of intercepted content or secondary data for examination is carried out only for the specified purposes if the intercepted content or secondary data is selected for examination only so far as is necessary for the operational purposes specified in the warrant in accordance with section 142.

In this subsection 'specified in the warrant' means specified in the warrant at the time of the selection of the intercepted content or secondary data for examination.

(3) The selection conditions referred to in subsection (1)(c) are—

(a) that the selection of the intercepted content for examination does not breach the prohibition in subsection (4);

(b) that the person to whom the warrant is addressed considers that the selection of the intercepted content for examination would not breach that prohibition;

(c) that the selection of the intercepted content for examination in breach of that prohibition is authorised by subsection (5);

(d) that the selection of the intercepted content for examination in breach of that prohibition is authorised by a targeted examination warrant issued under Chapter 1 of Part 2.

(4) The prohibition referred to in subsection (3)(a) is that intercepted content may not at any time be selected for examination if—

(a) any criteria used for the selection of the intercepted content for examination are referable to an individual known to be in the British Islands at that time, and

(b) the purpose of using those criteria is to identify the content of communications sent by, or intended for, that individual.

It does not matter for the purposes of this subsection whether the identity of the individual is known.

(5) The selection of intercepted content ('the relevant content') for examination is authorised by this subsection if—

(a) criteria referable to an individual have been, or are being, used for the selection of intercepted content for examination in circumstances falling within subsection (3)(a) or (b),

(b) at any time it appears to the person to whom the warrant is addressed that there has been a relevant change of circumstances in relation to the individual (see subsection (6)) which would mean that the selection of the relevant content for examination would breach the prohibition in subsection (4),

(c) since that time, a written authorisation to examine the relevant content using those criteria has been given by a senior officer, and

(d) the selection of the relevant content for examination is made before the end of the permitted period (see subsection (7)).

(6) For the purposes of subsection (5)(b) there is a relevant change of circumstances in relation to an individual if—

(a) the individual has entered the British Islands, or

(b) a belief by the person to whom the warrant is addressed that the individual was outside the British Islands was in fact mistaken.

(7) In subsection (5)—

'senior officer', in relation to a warrant addressed to the head of an intelligence service, means a member of the intelligence service who—

(a) is a member of the Senior Civil Service or a member of the Senior Management Structure of Her Majesty's Diplomatic Service, or

(b) holds a position in the intelligence service of equivalent seniority to such a member;

'the permitted period' means the period ending with the fifth working day after the time mentioned in subsection (5)(b).

(8) In a case where the selection of intercepted content for examination is authorised by subsection (5), the person to whom the warrant is addressed must notify the Secretary of State that the selection is being carried out.

153 Additional safeguards for items subject to legal privilege

(1) Subsection (2) applies if, in a case where intercepted content obtained under a bulk interception warrant is to be selected for examination—

(a) the selection of the intercepted content for examination meets any of the selection conditions in section 152(3)(a) to (c), and

(b) either—

(i) the purpose, or one of the purposes, of using the criteria to be used for the selection of the intercepted content for examination ('the relevant criteria') is to identify any items subject to legal privilege, or

(ii) the use of the relevant criteria is likely to identify such items.

(2) The intercepted content may be selected for examination using the relevant criteria only if a senior official acting on behalf of the Secretary of State has approved the use of those criteria.

(3) In deciding whether to give an approval under subsection (2) in a case where subsection (1)(b)(i) applies, a senior official must have regard to the public interest in the confidentiality of items subject to legal privilege.

(4) A senior official may give an approval under subsection (2) only if—

(a) the official considers that the arrangements made for the purposes of section 150 (safeguards relating to retention and disclosure of material) include specific arrangements for the handling, retention, use and destruction of items subject to legal privilege, and

(b) where subsection (1)(b)(i) applies, the official considers that there are exceptional and compelling circumstances that make it necessary to authorise the use of the relevant criteria.

(5) For the purposes of subsection (4)(b), there cannot be exceptional and compelling circumstances that make it necessary to authorise the use of the relevant criteria unless—

(a) the public interest in obtaining the information that would be obtained by the selection of the intercepted content for examination outweighs the public interest in the confidentiality of items subject to legal privilege,

(b) there are no other means by which the information may reasonably be obtained, and

(c) obtaining the information is necessary in the interests of national security or for the purpose of preventing death or significant injury.

(6) Subsection (7) applies if, in a case where intercepted content obtained under a bulk interception warrant is to be selected for examination—

(a) the selection of the intercepted content for examination meets any of the selection conditions in section 152(3)(a) to (c),

(b) the purpose, or one of the purposes, of using the criteria to be used for the selection of the intercepted content for examination ('the relevant criteria') is to identify communications that, if they were not made with the intention of furthering a criminal purpose, would be items subject to legal privilege, and

(c) the person to whom the warrant is addressed considers that the communications ('the targeted communications') are likely to be communications made with the intention of furthering a criminal purpose.

(7) The intercepted content may be selected for examination using the relevant criteria only if a senior official acting on behalf of the Secretary of State has approved the use of those criteria.

(8) A senior official may give an approval under subsection (7) only if the official considers that the targeted communications are likely to be communications made with the intention of furthering a criminal purpose.

(9) Where an item subject to legal privilege which has been intercepted in

accordance with a bulk interception warrant is retained following its examination, for purposes other than the destruction of the item, the person to whom the warrant is addressed must inform the Investigatory Powers Commissioner as soon as is reasonably practicable.

(For provision about the grounds for retaining material obtained under a warrant, see section 150.)

(10) Unless the Investigatory Powers Commissioner considers that subsection (12) applies to the item, the Commissioner must—

(a) direct that the item is destroyed, or

(b) impose one or more conditions as to the use or retention of that item.

(11) If the Investigatory Powers Commissioner considers that subsection (12) applies to the item, the Commissioner may nevertheless impose such conditions under subsection (10)(b) as the Commissioner considers necessary for the purpose of protecting the public interest in the confidentiality of items subject to legal privilege.

(12) This subsection applies to an item subject to legal privilege if—

(a) the public interest in retaining the item outweighs the public interest in the confidentiality of items subject to legal privilege, and

(b) retaining the item is necessary in the interests of national security or for the purpose of preventing death or significant injury.

(13) The Investigatory Powers Commissioner—

(a) may require an affected party to make representations about how the Commissioner should exercise any function under subsection (10), and

(b) must have regard to any such representations made by an affected party (whether or not as a result of a requirement imposed under paragraph (a)).

(14) Each of the following is an 'affected party' for the purposes of subsection (13)—

(a) the Secretary of State;

(b) the person to whom the warrant is or was addressed.

154 Additional safeguard for confidential journalistic material

Where—

(a) a communication which has been intercepted in accordance with a bulk interception warrant is retained, following its examination, for purposes other than the destruction of the communication, and

(b) it is a communication containing confidential journalistic material,

the person to whom the warrant is addressed must inform the Investigatory Powers Commissioner as soon as is reasonably practicable.

(For provision about the grounds for retaining material obtained under a warrant, see section 150.)

155 Offence of breaching safeguards relating to examination of material

(1) A person commits an offence if—

(a) the person selects for examination any intercepted content or secondary data obtained under a bulk interception warrant,

(b) the person knows or believes that the selection of that intercepted content or secondary data for examination does not comply with a requirement imposed by section 152 or 153, and

(c) the person deliberately selects that intercepted content or secondary data for examination in breach of that requirement.

(2) A person guilty of an offence under this section is liable—

(a) on summary conviction in England and Wales—

(i) to imprisonment for a term not exceeding 12 months (or 6 months, if the offence was committed before the commencement of section 154(1) of the Criminal Justice Act 2003), or

(ii) to a fine,

or to both;

(b) on summary conviction in Scotland—
(i) to imprisonment for a term not exceeding 12 months, or
(ii) to a fine not exceeding the statutory maximum,
or to both;
(c) on summary conviction in Northern Ireland—
(i) to imprisonment for a term not exceeding 6 months, or
(ii) to a fine not exceeding the statutory maximum,
or to both;
(d) on conviction on indictment, to imprisonment for a term not exceeding 2 years or to a fine, or to both.

(3) No proceedings for any offence which is an offence by virtue of this section may be instituted—

(a) in England and Wales, except by or with the consent of the Director of Public Prosecutions;

(b) in Northern Ireland, except by or with the consent of the Director of Public Prosecutions for Northern Ireland.

156 Application of other restrictions in relation to warrants

(1) Section 56 and Schedule 3 (exclusion of matters from legal proceedings etc.) apply in relation to bulk interception warrants as they apply in relation to targeted interception warrants.

(2) Sections 57 to 59 (duty not to make unauthorised disclosures) apply in relation to bulk interception warrants as they apply in relation to targeted interception warrants, but as if the reference in section 58(2)(c) to a requirement for disclosure imposed by virtue of section 41(5) were a reference to such a requirement imposed by virtue of section 149(4).

Interpretation

157 Chapter 1: interpretation

(1) In this Chapter—

'intercepted content', in relation to a bulk interception warrant, means any content of communications intercepted by an interception authorised or required by the warrant;

'overseas-related communications' has the meaning given by section 136;

'secondary data' has the meaning given by section 137, and references to obtaining secondary data from a communication are to be read in accordance with that section;

'senior official' means a member of the Senior Civil Service or a member of the Senior Management Structure of Her Majesty's Diplomatic Service;

'the specified operational purposes' has the meaning given by section 142(11).

(2) See also—

section 261 (telecommunications definitions),
section 263 (general definitions),
section 264 (general definitions: 'journalistic material' etc.),
section 265 (index of defined expressions).

EUROPEAN UNION (WITHDRAWAL) ACT 2018
(2018 c 16)

This Act is reproduced as amended by the European Union (Withdrawal Agreement) Act 2020. Provisions which were not in force at the time of going to press are in italics.

Repeal of the ECA

1 Repeal of the European Communities Act 1972
The European Communities Act 1972 is repealed on exit day.

[Savings for implementation period]

[1A Saving for ECA for implementation period
(1) Subsections (2) to (4) have effect despite the repeal of the European Communities Act 1972 on exit day by section 1.
(2) The European Communities Act 1972, as it has effect in domestic law or the law of a relevant territory immediately before exit day, continues to have effect in domestic law or the law of the relevant territory on and after exit day so far as provided by subsections (3) to (5).
(3) The Act of 1972 has effect on and after exit day as if—
(a) the definitions of 'the Treaties' and 'the EU Treaties' given by section 1(2) to (4) (interpretation)—
(i) included Part 4 of the withdrawal agreement (implementation period), other than that Part so far as it relates to, or could be applied in relation to, the Common Foreign and Security Policy, but
(ii) were otherwise limited to anything which falls within those definitions as at immediately before exit day so far as it is not excluded by regulations made on or after exit day by a Minister of the Crown under this sub-paragraph,
(b) the reference in section 2(2) to the objects of the EU were a reference to those objects so far as they are applicable to and in the United Kingdom by virtue of Part 4 of the withdrawal agreement,
(c) section 2(3) (payment of EU costs etc) were omitted,
(d) in section 3 (decisions on, and proof of, EU Treaties and EU instruments etc)—
(i) the references to the Treaties in subsections (1) and (2) included the withdrawal agreement, and
(ii) the words in brackets in subsection (1) only applied so far as they are in accordance with Part 4 of the withdrawal agreement,
(e) references in sections 5 and 6 (customs duties and common agricultural policy) to the common customs tariff of the EU, directly applicable EU provision, the exclusion of customs duties, EU arrangements and agricultural levies of the EU were to such things so far as they are applicable to and in the United Kingdom by virtue of Part 4 of the withdrawal agreement, and
(f) in Part 2 of Schedule 1 (general definitions in relation to the EU)—
(i) in the definition of 'EU customs duty', the reference to directly applicable EU provision were to such provision so far as it is applicable to and in the United Kingdom by virtue of Part 4 of the withdrawal agreement, and
(ii) in the definition of 'Member' in the expression 'member State', after 'EU' there were inserted and for the purposes of this expression the United Kingdom is to be treated as if it were a member of the EU during the implementation period (within the meaning given by section 1A(6) of the European Union (Withdrawal) Act 2018).
(4) In this section 'relevant territory' means the Isle of Man, any of the Channel Islands or Gibraltar.
(5) Subsections (1) to (4) are repealed on IP completion day.

(6) In this Act—

'the implementation period' means the transition or implementation period provided for by Part 4 of the withdrawal agreement and beginning with exit day and ending on IP completion day;

'IP completion day' (and related expressions) have the same meaning as in the European Union (Withdrawal Agreement) Act 2020 (see section 39(1) to (5) of that Act);

'withdrawal agreement' has the same meaning as in that Act (see section 39(1) and (6) of that Act).

(7) In this Act—

(a) references to the European Communities Act 1972 are to be read, so far as the context permits or requires, as being or (as the case may be) including references to that Act as it continues to have effect by virtue of subsections (2) to (4) above, and

(b) references to any Part of the withdrawal agreement or the EEA EFTA separation agreement include references to any other provisions of that agreement so far as applying to that Part.]

[1B Saving for EU-derived domestic legislation for implementation period

(1) Subsections (2) to (5) have effect despite the repeal of the European Communities Act 1972 on exit day by section 1.

(2) EU-derived domestic legislation, as it has effect in domestic law immediately before exit day, continues to have effect in domestic law on and after exit day, subject as follows.

(3) Any enactment which continues to have effect by virtue of subsection (2) is to be read, on and after exit day and so far as the context permits or requires, as if—

(a) any reference to an expression which is to be read in accordance with Schedule 1 to the Interpretation Act 1978 and is an expression defined by section 1 of, or Part 2 of Schedule 1 to, the European Communities Act 1972 were a reference to that expression as defined by that section or that Part of that Schedule as it continues to have effect by virtue of section 1A(2) to (4) of this Act,

(b) any reference (however expressed and subject to paragraph (a) above) to—

(i) EU law,

(ii) any particular EU Treaty or any part of it,

(iii) any EU instrument, or other document of an EU entity or of the EU, or any part of any such instrument or document,

(iv) any part of EU law not falling within sub-paragraph (ii) or (iii),

(v) any tax, duty, levy or interests of the EU, or

(vi) any arrangement involving, or otherwise relating to, the EU of a kind not falling within sub-paragraph (i), (ii), (iii), (iv) or (v),

were a reference to any such thing so far as it is applicable to and in the United Kingdom by virtue of Part 4 of the withdrawal agreement,

(c) any reference (however expressed and subject to paragraph (a) above) to the European Communities Act 1972 were or (as the case may be) included a reference to the Act of 1972 as it continues to have effect by virtue of section 1A (2) to (4) of this Act,

(d) any reference (however expressed) to the area of the EU or of the EEA included the United Kingdom,

(e) any reference (however expressed) to a citizen of the EU or a national of the EEA included a United Kingdom national (within the meaning given by Article 2(d) of the withdrawal agreement), and

(f) such other modifications were made as—

(i) are provided for by regulations under section 8A or Part 1A of Schedule 2, or

(ii) so far as not so provided, are necessary for any purpose of Part 4 of the withdrawal agreement and are capable of being ascertained from any such purpose or otherwise from that Part of that agreement.

(4) Any EU-derived domestic legislation which is an enactment passed or made on or after exit day and before IP completion day is, unless the contrary intention appears, to be read in accordance with subsection (3) (and anything done or omitted to be done in connection with any such enactment is to be understood, and has effect, accordingly).

(5) Subsections (2) to (4) are subject to any regulations made under section 8A or 23 or Part 1A of Schedule 2 or otherwise under this Act or under the European Union (Withdrawal Agreement) Act 2020.

(6) Subsections (1) to (5) are repealed on IP completion day.

(7) In this Act 'EU-derived domestic legislation' means any enactment so far as—

(a) made under section 2(2) of, or paragraph 1A of Schedule 2 to, the European Communities Act 1972,

(b) passed or made, or operating, for a purpose mentioned in section 2(2)(a) or (b) of that Act,

(c) relating to—

(i) anything which falls within paragraph (a) or (b), or

(ii) any rights, powers, liabilities, obligations, restrictions, remedies or procedures which are recognised and available in domestic law by virtue of section 2(1) of the European Communities Act 1972, or

(d) relating otherwise to the EU or the EEA,

but does not include any enactment contained in the European Communities Act 1972 or any enactment contained in this Act or the European Union (Withdrawal Agreement) Act 2020 or in regulations made under this Act or the Act of 2020.]

Retention of existing EU law

2 Saving for EU-derived domestic legislation

(1) EU-derived domestic legislation, as it has effect in domestic law immediately before [IP completion day], continues to have effect in domestic law on and after [IP completion day].

[. . .]

(3) This section is subject to section 5 and Schedule 1 (exceptions to savings and incorporation [and section 5A (Savings and incorporation: Supplementary)]).

3 Incorporation of direct EU legislation

(1) Direct EU legislation, so far as operative immediately before [IP completion day], forms part of domestic law on and after [IP completion day].

(2) In this Act 'direct EU legislation' means—

(a) any EU regulation, EU decision or EU tertiary legislation, as it has effect in EU law immediately before [IP completion day] and so far as—

[(ai) it is applicable to and in the United Kingdom by virtue of Part 4 of the withdrawal agreement,

(bi) it neither has effect nor is to have effect by virtue of section 7A or 7B,]

(i) it is not an exempt EU instrument (for which see section 20(1) and Schedule 6), and

[. . .]

(iii) its effect is not reproduced in an enactment to which section 2(1) applies,

(b) any Annex to the EEA agreement, as it has effect in EU law immediately before [IP completion day] and so far as—

(i) it refers to, or contains adaptations of, anything falling within paragraph (a), and

(ii) its effect is not reproduced in an enactment to which section 2(1) applies, or

(c) Protocol 1 to the EEA agreement (which contains horizontal adaptations that apply in relation to EU instruments referred to in the Annexes to that agreement), as it has effect in EU law immediately before [IP completion day] and so far as—

[(ai) it is applicable to and in the United Kingdom by virtue of Part 4 of the withdrawal agreement,

(bi) it neither has effect nor is to have effect by virtue of section 7A or 7B,]

(3) For the purposes of this Act, any direct EU legislation is operative immediately before [IP completion day] if—

(a) in the case of anything which comes into force at a particular time and is stated to apply from a later time, it is in force and applies immediately before [IP completion day],

(b) in the case of a decision which specifies to whom it is addressed, it has been notified to that person before [IP completion day], and

(c) in any other case, it is in force immediately before [IP completion day].

(4) This section—

(a) brings into domestic law any direct EU legislation only in the form of the English language version of that legislation, and

(b) does not apply to any such legislation for which there is no such version,

but paragraph (a) does not affect the use of the other language versions of that legislation for the purposes of interpreting it.

(5) This section is subject to section 5 and Schedule 1 (exceptions to savings and incorporation [and section 5A (savings and incorporation: supplementary)]).

4 Saving for rights etc under section 2(1) of the ECA

(1) Any rights, powers, liabilities, obligations, restrictions, remedies and procedures which, immediately before [IP completion day]—

(a) are recognised and available in domestic law by virtue of section 2(1) of the European Communities Act 1972, and

(b) are enforced, allowed and followed accordingly,

continue on and after [IP completion day] to be recognised and available in domestic law (and to be enforced, allowed and followed accordingly).

(2) Subsection (1) does not apply to any rights, powers, liabilities, obligations, restrictions, remedies or procedures so far as they—

(a) form part of domestic law by virtue of section 3,

[(aa) are, or are to be, recognised and available in domestic law [and enforced, allowed and followed accordingly) by virtue of section 7A or 7B,] or

(b) arise under an EU directive (including as applied by the EEA agreement) and are not of a kind recognised by the European Court or any court or tribunal in the United Kingdom in a case decided before [IP completion day] (whether or not as an essential part of the decision in the case).

(3) This section is subject to section 5 and Schedule 1 (exceptions to savings and incorporation [and section 5A (savings and incorporation: supplementary)]).

5 Exceptions to savings and incorporation

(1) The principle of the supremacy of EU law does not apply to any enactment or rule of law passed or made on or after [IP completion day].

(2) Accordingly, the principle of the supremacy of EU law continues to apply on or after [IP completion day] so far as relevant to the interpretation, disapplication or quashing of any enactment or rule of law passed or made before [IP completion day].

(3) Subsection (1) does not prevent the principle of the supremacy of EU law from applying to a modification made on or after [IP completion day] of any enactment or rule of law passed or made before [IP completion day] if the application of the principle is consistent with the intention of the modification.

(4) The Charter of Fundamental Rights is not part of domestic law on or after [IP completion day].

(5) Subsection (4) does not affect the retention in domestic law on or after [IP completion day] in accordance with this Act of any fundamental rights or principles which exist irrespective of the Charter (and references to the Charter in any

case law are, so far as necessary for this purpose, to be read as if they were references to any corresponding retained fundamental rights or principles).

(6) Schedule 1 (which makes further provision about exceptions to savings and incorporation) has effect.

[(7) Subsections (1) to (6) and Schedule 1 are subject to relevant separation agreement law (for which see section 7C).]

[5A Savings and incorporation: supplementary

The fact that anything which continues to be, or forms part of, domestic law on or after IP completion day by virtue of section 2, 3 or 4 has an effect immediately before IP completion day which is time-limited by reference to the implementation period does not prevent it from having an indefinite effect on and after IP completion day by virtue of section 2, 3 or 4.]

6 Interpretation of retained EU law

(1) A court or tribunal—

(a) is not bound by any principles laid down, or any decisions made, on or after [IP completion day] by the European Court, and

(b) cannot refer any matter to the European Court on or after [IP completion day].

(2) Subject to this and subsections (3) to (6), a court or tribunal may have regard to anything done on or after [IP completion day] by the European Court, another EU entity or the EU so far as it is relevant to any matter before the court or tribunal.

(3) Any question as to the validity, meaning or effect of any retained EU law is to be decided, so far as that law is unmodified on or after [IP completion day] and so far as they are relevant to it—

(a) in accordance with any retained case law and any retained general principles of EU law, and

(b) having regard (among other things) to the limits, immediately before [IP completion day], of EU competences.

(4) But—

(a) the Supreme Court is not bound by any retained EU case law,

(b) the High Court of Justiciary is not bound by any retained EU case law when—

(i) sitting as a court of appeal otherwise than in relation to a compatibility issue (within the meaning given by section 288ZA(2) of the Criminal Procedure (Scotland) Act 1995) or a devolution issue (within the meaning given by paragraph 1 of Schedule 6 to the Scotland Act 1998), or

(ii) sitting on a reference under section 123(1) of the Criminal Procedure (Scotland) Act 1995,

[(ba) a relevant court or relevant tribunal is not bound by any retained EU case law so far as is provided for by regulations under subsection (5A),] and

(c) no court or tribunal is bound by any retained domestic case law that it would not otherwise be bound by.

(5) In deciding whether to depart from any retained EU case law [by virtue of subsection (4)(a) or (b)], the Supreme Court or the High Court of Justiciary must apply the same test as it would apply in deciding whether to depart from its own case law.

[(5A) A Minister of the Crown may by regulations provide for—

(a) a court or tribunal to be a relevant court or (as the case may be) a relevant tribunal for the purposes of this section,

(b) the extent to which, or circumstances in which, a relevant court or relevant tribunal is not to be bound by retained EU case law,

(c) the test which a relevant court or relevant tribunal must apply in deciding whether to depart from any retained EU case law, or

(d) considerations which are to be relevant to—

(i) the Supreme Court or the High Court of Justiciary in applying the test mentioned in subsection (5), or

(ii) a relevant court or relevant tribunal in applying any test provided for by virtue of paragraph (c) above.

(5B) Regulations under subsection (5A) may (among other things) provide for—

(a) the High Court of Justiciary to be a relevant court when sitting otherwise than as mentioned in subsection (4)(b)(i) and (ii),

(b) the extent to which, or circumstances in which, a relevant court or relevant tribunal not being bound by retained EU case law includes (or does not include) that court or tribunal not being bound by retained domestic case law which relates to retained EU case law,

(c) other matters arising in relation to retained domestic case law which relates to retained EU case law (including by making provision of a kind which could be made in relation to retained EU case law), or

(d) the test mentioned in paragraph (c) of subsection (5A) or the considerations mentioned in paragraph (d) of that subsection to be determined (whether with or without the consent of a Minister of the Crown) by a person mentioned in subsection (5C)(a) to (e) or by more than one of those persons acting jointly.

(5C) Before making regulations under subsection (5A), a Minister of the Crown must consult—

(a) the President of the Supreme Court,

(b) the Lord Chief Justice of England and Wales,

(c) the Lord President of the Court of Session,

(d) the Lord Chief Justice of Northern Ireland,

(e) the Senior President of Tribunals, and

(f) such other persons as the Minister of the Crown considers appropriate.

(5D) No regulations may be made under subsection (5A) after IP completion day.]

(6) Subsection (3) does not prevent the validity, meaning or effect of any retained EU law which has been modified on or after [IP completion day] from being decided as provided for in that subsection if doing so is consistent with the intention of the modifications.

[(6A) Subsections (1) to (6) are subject to relevant separation agreement law (for which see section 7C).]

(7) In this Act—

'retained case law' means—

(a) retained domestic case law, and

(b) retained EU case law;

'retained domestic case law' means any principles laid down by, and any decisions of, a court or tribunal in the United Kingdom, as they have effect immediately before [IP completion day] and so far as they—

(a) relate to anything to which section 2, 3 or 4 applies, and

(b) are not excluded by section 5 or Schedule 1,

(as those principles and decisions are modified by or under this Act or by other domestic law from time to time);

'retained EU case law' means any principles laid down by, and any decisions of, the European Court, as they have effect in EU law immediately before [IP completion day] and so far as they—

(a) relate to anything to which section 2, 3 or 4 applies, and

(b) are not excluded by section 5 or Schedule 1,

(as those principles and decisions are modified by or under this Act or by other domestic law from time to time);

'retained EU law' means anything which, on or after [IP completion day], continues to be, or forms part of, domestic law by virtue of section 2, 3 or 4 or subsection (3) or (6) above (as that body of law is added to or otherwise modified by or under this Act or by other domestic law from time to time);

'retained general principles of EU law' means the general principles of EU law, as they have effect in EU law immediately before [IP completion day] and so far as they—

(a) relate to anything to which section 2, 3 or 4 applies, and

(b) are not excluded by section 5 or Schedule 1,

(as those principles are modified by or under this Act or by other domestic law from time to time).

7 Status of retained EU law

(1) Anything which—

(a) was, immediately before exit day, primary legislation of a particular kind, subordinate legislation of a particular kind or another enactment of a particular kind, and

(b) continues to be domestic law on and after exit day by virtue of section 2, continues to be domestic law as an enactment of the same kind.

(2) Retained direct principal EU legislation cannot be modified by any primary or subordinate legislation other than—

(a) an Act of Parliament,

(b) any other primary legislation (so far as it has the power to make such a modification), or

(c) any subordinate legislation so far as it is made under a power which permits such a modification by virtue of—

(i) paragraph 3, 5(3)(a) or (4)(a), 8(3), 10(3)(a) or (4)(a), 11(2)(a) or 12(3) of Schedule 8,

(ii) any other provision made by or under this Act,

(iii) any provision made by or under an Act of Parliament passed before, and in the same Session as, this Act, or

(iv) any provision made on or after the passing of this Act by or under primary legislation.

(3) Retained direct minor EU legislation cannot be modified by any primary or subordinate legislation other than—

(a) an Act of Parliament,

(b) any other primary legislation (so far as it has the power to make such a modification), or

(c) any subordinate legislation so far as it is made under a power which permits such a modification by virtue of—

(i) paragraph 3, 5(2) or (4)(a), 8(3), 10(2) or (4)(a) or 12(3) of Schedule 8,

(ii) any other provision made by or under this Act,

(iii) any provision made by or under an Act of Parliament passed before, and in the same Session as, this Act, or

(iv) any provision made on or after the passing of this Act by or under primary legislation.

(4) Anything which is retained EU law by virtue of section 4 cannot be modified by any primary or subordinate legislation other than—

(a) an Act of Parliament,

(b) any other primary legislation (so far as it has the power to make such a modification), or

(c) any subordinate legislation so far as it is made under a power which permits such a modification by virtue of—

(i) paragraph 3, 5(3)(b) or (4)(b), 8(3), 10(3)(b) or (4)(b), 11(2)(b) or 12(3) of Schedule 8,

(ii) any other provision made by or under this Act,

(iii) any provision made by or under an Act of Parliament passed before, and in the same Session as, this Act, or

(iv) any provision made on or after the passing of this Act by or under primary legislation.

(5) For other provisions about the status of retained EU law, see—

(a) section 5(1) to (3) (status of retained EU law in relation to other enactments or rules of law),

(b) section 6 (status of retained case law and retained general principles of EU law),

(c) section 15(2) and Part 2 of Schedule 5 (status of retained EU law for the purposes of the rules of evidence),

(d) paragraphs 13 to 16 of Schedule 8 (affirmative and enhanced scrutiny procedure for, and information about, instruments which amend or revoke subordinate legislation under section 2(2) of the European Communities Act 1972 including subordinate legislation implementing EU directives),

(e) paragraphs 19 and 20 of that Schedule (status of certain retained direct EU legislation for the purposes of the Interpretation Act 1978), and

(f) paragraph 30 of that Schedule (status of retained direct EU legislation for the purposes of the Human Rights Act 1998).

(6) In this Act—

'retained direct minor EU legislation' means any retained direct EU legislation which is not retained direct principal EU legislation;

'retained direct principal EU legislation' means—

(a) any EU regulation so far as it—

(i) forms part of domestic law on and after exit day by virtue of section 3, and

(ii) was not EU tertiary legislation immediately before exit day, or

(b) any Annex to the EEA agreement so far as it—

(i) forms part of domestic law on and after exit day by virtue of section 3, and

(ii) refers to, or contains adaptations of, any EU regulation so far as it falls within paragraph (a),

(as modified by or under this Act or by other domestic law from time to time).

[Further aspects of withdrawal]

[7A General implementation of remainder of withdrawal agreement

(1) Subsection (2) applies to—

(a) all such rights, powers, liabilities, obligations and restrictions from time to time created or arising by or under the withdrawal agreement, and

(b) all such remedies and procedures from time to time provided for by or under the withdrawal agreement,

as in accordance with the withdrawal agreement are without further enactment to be given legal effect or used in the United Kingdom.

(2) The rights, powers, liabilities, obligations, restrictions, remedies and procedures concerned are to be—

(a) recognised and available in domestic law, and

(b) enforced, allowed and followed accordingly.

(3) Every enactment (including an enactment contained in this Act) is to be read and has effect subject to subsection (2).

(4) This section does not apply in relation to Part 4 of the withdrawal agreement so far as section 2(1) of the European Communities Act 1972 applies in relation to that Part.

(5) See also (among other things)—

(a) Part 3 of the European Union (Withdrawal Agreement) Act 2020 (further provision about citizens' rights),

(b) section 20 of that Act (financial provision),

(c) section 7C of this Act (interpretation of law relating to withdrawal agreement etc.),

(d) section 8B of this Act (power in connection with certain other separation issues),

(e) section 8C of this Act (power in connection with the Protocol on Ireland/ Northern Ireland in withdrawal agreement), and

(f) Parts 1B and 1C of Schedule 2 to this Act (powers involving devolved authorities in connection with certain other separation issues and the Ireland/ Northern Ireland Protocol).]

[7B General implementation of EEA EFTA and Swiss agreements

(1) Subsection (2) applies to all such rights, powers, liabilities, obligations, restrictions, remedies and procedures as—

(a) would from time to time be created or arise, or (in the case of remedies or procedures) be provided for, by or under the EEA EFTA separation agreement or the Swiss citizens' rights agreement, and

(b) would, in accordance with Article 4(1) of the withdrawal agreement, be required to be given legal effect or used in the United Kingdom without further enactment,

if that Article were to apply in relation to the EEA EFTA separation agreement and the Swiss citizens' rights agreement, those agreements were part of EU law and the relevant EEA states and Switzerland were member States.

(2) The rights, powers, liabilities, obligations, restrictions, remedies and procedures concerned are to be—

(a) recognised and available in domestic law, and

(b) enforced, allowed and followed accordingly.

(3) Every enactment (other than section 7A but otherwise including an enactment contained in this Act) is to be read and has effect subject to subsection (2).

(4) See also (among other things)—

(a) Part 3 of the European Union (Withdrawal Agreement) Act 2020 (further provision about citizens' rights),

(b) section 7C of this Act (interpretation of law relating to the EEA EFTA separation agreement and the Swiss citizens' rights agreement etc),

(c) section 8B of this Act (power in connection with certain other separation issues), and

(d) Part 1B of Schedule 2 to this Act (powers involving devolved authorities in connection with certain other separation issues).

(5) In this section 'the relevant EEA states' means Norway, Iceland and Liechtenstein.

(6) In this Act 'EEA EFTA separation agreement' and 'Swiss citizens' rights agreement' have the same meanings as in the European Union (Withdrawal Agreement) Act 2020 (see section 39(1) of that Act).]

[7C Interpretation of relevant separation agreement law

(1) Any question as to the validity, meaning or effect of any relevant separation agreement law is to be decided, so far as they are applicable—

(a) in accordance with the withdrawal agreement, the EEA EFTA separation agreement and the Swiss citizens' rights agreement, and

(b) having regard (among other things) to the desirability of ensuring that, where one of those agreements makes provision which corresponds to provision made by another of those agreements, the effect of relevant separation agreement law in relation to the matters dealt with by the corresponding provision in each agreement is consistent.

(2) See (among other things)—

(a) Article 4 of the withdrawal agreement (methods and principles relating to the effect, the implementation and the application of the agreement),

(b) Articles 158 and 160 of the withdrawal agreement (jurisdiction of the European Court in relation to Part 2 and certain provisions of Part 5 of the agreement),

(c) Articles 12 and 13 of the Protocol on Ireland/Northern Ireland in the withdrawal agreement (implementation, application, supervision and enforcement of the Protocol and common provisions),

(d) Article 4 of the EEA EFTA separation agreement (methods and principles relating to the effect, the implementation and the application of the agreement), and

(e) Article 4 of the Swiss citizens' rights agreement (methods and principles relating to the effect, the implementation and the application of the agreement).

(3) In this Act 'relevant separation agreement law' means—

(a) any of the following provisions or anything which is domestic law by virtue of any of them—

(i) section 7A, 7B, 8B or 8C or Part 1B or 1C of Schedule 2 or this section, or

(ii) Part 3, or section 20, of the European Union (Withdrawal Agreement) Act 2020 (citizens' rights and financial provision), or

(b) anything not falling within paragraph (a) so far as it is domestic law for the purposes of, or otherwise within the scope of—

(i) the withdrawal agreement (other than Part 4 of that agreement),

(ii) the EEA EFTA separation agreement, or

(iii) the Swiss citizens' rights agreement,

as that body of law is added to or otherwise modified by or under this Act or by other domestic law from time to time.]

Main powers in connection with withdrawal

8 Dealing with deficiencies arising from withdrawal

(1) A Minister of the Crown may by regulations make such provision as the Minister considers appropriate to prevent, remedy or mitigate—

(a) any failure of retained EU law to operate effectively, or

(b) any other deficiency in retained EU law,

arising from the withdrawal of the United Kingdom from the EU.

(2) Deficiencies in retained EU law are where the Minister considers that retained EU law—

(a) contains anything which has no practical application in relation to the United Kingdom or any part of it or is otherwise redundant or substantially redundant,

(b) confers functions on, or in relation to, EU entities which no longer have functions in that respect under EU law in relation to the United Kingdom or any part of it,

(c) makes provision for, or in connection with, reciprocal arrangements between—

(i) the United Kingdom or any part of it or a public authority in the United Kingdom, and

(ii) the EU, an EU entity, a member State or a public authority in a member State,

which no longer exist or are no longer appropriate,

(d) makes provision for, or in connection with, other arrangements which—

(i) involve the EU, an EU entity, a member State or a public authority in a member State, or

(ii) are otherwise dependent upon the United Kingdom's membership of the EU [or Part 4 of the withdrawal agreement],

and which no longer exist or are no longer appropriate,

(e) makes provision for, or in connection with, any reciprocal or other arrangements not falling within paragraph (c) or (d) which no longer exist, or are no longer appropriate, as a result of the United Kingdom ceasing to be a party to any of the EU Treaties [or as a result of either the end of the implementation period or any other effect of the withdrawal agreement],

[(ea) is not clear in its effect as a result of the operation of any provision of Sections 2 to 6 or Schedule 1,]

(f) does not contain any functions or restrictions which—

(i) were in an EU directive and in force immediately before [IP completion day] (including any power to make EU tertiary legislation), and

(ii) it is appropriate to retain, or

(g) contains EU references which are no longer appropriate.

(3) There is also a deficiency in retained EU law where the Minister considers that there is—

(a) anything in retained EU law which is of a similar kind to any deficiency which falls within subsection (2), or

(b) a deficiency in retained EU law of a kind described, or provided for, in regulations made by a Minister of the Crown.

(4) But retained EU law is not deficient merely because it does not contain any modification of EU law which is adopted or notified, comes into force or only applies on or after [IP completion day].

(5) Regulations under subsection (1) may make any provision that could be made by an Act of Parliament.

(6) Regulations under subsection (1) may (among other things) provide for functions of EU entities or public authorities in member States (including making an instrument of a legislative character or providing funding) to be—

(a) exercisable instead by a public authority (whether or not established for the purpose) in the United Kingdom, or

(b) replaced, abolished or otherwise modified.

(7) But regulations under subsection (1) may not—

(a) impose or increase taxation or fees,

(b) make retrospective provision,

(c) create a relevant criminal offence,

(d) establish a public authority,

[. . .]

(f) amend, repeal or revoke the Human Rights Act 1998 or any subordinate legislation made under it, or

(g) amend or repeal the Scotland Act 1998, the Government of Wales Act 2006 or the Northern Ireland Act 1998 (unless the regulations are made by virtue of paragraph 21(b) of Schedule 7 to this Act or are amending or repealing any provision of those Acts which modifies another enactment).

(8) No regulations may be made under this section after the end of the period of two years beginning with [IP completion day].

(9) The reference in subsection (1) to a failure or other deficiency arising from the withdrawal of the United Kingdom from the EU includes a reference to any failure or other deficiency arising from [—

(a) any aspect of that withdrawal, including (among other things)—

(i) the end of the implementation period, or

(ii) any other effect of the withdrawal agreement, or

(b) that withdrawal, or any such aspect of it, taken together] with the operation of any provision, or the interaction between any provisions, made by or under this Act [or the European Union (Withdrawal Agreement) Act 2020].

[8A Supplementary power in connection with implementation period

(1) A Minister of the Crown may by regulations

(a) provide for other modifications for the purposes of section 1B(3)(f)(i) (whether applying in all cases or particular cases or descriptions of case),

(b) provide for subsection (3) or (4) of section 1B not to apply to any extent in particular cases or descriptions of case,

(c) make different provision in particular cases or descriptions of case to that made by subsection (3) or (4) of that section,

(d) modify any enactment contained in this Act in consequence of any repeal made by section 1A(5) or 1B(6), or

(e) make such provision not falling within paragraph (a), (b), (c) or (d) as the Minister considers appropriate for any purpose of, or otherwise in connection with, Part 4 of the withdrawal agreement.

(2) The power to make regulations under subsection (1) may (among other things) be exercised by modifying any provision made by or under an enactment.

(3) In subsection (2) 'enactment' does not include primary legislation passed or made after IP completion day.

(4) No regulations may be made under subsection (1) after the end of the period of two years beginning with IP completion day.]

[8B Power in connection with certain other separation issues

(1) A Minister of the Crown may by regulations make such provision as the Minister considers appropriate—

(a) to implement Part 3 of the withdrawal agreement (separation provisions),

(b) to supplement the effect of section 7A in relation to that Part, or

(c) otherwise for the purposes of dealing with matters arising out of, or related to, that Part (including matters arising by virtue of section 7A and that Part).

(2) A Minister of the Crown may by regulations make such provision as the Minister considers appropriate—

(a) to implement Part 3 of the EEA EFTA separation agreement (separation provisions),

(b) to supplement the effect of section 7B in relation to that Part, or

(c) otherwise for the purposes of dealing with matters arising out of, or related to, that Part (including matters arising by virtue of section 7B and that Part).

(3) Regulations under this section may make any provision that could be made by an Act of Parliament.

(4) Regulations under this section may (among other things) restate, for the purposes of making the law clearer or more accessible, anything that forms part of domestic law by virtue of—

(a) section 7A above and Part 3 of the withdrawal agreement, or

(b) section 7B above and Part 3 of the EEA EFTA separation agreement.

(5) But regulations under this section may not—

(a) impose or increase taxation or fees,

(b) make retrospective provision,

(c) create a relevant criminal offence,

(d) establish a public authority,

(e) amend, repeal or revoke the Human Rights Act 1998 or any subordinate legislation made under it, or

(f) amend or repeal the Scotland Act 1998, the Government of Wales Act 2006 or the Northern Ireland Act 1998 (unless the regulations are made by virtue of paragraph 21(b) of Schedule 7 to this Act or are amending or repealing any provision of those Acts which modifies another enactment).

(6) In this section references to Part 3 of the withdrawal agreement or of the EEA EFTA separation agreement include references to any provision of EU law which is applied by, or referred to in, that Part (to the extent of the application or reference).]

[. . .]

Devolution

10 Continuation of North-South co-operation and the prevention of new border arrangements

(1) In exercising any of the powers under this Act, a Minister of the Crown or devolved authority must—

(a) act in a way that is compatible with the terms of the Northern Ireland Act 1998, and

(b) have due regard to the joint report from the negotiators of the EU and the United Kingdom Government on progress during phase 1 of negotiations under Article 50 of the Treaty on European Union.

(2) Nothing in section 8, 9 or 23(1) or (6) of this Act authorises regulations which—

(a) diminish any form of North-South cooperation provided for by the Belfast Agreement (as defined by section 98 of the Northern Ireland Act 1998), or

(b) create or facilitate border arrangements between Northern Ireland and the Republic of Ireland after exit day which feature physical infrastructure, including border posts, or checks and controls, that did not exist before exit day and are not in accordance with an agreement between the United Kingdom and the EU.

[(3) A Minister of the Crown may not agree to the making of a recommendation by the Joint Committee under Article 11(2) of the Protocol on Ireland/Northern Ireland in the withdrawal agreement (recommendations as to North-South co-operation) to—

(a) alter the arrangements for North-South co-operation as provided for by the Belfast Agreement,

(b) establish a new implementation body, or

(c) alter the functions of an existing implementation body.

(4) In this section—

'the Belfast Agreement' has the meaning given by section 98 of the Northern Ireland Act 1998;

'implementation body' has the meaning given by section 55(3) of that Act.]

11 Powers involving devolved authorities corresponding to sections 8 and 9

Schedule 2 (which confers powers to make regulations involving devolved authorities which correspond to the powers conferred by sections 8 and 9) has effect.

12 Retaining EU restrictions in devolution legislation etc

(1), (2) *amend the Scotland Act 1998.*

(3), (4) *amend the Government of Wales Act 2006.*

(5), (6) *amend the Northern Ireland Act 1998.*

(7) Part 1 of Schedule 3 (which makes corresponding provision in relation to executive competence to that made by subsections (1) to (6) in relation to legislative competence) has effect.

(8) Part 2 of Schedule 3 (which imposes reporting obligations on a Minister of the Crown in recognition of the fact that the powers to make regulations conferred by subsections (1) to (6) and Part 1 of Schedule 3, and any restrictions arising by virtue of them, are intended to be temporary) has effect.

(9) A Minister of the Crown may by regulations—

(a) repeal any of the following provisions—

(i) section 30A or 57(4) to (15) of the Scotland Act 1998,

(ii) section 80(8) to (8L) or 109A of the Government of Wales Act 2006, or

(iii) section 6A or 24(3) to (15) of the Northern Ireland Act 1998, or

(b) modify any enactment in consequence of any such repeal.

(10) Until all of the provisions mentioned in subsection (9)(a) have been repealed, a Minister of the Crown must, after the end of each review period, consider whether it is appropriate—

(a) to repeal each of those provisions so far as it has not been repealed, or

(b) to revoke any regulations made under any of those provisions so far as they have not been revoked.

(11) In considering whether to exercise the power to make regulations under subsection (9), a Minister of the Crown must have regard (among other things) to—

(a) the fact that the powers to make regulations conferred by the provisions mentioned in subsection (9)(a), and any restrictions arising by virtue of them, are intended to be temporary and, where appropriate, replaced with other arrangements, and

(b) any progress which has been made in implementing those other arrangements.

(12) Part 3 of Schedule 3 (which contains amendments of devolution legislation not dealt with elsewhere) has effect.

(13) In this section—

'arrangement' means any enactment or other arrangement (whether or not legally enforceable);

'review period' means—

(a) the period of three months beginning with the day on which subsection (10) comes into force, and

(b) after that, each successive period of three months.

Parliamentary approval of outcome of EU negotiations

[. . .]

[13A Review of EU legislation during implementation period

(1) Subsection (2) applies where the European Scrutiny Select Committee of the House of Commons ('the ESC') publishes a report in respect of any EU legislation made, or which may be made, during the implementation period and the report—

(a) states that, in the opinion of the ESC, the EU legislation raises a matter of vital national interest to the United Kingdom,

(b) confirms that the ESC has taken such evidence as it considers appropriate as to the effect of the EU legislation and has consulted any Departmental Select Committee of the House of Commons which the ESC considers also has an interest in the EU legislation, and

(c) sets out the wording of a motion to be moved in the House of Commons in accordance with subsection (2).

(2) A Minister of the Crown must, within the period of 14 Commons sitting days beginning with the day on which the report is published, make arrangements for the motion mentioned in subsection (1)(c) to be debated and voted on by the House of Commons.

(3) Subsection (4) applies where the EU Select Committee of the House of Lords ('the EUC') publishes a report in respect of any EU legislation made, or which may be made, during the implementation period and the report—

(a) states that, in the opinion of the EUC, the EU legislation raises a matter of vital national interest to the United Kingdom,

(b) confirms that the EUC has taken such evidence as it considers appropriate as to the effect of the EU legislation, and

(c) sets out the wording of a motion to be moved in the House of Lords in accordance with subsection (4).

(4) A Minister of the Crown must, within the period of 14 Lords sitting days beginning with the day on which the report is published, make arrangements for the motion mentioned in subsection (3)(c) to be debated and voted on by the House of Lords.

(5) In this section—

'EU legislation' means—

(a) any amendment to the Treaty on European Union, the Treaty on the Functioning of the European Union, the Euratom Treaty or the EEA agreement,

(b) any EU directive, or

(c) any EU regulation or EU decision which is not EU tertiary legislation;

'[the European Scrutiny Select Committee of the House of Commons' means the Select Committee of the House of Commons known as the European Scrutiny Select Committee or any successor of that committee;

'the EU Select Committee of the House of Lords' means the Select Committee of the House of Lords known as the EU Select Committee or any successor of that committee.]

[13B Certain dispute procedures under withdrawal agreement

(1) Subsection (2) applies if a request has been made under Article 170 of the withdrawal agreement to the other party in a dispute (request to establish an arbitration panel in relation to a dispute between the EU and the United Kingdom).

(2) A Minister of the Crown must, within the 14 day period beginning with the day on which the request is made, make a statement in writing to each House of Parliament that the request has been made and setting out the details of it.

(3) Subsection (4) applies if the European Court has given a ruling in response to a request by an arbitration panel under Article 174(1) of the withdrawal agreement (request for ruling by European Court on certain questions arising in a dispute submitted to arbitration).

(4) A Minister of the Crown must, within the 14 day period beginning with the publication in the Official Journal of the European Union of the ruling of the European Court, make a statement in writing to each House of Parliament that the ruling has been made and setting out the details of it contained in the Official Journal.

(5) After the end of each reporting period, a Minister of the Crown must lay before each House of Parliament a report setting out the number of times within the reporting period that the Joint Committee has been provided with notice under Article 169(1) of the withdrawal agreement (notice concerning the commencement of consultations in the Joint Committee to resolve a dispute between the EU and the United Kingdom about the interpretation and application of the withdrawal agreement).

(6) In this section—

'reporting period' means—

(a) the period of one year beginning with the day on which IP completion day falls, and

(b) each subsequent year;

'the 14 day period' means—

(a) in relation to the House of Commons, the period of 14 Commons sitting days, and

(b) in relation to the House of Lords, the period of 14 Lords sitting days.]

Financial and other matters

14 Financial provision

(1) Schedule 4 (which contains powers in connection with fees and charges) has effect.

(2) A Minister of the Crown, government department or devolved authority may incur expenditure, for the purpose of, or in connection with, preparing for anything about which provision may be made under a power to make subordinate legislation conferred or modified by or under this Act, before any such provision is made.

(3) There is to be paid out of money provided by Parliament—

(a) any expenditure incurred by a Minister of the Crown, government department or other public authority by virtue of this Act, and

(b) any increase attributable to this Act in the sums payable by virtue of any other Act out of money so provided.

(4) Subsection (3) is subject to any other provision made by or under this Act or any other enactment.

15 Publication and rules of evidence

(1) Part 1 of Schedule 5 (which makes provision for the publication by the Queen's Printer of copies of retained direct EU legislation and related information) has effect.

(2) Part 2 of Schedule 5 (which makes provision about rules of evidence) has effect.

[15A Prohibition on extending implementation period

A Minister of the Crown may not agree in the Joint Committee to an extension of the implementation period.]

[15B Ministerial co-chairs of the Joint Committee

The functions of the United Kingdom's co-chair of the Joint Committee, under Annex VIII of the withdrawal agreement (rules of procedure of the Joint Committee and specialised committees), are to be exercised personally by a Minister of the Crown (and, accordingly, only a Minister of the Crown may be designated as a replacement under Rule 1(3)).]

[15C No use of written procedure in the Joint Committee

(1) The United Kingdom's co-chair of the Joint Committee may not consent to the Joint Committee using the written procedure provided for in Rule 9(1) of Annex VIII of the withdrawal agreement.

(2) In subsection the reference to the United Kingdom's co-chair of the Joint Committee includes a reference to any designee of the co-chair designated under Rule 1(3) of Annex VIII of the withdrawal agreement.]

[. . .]

17 Family unity for those seeking asylum or other protection in Europe

[(1) A Minister of the Crown must, within the period of two months beginning with the day on which the European Union (Withdrawal Agreement) Act 2020 is passed, lay before Parliament a statement of policy in relation to any future arrangements between the United Kingdom and the EU about—

(a) unaccompanied children, who make an application for international protection to a member State, coming to the United Kingdom where it is in their best interests to join a relative who—

(i) is a lawful resident of the United Kingdom, or

(ii) has made a protection claim which has not been decided, and

(b) unaccompanied children in the United Kingdom, who make a protection claim, going to a member State to join a relative there in equivalent circumstances.]

(2) For the purposes of subsection (1)(a)(i) a person is not a lawful resident of the United Kingdom if the person requires leave to enter or remain in the United Kingdom but does not have it.

(3) For the purposes of subsection (1)(a)(ii), a protection claim is decided—

(a) when the Secretary of State notifies the claimant of the Secretary of State's decision on the claim, unless the claimant appeals against the decision, or

(b) if the claimant appeals against the Secretary of State's decision on the claim, when the appeal is disposed of.

(4) In this section—

'application for international protection' has the meaning given by Article 2(h) of Directive 2011/95/EU of the European Parliament and of the Council on standards for the qualification of third-country nationals or stateless persons as beneficiaries of international protection, for a uniform status for refugees or for persons eligible for subsidiary protection, and for the content of the protection granted;

'protection claim' has the same meaning as in Part 5 of the Nationality, Immigration and Asylum Act 2002 (see section 82(2) of that Act);

'relative', in relation to an unaccompanied child, means—

(a) a spouse or civil partner of the child or any person with whom the child has a durable relationship that is similar to marriage or civil partnership, or

(b) a parent, grandparent, uncle, aunt, brother or sister of the child;

'unaccompanied child' means a person under the age of 18 ('the child') who is not in the care of a person who—

(a) is aged 18 or over, and

(b) by law or custom of the country or territory in which the child is present, has responsibility for caring for the child.

[. . .]

General and final provision

20 Interpretation

(1) In this Act—

'Charter of Fundamental Rights' means the Charter of Fundamental Rights of the European Union of 7 December 2000, as adapted at Strasbourg on 12 December 2007;

'devolved authority' means—

(a) the Scottish Ministers,

(b) the Welsh Ministers, or

(c) a Northern Ireland department;

'domestic law' means—

(a) in section 3, the law of England and Wales, Scotland and Northern Ireland, and

(b) in any other case, the law of England and Wales, Scotland or Northern Ireland;

'the EEA' means the European Economic Area;

'enactment' means an enactment whenever passed or made and includes—

(a) an enactment contained in any Order in Council, order, rules, regulations, scheme, warrant, byelaw or other instrument made under an Act,

(b) an enactment contained in any Order in Council made in exercise of Her Majesty's Prerogative,

(c) an enactment contained in, or in an instrument made under, an Act of the Scottish Parliament,

(d) an enactment contained in, or in an instrument made under, a Measure or Act of the National Assembly for Wales,

(e) an enactment contained in, or in an instrument made under, Northern Ireland legislation,

(f) an enactment contained in any instrument made by a member of the Scottish Government, the Welsh Ministers, the First Minister for Wales, the Counsel General to the Welsh Government, a Northern Ireland Minister, the First Minister in Northern Ireland, the deputy First Minister in Northern Ireland or a Northern Ireland department in exercise of prerogative or other executive functions of Her Majesty which are exercisable by such a person on behalf of Her Majesty,

(g) an enactment contained in, or in an instrument made under, a Measure of the Church Assembly or of the General Synod of the Church of England, and

(h) except in sections 2 and 7 or where there is otherwise a contrary intention, any retained direct EU legislation;

'EU decision' means—

(a) a decision within the meaning of Article 288 of the Treaty on the Functioning of the European Union, or

(b) a decision under former Article 34(2)(c) of the Treaty on European Union;

'EU directive' means a directive within the meaning of Article 288 of the Treaty on the Functioning of the European Union;

'EU entity' means an EU institution or any office, body or agency of the EU;

'EU reference' means—

(a) any reference to the EU, an EU entity or a member State,

(b) any reference to an EU directive or any other EU law, or

(c) any other reference which relates to the EU;

'EU regulation' means a regulation within the meaning of Article 288 of the Treaty on the Functioning of the European Union;

'EU tertiary legislation' means—

(a) any provision made under—

(i) an EU regulation,

(ii) a decision within the meaning of Article 288 of the Treaty on the Functioning of the European Union, or

(iii) an EU directive,

by virtue of Article 290 or 291(2) of the Treaty on the Functioning of the European Union or former Article 202 of the Treaty establishing the European Community, or

(b) any measure adopted in accordance with former Article 34(2)(c) of the Treaty on European Union to implement decisions under former Article 34(2)(c),

but does not include any such provision or measure which is an EU directive;

'exempt EU instrument' means anything which is an exempt EU instrument by virtue of Schedule 6;

'exit day' means 29 March 2019 at 11.00 p.m. (and see subsections (2) to (5));

'member State' (except in the definitions of 'direct EU legislation' and 'EU reference') does not include the United Kingdom;

'Minister of the Crown' has the same meaning as in the Ministers of the Crown Act 1975 and also includes the Commissioners for Her Majesty's Revenue and Customs;

'modify' includes amend, repeal or revoke (and related expressions are to be read accordingly);

'Northern Ireland devolved authority' means the First Minister and deputy First Minister in Northern Ireland acting jointly, a Northern Ireland Minister or a Northern Ireland department;

'primary legislation' means—

(a) an Act of Parliament,

(b) an Act of the Scottish Parliament,

(c) a Measure or Act of the National Assembly for Wales, or

(d) Northern Ireland legislation;

'public authority' means a public authority within the meaning of section 6 of the Human Rights Act 1998;

'relevant criminal offence' means an offence for which an individual who has reached the age of 18 (or, in relation to Scotland or Northern Ireland, 21) is capable of being sentenced to imprisonment for a term of more than 2 years (ignoring any enactment prohibiting or restricting the imprisonment of individuals who have no previous convictions);

'retained direct EU legislation' means any direct EU legislation which forms part of domestic law by virtue of section 3 (as modified by or under this Act or by other domestic law from time to time, and including any instruments made under it on or after exit day);

'retrospective provision', in relation to provision made by regulations, means provision taking effect from a date earlier than the date on which the regulations are made;

'subordinate legislation' means—

(a) any Order in Council, order, rules, regulations, scheme, warrant, byelaw or other instrument made under any Act, or

(b) any instrument made under an Act of the Scottish Parliament, Northern Ireland legislation or a Measure or Act of the National Assembly for Wales, and (except in section 7 or Schedule 2 or where there is a contrary intention) includes any Order in Council, order, rules, regulations, scheme, warrant, byelaw or other instrument made on or after exit day under any retained direct EU legislation;

'tribunal' means any tribunal in which legal proceedings may be brought;

'Wales' and 'Welsh zone' have the same meaning as in the Government of Wales Act 2006 (see section 158 of that Act);

'withdrawal agreement' means an agreement (whether or not ratified) between the United Kingdom and the EU under Article 50(2) of the Treaty on European Union which sets out the arrangements for the United Kingdom's withdrawal from the EU.

(2) In this Act references to before, after or on exit day, or to beginning with exit day, are to be read as references to before, after or at 11.00 p.m. on 29 March 2019 or (as the case may be) to beginning with 11.00 p.m. on that day.

(3) Subsection (4) applies if the day or time on or at which the Treaties are to cease to apply to the United Kingdom in accordance with Article 50(3) of the Treaty on European Union is different from that specified in the definition of 'exit day' in subsection (1).

(4) A Minister of the Crown may by regulations—

(a) amend the definition of 'exit day' in subsection (1) to ensure that the day and time specified in the definition are the day and time that the Treaties are to cease to apply to the United Kingdom, and

(b) amend subsection (2) in consequence of any such amendment.

(5) In subsections (3) and (4) 'the Treaties' means the Treaty on European Union and the Treaty on the Functioning of the European Union.

(6) In this Act references to anything which continues to be domestic law by virtue of section 2 include references to anything to which subsection (1) of that section applies which continues to be domestic law on or after exit day (whether or not it would have done so irrespective of that section).

(7) In this Act references to anything which is retained EU law by virtue of section 4 include references to any modifications, made by or under this Act or by other domestic law from time to time, of the rights, powers, liabilities, obligations, restrictions, remedies or procedures concerned.

(8) References in this Act (however expressed) to a public authority in the United Kingdom include references to a public authority in any part of the United Kingdom.

(9) References in this Act to former Article 34(2)(c) of the Treaty on European Union are references to that Article as it had effect at any time before the coming into force of the Treaty of Lisbon.

(10) Any other reference in this Act to—

(a) an Article of the Treaty on European Union or the Treaty on the Functioning of the European Union, or

(b) Article 10 of Title VII of Protocol 36 to those treaties,

includes a reference to that Article as applied by Article 106a of the Euratom Treaty.

21 Index of defined expressions

(1) In this Act, the expressions listed in the left-hand column have the meaning given by, or are to be interpreted in accordance with, the provisions listed in the right-hand column.

Expression	*Provision*
Anything which continues to be domestic law by virtue of section 2	Section 20(6)
Anything which is retained EU law by virtue of section 4	Section 20(7)
Article (in relation to the Treaty on European Union or the Treaty on the Functioning of the European Union)	Section 20(10)
Charter of Fundamental Rights	Section 20(1)
Devolved authority	Section 20(1)
Direct EU legislation	Section 3(2)
Domestic law	Section 20(1)
The EEA	Section 20(1)
EEA agreement	Schedule 1 to the Interpretation Act 1978
Enactment	Section 20(1)
The EU	Schedule 1 to the Interpretation Act 1978
EU decision	Section 20(1)
EU directive	Section 20(1)
EU entity	Section 20(1)
EU institution	Schedule 1 to the Interpretation Act 1978
EU instrument	Schedule 1 to the Interpretation Act 1978
Euratom Treaty	Schedule 1 to the Interpretation Act 1978
EU reference	Section 20(1)
EU regulation	Section 20(1)
European Court	Schedule 1 to the Interpretation Act 1978
EU tertiary legislation	Section 20(1)
EU Treaties	Schedule 1 to the Interpretation Act 1978
Exempt EU instrument	Section 20(1)
Exit day (and related expressions)	Section 20(1) to (5)
Former Article 34(2)(c) of Treaty on European Union	Section 20(9)
Member State	Section 20(1) and Schedule 1 to the Interpretation Act 1978
Minister of the Crown	Section 20(1)
Modify (and related expressions)	Section 20(1)
Northern Ireland devolved authority	Section 20(1)
Operative (in relation to direct EU legislation)	Section 3(3)
Primary legislation	Section 20(1)
Public authority	Section 20(1)
Public authority in the United Kingdom (however expressed)	Section 20(8)
Relevant criminal offence	Section 20(1) (and paragraph 44 of Schedule 8)
Retained case law	Section 6(7)
Retained direct EU legislation	Section 20(1)
Retained direct minor EU legislation	Section 7(6)
Retained direct principal EU legislation	Section 7(6)
Retained domestic case law	Section 6(7)
Retained EU case law	Section 6(7)
Retained EU law	Section 6(7)
Retained general principles of EU law	Section 6(7)
Retrospective provision	Section 20(1)

Expression	*Provision*
Subordinate legislation	Section 20(1)
Tribunal	Section 20(1)
Wales	Section 20(1)
Welsh zone	Section 20(1)
Withdrawal agreement	Section 20(1)

(2) See paragraph 22 of Schedule 8 for amendments made by this Act to Schedule 1 to the Interpretation Act 1978.

22 Regulations

Schedule 7 (which makes provision about the scrutiny by Parliament and the devolved legislatures of regulations under this Act and contains other general provision about such regulations) has effect.

23 Consequential and transitional provision

(1) A Minister of the Crown may by regulations make such provision as the Minister considers appropriate in consequence of this Act.

(2) The power to make regulations under subsection (1) may (among other things) be exercised by modifying any provision made by or under an enactment.

(3) In subsection (2) 'enactment' does not include primary legislation passed or made after the end of the Session in which this Act is passed.

(4) No regulations may be made under subsection (1) after the end of the period of 10 years beginning with exit day.

(5) Parts 1 and 2 of Schedule 8 (which contain consequential provision) have effect.

(6) A Minister of the Crown may by regulations make such transitional, transitory or saving provision as the Minister considers appropriate in connection with the coming into force of any provision of this Act (including its operation in connection with exit day).

(7) Parts 3 and 4 of Schedule 8 (which contain transitional, transitory and saving provision) have effect.

(8) The enactments mentioned in Schedule 9 (which contains repeals not made elsewhere in this Act) are repealed to the extent specified.

24 Extent

(1) Subject to subsections (2) and (3), this Act extends to England and Wales, Scotland and Northern Ireland.

(2) Any provision of this Act which amends or repeals an enactment has the same extent as the enactment amended or repealed.

(3) Regulations under section 8(1) or 23 may make provision which extends to Gibraltar—

(a) modifying any enactment which—

(i) extends to Gibraltar and relates to European Parliamentary elections, or

(ii) extends to Gibraltar for any purpose which is connected with Gibraltar forming part of an electoral region, under the European Parliamentary Elections Act 2002, for the purposes of such elections, or

(b) which is supplementary, incidental, consequential, transitional, transitory or saving provision in connection with a modification within paragraph (a).

25 Commencement and short title

(1) The following provisions—

(a) sections 8 to 11 (including Schedule 2),

(b) paragraphs 4, 5, 21(2)(b), 48(b), 51(2)(c) and (d) and (4) of Schedule 3 (and section 12(8) and (12) so far as relating to those paragraphs),

(c) sections 13 and 14 (including Schedule 4),

(d) sections 16 to 18,
(e) sections 20 to 22 (including Schedules 6 and 7),
(f) section 23(1) to (4) and (6),
(g) paragraph 41(10), 43 and 44 of Schedule 8 (and section 23(7) so far as relating to those paragraphs),
(h) section 24, and
(i) this section,

come into force on the day on which this Act is passed.

(2) In section 12—

(a) subsection (2) comes into force on the day on which this Act is passed for the purposes of making regulations under section 30A of the Scotland Act 1998,

. . .

(3) In Schedule 3—

(a) paragraph 1(b) comes into force on the day on which this Act is passed for the purposes of making regulations under section 57(4) of the Scotland Act 1998,

. . .

(d) paragraph 24(2) comes into force on that day for the purposes of making regulations under section 30A of the Scotland Act 1998,
(e) paragraph 24(3) comes into force on that day for the purposes of making regulations under section 57(4) of the Scotland Act 1998,
(f) paragraph 25 comes into force on that day for the purposes of making regulations under section 30A or 57(4) of the Scotland Act 1998,

. . .

and section 12(7) and (12), so far as relating to each of those paragraphs, comes into force on that day for the purposes of making the regulations mentioned above in relation to that paragraph.

(4) The provisions of this Act, so far as they are not brought into force by subsections (1) to (3), come into force on such day as a Minister of the Crown may by regulations appoint; and different days may be appointed for different purposes.

(5) This Act may be cited as the European Union (Withdrawal) Act 2018.

EARLY PARLIAMENTARY GENERAL ELECTION ACT 2019
(2019, c 29)

1 Early parliamentary general election

(1) An early parliamentary general election is to take place on 12 December 2019 in consequence of the passing of this Act.

(2) That day is to be treated as a polling day appointed under section 2(7) of the Fixed-term Parliaments Act 2011.

(3) This early parliamentary general election is to be treated as taking place in accordance with section 2 of that Act for the purposes of—

(a) section 96A(9) of the Welfare Reform Act 2012 (benefit cap: review), and
(b) section 23(8) of the Small Business, Enterprise and Employment Act 2015 (duty on Secretary of State to publish reports on economic impact on business activities of regulatory provisions).

(4) For the purposes of regulation 29(4) of the Representation of the People (Scotland) Regulations 2001 (which sets out a period for objecting to applications for registration), regulation 8(3) of those Regulations applies as if 2 December 2019 were not a bank holiday.

2 Commencement and short title

(1) This Act comes into force on the day it is passed.

(2) This Act may be cited as the Early Parliamentary General Election Act 2019.

CONTINGENCIES FUND ACT 2020
(2020, c 6)

1 Temporary increase of capital limit of Contingencies Fund

(1) Section 1(1) of the Contingencies Fund Act 1974 (which provides that the capital of the Contingencies Fund must not exceed 2 per cent of the authorised supply expenditure for the year ending on the previous 31 March) is modified as follows.

(2) The reference to 2 per cent is to be read as if it were a reference to 50 per cent.

(3) The modification made by subsection (2) has effect in relation to any time before 1 April 2021.

2 Short title

This Act may be cited as the Contingencies Fund Act 2020.

EUROPEAN UNION (WITHDRAWAL AGREEMENT) ACT 2020
(2020, c 1)

38 Parliamentary sovereignty

(1) It is recognised that the Parliament of the United Kingdom is sovereign.

(2) In particular, its sovereignty subsists notwithstanding—

(a) directly applicable or directly effective EU law continuing to be recognised and available in domestic law by virtue of section 1A or 1B of the European Union (Withdrawal) Act 2018 (savings of existing law for the implementation period),

(b) section 7A of that Act (other directly applicable or directly effective aspects of the withdrawal agreement),

(c) section 7B of that Act (deemed direct applicability or direct effect in relation to the EEA EFTA separation agreement and the Swiss citizens' rights agreement), and

(d) section 7C of that Act (interpretation of law relating to the withdrawal agreement (other than the implementation period), the EEA EFTA separation agreement and the Swiss citizens' rights agreement).

(3) Accordingly, nothing in this Act derogates from the sovereignty of the Parliament of the United Kingdom.

CORONAVIRUS (SCOTLAND) ACT 2020
(2020, asp 7)

12 Expiry

(1) Part 1 expires on 30 September 2020.

(2) Subsection (1) is subject to section 13.

(3) The Scottish Ministers may by regulations—

(a) amend subsection (1) so as to replace '30 September 2020' with '31 March 2021',

(b) further amend subsection (1) so as to replace '31 March 2021' with '30 September 2021'.

(4) The power conferred by subsection (3)(b) may be used only after 30 September 2020.

(5) Regulations under subsection (3) are subject to the affirmative procedure.

(6) Before laying a draft Scottish statutory instrument containing regulations under subsection (3) before the Scottish Parliament in accordance with section 29(2) of the Interpretation and Legislative Reform (Scotland) Act 2010, the Scottish Ministers must lay before the Parliament a statement of their reasons why the regulations should be made.

(7) Subsection (8) applies if the regulations are made in accordance with paragraph 23 of schedule 7.

(8) The Scottish Ministers must, at the same time as laying the regulations before the Parliament in accordance with paragraph 26 of that schedule, lay before the Parliament a statement of their reasons for making the regulations.

(9) The Scottish Ministers may by regulations make transitional, transitory or saving provision in connection with the expiry under subsection (1) of any provision of this Act.

(10) Regulations under subsection (9)—

(a) may make different provision for different purposes or areas,

(b) are subject to the negative procedure.

13 Power to bring forward expiry

(1) The Scottish Ministers may by regulations provide that any provision of Part 1—

(a) does not expire at the time when it would otherwise expire (whether by virtue of section 12 or previous regulations under this section), and

(b) expires instead at such earlier time as is specified in the regulations.

(2) Regulations under this section—

(a) may make different provision for different purposes or areas,

(b) may make transitional, transitory or saving provision.

(3) Regulations under this section are subject to the negative procedure.

PART II
OTHER MATERIALS

RULES OF THE COURT OF SESSION
Act of Sederunt (Rules of the Court of Session 1994), SI 1994/1443

CHAPTER 58
JUDICIAL REVIEW

The petition

58.3.(1) A petition may not be lodged in respect of an application if that application could be made by appeal or review under or by virtue of any enactment.

(2) For the purposes of calculating the time limit under section 27A of the Act of 1988, an application is made when a petition is lodged.

(3) A petition for judicial review is made in Form 58.3.

(4) A petition must—

(a) have lodged with it all relevant documents in the petitioner's possession or control;

(b) have appended to it a schedule specifying—

(i) any documents which the petition founds on that are not in the petitioner's possession or control; and

(ii) the person who has possession or control over those documents;

(c) where the decision, act or omission in question and the basis of the challenge is not apparent from the documents lodged, have lodged with it an affidavit stating the terms of that decision, act or omission and the basis of the challenge

The petition: intimation and service

58.4.(1) When a petition is lodged, the Lord Ordinary must make an order specifying—

(a) such intimation, service and advertisement as may be necessary;

(b) the date by which any respondent or interested party who intends to participate in the decision whether permission should be granted must, if so advised, lodge answers and any relevant documents (see rule 58.6(1)).

The permission stage

58.7.(1) Within 14 days from the end of the period for lodging answers the Lord Ordinary must—

(a) decide whether to grant permission (including permission subject to conditions or only on particular grounds); or

(b) order an oral hearing (for the purpose of deciding whether to grant permission) to take place within 7 days.

(2) Where permission is refused (or permission is granted subject to conditions or only on particular grounds) without an oral hearing, the Lord Ordinary must give reasons for the decision.

The permission stage: requesting an oral hearing

58.8.(1) A request to review a decision made without an oral hearing is made in Form 58.8.

(2) Where a request is granted, the oral hearing must take place within 7 days.

(3) The petitioner, respondent and any other person who has lodged answers to the petition must be given at least 2 days' notice of the oral hearing.

The permission stage: oral hearing
58.9.(1) Except on cause shown, an oral hearing must not exceed 30 minutes.

(2) Where permission is refused (or permission is granted subject to conditions or only on particular grounds) at an oral hearing, the Lord Ordinary must give reasons for the decision.

The permission stage: appeal to the Inner House
58.10. An appeal under section 27D(2) of the Act of 1988 (appeals following oral hearings) is made by reclaiming motion (see rule 38.8(d)).

The permission stage: where permission is granted
58.11.(1) When permission is granted, the Keeper of the Rolls must, in consultation with the Lord Ordinary, fix—

(a) a date for the substantive hearing, which must be no later than 12 weeks from the date on which permission is granted, except where the Lord Ordinary is satisfied that a longer period is necessary; and

(b) a date for the procedural hearing (unless the Lord Ordinary is satisfied that a procedural hearing is unnecessary), which must be no later than 6 weeks from the date on which permission is granted, except where the Lord Ordinary is satisfied that a longer period is necessary.

(2) When permission is granted, the Lord Ordinary must make such orders for further procedure as are appropriate for the speedy determination of the petition and in particular may order—

(a) service of the petition, answers and relevant documents, on a person not specified in the order made under rule 58.4;

(b) service of the decision granting permission and the date of the hearing on a person specified in the order made under rule 58.4 who lodged answers;

(c) service of the decision granting permission and the date of the hearing on a person specified in the order made under rule 58.4 who did not lodge answers but who did notify the court of an intention to contest the petition;

(d) answers and any relevant documents to be lodged by a party who notified the court of an intention to contest the petition, within such period as may be specified;

(e) adjustment of the pleadings within such period as may be specified;

(f) relevant documents to be marked up to indicate the parts the party intends to rely on;

(g) authorities to be lodged by a certain date, and to be marked up to indicate the parts the party intends to rely on;

(h) notes of argument to be lodged by a certain date;

(i) statements of issues to be lodged bya certain date;

(j) facts founded on by a party at the hearing to be supported by evidence on affidavit to be lodged within such period as may be specified;

(k) parties to write to the court to confirm whether they are ready to proceed to the substantive hearing by a certain date.

(3) Except where the Lord Ordinary orders otherwise, any intimation, service and advertisement must be ordered to take place within 7 days of the date of the interlocutor.

The substantive hearing
58.13.(1) At the substantive hearing the Lord Ordinary must hear the parties.

(2) In exercising the supervisory jurisdiction on a petition for judicial review, the Lord Ordinary may—

(a) grant or refuse any part of the petition, with or without conditions;

(b) make any order that could be made if sought in any action or petition including, in particular, an interim order or any order listed in paragraph (3) (whether or not such an order was sought in the petition).

(3) Those orders are—

(a) reduction;
(b) declarator;
(c) suspension;
(d) interdict;
(e) implement;
(f) restitution; and
(g) payment (whether of damages or otherwise).

Public interest intervention

58.17.(1) This rule applies to a person who—

(a) was not specified in an order made under rules 58.4(1), 58.11(2) or 58.12 (2) as a person who should be served with the petition; and
(b) is not directly affected by any issue raised in the petition.

(2) That person may apply by application for leave to intervene—

(a) in the decision whether to grant permission;
(b) in a petition which has been granted permission; or
(c) in an appeal in connection with a petition for judicial review.

(3) In rules 58.18 to 58.20, 'court' means the Lord Ordinary or the Inner House, as the case may be.

Public interest intervention: the minute of intervention

58.18.(1) An application for leave to intervene is made by minute of intervention in Form 58.18.

(2) The minute of intervention must set out—

(a) the name and description of the applicant;
(b) a brief statement of the issue in the proceedings which the applicant wishes to address and the applicant's reasons for believing that this issue raises a matter of public interest; and
(c) a brief statement of the propositions to be advanced by the applicant and the applicant's reasons for believing that they are relevant to the proceedings and that they will assist the court.

(3) The applicant must—

(a) send a copy of the minute to all parties; and
(b) lodge the minute, certifying on it that it has been sent to all parties.

Public interest intervention: the decision of the court

58.19.(1) The court may, in an application for leave to intervene—

(a) refuse leave without a hearing;
(b) grant leave without a hearing (unless a hearing is requested); or
(c) refuse or grant leave after a hearing.

(2) A hearing may be held if one of the parties lodges a request for a hearing—

(a) in an application to intervene where the court has not yet granted permission, within 2 days from the date that the minute of intervention was lodged; or
(b) in any other case, within 14 days from the date that the minute of intervention was lodged.

(3) At a hearing, the parties may address the court on whether the intervention will unduly delay or otherwise prejudice the rights of the parties, including their potential liability for expenses.

(4) The court may grant leave only if it is satisfied that—

(a) the proceedings raise a matter of public interest;
(b) the issue in the proceedings which the applicant wishes to address raises a matter of public interest;

(c) the propositions to be advanced by the applicant are relevant to the proceedings and are likely to assist the court; and

(d) the intervention will not unduly delay or otherwise prejudice the rights of the parties, including their potential liability for expenses.

(5) The court may, when granting leave, impose such terms and conditions as it considers desirable in the interests of justice, including making provision in respect of additional expenses incurred by the parties as a result of the intervention.

(6) The clerk of court must give written intimation of a grant or refusal of leave to the applicant and all parties.

Public interest intervention: form of intervention

58.20.(1) An intervention is by written submission.

(2) The written submission (including appendices) must not exceed 5000 words.

(3) The applicant must lodge the written submission and send a copy of it to all parties by such time as the court may direct.

(4) The court may, in exceptional circumstances—

(a) allow a longer written submission;

(b) allow an oral submission.

UN UNIVERSAL DECLARATION OF HUMAN RIGHTS

Article 1

All human beings are born free and equal in dignity and rights. They are endowed with reason and conscience and should act towards one another in a spirit of brotherhood.

Article 10

Everyone is entitled in full equality to a fair and public hearing by an independent and impartial tribunal, in the determination of his rights and obligations and of any criminal charge against him.

Article 11

(1) Everyone charged with a penal offence has the right to be presumed innocent until proved guilty according to law in a public trial at which he has had all the guarantees necessary for his defence.

EUROPEAN CONVENTION FOR THE PROTECTION OF HUMAN RIGHTS AND FUNDAMENTAL FREEDOMS

Article 1 – Obligation to respect Human Rights

The High Contracting Parties shall secure to everyone within their jurisdiction the rights and freedoms defined in Section I of this Convention.

SECTION I
RIGHTS AND FREEDOMS

Article 2 – Right to life

1. Everyone's right to life shall be protected by law. No one shall be deprived of his life intentionally save in the execution of a sentence of a court following his conviction of a crime for which this penalty is provided by law.
2. Deprivation of life shall not be regarded as inflicted in contravention of this Article when it results from the use of force which is no more than absolutely necessary:

(a) in defence of any person from unlawful violence;
(b) in order to effect a lawful arrest or to prevent the escape of a person lawfully detained;
(c) in action lawfully taken for the purpose of quelling a riot or insurrection.

Article 3 – Prohibition of torture
No one shall be subjected to torture or to inhuman or degrading treatment or punishment.

Article 4 – Prohibition of slavery and forced labour
1. No one shall be held in slavery or servitude.
2. No one shall be required to perform forced or compulsory labour.
3. For the purpose of this Article the term 'forced or compulsory labour' shall not include:
(a) any work required to be done in the ordinary course of detention imposed according to the provisions of Article 5 of this Convention or during conditional release from such detention;
(b) any service of a military character or, in case of conscientious objectors in countries where they are recognised, service exacted instead of compulsory military service;
(c) any service exacted in case of an emergency or calamity threatening the life or well-being of the community;
(d) any work or service which forms part of normal civic obligations.

Article 5 – Right to liberty and security
1. Everyone has the right to liberty and security of person. No one shall be deprived of his liberty save in the following cases and in accordance with a procedure prescribed by law:
(a) the lawful detention of a person after conviction by a competent court;
(b) the lawful arrest or detention of a person for non-compliance with the lawful order of a court or in order to secure the fulfilment of any obligation prescribed by law;
(c) the lawful arrest or detention of a person effected for the purpose of bringing him before the competent legal authority on reasonable suspicion of having committed an offence or when it is reasonably considered necessary to prevent his committing an offence or fleeing after having done so;
(d) the detention of a minor by lawful order for the purpose of educational supervision or his lawful detention for the purpose of bringing him before the competent legal authority;
(e) the lawful detention of persons for the prevention of the spreading of infectious diseases, of persons of unsound mind, alcoholics or drug addicts or vagrants;
(f) the lawful arrest or detention of a person to prevent his effecting an unauthorised entry into the country or of a person against whom action is being taken with a view to deportation or extradition.
2. Everyone who is arrested shall be informed promptly, in a language which he understands, of the reasons for his arrest and of any charge against him.
3. Everyone arrested or detained in accordance with the provisions of paragraph 1 (c) of this Article shall be brought promptly before a judge or other officer authorised by law to exercise judicial power and shall be entitled to trial within a reasonable time or to release pending trial. Release may be conditioned by guarantees to appear for trial.
4. Everyone who is deprived of his liberty by arrest or detention shall be entitled to take proceedings by which the lawfulness of his detention shall be decided speedily by a court and his release ordered if the detention is not lawful.
5. Everyone who has been the victim of arrest or detention in contravention of the provisions of this Article shall have an enforceable right to compensation.

Article 6 – Right to a fair trial

1. In the determination of his civil rights and obligations or of any criminal charge against him, everyone is entitled to a fair and public hearing within a reasonable time by an independent and impartial tribunal established by law. Judgment shall be pronounced publicly but the press and public may be excluded from all or part of the trial in the interests of morals, public order or national security in a democratic society, where the interests of juveniles or the protection of the private life of the parties so require, or to the extent strictly necessary in the opinion of the court in special circumstances where publicity would prejudice the interests of justice.
2. Everyone charged with a criminal offence shall be presumed innocent until proved guilty according to law.
3. Everyone charged with a criminal offence has the following minimum rights:

(a) to be informed promptly, in a language which he understands and in detail, of the nature and cause of the accusation against him;

(b) to have adequate time and facilities for the preparation of his defence;

(c) to defend himself in person or through legal assistance of his own choosing or, if he has not sufficient means to pay for legal assistance, to be given it free when the interests of justice so require;

(d) to examine or have examined witnesses against him and to obtain the attendance and examination of witnesses on his behalf under the same conditions as witnesses against him;

(e) to have the free assistance of an interpreter if he cannot understand or speak the language used in court.

Article 7 – No punishment without law

1. No one shall be held guilty of any criminal offence on account of any act or omission which did not constitute a criminal offence under national or international law at the time when it was committed. Nor shall a heavier penalty be imposed than the one that was applicable at the time the criminal offence was committed.
2. This Article shall not prejudice the trial and punishment of any person for any act or omission which, at the time when it was committed, was criminal according to the general principles of law recognised by civilised nations.

Article 8 – Right to respect for private and family life

1. Everyone has the right to respect for his private and family life, his home and his correspondence.
2. There shall be no interference by a public authority with the exercise of this right except such as is in accordance with the law and is necessary in a democratic society in the interests of national security, public safety or the economic well-being of the country, for the prevention of disorder or crime, for the protection of health or morals, or for the protection of the rights and freedoms of others.

Article 9 – Freedom of thought, conscience and religion

1. Everyone has the right to freedom of thought, conscience and religion; this right includes freedom to change his religion or belief and freedom, either alone or in community with others and in public or private, to manifest his religion or belief, in worship, teaching, practice and observance.
2. Freedom to manifest one's religion or beliefs shall be subject only to such limitations as are prescribed by law and are necessary in a democratic society in the interests of public safety, for the protection of public order, health or morals, or for the protection of the rights and freedoms of others.

Article 10 – Freedom of expression

1. Everyone has the right to freedom of expression. This right shall include freedom to hold opinions and to receive and impart information and ideas without

interference by public authority and regardless of frontiers. This Article shall not prevent States from requiring the licensing of broadcasting, television or cinema enterprises.

2. The exercise of these freedoms, since it carries with it duties and responsibilities, may be subject to such formalities, conditions, restrictions or penalties as are prescribed by law and are necessary in a democratic society, in the interests of national security, territorial integrity or public safety, for the prevention of disorder or crime, for the protection of health or morals, for the protection of the reputation or rights of others, for preventing the disclosure of information received in confidence, or for maintaining the authority and impartiality of the judiciary.

Article 11 – Freedom of assembly and association

1. Everyone has the right to freedom of peaceful assembly and to freedom of association with others, including the right to form and to join trade unions for the protection of his interests.
2. No restrictions shall be placed on the exercise of these rights other than such as are prescribed by law and are necessary in a democratic society in the interests of national security or public safety, for the prevention of disorder or crime, for the protection of health or morals or for the protection of the rights and freedoms of others. This Article shall not prevent the imposition of lawful restrictions on the exercise of these rights by members of the armed forces, of the police or of the administration of the State.

Article 12 – Right to marry

Men and women of marriageable age have the right to marry and to found a family, according to the national laws governing the exercise of this right.

Article 13 – Right to an effective remedy

Everyone whose rights and freedoms as set forth in this Convention are violated shall have an effective remedy before a national authority notwithstanding that the violation has been committed by persons acting in an official capacity.

Article 14 – Prohibition of discrimination

The enjoyment of the rights and freedoms set forth in this Convention shall be secured without discrimination on any ground such as sex, race, colour, language, religion, political or other opinion, national or social origin, association with a national minority, property, birth or other status.

Article 15 – Derogation in time of emergency

1. In time of war or other public emergency threatening the life of the nation any High Contracting Party may take measures derogating from its obligations under this Convention to the extent strictly required by the exigencies of the situation, provided that such measures are not inconsistent with its other obligations under international law.

. . .

3. Any High Contracting Party availing itself of this right of derogation shall keep the Secretary General of the Council of Europe fully informed of the measures which it has taken and the reasons therefor. It shall also inform the Secretary General of the Council of Europe when such measures have ceased to operate and the provisions of the Convention are again being fully executed.

Article 16 – Restrictions on political activity of aliens

Nothing in Articles 10, 11 and 14 shall be regarded as preventing the High Contracting Parties from imposing restrictions on the political activity of aliens.

Article 17 – Prohibition of abuse of rights

Nothing in this Convention may be interpreted as implying for any State, group or person any right to engage in any activity or perform any act aimed at the destruction of any of the rights and freedoms set forth herein or at their limitation to a greater extent than is provided for in the Convention.

Article 18 – Limitation on use of restrictions on rights
The restrictions permitted under this Convention to the said rights and freedoms shall not be applied for any purpose other than those for which they have been prescribed.

SECTION II
EUROPEAN COURT OF HUMAN RIGHTS

Article 19 – Establishment of the Court
To ensure the observance of the engagements undertaken by the High Contracting Parties in the Convention and the Protocols thereto, there shall be set up a European Court of Human Rights,

hereinafter referred to as 'the Court'. It shall function on a permanent basis.

Article 34 – Individual applications
The Court may receive applications from any person, non-governmental organisation or group of individuals claiming to be the victim of a violation by one of the High Contracting Parties of the rights set forth in the Convention or the Protocols thereto. The High Contracting Parties undertake not to hinder in any way the effective exercise of this right.

Article 41 – Just satisfaction
If the Court finds that there has been a violation of the Convention or the Protocols thereto, and if the internal law of the High Contracting Party concerned allows only partial reparation to be made, the Court shall, if necessary, afford just satisfaction to the injured party.

Article 46 – Binding force and execution of judgments

1. The High Contracting Parties undertake to abide by the final judgment of the Court in any case to which they are parties.
2. The final judgment of the Court shall be transmitted to the Committee of Ministers, which shall supervise its execution.
3. If the Committee of Ministers considers that the supervision of the execution of a final judgment is hindered by a problem of interpretation of the judgment, it may refer the matter to the Court for a ruling on the question of interpretation. A referral decision shall require a majority vote of two-thirds of the representatives entitled to sit on the committee.
4. If the Committee of Ministers considers that a High Contracting Party refuses to abide by a final judgment in a case to which it is a party, it may, after serving formal notice on that Party and by decision adopted by a majority vote of two-thirds of the representatives entitled to sit on the committee, refer to the Court the question whether that Party has failed to fulfil its obligation under paragraph1.
5. If the Court finds a violation of paragraph 1, it shall refer the case to the Committee of Ministers for consideration of the measures to be taken. If the Court finds no violation of paragraph 1, it shall refer the case to the Committee of Ministers, which shall close its examination of the case.

Article 50 – Expenditure on the Court
The expenditure on the Court shall be borne by the Council of Europe.

PROTOCOL NO 1

Article 1 – Protection of property
Every natural or legal person is entitled to the peaceful enjoyment of his possessions. No one shall be deprived of his possessions except in the public interest and

subject to the conditions provided for by law and by the general principles of international law.

The preceding provisions shall not, however, in any way impair the right of a State to enforce such laws as it deems necessary to control the use of property in accordance with the general interest or to secure the payment of taxes or other contributions or penalties.

Article 2 – Right to education
No person shall be denied the right to education.

In the exercise of any functions which it assumes in relation to education and to teaching, the State shall respect the right of parents to ensure such education and teaching in conformity with their own religious and philosophical convictions.

Article 3 – Right to free elections
The High Contracting Parties undertake to hold free elections at reasonable intervals by secret ballot, under conditions which will ensure the free expression of the opinion of the people in the choice of the legislature.

PROTOCOL NO 4

Article 2 – Freedom of movement

1 Everyone lawfully within the territory of a State shall, within that territory, have the right to liberty of movement and freedom to choose his residence.
2 Everyone shall be free to leave any country, including his own.
3 No restrictions shall be placed on the exercise of these rights other than such as are in accordance with law and are necessary in a democratic society in the interests of national security or public safety, for the maintenance of ordre public, for the prevention of crime, for the protection of health or morals, or for the protection of the rights and freedoms of others.
4 The rights set forth in paragraph 1 may also be subject, in particular areas, to restrictions imposed in accordance with law and justified by the public interest in a democratic society.

PROTOCOL NO 6

Article 1 – Abolition of the death penalty
The death penalty shall be abolished. No-one shall be condemned to such penalty or executed.

Article 2 – Death penalty in time of war
A State may make provision in its law for the death penalty in respect of acts committed in time of war or of imminent threat of war; such penalty shall be applied only in the instances laid down in the law and in accordance with its provisions. The State shall communicate to the Secretary General of the Council of Europe the relevant provisions of that law.

PROTOCOL NO 12

Article 1 – General prohibition of discrimination

1 The enjoyment of any right set forth by law shall be secured without discrimination on any ground such as sex, race, colour, language, religion, political or other opinion, national or social origin, association with a national minority, property, birth or other status.
2 No one shall be discriminated against by any public authority on any ground such as those mentioned in paragraph 1.

PROTOCOL NO 13

Article 1 – Abolition of the death penalty
The death penalty shall be abolished. No one shall be condemned to such penalty or executed.

Article 2 – Prohibition of derogations
No derogation from the provisions of this Protocol shall be made under Article 15 of the Convention.

Article 3 – Prohibition of reservations
No reservation may be made under Article 57 of the Convention in respect of the provisions of this Protocol.

INDEX OF STATUTES

EU representative:
Easy Access System Europe
Mustamäe tee 50, 10621 Tallinn, Estonia
Gpsr.requests@easproject.com

www.ingramcontent.com/pod-product-compliance
Lightning Source LLC
LaVergne TN
LVHW050754061126
851857LV00012B/560
9781474473934